Patient Care Case Law: Ethics, Regulation, and Compliance

George D. Pozgar, MBA, CHE

Consultant
GP Health Care Consulting
Annapolis, MD

JONES & BARTLETT
LEARNING

World Headquarters
Jones & Bartlett Learning
5 Wall Street
Burlington, MA 01803
978-443-5000
info@jblearning.com
www.jblearning.com

Jones & Bartlett Learning books and products are available through most bookstores and online booksellers. To contact Jones & Bartlett Learning directly, call 800-832-0034, fax 978-443-8000, or visit our website, www.jblearning.com.

Substantial discounts on bulk quantities of Jones & Bartlett Learning publications are available to corporations, professional associations, and other qualified organizations. For details and specific discount information, contact the special sales department at Jones & Bartlett Learning via the above contact information or send an email to specialsales@jblearning.com.

Copyright © 2013 by Jones & Bartlett Learning, LLC, an Ascend Learning Company

All rights reserved. No part of the material protected by this copyright may be reproduced or utilized in any form, electronic or mechanical, including photocopying, recording, or by any information storage and retrieval system, without written permission from the copyright owner.

This publication is designed to provide accurate and authoritative information in regard to the Subject Matter covered. It is sold with the understanding that the publisher is not engaged in rendering legal, accounting, or other professional service. If legal advice or other expert assistance is required, the service of a competent professional person should be sought.

Production Credits

Publisher: Michael Brown
Managing Editor: Maro Gartside
Editorial Assistant: Kayla Dos Santos
Production Assistant: Rebekah Linga
Senior Marketing Manager: Sophie Fleck Teague
Manufacturing and Inventory Control Supervisor:
  Amy Bacus

Composition: Cenveo Publisher Services
Cover Design: Scott Moden
Cover Image: Wooden gavel for a judge: © Pilar
  Echevarria/ShutterStock, Inc.; Santiago Hospital:
  © bruno ismael da silva alves/ShutterStock, Inc.
Printing and Binding: Malloy, Inc.
Cover Printing: Malloy, Inc.

Library of Congress Cataloging-in-Publication Data
Pozgar, George D.
  Patient care case law : ethics, regulation, and compliance / George Pozgar.
    p. cm.
  Includes bibliographical references and index.
  ISBN-13: 978-1-4496-0458-5 (pbk.)
  ISBN-10: 1-4496-0458-7 (ibid.)
  1. Medical care—Law and legislation—United States. I. Title.
  KF3821.P695 2012
  344.7304'1—dc23
                                      2011044600

6048
Printed in the United States of America
16 15 14 13 12   10 9 8 7 6 5 4 3 2 1

Contents

Preface

Patient Care Case Law: Ethics, Regulation, and Compliance is both a unique stand-alone book and a companion guide for a wide variety of texts utilized in educational settings. It is an independent compendium of a broad variety of case studies covering various legal and ethical issues.

The emphasis of *Patient Care Case Law: Ethics, Regulation, and Compliance* is the patient's progression from admission through discharge including chapters on patient rights, the screening and assessment process, diagnostic services, diagnosis, treatment, universal protocols, discharge planning, and follow-up care. The book continues with a review of cases pertinent to employee and patient safety, human resources, and criminal acts. There's a summary case written as a *closet drama*, as well as a chapter that describes a healthcare system that may be just "Too Big to Fail," in addition to an appendix containing a list of suggested websites that includes a brief description of what can be found on each website to help the reader conduct further research into the legal and ethical issues of health care. The text also provides a glossary of terminology and summary notes for various health professionals and the general public. There is an assessment template that healthcare organizations can use to assist in evaluating the quality of care in their organizations. The Code of Federal Regulations (CFR) Chapter 42 for hospitals is provided in Appendix A for easy reference. Prior to reading this book, the reader should become familiar with the contents of CFR Chapter 42.

This book has been designed for use by students and practicing healthcare professionals. It is written using terminology focused on the layperson and provides healthcare professionals with the necessary knowledge to become conversant in legal issues pertinent to their jobs.

The information contained in the casebook is based on applicable statutory and decisional authority, as well as the author's specialized knowledge gained through extensive experience in the healthcare field, including standards and regulatory compliance surveys and consultations at more than a 1,000 healthcare sites throughout the United States and Puerto Rico.

In the litigious environment that exists in the United States, wherein negligence suits continue to plague the healthcare industry, it is imperative that healthcare professionals understand their rights and responsibilities under the law and the legal ramifications of their actions. A review of a wide variety of cases over the years has revealed that the same or similar negligent acts have been repeated. The passage of time has merely changed the names of the litigants.

The reader will note that there is not a citation associated with every case. Many high profile cases are settled out of the courtroom due to the negative impact they can have on a healthcare provider. Therefore, secondary sources such as newspaper articles and personal experiences by those who wish to retain their anonymity have been digested and adapted into a variety of formats to encourage the learning process.

Each case has been given a title that signals the type of case about to be reviewed. Citations are helpful to students who wish to conduct further research on a particular case or topic. A case citation describes the identity of the parties in the case, the legal reporter in which the case can be found, the volume and page number, and the year in which the case was decided.

The court cases discussed provide: (1) a review of the facts of the case; (2) the issues discussed in any given case, selected for review on the basis of pertinence to healthcare professionals (although any one case in this text may have multiple issues, emphasis is placed on selecting those issues considered to be most relevant to the reader); and (3) the court's ruling and rationale for its decision based on the facts, issues, and applicable laws pertaining to the case. Discussion questions are also provided at the end of each case.

chapter one

Regulatory and Accrediting Bodies

This chapter focuses on the *Centers for Medicare and Medicaid Services* (CMS) *Conditions for Participation*, which must be met in order for healthcare organizations to be eligible for Federal funding of services rendered to Medicare and Medicaid recipients. CMS requirements for hospitals can be found in Appendix A "U.S. Code of Federal Regulations." Appendix B "Centers for Medicare and Medicaid Certification Process" provides an overview of the *CMS Certification Process*. Although there are a plethora of regulatory agencies on the federal, state, and local levels, emphasis is placed on CMS requirements for hospitals.

There are also a variety of accreditation agencies. Again, the emphasis is on the Joint Commission (TJC), which is the largest non-profit accrediting body that requires compliance with CMS requirements in its standards. TJC was the first accrediting body written into the law to be granted *deemed status* to accredit hospitals and other healthcare organizations. Deemed status refers to a provider or supplier that has been accredited by a CMS-approved national accreditation program and, through such accreditation, demonstrates compliance with the applicable conditions of participation, conditions for coverage, conditions for certification or requirements.[1]

A provider may select CMS or another CMS body with deemed status to conduct the accreditation survey and certification process. The various states generally carry out the accreditation survey for CMS if the provider decides not to select an accrediting body with deemed status, such as TJC. It should be noted that CMS also conducts validation surveys to determine the effectiveness of surveys conducted by other accrediting bodies with deemed status.

The survey is an evaluative process in which a healthcare provider undergoes an examination of its policies, procedures, practices, patient care, and performance to ensure that it meets CMS Conditions for Participation and, where applicable, the standards of the organization chosen by the provider to conduct the survey. TJC in its Hospital Accreditation Standards LD.04.01.01 requires hospitals to comply with laws and regulations that include CMS Conditions for Participation.

The cases presented in each chapter illustrate the importance of complying with the requirements of CMS Conditions of Participation for Medicare and Medicaid reimbursement purposes and, where applicable, if the organization so chooses, the accreditation standards of the surveying body (e.g., TJC). Some healthcare organizations choose to be surveyed by the various states for CMS Conditions of Participation for compliance purposes. It should be emphasized here that healthcare organizations that choose TJC to conduct its accreditation survey must comply with both the CMS Conditions of Participation, as well as, the standards of the TJC. State and local laws are often referred to in the various cases to illustrate how an unfortunate outcome might have been prevented if the laws and regulations that apply to the case had been followed. Laws, rules, regulations, and standards are written to help ensure the quality of care provided to patients and prevent unwanted outcomes.

Regulators Penalize Some Maryland Hospitals for Complication Rates

One of five Maryland hospitals failed to meet targets set for them by the state for rates of infections, pneumonia, and other complications last year, and most of those medical centers will suffer financial penalties as a result, regulators say.

Nine hospitals in the state will face a combined $2.1 million cut in their allowed rate increases for the coming fiscal year. Maryland, alone among the states, regulates what hospitals can charge.

Twenty-three hospitals had better-than-average complication rates and will see small bonuses as a result. Scores for all 45 hospitals being tracked are posted online.

Julie Appleby, Kaiser Health News, *February 24, 2011*[2]

The laws, rules, regulations, and accreditation standards involved in the delivery of health care is dramatically increasing the costs for providers, and yet the insurance industry continues to profit in billions of dollars. One needs only to go to a Marriott hotel in Los Angeles and look *up* from a top floor window at the towering headquarters of insurance companies to realize where all the money is going and why it is difficult for patients to receive insurance benefits. And after looking at these mammoth structures, one could then visit local hospitals for the sake of comparison. Which buildings are more modern and lavishly built? A picture is worth a thousand words.

CMS CONDITIONS FOR PARTICIPATION

CMS develops Conditions of Participation (CoPs) and Conditions for Coverage (CfCs) that healthcare organizations must meet in order to participate in the Medicare and Medicaid programs. These minimum health and safety standards are the foundation for improving quality and protecting the health and safety of beneficiaries. CMS also ensures that the standards of accrediting organizations recognized by CMS (through the "deeming" process) meet or exceed the Medicare standards set forth in CoPs and CfCs.

CoPs and CfCs are the minimum health and safety standards that providers and suppliers must meet in order to be Medicare and Medicaid certified. CoPs and CfCs apply to Ambulatory Surgical Centers, Critical Access Hospitals, Home Health Agencies, Hospices, Hospitals, Providers of Outpatient Services, Skilled Nursing Facilities, and a variety of other care providers.[3]

The CoPs for hospitals can be found in the Code of Federal Regulations (CFR 42).

Code of Federal Regulations (CFR 42) Public Health
CHAPTER IV—CENTERS FOR MEDICARE & MEDICAID SERVICES, DEPARTMENT OF HEALTH AND HUMAN SERVICES
    Part 482—Conditions of Participation for Hospitals
    Subpart A— General Provisions
    § 482.1 Basis and Scope
(a) *Statutory basis.* (1) Section 1861 (e) of the act provides that—
    (i) Hospitals participating in Medicare must meet certain specified requirements; and
    (ii) The Secretary may impose additional requirements if they are found necessary in the interest of the health and safety of the individuals who are furnished services in the hospital.
(5b) *Scope.* Except as provided in subpart A of part 488 of this chapter, the provisions of this part serve as the basis of survey activities for the purpose of determining whether a hospital qualifies for a provider agreement under Medicare and Medicaid.

See Appendix A "U.S. Code of Federal Regulations" for details of conditions of participation that apply to hospitals.

STATE OPERATIONS MANUAL

The *Observation* section of the *State Operations Manual for the Survey Protocol, Regulations and Interpretive Guidelines for Hospitals* is quoted next to assist the reader in obtaining a general sense of how the survey process is conducted. For the complete set of guidelines, see the web link provided at the end of the following quote:

Observations

Observations provide first-hand knowledge of hospital practice. The regulations and interpretive guidelines offer guidance for conducting observations. Observation of the care environment provides valuable information about how the care delivery system works and how hospital departments work together to provide care. Surveyors are encouraged to make observations, complete interviews, and review records and policies/procedures by stationing themselves as physically close to patient care as possible. While completing a chart review, for instance, it may be possible to also observe the environment and the patients, as far as care being given, staff interactions with patients, safety hazards, and infection control practices. When conducting observations, particular attention should be given to the following:

- Patient care, including treatments and therapies in all patient care settings
- Staff member activities, equipment, documentation, building structure, sounds and smells
- People, care, activities, processes, documentation, policies, equipment, etc., that are present that should not be present as well as those that are not present that should be present
- Integration of all services, such that the facility is functioning as one integrated whole
- Whether quality assessment and performance improvement (QAPI) is a facility-wide activity, incorporating every service and activity of the provider and whether every facility department and activity reports to, and receives reports from, the facility's central organized body managing the facility-wide QAPI program
- Storage, security, and confidentiality of medical records

A surveyor should take complete notes of all observations and should document: the date and time of the observation(s), location, patient identifiers, individuals present during the observation, and the activity being observed (e.g., therapy, treatment modality).

A surveyor should have observations verified by the patient, family, facility staff, other survey team member(s), or by another mechanism. For example, when finding an outdated medication in the pharmacy, ask the pharmacist to verify that the drug is outdated.

In addition, a surveyor should integrate the data from observations with data gathered through interviews and document reviews.

Surveyors must not examine patients by themselves, although in certain circumstances, in order to determine a patient's health status and whether appropriate health care is being provided, especially to ensure a patient's welfare where he/she appears to be in immediate jeopardy, it is permissible and necessary to examine the patient. After obtaining permission from the patient, the surveyor should request that a staff member of the facility examine the patient in the surveyor's presence. The health and dignity of the patient is always of paramount concern. A surveyor must respect the patient's right to refuse to be examined.

http://www.cms.gov/manuals/downloads/som107ap_a_hospitals.pdf

ACCREDITATION AGENCIES

The accrediting bodies that follow are a few examples of those that have been awarded deemed status with CMS. DNV is one of the more recent bodies to receive deemed status. TJC was the first to be written into law.

DNV Healthcare Inc.

The Centers for Medicare and Medicaid Services (CMS) has granted DNV Healthcare Inc. deemed status to conduct accreditation surveys. DNV Healthcare is a division of Hovik, Norway-based Det Norske Veritas, which was established in 1864 as an inspector of ships but which now conducts reviews for many other industries.

The prestigious DNV Accreditation symbol signifies adherence both to CMS CoPs and to ISO 9001 quality management system under one, seemless program named National Integrated Accreditation for Healthcare Organizations (NIAHO).[4] NIAHO requires surveys on an annual basis and is designed to drive quality transformation into the core processes of running a hospital.

TJC

TJC is a not-for-profit independent organization dedicated to improving the quality of health care in organized healthcare settings.

1965 Congress passed the Social Security Amendments of 1965 with a provision that hospitals accredited by the *Joint Commission on*

Accreditation of Hospitals (then known as JCAH but, today, is named *the Joint Commission* or TJC) would be deemed in compliance with most of the Medicare Conditions of Participation for Hospitals and, thus, would be eligible to participate in the Medicare and Medicaid programs.

1972 The Social Security Act was amended to require that the Secretary of the U.S. Department of Health and Human Services (DHHS) validate JCAH findings. The law also required the Secretary to include an evaluation of JCAH's accreditation process in the annual DHHS report to Congress.[5]

TJC currently accredits over 19,000 healthcare organizations and programs in the United States. The major functions of TJC include developing organizational standards, awarding accreditation decisions, and providing education and consultation to healthcare organizations. TJC surveys hospitals on an unannounced triennial basis.

HEALTH INSURANCE PORTABILITY AND ACCOUNTABILITY ACT

The Health Insurance Portability and Accountability Act (HIPAA) of 1996 (Public Law 104-191) was designed to protect the privacy, confidentiality, and security of patient information. HIPAA standards are applicable to all health information in all of its formats (e.g., electronic, paper, verbal), and they apply to both electronically maintained and transmitted information. HIPAA privacy standards include restrictions on access to individually identifiable health information and to the use and disclosure of that information, and they set requirements for such administrative activities as training, compliance, and enforcement of HIPAA mandates.

THE PATIENT PROTECTION AND AFFORDABLE CARE ACT

The Patient Protection and Affordable Care Act (PPACA), was passed by Congress and signed into law by the President in March 2010. Its design and purpose is to provide better health security by putting into place comprehensive health insurance reforms that hold insurance companies accountable, lower healthcare costs, guarantee more choice, and enhance the quality of care for all Americans. The battle continues as to the costs of implementing this Act in its entirety. The reader can locate more detailed information on this Act at http://democrats.senate.gov/pdfs/reform/patient-protection-affordable-care-act-as-passed.pdf

REGULATORY CONFLICTS OF INTEREST ABOUND

Food Inspection Is Often Flawed

The voluntary quality control system widely used in the nation's $1 trillion domestic food industry is rife with conflicts of interest, inexperienced auditors, and cursory inspections that produce inflated ratings, according to food retail executives and other industry experts.

Recent outbreaks of salmonella illness . . . have focused new attention on weaknesses in the decades–old system, which relies on private-sector auditors hired by food makers.

. . . But experts agree that the inspections often do not translate into safer products for consumers.

"It's a business strategy, not a public health strategy," . . . .

Suppliers "will hunt down the fastest, cheapest, easiest and least-intrusive third-party auditors that will provide the certificate" that will allow them to sell their product . . . until that model flips, there will continue to be a false sense of security in terms of what these systems offer."

Lena H. Sun, The Washington Post, *October 22, 2010*

The mission of accrediting bodies is to improve the quality of care rendered in hospitals through its survey process. Accrediting bodies are dependent upon the hospitals it surveys/inspects to reimburse it for the costs of those surveys. This means they need to maintain satisfied clients, and in so doing, a conflict arises. How credible can a survey be when the accrediting body is dependent on the organizations it surveys for financial survival and the organizations being surveyed are dependent on the accrediting body for financial survival? Further, hospitals evaluate the performance of the surveyors. The survival of the surveyor in his or her job is dependent upon good evaluations from the contracting hospitals. Conflicting interests here encourage surveyors/inspectors to be careful about what he/she scores due to fear of retaliation by both the organizations surveyed and the accrediting body.

Inspections within the food service industry are somewhat similar to the hospital accreditation survey process.

- Food makers often know when inspectors will audit their facilities, and they vigorously prepare for those inspections. This was also true with hospitals until several years ago when TJC, for example, decided to conduct unannounced surveys. This change occurred mostly because of criticism from its own surveyors, the public, and even some of the surveyed organizations.

- Most food makers score high on their inspections, and yet they still have outbreaks and recalls. Until several years ago, TJC scored hospitals, but they have discontinued the scoring process, in part due to criticism from surveyors and healthcare providers. Because of the competition between hospitals, surveyors had been pressured by the organizations they inspected to give high scores. Large billboards on Florida highways advertised scores of 100, yet in actuality, those hospitals may have provided no better quality of care than a hospital that had scored an 80.

  (1) One small town hospital advertised in a newspaper that it scored 100 on its TJC survey. The same hospital had no full-time emergency department physician. An uncle's niece said, "I would not take my dog to that hospital. They killed my mom."

  (2) Bob's dad was having difficulty breathing, and Bob convinced him to go to the emergency department of a hospital that sported a score of 98. The emergency department physician, after examining an X-ray of the patient, told Bob, "It's people like your dad that drive up the costs of health care. By the way, your dad is okay." Even though Bob was disturbed by the physician's first remark, he went home pleased that his dad had been given a clean bill of health. Unfortunately, the hospital called Bob's dad the next day to say that he should see his family doctor because he had a suspicious lesion on his lung. It was cancer, and he has since passed away.

  (3) Addy was at a hospital with a score of 99. She had colon cancer and, after surgery, was told she would be on a soft diet. Shortly thereafter, Addy was served pork chops at mealtime, so she queried her nurse about this and explained that she had been told she would receive a soft diet. The nurse responded that the diet could not be changed and that until she got a soft diet order from the physician, Addy would have to remain on a regular diet, which of course meant that Addy had to go without eating.

  (4) Annie had continual headaches for more than a year. The doctor had diagnosed migraines and said they were stress-related. More than 2 years later, a brain scan was finally ordered, and it revealed Annie had had a brain tumor. She has since passed away.

  (5) Nancy went to her doctor's appointment. The doctor said, "Please lay down on the examining table." She reached for the doctor's hand for help in easing down onto the table. The doctor did not extend a helping hand. When the exam was over, Nancy again reached for the doctor's hand. The doctor looked away from her and said, "You got down by yourself, you can get up by yourself."

(6) The anesthesiologist who attended Auntie (a happy, elderly lady) during anesthesia said to Auntie's daughter Susie that he had not seen Auntie's medical files. He was not aware of her diagnoses (hiatal hernia, asthma . . .) and test results (e.g., EKG). He said to the daughter, "If I had seen all of the test results, I would have administered a local anesthetic instead of a general anesthetic." Auntie had to be placed on a ventilator because she developed pneumonia after surgery, and she was eventually transferred to a nursing home. Three days later, during Susie's third visit to her mother at the nursing home, the daughter noticed alarming signs that her mother might be dying, so she hurried to the nursing station and reported this. The nurse who went to the room with Susie asked, "How do you know she is dying?" Susie said, "Look at her feet, they are purple." The nurse then took Auntie's blood pressure, which was too low, but the nurse seemed unconcerned about the reading or about Auntie's extreme restlessness. Susie said to the nurse, "My mother is dying. I see you gave her morphine. You are never supposed to give her morphine unless she is on a ventilator." (They had given her morphine and a relaxant medication.) At that point, the nurse began preparing a bath for Auntie and ordered food for her. Susie cried out, "I am not a freaking nurse, but I know my mother is dying, and here you are figuring to give her a bath and feed her." The nurse again said, "How do you know she is dying?" Susie again said, "Look, her feet are purple, and I can tell by the way she's breathing." Auntie passed away shortly thereafter.

- As with hospitals, the food companies typically pay food industry inspectors, creating a conflict of interest for inspectors who might fear they will lose business if they don't hand out high ratings.

The industries presented earlier raise some disturbing issues. For instance, there is a blatant conflict of interest for the various inspecting agencies and for those entities they are inspecting, and this places public health at risk in order to benefit the bottom line of those agencies and healthcare providers. The question arises: should someone regulate the regulators? But even if so, one must ask at what point standards and regulations become important enough that caregivers understand them and adhere to them. It is likely that managers and caregivers would agree there is inconsistency in knowing what the standards and expectations are, interpreting them consistently—and in scoring them.

Continuous Stream of New Laws and Regulatory Requirements

Although regulations are generally enacted out of public concern—as well as legal and ethical reasoning—the continuous flow of new regulations often create new problems even as they help resolve earlier ones. For example, do HIPPA regulations that aim to protect patient privacy also affect patient care negatively? Two anonymous opinions are provided next.

Con

Ever since hospitals started increasing their compliance to HIPAA regulations, a lot of subtle and not-so subtle changes have been taking place in the way patient information is communicated (at least at the hospitals I have rotated at). Patient names are now often reduced to initials on checkout sheets. At the ER, a patient's chief complaints are no longer noted on the board. No one is allowed to photocopy any progress notes or order sheets containing patient information anymore. While I feel strongly that patient confidentiality is very important and should be protected within reason, I also feel that some of the regulations are getting out of hand, making it much more difficult for residents, students, and others involved in patient care to share important communications, even within a closed system. It seems that these regulations are hell-bent on blindfolding and gagging healthcare workers in an effort to protect confidentiality at the expense of clear communication between colleagues about important patient issues.

Pro

I haven't had to do anything with patient care under HIPPA, but something had to be done about patient privacy, so I don't know how difficult it is. However, something had to be done about protecting patient privacy. In a university hospital, where I worked in a lab, patient records were often left on carts in the hallway unattended for hours. Conversations about patients were common in the elevators even when it was obvious that some of the occupants were visitors. In a horrifying incident for me, I was molested when I was a patient, and the hospital administrator gave the police my chart! Because the administrator had no legal responsibility to maintain my privacy, she suffered NO repercussions for her devastating actions.

Commentary

The regulatory effect on the hospital's bottom line is incalculable. There are conservatively more than 100 regulatory agencies that affect hospital operations. Various attempts have been made to list and describe how many of them overlap. Discussed in this casebook are the regulatory requirements that affect providers participating in Medicare programs, which is a majority of providers.

Discussion

1. Discuss how the constant flow of regulatory requirements can harm the quality of care provided in the nation's hospitals.
2. Discuss how the constant flow of regulatory requirements can improve the quality of care provided in the nation's hospitals.

Standards and regulations are helpful in establishing the "Standard of Care" expected in a particular case. Standards and regulations are written—and healthcare organizations are required to comply with them—to help minimize the numerous mistakes and injures that occur on a daily basis in the delivery of patient care.

The intent of laws, rules, and regulations are often broken, misinterpreted, or even applied indiscriminately based on the knowledge and ethical character of the reviewer. The preceding article describes how pervasive conflicts of interest are between inspected agencies and accrediting bodies.

Accreditation Surveys and State Enforcement of Standards

Citation: *Evelyn V. v. Kings County Hosp. Ctr.*, 956 F. Supp. 288 (1997)

The essence of the plaintiffs' claim in this case is that reasonable steps were not taken to ensure that Kings County Hospital complied with established state health standards. The plaintiffs submitted that 42 U.S.C. § 1396a(a)(9) gives them a federal right to such enforcement of state standards. 42 U.S.C. § 1396a(a)(9) states: "A state plan for medical assistance must provide that the State health agency, or other appropriate State medical agency, shall be responsible for establishing and maintaining health standards for private or public institutions in which recipients of medical assistance under the plan may receive care or services."

Kings County Hospital Center had a history of noncompliance with healthcare standards. In January and February 1989, Health and Human Services (HHS) requested that the New York State Department of Health (Department of Health) conduct an allegation survey of the hospital. Based on the survey report, HHS concluded that the hospital was not in compliance with five CoPs in Medicare and Medicaid. In April 1989, HHS advised the hospital that a complete Medicare survey would be conducted by the Department of Health, after which the hospital would be expected to submit a plan for correction. HHS warned that if the hospital were unable to achieve compliance with the Medicare conditions, termination action would be pursued.

Before conducting the complete Medicare survey, the Department of Health settled its state enforcement action with the hospital. On April 19,

1989, the hospital agreed to pay a fine and to implement a detailed plan of correction.

In June 1989, the Department of Health conducted the requested survey of the hospital. The hospital was found to be out of compliance with seven CoPs in Medicaid and Medicare. Efforts were undertaken by the hospital to correct the cited deficiencies. The Department of Health conducted a follow-up survey in August 1989, and based on its report, HHS concluded that the hospital had attained compliance with all CoPs in Medicare and Medicaid, except those relating to physical environment. HHS accepted the hospital's long-range plan for correction of environment deficiencies. It did, however, advise the hospital that it would no longer be deemed eligible for Medicare and Medicaid participation based on its TJC accreditation. Rather, it would be closely monitored by the Department of Health. Department of Health monitoring reports from September, October, and November 1989 indicate that although the hospital was still experiencing compliance difficulties, significant improvements were being made.

The Department of Health did not conduct, nor does it appear that HHS requested, any comprehensive survey of the hospital in 1990. During that year, the Department of Health investigated 29 specific complaints about the hospital's care and conditions. On-site investigations resulted in the issuance of 11 statements of deficiencies requiring corrections.

From January 7 to January 18, 1991, the Department of Health conducted a federal monitoring survey at the hospital. Based on findings that the hospital was out of compliance with five conditions for participation in Medicare and Medicaid, HHS notified the hospital on March 19, 1991, that its "participation in the Medicare program is being terminated as of May 19, 1991." The hospital was advised that the termination order would be rescinded if it brought itself back to condition-level compliance before the scheduled termination date.

On April 5, 1991, the hospital submitted to the Department of Health a plan of correction and a request for resurvey. The resurvey revealed that although problems had not been completely eliminated, the hospital had managed to achieve condition-level compliance with all federal standards for participation in Medicare and Medicaid except those relating to physical environment. On May 1, 1991, the Department of Health recommended to HHS that the hospital be permitted to continue to participate in the Medicare and Medicaid programs. HHS agreed and, on May 8, 1991, notified the hospital that it was rescinding its previous termination decision. The hospital was warned that, because it had not demonstrated the ability to sustain the corrective action outlined in the plan submitted in 1989, the time frames in the April 1991 submission would be closely monitored, and the facility would remain under state survey jurisdiction.

A few days later, on May 10, 1991, the Department of Health issued a report finding that the deficiencies noted at the hospital in the January 1991 survey constituted violations of both state and federal standards. A formal enforcement action was commenced. Negotiations to settle this action were interrupted when the death of a stabbing victim at the hospital raised further questions about the hospital's delivery of care. The Department of Health conducted an investigation into the victim's treatment at the hospital and, in the fall of 1991, cited the hospital for further violations of state health standards.

In October 1991, the Department of Health conducted another federal survey of the hospital and again found several serious departures from federal and state standards. HHS again threatened to terminate the hospital from participation in the Medicare and Medicaid programs, and the Department of Health formally cited the hospital for violations, demanding a plan of correction by November 22, 1991.

The Department of Health resurveyed the hospital in early December 1991 and issued its report to HHS on December 6, 1991. On December 16, 1991, HHS decided once again to rescind its termination of the hospital from the Medicare and Medicaid programs, finding that in the resurvey the hospital had managed to demonstrate condition-level compliance with all requirements except physical environment.

On February 3, 1992, the Department of Health advised the hospital that it was amending the pending state enforcement action to add the deficiencies cited during the October 1991 survey. This action was settled on July 10, 1992. The hospital again agreed to implement a plan of correction. To monitor the hospital's compliance with the plan of correction, the Department of Health was to conduct monitoring visits in October 1992, February 1993, and July 1993. Soon after the October 1991 Department of Health survey, the hospital was surveyed by TJC to determine whether the hospital should be reaccredited. In January 1992, TJC notified the hospital that it was recommending against accreditation. TJC ultimately permitted the hospital to operate with conditional accreditation.

In October 1992, the Department of Health conducted its first monitoring visit of the hospital pursuant to its July 1992 order of settlement with the hospital. The hospital was cited for numerous specific and general violations. The Department of Health demanded that the hospital provide a plan for correction.

In January 1993, the Department of Health conducted a comprehensive state and federal survey of the hospital. Although numerous deficiencies were cited, HHS did not take any action against the hospital. On March 17, 1993, the hospital submitted a plan to the Department of Health to correct the noted deficiencies. Parts of the plan were deemed unacceptable, prompting resubmissions by the hospital in June and July 1993. In July 1993, the Department of Health conducted a monitoring visit of the hospital. Various deficiencies were again noted. In August 1993, the Department of Health accepted the hospital's most recent plan for correction.

In November 1994, the hospital was scheduled to be reviewed by TJC. Having run the hospital for some time with only conditional accreditation, management understood that the institution would have to pass TJC review or lose its accreditation and its status as a Medicare and Medicaid provider. To assist the hospital in preparing for the review, New York City's Health and Hospitals Corporation arranged for a mock survey to be conducted in May 1994. In July 1994, the results were announced: numerous problems still existed. Some changes in management were made and the Health and Hospitals Corporation authorized a one-time allocation of over $1 million to the hospital to address various needs that would be pertinent to TJC review. These efforts proved successful and TJC again accredited the hospital.

In moving for summary judgment in their favor, the defendants submitted that the plaintiffs failed to state a claim because 42 U.S.C. § 1396a(a)(9) does not confer the right to enforcement of state standards, and even if the court were to find such an enforceable federal right, their actions suffice to satisfy their legal obligations.

As evidence that the state agencies were failing to meet their obligations pursuant to 42 U.S.C. § 1396a(a)(9) with respect to the hospital, the plaintiffs pointed to the various surveys of the hospital over the years revealing noncompliance with health standards. The Department of Health surveyed the hospital to ensure compliance with both federal and state law. 42 U.S.C. § 1395aa(a), expressly referred to in § 1396a(a)(9), provides for the Secretary of HHS to contract with state health agencies to certify those institutions qualifying for Medicaid participation. This law states

---

The Secretary shall make an agreement with any State which is able and willing to do so under which the services of the State health agency or other appropriate State agency (or the appropriate local agencies) will be utilized by him for the purpose of determining whether an institution therein is a hospital or skilled nursing facility, or . . . a home health agency, or . . . a hospice program or . . . a rural health clinic, [or] a rural primary care hospital, . . . or a comprehensive outpatient rehabilitation facility. . . .

To the extent that the Secretary finds it appropriate, an institution or agency which such a State (or local) agency certifies is a hospital, skilled nursing facility, rural health clinic, comprehensive outpatient rehabilitation facility, home health agency, or hospice program (as those terms are defined in section 1395x of this title) may be treated as such by the Secretary.

Further, 42 U.S.C. § 1395aa(c) provides for the Secretary of HHS to use state health agencies to conduct surveys of hospitals participating in the Medicaid program. It states

The Secretary is authorized to enter into an agreement with any State under which the appropriate State or local agency which performs the certification function described in subsection (a) of this section will survey, on a selective sample basis (or where the Secretary finds that a survey is appropriate because of substantial allegations of the existence of a significant deficiency or deficiencies which would, if found to be present, adversely affect health and safety of patients), hospitals which have an agreement with the Secretary under 1395cc of this title and which are accredited by the Joint Commission on Accreditation of Hospitals. The Secretary shall pay for such services in the manner prescribed in subsection (b) of this section.

42 C.F.R. § 488.26(c)(1) describes the survey process as the means to assess compliance with federal health, safety, and quality standards.

The Secretary of HHS entered into an agreement with the Department of Health to perform the certifications and surveys provided for in these statutes and regulations. It was expressly recognized in the agreement that, in performing its contractual duties, the State acted on behalf of the Secretary.

As a general rule, institutions accredited as hospitals by TJC are deemed qualified to participate in Medicare and Medicaid. The Secretary of HHS may, however, request a state agency such as the Department of Health to conduct a validation survey to determine whether an accredited hospital does meet Medicare and Medicaid participation standards. The Secretary of HHS may also request that the Department of Health conduct allegation surveys when HHS receives information indicating that a hospital may be out of compliance with the conditions for participation in Medicaid and Medicare and that it conduct monitoring surveys to determine if past noted deficiencies have been corrected. Survey reports are submitted to HHS, which makes the final determination as to whether a hospital may continue to participate in the Medicare and Medicaid programs.

Accreditation survey reports constitute recommendations to the Health Care Financing Administration. Based on these recommendations, HHS takes appropriate action. If a survey reveals that a hospital is not in

compliance with one or more federal standards, its ability to continue participating in Medicare and Medicaid programs depends on its submission of an
acceptable plan of correction for achieving compliance within a reasonable
period of time acceptable to the Secretary of HHS. Ordinarily, a deficient
hospital is expected to bring itself into compliance with federal conditions
within 60 days, but the Secretary of HHS may grant additional time when
appropriate. Where noncompliance is acute or persistent, the Secretary of
HHS is empowered to terminate a hospital from participation in Medicare
and Medicaid programs. The parties agree that such termination would
effectively shut down a public hospital, because it could not operate without
federal funds.

In addition to conducting federally requested surveys, the Department
of Health also uses on-site surveys to assess hospitals' compliance with state
standards of care. Should deficiencies be detected with respect to these
standards, hospitals are required to submit plans of correction, which are
reviewed through follow-up surveys. Where appropriate, the Department of
Health can commence an enforcement proceeding against a deficient hospital, with possible penalties ranging from a fine to revocation of a hospital's
operating certificate and closure.

Issue

Does 42 U.S.C. § 1396a(a)(9) confer on the plaintiffs a federal right enforceable through 42 U.S.C. § 1983 to have the New York State Department of
Social Services and the New York State Department of Health take reasonable steps to ensure that hospitals operating as Medicaid providers comply
with state standards of operation?

Holding

Because the plaintiffs have no federal right to state enforcement of state
standards of health care at hospitals participating in the Medicaid program,
summary judgment was granted in favor of the defendants.

Reason

The court had to determine if this case really involved a federal right, as
opposed to a claimed violation of federal law. The problem in this case was
in deciding precisely what it is Congress mandated in § 1396a(a)(9) for
the benefit of Medicaid recipients. Congress requires state Medicaid plans
to provide for a state health agency to be responsible for establishing and

maintaining health standards for institutions that operate as Medicaid providers. The parties agree that the New York plan provides for the Department of Health to serve this statutory function. They agree that the Department of Health has established standards for state hospitals. Where the parties disagree is in their interpretation of the statute's requirement with respect to maintaining health standards. A thing is "maintained" when it is kept "in a state of repair, efficiency, or validity," when it is "preserve[d] from failure or decline" [Webster's Third New International Dictionary 1362 (1986)]. The defendants submitted that the statute thus obligated them to review their health standards and, when necessary, update them to ensure that they remain valid and consistent with current medical practice. The plaintiffs submitted that the statutory obligation is broader—that reasonable efforts must be made to ensure that state hospitals participating in the Medicaid program operate in compliance with established state standards. The court rejected the plaintiffs' construction.

The court noted that, although § 1983 has been used as a vehicle to enforce federal rights embodied in federal regulations as well as statutes, it would be quite remarkable for Congress to federalize a whole body of unspecified state rules and regulations and thereby make the state's enforcement of its own standards a federal right that parties could pursue through private § 1983 actions. The language of § 1396a(a)(9) does not suggest such a sweeping congressional intent. The statute requires simply that a state agency be responsible for establishing and maintaining health standards for participating institutions. An agency can maintain appropriate standards for institutions without having any enforcement powers over those institutions. Few fields have changed as rapidly in this century as medicine. Surgical procedures, professional training requirements, medication protocols, and methods for handling and storing blood have all evolved considerably, such that standards considered exemplary when § 1396a(a)(9) was first enacted would not be deemed adequate today. Congress wished to ensure that states did not view their § 1396a(a)(9) obligation as static. Rather, they would be expected to maintain, review, and update the health standards they established to ensure that they remained consistent with modern medical practice.

If Congress had wished to mandate enforcement of the state standards, it could easily have expressed this intent by drafting § 1396a(a)(9) to require maintenance of health standards at all institutions, rather than simply for participating institutions. As the parties have noted, when the federal government did wish to impose an enforcement obligation on the states with respect to standards for nursing homes, this was plainly expressed. 42 U.S.C.

§ 1396a(a)(26) requires states to have "medical review teams" conduct "periodic inspections" of such facilities. From 1978 to 1994, 42 C.F.R. § 449.33(5)(iii) required states to review the reports of such medical teams "as they reflect on health and safety requirements and as necessary take appropriate action to achieve compliance or withdraw certification." No such survey or compliance obligation has ever been imposed on states with respect to hospitals.

The plaintiffs submitted that it made no sense that Congress simply wished to require state agencies to promulgate standards and update them from time to time without also contemplating their enforcement. The legislative history reveals that Congress did contemplate local enforcement of state standards, but it did not mandate such enforcement. A senate report indicated that Congress wished to encourage states to improve healthcare standards while interfering as little as possible in a state's actual articulation or supervision of those standards. Congressional expectations and hopes do not create unambiguous federal rights enforceable through § 1983.

The overall scheme for review of hospitals participating in Medicare and Medicaid is also at odds with the plaintiffs' claim of a federal right to sue state defendants to compel enforcement of state healthcare standards with respect to hospitals. There is no federal requirement that state agencies ever survey hospitals to assess compliance with their own standards. Instead, the focus of the statute and regulations is on the promulgation and enforcement of federal standards. It is the Secretary of HHS who has sole responsibility for promulgating federal health, safety, and quality standards applicable to hospitals participating in Medicare and Medicaid programs [see 42 U.S.C. § 1395x(e)(9)] and who is charged with enforcing these standards by threatening termination.

The focus of this statutory and regulatory scheme on the responsibilities of the Secretary of HHS for the promulgation and enforcement of federal standards of health care necessarily supports the conclusion that a state agency satisfies its § 1396a(a)(9) obligations to "establish and maintain" local standards for healthcare providers simply by promulgating and then updating these standards. In this way, Congress certainly hoped to encourage better standards of local health care and even their enforcement. Sensitive to differences in regional capabilities, Congress did not create a federal right to any particular state standard or to any level of local enforcement. The core responsibility for ensuring that Medicare and Medicaid providers meet some minimum standard of care remains exclusively with the federal government.

Discussion

1. What was the court's reasoning for not granting the plaintiffs a federal right enforceable through 42 U.S.C. § 1983 to have the New York State Department of Social Services and the New York State Department of Health take reasonable steps to ensure that hospitals operating as Medicaid providers comply with state standards of operation?
2. What are the implications for hospitals that lose their accreditation?

TJC Reports: Privileged Communications

Citation: *Humana Hosp. Corp. v. Spears-Petersen*, 867 S.W.2d 858 (Tex. Ct. App. 1993)

The underlying suit in this petition involved a plaintiff, Ms. Garcia, who was scheduled to undergo an epidural steroid injection but was administered a lumbar epidural steroid injection instead by the defendant, Dr. Garg. The plaintiff sued Dr. Garg on the basis of negligence, lack of informed consent, battery, and fraud. She also sued Humana Hospital Corporation (Humana) for negligence in credentialing, supervising, and monitoring Dr. Garg's clinical privileges. The plaintiff's attorney requested documents from Humana, including reports prepared by TJC.

TJC is a voluntary organization that surveys various healthcare organizations for the purpose of accreditation. The organization's governing body consists of members representing such organizations as the American Medical Association, the American College of Physicians, and the American Hospital Association.

Humana objected to releasing TJC reports and filed for a protective order preventing disclosure. TJC reports contained recommendations describing the hospital's noncompliance with certain of its published standards. Humana argued that TJC reports are privileged information under Texas statute. Under Texas law, the records and proceedings of a medical committee are considered confidential and are not subject to a court subpoena. The plaintiff argued that TJC is not a medical committee as defined in the Texas statute. The hospital's chief operating officer, Mr. Williams, testified that TJC surveys and accredits hospitals across the country. The accreditation is voluntary, and the hospital chooses to have the accreditation survey. During the survey, TJC looks at certain standards it has developed for hospitals to abide by in maintaining quality care. The hospital's executive committee is charged in its bylaws with keeping abreast of the accreditation process. Humana argued that release of TJC's recommendations would do more than "chill" the effectiveness of such accreditation—no prudent hospital would discuss or release any information to TJC knowing that it could be used against it in malpractice suits. Id. at 861. Humana argued further that even if the information was privileged, it had already been disclosed to a third party, the hospital, thus waiving its rights to nondisclosure. The trial court denied Humana's motion for a protective order that, if granted, would have permitted it to withhold from discovery any information pertaining to credentialing, monitoring, or supervision practices of the hospital regarding its physicians. Humana appealed.

Issue

Were TJC Accreditation reports considered privileged?

Holding

The Court of Appeals of Texas held that the accreditation reports were privileged because (1) TJC was a "joint committee" as created by statute creating a privilege from discovery for hospital review committee deliberations, (2) the disclosure of TJC's reports to the hospital did not result in waiver of the privilege, and (3) the reports reflected a deliberative process by TJC and were therefore privileged.

Reason

The purpose of privileged communications is to encourage open and thorough review of a hospital's medical staff and operations of a hospital with the objective of improving the delivery of patient care. The plaintiff argued that TJC is not a medical committee as defined in the Texas statute. The court of appeals found that

the determinative factor is not whether the entity is known as a "committee," or a "commission," or by any other particular term, but whether it is organized for the purposes contemplated by the statute and case law. We think it is clear from the evidence we have detailed that the Joint Commission is a joint committee made up of representatives of various medical organizations and thus fits within the statutory definition. . . . Further, it is organized, as are the various in-house medical committees that indisputably come within the statute, for the laudable purposes of improving patient care. Both the statute and case law recognize that the open, thorough, and uninhibited review that is required for such committees to achieve their purpose can only be realized if the deliberations of the committee remain confidential. Id. at 862.

As to TJC's disclosing its report to the hospital, the

only disclosure . . . was to the hospital as the intended beneficiary of the committee's findings. The only disclosure made to the outside world was the accreditation certificate, which merely declares that the hospital has been awarded accreditation by the Joint Commission. Id. at 862.

Discussion

1. How might TJC's new "public disclosure policy" to make available certain information to the public affect the "privilege" of other information surrounding the accreditation process (e.g., interviews, notes, minutes, and reports)?
2. Does privilege from discovery extend to all documents maintained in the normal course of business?

Failure to Report Patient Incident

Citation: *Westin v. Shalala*, 845 F. Supp. 1446 (D. Kan. 1994)

Facts

On December 17, 1984, Ms. Grundmeier, a patient in a nursing facility, was found unconscious and wedged between the mattress and the bedrail in her room. After emergency resuscitation, she was airlifted to a hospital, where she died later that same day.

On November 18, 1985, a grand jury convened and returned an indictment against Ms. Westin in her capacity as the nursing facility's administrator. The indictment charged Ms. Westin with one felony and four misdemeanors.

The Colorado Department of Health, Pursuant to the Code of Colorado

Regulations at 6 CCR 1011-1 ch. V § 4.5.4, require that

. . . accidents and incidents resulting in possible patient injury shall be reported on special report forms. The report shall include date, time, and place of incident; circumstances of the occurrence; signature of witness; time doctor was notified; physician's report; and signature of person making the report. A copy of the report shall be filed in the patient's medical record.

Despite these requirements, no incident report was prepared.

On March 13, 1990, upon motion of the district attorney, the court dismissed the case against Ms. Westin. On May 24, 1991, the Inspector General notified Ms. Westin that she was going to be excluded for 5 years from participation in Medicare and any state healthcare program because of her conviction of a criminal offense relating to the neglect or abuse of patients. Ms. Westin appealed the Inspector General's decision to the Department of HHS, Departmental Appeals Board (DAB), and an administrative law judge (ALJ) sustained the exclusion imposed. Ms. Westin appealed, and the DAB, Appellate Division, affirmed the ALJ's decision. Ms. Westin appealed Appellate Division's decision, claiming there was not sufficient evidence to support the exclusion of her from participating in the Medicare program.

Issue

Was there substantial evidence to support an order excluding Ms. Westin from participation in the Medicare program?

Holding

The United States District Court for the District of Kansas held that there was substantial evidence to support an order excluding Ms. Westin from participation in the Medicare program.

Reason

There was no requirement that the Secretary of HHS demonstrate that actual neglect or abuse of patients occurred, nor was there a requirement that the individual or entity be convicted of an actual offense of patient neglect or abuse. Under Colorado law, Ms. Westin, as an administrator of a nursing home, was required to (1) report all accidents and injuries "resulting in possible patient injury" to the Colorado Department of Health, and (2) file a copy of that report in the patient's medical record. The evidence was clear from the record that the conviction for failing to report the incident occurred while Ms. Grundmeier was a patient at the nursing facility, and that the conviction was connected to the medical services the nursing facility and its employees provided to Ms. Grundmeier. Id. at 1452.

Discussion

1. Do you believe the court was too harsh in its decision to exclude the administrator of the nursing facility from participating in the Medicare program for a period of 5 years? Explain.

2. Why have statutes been enacted that require the reporting of accidents and incidents that result in patient injuries?

Breaking State Law—Administering Nitrous Oxide

Citation: *Lowenberg v. Sobol*, 594 N.Y.S.2d 874 (N.Y. App. Div. 1993)

Facts

This case arises from a complaint by a dental hygienist against a former employer, Lowenberg and Lowenberg Corporation. The dental hygienist alleged that the defendant allowed the dental hygienists to administer nitrous oxide to patients. Under state law, dental hygienists may not administer nitrous oxide. The Department of Education's Office of Professional Discipline investigated the complaint by using an undercover investigator. The investigator made an appointment for teeth cleaning. At the time of her appointment, she requested that nitrous oxide be administered. Agreeing to the investigator's request, the dental hygienist administered the nitrous oxide. After the procedure was completed, the investigator paid her bill and left the office. There were no notations in the patient's chart indicating that she had been administered nitrous oxide.

The hearing panel found the dental hygienist guilty of administering nitrous oxide without being properly licensed. In addition, the hearing panel found that the dental hygienist had failed to accurately record on the patient's chart that she had administered nitrous oxide. Lowenberg and Lowenberg Corporation were reprimanded and fined $750 each. The plaintiffs/petitioners, the dental hygienist and Lowenberg and Lowenberg, Corporation commenced proceedings for review of the determination.

Issue

Was there sufficient evidence to support a determination that the petitioners engaged in professional misconduct?

Holding

The New York Supreme Court, Appellate Division, held that the investigator's report provided sufficient evidence to support the hearing panel's determination that the petitioners had committed professional misconduct by permitting an unlicensed individual to administer nitrous oxide.

Reason

The Lowenberg's's actual knowledge of the hygienist's illegal conduct is not a prerequisite to a finding of misconduct based on a failure to supervise. There is adequate support in the record to support a finding that the Lowenberg's conduct was such that it could reasonably be said that he permitted the dental hygienist to perform acts she was not licensed to perform.

Discussion

1. What issues does this case raise for healthcare organizations that fail to provide properly licensed personnel in patient care settings, as required by law (e.g., the availability of registered nurses on nursing units)?
2. Do you agree that there was sufficient evidence to support a determination of professional misconduct?

Code Violation and Revocation of License

Citation: *Henley v. Alabama Bd. of Nursing*, 607 So.2d 56 (Ala. Civ. App. 1992)

Facts

A registered nurse sought review of a decision by the State Board of Nursing revoking her license. The board filed a complaint against the nurse alleging that she had violated Ala. Code 1975, § 34-21-25 and § 610-X-8-.05(c)(d) (e) of the Alabama Board of Nursing Administrative Code. These provisions allow the revocation of a nursing license if (1) the licensee is found unfit or incompetent because of the use of alcohol or is addicted to the use of habit-forming drugs to such an extent as to render the licensee unsafe or unreliable; (2) the licensee is mentally incompetent; or (3) the licensee is guilty of unprofessional conduct of a character likely to deceive, defraud, or injure the public in matters pertaining to health care. This complaint was filed after the nurse was subjected to a series of arrests beginning in November 1986, when she was arrested and charged with disorderly conduct and public intoxication.

A hearing officer reviewed the evidence of the allegations and recommended revocation of the nurse's license. The hearing officer's findings of fact and conclusions of law were adapted by the board, and the nurse's license was revoked. That decision was appealed to the trial court, which upheld the decision of the board. The nurse appealed pro se, claiming the evidence did not support revocation of her license.

Issue

Did the evidence of the nurse's arrests and conviction for disorderly conduct and public intoxication support revocation of her license, absent evidence from a treating physician regarding her competence?

Finding

The Alabama Court of Civil Appeals found that the evidence of the nurse's arrests and conviction for disorderly conduct and public intoxication supported revocation of her license, absent evidence from a treating physician regarding her competence.

Reason

Appellate review of administrative actions is limited to determinations of "whether the agency acted within the powers conferred upon it by law and the constitution, whether its decision is supported by substantial evidence, and whether the agency's decision is reasonable and not arbitrary." *Alabama Bd. of Nursing v. Herrick*, 454 So.2d 1041, 1043 (Ala. Civ. App. 1984). The allegations were that the nurse suffered from alcohol addiction and mental incompetency, which rendered her incompetent to assume all of the responsibilities of the practice of nursing. The record contained substantial evidence supporting those allegations, and the nurse presented nothing to sufficiently rebut them.

Discussion

1. What other alternatives might the hospital consider in its disciplinary process?
2. Do you agree with the court's decision? Explain.

NOTES

1. http://hospitalcompare.hhs.gov/%28S%28pvan5rfwa0sta1iajui30h45%29%29/staticpages/help/hospital-glossary.aspx?Choice=D
2. http://www.kaiserhealthnews.org/Stories/2011/February/24/maryland-hospitals-infection-control.aspx
3. https://www.cms.gov/CFCsAndCoPs/
4. http://www.dnv.com/industry/healthcare/
5. http://www.jointcommission.org/assets/1/18/Joint_Commission_History_20111.PDF

chapter two

Communications and Information Management

My words fly up, my thoughts remain below:
Words without thoughts never to heaven go.

William Shakespeare, English Dramatist & Poet (*1564–1616*), Hamlet, *Act 3 Scene 3*

Communication is the exchange of thoughts, messages, or information as by speech, signals, writing, or behavior. It is the art and technique of using words effectively to impart information or ideas.[1] The process of communication includes both verbal and nonverbal messages. Communication requires a sender, a message, and an intended recipient, the receiver.

Communications can be transmitted verbally through words, which are the tools of thought. The more words you thoroughly understand, the more effectively you can articulate your thoughts and ideas to other people. The sender of information can also transmit a message through body language, posture, gestures, facial expressions, and eye contact. Clothing styles, hairstyles, and tone of voice are forms of nonverbal communication. Nonverbal communication has been called the *silent language* and plays a key role in day-to-day life from, for example, employment relationships to romantic gestures. During face-to-face communication, body language and the tone of one's voice play a significant role, and they may have greater impact on the listener than the intended content of spoken words.

The problems of effective communication have existed since the creation of the first man and woman. Just as Eve trusted her first impression regarding the serpent's temptation that eating the fruit of a certain tree would make her and Adam "as gods, knowing good and evil" (Genesis 3:1–24), each person often accepts first impressions as reality. It takes time for individuals to understand one another, and it seems that few are willing to make that commitment.

Both managers and employees tend to perceive each new experience as reinforcing preconceived notions and biases and, at the same time, screening out those things that do not strengthen their ideas or individual conceptions of the real world. There is a tendency to make value judgments from one's own perspective and to evaluate all new knowledge according to its positive or negative impact on preconceived beliefs.

Barriers to successful communication include *message overload*, which can occur when a person receives too many messages at the same time. Employees, for example, may spill out to a manager those things that have been bothering them for weeks or even years during a conversation. It is important the manager focus on one issue at a time and keep the conversation on track. Employees often need reassurance that the manager understands the employees have other concerns that will be heard—not forgotten or ignored—and worked out. Managers who develop a trust relationship with their employees will be more able to keep conversations in focus. Effective communication requires that one take the time to clearly communicate his or her thoughts in order to save time later having to clear up misunderstandings.

The process of communication is more difficult in multilingual and multicultural environments. A simple whistle may be a gesture of approval in one culture, whereas it may be a sign of disapproval in another. The various dialects and semantic differences within a given language further complicate the process of meaningful communication.

The sender's personal filters and the receiver's personal filters may vary based on different religious beliefs, regional traditions, cultures, gender, race, and more, which may alter the intended meaning of the message. Barriers to effective communication include the *noise interferences* (1) environmental (e.g., disruption of communication by a barking dog); (2) physiological-impairment (e.g., deafness, blindness, pain); (3) semantic (e.g., "coke" could refer to coal, cocaine, or a certain cola); (4) syntactical (e.g., mistakes in grammar); (5) organizational (e.g., corporate policies on grievance procedures that differ with the employee handbooks); (6) cultural (e.g., stereotyping the followers of a particular religion because of extremists); and (7) psychological (e.g., stress, fear, anger, or sadness that may cause someone to lose focus in the moment and thus distort effective communications).

The American Academy on Communications in Healthcare provides programs for helping caregivers improve communications among one another and among themselves, patients, and family.

It's all about communication. And relationships.

Whether you are an RN or the CEO of a health system, a practicing physician or a first-year doctoring course teacher, a researcher or a student, a patient or a caregiver, you know that communication is the key to exceptional patient care.

For more than 30 years, the American Academy on Communication in Healthcare (AACH) has been in the forefront of research, teaching relationship-centered healthcare communication.

If you are looking for ways to improve patient safety, interdisciplinary teamwork, patient satisfaction scores, or just want to work on individual communication skills, AACH can help.

AACH improves health care through education, research, and practice that focuses on communication and relationships with patients, families, and healthcare teams.

For more research information into improving communications in health care refer to the AACH website http://www.aachonline.org/.

Words convey our thoughts to others. Our ears hear varying sounds and our brains translate them into meanings or thoughts. The written word is only a symbol to the eye of the spoken word heard by the ear. The spoken word dies as soon as it is spoken; but the written word remains for others to see and interpret. Many words suggest more than they literally mean. Think of the associations called up in one's mind by the word "home." It can remind us of both happy and sad moments.

It is through words that we communicate our thoughts and stir our emotions. Consider the following quote when thinking of the power of words, while each person looks inwardly into himself or herself:

I am Me. In all the world, there is no one else exactly like me. Everything that comes out of me is authentically mine, because I alone chose it—I own everything about me: my body, my feelings, my mouth, my voice, all my actions, whether they be to others or myself. I own my fantasies, my dreams, my hopes, my fears. I own my triumphs and successes, all my failures and mistakes. Because I own all of me, I can become intimately acquainted with me. By so doing, I can love me and be friendly with all my parts. I know there are aspects about myself that puzzle me, and other aspects that I do not know—but as long as I am friendly and loving to myself, I can courageously and hopefully look for solutions to the puzzles and ways to find out more about me. However I look and sound, whatever I say and do, and whatever I think and feel at a given moment in time is authentically me. If later some parts of how I looked, sounded, thought, and felt turned out to be unfitting, I can discard that which is unfitting, keep the rest, and invent something new for that which I discarded. I can see, hear, feel, think, say, and do. I have the tools to survive, to be close to others, to be productive, and to make sense and order out of the world of people and things outside of me. I own me, and therefore, I can engineer me. I am me and I am Okay.

Virginia Satir, American Psychologist and Educator *(1916–1988)*

E-mails have become a major means of communication, but they often seem "flat" without tone-of-voice and timing cues and do not adequately transfer the intent of the communication. Telephone conference calls are also at a disadvantage (unless those calls include video linkup), because important body language cues are missing between/among the parties on the line. Direct verbal communications are the most effective way to communicate with others.

For good or ill, your conversation is your advertisement. Every time you open your mouth, you let men look into your mind. Do they see it well- clothed, neat, businesslike?

Bruce Barton, American Author and Politician *(1886–1967)*

The following *closet drama* should help the reader better understand communications and the real world of working relationships. It is anticipated that legal and ethical issues will be applied here. Many professionals, regardless of their field of training, will undoubtedly face similar issues during their career. This drama ends with a variety of thought-provoking questions.

Leadership Fails the Communications Test

Organizational leadership must develop a strategy for effectively communicating with managers and employees on a continuing basis. Communication is an ongoing process and not a one-time campaign.

Gp

Jack, a nurse at Community Hospital, had exercised his right to appeal a decision of his manager and the human resources department. Level III of the appeal process allowed for a meeting with the hospital's Vice President of Operations, and it did so at a hospital that touted the importance of communications between employees and management. Although Jack had reached the third level of his appeal, the human resources director stated that the VP would not be available to meet directly with the nurse but would be available to conduct a conference call with him on the phone, to which Jack reluctantly agreed (not that he had much of a choice).

Body language, tone of voice, background noise that included other unknown listeners, and the drawn out appeal process served only to frustrate Jack. *The appeal process and the hospital's management team appeared to be window dressing to Jack.*

The final step in the process allowed for Jack to take his appeal to the CEO of the hospital. The CEO was as untimely in responding to the appeal as other managers involved in the appeal process had been. Ultimately, the CEO refused to meet with Jack, even though the two men had previously met on a more personal basis in Los Angeles.

The remaining events of Jack's grievance are presented next in conversational form.

Shirley: Jack, you said that you never received a copy of the Grievance Policy. In one of our conversations, I indicated that you could find the policy on our dedicated website. For your convenience, I have printed a copy for you.

Jack: I was referred to the online employee handbook for information regarding the grievance procedure. The online copy of the handbook is dated January 2011. During our conference call you stated that you believed it to be out of date. You now provide me with a copy of "Grievance Process" that was effective November 2005. Which of the two documents is in effect?

Shirley: Jack, official policy always takes precedence over the handbook. We have had some technical issues with the handbook in that when we update one section, other sections revert back to older editions. I am not sure if this is human error or technology.

Jack: Computers don't edit handbooks. My email from my manager referred me to the "Employee Handbook," which was signed with a letter by the CEO to employees. It did not mention anything about a policy. Actually, you remain out of compliance even with the policy. The grievance policy to which you are referring provides "Informal Process" steps, which you failed to follow.

Shirley: What are you talking about?

Jack: The policy states in Step I of the grievance process that the manager is to meet with the employee within 5 working days following receipt of notification of a grievance. It also provides that the employee making the grievance has a right to appear before a committee of his or her peers to explain his or her grievance and obtain a recommendation from the committee as to any right or wrong committed by the hospital. That never happened! So you were out of compliance with your own policy.

Shirley: Well, it is your responsibility to follow hospital policy.

Jack: This should not be an adversarial process. As HR director, one would expect that you would have helped guide me, the employee, and kept the appeal process on course. Explaining to me 5 months into the grievance that I was not in compliance with policy was not a good-faith gesture. Your failure has served only to cause a rift between senior management and myself. No one seems to want to come forward and accept responsibility for not leading. We call it leadership. Leaders lead, they do not sit back and watch an employee follow a wrong path for 5 months.

Shirley: Well it is up to you to follow the policy.

Jack: Then if I was following the wrong policy, why did you allow me to proceed under the wrong grievance policy?

Shirley: Well, ugh.

Jack: That policy also provides that immediately after the discussion with the manager, the employee is then provided with a written response. As you know I have been requesting the written response, as was promised months ago. Further, the written information outlined as a requirement in your policy is required to be provided.

Shirley: Well, we never had a grievance like this before.

Jack: Wow, I wonder why? By the way, don't you think employees should receive clarification when discrepancies exist between hospital policy and what appears in the employee handbook? Employees should understand that you intend policy to take precedence over the handbook. I would suggest that you pull the handbook off line until such time as you can match it up with policy.

Shirley: Well, I will be sure this is addressed.

Jack: This grievance could have been handled with transparency and fairness from the beginning. I still remain hopeful that, going forward, apologies will be forthcoming from the managers and that this grievance will be handled in accordance with the purpose of the policy which states, "To provide employees with a formal process for the fair review and equitable resolution of employment concerns."

Shirley: Earlier this week, I received your request to forward your grievance information to the CEO. I will give him a package on Monday and will ask him, at that time, approximately when his review will be completed. Meanwhile, I will place you on an unpaid leave of absence until this issue is resolved.

Jack: I would assume that you would not threaten me with a retaliatory action by placing me at this time on an unpaid leave of absence. It sounds as though you are being presumptuous in knowing the CEO's response. You have given yourselves months to conduct a mysterious investigation, and now, you cannot wait for the CEO's decision regarding my grievance and want to place me on an unpaid leave of absence.

Shirley: Well, you should have followed the grievance policy procedure.

Jack: I think we are traveling in circles at this point. So you take no responsibility for failing to assure that the grievance process was on track?

Shirley: I think that I already answered that question.

Jack: As you know, this is the second time that HR, managers, in-house counsel, the compliance officer, and outside counsel have wrongfully advised the CEO. As you recall, after your incorrect advice to the CEO, it took the Department of Labor to correct your wrong when you financially penalized me for taking Family Medical Leave. I await the CEO's response to my grievance.

[In the meantime, Jack speaks with Frank, a CEO from another hospital, in New York City.]

Frank: Hey Jack, how is it going?

Jack: I am fine.

Frank: I can't stop thinking about the shabby treatment you have been getting from the hospital. I sure hope that something good will come of all this. They certainly do know how to fabricate a storyline. Sounds like a trumped-up nonissue that became an issue, and as the snowball ran down hill, they had to cover-up their mistakes to protect their jobs. Unfortunately, you became the victim. I think they became obsessed with defending their actions.

[Four weeks later, Jack receives a follow-up communication from Shirley.]

Shirley: The CEO has requested that I communicate his decision regarding your grievance, as he decided it is not necessary to speak with you. He confers with the Vice President's decision. As you know, they are both new to the hospital and, therefore, had to rely on our decisions.*

The playwright who wrote this closet drama remains anonymous and retains the rights of ownership of the information contained herein.

Discussion

1. Based on the facts presented, describe how you would have handled Jack's grievance.
2. Was the grievance process an illusion? Did leadership merely go through the motions of a grievance? Was it somewhat like advertising a position when you already know whom you are going to pick? Is this an example of *don't confuse me with the facts—I've already had others make up my mind*? Discuss your answer.
3. Discuss the communication issues in this case.

The key to success in management is the ability to understand, and to respond appropriately to, communications. The communication of thoughts and ideas are made possible by a common language. Although the spoken word is not the only method of conveying a thought or idea, it is the most useful, sophisticated method. Human beings are the only mammals that have developed the ability to communicate by spoken language. Can you imagine how difficult it would be if a manager and employee had to act out a message, as do certain species of bees, by means of a complex dance to describe the location of nearby nectar?

The damage that can result from unskilled communications is incalculable, and *the supervisor may find that the poor communication experience with one employee is compounded by its effect on other employees.* As noted by Patrick Delany, "Think all you speak, but speak not all you think. Thoughts are your own; your words are so no more."[2]

Figure 2-1 is a model of the *process of communication* by way of formation, transmission, and translation between two persons. The addition of multiple personalities in group conversations can give rise to an exponential growth in the distortion factor. The reader should review the model carefully to obtain a general understanding of the complex nature of the communication process.

The development of one's character depends on many lifetime influences (e.g., language, education, religion, past and present experiences, culture, environment, work, and physical traits) as presented in Figure 2-1.

There are 16 selected, individual, personality and ability traits listed in the figure, which describes certain characteristics of a communicator and a receiver at stated times in their lives. The figure illustrates how each individual has developed each particular trait; for example, the communicator is an introvert and the receiver is an extrovert. The percentiles at the top of the columns indicate the degree to which each person in the communication process has developed a specific trait.

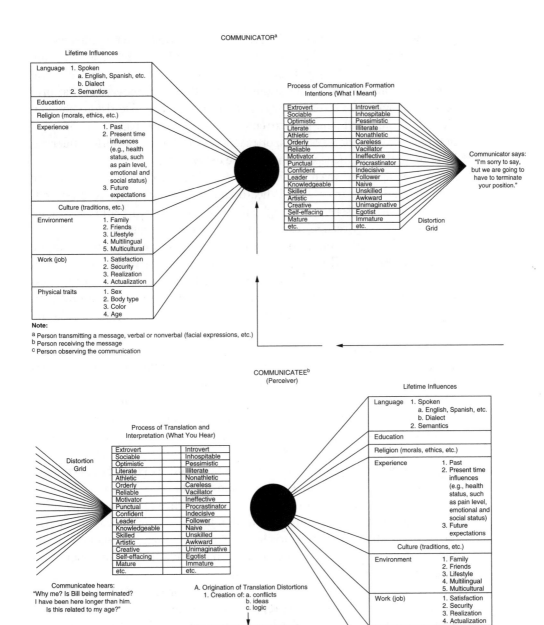

Figure 2-1 The Process of Communication

It should be noted that ability and personality traits are not independent of one another, illustrated by the distortion grid in Figure 2-1. The distortion grid represents a melting pot for an individual's wants, needs, and expectations. The interaction of the various traits within each individual that processes and acts on a given message at a given time can give rise to conflict, ideas, logic, and so forth. It is extremely important each party to a conversation realizes that one's response or reactions will be significantly influenced by both lifetime influences and recent life experiences.

A message conceived of, and conveyed by, the communicator can be somewhat different from what is heard and understood by the receiver and/or a third-party observer, although an individual observing a two-way conversation generally recognizes more readily what message each party to the conversation is attempting to convey. That varying interpretations can be made of a transmitted message illustrates the need for feedback, which in turn can be useful in developing a framework for understanding the message. Without such a framework, problem solving becomes more difficult due to intentional or unintentional distortions that can occur during the communication process.

Managers who do not provide a setting for feedback are providing, instead, an environment for unmotivated and disgruntled staff. As one studies the communication model, it quickly becomes evident that there are thousands of factors affecting each individual's behavior and communication.

Each party in a conversation should request clarification when he or she is not sure of the true intent of the message conveyed. Failure to request clarification can lead to misunderstandings and inappropriate actions.

Managers should provide a setting for both informal and formal communications, and each party in a conversation should be put at ease. The manager should remember that the stress factor present in a given conversation causes a proportionate rise in the distortion factor. If a message is emotional, the manager should take time to clear the air. One's ability to communicate with the manager is certainly much easier in a sympathetic setting than in an antagonistic setting.

If a message is not clear to the manager, he or she should request that the message be rephrased. The rephrased message may provide clarity and perhaps even convey a completely different meaning than what the unclear original message seemed to imply. The manager, to reassure the employee that the message is clearly understood, should repeat back to the employee the question raised or comment made.

Don't Let Hospitals Make You Sick

The problem is not that we have an epidemic of negligent doctors. Rather, it's that the healthcare system has grown so complicated that there is a greater chance than ever of things falling through the cracks.

Another problem is that hospitals produce massive amounts of data including lab and X-ray reports, medication lists, doctors' orders, and dietary restrictions. It is easier than ever for critical communications to get lost, and hospitals often don't have thorough backup systems.

Dr. Ranit Mishori, The Washington Post, [Parade Magazine], *February 8, 2009*

Communications: Documentation Sparse and Contradictory

Citation: *Feeney v. New England Med. Ctr. Inc.,* 615 N.E.2d 585 (Mass. App. Ct. 1993)

Facts

The plaintiff, an administrator, alleging that the death of his son was caused by medical malpractice, commenced this action against the emergency department physician, the nurse on duty, and the hospital.

On December 1, 1987, at 10:16 p.m., an ambulance team of the Boston Department of Health and Hospitals found 26-year-old Mr. Feeney intoxicated, sitting on a street corner in South Boston. Mr. Feeney admitted to alcohol abuse but denied that he used drugs. He was physically and verbally combative and had trouble walking and speaking intelligibly. His condition interfered with the team's conducting an examination of him, so his vital signs were not taken.

At 10:45 p.m. Mr. Feeney was picked up by the ambulance and arrived at the hospital. No observer could doubt that the patient was highly intoxicated with alcohol. The autopsy report in fact revealed an ethyl alcohol blood level of 0.39%, a very dangerous condition. A physician or nurse could readily recognize a grave risk to the patient through depression of the respiratory system: "in the short run, the systemic effects [of the ingestion of ethanol] with the potential for the greatest negative outcome involves depression of the respiratory system." Id. at 586–587.

The documentation for the period between 10:45 p.m. and 11:30 p.m. was *"sparse and contradictory,"* as stated by Dr. McGoey, one of the experts. Id. at 587. The next entry on the emergency department record after 10:45 p.m.

is at 11:30 p.m., made when the patient was brought to the examining room. He was then without respiration and was cyanotic with his pupils fixed and dilated. On the physician documentation record, in which the emergency department physician wrote out the course of the case to the end, he reported (secondhand) that a nurse returned 20 minutes after 10:45 p.m. and found the patient unresponsive and without respiration.

The record goes on to report that the patient was pronounced dead after about 30 minutes of "code." If (referring to the emergency department record) the nurse returned to the patient at 11:30 p.m., then, inferentially, the patient had not been monitored for 45 minutes. On the other hand, if (referring to the physician documentation record) the patient was seen at 11:05 p.m., there was room for the inference that a lapse of 25 minutes intervened between that visit and the commencement of "code." An expert suggested that the former was the "more probable scenario." On either basis, a gap appears, needing explanation. Id. at 587.

A Suffolk County medical tribunal found the administrator's offer of proof insufficient and entered judgment against the physician, dismissing his complaint. The administrator appealed.

Issue

Was the offer of proof made by the administrator sufficient to support a medical malpractice action against the hospital and the emergency department physician and nurse?

Holding

The Appeals Court of Massachusetts held that the administrator's offer of proof was sufficient to sustain his cause of action.

Reason

The minimum standard of care for nursing required monitoring the respiratory rate of the patient every 15 minutes; this "would more likely have permitted the nursing staff to observe changes in the patient's breathing patterns and/or the onset of respiratory arrest." As for the emergency department physician, he failed to evaluate the patient and to initiate care within the first few minutes of Mr. Feeney's entry into the emergency facility. The emergency physician had an obligation to determine who was waiting for physician care and how critical was the need for that care. Had the standards been maintained, respiratory arrest might have been averted.

According to the autopsy report, respiratory arrest was the sole cause of death.

The failure to provide adequate care could be rationally attributed to the staff nurse assigned to the area in which the patient lay, as well as to the physicians in charge. The hospital was implicated on the basis of the acts or omission of its staff.

Discussion

1. Do you agree with the court's finding?
2. What effect, if any, might cases of this sort have on the care being rendered in emergency departments?

Communications: Failure to Communicate with the Patient

Citation: *Follett v. Davis*, 636 N.E.2d 1282 (Ind. Ct. App. 1994)

In 1987, the plaintiff, Ms. Follett, had her first office visit with Dr. Davis. In the spring of 1988, Ms. Follett discovered a lump in her right breast and made an appointment to see Dr. Davis. The clinic had no record of her appointment. The clinic's employees directed her to radiology for a mammogram. Neither Dr. Davis, nor any other physician at the clinic, offered Ms. Follett an examination. In addition, she was not scheduled for a physician's examination as a follow-up to the mammogram. A technician examined Ms. Follett's breast and confirmed the presence of a lump in her right breast. After the mammogram, clinic employees told her that she would hear from Dr. Davis if there were any problem with her mammogram.

The radiologist explained in his deposition that the mammogram was not normal. Dr. Davis received and reviewed the mammogram report and considered it to be negative for malignancy. He did not know of the new breast lump because none of the clinic employees had informed him about it. The clinic, including Dr. Davis, never contacted Ms. Follett about her lump or the mammogram. On April 6, 1990, Ms. Follett called the clinic and was told that there was nothing to worry about unless she heard from Dr. Davis. On September 24, 1990, Ms. Follett returned to the clinic after she had developed pain associated with that same lump. A mammogram performed on that day gave results consistent with cancer. Three days later, Dr. Davis made an appointment for Ms. Follett with a clinic surgeon for a biopsy and treatment. She kept her appointment with the surgeon. Nevertheless, this was her last visit with the clinic, as she subsequently transferred her care to other physicians.

In October 1990, the biopsy confirmed the diagnosis of cancer. Ms. Follett filed a lawsuit, and the superior court, in a medical malpractice action, entered summary judgment for the physician and clinic on the grounds that the statute of limitations had tolled, and the patient appealed.

Issue

Was the doctrine of continuing wrong applicable so that the period of limitations did not begin to run until the patient's last visit to the clinic?

Holding

The Court of Appeals of Indiana held that the doctrine of continuing wrong was applicable so that the period of limitations did not begin to run until the patient's last visit to the clinic.

Reason

Ms. Follett claimed the wrong she suffered was a continuing wrong. The doctrine of continuing wrong is simply a legal concept used to define when an act, omission, or neglect took place. The statutory period of limitations begins to run at the end of the continuing wrongful act. The evidence shows that, after she had found a lump in her breast, she went to Dr. Davis, her regular obstetrician/gynecologist, and the clinic for aid. Dr. Davis and the clinic, through the clinic's employees and agents, undertook to treat her ailment. That undertaking ended only when the clinic's surgeon performed the biopsy and therefore was continuous in nature. When the sole claim of medical malpractice is a failure to diagnose, the omission cannot as a matter of law extend beyond the time the physician rendered a diagnosis. When Ms. Follett last visited Dr. Davis on September 24, 1990, and last visited the clinic on September 27, 1990, the evidence most favorable to her demonstrated that, had clinic procedures been followed, Dr. Davis or another doctor at the clinic would have had occasion to diagnose her problem before either of those dates. On August 20, 1992, Ms. Follett timely filed her proposed complaint within 2 years of the last visits to Dr. Davis and the clinic.

Discussion

1. What are the pros and cons as to when the statute of limitations should reasonably begin to run?

2. Do you think all of the 50 states should agree as to when the statute of limitations should begin to toll?

3. What are the communications issues involved in this case?

Communications: Failure to Report Patient's Deteriorating Condition

Citation: *Flores v. Cyborski*, 629 N.E.2d 74 (Ill. App. Ct. 1993)

The patient was admitted to the hospital after having complained of abdominal and lower back pain. She was given tests, after which she was diagnosed as having kidney infection and possible pneumonia. A physician was called in to see the patient. Diagnostic tests were ordered, including blood, sputum, and urine cultures. The physician visited the patient soon after the phone call. The patient complained that she was experiencing chest pain and had a congestive cough. Her white blood count was elevated, which indicated the patient had a possible infection. After studying the results of the patient's tests and chest X-rays, the physician concluded that the patient had lower-lobe pneumonia. He prescribed the broad-spectrum antibiotic Keflin. The next day, the patient said she was feeling better, her lungs sounded better, and her elevated temperature had decreased. Two days later, she told the nurses she was experiencing shooting pains and shortness of breath. She also had a pulse rate of 180, but the nurses did not notify the physician until the patient was in cardiac arrest. She died later that day.

The patient's estate sued the physician for negligence in treating the patient. Dr. Sharp, who was the brother of an associate at the plaintiff's law firm, testified that the defendant had deviated from the standard of care. He stated that the defendant failed to obtain blood gas tests, prescribe an appropriate antibiotic, and prescribe that the antibiotic be administered intravenously. He further testified that the lowering of the patient's temperature was due to the administration of Tylenol, not to an improvement in the patient's condition. The defendant's experts stated that the physician had complied with the applicable standard of care and that the death was unexpected and sudden. Her decreased white blood cell count and the data that had been collected from all who had examined her indicated that she was getting better. The jury returned a verdict for the defendant, and the plaintiff appealed.

Issue

For impeachment purposes, did the court have a right to allow into evidence the testimony regarding the sibling relationship between the plaintiff's expert and attorney during cross-examination?

Holding

The Appellate Court of Illinois affirmed the verdict for the defendant. The court, for impeachment purposes, had a right to allow into evidence the testimony regarding the sibling relationship between the plaintiff's expert and attorney during cross-examination.

Reason

The physician's testimony may have been colored by his relationship with his brother. The jury was correctly permitted to consider that possibility in order to judge the credibility of the physician as a witness.

The issue of whether the nurses' failure to respond to the change in the patient's condition constituted the proximate cause of the patient's death was for the jury to decide. Moreover, there was no evidence that the physician caused the patient's suffering and death.

Discussion

1. Take the position of the defense attorney and explain, giving specific reasons, why the physicians did not breach the applicable standard of care.
2. Discuss what additional evidence would have been helpful to the plaintiff's case.
3. What action should the nurses have taken upon discovering a significant change in the patient's condition?
4. Describe those changes in a patient's condition that would trigger a need to notify a patient's attending physician.
5. What educational processes should an organization have in place to prevent similar incidents from reoccurring?

Communications: Progress Notes and Office Records

Citation: *Dardeau v. Ardoin*, 703 So.2d 695, 97-144 (La. App. 1997)

The plaintiff, Ms. Dardeau, alleges that when she was 28 years old, she came under the care of Dr. Ardoin for routine examinations. She contends that after her first visit with Dr. Ardoin, he recommended and performed radical surgery consisting of a bladder suspension, cystocele repair, rectocele repair, complete hysterectomy, and removal of her ovaries. According to the plaintiff, Dr. Ardoin injured her obturator nerve during the cystocele surgery, and that as a result, she has sustained permanent paralysis in her right leg.

The Louisiana Medical Mutual Insurance Company (LAMMICO) contends that when Ms. Dardeau was first seen by Dr. Ardoin, she complained that coughing, sneezing, jumping, or running caused a loss of urine, and she related a history of a tubal ligation after the birth of her second child. Dr. Ardoin noted a cystocele (or herniation of the bladder), a rectocele (or herniation of the rectum through the vagina), and some uterine descensus (or falling of the uterus). He recommended conservative treatment and advised Ms. Dardeau to return in one month.

According to the defendant, the plaintiff's complaints persisted and Dr. Ardoin recommended diagnostic studies. After review of the diagnostic studies, he suggested surgery to correct the urinary incontinence and to repair the cystocele and rectocele. Dr. Ardoin also recommended a hysterectomy due to the uterine descensus and complaints of dyspareunia (or pain with intercourse) and dysmenorrhea (or painful menstruation). After a discussion of the procedures, the plaintiff executed three consent forms, which were introduced into the record. A second opinion was obtained from Dr. Cantu who agreed with Dr. Ardoin's findings and recommendation for surgery.

After surgery, the plaintiff complained of leg pain. It was determined by the defendant that she suffered from a rare, but known, complication of injury to the obturator nerve. The record reflects that a medical review panel rendered a unanimous opinion that Dr. Ardoin did not breach the standard of care in his treatment of Ms. Dardeau, and that Dr. Ardoin had adequately informed her that serious complications could occur in connection with the surgical procedures. Furthermore, the panel found that Dr. Ardoin recognized the complication early and addressed it appropriately.

The jury concluded that Dr. Ardoin obtained Ms. Dardeau's informed consent prior to surgery; that a reasonable person would have accepted the risk of nerve injury based upon the medical condition of the plaintiff at the time of the surgery; that Dr. Ardoin was not guilty of substandard conduct constituting malpractice; and that the plaintiff's injury was not caused by any substandard conduct on the part of Dr. Ardoin.

Dr. Ardoin passed away prior to trial. The plaintiff complained in brief that the introduction of progress notes or office chart by Dr. Ardoin constituted hearsay evidence. She argued that LAMMICO defended this case on unauthenticated progress notes that claimed to be made by Dr. Ardoin.

Issue

Was there error on the part of the trial court as to the admissibility of the physician's progress notes or office chart?

Holding

The appeals court found no error on the part of the trial court as to the admissibility of the physician's progress notes or office chart and affirmed the jury verdict and the judgment of the trial court.

Reason

The plaintiff's own expert testified that he relied upon Dr. Ardoin's office chart to render his opinion in the case. Ms. Dardeau argues that LAMMICO attempted to introduce Dr. Ardoin's office chart through Ms. Fontenot, Dr. Ardoin's receptionist, who could not provide any of the qualifying circumstances set forth in La. Code Evid. arts. 803 and 804 that could ensure the trustworthiness of these records. More specifically, plaintiff argued that Ms. Fontenot did not have personal knowledge of the information contained in the progress notes and had no recollection of anything in the office chart.

A significant portion of Dr. Ardoin's chart was included in the records of Humana Hospital of Ville Platte, which were introduced at trial without objection. Dr. Ardoin's office chart was admissible because it was created during the course of his treatment of the plaintiff and constituted a record maintained in the course of a regularly conducted business activity [La. Code Evid. art. 803(6)]. Dr. Ardoin's receptionist, Ms. Fontenot, testified at trial that the office chart was created in connection with Dr. Ardoin's business, that the entries in the chart were made at the time of treatment, and that the entries were made by Dr. Ardoin who had personal knowledge of the information in the chart. Ms. Fontenot testified that she never saw any chart being altered or falsified by Dr. Ardoin, nor did Dr. Ardoin request that she alter any office chart. There was no evidence presented by the plaintiff that would indicate that Dr. Ardoin's records were untrustworthy.

Discussion

1. What was the appeals court's reasoning for allowing the physician's progress notes and office records to be admissible as evidence?
2. What is the danger of allowing written records admitted into evidence when the author of such records is not available for cross-examination?
3. What is the danger of not allowing written records to be admitted into evidence when the author of such records is not available for cross-examination?

Communications: Inadequate Record Keeping

Citation: *United States v. Veal*, 23 F.3d 985 (6th Cir. 1994)

Facts

In October 1990, United States Drug Enforcement Administration (DEA) investigators received reports from drug wholesalers that the defendant, Mr. Veal, was making inordinately large purchases of Doriden and Tylenol 4. Doriden, a sleeping medication, and Tylenol 4, a pain medication containing codeine, are Schedule III controlled substances. These drugs have a heroin-like effect when ingested in combination. The combination is commonly referred to in the illegal drug market as "fours and doors." Although a registered pharmacist pays anywhere from four to seven cents a pill of either variety, a single dose of the "fours and doors" combination costs about $20 on the street.

On October 5, 1990, DEA investigators went to the defendant's pharmacy to serve him with a notice of intent to inspect his records, prescriptions, and inventory. The defendant agreed that the agents could perform the inspection 4 days later, at which time he said he would turn over his records. When the agents returned on October 9, 1990, the defendant asked them whether they would be removing the records. The officers answered that the records would be seized only if they were found to contain incriminating evidence. The defendant responded, "So you'll take my records." The officers reiterated that they would only take the records if they were incriminating; the defendant then withdrew his consent to the search, and the officers left the premises. The officers subsequently obtained a search warrant pursuant to which they went through the defendant's pharmacy records. They discovered significant discrepancies between his controlled substance purchases and quantities accounted for. The records also revealed that the defendant had filled numerous phony prescriptions for Doriden and Tylenol 4. Some of the prescriptions bore the name of a fictitious physician, and others bore the names of actual physicians who testified at trial that they had not written the prescriptions.

The defendant was tried on a 13-count indictment. The jury returned a verdict of guilty on six counts and not guilty on the remaining counts. A motion for acquittal or a new trial was denied, and the defendant appealed.

Issue

(1) Did the evidence support a conviction for the possession and illegal distribution of controlled substances? (2) Did the evidence support a conviction

on record-keeping charges? (3) Was there ample evidence to support a finding that the fraudulent character of the prescriptions should have been obvious to the defendant?

Holding

The Court of Appeals for the Sixth Circuit held that (1) the evidence supported a conviction for the possession and illegal distribution of controlled substances, (2) the evidence supported conviction on record-keeping charges, and (3) there was ample evidence to support a finding that the fraudulent character of the prescriptions should have been obvious to the defendant.

Reason

The government established that a fictitious physician issued some prescriptions and that other prescriptions were facially invalid. Several experts testified about the well-known combination of "fours and doors" and stated that any reasonable pharmacist should have been suspicious of prescriptions calling for that combination. A pharmacist acting in good faith would have called to verify the prescriptions, according to the government's evidence, and the defendant did not do so.

The evidence against the defendant was also sufficient to support the finding of guilt on the charges of inadequate record keeping. In order to convict Mr. Veal on these charges, the government was required to show only that the defendant under:

21 U.S.C. §§ 827(a)(3) and 843(a)(4)(A) had not kept a complete and accurate record of each [controlled] substance manufactured, received, sold, delivered, or otherwise disposed of by him....

The evidence introduced at trial included the results of an extensive audit that tended to show that the defendant had failed to account for significant quantities of the controlled substances he handled. The audit assumed the validity of all of the distributions documented by the defendant, and it demonstrated that the defendant had failed to account for 951 Doriden tablets (9% of his total purchases of Doriden during the audit period), nearly 1,600 Tylenol 4 tablets (19% of his total purchases of Tylenol 4 during the audit period), and 3,227 Tylenol 3 tablets (21% of his total Tylenol 3 purchases). The government was not required to prove that the missing tablets were dispensed illegally; what actually happened to those substances had no bearing on the record-keeping charges.

Discussion

1. When a pharmacist is charged with filling invalid prescriptions, what must be proven to sustain a conviction?
2. What are the causes of the wide variety of billing scams committed across the nation?
3. Do you think that the use of generic medications increases or decreases the likelihood of such scams? Explain.

Communications: Alteration of Records

Citation: *Dimora v. Cleveland Clinic Found.*, 683 N.E.2d 1175 (Ohio App. 8 Dist. 1996)

Facts

Ms. Dimora, a 79-year-old woman, was admitted on October 18, 1993, as a patient at the Cleveland Clinic. She had difficulty in ambulating and transferring, requiring an attendant while using a walker. Her condition was noted numerous times on her chart. She was evaluated as high risk for falls.

On November 5, 1993, Ms. Dimora was preparing to be discharged from the clinic. After using the toilet with the assistance of a student nurse, she lost her balance and fell backward. The fall caused a severe bruising to her thorax and resulted in the breaking of five or six ribs. Mrs. Dimora's fall was noted in the nursing notes, and in the discharge summary by the attending physician, who examined her subsequent to the fall. Upon examination, Ms. Dimora was "found to have good strength in all four extremities," was "without pain of movement," and had a "small 5 × 8 cm area" on the right posterior thorax "slightly scraped." The area was noted to be "non-tender with deep palpitation and there was no evidence of crepitus." Ice and lotion were applied to the abraded area. No X-rays were taken at the clinic after the fall, and no further treatment was administered by the clinic. Ms. Dimora's broken ribs were not diagnosed until the following day, when X-rays were taken at Marymount Hospital.

Ms. Dimora's daughter, granddaughter, and caregiver testified that when they arrived at the hospital to pick up Ms. Dimora, she was crying and complaining of pain, and her side was all red. Ms. Dimora's daughter testified that one of the nurses said Ms. Dimora had fallen when she was left alone in the bathroom. The three women each testified that they had difficulty getting Ms. Dimora in and out of the car because she was in so much pain. Both movement and breathing caused Ms. Dimora pain for a few weeks.

Subsequent to this fall, Ms. Dimora required much more care, and she was unable to enjoy many of her former activities.

The plaintiff–appellee Ms. Dimora filed a complaint against defendant–appellant Cleveland Clinic Foundation (the Clinic) alleging that the Clinic negligently provided medical care and treatment for her during her confinement there. Ms. Dimora further claimed punitive damages, alleging that the Clinic and/or its agents and/or employees intentionally falsified her medical records or inaccurately reported her condition to avoid liability for their negligence.

The defendant moved for a directed verdict, claiming that the plaintiff had failed to demonstrate alteration of the record and malice on the part of the Clinic, asserting, therefore, that the claim for punitive damages must fail. The trial court denied this motion. The jury awarded a verdict in favor of Ms. Dimora in the amount of $25,000 for compensatory damages and $25,000 in punitive damages.

Issue

(1) Did the trial court properly determine that reasonable minds could differ on the issue of whether the progress notes and the discharge notes were falsified or inaccurately reported to avoid liability for the medical malpractice or negligence of hospital personnel? (2) Did the trial court err when it denied the appellant's motions for directed verdicts on the appellee's claims for negligence and for punitive damages?

Holding

The trial court properly determined that reasonable minds could differ on the issue of whether the progress notes and the discharge notes were falsified or inaccurately reported to avoid liability for the medical malpractice or negligence of hospital personnel. Therefore, the trial court did not err when it denied the appellant's motions for directed verdicts on the appellee's claims for negligence and for punitive damages.

Reason

The claim of the appellee for punitive damages alleges that the clinic, through its agents and/or employees, intentionally falsified her medical records or inaccurately and improperly reported the fall incident to avoid liability for its medical malpractice or negligence.

In a case involving medical malpractice where liability is determined and compensatory damages are awarded, punitive damages pled in connection with the claim for malpractice may be awarded upon a showing of actual malice, defined as: the intentional alteration, falsification, or destruction of medical records by a physician to avoid liability for his or her medical negligence.

At trial, the testimony presented by witnesses for the appellee indicated that the right side of Ms. Dimora's body was red, bruised, and painful after the fall. Three witnesses testified that Ms. Dimora was crying and in pain approximately 45 minutes after the incident, while she was still in the hospital.

Testimony was offered that broken ribs would be painful upon deep palpation. Pictures were offered into evidence indicating large areas of bruising on Ms. Dimora's body on the day after the event.

Appellant contends that this record accurately reflects the incident. However, the testimony presented by the appellee is in apparent conflict with the description of the incident, the injury, and Ms. Dimora's demeanor. The evidence showed that Ms. Dimora had fallen and broken five or six ribs; yet, upon examination, the physician noted that she was smiling and laughing pleasantly with no pain upon deep palpation of the area. Other testimony indicated that she was in pain and crying. The discrepancy between the written progress notes and the testimony of the witnesses who observed Ms. Dimora was sufficient to raise a question of fact as to the possible falsification of documents by the physician to minimize the nature of the incident and the injury of the patient due to the possible negligence of hospital personnel. The testimony of the witnesses, if believed, would be sufficient to show that the physician falsified the record or intentionally reported the incident inaccurately to avoid liability for the negligent care. Such conduct is the type of intentional and deceptive behavior more indicative of actual malice. If such evidence is believed, the jury could award punitive damages. With the proper caution exercised in instructing the jury as to when punitive damages are proper, the issue of punitive damages should have been submitted to the jury.

The trial court properly determined that reasonable minds could differ on the issue of whether the progress notes and the discharge notes were falsified or inaccurately reported to avoid liability for the medical malpractice or negligence of hospital personnel. Therefore, the trial court did not err when it denied the appellant's motions for directed verdicts on the appellee's claims for negligence and for punitive damages.

Discussion

1. Do you agree with the court's finding? Why?
2. What would you have done differently if you were the hospital? Nurse? Physician?

Communications: Falsification of Records

Citation: *Moskovitz v. Mount Sinai Med. Ctr.*, 635 N.E.2d 331 (Ohio 1994)

Facts

The facts giving rise to this appeal involved the conduct of Dr. Figgie, who failed to timely diagnose and treat a malignant tumor on Mrs. Moskovitz's left leg and altered certain records to conceal the fact that malpractice had occurred.

In 1978, Mrs. Moskovitz was treated by Dr. Gabelman for a tumor on her left leg. The tumor was removed and found to be benign. In 1984, Dr. Gabelman completely and successfully removed a second mass. In 1985, Mrs. Moskovitz was referred to Dr. Figgie, an orthopaedic surgeon, for treatment of a degenerative arthritic condition in her knees. In October 1985, Dr. Figgie performed surgery on Mrs. Moskovitz. Mrs. Moskovitz underwent additional knee surgery performed by Dr. Figgie in May 1986.

On October 2, 1986, Mrs. Moskovitz visited Dr. Figgie's office, complaining of a lump on her leg. Dr. Figgie did not recommend a biopsy of the lesion.

On November 3, Mrs. Moskovitz was admitted to University Hospitals for a right knee revision. Prior to surgery, Mr. Magas, a registered nurse, examined Mrs. Moskovitz. Mr. Magas's written report of the examination, signed by Dr. Figgie, noted the existence of a firm nodule measuring 1 cm × 1 cm on Mrs. Moskovitz's left Achilles tendon. Dr. Figgie performed the right knee revision on November 5. Following surgery, Dr. Balourdas, a resident physician at University Hospitals, examined Mrs. Moskovitz on Dr. Figgie's behalf. A discharge summary prepared by Dr. Balourdas (and signed by Dr. Figgie) noted the existence of a "left Achilles tendon mass, [1] × 1 cm. nodule." The report indicated that the mass had been present for some time.

On November 10, 1987, Dr. Figgie removed the mass. On November 13, the tumor was found to be an epithelioid sarcoma, a rare form of malignant soft-tissue cancer. A bone scan revealed that the cancer had metastasized to Mrs. Moskovitz's shoulder and right femur.

Following the diagnosis of cancer, Mrs. Moskovitz's care was transferred to Dr. Figgie's partner at University Orthopaedic, Dr. Makley, an orthopaedic surgeon specializing in oncology. Dr. Makley received Dr. Figgie's original office chart, which contained seven pages of notes documenting Mrs. Moskovitz's course of treatment from 1985 through November 1987. Dr. Makley thereafter referred Mrs. Moskovitz to radiation therapy at University Hospitals. Apparently, in November 1987, without Dr. Figgie's knowledge, Dr. Makley sent a copy of page 7 of Dr. Figgie's office notes to the radiation department at University Hospitals.

In December 1987, Dr. Figgie, or someone on his behalf, requested that Dr. Makley return Dr. Figgie's office chart pertaining to the care of Mrs. Moskovitz. In December 1987, Dr. Makley was Mrs. Moskovitz's primary treating physician, and Dr. Figgie was no longer directly involved in Mrs. Moskovitz's care and treatment.

Dr. Makley's secretary forwarded the chart to Dr. Figgie's office. Dr. Figgie's secretary then sent a copy of the chart to Dr. Ashenberg, Mrs. Moskovitz's psychologist. Dr. Ashenberg received the copy sometime between December 14 and 18, 1987.

In January 1988, Dr. Makley's secretary requested that Dr. Figgie's office return the chart to Dr. Makley. At this time, it was discovered that the original chart had mysteriously vanished. On October 21, 1988, Mrs. Moskovitz filed a complaint for discovery in the Court of Common Pleas seeking to ascertain information relative to a potential claim for medical malpractice. Mrs. Moskovitz died on December 5, 1988, as a result of the cancer. Prior to her death, her testimony was preserved by way of videotaped deposition.

Dr. Makley, in his January 30, 1989, deposition, produced a copy of page 7 of Dr. Figgie's office chart. That copy was identical to the copy ultimately recovered by the plaintiff's counsel from the radiation department records at University Hospitals. The copy produced by Dr. Makley contained a typewritten entry dated September 21, 1987, which states: "Mrs. Moskovitz comes in today for her evaluation on the radiographs reviewed with Dr. York. He was not impressed that this [the mass on Moskovitz's left leg] was anything other than a benign problem, perhaps a fibroma. We [Figgie and York] will therefore elect to continue to observe." However, the photostatic copy revealed that a line had been drawn through the sentence "We will therefore elect to continue to observe." The copy further revealed that beneath the entry Dr. Figgie had interlineated a handwritten notation: "As she does not want excisional Bx [biopsy] we will observe." The September 21, 1987, entry was followed by a typewritten entry dated September 24, 1987, which states: "I [Figgie] reviewed the X-rays with Dr. York. I discussed the clinical findings with him. We [Figgie and York] felt this to be benign, most likely a fibroma. He [York] said that we could observe and I concur." At some point, Figgie had also added to the September 24, 1987, entry a handwritten notation, "see above," referring to the September 21, 1987, handwritten notation that Mrs. Moskovitz did not want an excisional biopsy. Id. at 336.

Dr. Figgie, at his deposition on March 2, 1989, produced records, including a copy of page 7 of his office chart. As his original chart had been lost in December 1987 or January 1988, Dr. Figgie had this copy made from the copy of the chart that had been sent to Dr. Ashenberg in December 1987. The September 21, 1987, entry in the records produced by Dr. Figgie did not contain the statement "We will therefore elect to continue to observe." Apparently, that sentence had been deleted (whited out) on the original office chart from which Dr. Ashenberg's copy (and, in turn, Dr. Figgie's copy) had been made, in a way that left no indication on the copy that the sentence had been removed from the original records. Id. at 336.

During his deposition, Dr. Figgie maintained that he did not discover the mass on the left Achilles tendon until February 23, 1987, and that Mrs. Moskovitz had continually refused a workup or biopsy.

During discovery, another copy of page 7 of Dr. Figgie's office chart, identical to the copy produced by Dr. Makley during his deposition, was recovered from the radiation department records at University Hospitals, this copy of the record had been received by the radiation department in November 1987, when Dr. Makley referred Mrs. Moskovitz to radiation therapy. It became apparent that the final sentence in the September 21, 1987, entry had been deleted from Dr. Figgie's original office chart sometime between November 1987, when the radiation department obtained a copy of the record, and mid-December 1987, when Dr. Ashenberg received a copy of the record from Dr. Figgie's office. Presumably, that alteration occurred in December 1987 while the original chart was in the possession of Dr. Figgie.

Eventually, Dr. Figgie's entire office chart was reconstructed from copies obtained through discovery. The reconstructed chart contains no indication that a workup or biopsy was recommended by Dr. Figgie and refused by Mrs. Moskovitz at any time prior to August 10, 1987.

In her videotaped deposition, Mrs. Moskovitz claimed that she never refused to have the tumor biopsied. The panel found in favor of all defendants participating in that proceeding with the exception of Dr. Figgie. The panel made the following findings regarding Dr. Figgie:

The jury believed the decedent would have had a very good chance of long-term survival had the tumor been found to be malignant before it exceeded one centimeter in size. The trial court entered judgment in accordance with the jury's verdict.

The court of appeals upheld the finding of liability against Dr. Figgie on the wrongful death and survival claims. The court of appeals found that the appellant was not entitled to punitive damages as a matter of law.

Issue

(1) Is an intentional alteration or destruction of medical records to avoid liability sufficient to show actual malice? (2) Can punitive damages be awarded whether or not the act of altering or destroying records directly causes compensable harm?

Holding

The Supreme Court of Ohio held that the evidence regarding the physician's alteration of the patient's records supported an award of punitive damages, regardless of whether the alteration caused actual harm.

Reason

The jury's award of punitive damages was based on Dr. Figgie's alteration or destruction of medical records. Dr. Figgie's alteration of records was inextricably intertwined with the claims advanced by the appellant for medical malpractice, and the award of compensatory damages on the survival claim formed the necessary predicate for the award of punitive damages based on the alteration of medical records.

The purpose of punitive damages is not to compensate a plaintiff but to punish and deter certain conduct. If the act of altering and destroying records to avoid liability is to be tolerated in our society, the court could think of no better way to encourage it than to hold that punitive damages were not available in this case. Dr. Figgie's conduct of altering records should not go unpunished. The court warned others to refrain from similar conduct through an award of punitive damages.

Dr. Figgie's alteration of records exhibited a total disregard for the law and the rights of Mrs. Moskovitz and her family. Had the copy of page 7 of Dr. Figgie's office chart not been recovered from the radiation department records at University Hospitals, the appellant would have been substantially less likely to succeed in this case. The copy of the chart and other records produced by Dr. Figgie would have tended to exculpate Dr. Figgie for his medical negligence while placing the blame for his failures on Mrs. Moskovitz.

A unanimous panel of arbitrators determined that records were altered with bad motive and that Dr. Figgie was the responsible party. The Supreme

Court believed that the appellate court simply substituted its judgment for that of the jury and, thereby, invaded the province of the finder of fact.

Discussion

1. Do you consider the evidence sufficiently adequate to establish that the surgeon intentionally altered, falsified, or destroyed the patient's medical records to avoid liability for medical negligence? Explain.
2. If you found it necessary to clarify an entry that you made in a patient's medical record, what procedure would you follow?
3. Is the use of correction fluid the preferred way to clarify your entries?

Communications: Charting by Exception Risky Business

Citation: *Lama v. Borras*, 16 F.3d 473 (1st Cir. 1994)

Facts

In 1985, the patient, Mr. Lama, was suffering from back pain. Dr. Alfonso, the patient's family physician, provided some treatment but then referred him to Dr. Borras, a neurosurgeon. Dr. Borras concluded that the patient had a herniated disc and scheduled surgery. Prior to surgery Dr. Borras neither prescribed nor enforced a regimen of absolute bed rest, nor did he offer other key components of conservative treatment.

On April 9, 1986, while operating on the patient, Dr. Borras discovered that the patient had an extruded disc and attempted to remove the extruded material. Either because Dr. Borras failed to remove the offending material or because he operated at the wrong level, the patient's original symptoms returned in full force several days after the operation. Dr. Borras concluded that a second operation was necessary to remedy the recurrence.

On May 15, Dr. Borras operated again on the patient. Dr. Borras did not order pre- or postoperative antibiotics. It is unclear whether the second operation was successful in curing the herniated disc. On May 17, a nurse's note indicated that the bandage covering the patient's surgical wound was "very bloody," a symptom which, according to expert testimony, indicates the possibility of infection. On May 18, the patient was experiencing local pain at the site of the incision, another symptom consistent with an infection. On May 19, the bandage was soiled again. A more complete account of the patient's evolving condition was not available, because the hospital instructed nurses to engage in charting by exception, a system whereby nurses did not record qualitative observations for each of a day's three shifts but, instead, made such notes only when necessary to chronicle important changes in a patient's condition.

On May 21, Dr. Piazza, an attending physician, diagnosed the patient's problem as discitis—an infection of the space between discs—and responded by initiating antibiotic treatment. Mr. Lama was hospitalized for several additional months while undergoing treatment for the infection.

After moving from Puerto Rico to Florida, Mr. Lama filed a tort action in United States District Court for the District of Puerto Rico. While the plaintiff did not claim that the hospital was vicariously liable for any negligence on the part of Dr. Borras, he alleged that the hospital was itself negligent in two respects: (1) failure to prepare, use, and monitor proper medical records; and (2) failure to provide proper hygiene at the hospital premises.

At the close of the plaintiff's case and at the close of all the evidence, the defendants moved for judgment as a matter of law. After the jury returned a verdict awarding plaintiff $600,000 in compensatory damages, the defendants again sought judgment as a matter of law. The district court ruled that the evidence was legally sufficient to support the jury's findings, and an appeal was taken.

Issue

Did the evidence support a jury conclusion that the hospital had been negligent in pursuing a charting by exception policy in the postoperative monitoring of the patient, whereby records were entered in the patient's chart only when necessary to chronicle important changes in the patient's condition?

Holding

The United States Court of Appeals for the First Circuit held that the evidence supported a jury conclusion that the hospital had been negligent by maintaining a charting by exception method of recording notes in the patient's record, which involved charting only important changes in the patient's condition.

Reason

The defendants argued that the plaintiff failed to prove a general medical standard governing the need for conservative treatment. The court disagreed. The plaintiff's chief expert witness, Dr. Udvarhelyi, testified that, absent an indication of neurological impairment, the standard practice is for a neurosurgeon to postpone lumbar disc surgery while the patient undergoes conservative treatment, with a period of absolute bed rest as the prime ingredient.

The hospital could not seriously dispute that the plaintiff introduced sufficient evidence on the elements of duty and breach. The hospital did not contest the plaintiff's allegation that a regulation of the Puerto Rico Department of Health, in force in 1986, requires qualitative nurses' notes for each nursing shift. Nor did the hospital dispute the charge that, during the patient's hospital stay, the nurses attending to him did not supply the required notes for every shift but, instead, followed the hospital's official policy of charting by exception. The sole question, then, was whether there was sufficient evidence for the jury to find that the violation of the regulation was a proximate cause of harm to Mr. Lama.

The hospital questioned the plaintiff's proof of causation in two respects. First, the hospital claimed that the plaintiff did not prove that the charting by exception policy was a proximate cause of the delayed detection of the patient's infection. Second, the hospital argued that there was no causal relationship between the belated diagnosis of the infection and any unnecessary harm suffered.

There was evidence from which the jury could have inferred that, as part of the practice of charting by exception, the nurses did not regularly record certain information important to the diagnosis of an infection, such as the changing characteristics of the surgical wound and the patient's complaints of postoperative pain. Indeed, one former nurse at the hospital who attended to the patient in 1986 testified that, under the charting by exception policy, she would not report a patient's pain if she either did not administer any medicine or simply gave the patient an aspirin-type medication (as opposed to a narcotic). Further, since there was evidence that the patient's hospital records contained some scattered possible signs of infection that, according to Dr. Udvarhelyi, deserved further investigation (e.g., an excessively bloody bandage and local pain at the site of the wound), the jury could have reasonably inferred that the intermittent charting failed to provide the sort of continuous danger signals that would be the most likely to spur early intervention by the physician.

The hospital claimed that even if faulty record keeping was a cause of the delayed diagnosis, the plaintiff failed to demonstrate a link between the timing of the diagnosis and the harm the patient eventually suffered. Drawing all inferences in favor of the plaintiff, it appeared that he acquired a wound infection as early as May 17 (when a nurse noted a "very bloody" bandage) or May 19 (when Mr. Lama complained of pain at the site of the wound).

The wound infection then developed into discitis on or about May 20 (when Mr. Lama began experiencing excruciating back pain). While there may have been no way to prevent the initial wound infection, the key question then becomes whether early detection and treatment of the wound infection could have prevented the infection from reaching the disc interspace in the critical period prior to May 20. Dr. Udvarhelyi testified that "time is an extremely important factor" in handling an infection. A 24-hour delay in treatment can make a difference, and a delay of several days "carries a high-risk . . . that the infection will [not be] properly controlled." Id. at 481.

The jury could have reasonably inferred that the diagnosis and treatment were delayed at least 24 hours (May 19 to 20), and perhaps 72 hours (May 17 to 20). As a result, the jury could have reasonably concluded that the delayed timing of the diagnosis and treatment of the wound infection was a proximate cause of the patient's discitis.

Discussion

1. What is charting by exception?
2. What are the pros and cons of charting by exception?

Communications: Failure on Multiple Levels

Citation: *Martin v. Ricotta*, NY Slip Op 32976(U) (N.Y. Sup. Ct., 12/15/2009)

Facts

The decedent infant was admitted to Stony Brook University Hospital, PICU, to the service of the attending PICU specialist, Dr. Fenton, to determine why the infant developed respiratory dysfunction. During that admission, the infant underwent a tracheostomy based on the need for chronic ventilation. She also had placement of a gastrostomy tube for nutritional support for failure to thrive. Dr. Fenton performed a right femoral central line placement but inadvertently cannulated the artery and immediately removed the line. Thereafter, the infant's right leg was allegedly pale but had a positive femoral pulse; however, decreased and inadequate perfusion of blood through the arterial system of the leg was noted. Ultimately, the infant was seen by Dr. Ricotta, who performed an emergent thrombectomy on the infant's right lower extremity but found no clot. Dr. Jacob was the anesthesiologist who administered anesthesia to the infant plaintiff.

It is claimed that Dr. Ricotta administered 162 mg Papaverine, intraoperatively, which dosage was 27 times the recommended dose. It is further claimed that in addition to the alleged incorrect dose of Papaverine being administered, the Papaverine was contraindicated as the infant was receiving beta-blockers. Shortly after the administration of the Papaverine, the infant went into cardiac arrest. Attempts at resuscitation were unsuccessful, and the infant was pronounced dead in the operating room. It is claimed that these aforementioned alleged departures proximately caused the death of the infant. The plaintiffs subsequently commenced an action against Dr. Fenton, Dr. Jacob, and Dr. Ricotta.

Dr. Fenton and Dr. Jacob claim that it was later learned that the surgical technician employed by Stony Brook University Hospital, Jack Levine, ORT, had "improperly" accepted a vial containing Papaverine, requested by Dr. Ricotta, and that although Levine was not authorized to accept or prepare medications, he failed to advise Dr. Jacob, the anesthesiologist, of that fact. Drs. Fenton and Jacob claim that Levine drew the contents of the vial into a syringe and placed it at the end of the operating table, allegedly without diluting it, and the patient received a lethal dose when the medication was administered by Dr. Ricotta.. Dr. Jacob had advised Dr. Ricotta of the proper dosage of the Papaverine for the infant when asked by Dr. Ricotta. Drs. Fenton and Jacob argue that it was the duty of the circulating nurse, Mr. Cruz, to dilute the medication, and Cruz did not do so that day. Therefore, Drs. Fenton and Jacob argue that they bear no liability in this action.

As per the summary judgment request by defendents Drs. Fenton and Jacob, an order granting summary judgment dismissing plaintiffs' complaint was granted, and the complaint was dismissed with prejudice as asserted against them. The summary judgment request by the defendant Dr. Ricotta to dismiss the plaintiffs' complaint was denied.

Issue

(1) Did the plaintiffs raise factual issues with regard to Dr. Ricotta's use and administration of the Papaverine precluding summary judgment? (2) Did the plaintiffs' expert raise a factual issue with regard to the defendants Dr. Fenton or Dr. Jacob to preclude summary judgment being granted to them?

Holding

It was determined that the plaintiffs have raised factual issues with regard to Dr. Ricotta's use and administration of the Papaverine to preclude summary judgment in this action. It was also determined that the plaintiffs' expert does not raise a factual issue with regard to the defendants Dr. Fenton or Dr. Jacob to preclude summary judgment being granted to them.

Reason

It is claimed by Dr. Ricotta that he determined in the operating room there was no specific blood clot causing the lack of perfusion and ordered Papaverine to dilate the blood vessel and increase the blood flow. He therefore requested that anesthesia determine the correct dosage of the Papaverine for the infant, and Dr. Jacob, the anesthesiologist, determined a dosage of upwards of 9 mg but eventually agreed on 7 mg. Dr. Ricotta claims it was the responsibility of the operating room staff, specifically the circulating nurse, to procure the medication and to ensure the appropriate dosage was aspirated into the syringe for administration. Dr. Ricotta also claims that the person who scrubbed in, and was later determined to be a surgical technician, prepared the syringe in violation of hospital policy. Dr. Ricotta claims he administered the Papaverine provided in the syringe intravenously over a 5- to 10-minute period, not knowing of the incorrect dosage. When he thereafter left the operating room to speak with the infant's mother, the infant experienced cardiac arrest. Therefore, Dr. Ricotta argues he bears no liability in this action.

Dr. Ricotta did not know who was discharged with the responsibility of drawing up the 7 mg of Papaverine, and stated that normally the nurse draws up the medication. He subsequently learned that Mr. Levine the scrub technician drew up the Papaverine. He believed that Mr. Levine stepped out of protocol by drawing up the medication. Dr. Ricotta testified that the operating room nurse was not in the operating room at the time and he trusted that the syringe he had received was of the correct dosage. He stated that usually the Papaverine is diluted to 1 mg per cc, so when he saw the 7cc syringe and knew they were going to give 7 mg of Papaverine, he made an assumption that it was 7 mg of Papaverine. He infused the drug slowly over 8 to 10 minutes. He and Dr. Jacobs were watching the infant's blood pressure and there were no changes in her vital signs. He let Dr. Rubin, the resident, close the wound and had left to speak to Mrs. Martin but was called back in when the infant went into cardiac arrest. Dr. Fenton was also called in. Resuscitation was not successful. He, Dr. Fenton, and Dr. Jacob thereafter spoke to Mrs. Martin. Dr. Ricotta learned later that the Papaverine had not been diluted, and after that, he was instructed by the hospital not to have further contact regarding the situation. Hospital representatives took over management of the situation; spoke to the infant's pediatrician (Dr. Martinez), jointly came to the conclusion that there had been a medication error, and through Dr. Biancaniello, strongly encouraged staff not to speak further with the family.

The plaintiffs' expert opined within a reasonable degree of medical certainty that Dr. Ricotta departed from accepted standards in his care and treatment of the decedent infant on May 12 and 13, 2006, firstly, when he ordered and administered Papaverine for the infant, and secondly, when he failed to confirm the dose of Papaverine prior to administering the drug, resulting in the administration of 162 mg, or 27 times the recommended dose. It is the expert's further opinion that the failure of Dr. Ricotta to ascertain the correct dose of the Papaverine, and his administration of the incorrect dose of Papaverine (which could have been avoided), were substantial factors in the cause of the infant's death.

Discussion

1. Do you agree with the court's decision?
2. Should the staff have been encouraged not to speak to the family? Discuss your answer.
3. Should the hospital bear any fault?
4. From an ethical point of view, what trust issues do you see at play in this case?

Communications: X-Ray Findings

Citation: *Bouley v. Reisman*, 645 N.E.2d 708 (1995)

Facts

On February 16, 1986, Ms. Bouley was involved in an automobile accident. That afternoon she went to the emergency department at the Malden Hospital because she had been experiencing pain in the area of her left ribs, which were injured in the accident. Ms. Bouley was seen by the defendant, Dr. Reisman, a specialist in emergency medicine and an employee of Emergency Care, Inc. (ECI).

After Dr. Reisman conducted a physical examination of Ms. Bouley, he ordered X-rays taken of Ms. Bouley's left ribs. She went to the X-ray department where four X-rays were taken: three showing the left ribs at different angles, and one a posterior, anterior chest X-ray. She then returned with her X-rays to the emergency department. Because it was after 5 p.m. on Sunday, there was no radiologist on duty when the X-rays were taken.

Dr. Reisman read and interpreted the X-rays, including the chest X-ray. He wrote "OK" on the reading form and discharged Ms. Bouley. He made a discharge diagnosis of "contusion left ribs" and wrote that her condition upon discharge was "good." He then referred her X-rays to the radiology department for review by a radiologist the following day.

The defendant, Dr. Sitzman, a radiologist, was on duty the next day. He read all of Ms. Bouley's X-rays that morning. When he read Ms. Bouley's chest X-ray, he saw an indeterminate density in the right upper lobe of her lung. It was Dr. Sitzman's opinion that the density represented a "significant positive finding" that required further investigation. However, no physician at the Malden Hospital, including Drs. Reisman and Sitzman, informed Ms. Bouley of the presence of the density. Ten months later at the Lahey Clinic, the density seen by Dr. Sitzman was diagnosed as a malignant lung cancer. Ms. Bouley died from lung cancer on February 19, 1987.

Issue

Did the judge have discretion to give detailed instructions to the jury about its role in determining the credibility of witnesses and the inferences it might draw from the direct and circumstantial evidence presented at the trial?

Holding

The judge had discretion to decide whether or not to include the instruction. The appeals court found no abuse of that discretion; the judge gave detailed instructions to the jury about their role in determining the credibility of witnesses and the inferences that they might draw from the direct and circumstantial evidence presented at the trial.

Reason

Dr. Sitzman testified that when the emergency department refers a patient to him, it is his personal practice to report significant positive findings (such as that he saw in Ms. Bouley's chest X-ray) both through a written report and through a telephone report to the emergency department. It was his practice not to ask for anyone in particular when he called but, rather, to give the information to whoever answered the telephone. It was Dr. Sitzman's impression that his oral report of a significant positive finding would always be written down by the person receiving the telephone call in the emergency department. Dr. Sitzman had no actual memory of making a telephone call concerning the Bouley matter but testified that he consistently telephoned in such situations and must have done so then. The physician who had been on duty in the emergency department the day that Dr. Sitzman read Ms. Bouley's X-rays could not remember any such telephone call. If Dr. Reisman had received a telephone call from Dr. Sitzman, there should have been some notation made in Ms. Bouley's medical record about the contents of the telephone message. No such notation appeared in Ms. Bouley's record.

The plaintiff submitted the following request for an instruction by the judge to the jury:

If you find that it was required of all personnel in the emergency department at the Malden Hospital on February 16, 1986 to make a written record of any telephone calls made by a radiologist reporting abnormal X-rays and that this written record would be made in the emergency department record of the patient or in an addendum to the patient's emergency department record, you may find from the lack or absence of a written record of such a telephone call in the Lillian Bouley's emergency department records or in the addendum to it, that no such telephone call was ever made by the radiologist in this case.

The judge did not include the instruction in his charge to the jury. The plaintiff renewed her request. The evidence, however, that there was no notation in Ms. Bouley's record of Dr. Sitzman's telephone call would not necessarily warrant the jury's drawing the inference that Dr. Sitzman did not make the call. The lack of a notation in Ms. Bouley's record could have meant that (1) Dr. Sitzman did not call; (2) Dr. Sitzman did call, but the message he left was not passed on to the emergency department physician; or (3) Dr. Sitzman did call, the message was passed on to a physician, but no notation was made on the record. Therefore, several inferences were possible from the lack of a notation, not just the one that was the subject of the requested instruction.

Further, there was conflicting evidence concerning whether the standard of care expected of a qualified radiologist required a telephone call to the emergency department about the significant positive finding in Ms. Bouley's X-ray. While plaintiff's expert and Dr. Sitzman himself testified that the standard of care required a telephone call, there was evidence from Dr. Sitzman's expert and from Dr. Sitzman (he contradicted his earlier testimony) that the standard of care required only a written report, not an oral report. Consequently, a finding that no phone call was made was not decisive on the issue of Dr. Sitzman's negligence because the jury would still have had to determine whether the standard of care required that he make such a call.

Discussion

1. Do you consider this case a people problem or a systems failure? Why?
2. What safeguards might the hospital and physicians implement to prevent similar occurrences in the future?

Communications: Retention of X-Ray Records

Citation: *Rodgers v. St. Mary's Hosp. of Decatur*, 597 N.E.2d 616 (Ill. 1992)

Facts

Mr. Rodgers filed a medical malpractice action in the circuit court of Macon County on May 27, 1986, alleging the wrongful death of his wife, who died at the hospital 2 days after giving birth to their son. Named as defendants in the medical malpractice action were Mrs. Rodgers's obstetricians, her radiologists, and the hospital.

Mr. Rodgers filed a complaint for damages against the hospital alleging that the hospital breached its statutory duty to preserve for 5 years all of the X-rays taken of Mrs. Rodgers (see Ill. Rev. Stat. 1987, ch. 111 1/2, ¶ 157-11 [X-Ray Retention Act]). He claimed that the X-rays were crucial to proving his case against the obstetricians and radiologists.

On April 12, 1988, on motion of the hospital, the circuit court dismissed that complaint without prejudice. Mr. Rodgers amended his complaint and brought a medical malpractice action against the hospital on May 25, 1989, the day after he reached an $800,000 settlement with the obstetricians. In his complaint, Mr. Rodgers alleged that his wife's death was caused by a sigmoid colonic volvulus, and that the condition appeared on an X-ray that the hospital had a duty to preserve. He alleged that the hospital's failure to preserve the X-ray was a breach of its duty arising from the X-Ray Retention Act and from the hospital's internal regulations. Mr. Rodgers asserted that because the hospital failed to preserve the X-ray, he was unable to prove his case against the radiologists. The circuit court entered judgment in favor of the hospital, and Mr. Rodgers appealed.

Issue

Was there a private cause of action that existed under the X-Ray Retention Act, and did Mr. Rodgers state a claim under the Act?

Holding

The Supreme Court of Illinois held that a private cause of action existed under the X-Ray Retention Act, and Mr. Rodgers stated a claim under the Act.

Reason

The X-Ray Retention Act provides that "Hospitals which produce photographs of the human anatomy by the X-ray or roentgen process on the request of licensed physicians for use by them in the diagnosis or treatment of a patient's illness or condition shall retain such photographs or films as part of their regularly maintained records for a period of 5 years. . . ." (Ill. Rev. Stat. 1987, ch. 111 1/2, ¶ 157-11).

The hospital argued that the statute is merely an administrative regulation to be enforced exclusively by the Public Health Department. The court disagreed. Nothing in the statute suggests that the legislature intended to limit the available remedies to administrative ones. "The threat of liability is a much more efficient method of enforcing the regulation than requiring the Public Health Department to hire inspectors to monitor the compliance of hospitals with the provisions of the Act." Id. at 619.

The hospital also argued that its loss of one X-ray out of a series of six should be considered de minimus and not a violation of the statute. The court disagreed, finding that the statute requires that all X-rays be preserved, not just some of them. The court concluded that Mr. Rodgers had stated a cause of action against the hospital for failure to preserve the X-ray for use in litigation. Whether the missing X-ray proximately caused Mr. Rodgers to lose his case against the radiologists and to settle for less than the full amount of the judgment is a question for the trier of fact.

Discussion

1. What records should a hospital maintain?
2. How long should patient records of X-rays, electrocardiograms (ECGs), etc., be maintained?

Failure to Record Treatment: Below Standard of Care

Citation: *Pellerin v. Humedicenters Inc.*, 696 So.2d 590, 96-1996 (La. App. 1997)

Facts

The plaintiff had gone to the emergency department at Lakeland Medical Center complaining of chest pain on February 22, 1988. An emergency department physician, Dr. Gruner, examined her and ordered a nurse, Ms. Tangney, to give her an injection consisting of 50 mg of Demerol and

25 mg of Vistaril. Although Ms. Tangney testified she did not recall giving the injection, she did not deny giving it, and her initials are present in the emergency department record. Ms. Tangney further testified to what she routinely does when administering injections such as the one plaintiff received. Ms. Tangney admitted she failed to record the site and mode of injection in the emergency department records. She said she may have written this information in the nurse's notes, but no such notes were admitted into evidence.

A medical review panel rendered an opinion in favor of Dr. Gruner, Ms. Tangney, and the hospital, finding no breach of the standard of care. However, at trial in 1996, the jury returned a verdict in favor of plaintiff and against Ms. Tangney and awarded $90,304.68 in damages.

Issue

Did the evidence show that the plaintiff's injury was caused by Ms. Tangney's breaching the standard of care required of nurses?

Holding

The appeals court found that there was sufficient evidence to support a jury finding that Ms. Tangney had breached the applicable standard of care in administering an injection of Vistaril into Ms. Pellerin's hip.

Reason

"To prove medical malpractice, the plaintiff must establish by a preponderance of the evidence: the standard of care, a breach of that standard, causation, and damages." A determination of whether a hospital has breached the duty of care owed to a particular patient depends on the facts and circumstances of the case, and in finding or refusing to find a breach of duty, the fact finder has great discretion.

The plaintiff's expert in pharmacology, Dr. Krefft, testified that Vistaril could cause tissue damage if it is not injected into the muscle. Dr. Krefft testified that the plaintiff had nerve damage, that damage to the nerve is consistent with damage to subcutaneous tissue, and that such damage can occur from injection of Vistaril. Dr. Krefft qualified this, however, by stating an injection of anything could cause nerve damage, because the needle itself could be responsible. Both Dr. Krefft and Dr. Chugden (a member of the medical review panel and defense expert in emergency department medicine) testified that cutaneous neuropathy is more likely to be caused by the mechanics of injecting a needle than by the drug being injected.

The verdict of the jury is very much supported by the record. Ms. Tangney admitted that she failed to record the site and mode of injection in the emergency department records. According to the testimony of two experts in nursing practice, failing to record this information is below the standard of care for nursing. While these omissions could not have affected the administration of the injection, they tend to indicate that in this instance Ms. Tangney did not follow accepted procedure while performing her job. The nurses' testimony alone would not necessarily be enough to support the jury's decision, but when it is added to the other evidence presented, the jury's verdict cannot be said to be erroneous.

Discussion

1. Discuss the theory upon which the hospital is liable.
2. If the nurse had maintained more accurate records, would she have been excused from liability? Discuss your answer.

NOTES

1. *The American Heritage Dictionary of the English Language*, 4th ed. (New York: Houghton Mifflin Company, 2000), 373.
2. Edwards, T. et al., *The New Dictionary of Thoughts* (Cincinnati, Ohio: Standard, 1977), 636.

chapter three

Patient Rights and Responsibilities

Prior to care and treatment, providers generally present patients with written copies of healthcare and decision-making rights that are often referred to as "The Patient's Bill of Rights."

The continuing trend of consumer awareness, coupled with increased governmental regulations, makes it advisable for caregivers to understand both the scope of patient rights and how to ensure them. The Patient Self-Determination Act of 1990 (PSDA),[1] for example, made a significant advance in protecting the right of a patient to make decisions regarding his or her own health care. Healthcare organizations may no longer passively permit patients to exercise their rights but must protect and promote such rights.

Patients have a right to informed consent; to receive a clear explanation of tests, diagnoses, treatment options, prescribed medications, and prognosis; to participate in healthcare decisions; to understand treatment options; and to discontinue or refuse treatment. The Code of Federal Regulations requires that hospitals promote each patient's rights.

The rights of patients continue to expand, as noted for example in *The Affordable Care Act's New Patient's Bill of Rights*. These rights regulations detail the following set of protections that apply to health insurance coverage:

No Pre-Existing Condition Exclusions for Children Under Age

A Texas insurance company denied coverage for a baby born with a heart defect that required surgery. Friends and neighbors rallied around the family to raise the thousands of dollars needed to pay for the surgery and put pressure on the insurer to pay for the needed treatment. A week later the insurer restored coverage for the baby.

No Arbitrary Rescissions of Insurance Coverage

In Los Angeles, a woman undergoing chemotherapy had her coverage cancelled by an insurer who insisted her cancer existed before she bought coverage. She faced more than $129,000 in medical bills and was forced to stop chemotherapy for several months after her insurance was rescinded.

No Lifetime Limits on Coverage

A teenager was diagnosed with an aggressive form of leukemia, the costly treatment of which included chemotherapy and a stay in the intensive care unit. In less than a year, he had reached the $1 million lifetime limit of his family's insurance plan. His parents had to turn to the public for help when the hospital informed them it needed either $600,000 in certified insurance or a $500,000 deposit to perform the bone marrow transplant needed by their son.

Restricted Annual Dollar Limits on Coverage

The rules will phase out the use of annual dollar limits over the next 3 years; in 2014 the Affordable Care Act bans annual dollar limits for most plans.

Protecting Your Choice of Doctors

The new rules make clear that health plan members are free to designate any available participating primary care provider as their provider.[2]

Right to Freedom From Abuse

Ex-Delaware Pediatrician Guilty of Child Sex Abuse

Georgetown, Del.—A former Delaware pediatrician who decorated his office with Disney characters and miniature amusement park rides was found guilty Thursday of sexually abusing scores of his young patients.

Earl Bradley, 58, recorded homemade videos of the abuse, said prosecutors, who presented the judge with more than 13 hours of videos showing sex crimes against more than 80 victims, most of whom were toddlers.

Superior Court Judge William Carpenter Jr. announced the verdict in business-like fashion, avoiding any personal remarks about Bradley. An indictment against Bradley initially contained 470 counts, but attorneys agreed before the trial to consolidate them into 24 counts.

Bradley was found guilty on 14 counts of first-degree rape and five counts each of second-degree assault and sexual exploitation of a child.

Bradley, who will be sentenced on Aug. 26, faces up to life in prison on each rape charge.

He showed no reaction when the verdict was announced, but some of the spectators cried.

Carpenter presided over a 1-day trial in which prosecutors called two witnesses and presented the judge with an external hard drive containing the videos, recorded from December 1998 to Dec. 13, 2009. Bradley was arrested after a 2-year-old girl told her mother the doctor hurt her after an office visit, an accusation that came just days before the last video was recorded.

Randall Chase, Associated Press, June 23, 2011[3]

Patients have the right to be free from abuse from birth to death. Unfortunately there are many depraved persons who do not recognize this right, as noted in the preceding news article. Criminal law, CMS Conditions of Participation, and the various accreditation bodies recognize this right.

---

42 CFR § 482.13 Condition of Participation: Patient's Rights

A hospital must protect and promote each patient's rights.
   (c) *Standard: Privacy and safety*
       (1) The patient has the right to personal privacy.
       (2) The patient has the right to receive care in a safe setting.
       (3) The patient has the right to be free from all forms of abuse or harassment.

Patients have a right to be free from abuse by caregivers. The preceding article describes one of the most horrendous cases of abuse on multiple occasions by a physician who was trained and licensed to care for infants and children.

The cases that follow illustrate the importance of caregivers being aware of patient's rights and the legal consequences for failing to adhere to those rights.

Treatment with Dignity

Citation: *State v. Cunningham*, 493 N.W.2d 884 (Iowa Ct. App. 1992)

Facts

Iowa Code: Section 726.7 (1989)

A person commits wanton neglect of a resident of a healthcare facility when the person knowingly acts in a manner likely to be injurious to the physical, mental, or moral welfare of a resident of a healthcare facility. . . . Wanton neglect of a resident of a healthcare facility is a serious misdemeanor.

The defendant, who is owner and administrator of a residential care facility, housed 30 to 37 mentally ill, mentally retarded, or elderly residents. The Iowa Department of Inspections and Appeals conducts routine inspections of healthcare facilities. All inspections are unannounced, and deficiency statements are sent to the administrator of the facility surveyed.

Various surveys were conducted at the defendant's facility between October 1989 and May 1990. All of the surveys except one resulted in a $50 daily fine assessed against the defendant for violations of the regulations. On August 16, 1990, a grand jury filed an indictment charging the defendant with several counts of wanton neglect of a resident in violation of Iowa Code. section 726.7 (1989).

The district court held that the defendant had knowledge of the dangerous conditions in the healthcare facility but that he willfully and consciously refused to provide or exercise adequate supervision to remedy or attempt to remedy those dangerous conditions. The residents were exposed to physical dangers (unhealthy and unsanitary physical conditions) and were grossly deprived of much needed medical care and personal attention. The conditions were likely to and did cause injury to the physical and mental well-being of the facility's residents. The defendant was found guilty on five counts of wanton neglect. The district court sentenced the defendant to 1 year in jail for each of the five counts, to run concurrently. The district court suspended all but 2 days of the defendant's sentence, ordered him to pay $200 for each count (plus a surcharge and costs), and to perform community service. A motion for a new trial was denied, and the defendant appealed.

Issue

Was there sufficient evidence to convict the defendant of the charges?

Holding

The Court of Appeals of Iowa held that there was substantial evidence to support a finding that the defendant was responsible for not properly maintaining the nursing facility, which led to prosecution for wanton neglect of the facility's residents.

Reason

The defendant knowingly acted in a manner likely to be injurious to the physical or mental welfare of the facility's residents by creating, directing, or maintaining the following five hazardous conditions and unsafe practices:

1. There were fire hazards and circumstances that impeded safety from fire.
   - Cigarette stubs found in a cardboard box
   - Burn holes found in patient clothing
   - Burn holes found in furniture
   - Cigarette burns noted in nonsmoking areas
   - A rusted fire door that was bent and would not close or latch
   - Exposed electrical wiring
2. The facility was not properly maintained.
   - Broken glass in patients' rooms
   - Excessively hot water in faucets
   - Dried feces on public bathroom walls and grab bars
   - Insufficient towels and linens
   - Dead and live cockroaches and worms in the food preparation area
   - Debris, bugs, and grease throughout the facility
   - No soap available in the kitchen
   - At one point only one bar of soap and one container of shampoo found in the entire facility
   - Entire facility in a general state of disrepair
3. Dietary facilities were unsanitary and inadequate to meet the dietary needs of the residents.
   - An ordered, no-concentrated-sweets diet for a diabetic patient not followed, subjecting him to life-threatening blood sugar levels
4. There were inadequate staffing patterns and supervision in the facility.
   - No funds spent on employee training (only one of three kitchen employees was properly trained)
   - Defendant did not spend the minimum amount of time at the facility, as required by administrative standards

5. Improper dosages of medications were administered to the residents.
   - Distributing an ongoing overdose of heart medication to one resident
   - Failure to administer medication, resulting in one resident suffering a seizure
   - Failure to treat residents' skin lesions and herpes (Id. at 887–888)

The defendant argued that he did not "create" the unsafe conditions at the facility. The court of appeals disagreed. The statute does not require that the defendant create the conditions at the facility to sustain a conviction. The defendant was the administrator of the facility and responsible for the conditions that existed. The defendant also argued that some of the deficiencies cited had been corrected. The statute, however, does not require failure or refusal to remedy the found conditions in order to sustain a conviction.

Discussion

1. The lessons in this case are numerous. As a classroom activity, in groups of three to five, brainstorm the numerous ramifications.
2. Was the sentencing of the court adequate? Explain.

42 CFR § 482.24 (c)(2)(v) Condition of Participation: Medical Record Services

(c) *Standard: Content of record.* The medical record must contain information to justify admission and continued hospitalization, support the diagnosis, and describe the patient's progress and response to medications and services.

(2) All records must document the following, as appropriate:

(v) Properly executed informed consent forms for procedures and treatments specified by the medical staff, or by Federal or State law if applicable, to require written patient consent.

The Joint Commission: RI.01.03.01–RI.01.03.05

See the Joint Commission requirements, Standards and Elements of Performance and/or conduct a search for "informed consent" at http://www.jointcommission.org/.

Lack of Informed Consent

Citation: *Greynolds v. Kurman*, 632 N.E.2d 946 (Ohio Ct. App. 1993)

Facts

Mr. Greynolds and his wife brought a medical malpractice action against a physician arising from Mr. Greynolds's stroke caused by an angiogram.

On July 29, 1987, Mr. Greynolds suffered from a transient ischemic attack (TIA). A TIA is a sudden loss of neurological function caused by vascular impairment to the brain. As a result of the TIA, Mr. Greynolds had garbled speech and expressive and perceptive aphasia (a medical term used to describe the loss of the power of expression by speech, writing, or signs, or of comprehending spoken or written language). Mr. Greynolds was taken to a hospital's emergency department where Dr. Litman, a cardiologist, met him. At Dr. Litman's request, Dr. Rafecas, a cardiologist, examined him. Dr. Rafecas determined that Mr. Greynolds was at a high risk for a stroke because of his past medical history (which included previous TIAs) and sought to pinpoint the exact source of vascular insufficiency to the brain.

On August 3, 1987, after receiving the results of noninvasive tests, Dr. Rafecas ordered a cerebral angiogram. Dr. Kurman performed the angiogram. Mr. Greynolds suffered a stroke during the procedure that left him severely disabled.

Mr. Greynolds and his wife filed a medical malpractice action against Dr. Rafecas and Dr. Kurman, asserting that Dr. Rafecas had negligently recommended the procedure and that Dr. Kurman had performed the procedure without obtaining the informed consent of the patient.

Dr. Kurman argued that the trial court erred by refusing to enter judgment for him consistent with the answer to jury Interrogatory No. 3.

Interrogatory No. 1: Do you find there was a failure to obtain informed consent?

Answer: Yes.

Interrogatory No. 2: If you answered Interrogatory No. 1 yes, then state specifically in what manner Dr. Kurman's care fell below the recognized standards of the medical community?

Answer: Mr. Greynolds was not in our estimation capable of comprehending the consent form. Therefore, Dr. Kurman should have obtained consent from the next-of-kin, specifically, Mrs. Greynolds.

Interrogatory No. 3: If you answered yes to interrogatory No. 1, and you found that Mr. Greynolds did not consent to the procedure, do you find that a reasonable person would have consented to the procedure?

Answer: Yes. Id. at 949.

Dr. Kurman moved the trial court to grant him a judgment notwithstanding the verdict because the jury's answer to Interrogatory No. 3 was inconsistent with the jury's general verdict. The trial court overruled Dr. Kurman's motion and entered judgment for the plaintiffs. Dr. Kurman appealed.

Issue

Was there sufficient evidence to support a judgment for the plaintiffs?

Holding

The Court of Appeals of Ohio held that the evidence was sufficient to support a judgment in favor of the plaintiffs.

Reason

In determining whether a judgment in a civil case is supported by sufficient evidence, the court examines whether the judgment is supported by credible evidence going to all the essential elements of the case. The jury needed to determine that the risks involved in the cerebral angiogram were not disclosed to Mr. Greynolds, that the risks involved in the procedure materialized and caused his stroke, and that a reasonable person in the position of Mr. Greynolds would have decided against having the angiogram had the risks associated with the procedure been disclosed to him. The jury concluded that Mr. Greynolds did not consent to the angiogram because he "was not . . . capable of comprehending the consent form," and further noted that Dr. Kurman should have sought consent from the next of kin, specifically, Mrs. Greynolds. Id. at 951. Given the evidence of Mr. Greynolds's condition when he signed the consent forms, his past medical history, and the fact that he was at an increased risk to suffer complications during an angiogram, the court found that there was sufficient evidence to support a finding of lack of informed consent.

Discussion

1. What would constitute informed consent?
2. Who should describe the risks associated with a procedure to the patient?

Physician Failed to Obtain Informed Consent

Citation: *Riser v. American Medical Intern Inc.*, 620 So. 2d 372 (La. Ct. App. 1993)

Facts

Four siblings brought a medical malpractice action against Dr. Lang, a physician who performed a femoral arteriogram on their 69-year-old mother, Mrs. Riser, who expired 11 days following the medical procedure. Mrs. Riser had been admitted to De La Ronde Hospital experiencing impaired circulation in her lower arms and hands. The patient had multiple medical diagnoses, including diabetes mellitus, end-stage renal failure, and arteriosclerosis. Her physician, Dr. Sottiurai had ordered bilateral brachial arteriograms in order to determine the cause of the patient's impaired circulation. Because De La Ronde Hospital could not accommodate Dr. Sottiurai's request, Mrs. Riser was transferred to St. Jude Hospital and Dr. Lang, a radiologist at St. Jude, performed a femoral arteriogram, not the bilateral brachial arteriograms ordered by Dr. Sottiurai. The procedure seemed to go well, and the patient was prepared for transfer back to De La Ronde Hospital. However, shortly after the ambulance departed the hospital, the patient suffered a seizure in the ambulance and was returned to St. Jude. Mrs. Riser's condition deteriorated and she expired 11 days later. The plaintiffs claimed in their lawsuit that Mrs. Riser was a poor risk for the procedure. The District Court ruled for the plaintiffs, awarding damages in the amount of $50,000 for Mrs. Riser's pain and suffering and $100,000 to each child. Dr. Lang appealed.

Issue

Did Dr. Lang fail to obtain informed consent from the patient and was the damage award excessive?

Holding

The Court of Appeal of Louisiana held that Dr. Lang failed to obtain informed consent from the patient, and that the damage award was not excessive.

Reason

Informed consent requires that the physician reveal to the patient all material risks. The patient's consent to an arteriogram was vitiated by Dr. Lang's failure to disclose such a possibility. Furthermore, the consent form itself did not contain express authorization for Dr. Lang to perform the femoral arteriogram. Dr. Sottiurai ordered bilateral brachial arteriograms, not a femoral arteriogram. Mrs. Riser was under the impression that she was about to undergo bilateral brachial arteriograms, not a femoral arteriogram. Two consent forms were signed; neither form authorized the performance of a femoral arteriogram. Mrs. O'Neil, one of Mrs. Riser's daughters, claimed that her mother said, following the arteriogram, "Why did you let them do that to me?" Id. at 380. Although Dr. Lang claims that he explained the femoral procedure to Mrs. Riser and Mrs. O'Neil, the trial court, faced with this conflicting testimony, chose to believe the plaintiffs.

Discussion

1. Describe what information a patient should be provided prior to undergoing a risky procedure in order for consent to be "informed."
2. Why is it important to obtain consent from a patient prior to proceeding with a risky procedure?

Informed Consent: Physican Must Warn of Risks

Citation: *Warren v. Schecter*, 57 Cal. App.4th 1189 (C1997)

Facts

Ms. Warren was diagnosed as having a stomach ulcer in December 1981. Dr. Feldman, who referred her to Dr. Schecter, a surgeon, initially treated her. Dr. Schecter sought to perform surgery to remove the portions of the stomach containing the ulcer, which was not healing completely. One of the significant risks of gastric surgery is decreased calcium absorption, leading to early and severe metabolic bone disease (e.g., osteoporosis, osteomalacia, or bone pain). Studies have reported that up to 38% of patients develop early severe osteoporosis following such surgery. It was Dr. Schecter's role as the surgeon to advise Ms. Warren of the risks of surgery in order to obtain her informed consent. Dr. Schecter did not believe osteoporosis, osteomalacia, and bone pain were risks of the surgery, and he did not discuss those substantial risks with her. Dr. Schecter did advise Ms. Warren that she might experience bowel obstructions. Dr. Schecter also informed Ms. Warren of other risks, including "dumping syndrome," which involves nausea and the slight risk of death from the administering of anesthesia during any operation. Based on the limited risks disclosed to Ms. Warren, she consented to the surgery, which Dr. Schecter performed on September 10, 1982.

The surgery recommended by Dr. Schecter was elective. Ms. Warren had nonsurgical options for her ulcers, namely, to discontinue the use of Advil and aspirin, to cease smoking, and to continue with her ulcer medications.

Following the surgery, Ms. Warren developed dumping syndrome, a side effect that occurs in about 1% of the patients who undergo this procedure. Ms. Warren also developed alkaline reflux gastritis, a condition involving the movement of alkaline fluid back into the stomach.

After Ms. Warren was diagnosed with these complications, she returned to Dr. Schecter, who recommended a second surgery. The purpose of the second surgery was to relieve the pain and discomfort from the first surgery. The second surgery would enhance the risk of bone disease. However, Dr. Schecter again failed to advise Ms. Warren of the risk of metabolic bone disease.

The first manifestation of bone disease occurred on May 4, 1990, when Ms. Warren fractured her back from the mere act of turning over in bed. Until then, there had been no objective evidence of bone disease, and no symptoms. Ms. Warren was taken to emergency at UCLA Hospital and there advised she had suffered a fracture of one of the lumbar vertebrae. At that time, she first learned that severe metabolic bone disease was a common side effect of the surgeries she had undergone. Dr. Saleh at UCLA advised Ms. Warren that the surgeries had caused the osteoporosis that had led to the fracture. A bone density scan confirmed that Ms. Warren's bones were both soft and brittle and that she had lost a lot of bone mass. From the onset of bone disease, Ms. Warren's condition continued to deteriorate.

In January 1991, Ms. Warren filed an action for medical negligence, alleging Dr. Schecter is liable under an informed consent theory for performing surgery without advising her of the risk of bone disease. Ms. Warren claimed that had Dr. Schecter warned her of the risk of metabolic bone disease, she would not have consented to surgery. The jury found on special verdict that (1) Dr. Schecter did not disclose to Ms. Warren all relevant information that would enable her to make an informed decision regarding surgery, (2) a reasonably prudent person in Ms. Warren's position would not have consented to surgery if adequately informed of all the significant perils, and (3) Dr. Schecter's negligence was a cause of injury to Ms. Warren.

Issue

Was the defendant–physician liable under an informed consent theory for performing surgery without advising the plaintiff of the risk of bone disease?

Holding

The court of appeals found that the plaintiff was entitled to compensation for all damages proximately resulting from the physician's failure to give full disclosure of the risks of surgery. The patient was entitled to recover not only for the undisclosed complications but also for the disclosed complications, because she would not have consented to any surgery had the true risk been disclosed, and therefore she would not have suffered those complications.

Reason

There must be a causal relationship between the physician's failure to inform and the injury to the plaintiff. Such causal connection arises only if it were established that had revelation been made, consent to treatment would not have been given. Because the uncommunicated hazard had materialized at the time of trial, it would be surprising if the patient did not claim that had he or she been informed of the dangers, he or she would have declined treatment. "Subjectively" he or she may believe so, with the benefit of hindsight. Thus an "objective test" is preferable: that is, what would a prudent person in the patient's position have decided if adequately informed of all significant perils? The prudent person test for causation was established to protect defendant physicians from the unfairness of having a jury consider the issue of proximate cause with the benefit of hindsight.

A plaintiff meets the burden of establishing a causal relationship between the physician's failure to inform and the injury to the plaintiff by demonstrating that a prudent person in the plaintiff's position would have declined the procedure if adequately informed of the risks. The objective standard, which in effect equates the plaintiff with a reasonable person, is appropriate because it protects the defendant–physician from the self-serving testimony of a plaintiff who will inevitably assert at trial that he or she would have refused the procedure if duly advised of the risk(s). The objective test required of the plaintiff does not prevent the physician from showing, by way of defense, that even though a reasonably prudent person might not have undergone the procedure if properly informed of the perils, this particular plaintiff still would have consented to the procedure. In sum, it was not Ms. Warren's burden to establish that she would have refused consent to the surgery even if adequately informed. Under the objective standard, Ms. Warren only had to prove a prudent person in her position would not have consented if adequately informed of the risks. Dr. Schecter failed to provide Ms. Warren with the risks and benefits of the surgical procedures prior to obtaining her consent for the operations. Ms. Warren testified that she would not have consented to either surgery if duly advised of the risks.

Discussion

1. How much information is sufficient in order for informed consent to be effective?
2. Discuss the implications of the following statement: "Patients are generally persons unlearned in the medical sciences and, therefore, except in rare instances, the knowledge of patient and physician are not in parity."

Informed Consent: Physician Must Provide—Not Nurses

Citation: *Davis v. Hoffman*, 972 F. Supp. 308 (E.D. Pa. 1997)

Facts

The plaintiff, Ms. Davis, experienced pain in her lower abdomen and consulted Dr. Hoffman. He diagnosed her to be suffering from a fibroid uterus and prescribed a dilation and curettage procedure designed to remove the fibroids. The physician further suggested a laparoscopy and hysteroscopy to search for cancer. The physician's nurse, Ms. Puchini, conducted a presurgical interview with the plaintiff, in which she described a video hysteroscopy, a dilation and curettage procedure, a resectoscopic removal of submucous fibroids, a laparoscopy, and a laser myomectomy. The plaintiff claimed that she specifically informed Dr. Hoffman and Ms. Puchini that she did not consent to a hysterectomy. They responded that they would awaken her during the operation to obtain her consent before proceeding to a hysterectomy. At no time did they inform the plaintiff that the physician intended to perform a hysterectomy. The plaintiff underwent a procedure that resulted in a hysterectomy, during which no one awakened her to discuss and explore possible alternatives, or if there was to be a hysterectomy, to first obtain her consent. Claiming that the hysterectomy caused her substantial injuries, the plaintiff brought an action against Dr. Hoffman, Ms. Puchini, and the hospital for lack of informed consent.

Issue

Was the nurse or hospital responsible for informing and obtaining consent from the patient as to the surgical procedures to be performed by the surgeon?

Holding

Responsibility for obtaining informed consent for surgery lies with the operating surgeon, not the hospital or nurse.

Reason

In response to the plaintiff's allegation that the hospital committed battery by lack of informed consent to the hysterectomy, the hospital asserted that Pennsylvania law places no duty on a hospital to obtain a patient's consent to an operation. The hospital argued that Pennsylvania courts have applied the doctrine of informed consent only to physicians, not to hospitals.

The plaintiff responded that the hospital gratuitously undertook to obtain her consent prior to the operation. Although the consent form used was authored and printed by the hospital, there was no suggestion in the form that the deficiency in consent was in any way causally inadequate. Rather, any failure is attributed to the omissions in the way the form was completed, or in the way the patient was not informed as to what was to be the next phase of the operation. Thus, the form was causally irrelevant and could not be a basis for finding liability.

Because nurses do not have a duty to obtain informed consent, the plaintiff has not stated a claim for battery by lack of informed consent against Ms. Puchini. Pennsylvania law generally imposes no duty on persons other than surgeons to obtain informed consent before performing surgery. Thus, courts have not imposed the duty on nurses. Persons who assist the primary treating physician have no duty to obtain the patient's informed consent.

Discussion

1. Under what circumstances might a hospital be responsible for ensuring that a patient's informed consent is obtained prior to a medical or surgical intervention (e.g., research protocols, hospital-owned physician practices)?
2. Discuss the circumstances under which a nurse might be responsible for obtaining a patient's informed consent.

Informed Consent: Right to Know Alternative Procedures
Citation: *Stover v. Surgeons*, 635 A.2d 1047 (Pa. Super. Ct. 1993)

Facts

A patient suffered damage to her heart valves as a result of childhood rheumatic fever. Dr. Ford, one of a group of physicians the patient consulted after her condition had worsened, informed the patient that she needed a heart valve replacement. Testimony from Dr. Ford revealed that he briefly reviewed the details of the surgery with the patient, who claimed Dr. Ford told her only that mechanical valves outlasted natural tissue valves. The patient further stated that she was never informed about the risks associated with installing mechanical valves, including the Beall valve that was implanted in her. She stated that thromboemboli, strokes, and the lifelong use of anticoagulants, which are common side effects of valve replacements, were never discussed with her. Dr. Zikria performed the surgery, and could not recall discussing any risks other than clotting risks associated with the implantation. After the surgery, the patient suffered severe, permanent brain damage from multiple episodes of thromboemboli directly caused by the valve implantation. She then sued for lack of informed consent, and the jury returned a verdict for her. The physicians appealed.

Issue

Does, in this case, the doctrine of informed consent apply when selecting a heart valve to be surgically placed in the patient?

Holding

The Superior Court held that the physicians had to discuss with the patient prostheses that represented recognized, medically sound alternatives. Evidence that the Beall heart valve actually implanted was no longer in general use at the time of operation was deemed relevant and material to the issue of informed consent.

Reason

Although the physicians argued that the choice of prosthesis should belong to them, the court held that if there are other recognized, medically sound alternatives, the patient must be informed about the risks and benefits of them in order to make a sound treatment judgment, including the desire to execute a waiver of consent. The agreement between the physician and the patient is contractual. Therefore, in order for valid consent to occur, there must be a finding that both parties understood the nature of the procedure, including any possible and expected results. The consent is not valid if the patient did not understand the operation to be performed, its seriousness, the disease or incapacity, and the possible results. Physicians must disclose risks that a reasonable person would consider material to his or her decision of whether to undergo treatment. In the instant case, the physicians failed to inform the patient about the recognized risks of the valve that was implanted.

Finally, the court reasoned that there were alternative valves available that were never discussed with the patient. In order to arrive at an informed decision concerning her treatment, it was material for her to have been told about the alternatives and their risks and benefits.

Discussion

1. What are the elements of informed consent, including the responsibilities of the physician and patient?
2. What are the responsibilities of the hospital in ensuring that informed consent has been obtained from the patient?

Informed Consent: Hospitals Can Be Responsible in Some Cases

Citation: *Keel v. St. Elizabeth Med. Ctr.*, 842 S.W.2d 860 (Ky. 1992)

Facts

The plaintiff, Mr. Keel, alleged that St. Elizabeth Medical Center Hospital performed a medical procedure without his informed consent, which resulted in medical complications. The plaintiff went to the medical center for a computed tomography (CT) scan, which was to include the injection of a contrast dye material. Prior to the test, he was given no information concerning any risks attendant to the procedure. The dye was injected and the scan was conducted. However, the plaintiff developed a thrombophlebitis at the site of the injection.

Mr. Keel argued for recovery for damages due to a lack of informed consent. Moreover, the plaintiff argued that expert medical testimony was not required in order to prove the absence of informed consent. The hospital argued that the question of informed consent, like the question of negligence, must be determined against the standard of practice among members of the medical profession.

The circuit court granted summary judgment to the hospital on the grounds that the plaintiff failed to present expert testimony on the issue. The plaintiff appealed.

Issue

Was expert medical testimony required with respect to risks associated with a CT scan, and did the hospital have a duty to inform the patient as to the risks of the CT scan?

Holding

The Supreme Court of Kentucky held that expert testimony was not required to establish lack of informed consent and that the hospital had a duty to inform the patient of the risks of the procedure. Responsibility did not lie solely with the patient's personal physician. The circuit court's summary judgment for the hospital was reversed, and the matter was remanded for further proceedings.

Reason

In most cases, expert medical evidence will likely be a necessary element of a plaintiff's proof in negating informed consent. In view of the special circumstances of this case, the court found it significant that

St. Elizabeth offered Keel no information whatsoever concerning any possible hazards of this particular procedure, while at the same time the hospital admits that it routinely questions every patient about to undergo a dye injection as to whether he/she has had any previous reactions to contrast materials. If we are to analogize consent actions to negligence actions, we must also acknowledge that a failure adequately to inform the patient need not be established by expert testimony where the failure is so apparent that laymen may easily recognize it or infer it from evidence within the realm of common knowledge. Id. at 862.

A juror might reasonably infer from the nontechnical evidence that St. Elizabeth's utter silence as to the risks amounted to an assurance that there were none. The hospital's own questions to patients regarding reactions to the CT scan procedure demonstrated that the hospital recognized the substantial possibility of complications. These inconsistencies are apparent without recourse to expert testimony.

Although not strictly at issue in this case, the court noted under KRS 304.40-320 that the duty to provide informed consent is upon "healthcare providers"; and KRS 304.40-260 expressly includes hospitals within the definition of that term. The court had no doubt that the duty exists and is breached at peril. Id. at 862.

Discussion

1. What procedures should hospitals have in place to ensure that patients are properly informed as to procedures they have been advised to consider undergoing?

2. What are the pros and cons of general and specific consent? Which is more effective?

3. What liability, if any, should be imparted to the physician ordering the CT scan? Discuss your answer.

Duty Lies with the Physician to Provide Informed Consent

Citation: *Mathias v. St. Catherine's Hosp. Inc.*, 569 N.W.2d 330 (Wis. Ct. App. 1997)

Facts

Ms. Mathias, a patient of Dr. Witt's at St. Catherine's Hospital, delivered a full-term son by Caesarean section on February 2, 1993, while she was under general anesthesia. While in the operating room, Dr. Witt indicated that he needed a particular instrument that would be used in a tubal ligation. The nurses, Ms. Snyder and Ms. Perri, employees of St. Catherine's, looked at Ms. Mathias's chart. Ms. Snyder informed Dr. Witt that she did not see a signed consent form for that procedure. In deposition testimony, Ms. Snyder stated that Dr. Witt replied, "Oh, okay."

Dr. Witt performed a tubal ligation anyway. Three days after the procedure, a nurse brought Ms. Mathias a consent form for the procedure. This nurse told Ms. Mathias that the form was "just to close up our records." The nurse testified in her deposition that she signed Ms. Perri's name on that same consent form and backdated it to February 2, 1993, the day the surgery was performed. As the trial court noted in its oral decision granting summary judgment, these actions after the surgery are immaterial to the issue of the hospital's duty to Ms. Mathias. The trial court granted summary judgment dismissing St. Catherine's from their medical malpractice action and from an order denying reconsideration. Mr. and Ms. Mathias appealed the summary judgment, contending that the hospital owed a duty to Ms. Mathias to prevent her physician from performing a tubal ligation for which there was no signed consent form.

Issue

Did the hospital owe a duty to Ms. Mathias to prevent her physician from performing a tubal ligation for which there was no consent, and if so, did the trial court err in granting summary judgment to St. Catherine's?

Holding

The Appeals Court determined that St. Catherine's fulfilled its duty of ordinary care to Ms. Mathias and therefore is not liable. The trial court's grant of summary judgment was affirmed.

Reason

The law in Wisconsin on informed consent is well settled. In *Scaria v. St. Paul Fire & Marine Ins. Co.*, 68 Wis. 2d 1, 18, 227 N.W.2d 647, 651, 656 (1975), the court held that the duty to advise a patient of the risks of treatment lies with the physician. In that case, a patient became paralyzed from the waist down after a diagnostic test that involved injecting dye into his system. The court was explicit in pointing out that the duty to obtain informed consent lay with the physician, not the hospital.

The duty of the physician to ensure that a patient gives an informed consent to any medical treatment is codified in § 448.30 Wis. Stat., which requires

(a)ny physician who treats a patient shall inform the patient about the availability of all alternate, viable medical modes of treatment and about the benefits and risks of these treatments. The physician's duty to inform the patient under this section does not require disclosure of

1. information beyond what a reasonably well-qualified physician in a similar medical classification would know,
2. detailed technical information that in all probability a patient would not understand,
3. risks apparent or known to the patient,
4. extremely remote possibilities that might falsely or detrimentally alarm the patient,
5. information in emergencies where failure to provide treatment would be more harmful to the patient than treatment,
6. information in cases where the patient is incapable of consenting.

This statute is the cornerstone of the hospital's duty in this case. The court noted that the legislature limited the application of the duty to obtain informed consent to the treating physician. While the record is littered with semantic arguments about whether this is a case of nonconsent or lack of informed consent, what The Mathiases seek is to extend the duty of ensuring informed consent to the hospital.

The duty to inform rests with the physician and requires the exercise of delicate medical judgment. A cogent explanation of the reasons for adopting this principle was set out in *Kelly v. Methodist Hosp.*, 444 Pa. Super. 427, 664 A.2d 148, 151 (1995), in which the court held

---

(b)eyond our conclusion Pennsylvania law does not recognize the cause of action asserted by appellants, we find compelling reasons for not imposing upon hospitals the duty of obtaining informed consent. It is the surgeon and not the hospital who has the education, training and experience necessary to advise each patient of risks associated with the proposed surgery. Likewise, by virtue of his relationship with the patient, the physician is in the best position to know the patient's medical history and to evaluate and explain the risks of a particular operation in light of the particular medical history.

The Wisconsin statute, § 448.30, specifies only that a physician obtain informed consent. The legislature could have enumerated other responsible entities had it chosen to do so. It did not. Furthermore, under the plain language of the statute, buttressed by Wisconsin case law and the reasoning of other courts, the appeals court concluded that under the facts of this case summary judgment in favor of St. Catherine's was appropriate.

The Mathiases, however, contend that the nurses had a duty to act under a theory of foreseeability. They argue that "[w]hen one assumes a duty towards another person, one becomes responsible as a participant if the duty is not carried out with reasonable care and caution." According to the Mathiases, "[t]he duty arises when Nurse Perri realizes that the consent form for sterilization is the only form that is not signed, which is a red flag to her, and should have been to any healthcare provider in a modern hospital context."

An act or the omission of an act may form the foundation of a cause of action only when it appears that a duty was owed. At issue here is a determination of what is encompassed by the nurse's duty of ordinary care in this situation. Therefore, having concluded that St. Catherine's did not have a legal duty to ensure that Dr. Witt had obtained informed consent from the patient, the issue presented is whether, under the circumstances of this case, the actions of the nurses conformed to the standard of ordinary care.

The duty to explain the procedure to Ms. Mathias and to obtain her informed consent lay with Dr. Witt. The nurses in the operating room checked Ms. Mathias's medical chart to ascertain whether there were appropriate signed consent forms. Ms. Snyder informed Dr. Witt that a written consent form for the tubal ligation was not in Ms. Mathias's chart. According to Ms. Snyder's deposition, Dr. Witt acknowledged having heard her comment. Although Ms. Mathias's chart did not contain the signed form, that fact alone would not lead a reasonable person to conclude that Dr. Witt was performing a nonconsensual procedure. Based on Dr. Witt's response and the information they had available to them, the nurses had no reason to conclude that the absence of the form was anything more than a clerical error. Ms. Snyder informed Dr. Witt that the chart did not contain a signed consent form; in this instance, neither Ms. Snyder nor Ms. Perri had any duty to take further action.

There were allegations regarding the hospital's obtaining a signed consent form from Ms. Mathias 3 days after the surgery. This issue was argued extensively in the plaintiffs' affidavits in opposition to the summary judgment motion. Furthermore, evidence of what occurred relating to a consent form after the tubal ligation was performed is immaterial to the legal issue of St. Catherine's duty to Ms. Mathias. The appeals court concurred with the trial court that any evidence as to these actions was merely cumulative.

Discussion

1. Do you agree with the court's finding that the hospital had no legal duty to ensure that Dr. Witt obtain informed consent from Ms. Mathias? Explain.
2. What finding would the Joint Commission on Accreditation of Healthcare Organizations (Joint Commission) make during an accreditation survey if its hospital surveyors found that Ms. Mathias had undergone surgery without informed consent? Should the hospital be penalized by the Joint Commission for the surgeon's failure to obtain informed consent? Explain.
3. What issues do you see in another nurse's decision to sign Ms. Perri's name on the consent form and then backdate it to February 2, 1993?

Right to Refuse Emergency Treatment

Citation: *Matthews v. DeKalb County Hosp. Auth.*, 211 GA. App. 858 440 S.E. 2d 743 (1994)

Facts

On August 10, 1988, Mrs. Mathews had gone unassisted to the emergency department of DeKalb County Hospital complaining of a burning pain in her upper chest that had radiated down her right side that evening and on the previous evening. Upon arriving at the hospital's emergency department at about 11:25 p.m., she was triaged by a nurse who took her vital signs, recorded her medical history, and made an assessment of her immediate medical needs. Although slightly elevated, Mrs. Matthews's vital signs were within normal limits. She explained to the triage nurse that after her pain had subsided, she needed to have a bowel movement. The triage nurse classified Mrs. Matthews as a "category two," which designates a nonthreatening condition. It was explained to Mrs. Matthews that she would have a long wait because the emergency department was very busy. (A social services representative later testified that he spoke to Mrs. Matthews between six and eight times during her wait in the emergency department. He indicated that she had been in no apparent distress during those times he spoke to her.) Following a 4.5-hour wait, Mrs. Matthews left the emergency department without being treated. The social services representative stated that he told Mrs. Matthews a treatment room was ready for her, and she could be attended to shortly. Mrs. Matthews responded that she had already waited long enough, and she was leaving. The social services representative stated that he pleaded with her to stay, but she refused, claiming that she would see her own physician in the morning. Mrs. Matthews went to work the following day without having seen her physician. She expired on August 12, 1988. The DeKalb Superior Court granted the hospital's motion for summary judgment, and an appeal was taken.

A malpractice action by the appellants, Callahan and Michael T. Bennett, and Robert L. Callahan, III, was brought against DeKalb County Hospital Authority arising out of the death of Mrs. Matthews.

Issue

Could the hospital be held liable for the patient's subsequent death following her voluntary termination of her visit to the hospital's emergency department?

Holding

The Court of Appeals held that the patient's voluntary termination of her relationship with the hospital's emergency department effectively severed any relationship between her and the hospital. Accordingly, the hospital could not be held liable for the death of the patient. The court also held that the appeal was frivolous and required the imposition of a $250 penalty.

Reason

> [T]o recover damages in a tort action, a plaintiff must prove that the defendant's negligence was both the 'cause in fact' and the 'proximate cause' of the injury. The requirement of proximate cause constitutes a limit on legal liability; it is a policy decision . . . that, for a variety of reasons (e.g., intervening act, the defendant's conduct, and the plaintiff's injury) are too remote for the law to countenance recovery.
>
> *Atlanta Obstetrics, etc., v. Coleman, 260 Ga. 569, 398 S.E.2d 16 (1990).*

Mrs. Matthews left the hospital on her own cognizance when the hospital's emergency department physician was about to see her. She went to work the following morning without seeing her own physician, contrary to what she had indicated upon leaving the emergency department. The fact that Mrs. Matthews voluntarily terminated her relationship with the emergency department personnel at DeKalb General effectively severed any causal relationship that might have existed between DeKalb General's act of classifying Mrs. Matthews as a category two patient and her death. The appeal was found to be without any arguable merit and a penalty of $250 was imposed against the appellants.

Discussion

1. What elements must a plaintiff establish in a malpractice case in order to establish liability for negligence?
2. Was there adequate evidence to discredit the plaintiff's claim of causation?
3. What steps might the hospital consider taking in the future in order to reduce the risks of lawsuits similar to those in the Matthews case?
4. What are the inherent risks when utilizing a triage nurse in making the initial assessment and prioritizing emergency department patients based on their presenting complaints?
5. In the emergency department setting, at what point should a physician become involved in assessing a patient's needs? Should a physician perform the initial assessment? Explain.

Assisted Suicide Limited by State Statute

Citation: *Kevorkian v. Thompson*, 947 F. Supp. 1152 (E.D. 1997)

Facts

In this action, plaintiffs Dr. Kevorkian and Ms. Good sought a court order enjoining defendant Mr. Thompson and his successor in the office of Oakland County Prosecutor from prosecuting Dr. Kevorkian for his assisted-suicide activities. At the heart of both plaintiffs' amended complaint for declaratory and injunctive relief and their motion for summary judgment is their contention that the statutes and the common law under which Dr. Kevorkian has been prosecuted in the past are unconstitutional, and therefore, any future prosecutions of Dr. Kevorkian will result in the deprivation of their constitutional rights.

The plaintiffs asked the court to declare that mentally competent adults who are terminally ill or intractably suffering have a liberty interest protected by the Fourteenth Amendment's due process clause to end their suffering by committing suicide and seeking physician aid in doing so. The plaintiffs claimed that any unwritten common law violates the equal protection clause of the Fourteenth Amendment if it affords adult patients who are attached to life support systems the right to terminate that life support, but then denies mentally competent adults who are terminally ill or intractably suffering (without being on life support systems) the right to commit suicide with the assistance of a physician.

The Michigan Supreme Court found that a Michigan statute on assisted suicide was validly enacted, that the United States Constitution does not prohibit states from imposing criminal penalties for assisting someone in committing suicide, and that assisted suicide is a common law crime in Michigan that may be prosecuted under the common law. Dr. Kevorkian petitioned the United States Supreme Court, seeking to overturn the Michigan Supreme Court's decision.

Issue

(1) Is there is a constitutional right to assisted suicide? Are persons seeking physician-assisted suicide denied equal protection under the Fourteenth Amendment, in light of the fact that the law protects the right to reject medical treatment for those on life support but denies a right to assistance with suicide for those not on life support?

Finding

The United States Supreme Court denied that petition for certiorari. The Court held that there is no constitutional right to assisted suicide and that the statute barring assisted suicide does not violate the equal protection clause of the Fourteenth Amendment.

Reason

The plaintiffs contended that there is a constitutional right to assisted suicide and that a mentally competent adult has a protected liberty interest to a physician-assisted suicide under the due process clause of the Fourteenth Amendment. The plaintiffs specifically attacked the Michigan Supreme Court's ruling that these cases do not suggest any inclination on the part of the Supreme Court to expand the notion of constitutionally protected liberty interests to encompass a right to suicide (such a right is not expressly recognized anywhere in the United States Constitution or in the decisions of the United States Supreme Court and cannot be reasonably inferred).

In resolving these issues, the Supreme Court acknowledged "the principle that a competent person has a constitutionally protected liberty interest in refusing unwanted medical treatment may be inferred from our prior decisions." 497 U.S. at 277, 110 S. Ct. at 2851. The Court went on, however, to make clear that "determining that a person has a liberty interest under the Due Process Clause does not end our inquiry; 'whether respondent's constitutional rights have been violated must be determined by balancing [her] liberty interests against the relevant state interests.'" Id. at 279, 110 S. Ct. at 2851-52.

Essentially, the judges were being asked to declare unconstitutional a law that prohibits assistance in taking a viable, self-sustaining life. This struck the Supreme Court as not merely a request to venture into uncharted legal territory but also into uncharted moral and ethical territory.

Viewed in this context, it seems particularly critical for the policy branches of government to establish such a right, if one is to be established. Given the historical treatment of suicide and assisted suicide, the Supreme Court was loath to find or create new constitutional rights where none existed before. The Court did not accept the plaintiffs' argument that, because the policy branches of government have not acted, the courts must.

The plaintiffs asked the Court to strike down a law adopted by the State of Michigan, through its Supreme Court, in an area that has traditionally been left to the states: the regulation of medical and ethical conduct and the definition of crimes involving the taking of life. The regulation of this area goes to the heart of a state's traditional responsibility to define crimes and make determinations governing general health and welfare issues. Before federal courts invade and preempt this province of the states, it must be shown that there is an overriding federal constitutional interest that dictates such extraordinary action. In this case there has been no showing made of an overriding federal interest that would require displacement of state law.

The Court declined the plaintiffs' request to find a due process liberty interest right in the Constitution that confers constitutionally protected status upon assisted suicide.

The plaintiffs argued that a withdrawal of life-supporting nutrition and hydration is indistinguishable from assisted suicide. They contended that the withdrawal of food, water, and respiration were overt acts, not omissive conduct. They argued that because these acts were overt, there is no rational distinction between them and acts to hasten death by means of assisted suicide.

There is a rational basis for distinguishing withdrawal of life support from assisting at a suicide. As the Michigan Supreme Court explained:

[W]hereas suicide involves an affirmative act to end a life, the refusal or cessation of life-sustaining medical treatment simply permits life to run its course, unencumbered by contrived intervention. Put another way, suicide frustrates the natural course by introducing an outside agent to accelerate death, whereas the refusal or withdrawal of life-sustaining medical treatment allows nature to proceed, e.g., death occurs because of the underlying condition. 527 N.W.2d at 728.

The equal protection clause of the Fourteenth Amendment requires only that states treat in a similar manner all individuals who are similarly situated.

Discussion

1. Examine the plaintiffs' arguments for asking the court to decide that prohibiting assisted suicide violates the equal protection clause.
2. For what specific reasons did the court decide there is no constitutional right to assisted suicide?
3. On October 27, 1997, Oregon enacted the Death with Dignity Act, which allows terminally ill Oregonians to end their lives through the voluntary self-administration of lethal medications expressly prescribed by a physician for that purpose. Oregon is the first state—and one of the first jurisdictions in the world—to permit some terminally ill patients to determine the time of their own death. Discuss whether this Act has any bearing on Michigan statutes.

"Right to Die" and "Making One Die" Distinguished

Citation: *Quill v. Vacco,* 117 S. Ct. 2293 (1997)

Facts

The plaintiffs–appellants, Drs. Quill, Klagsbrun, and Grossman, challenged the constitutionality of two New York State statutes penalizing assisted suicide. The physicians contended that each statute is invalid to the extent that it prohibits them from acceding to the requests of mentally competent, terminally ill patients for help in hastening death.

The physician respondents alleged that they encountered, in the course of their medical practices, mentally competent, terminally ill patients who requested assistance in the voluntary self-termination of life. Many of these patients apparently experienced chronic, intractable pain and/or intolerable suffering and sought to hasten their deaths for those reasons. The physicians alleged that they were unable to exercise their best professional judgment to prescribe requested drugs, and the other plaintiffs alleged that they were unable to receive the requested drugs, because of the prohibitions contained in sections 125.15(3) and 120.30 of the New York Penal Law, all respondents being residents of New York.

Section 125.15 of the New York Penal Law

A person is guilty of manslaughter in the second degree when . . . He intentionally . . . aids another person to commit suicide.

A violation of this provision is classified as a class C felony. Id.

Section 120.30 of the New York Penal Law

A person is guilty of promoting a suicide attempt when he intentionally . . . aids another person to attempt suicide.

Respondents argued that "[t]he Fourteenth Amendment guarantees the liberty of mentally competent, terminally ill adults with no chance of recovery to make decisions about the end of their lives." It also included an allegation that the Fourteenth Amendment guarantees the liberty of physicians to practice medicine consistent with their best professional judgment, including the use of their skills and powers in prescribing suitable medications for self-administration by mentally competent, terminally ill adult patients who have exercised the decision to hasten inevitable death.

Respondents further urged that the relevant portions of the New York Penal Law deny the patient–plaintiffs and the patients of the physician–plaintiffs the equal protection of the law by denying them the right to choose to hasten inevitable death, while terminally ill persons whose treatment includes life support are able to exercise this choice with necessary medical assistance by directing termination of such treatment.

The district court concluded that physician-assisted suicide at issue in this case does not involve a fundamental liberty interest protected by the Due Process Clause of the Fourteenth Amendment.

The district court identified a reasonable and rational basis for the distinction drawn by New York law between the refusal of treatment at the hands of physicians and physician assisted suicide.

[I]t is hardly unreasonable or irrational for the State to recognize a difference between allowing nature to take its course, even in the most severe situations, and intentionally using an artificial death-producing device. The State has obvious legitimate interests in preserving life, and in protecting vulnerable persons. The State has the further right to determine how these crucial interests are to be treated when the issue is posed as to whether a physician can assist a patient in committing suicide. Id. at 84–85.

Issue

Did the assisted suicide ban and the law permitting patients to refuse medical treatment in this case treat anyone differently from anyone else or draw any distinctions between persons?

Finding

The Supreme Court decided on appeal that neither the assisted suicide ban nor the law permitting patients to refuse medical treatment treats anyone differently from anyone else or draws any distinctions between persons. It explained that there is a distinction between "letting a patient die," and "making one die." Most legislatures have allowed the former but have prohibited the latter. The Supreme Court disagreed with the respondents' claim that the distinction is arbitrary and irrational.

Reason

In its decision, the Supreme Court determined that New York had valid reasons for distinguishing between "refusing treatment" and "assisting suicide." Those reasons included prohibiting intentional killing and preserving life; preventing suicide; maintaining the physician's role as his or her patient's healer; and protecting vulnerable people from indifference, prejudice, and psychological and financial pressure to end their lives. All of those reasons, the Court decided, constitute valid and important public interests fulfilling the constitutional requirement that a legislative classification bear a rational relation to a legitimate end.

Discussion

1. For what reasons did the Supreme Court disagree with the second circuit and find that New York's statute prohibiting assisted suicide did not violate the equal protection clause?
2. Describe what you think the Supreme Court meant when it stated that there is a difference between letting and making a person die. Cite examples to explain the difference.

Right to Have Care Requests Honored

Citation: *In re Martin,* 517 N.W.2d 749 (Mich. Ct. App. 1994)

Facts

Mr. Martin sustained debilitating injuries as the result of an automobile accident. He suffered severe subcortical brain damage that significantly impaired his physical and cognitive functioning. His injuries left him totally paralyzed on the left side, with limited but nonfunctional movement in his right limbs. He could not speak or eat and had no bladder or bowel control. Mr. Martin remained conscious and had some awareness of his surroundings. He could communicate to a very minimal degree through head nods.

The trial court determined that Mr. Martin did not have nor would he ever have the requisite capacity to make decisions regarding the withdrawal of life-supporting medical equipment. The evidence demonstrated that Mr. Martin's preference would have been to decline life support equipment, given his medical condition and prognosis.

The trial court's decision was based on the following four-part test for determining if a person has the requisite capacity to make a decision:

[W]hether the person (1) has sufficient mind to reasonably understand the condition, (2) is capable of understanding the nature and effect of the treatment choices, (3) is aware of the consequences associated with those choices, and (4) is able to make an informed choice that is voluntary and not coerced. Id. at 751.

The trial court determined that Mrs. Martin, the patient's spouse, was a suitable guardian for him. Mrs. Martin petitioned to withdraw her husband's life support. Mr. Martin's mother and sister counter petitioned to have Mrs. Martin removed as the patient's guardian.

Issue

(1) Was the evidence sufficient to support a finding that the patient lacked capacity to make decisions regarding the withholding or withdrawal of life-sustaining medical treatment? (2) Was there sufficient evidence to show that the patient had a medical preference to decline medical treatment? (3) Was there sufficient evidence to show that the patient's spouse was a suitable guardian?

Holding

(1) The Michigan Court of Appeals on appeal held that the evidence was sufficient to support a finding that the patient lacked capacity to make decisions regarding the withholding or withdrawal of life-sustaining medical treatment. (2) As to the patient's desire not to be placed on life-supporting equipment, there was sufficient evidence to show that the patient had a medical preference to decline medical treatment under circumstances such as those that occurred. (3) There was also sufficient evidence to show that the patient's spouse was a suitable guardian.

Reason

The test for determining if Mr. Martin had the requisite capacity to make a decision regarding the withholding or withdrawal of life-supporting medical treatment was clear and convincing—he did not have sufficient decision-making capacity. The evidence was just as clear that he never would regain sufficient decision-making capacity that would enable him to make such a decision. It was the general consensus of all of the experts that Mr. Martin's condition and cognitive level of functioning would not improve in the future.

Testimony from two of Mr. Martin's friends described statements made by him that he would never want to be maintained in a coma or in a vegetative state. In addition, Mrs. Martin described numerous statements made to her by Mr. Martin prior to the accident that he would not want to be maintained alive given the circumstances described earlier. The trial court found that Mrs. Martin was "credible, if not the most credible witness the court has heard throughout these proceedings." Id. at 753. The court of appeals found no reason to dispute the trial court's finding as to Mrs. Martin's credibility.

Contrary to allegations made by the patient's mother and sister, the evidence was clear that Mrs. Martin's testimony was credible. There was no evidence of financial considerations or pressure from any other individual that would show Mrs. Martin's testimony was influenced by other individuals, no evidence that she had anything but her husband's best interest at heart.

Discussion

1. Knowing that the patient had some ability to interact with his environment, discuss the four-part test for determining the patient's ability to make a decision.
2. Do you agree with the court's decision? Explain.
3. Should the concern of the patient's mother and sister have carried more weight in removing custody from Mrs. Martin?
4. What influence do you believe the mother and sister might have had on Mrs. Martin?

Patient Wishes Must Be Established

Citation: *Grace Plaza of Great Neck v. Elbaum*, 623 N.E.2d 513 (N.Y. 1993)

Facts

In September 1986, the plaintiff, Grace Plaza, a long-term care facility, admitted Ms. Elbaum, who had been treated for a stroke by North Shore University Hospital. She was admitted in a persistent vegetative state, necessitating a gastrostomy tube. Her husband informed the nursing home that he wanted them to remove the feeding tube because his wife had told him she wanted to die naturally. When the facility refused to remove the tube, Mr. Elbaum refused to pay for further treatment. When the plaintiff sued to recover the money, Mr. Elbaum was granted summary judgment. The New York Supreme Court, Appellate Division, reversed, and Mr. Elbaum then appealed.

Issue

(1) If there is a disagreement between the facility and the family of the patient, is it the family who must seek legal determination of the patient's wishes? (2) Did the defendant present any documentary evidence of his wife's intentions? (3) Was the patient competent to communicate her treatment wishes?

Holding

(1) The court found that if there is a disagreement between the facility and the family of the patient, it is the family who must seek legal determination of the patient's wishes. (2) The defendant did not present any documentary evidence of his wife's intentions. (3) Although New York recognizes the right of competent patients to decide what happens to their bodies, including preventing life-sustaining treatment, the patient was incompetent and thus could not communicate her lack of consent to treatment.

Reason

Since there were no proxy or living will laws in effect at the time of this case, only the patient had the right to decide what her course of treatment would be, if any. Families of incompetent patients must establish, by clear and convincing evidence, the patient's wishes regarding continuation of care. If there is a dispute over the wishes, the provider may refuse to discontinue treatment until the matter is resolved legally. If the provider continues treatment, it may be paid for services rendered, because the refusal to discontinue does not constitute a breach of contract. The request to terminate life support is treated differently than a routine change in treatment. The family of an incompetent patient has the most access to necessary evidence to submit to the court.

Discussion

1. Do you agree with the court's decision? Explain.
2. What role could an ethics committee have played in this scenario?

Right of Bodily Self-Determination

Citation: *Stamford Hosp. v. Vega*, 236 Conn. 646, 674 A.2d 821 (Conn. Super. Ct. 1996)

Facts

On August 26, 1994, Ms. Vega was admitted as a patient to Stamford Hospital to deliver her first child. That evening, Ms. Vega, a Jehovah's Witness, executed a release requesting that no blood or its derivatives be administered to her during her hospitalization and relieving the hospital and its personnel of liability for any adverse effects that might result from her refusal to permit the use of blood in her treatment. Ms. Vega's husband also signed the release.

On August 27, 1994, Ms. Vega delivered a healthy baby. Following the delivery, Ms. Vega bled heavily as a result of a retained piece of the placenta. Her obstetrician, Dr. Sood, recommended a dilation and curettage in order to stop the bleeding. Although Ms. Vega agreed to permit Dr. Sood to perform the dilation and curettage, she refused to allow a blood transfusion. Prior to undergoing the procedure, she signed another release requesting that she be given no transfusions and releasing the hospital from liability. Despite the dilation and curettage, Ms. Vega continued to hemorrhage.

Ms. Vega's physician tried a number of alternatives to the use of blood, but her condition continued to worsen. Eventually, when she was having difficulty breathing, her physicians placed her on a respirator in the intensive care unit. Ms. Vega and her husband maintained throughout these events that, although she might die without blood transfusions, it was against their religious beliefs to allow the use of blood. Because Dr. Sood and the other physicians involved in Ms. Vega's care believed it was essential that she receive blood in order to survive, the hospital filed a complaint against Ms. Vega on August 28, 1994, requesting that the court issue an injunction that would permit the hospital to administer blood transfusions to her.

The trial court convened an emergency hearing at the hospital on August 28. Although Ms. Vega's attorney was en route to the hospital, the court appointed Ms. Vega's husband as her guardian ad litem and began hearing testimony. Ms. Vega's physicians testified that they had exhausted all nonblood alternatives and that, with reasonable medical certainty, she would die without blood transfusions. Her husband testified that, on the basis of his religious beliefs as a Jehovah's Witness, he continued to support his wife's decision to refuse transfusions and believed she would take the same position if she were able to participate in the hearing.

The court, relying on the state's interests in preserving life and protecting innocent third parties, and noting that Ms. Vega's life could be saved by a blood transfusion, granted the hospital's request for an injunction permitting it to administer blood transfusions to her. The court then stayed the order until Ms. Vega's attorney could arrive and be given the opportunity to present argument and additional evidence, after which the court reinstated its judgment permitting the hospital to administer blood transfusions to Ms. Vega. Ms. Vega was then given blood transfusions; she recovered and was discharged from the hospital.

Ms. Vega appealed the trial court's judgment in Appellate Court.

Issue

Was the hospital's move to dismiss the appeal sustainable on grounds that it was moot?

Holding

The Appellate Court granted the hospital's motion.

Reason

Ms. Vega argued that if her refusal of blood transfusions interfered with certain state interests, it should be the state itself, not a private hospital, that asserts the state's interests. The hospital responded that, because it was charged with Ms. Vega's care, and because it was required to choose between disregarding either Ms. Vega's wishes or her physicians' recommendations that she receive the transfusions, it had a direct stake in the outcome of the controversy and was a proper party to bring this action.

The court determined that the case was not moot; insofar as the hospital's claims are founded on its own interests, rather than those of the state, the court agreed with the hospital that it had standing to bring those claims; and the court concluded that, under the circumstances of this case, the hospital's legitimate interest in protecting its patients does not extend that far.

The hospital later conceded that this case is not moot, because it is capable of repetition. Notwithstanding the hospital's concession and the resulting lack of dispute between the parties, the court considered the issue of mootness.

A challenge to the issuance of an injunction permitting the administration of nonconsensual blood transfusions will virtually always become moot long before appellate litigation can be concluded (or even initiated). Obviously, a medically necessary blood transfusion must be accomplished, if at all, as soon as reasonably possible after its need becomes apparent to the patient's healthcare provider. Once a court order is issued permitting such a transfusion against the patient's will, and once the court lifts any stay of that order (as it inevitably does), the healthcare provider that sought the order cannot be expected to await the outcome of an appeal before giving the urgently needed transfusion. Any order that is challenged on appeal is, by its very nature, of such limited duration that it is virtually certain it will become moot before appellate litigation can be concluded.

The hospital had a legitimate interest in receiving official guidance in resolving the ethical dilemma it faced: whether to practice medicine by trying to save a patient's life despite that patient's refusal to consent to treatment, or to practice medicine in accordance with the patient's wishes and likely watch the patient die, knowing nonetheless that it had the power to save her life. The hospital had conflicting interests and was in the role not of opposing its patient but of seeking the court's guidance in determining its obligations under the circumstances.

Conferring standing only on the state and denying it to the hospital, in this case, however, would have had the practical effect of requiring the hospital to abandon its own legitimate interests. Such action would have effectively insulated the patient's choice from any official scrutiny, because it would have been extremely difficult for the state to initiate judicial proceedings in time to do any good, and even if the state could have done so, it would likely have been unfamiliar both with the medical options available and with the facts and circumstances surrounding the patient's desires. Under these circumstances, the hospital was the best-informed and most feasible candidate to set judicial machinery in motion. The court concluded that, for these reasons, the hospital had standing to challenge Ms. Vega's refusal of blood transfusions.

Ms. Vega claimed that the state's interest in the welfare of her child is not sufficiently compelling as to outweigh her interest in refusing blood transfusions. Ms. Vega maintains that the trial court's injunction, issued at the behest of the hospital, violated her common law right of self-determination, her federal constitutional right to bodily self-determination, her federal constitutional right to free exercise of religion, and her state constitutional right of religious liberty. The court concluded that, under the circumstances of this case, the issuance of the injunction, followed by administration of the blood transfusions, violated Ms. Vega's common law right of bodily self-determination.

Once the infant was born, Ms. Vega's decision to refuse a blood transfusion posed no risk to the infant's physical health. Ms. Vega's claim centers on her common law right of bodily self-determination. The only question, therefore, is whether the hospital and the trial court were obliged to respect Ms. Vega's decision to refuse blood transfusions, even though her decision would likely have led to her death.

Although the hospital's interests are sufficient to confer standing in this case, they are not sufficient to take priority over Ms. Vega's common law right to bodily integrity, even when the assertion of that right threatens her own life. The hospital had no common law right or obligation to thrust unwanted medical care on a patient who, having been sufficiently informed of the consequences, competently and clearly declined that care. The hospital's interests were sufficiently protected by Ms. Vega's informed choice, and neither it nor the trial court was entitled to override that choice. Ms. Vega's common law right of bodily self-determination was entitled to respect and protection. The trial court improperly issued an injunction that permitted the hospital to administer blood transfusions to Ms. Vega.

Discussion

1. Does a hospital have standing to assert the state's parens patriae interest in the welfare of a minor child whose adult parent is hospitalized and is refusing allegedly lifesaving medical treatment?
2. Is the state's alleged parens patriae interest in the welfare of a minor child whose parent is refusing allegedly lifesaving treatment for religious and medical reasons a compelling state interest that overrides the parent's common law right of bodily self-determination, federal constitutional rights of bodily self-determination and religious free exercise, and state constitutional right of religious liberty?
3. Is the forcible administration of unwanted medical treatment to a competent adult the least restrictive, least intrusive means of protecting the state's alleged parens patriae interest in the welfare of that adult's minor child?

Right to Refuse Treatment on Religious Grounds
Citation: *Matter of Dubreuil*, 629 So. 2d 819 (Fla. 1993)

Facts

A patient was in an advanced stage of pregnancy when she was admitted through the emergency department of the hospital. At the time of her admission, she signed a standard consent form that included her agreement to have a blood transfusion if necessary. On the next day, however, she would not consent to a blood transfusion (because of her religious beliefs) before undergoing Caesarean section. During the course of the delivery, after the patient had lost a significant amount of blood, her physicians determined that she needed a transfusion to save her life, but she again refused consent. Her estranged husband was contacted, and upon his arrival at the hospital, he gave his consent for the transfusion. After the first transfusion, physicians determined that she would need more, so they petitioned the circuit court for an emergency declaratory judgment hearing to determine if they could give the transfusion in spite of the patient's lack of consent. Although no testimony was given at the hearing, there was a telephone call advising the court that the patient had just regained consciousness and that she continued to withhold her consent.

The trial court decided to allow the hospital to administer blood, for they felt it was necessary. The patient moved for a rehearing, and the circuit court denied it. The patient then sought review by the Florida Supreme Court, arguing that her federal and state constitutional rights of privacy, self-determination, and religious freedom had been denied.

Issue

Does a competent person have the right to choose or refuse medical treatment, including all decisions relevant to his or her health?

Holding

A competent person has the right to choose or refuse medical treatment, including all decisions relevant to his or her health.

Reason

A competent person has the right to choose or refuse medical treatment, including all decisions relevant to his or her health. That right includes the right to refuse a blood transfusion and merges with the right to exercise one's religious beliefs. A healthcare provider must comply with the patient's wishes unless supported by a court order to do otherwise. Here, the state interest was the protection of the children as innocent third parties. However, in this case there would have been no abandonment, because under Florida law, when there are two living parents, they share equally in the responsibilities of parenting. Had the patient died, her husband would have assumed care of the children.

Discussion

1. What are the competing rights of the state and patient with regard to refusing blood transfusions because of the patient's religious beliefs?
2. Do you agree with the court's decision? Explain.

Right to Refuse Blood Transfusion

Citation: *Harrell v. St. Mary's Hosp. Inc.*, 678 So. 2d 455 (1996)

Facts

The appellee, St. Mary's Hospital, filed an emergency petition in circuit court regarding the health care of the appellant, Mrs. Harrell, a Jehovah's Witness. Mrs. Harrell was 6-months pregnant when the physicians discovered a life-threatening blood condition that could rapidly deteriorate and place both her life and the life of the fetus in jeopardy. Because of her religious beliefs, Mrs. Harrell objected to any blood transfusion. After an emergency hearing at which The Harrells could not summon an attorney, the court ruled that a blood transfusion could be given to Mrs. Harrell if it was necessary to save the life of the fetus and that, after the child was born, a blood transfusion could be given to the child if necessary to save the child's life. However, the child was delivered by Caesarean section and died 2 days later. No blood transfusion was given to Mrs. Harrell or to the child. As a result, St. Mary's Hospital and the state claim that the appeal of the trial court's order is moot. Because of the hospital's serious misunderstanding about its standing to bring such proceedings, the court addressed the issue of standing as capable of repetition yet evading review.

Issue

Does a medical provider have standing to assert state interests in a petition to require treatment for its patient?

Holding

The Florida District Court of Appeals determined that a medical provider does not have standing to assert state interests in a petition to require treatment for its patient.

Reason

Article I, Section 23 of the Florida Constitution guarantees that a competent person has the constitutional right to choose or refuse medical treatment, and that right extends to all relevant decisions concerning one's health. In cases where these rights are litigated, a party generally seeks to invoke the power of the state, through the exercise of the court's judicial power, either to enforce the patient's rights or to prevent the patient from exercising those rights. The state has a duty to ensure that a person's wishes regarding medical treatment are respected. That obligation serves to protect the rights of the individual from intrusion by the state unless the state has a compelling interest great enough to override this constitutional right (e.g., protection of innocent third parties). The means to carry out any such compelling state interest must be narrowly tailored in the least intrusive manner possible to safeguard the rights of the individual.

Mrs. Harrell argued that the hospital should not have intervened in her private decision to refuse a blood transfusion. She claimed that the state had never been a party in this action, had not asserted any interest, and that the hospital had no authority to assume the state's responsibilities.

The court concluded that a healthcare provider must not be forced into the position of having to argue zealously against the wishes of its own patient, seeking deference to the wishes or interests of nonpatients—in this case, the patient's husband, her brothers, the children, and the state itself. Patients do not lose their right to make decisions affecting their lives when they enter into the care of a healthcare facility. A healthcare provider's function is to provide medical treatment in accordance with the patient's wishes and best interests, not to supervene the wishes of a competent adult. A healthcare provider must comply with the wishes of a patient who refuses medical treatment, unless the provider is ordered to do otherwise by a court of competent jurisdiction. A healthcare provider cannot act on behalf of the state to assert state interests.

In situations like these, healthcare providers generally have sought judicial intervention to determine their rights and obligations so as to avoid liability. When terminating life support in accordance with a patient's wishes, healthcare providers are relieved of potential civil and criminal liability as long as they act in good faith and do not require prior court approval of that termination. When a healthcare provider acts in good faith and follows the wishes of a competent and informed patient to refuse medical treatment, the provider is acting appropriately and cannot be subjected to civil or criminal liability.

Although this procedure absolves the healthcare facility of any obligation to go to court, the court recognizes the need for the state and interested parties to have the opportunity to seek judicial intervention, if appropriate. A healthcare provider wishing to override a patient's decision to refuse medical treatment must immediately provide notice to the State Attorney presiding in the circuit where the controversy arises and to interested third parties known to the healthcare provider. The extent to which the State Attorney chooses to engage in a legal action (if any) is discretionary, based on the law and facts of each case. This procedure should eliminate needless litigation by healthcare providers while honoring the patient's wishes and giving other interested parties the right to intervene if there is a good faith reason to do so.

The hospital's contention that it had standing to seek judicial intervention to determine its "obligations, duties, and responsibilities" concerning the delivery of medical health care and treatment was rejected. If the hospital wished to override Mrs. Harrell's decision to refuse medical treatment, it was required to immediately provide notice to the State Attorney so that the State Attorney could determine whether it would take legal action to compel the transfusion.

Discussion

1. Describe those circumstances in which a state might have a right to interfere with a patient's decision to forgo emergency care.
2. When considering a person's religious beliefs, should the state have a right to interfere with a mother's decision to refuse a blood transfusion? Why?
3. Should a hospital be able to raise whatever interest the state itself may have in seeking to compel an unwilling patient to undergo a routine, lifesaving medical procedure? Explain.

Right to Have a Guardian Appointed

Citation: *Matter of Hughes*, 611 A.2d 1148 (N.J. Super. Ct. 1992)

Facts

On May 13, 1991, a 39-year-old and devout Jehovah's Witness named Mrs. Hughes was admitted to the hospital to undergo a hysterectomy. A principal tenet of Jehovah's Witnesses is the belief that receiving blood or blood products into one's body precludes resurrection and everlasting life after death. At the time of her admission to the hospital, Mrs. Hughes signed forms expressing her desire not to receive any blood or blood products. She also verbally expressed this intention to her treating physician, Dr. Ances. Unanticipated problems arose during surgery that, in the opinion of Dr. Ances, required blood transfusions to save Mrs. Hughes's life. Dr. Ances contacted the patient's husband to discuss the emergency situation and his wife's consequent need for blood. Mr. Hughes, also a Jehovah's Witness, authorized transfusions when Dr. Ances spoke with him by phone.

On May 14, 1991, the hospital initiated an emergency hearing before a judge for the purpose of having a temporary guardian appointed for Mrs. Hughes to allow additional transfusions after the surgery. Mrs. Hughes was unconscious and incapable of expressing her desires at the time.

Dr. Ances testified that Mrs. Hughes, who had been his patient for 6 weeks at the time of her hysterectomy, told him that she did not want blood products. He informed her that a situation could arise requiring blood to save her life. He also told her that, given the procedure and the size of the uterus, it was unlikely that she would need blood during the surgery. Dr. Ances was aware that Mrs. Hughes had signed hospital forms refusing blood and assumed Mrs. Hughes was aware of the ramifications of refusing the blood, so he did not specifically discuss those ramifications with her. After hearing testimony from Dr. Ances and Mrs. Hughes's family, the judge found the evidence unclear as to whether she would want blood or blood products if it meant saving her life. As a result, the judge appointed the hospital's risk manager as temporary guardian for the limited purpose of giving consent to the administration of blood and blood products. The order explicitly extended only until Mrs. Hughes regained consciousness and became competent to make her own decisions. Mrs. Hughes received blood transfusions and recovered. Upon regaining competency, she withdrew the hospital's right to transfuse blood.

Issue

Was the judge's decision to appoint a temporary medical guardian for Mrs. Hughes legally supportable?

Holding

The Superior Court of New Jersey held that the judge's decision to appoint a temporary medical guardian for Mrs. Hughes was legally supportable.

Reason

The doctrine of informed consent was developed to protect the right of self-determination in matters of medical treatment. Self-determination encompasses the right to refuse medical treatment and is a right protected by common law and by the federal and state constitutional right to privacy. The New Jersey Supreme Court has repeatedly addressed the right to decline medical treatment in situations where the patient is opposed to prolonging an otherwise irreversible condition. The distinguishing factor in this case, however, is that the transfusion can preserve a healthy young woman's life, not prolong a painful and imminent death. The Pennsylvania Supreme Court affirmed a trial judge's decision to appoint a temporary guardian to consent to blood transfusions when a patient is unconscious. The court reasoned that medical intervention necessary to preserve life requires nothing less than a "fully conscious contemporaneous decision by the patient . . ." *In re Estate of Darone*, 349 Pa. Super. Ct. 59, 502 A.2d 1271 (1985), aff'd, 517 Pa. 3, 534 A.2d 452, 455 (1987). In New Jersey, the decision maker must determine and effectuate, insofar as possible, the decision that the patient would have made if competent. Any information bearing on the person's intent may be an appropriate aid in determining what course of treatment the patient would have wished to pursue.

A subjective standard was held by the Supreme Court of New Jersey to be "applicable in every surrogate-refusal-of-treatment case, regardless of the patient's medical condition or life-expectancy." Under this standard, life-sustaining treatment may be withdrawn or withheld when there is clear and convincing evidence that the patient, if competent, would decline the treatment. Id. at 1152. The present facts indicate that Mrs. Hughes specifically advised Dr. Ances and family members of her desire not to receive blood or blood products. She further directed the hospital and her physician, in writing, to refrain from giving her a transfusion. Yet, some uncertainty remained as to what Mrs. Hughes may have desired had she been competent and understood the gravity of the life-threatening situation that developed. Mrs. Hughes's statements were made in the context of an impending hysterectomy—a procedure Dr. Ances advised would probably not require a transfusion. At no time did Mrs. Hughes discuss with Dr. Ances the risk of complications during surgery (such as bleeding to death) during a routine hysterectomy. Therefore, a doubt existed as to whether Mrs. Hughes had made a fully informed and knowing decision to refuse blood *even* if this meant her death. Any glimmer of uncertainty as to Mrs. Hughes's desires in an emergency situation should be resolved "in favor of preserving life." *In re Conroy*, 98 N.J. at 368, 486 A.2d 1209 (1985).

An approach to reinforce a patient's wishes is to have the patient sign forms prior to medical treatment. These suggested forms should be distinguished from those signed by Mrs. Hughes prior to her surgery. Mrs. Huges signed a standard hospital form entitled "Refusal to Permit Blood Transfusion," which used a fill-in-the-blanks type approach. The form stated

---

I request that no blood or blood derivatives be administered to Alice Hughes [typewritten on original form] during the hospitalization. I hereby release the hospital, its personnel, and the attending physician from any responsibility whatever for unfavorable reactions or any untoward results due to my refusal to permit the use of blood or its derivatives and I fully understand the possible consequences of such refusal on my part. The consequences of this refusal have been explained to me by———. Id. at 1153.

Mrs. Hughes and a witness signed the form, but there was no indication in the space provided that the consequences of her refusal had been explained to her in the context of this particular operation. These proposed forms must contain an unequivocal statement that blood is not to be used under any and all circumstances and an acknowledgment that the consequences of the refusal were fully supplied to the patient. The form should fully release the physician, all other medical personnel, and the hospital from liability should complications arise from the failure to administer blood, thereby resolving any doubt as to the physician's responsibility to his patient. If a patient refuses to sign such a form, the physician should then decide whether to continue with treatment or to aid the patient in finding another physician. Id. at 1153.

The court emphasized that this case arose in the context of elective surgery. This was not an emergency situation that prevented the physician and patient from having time to fully discuss the potential risks of the surgery and the depth of the patient's religious beliefs. A Jehovah's Witness patient has an obligation to make medical preferences unequivocally known to the treating physician, including the course to follow if life-threatening complications should arise. This protects not only the patient's rights to freedom of religion and self-determination but also the hospital's obligation to preserve life whenever possible. Id.

Discussion

1. Do you agree with the court's finding? Explain.
2. Under what conditions might it be reasonable to administer blood to a Jehovah's Witness?

Prolonging Life Not Actionable

Citation: *Anderson v. St. Francis–St. George Hosp.*, 614 N.E.2d 841 (Ohio Ct. App. 1992)

Facts

The administrator of the deceased patient's estate brought suit against the hospital, alleging battery, negligence, and "wrongful living." The administrator's original complaint alleged that on May 25, 1988, the deceased, Mr. Winter, was admitted to the hospital with chest pain. After initial treatment in the emergency department, Mr. Winter was given additional care in the hospital's coronary unit. The administrator alleged that Mr. Winter had a discussion with his family and his private physician, Dr. Russo, about the type of treatment that he was to receive while at the hospital; in addition, there was evidence that Dr. Russo entered the instruction in the hospital record "No Code Blue" as a result of that discussion. In his complaint, the administrator claimed that this no-code-blue entry indicated that Dr. Russo specifically instructed that Mr. Winter not be resuscitated.

During Mr. Winter's subsequent treatment at the hospital, he suffered a ventricular fibrillation. The administrator alleged that a nurse resuscitated Mr. Winter by shocking his heart with an electric current, despite Dr. Russo's instructions, and that the nurse's act of resuscitation constituted battery. The administrator also maintained that the hospital caused Mr. Winter "great pain, suffering, emotional distress, and disability" along with medical and other financial expenses by keeping him alive as they did.

The Court of Common Pleas granted summary judgment for the hospital, and the administrator appealed.

Issue

(1) Were there questions of fact as to consent? (2) Did the patient's harms caused by defibrillation preclude summary judgment on the battery claim? (3) Was prolonging the patient's life wrongful living? (4) Did questions of fact preclude summary judgment on the negligence claim?

Holding

The Court of Appeals of Ohio held that there were questions of fact as to consent and whether the patient's later harms were proximately caused by defibrillation, thus precluding summary judgment on the battery claim. Prolonging of the patient's life was not wrongful living, and questions of fact precluded summary judgment on the negligence claim.

Reason

In the appellant's assignment of error, he claims that the decedent's life was prolonged by the defibrillation but that life "was, for him, not worth living." Appellant coins the name for the cause of action for the life that was forced on decedent by the resuscitation as wrongful living. This rather novel notion has not been addressed directly in Ohio courts. Nonetheless, it is possible to determine that life is not a compensable harm; therefore, there is no cause of action for wrongful living. Id. at 845.

The Ohio Supreme Court has referred to the joy of life as an "intangible benefit" that cannot be valued monetarily. *Johnson v. Univ. Hosp. of Cleveland* (1989), 44 Ohio St. 3d 49, 55, 540 N.E.2d 1370, 1375. Damages are not those things that add to life but those that subtract. Even though a victim must have some legally recognized harm to recover actual damages, nonconsensual medical treatment that prolongs a person's life may still be a battery. Therefore, as in any battery, the plaintiff is entitled to some relief. When, however, the nonconsensual treatment is harmless or beneficial, damages for the wrongful act are nominal only, not actual.

There are, however, questions of fact concerning the possible breach of that duty. There was evidence in the record that indicates that the decedent requested limitations on his care while at the hospital. There was also evidence that the decedent's private physician ordered that the decedent not be resuscitated. Also, there was evidence that either the hospital or the nurse, or both, were negligent in preventing or causing the nonconsensual treatment. Therefore, two issues remain for the trier of fact. First, was the defibrillation precluded by the no-code-blue instruction? Second, if the defibrillation was within the ambit of the instruction, was either the hospital or the attending nurse negligent by resuscitating the decedent? If the trier of fact determines that either the hospital or the nurse breached a duty to the decedent, then just as in battery, the appellant must prove that later harms were proximately caused by the negligent act. In addition, if there were proximately caused harms, the court should allow compensation only for damages that are recognized by Ohio law. In contrast to battery, however, if the court finds negligence, but no compensable harm, it should not allow nominal damages. In this case, genuine issues remained on the question of the defendant's negligence. Therefore, the trial court erred by granting summary judgment on that portion of the case.

The court of appeals affirmed the trial court's judgment dismissing the cause of action for wrongful living. For the issues in both battery and negligence, the case was remanded to the trial court for further proceedings.

Discussion

1. What did the administrator in this lawsuit mean by wrongful living?
2. Do you agree with the court's decision? Explain.

Right to Know Physician's HIV Status

Citation: *Application of Milton S. Hershey Med. Ctr.*, 639 A.2d 159 (Pa. 1993)

Facts

Physician "Dr. John Doe" was a resident in obstetrics and gynecology at the Milton S. Hershey Medical Center. In 1991, he cut his hand with a scalpel while he was assisting another physician. Because of the uncertainty that blood had been transferred from Dr. Doe's hand wound to the patient through an open surgical incision, he agreed to have a blood test for HIV. His blood tested positive for HIV, and he withdrew himself from participation in further surgical procedures. The date and means by which Dr. Doe contracted HIV could not be determined. The Hershey Medical Center and Harrisburg Hospital, where Dr. Doe also participated in surgery, identified those patients who could be at risk. Hershey identified 279 patients and Harrisburg identified 168 patients who fell into this category. Because the hospital records did not identify those surgeries in which physicians may have accidentally cut themselves, the hospitals filed petitions in the Court of Common Pleas alleging that, under the Confidentiality of HIV-Related Information Act [35 P.S. § 7608(a)(2)], there was a "compelling need" to disclose information regarding Dr. Doe's condition to those patients who conceivably could have been exposed to HIV. Dr. Doe argued that there was no compelling need to disclose the information and that he was entitled to confidentiality under the Act.

The court issued an order for the selective release of information by providing the name of Dr. Doe to physicians and residents in the Department of Obstetrics and Gynecology, by providing the name of Dr. Doe to physicians with whom he had participated in a surgical procedure or obstetrical care, by providing a letter to the patients at risk describing Dr. Doe as a resident in obstetrics and gynecology, and by setting forth the relevant period of such service. The physicians were reminded that they were prohibited under the HIV Act from disclosing Dr. Doe's name. The superior court affirmed the decision of the trial court.

Issue

Was there a compelling need for at least a partial disclosure of the physician's HIV status?

Holding

There is no question that Dr. Doe's HIV-positive status fell within the HIV Act's definition of confidential information. There were, however, exceptions within the HIV Act that allowed for limited disclosure of the information.

Reason

In this case, there was a compelling reason to allow disclosure of the information. Although a definition of compelling reason is not included in the Act, a balancing analysis needs to be applied.

The "court shall weigh the need for disclosure against the privacy interest of the individual and the public interests which may be harmed by disclosure" [35 P.S. § 7608(c)].

The medical experts who testified agreed that there was some risk to exposure and that some form of notice should be given to the patients at risk. "Even the expert witness presented by Dr. Doe agreed that there was at least some conceivable risk of exposure and that giving a very limited form of notice would not be unreasonable." Id. at 162. Failure to notify the patients at risk could result in the spread of the disease to other individuals not infected through sexual contact but through exposure to other body fluids. Dr. Doe's name was not revealed to the patients, only the fact that a resident physician who participated in their care had tested HIV-positive. "No principle is more deeply embedded in the law than that expressed in the maxim Salus populi suprema lex, . . . (the welfare of the people is the supreme law), and a more compelling and consistent application of that principle than the one presented would be quite difficult to conceive." Id. at 163.

Discussion

1. What steps should healthcare organizations take to reduce unauthorized access to the medical records of patients who have been diagnosed with HIV, if any?
2. Should the confidentiality of all medical records be treated in the same manner?

Patient Responsibility to Disclose Health Information

Citation: *Oxford v. Upson County Hosp. Inc.*, 438 S.E.2d 171 (Ga. Ct. App. 1993)

Facts

Ms. Oxford brought a lawsuit against Upson County Hospital and nurses, claiming that their medical malpractice caused her injury from a fall in the hospital bathroom. Ms. Oxford had been admitted to the hospital after having been diagnosed with gastroenteritis and dehydration. Nothing on her chart indicated that she had experienced dizziness. Testimony at the trial indicated that Ms. Oxford had told her nurse that she had to go to the bathroom. Ms. Oxford did not inform the nurse that she felt dizzy. After the nurse escorted her to the bathroom, Ms. Oxford fainted while sitting on the toilet. As she fainted, she hit her head on the bathroom wall.

Two nurse experts testified that it is a patient's responsibility to communicate to the staff any symptoms the patient is experiencing. Ms. Oxford had told her physician prior to her hospitalization about feeling dizzy, but he had not related this information to the hospital's staff.

After a jury verdict for the hospital, Ms. Oxford appealed, arguing that the trial court's jury charges on causation, failure to exercise ordinary care, and comparative negligence were wrong.

Issue

Were the jury's verdict and the judge's charges on the issues sufficient?

Holding

The Georgia Court of Appeals affirmed the jury verdict and found that the judge's charges on the issues had been sufficient.

Reason

The court followed its determination in Harper, 196 Ga. Ct. App. 658, 659, 396 S.E.2d 587 (1990) that when a patient fails to disclose all information related to her condition and fails to exercise ordinary care for her safety by seeking medical attention for her worsening condition, a charge of comparative negligence is applicable. In this case, the court did not require that Ms. Oxford diagnose herself, but she should have told the staff about her symptoms so that they could have treated her using their professional judgment.

Discussion

1. What precautions should the admitting physician and nurses take to help prevent similar injuries from occurring in the future?
2. Do you agree with the appellate court's decision?

NOTES

1. 42 U.S.C. 1395cc(a)(1).
2. http://www.healthreform.gov/newsroom/new_patients_bill_of_rights.html
3. http://www.miamiherald.com/2011/06/23/2280324/verdict-to-be-announced-in-del.html

chapter four

Screenings, Assessments, and Reassessments

Doctor's Suit Faults Care at 2 Clinics

The lawsuit says medical care at the clinics did not meet the requisite standard. There was no policy or procedure, for example, for evaluating how sick "walk-in" patients were. In several cases, patients in critical condition were not seen by medical providers for hours, the lawsuit says.

In a Nov. 8, 2009, e-mail to the Rev. Mario Dorsonville of the Spanish Catholic Center, Briggs wrote that he had been pushing for implementation of policies and procedures for 14 months but that problems were not being addressed.

Lena H. Sun, The Washington Post, *April 8, 2011*

Although the preceding newspaper article describes the need for appropriate policies and procedures to identify the severity of illness of walk-in patients in two clinics, the same need also requires that all patients (e.g., in-patients, emergency patients, ambulatory patients) be properly screened, assessed, and reassessed.

Patient assessments involve the systematic collection and analysis of patient-specific data necessary to determine patient care and treatment plans. The patient's plan of care can only be as good as assessments conducted by practitioners of the various disciplines (e.g., physicians, nurses, dietitians, physical therapists).

The *physician's assessment* involves an evaluation of the patient's history, symptoms, and physical examination results. It must be conducted within 24 hours of a patient's admission to the hospital. The findings of the clinical examination are used to determine the patient's plan of care. The assessment is the process by which a doctor investigates the patient's state of health, looking for signs of trauma and disease. It sets the stage for accurately diagnosing the patient's medical problems. A cursory and negligent assessment can lead to a misdiagnosis of the patient's health problems and/or care needs and, consequently, to poor care.

The *nurse assessment* is conducted at the time of the patient's admission and is used to determine the patient's nursing care needs. A form is generally used to help guide the nurse through the screening and assessment process. Included in the assessment are questions that might lead the nurse, for example, to suggest nutritional and functional assessments by a dietitian and/or physical therapist.

Nutritional assessments are often triggered by risk criteria that can include recent change in body weight; swallowing problems; vomiting and diarrhea; signs of malnutrition; obesity; religious, cultural, or ethnic eating practices; and so on.

Mobility problems that result from accidents, or diagnoses associated with various diseases (e.g., multiple sclerosis, Parkinson's disease) can trigger the need for a functional assessment.

ASSESSMENTS REQUIRED BY REGULATIONS AND STANDARDS

42 CFR ch. IV § 482.22 (b) Conditions of Participation

Standard: Medical staff organization and accountability. The medical staff must be well-organized and accountable to the governing body for the quality of medical care provided to patients.

42 CFR ch. IV § 482.22(c)(5)(i)

A medical history and physical examination is to be completed and documented for each patient no more than 30 days before or 24 hours after admission or registration but prior to surgery or a procedure requiring anesthesia services. The medical history and physical examination must be completed and documented by a physician (as defined in Section 1861(r) of the Act), an oromaxillofacial surgeon, or other qualified licensed individual in accordance with State law and hospital policy.

42 CFR ch. IV § 482.55 (3) Conditions of Participation: Emergency Services

The policies and procedures governing medical care provided in the emergency service or department are established by and are a continuing responsibility of the medical staff.

TJC 2010 Hospital Accreditation Standards, Provision of Care, Treatment, and Services (PC-1)

This section of the Joint Commission standards describes the screening and assessment process for patients. See the Joint Commission requirements, Standards and Elements of Performance for screenings and assessments at http://www.jointcomission.org/.

Need for Patient Assessment

Citation: *Delaney v. Cade*, 873 P.2d 175 (Kan. 1994)

Facts

The car of Ms. Delaney (plaintiff) collided with another automobile, and an ambulance transported her to Memorial Hospital. Ms. Delaney complained of chest pain. Dr. Cade, a member of the hospital's staff and the physician on call, began treating her. The plaintiff alleged Dr. Cade commenced suturing the lacerations on her knees without performing a physical examination, ordering X-rays, or starting an IV. After Ms. Delaney had been at Memorial 2 hours, Dr. Cade transferred her to Central Kansas Medical Center (CKMC). Ms. Delaney alleged she had feeling and movement in her legs when she left Memorial Hospital but had lost that feeling by the time she arrived at CKMC.

At the medical center, a physician performed an aortogram that showed the plaintiff had a transected aorta that had thrombosed. The physician operated on the plaintiff to repair the transected aorta. The plaintiff claimed that she was permanently paralyzed as a result of the thrombosed aorta. She contended Dr. Cade's treatment and his delay in transferring her to a facility that was equipped to treat her injuries deprived her of a significant chance to better recover from what became permanent injuries. The plaintiff supported her claims with the deposition testimony of three expert witnesses who agreed the thrombosis of her aorta caused the plaintiff's paralysis.

The defendants contend that a Dr. Harrison was the only witness to testify regarding any loss of chance the plaintiff may have suffered. In his deposition testimony, Dr. Harrison explained that 10% of patients with thoracic aortic injuries like Ms. Delaney's will suffer permanent paralysis regardless of how the injury is managed. If the plaintiff was in that 10%, she would have been a paraplegic no matter how much time passed between the accident and surgery. In addition, Dr. Harrison testified he had no way of determining whether the plaintiff was in that 10% or in the other 90%. However, Dr. Harrison did state that the plaintiff's risk of cord injury was increased 5 to 10% by the prolonged period of shock that she suffered prior to surgery. Id. at 178.

The trial court granted partial summary judgment for Dr. Cade, holding Kansas did not recognize the doctrine of significant chance of recovery. Ms. Delaney appealed.

Issue

Does Kansas recognize a medical malpractice cause of action for loss of chance of recovery?

Holding

The Supreme Court of Kansas held that Kansas recognizes a medical malpractice cause of action for loss of chance of recovery.

Reason

The loss of chance doctrine serves to fairly compensate the plaintiff for the tortious deprivation of an opportunity to live longer or recover from a physical injury or condition inflicted by the defendant's wrongful act or omission. In the medical malpractice context, lost chance endeavors to allow a plaintiff to recover for the diminished chances of surviving or recovering from a disease or malady which results from the health care defendant's malpractice.

Keith, Loss of Chance: A Modern Proportional Approach to Damages in Texas, 44 Baylor L. Rev. 759, 760 (1992).

The trial court made a determination that Kansas would not recognize such a cause of action in a loss of better recovery case even though it had recognized it in loss of chance for survival cases. The Supreme Court of Kansas found no support for the trial court's position. Although several jurisdictions have refused to recognize such a cause of action in either type of case, the court found no jurisdiction that has applied the theory to one type of case and denied it in the other. As noted by the plaintiff in her brief: "There is certainly nothing in that . . . rationale to justify leaving the season open on persons who suffer paralysis, organ loss, or other serious injury short of death while protecting only those who do not survive the negligence." Id. at 183. The court found that although most cases have involved death of the patient, and damages may be difficult to resolve in a loss of a better recovery case, this should not be grounds to refuse to recognize the doctrine whenever medical malpractice has substantially reduced a person's chance of a better recovery.

In conclusion, the court found

---

(1) Kansas does recognize a cause of action for the lost chance for a better recovery due to medical malpractice; (2) to withstand summary judgment, a plaintiff must show that the lost chance for a better recovery was a substantial loss of chance as opposed to a theoretical or de minimis loss; (3) the resulting injury or lessened degree of recovery suffered by the plaintiff as the result of the malpractice must be substantial; and (4) the finder of fact shall calculate the monetary recovery on the basis of the proportional damage approach. Id. at 187.

The court felt compelled to express a caveat.

In adopting and applying the loss of chance theory to medical malpractice cases, it must always be kept in mind that the practice of medicine and the furnishing of appropriate health care is not an exact science. In many, if not most, instances there is more than one acceptable approach to treatment, and the fact that one doctor selects one method as opposed to another does not in and of itself mean that one method is better than or preferable to another. For every treatment there are undoubtedly other doctors who might have performed or used a different one. The courts should use extreme caution in second-guessing the methods used by medical care providers, particularly in an area as nebulous as the loss of a chance for a better or more satisfactory recovery. Id. at 187.

Discussion

1. What was lacking in the assessment of the patient's immediate needs?
2. Discuss the loss of chance of recovery and the concept of loss of chance of better recovery.
3. What can be done to lessen the likelihood of injuries of this nature?
4. What is the importance of collaboration among caregivers in the treatment of patients in the emergency department setting?

Careless Assessment Results in Patient's Death

Citation: *Gibson v. Moskowitz*, M.D., 523 F.3d 657 (2008)

Facts

On Friday, January 25, 2002, Vaughn, an inmate in the Riverside Correctional Facility in Ionia, Michigan, began acting strangely. Concerned about his behavior, prison officials moved him from his prison cell to an observation room. Each inmate placed in an observation room is looked after by a "treatment team," which includes a psychiatrist, team of nurses and other trained personnel. For reasons that the record does not fully explain, the temperature in the observation room exceeded 90 degrees.

After moving Vaughn to the observation room, prison officials placed Dr. Moskowitz, a psychiatrist, on Vaughn's treatment team. That Friday, Moskowitz met with Vaughn, assessed his condition and proposed treatment— psychiatric medication and observation—to help Vaughn through the weekend.

When Moskowitz returned to work on Monday, he learned that Vaughn's condition had worsened. Although Moskowitz left open the possibility that Vaughn might have a "heat problem," his plan on Monday morning was to "keep observing Mr. Vaughn" and to give the medication more time to work.

Vaughn's condition continued to deteriorate on Monday. At 12:30 p.m., Foster, a prison guard, reported to the treatment team that Vaughn vomited in the bathroom after trying to drink a large amount of water from the bathroom sink. By Monday afternoon, Vaughn's room had reached 96 degrees. At the end of his Monday shift, Moskowitz concluded that "with cool temperature and more fluids Vaughn could be taken care of and . . . the dehydration could be prevented." Moskowitz's plan was to give the medication still more time to work, to transfer Vaughn to a cooler room and eventually to move Vaughn to a psychiatric hospital. Moskowitz "didn't feel that Vaughn's status was life threatening."

By the time Vaughn made it to a cooler room on Monday evening his condition had taken yet another turn for the worse. Vaughn began vomiting and dry-heaving, both of which continued into the night until he died from dehydration early Tuesday morning.

Gibson, the representative of Vaughn's estate, filed this an action against Moskowitz and other defendants, alleging deliberate indifference in violation of the Eighth and Fourteenth Amendments and raised several state law claims. The estate settled its claims against the 14 defendants, with the exception of Moskowitz, for $600,000. The estate took its claims against Moskowitz to trial, and the jury returned a verdict against Moskowitz awarding Gibson $2 million in compensatory damages, later reduced by $500,000 to account for settlements with the other defendants, and $3 million in punitive damages.

Moskowitz conceded that Vaughn's medical needs had become serious by Monday, January 28; he argued that they were not serious on Friday, January 25— when officials moved Vaughn to the observation room, when Moskowitz began treating Vaughn and when the jury ascribed initial liability to Moskowitz.

Dr. Shiener, the estate's psychiatric expert, explained to the jury that the drugs Moskowitz prescribed to treat Vaughn's schizophrenia "also affect the part of the brain that regulates temperature." When patients on this type of medication are put into a hot environment, they develop a "positive feed-back," which means they can't convect the heat or get rid of the heat and their body heats up out of control, which leads to a dangerous situation. Dr. Burns, another expert, corroborated Shiener's testimony by describing how some people can't deal with heat as well as other people due to the impact of the heat dissipation center in their brains.

Vaughn had a weight loss of 42 pounds over several days, which led to his death. A reasonable jury could find that Vaughn's medical needs were serious on Friday the 25th.

Issue

Did Moskowitz subjectively ignore Vaughn's medical needs? Does the evidence support the compensatory and punitive damages award?

Holding

The United States Court of Appeals, Sixth Circuit found that Moskowitz subjectively ignored Vaughn's medical needs and the evidence supported the compensatory damages award.

Reason

The risk was obvious and shows the employee must have understood the nature of the risk. A reasonable jury could fairly conclude that Moskowitz knew of and disregarded the risk to Vaughn's health.

All of this was enough for Nurse Blankstrom to reach the conclusion— which she initially shared with Moskowitz at noon on Monday—that Vaughn was suffering from severe dehydration. She informed him that she had taken Vaughn's vitals, which were all abnormal. And she relayed her opinion that "the vomiting ultimately points to a possibility that he was becoming dehydrated."

Blankstrom also asked Moskowitz to examine Vaughn—which he did, concluding that the problem "was not the medication or symptoms or side effects from the medication" and she arranged for Vaughn's medical team to meet to discuss Vaughn's treatment. Blankstrom described for the team that Vaughn was exhibiting signs of dehydration and needed immediate medical help. And she asked Moskowitz to evaluate Vaughn one more time because Vaughn was deteriorating and might be dehydrated. Despite this request, Moskowitz never examined Vaughn again.

Even if sufficient evidence supported the jury's liability determination, Moskowitz argues that the evidence does not support the amount of compensatory damages.

The district court was found not to have abused its discretion in letting this $1.5 million award stand. Vaughn's condition deteriorated over the course of several days, beginning late Thursday/early Friday and ending with his death early Tuesday morning. He suffered cramping, vomiting, confusion, delirium and disorientation during this time. He did not sleep, he sweated profusely and he looked physically ill. His vital signs were all abnormal, and he lost over 40 pounds from the onset of his dehydration until his death. Along with this physical pain, his experts testified, Vaughn would have suffered extreme mental anguish as well.

Moskowitz's failure to respond to Vaughn's deteriorating condition on Monday, when others testified that Vaughn's condition would have been apparent and shocking, supports the award. The evidence of Moskowitz's conduct supports a substantial award.

Discussion

1. Was the staff negligent when they placed the patient in a 90 degree room?
2. Do you agree with the court's finding that Moskowitz's conduct supported a substantial award? Explain your answer.
3. Describe the ethical and legal issues common to both the staff and the physician in the treatment of the patient?
4. Discuss why you think Moskowitz's assessment of the patient's condition was inattentive.

Failure to Correct Assessment

Citation: *Giles, v. Continental Casualty Company, et al.*, No. 4:11-CV-239 CAS (U.S. District Court, E.D. Missouri, Eastern Division, April 13, 2011)

Facts

The plaintiff began receiving Long-Term Disability (LTD) benefits in 2004. The benefits were terminated two years later based on a functional assessment by the defendant Dr. Barrack, the plaintiff's treating orthopedic surgeon. The assessment indicated that the plaintiff was able to perform sedentary work. The plaintiff believes the assessment was erroneous and that he was unable to perform any work. As a result, he claimed that he was entitled to lifetime LTD benefits. The plaintiff asserts that Dr. Barrack acknowledged that the assessment was incorrect and had been signed by someone in his office without his authority. The plaintiff alleges Dr. Barrack failed to correct the assessment or submit a new assessment to the disability insurance carrier. The plaintiff alleges that Dr. Barrack negligently failed to conduct a complete evaluation so as to provide an accurate assessment of his condition.

The plaintiff brought a lawsuit four years after the alleged negligently handled functional assessment against Dr. Barrack and Washington University Medical Center (WUMC). The plaintiff asserts that WUMC is also liable for Dr. Barrack's negligence because he was acting as WUMC's agent.

The defendants filed a motion to dismiss the case, asserting it was time-barred under Missouri's two-year statute of limitations.

Issue

Was the motion to dismiss the plaintiff's action based on the tolling of Missouri's revised statute of limitations § 516.105 a valid motion?

Holding

Based on the running of the statute of limitations, the U.S. District Court for the Eastern Division dismissed the suit on the basis of the tolling of the statute of limitations.

Reason

Missouri Revised Statute § 516.105 provides in pertinent part:

All actions against physicians, hospitals, dentists, registered or licensed practical nurses, optometrists, podiatrists, pharmacists, chiropractors, professional physical therapists, and any other entity providing healthcare services and all employees of any of the foregoing acting in the course and scope of their employment, for damages for malpractice, negligence, error or mistake related to health care shall be brought within two years from the date of occurrence of the act of the neglect complained of.

Missouri courts have rejected attempts to "plead around" the two-year statute by denominating a claim that is essentially for malpractice as one for general negligence. In this case, the complaint alleges that Dr. Barrack was negligent when he failed to accurately prepare a physical disability report concerning plaintiff, and failed to conduct a complete evaluation of plaintiff so as to provide an accurate functional assessment as to his disability and ability to perform work. These allegations plainly seek damages for malpractice, negligence, error, or mistake related to health care, and are subject to the two-year limitation period of § 516.105.

Discussion

1. Do you agree with the court's finding? Explain your answer.
2. If the patient was correct in the allegations made, should the patient continue receiving LTD.

Patient Screening

Citation: *Ballachino v. Anders*, 811 F. Supp. 121 (W.D. N.Y. 1993)

Facts

The decedent presented himself to a hospital on May 15, 1990, with complaints of chest pain and repeated episodes of loss of consciousness. Allegedly, the physicians negligently failed to provide an appropriate medical screening examination and failed to determine whether or not an emergency medical condition existed. The patient's survivor and representative brought an action against the hospital and physicians alleging violations of the Emergency Medical Treatment and Active Labor Act (EMTALA) and medical malpractice. EMTALA requires that a Medicare provider hospital must provide an appropriate medical screening examination to determine whether an emergency medical condition exists for any individual who presents to the emergency department seeking examination or treatment. If the hospital determines that an emergency medical condition exists, then it must either stabilize the patient or provide for transfer of the patient to a facility capable of meeting the patient's medical needs.

Issue

Was there a right of action against the physicians and was a claim appropriately stated against the hospital?

Holding

The United States District Court for the Western District of New York held that there is no private right of action against the individual physicians under EMTALA. However, the representative's complaint did state a claim against the hospital under EMTALA.

Reason

No private right of action exists against individual physicians under EMTALA. The enforcement provision of EMTALA is explicitly limited to actions against a Medicare participating hospital. While the physicians were alleged to have acted in concert in rendering professional medical and surgical care and treatment to the decedent while at the hospital, the physicians importantly are nowhere alleged to have provided any "emergency screening examination." The plaintiff clearly alleged that these defendants negligently failed to provide an appropriate medical screening examination and failed to determine whether an emergency medical condition existed for the decedent. The court was faced with the question of whether any emergency screening examination occurred at all.

The plaintiff also alleged that the hospital failed in its stabilization and transfer procedures. The district court determined that all of the allegations taken together stated a claim against the hospital under EMTALA.

Failure to Assess and Treat

Citation: *NKC Hosps, Inc. v. Anthony*, 849 S.W.2d 564 (Ky. Ct. App. 1993)

Facts

Decedent Mrs. Anthony was in her first pregnancy under the primary care of Dr. Hawkins, her personal physician and an obstetrician. Mrs. Anthony was in good health, 26 years of age, employed, and about 30 weeks along in her noneventful pregnancy.

On September 5, 1989, Mrs. Anthony went to the emergency department of Norton Hospital with her husband. She was experiencing nausea, vomiting, and abdominal pain, and because of her pregnancy, she was referred to the hospital's obstetrical unit. In the obstetrical unit, Mrs. Anthony came under the immediate care of Ms. Moore, a nurse, who performed an assessment.

Dr. Hawkins was called later that evening. He issued several orders, including an IV start, blood work, urinalysis, and a prescription for nausea. Later that night, a second call was made to Dr. Hawkins, giving her the test results and informing her that the patient was in extreme pain. Believing Mrs. Anthony had a urinary tract infection, antibiotics were ordered along with an order for her discharge from the hospital.

That same night a third call was made to Dr. Hawkins because of the pain Mrs. Anthony was experiencing, as observed by Ms. Moore. Mr. Anthony also talked with Dr. Hawkins about his wife's pain. Ms. Moore became concerned about Dr. Hawkins's discharge order. Although aware of Ms. Moore's evaluation, Dr. Hawkins prescribed morphine sulfate but was unrelenting in her order of discharge.

At approximately 2:00 a.m. on Sept. 6, a prescription for the morphine was ordered and administered pursuant to the telephoned directions of Dr. Hawkins, but the resident physician on duty, Dr. Love, did not see or examine the patient. It is not clear from the record, but it is assumed Dr. Love wrote the morphine prescription. It was administered to Mrs. Anthony, and she rested comfortably for several hours but awakened in pain again. At 6:00 a.m., the patient was discharged in that condition.

During trial testimony, a nursing supervisor named Ms. Hale admitted that it was a deviation from the standard of nursing care to discharge a patient in significant pain. Ms. Moore, who was always concerned with the patient's pain, had grave reservations about her discharge in that condition. She suggested that Dr. Love examine Mrs. Anthony. She even consulted her supervisor, Nurse Hale. The major allegation of the hospital's negligence in this case is the undisputed fact that Mrs. Anthony was never clinically seen or examined by a physician prior to her discharge.

At approximately 10:00 a.m., Mrs. Anthony was readmitted to the hospital, and Dr. Hawkins began personal supervision of her patient. On Sept. 7, Dr. Hawkins determined that Mrs. Anthony had a serious respiratory problem and then, on Sept. 8, had the patient transferred to the hospital's intensive care unit.

On Sept. 9, Mrs. Anthony's baby was delivered by Caesarean section. It was then belatedly determined that Mrs. Anthony's condition was caused by a perforation of the appendix at the large bowel, a condition not detected by anyone at the hospital during Mrs. Anthony's first admission. Almost 3 weeks later, while still in Norton Hospital, Mrs. Anthony died of acute adult respiratory distress syndrome (ARDS), a complication resulting from the delay in the diagnosis and treatment of her appendicitis.

A medical negligence judgment was brought against the hospital. At trial, an expert witness for the estate of Mrs. Anthony by the name of Dr. Fields (board certified in obstetrics and gynecology) testified in no uncompromising terms that the hospital deviated from the standard of care. Pertinent testimony of Dr. Fields follows from the trial transcript:

Question: Had Margaret [Anthony] received care at Norton's Hospital which was within, which would have been within the standard of care, what would have been the outcome?

Answer: She would have had a prompt appendectomy performed following ruling out of various other conditions, such as kidney infection, and the appendix would have been removed, the antibiotic therapy instituted promptly in the intravenous fashion, her dehydrated state would have been corrected, she would never have suffered the pulmonary complication known as acute adult respiratory distress syndrome.

Question: Within a degree of medical probability, sir, would she be alive today?

Answer: Yes.

Question: Was the discharge of Margaret Anthony from the hospital on the early morning hours of September 6, 1989, a deviation from the standard of care for the hospital?

Answer: Yes, sir. Id. at 566.

Dr. Fields's testimony tagged Norton Hospital with negligence as its actions were ". . . below the standard of care for any institution . . ." and he explained

---

Every patient who presents herself to the labor and delivery area, the emergency room, or any area of the hospital, would be seen by a physician before anything is undertaken, and certainly before she is allowed to leave the institution. Furthermore, to provide the patient with medication in the form of a prescription without the physician ever seeing the patient is below any standard I'm acquainted with. Id. at 567.

The jury was instructed on the comparative negligence of Dr. Hawkins and the hospital. An award of $2,265,923.70 was returned with an apportionment of causation attributable to Dr. Hawkins of 65% and to the hospital of 35%. The hospital argued that the trial court erred in failing to grant its motions for directed verdict and for judgment notwithstanding the verdict because of the lack of substantial causation in linking the negligence of the hospital to Mrs. Anthony's death.

Issue

Was the negligence of the hospital superseded by the negligence of the patient's primary care physician, and was the award excessive?

Holding

The Court of Appeals of Kentucky held that negligence of the hospital was not superseded by the negligence of the patient's primary care physician and that the award for 20 days of pain and suffering prior to the patient's death was not excessive.

Reason

The hospital's negligence is based on acts of omission, by failing to check Mrs. Anthony's lungs or to have her examined by a physician, and on positive acts of negligence, such as discharging her in pain. The hospital certainly should have foreseen the injury to Mrs. Anthony because its own staff was questioning the judgments of Dr. Hawkins while at the same time failing to follow through with the standard of care required of it. All qualified healthcare providers, within the range of care for the patient, were under a duty to exercise their senses and intelligence to investigate and inspect for potential dangers to her. They did not. Their voluntary ignorance of her condition will grant no relief because voluntary ignorance is negligence. The defense that the hospital's nurses were only following a "chain of command" by doing what Dr. Hawkins ordered is not persuasive. The nurses were not the agents of Dr. Hawkins. All involved had their independent duty to Mrs. Anthony.

The court concluded that

---

§ 442 B. of the Restatement of Torts, Second satisfies our inquiry whether to hold the hospital liable. It states: Where the negligent conduct of the actor [here, the hospital] creates or increases the risk of a particular harm and is a substantial factor in causing that harm, the fact that the harm is brought about through the intervention of another force [here, Dr. Hawkins] does not relieve the actor of liability, except where the harm is intentionally caused by a third person and is not within the scope of the risk created by the actor's conduct.

The evidence was of a woman conscious of her last days on earth, swollen beyond recognition, in severe pain, with tubes exiting almost every orifice of her body, and deteriorated to the point that she could not verbally communicate with loved ones. Among the last things she did was write out instructions about the care for her newborn child. The trial court, if confronted with a motion for a new trial under CR 59.01(d) on excessive damages, must evaluate the award mirrored against the facts. It is said that if the trial judge does not blush, the award is not excessive. No question, the award was monumental but so was the injury. Clearly, the relationship between the award and the injury in this case is not bizarre. The factual basis supporting the award convinces us there was no error or abuse of discretion in the denial of a new trial on this ground.

Discussion

1. Was Dr. Hawkins's "telephone" assessment of the patient appropriate?
2. How would you apportion negligence among the attending physician, resident, obstetrical nurse, nursing supervisor, and hospital?
3. What are the lessons that should be learned from this case?
4. What educational issues are apparent?
5. What is the importance of the screening and assessment procedures that should be in place for emergency department patients?

Physician Fails to Conduct Complete Assessment

Citation: *Moheet v. State Bd. of Regis. for Healing Arts*, 154 SW 3d 393 (Mo. Ct. App. 2005).

Facts

J.D., a 40-year-old male suffering from high blood pressure, felt a sudden and severe headache while driving. Soon after he returned home, he asked his son Jason to call an ambulance. When the paramedics arrived, they took J.D.'s history, which included hypertension (high blood pressure), and a list of J.D.'s medications, one of which was to treat the hypertension.

The nurse manager of the emergency department, Bouldin, R.N., was waiting to perform triage on J.D. when he arrived. Bouldin filled in an Emergency Room Record form (the "E.R. form") with J.D.'s vital signs. J.D.'s blood pressure was 170/130 at 4:50 p.m. J.D.'s wife gave Nurse Brooks J.D.'s medical history, which in addition to high blood pressure, included depression, alcoholism, and left arm numbness.

Dr. Moheet was on duty in the emergency room that day. At 5:05 p.m., Dr. Moheet began examining and taking a history from J.D. He observed that J.D. was lying on a backboard in a cervical collar, holding onto the side rails of the gurney, clenching his teeth, and going into spasms. When asked why he was in the emergency room, J.D. responded that he was having neck pain that radiated into the back part of his head. Dr. Moheet asked J.D. if he had hurt himself, and he said that he fell while sledding in the snow (referring to an incident the previous day when sledding with his children). He complained of numbness in the left arm. Dr. Moheet was hampered in taking J.D.'s medical history because J.D. was unhappy with the questions and repeatedly requested pain medication.

Dr. Moheet checked J.D.'s breathing, pulse, lung sounds, and abdomen. He then did a neurological check, which included checking his ability to feel sensations. J.D. had decreased sensation in the thumb, outer forearm, middle finger, and on the inner side of the left hand. To Dr. Moheet, these sensory changes suggested radiculopathy (nerve impingement due to a cervical disc problem). J.D. was given an injection for pain. Dr. Moheet sent J.D. for X-rays. Although J.D. had informed the nurse of a sudden onset of head pain, Dr. Moheet did not order a CT scan of the head. J.D.'s reflexes were normal. When it was determined that J.D. did not have a neck fracture, the collar, cushion, and backboard were removed, and he was returned to the emergency room.

At 6:40 p.m., Dr. Moheet again examined J.D. and checked his neurological responses. At this time, J.D. was sitting upright on the gurney and told Dr. Moheet that he was feeling 50% better. Dr. Moheet told J.D. of his diagnosis of a C-6 radiculopathy (pinched sixth nerve) on the left side. He told J.D. that the X-ray was negative and that he was being discharged with a muscle relaxant and an anti-inflammatory painkiller. J.D.'s wife asked whether those medications would cause a problem with J.D.'s blood pressure. Dr. Moheet said they would not. Dr. Moheet did not consider this mention of blood pressure to be a reason to further examine the patient. J.D. was given a soft collar for his neck and was released to go home.

Dr. Moheet later charted his findings for J.D. based on his notes. Dr. Moheet did not know J.D.'s blood pressure when he treated him and did not review the ambulance records or the E.R. form. Dr. Moheet expected his nurses to inform him of any abnormalities in the patient's vital signs. J.D. did not inform Dr. Moheet that he had high blood pressure nor did he mention that he had stopped taking his medication.

At approximately 6:30 the next morning, J.D.'s wife found J.D. unconscious on the bedroom floor and could not revive him. An ambulance crew responded and took J.D.'s blood pressure four times between 7:16 and 7:50 a.m. The readings were extremely high: 220/120; 200/128; 210/118; and 228/108. The ambulance crew gave J.D. a drug for hypertension and took him to the hospital.

At the hospital, a CT scan was taken, and emergency room personnel informed Dr. Boland, a neurosurgeon, that J.D. had an abnormal CT scan, was comatose, and needed emergency neurosurgical treatment. Dr. Boland diagnosed a spontaneous intraventricular hemorrhage in the fourth ventricle of his brain (a hemorrhagic stroke). The blood from the hemorrhage had clotted and blocked the flow of spinal fluid. The excess fluid in his brain built up tremendous pressure, causing J.D. to lapse into a coma. Dr. Boland believed that J.D. had already suffered the hemorrhage and had stopped bleeding by the time he arrived at the emergency room the first time and was seen by Nurse Bouldin and Dr. Moheet.

Dr. Boland told J.D.'s wife that J.D. needed an emergency procedure to avoid imminent death. His wife authorized the procedure. The procedure was performed in the emergency department due to the urgency. J.D. spent a week in neuro-intensive care, a week in a step-down area, and a week on a rehabilitation floor. At the time of the hearing, J.D. was deceased; but neither party has discussed whether the cause of death was related to the stroke.

The State Board of Registration for the Healing Arts Administrative Hearing Commission found cause to discipline Dr. Moheet's medical license by subjecting it to a public reprimand.

The pertinent parts of the Board's complaint alleged

---

13. While J.D. was in the emergency room the day before the admission, licensee knew or should have known that J.D.'s blood pressure was very high.

14. Failure to ascertain a patient's vital signs, including blood pressure, in the practice of emergency medicine is below the standard of care.

15. Licensee's failure to assess J.D.'s blood pressure in the emergency room constitutes gross negligence.

16. Because of licensee's failure to assess J.D.'s blood pressure in the emergency room, J.D. was deprived of timely diagnosis and treatment of the bleed, reducing the likelihood of a favorable clinical outcome.

17. While J.D. was in the emergency room the day before the admission, licensee failed to do a complete physical examination of the patient.

18. While J.D. was in the emergency room the day before the admission, licensee failed to obtain appropriate laboratory tests.

19. Licensee's failure to adequately assess, diagnose and treat J.D. when he presented in the emergency room was below the standard of care for an emergency department physician.

20. Licensee's conduct, as set forth herein, constitutes incompetency and gross negligence in the practice of medicine.

Dr. Moheet appealed.

Issue

Dr. Moheet appealed the decision of the Administrative Hearing Commission in which it found cause to discipline his medical license by subjecting it to a public reprimand.

Holding

The Missouri Court of Appeals affirmed the Administrative Hearing Commission's decision.

Reason

Dr. Moheet had adequate notice of the charges against him in that he was fully aware of the link between his failure to obtain an adequate medical history and the possibility of harm to the patient. He had sufficient notice of the allegation of his failure to obtain an adequate patient history, and his own pleading showed that he knew the charges he would be defending against. The testimony of the expert witnesses, combined with the other evidence in the record, constituted competent and substantial evidence to support the commission's finding of conduct that might be harmful to a patient. There is ample evidence in the record to support a finding of gross negligence.

Discussion

1. Discuss why physicians often fail to conduct complete assessments of ED patient care needs.
2. What actions can hospitals and their medical staffs take to improve the quality of patient assessments (e.g., develop a less lengthy assessment process by concentrating on emergent and urgent patient care needs)?

Inadequate Assessment: Mother Dies

Citation: *Foley v. Bishop*, 173 N.W.2d 881 (Neb. 1970).

Facts

Failure to obtain an adequate history and perform an adequate physical examination violates a standard of care owed to the patient. In *Foley v. Bishop* the spouse sued the hospital for the death of his wife, Mrs. Foley. During her pregnancy, Mrs. Foley was under the care of a private physician. She gave birth in the hospital on August 20, 1964, and died the following day, having developed a severe beta hemolytic streptococcus infection. During July and August, her physician had treated her for a sore throat. There was no evidence in the hospital record that the patient had complained about a sore throat while in the hospital. Hospital rules, however, required that a history and physical examination be completed and assessed in writing promptly (within 24 hours of admission). No history had been taken, although the patient had been examined several times in regard to the progress of her labor. The trial judge directed a verdict in favor of the hospital.

Issue

Should this case have been submitted to the jury for determination?

Holding

The appellate court held that the case should have been submitted to the jury for determination.

Reason

Hospital rules require that a history and physical examination shall be done and written with 24 hours of admission. One-rule states: "All necessary admission information is collected with particular attention to possibility of infection. Suspicion of infection is reported to the physician immediately." No history was taken, although Mrs. Foley was examined several times in regard to the progress of child labor.

A jury might reasonably have inferred that, if a history and physical examination had been promptly performed when Mrs. Foley was admitted to the hospital, the sore throat would have been discovered and hospital personnel alerted to watch for possible complications of the nature that later developed. Quite possibly, this attention also would have helped in diagnosing the patient's condition, especially if it had been apparent that she had been exposed to a strep throat infection. The court held that a hospital must guard not only against known physical and mental conditions of patients but also against conditions that reasonable care should have uncovered.

Hospitals now employ medical students, interns, and residents and physicians. The evidence discloses that it is customary for employees to take a medical history and conduct a physical examination of patients on admission for the purpose of protecting the patient and guarding against complications. This means taking the history before surgery, delivery, or treatment, not afterwards when it may be too late. We adopt the minority rule and overrule any prior conflicting Nebraska decisions. A jury question was presented. The judgment of the district court is therefore reversed and the cause remanded for a new trial.

Discussion

1. In light of this case, discuss the importance of conducting a complete history and physical examination.
2. Review the TJC website and Conditions for Participation (Appendix A) as they discuss various aspects of the assessment process for patients. Based on you review, do you agree with the court's decision to remand the case for a new trial? Discuss your answer.

Assessment: Physician Negligent and License Revoked

Citation: *Solomon v. Connecticut Medical Examining Bd*, 85 Conn. App. (Conn. App. Ct. 2004).

Facts

The Connecticut Medical Examining Board determined that a physician was negligent and incompetent in the practice of medicine in 9 out of 10 patient cases reviewed. Following a 6-day hearing, his license to practice medicine was revoked. The Board determined that the physician failed to adequately document patient histories, to perform adequate physical examinations, to assess a patient's condition appropriately, or to order appropriate laboratory tests or secure appropriate consultations. It further found that the physician had administered contraindicated medications to patients. The Board found that the physician did not practice medicine with reasonable skill and safety and that his practice of medicine poses a threat to the health and safety of any person. The physician ultimately appealed to the Connecticut Appellate Court.

Issue

Was there substantial evidence in the record to support the Board's finding that the plaintiff was negligent and incompetent in the practice of medicine?

Holding

The court concluded that there was substantial evidence in the record to support the Board's finding that the plaintiff was negligent and incompetent in the practice of medicine in 9 out of the 10 cases reviewed.

Reason

The plaintiff's testimony was not credible, as his answers to questions posed at the hearing frequently were unresponsive, self-contradictory, and evasive.

His recollection was contradicted by a review of information in the charts of the patients under his care. With respect to the expert testimony, the department's expert was more credible than one of the physician's.

The second count of the statement of charges alleged that the plaintiff was incompetent or negligent in the course of his duties as an emergency department physician at two hospitals in New York during 1999, it further alleged specific ways in which his medical conduct was negligent or incompetent. The defendant is "authorized to restrict, suspend or revoke the license or limit the right to practice of a physician . . . for any of the following reasons . . . (4) illegal, incompetent or negligent conduct in the practice of medicine . . . ." General Statutes § 20-13c.

There was substantial evidence to support disciplinary action against the physician, because the record indicated that he had failed to adequately document patient histories, to perform adequate physical examinations, to assess the patient's condition appropriately, or to order appropriate laboratory tests or secure appropriate consultations. The Connecticut Medical Examining Board found that the physician had administered contraindicated medications to patients, that he did not practice medicine with reasonable skill and safety, and that his practice of medicine posed a threat to the health and safety of any person. The board had concluded that there was a basis on which to subject the physician's license to disciplinary action.

Judicial review of an administrative agency decision requires a court to determine whether there is substantial evidence in the administrative record to support the agency's findings of basic fact and whether the conclusions drawn from those facts are reasonable . . . The substantial evidence standard is satisfied if the record provides a substantial basis of fact from which the fact in issue can be reasonably inferred.

The court reasoned that the Board's determinations were matters of credibility, particularly with respect to the experts who testified before the panel and the physician. It is not the function of the trial court or the Appellate Court to assess the credibility of witnesses, as that is the province of the trier of fact. The Appellate Court concluded that there was substantial evidence in the record to support the Board's decision.

Discussion

1. Do you believe the board's findings were too harsh? Discuss your answer.

2. Discuss why assessments in emergency departments are often too cursory.
3. What would happen to hospital costs if ED physicians were to conduct complete history and physical examinations?
4. Would more complete assessments ultimately reduce the costs of care if fewer malpractice suits were filed as a result?

Assessment: Delayed Follow-Up

Citation: *Rowe v. Sisters of the Pallottine Missionary Society*, No. 29161 (WV 2001).

Facts

Seventeen-year-old Brian W. Rowe lost control of his motorcycle. The motorcycle tumbled, injuring his knee. He was transported by ambulance to the emergency room of the appellant, Pallottine Missionary Society (the appellant is the Sisters of Pallottine Missionary Society, which does business as St. Mary's Hospital). Over the course of 2.5 hours, the nurses made extensive notes in Mr. Rowe's record indicating that he complained of severe pain in his left knee and numbness in his foot. The nurses repeatedly were unable to find a pulse in his lower left leg and foot. Mr. Rowe was also examined by a St. Mary's Hospital emergency room physician, Dr. Daniels, who noted tenderness and swelling in the left knee and lower left leg and had difficulty finding—but claims to have ultimately found—a pulse. A nurse testified she told Dr. Daniels that she was unable to detect a pulse in Mr. Rowe's foot, that she asked Dr. Daniels why she wasn't getting a pulse, and that Dr. Daniels replied, "I don't know." Although X-rays showed fragments of bone in Mr. Rowe's knee joint, Dr. Daniels noted in the patient file that Mr. Rowe had a severe sprain of his left knee.

Mr. Rowe was discharged and taken home by his mother. He was given instructions to make an appointment with an orthopaedist several days later and was told that, if his pain continued or became worse in the meantime, he should return to St. Mary's emergency room.

That night, Mr. Rowe's knee and leg continued to swell, and the pain intensified. His parents called several physicians by phone, and one agreed to see Mr. Rowe at 10:00 a.m. the next morning at Huntington Hospital's emergency room.

An examination revealed that Mr. Rowe had a dislocated knee and a lacerated popliteal artery, which passes behind the knee joint and provides circulation to the lower leg. Due to the loss of blood flow, the physician contemplated amputation of Mr. Rowe's lower left leg. However, after extensive surgery to repair the knee and artery, to relieve pressure on the leg, and to remove dead tissue, the lower leg was saved. Mr. Rowe was hospitalized for 35 days, and currently has significant impairment to the use of his left leg.

Mr. Rowe subsequently brought a lawsuit against Dr. Daniels and against St. Mary's Hospital for negligence. In October 1996, after 8 years of litigation, he settled his cause of action against Dr. Daniels for $270,000.00, and the case proceeded to trial against the hospital.

At trial, Mr. Rowe asserted that St. Mary's nurses had breached the standard of care by not adequately advocating his interests when he was discharged with unexplained and unaddressed symptoms. He presented evidence that St. Mary's policy—and the guiding standard of care for all emergency room nurses—is that when a nurse believes that appropriate care is not being administered to a patient by a physician, the nurse is expected to report the situation to a supervisor who would then discuss it with the doctor. If that did not alleviate the problem, the matter is to be referred up the chain of command so that another doctor can evaluate the problem.

The plaintiff's expert stated the nurses at St. Mary's Hospital failed to advocate for Brian Rowe in the sense that they knew that he had compromised circulation to his left leg, that he had no pulse in the leg, that he was not able to move his left foot, and that he had no sensation in the foot. The evidence showed that, instead of following the hospital's policy, the emergency room nurses simply made notes of their findings in Mr. Rowe's medical file, with the intention that one nurse admitted "I guess basically to cover myself."

A jury returned a verdict against the hospital, and the hospital appealed the circuit court's judgment order.

Issue

Was there error in the circuit court's rulings for Mr. Rowe?

Holding

Finding no error in the circuit court's rulings, the Supreme Court affirmed the judgment order for the appellee.

Reason

The parties presented the following stipulation, in part, to the jury:

[S]hould there be an occasion when an RN believes that appropriate care is not being administered to a patient by a physician, the following procedure shall occur:

One, the RN will discuss her concerns with the physician. If, after the discussion, she still feels that the care is inappropriate, she will report it to the clinical manager, if available, or the patient care coordinator on duty.

Secondly, the clinical manager or patient care coordinator will weigh the factors involved and if she feels that the concern is valid, she will discuss it with the physician. If nothing is done to ease her concern, she will contact nursing administration.

Thirdly, nursing administration will discuss it with the clinical manager and contact the chief of service for guidance and assistance. If nursing administration, after discussion with the chief of services, feels that appropriate action still has not been taken, the problem will then be referred to the assistant executive director of medical affairs.

The director of medical affairs will contact the attending physician and/or chief of service. Should appropriate action not be taken at this level, the director of medical affairs will contact the president of the medical staff.

Nursing administration may at any point in time request the assistance from administration.

Discussion

1. Do you agree with the Supreme Court's decision? Explain your answer.
2. Discuss what steps the hospital can take to prevent similar incidents in the future.
3. Should the nurses have initially pressed for further action or treatment? If so, what action should they have taken?

Shifting the Risk

A 2008 study published in the *Journal of the American Medical Association* found that patients who suffered a heart attack in the hospital door and off hours—were less likely to survive than those who had a cardiac arrest during normal business hours. Last year researchers at the University of Pennsylvania found that the quality of cardiopulmonary resuscitation at three urban teaching hospitals was poorer at night than during the day. And the president of New York's Beth Israel Medical Center decried the "stark discrepancy in quality between daytime and nighttime inpatient services" in a 2008 article in the *New England Journal of Medicine*.

Sandra G. Boodman, The Washington Post, *June 7, 2011*

Reassessment: Nurse's Untimely Response

Citation: *Fairfax Hosp. Sys. Inc. v. McCarty*, 419 S.E.2d 621 (Va. 1992)

Facts

At 7:30 a.m. on June 3, 1987, a pregnant Ms. McCarty was admitted to the hospital after spontaneous rupture of her membranes. During the patient's 7:10 p.m. assessment, Dr. Burka examined the mother and found that she "had made excellent progress . . . in the active phase of labor." An hour later, the second phase of labor began and lasted until the 9:17 p.m. delivery. The significant events in this case occurred during this second phase, 67-minute period. Dr. Burka was in the labor room many times between 8:10 p.m. and 8:25 p.m. Then, from 8:25 p.m. until nearly 8:58 p.m., he was not in the labor room but in a nearby physicians' lounge.

At 8:27 p.m., the evidence established that the fetus began experiencing trouble. At 8:29 p.m., a broad-based deceleration of the fetal heart rate began to register on the monitor. The mother began abnormal labor. At 8:37 p.m., the baby was sick and getting sicker, as indicated by the monitor's fetal heart rate tracings. At this point, according to the plaintiffs' expert witness, the applicable standard of care required the nurse to institute certain nursing procedures, including "to call for help to get this baby delivered." At that time, according to the witness, the delivery could have taken place in 10 to 12 minutes if the mother had been unhooked from the monitor and moved from the labor room to the delivery room 40 feet away. Dr. Burka was unaware of the heart rate fluctuations during this critical period both because he was in the physicians' lounge and because none of the remote terminals displaying fetal heart-rate tracings for the labor room were working. Id. at 624.

At 8:42 p.m., the fetus had exhausted its oxygen supply and began relying on its emergency reserve, a 4-minute back-up system that helps the fetus survive the stress of labor. Four minutes later, damage to the brain began. At 8:51 p.m., delivery became necessary to avoid injury to the baby. By 8:53 p.m., brain damage had occurred that was outside the limit for birth of a neurologically normal baby.

Between 8:50 p.m. and 9:00 p.m., Ms. McClure, employed by the Hospital as a labor and delivery nurse, went to get Dr. Burka, and he may have briefly appeared at the labor room door several minutes before 9:00 p.m. Based on what Ms. McClure told him at the time, Dr. Burka understood there had been a decline in the fetal heart rate and that this deceleration "had just happened." According to Dr. Burka, who testified as a witness for the plaintiffs, "there was no indication that there was an immediate emergency with the baby from Ms. McClure." Dr. Burka testified that if he had been watching the heart-rate tracings, he "would have moved to deliver Mrs. McCarty shortly before 8:40 p.m." Dr. Burka based this conclusion on the fact that during "the previous 10 minutes there had been a dramatic qualitative change in the fetal heart rate tracing from what had previously transpired." There were "progressively longer, deeper, more widely based heart rate decelerations with maternal contractions and pushing efforts." Id. at 624. Dr. Burka first realized the baby was in trouble shortly after 9:00 p.m., when the mother had been transferred to the delivery room.

At birth, the infant was neurologically impaired. The evidence established that the cause of this condition at delivery was a "prolonged episode of relatively severe hypoxia or lack of oxygen" that had occurred from 8:40 p.m. until delivery. According to the evidence, the otherwise normal and healthy fetus did not receive sufficient oxygen or nutrition because of "placental separation and abruption of the placenta which took away his oxygen supply in part and his ability to be nourished by his mother in part for a period of time before birth." Id. The plaintiffs' expert testified that Ms. McClure's failure to "take action or notify the physician delayed delivery and consequently contributed in a causative manner to the eventual outcome for this infant." Id.

Issue

Did the nurse's breach of the standard of care required result in the injuries sustained?

Holding

The Supreme Court of Virginia held that whether the nurse's breach of duty was the proximate cause of the infant's injuries presented a question for the jury.

Reason

The mere recital of the facts in the light most favorable to the plaintiffs shows there was abundant, credible evidence, which the jury was entitled to accept, establishing that Ms. McClure's breach of the standard of care was a proximate cause of the injuries and damages sustained; no further analysis of the evidence is necessary. It is sufficient to state that a jury issue was presented on the question of whether Ms. McClure's delay in recognizing and reacting to fetal distress, and in performing appropriate nursing intervention, including timely notice to the attending physician, were substantial breaches of the standard of care. It was for the jury to say whether these breaches by the hospital's employee constituted an efficient cause of the losses suffered by the plaintiffs.

Discussion

1. Analyzing the time elements in this case, do you agree with the court's decision? Explain.
2. How would you, as the nurse, defend your actions in this case?

Assessment: Failure to Report Fetal Distress

Joint Commission Standard

The Joint Commission National Patient Safety Goal #2 requires that there be effective communications amongst caregivers. In the case that follows, there was a breakdown in communications between the lab and physician and, ultimately, the patient. The lesson here is for all caregivers to communicate across all disciplines.

Citation: *Greer v. Bryant*, 621 A.2d 999 (Pa. Super. Ct. 1993)

Facts

Mrs. Greer, while at the Philadelphia College of Osteopathic Medicine (PCOM) and under the care of her physician, Dr. Bryant, was diagnosed with pre-eclampsia, a condition characterized by high blood pressure in the mother that poses a risk to her unborn child. On September 20, the patient suffered symptoms of fetal distress and was examined by the hospital's interns and residents. Tests ordered at the time of her visit revealed that the fetus was suffering from decelerations, a periodic lowering of the heartbeat. Following her examination, Mrs. Greer was instructed to return to the hospital on September 23. During her second appointment, it was noted that the fetus was experiencing "poor beat to beat variability." Mrs. Greer was once again sent home with instructions to return to the hospital on September 27. However, Mrs. Greer called the hospital emergency department on September 26, experiencing severe pains. She was told to wait until her scheduled appointment the following day. Her appointment was subsequently canceled because of inclement weather. Upon the insistence of her sister, Mrs. Greer went to the hospital anyway on September 27, where she delivered her child. The infant suffered from severe meconium aspiration (inhalation by the fetus of its own fecal matter while in utero) and died several days later.

The plaintiff alleged that the hospital, through its negligence, had contributed to her child's death. Mrs. Greer sued Dr. Bryant and PCOM separately. She alleged that based on the prenatal test results during her September 23 visit to PCOM, she should have been delivered on that date by Dr. Bryant. Questions were raised as to whether Dr. Bryant was aware of the test results. The plaintiff argued that, even if the test results had been communicated to Dr. Bryant and he decided to send her home, the residents should have recognized the serious condition of the fetus and, if necessary, sought approval from their superiors to keep the child at the hospital.

Dr. Bryant made an offer to settle, and the plaintiff accepted. The Court of Common Pleas, upon jury verdict, entered judgment for the mother and found PCOM 41% liable to the plaintiff. PCOM appealed.

Issue

(1) Was the hospital staff negligent by not reporting the fetal distress to Dr. Bryant? (2) Did the plaintiff's expert witness, Dr. Gabrielson, exceed her scope of opinion in her medical report?

Holding

The Superior Court of Pennsylvania found that the jury could find the hospital staff negligent by not reporting the fetal distress of the unborn child to Dr. Bryant and that the plaintiff's expert witness, Dr. Gabrielson, did not exceed her scope of opinion in her medical report.

Reason

Although a resident and intern claimed they had called Dr. Bryant, neither could testify as to the content of their conversation with him. Dr. Bryant testified that he did not recall receiving any telephone calls. He stated that if he had been aware of the decelerated heart rate, he would have ordered delivery of the child. "Since many of the critical events occurred on September 23, the jury could have determined that PCOM's employees' crucial nonfeasance occurred on that date . . . we must assume that the jury drew this inference." Id. at 1002.

Dr. Gabrielson, in three written reports and through oral testimony, testified that if the test results had not been reported to Dr. Bryant, such conduct, in her opinion, fell below the required standard of care. PCOM argued that "this new 'failure to override [Dr. Bryant's possible orders to send Rachel home] theory' was not contained in the reports and that they were unfairly surprised by the opinion." Id. at 1003. The superior court did not agree. The following is an excerpt from a report that presents questioning of Dr. Gabrielson by the plaintiff's counsel:

Question: Ms. Greer was sent to Osteopathic Hospital on three occasions for nonstress and contraction stress testing. On the second occasion . . . it was noted that the baby's heart rate showed poor variability. . . . Could you explain the significance of this finding with regard to the health and well-being of the fetus?

Answer: The episode of bradycardia observed on September 20 was a very ominous sign and very suggestive of cord compression probably resulting from oligohydramnios. This would result in fetal distress with meconium passage and aspiration. It could result in sudden intrauterine death.

Question: Once the fetal distress was detected, did the hospital act appropriately by sending Ms. Greer home?

Answer: No.

Question: What measures, if any, should have been taken to ensure the health and well-being of the fetus?

Answer: Ms. Greer should have been admitted and delivered. Id. at 1004.

The question of hospital negligence in sending the plaintiff home was within the fair scope of Dr. Gabrielson's oral testimony and written reports. "PCOM's decision to send Rachel home was contemplated, and counsel should have anticipated that the 'failure to override theory' was looming." Id. at 1004.

Discussion

1. What steps should hospitals take when a patient is faced with life-threatening test results, and the attending physician makes a determination to send the patient home?

2. What effect, if any, should such cases have upon the training of students and residents?

3. What action should a nurse take when faced with questionable actions by physicians and residents?

4. What policies and procedures should be in place to address similar issues in other patient care settings (emergency departments and ambulatory care centers)?

Reassessment: Negligent Monitoring

Citation: *Luthart v. Danesh*, 609 N.Y.S.706, 201 A.D.2d 9302d (N.Y. App. Div. 1994)

Facts

The estate executrix of the deceased brought an action alleging that the hospital nurses were negligent in monitoring the decedent's leg pulse. The executrix also alleged that the hospital was negligent for failing to have an ultrasonic stethoscope available. The trial court granted the hospital's motion for summary judgment, and an appeal was taken.

Issue

Was there a material issue of fact regarding the alleged negligence of the hospital nurses in monitoring the decedent's leg pulse and the alleged negligence of the hospital in failing to have an ultrasonic stethoscope available?

Holding

The New York Supreme Court, Appellate Division, held that there was a material issue of fact regarding the alleged negligence of the hospital nurses in monitoring the decedent's leg pulse, thus precluding summary judgment for the hospital. There are also factual issues, raised by conflicting expert opinions, as to whether the Hospital was negligent in failing to have a Doppler ultrasonic stethoscope available and whether that failure contributed to decedent's injury.

Reason

The facts relied upon by the hospital's expert in rendering his expert medical opinion conflicted with the deposition testimony of the defendants, Rathor and Danesh. Thus, credibility issues were raised concerning the expert's opinion that could not be resolved on a summary judgment motion. There was a factual issue regarding the alleged negligence of the hospital nurses in monitoring the pulse in the decedent's lower left leg. There were also factual issues, raised by conflicting expert opinions, as to whether the hospital was negligent in failing to have a Doppler ultrasonic stethoscope available and whether that failure contributed to the decedent's injury.

Discussion

1. What are the factual differences between *Luthart v. Danesh* and *Porter v. Lima Mem'l Hosp.*?

2. What issues should an organization consider when addressing the assessment and reassessment of a patient?

Nutritional Screening: Negligent Care

Citation: *Caruso v. Pine Manor Nursing Ctr*, 538 N.E.2d 722 (Ill. App. Ct. 1989)

Facts

In Illinois, a nursing facility by statute has a duty to provide its residents with proper nutrition. Under the Nursing Home Care Reform Act (the Act)

[T]he owner and licensee [of a nursing home] are liable to a resident for any intentional or negligent act or omission of their agents or employees which injured the resident. [Ill. Rev. Stat. 1981, ch. 1111/2, ¶ 4153-601.] The Act defines neglect as a failure in a facility to provide adequate medical or personal care or maintenance, which failure results in physical or mental injury to a resident or in the deterioration of the resident's condition. [Ill. Rev. Stat. 1981, ch. 111 1/2, ¶ 4151-116, 4151-117.] Personal care and maintenance include providing food and water and assistance with meals necessary to sustain a healthy life. [Ill. Rev. Stat. 1981, ch. 111 1/2, ¶ 4151-116, 4151-120.] Id. at 724.

Breach of Duty: The nursing facility maintained no records of the resident's fluid intake and output. A nurse testified that such a record was a required, standard nursing facility procedure that should have been followed for a person in the resident's condition but was not. The resident's condition deteriorated after a stay at the facility of 6.5 days. Upon leaving the facility and entering a hospital emergency department, the resident's treating physician diagnosed him as suffering from severe dehydration caused by an inadequate intake of fluids. The nursing facility offered no alternative explanation for the resident's dehydrated condition and failed to keep a chart of fluid intake and output as required by the applicable statute.

Injury: As a result of the facility's failure to maintain adequate records, the resident suffered severe dehydration requiring hospital treatment.

Causation: The evidence presented clearly demonstrated that the proximate cause of the resident's dehydration was the nursing facility's failure to administer proper nourishment to him. It was not unreasonable for the jury to conclude that the resident suffered dehydration and that the nursing facility's treatment of him caused the dehydration.

The trial court found that the record supported a finding that a resident had suffered from dehydration as a result of the nursing facility's negligence. The defendant appealed from a jury verdict awarding $65,000 in damages to the plaintiff. The trial court increased this amount to $195,000 (three times the actual damages) pursuant to Section 3-602 of the Nursing Home Reform Act. Ill. Rev. Stat. ch. 111 1/2, ¶ 4153-602 (1987).

Issue

The question before the Appellate Court of Illinois was whether or not the nursing facility resident suffered harm as a result of its negligence?

Holding

The Appellate Court of Illinois upheld the trial court's finding that the resident suffered dehydration as a result of the nursing facility's negligence.

Reason

The evidence presented clearly demonstrated that the proximate cause of the resident's dehydration was the nursing facility's failure to administer proper nourishment to him. It was not unreasonable for the jury to conclude that the resident suffered dehydration and that the nursing facility's treatment of him caused the dehydration.

Discussion

1. What steps could the nursing facility have taken in order to prevent such occurrences?
2. What record-keeping requirements did the nursing facility fail to follow?
3. What is the importance of timely nutritional screenings and assessments?
4. How does one monitor the appropriateness and effectiveness of nutritional care?
5. What is the mechanism for screening and assessing the nutritional needs of patients in your organization?

Reassessment: Monitoring Vital Signs

Citation: *Porter v. Lima Mem'l Hosp.*, 995 F.2d 629 (6th Cir. 1993)

Facts

On December 1, 1979, the automobile in which infant Liesl was traveling spun out of control, and she was thrown to the floor of the car. The rescue squad personnel examined the infant and found nothing seriously wrong. A rescue squad member then held Liesl in his arms while she and her mother, Mrs. Porter, were transported to Lima Memorial Hospital (Lima), the hospital nearest the scene of the accident.

The rescue squad took Liesl to the Lima emergency department where she lay on a hospital table awaiting examination by Dr. Singh, an emergency department physician. Ms. Ogelsbee, a registered nurse, took Liesl's vital signs and recorded them on the medical chart. She reported them to Dr. Singh upon his arrival for examination and treatment. At this point, the only observable sign of injury was a small bruise or hematoma on the right side of Liesl's head. Ms. Ogelsbee also reported this to Dr. Singh, and he then assumed primary responsibility for treating Liesl. Dr. Singh found all of Liesl's extremities functioning normally and ordered several laboratory tests and numerous X-rays. He did not, however, order any spinal X-rays and failed to diagnose spinal instability. Ms. Ogelsbee did not repeat the vital signs during or after Dr. Singh's examination, claiming that she received no doctor's instruction in this regard. After reviewing the X-rays and laboratory tests, Dr. Singh discharged Liesl and provided her mother with written instructions concerning her head injuries.

After Dr. Singh discharged Liesl, she and her mother remained at the hospital while awaiting a ride home. During a period of more than 2 hours, Liesl apparently displayed no additional signs of serious injury as observed by her mother. Her mother did report a short period of irregular breathing to one of the nurses at Lima. The nurse examined Liesl, determined that nothing was wrong, and returned Liesl to her mother. Mrs. Porter made no further inquiries; she testified that the nurse told her "babies just breathe funny." When she reached home, the mother noted that Liesl's condition was worsening, and she then took Liesl to Defiance Hospital, where doctors determined for the first time that Liesl's legs were not moving. They ordered numerous X-rays and laboratory tests, and eventually, another hospital staff doctor diagnosed a subluxation at her first and second lumbar vertebrae, which resulted in Liesl's paralysis from the waist down. Porter filed a lawsuit against Lima Memorial Hospital.

The experts who testified in the trial agreed that Liesl suffered paralysis sometime after Dr. Singh's examination and before her arrival, hours later, at Defiance Hospital. The experts also appeared to agree that Dr. Singh was the primary person who could have prevented the spinal injury by diagnosing Liesl's unstable spine before it became critically injured. Dr. Singh settled for $2,500,000.

Proximate cause was the crucial issue upon which Lima's asserted liability depended. There was evidence that both Dr. Singh and the Lima nurses breached a duty of care, and this evidence of negligence was sufficient to survive Lima's motion for a new trial. The pertinent question was whether the nurses' conduct proximately caused Liesl's paralysis. The district court, after the mother settled with the physician, denied the hospital's motion for judgment, notwithstanding the verdict in favor of the mother, but ordered a new trial at which the jury found the hospital not liable for the infant's injuries. Appeals were filed.

Issue

Was the nurses' failure to repeat vital signs legally insufficient to establish a connection between the failure to repeat vital signs and the eventual paralysis?

Holding

On appeal, the United States Court of Appeals for the Sixth Circuit held that the nurses' failure to repeat vital signs was legally insufficient to establish a connection between the failure to repeat vital signs and the eventual paralysis.

Reason

After the accident, Liesl was not immobilized while being transported to Lima. Dr. Singh did not direct that she be immobilized at any time while examining, testing, and treating her but notes that she was moving her extremities. Liesl demonstrated no signs of paralysis while he was examining her, and this would seem to eliminate any failure of this kind, which may have previously occurred, as a proximate cause of the paralysis. The experts on both sides generally agreed that the Lima nurses had no independent duty, apart from a doctor's instructions, to immobilize the infant.

The plaintiff's expert, Dr. Hall, changed his original, unequivocal opinion that the Lima nurses acted appropriately in the care of Liesl, but he made it clear, nonetheless, that the doctor was the ultimate person responsible from the standpoint of proximate cause.

Question: Now, Doctor [Hall], generally speaking, it's the role and responsibility of the emergency room physician to determine the patient's medical diagnosis and then to order the necessary and appropriate medical treatment, is it not?

Answer: Yes, it is.

Question: And, Doctor, in this case, where the emergency room doctor did not diagnose any spinal cord injury and discharged the baby after examining and X-raying the infant, you're not criticizing the nurses for not diagnosing and treating the spinal cord injury, are you?

Answer: That's correct.

Question: And that's because it was Dr. Singh's role and responsibility to do that, correct?

Answer: Yes.

Question: And what you're telling the jury is that, in your opinion, it was Dr. Singh who was responsible for treating Liesl's spinal cord injury, or at least he was responsible for ordering Liesl to be immobilized and hospitalized for further care and work up, isn't that the thrust of your testimony in this case?

Answer: Yes.

Question: So you are not saying that the conduct of the nurses or other hospital personnel caused any permanent harm or injury [to Liesl Fitzenrider], are you?

Answer: That's correct. Id. at 634.

Dr. Aranosian, another of the plaintiff's experts, opined that the Lima nurses should have repeated vital signs. Like Dr. Hall, however, he believed it was Dr. Singh's failure rather than the nurses' failure to repeat vital signs or to immobilize Liesl that proximately caused Liesl's injuries.

Question: Okay. And it's your testimony that Dr. Singh should have ordered Liesl to be immobilized after she arrived at the emergency room, isn't that correct?

Answer: Yes, sir.

Question: And it's your opinion that as far as responsibility for ordering immobilization in the emergency room in 1979 that would be the duty of the emergency room physician involved in the care of the patient, isn't that true?

Answer: Yes, sir.

Question: And it's also true—now, generally speaking, I will go on. Now, generally speaking, isn't it the real object and responsibility of the emergency room physician to determine the patient's medical diagnosis and then to order the necessary and appropriate medical treatment?

Answer: Yes, sir.

Question: And, Doctor, in this case, where the emergency room doctor did not diagnose any spinal cord injury and then discharged the baby after examining and X-raying the infant, you certainly are not criticizing the nurses for not diagnosing and treating the spinal cord injury, are you?

Answer: Well, that's correct. I mean, the nurse would not make the diagnosis on the child. That's correct.

Question: And that's because it was Dr. Singh's role and responsibility to determine the medical diagnosis and then order the necessary and appropriate medical treatment, isn't that correct?

Answer: Yes, sir. Id. at 634.

Dr. Kiehl's testimony as to vital signs was to the same effect. Still another of the plaintiff's experts, Dr. Kytja Voeller, was even more specific in stating: "I don't think the vital signs had any causal relationship" to the paralysis. Id.

Discussion

1. What is the importance of patient assessment and documentation?
2. What is the importance of collaboration between the nurse and physician as it relates to this case?

Reassessments Vital to Survival

Citation: *Stokes v. Spartanburg Reg. Med. Ctr,* 629 S.E.2d 675 (S.C. App. 2006)

Facts

On June 10, 1998, Mr. Stokes underwent surgery to remove his thyroid and lymph nodes, which were cancerous. Dr. Hull performed the surgery. No complications arose during the surgery, and according to Dr. Hull, Stokes's prognosis was very good.

From the recovery room, Stokes was transferred to the third floor of the hospital, which is designated "Pediatrics." While on the third floor, Stokes no longer had an oxygen mask and was not being monitored with a pulse oximeter. According to the nurse's notes, Stokes arrived on the third floor at 6:45 p.m. and, by 7:30 p.m., his neck was "swollen" and his wound dressing was "saturated." Thirty minutes later, Stokes complained of pain and received Demerol combined with Phenergan. According to the nurse,

Stokes began having "difficulty breathing" at 8:30 p.m., and at 8:55 p.m., his breathing stopped. Five minutes later, a "code" was initiated.

During the code, a nurse anesthetist tried to intubate Stokes in order to provide him with oxygen, but the intubation was unsuccessful. The nurse anesthetist called the anesthesiologist for help. Dr. Cochran, a partner of Dr. Hull's, was also notified of the code, and took charge of the resuscitation. At 9:21 p.m., Dr. Long, the anesthesiologist, arrived and successfully intubated Stokes. Despite the intubation, Stokes could not be revived. Dr. Cochran signed the death certificate, stating the cause of death was "respiratory failure."

After Stokes died, his son Terry E. Stokes, as Personal Representative of the Estate of Jennings E. Stokes, Appellant, brought a survivorship action and wrongful death action against the hospital. The appellant argued that Stokes died from a lack of oxygen, which could have been prevented if the hospital's staff had not deviated from the standard of care for a patient recovering from a thyroidectomy. According to the appellant's experts, a well-known complication of this type of surgery is airway obstruction caused by the swelling of soft tissue in the patient's neck. To decrease the chance of a patient's airway being obstructed, these experts testified that the patient should be on supplemental oxygen and "vigilantly monitored" for signs of respiratory distress.

The hospital argued that Stokes probably died of a heart attack. During trial, the appellant pointed out two pieces of medical documentation that were missing from Stokes's medical records: (1) the results of a blood test to determine whether oxygen was reaching Stokes's bloodstream, even though there was evidence that blood had been drawn from Stokes's artery during the code for this purpose; and (2) the vital signs flow chart prepared by the floor nurse at the time of Stokes's death. The hospital was unsure why the chart was missing but speculated that it was misplaced during the code.

At trial, the judge held a conference to discuss jury charges. One of the plaintiffs requested a "spoliation of evidence" charge, which allowed jurors to draw a negative inference if it found the hospital's explanation regarding the missing records unsatisfactory. The trial judge agreed to the charge, and the hospital did not object. However, when it came time to charge the jury, the trial judge failed to give the "spoliation of evidence" instruction.

When the jury came back with a verdict for the defense, appellant's counsel moved for a new trial based on the jury charge. The trial judge denied the motion and an appeal was filed.

Issue

Did the trial court err by failing to instruct the jury on "spoliation of evidence," especially when the hospital did not object to the proposed charge?

Holding

The appellant had requested that the trial court charge the jury

---

I charge you that when a party fails to preserve material evidence for trial, it is for you to determine whether the party has offered a satisfactory explanation for that failure. If you find the explanation unsatisfactory, you are permitted—but not required—to the inference that the evidence would have been unfavorable to the party's claim.

The appeals court believed this language reflected the law of South Carolina and should have been charged based on the evidence presented in this case. The charge as given made no mention of missing evidence at all.

Reason

The appellant's malpractice claim against the hospital hinged on the jury believing Stokes died from lack of oxygen rather than from a sudden and unexpected heart attack. Both pieces of evidence the appellant alleges are missing would have helped determine how Stokes died. Thus, it was crucial to appellant's case that the jury know it could draw a negative inference from the hospital's failure to produce those important pieces of evidence. Thus the appeals court found that the appellant was prejudiced by the trial court's failure to instruct the jury on "spoliation of evidence." The appeals court, therefore, reversed and remanded the case for a new trial.

Discussion

1. Discuss why the appellant wanted the judge to charge the jury as to "spoliation of evidence."
2. If you determined that the "spoliation of evidence" would not have changed the outcome of the case, thus favoring the hospital, what additional discussion do you think might have occurred in the jury room during deliberations (e.g., transfer of the patient to a pediatric unit, the experience of the pediatric nursing staff in treating this type of adult post-operative patient, the effect of pain medication on the patient's respiratory system, failure of the staff to closely monitor the patient, poor record keeping)?

3. What steps might the hospital take to prevent such occurrences (e.g., retraining the staff as to the importance of continuous patient monitoring and reassessments)?

Screening and Discharge Appropriate

Citation: *Marshall v. East Carroll Parish Hosp. Serv. Dist.*, 134 F.3d 319 (5th Cir. 1998)

Facts

Fifteen-year-old Nydia Marshall was brought by ambulance to the East Carroll Parish Hospital emergency department on October 18, 1994, because she "wouldn't move" while at school after the bell rang. Upon her arrival, hospital personnel took her history and vital signs. She was unable to communicate verbally while at the emergency department but cooperated when removing her clothing and watched movement of persons coming in and out of the emergency department. She was examined by Dr. Horowitz, who also had several medical tests performed on her.

Dr. Horowitz diagnosed Nydia as having a respiratory infection and discharged her. He informed Nydia's mother, Ms. Marshall, that her daughter's failure to communicate was of unknown etiology, and he advised her to continue administering the medications that had been prescribed by the family physician on the previous day and to return to the emergency department if the condition deteriorated. The complaint alleged that, later that same day, Nydia's symptoms continued to worsen, and she was taken to the emergency department at a different hospital, where she was diagnosed as suffering from a cerebrovascular accident consistent with a left middle cerebral artery infarction.

This action claimed that the hospital violated EMTALA, 42 U.S.C. § 1395dd, by failing to provide Nydia with an appropriate medical screening examination and failing to stabilize her condition prior to discharge. The hospital moved for summary judgment and submitted supporting affidavits from Dr. Horowitz and a registered nurse who had participated in Nydia's treatment in the hospital's emergency department.

The district court allowed Ms. Marshall 3 months in which to conduct discovery necessary to respond to the motion. In opposition to that motion, Ms. Marshall submitted a statement of contested facts and the sworn affidavit of Ms. Middlebrooks, a licensed practical nurse who had been on duty at the hospital emergency department when Nydia was treated.

The district court granted summary judgment for the hospital on the grounds that no material fact issues were in dispute. Ms. Marshall contends that Ms. Middlebrooks's affidavit created a genuine issue of material fact.

Issue

Did the trial court err in granting summary judgment to the hospital?

Holding

The U.S. Circuit Court of Appeals, Fifth Circuit, found that the trial court did not err in granting summary judgment for the hospital.

Reason

42 U.S.C. § 1295dd(a)

EMTALA provides in relevant part

In the case of a hospital that has a hospital emergency department, if any individual . . . comes to the emergency department and a request is made on the individual's behalf for examination or treatment for a medical condition, the hospital must provide for an appropriate medical screening examination within the capability of the hospital's emergency department, including ancillary services routinely available to the emergency department, to determine whether or not an emergency medical condition . . . exists. 42 U.S.C. § 1295dd(a).

42 U.S.C. § 1395dd(e)(1)

The Act defines an "emergency medical condition," in pertinent part, as a medical condition manifesting itself by acute symptoms of sufficient severity (including severe pain) such that the absence of immediate medical attention could reasonably be expected to result in

> (i) placing the health of the individual (or, with respect to a pregnant woman, the health of the woman or her unborn child) in serious jeopardy,
> (ii) serious impairment to bodily functions, or
> (iii) serious dysfunction of any bodily organ or part. . . .

42 U.S.C. § 1395dd(e)(1).

42 U.S.C. § 1395dd(b)(1)

And, if the hospital determines that the individual has an "emergency medical condition," then the hospital must provide either

(A) within the staff and facilities available at the hospital, for such further medical examination and such treatment as may be required to stabilize the medical condition, or

(B) for transfer of the individual to another medical facility. . . .

42 U.S.C. § 1395dd(b)(1).

Ms. Marshall contends that Ms. Middlebrooks's affidavit demonstrates that hospital personnel knew that Nydia had an emergency medical condition and were very concerned about the cursory examination provided by Dr. Horowitz; that Dr. Horowitz should have performed a fundoscopic examination, cranial nerve testing, motor strength testing, and deep tendon reflex testing; and that Nydia should have been admitted to the hospital for observation of her unexplained altered mental status. In essence, Ms. Marshall is contending that Dr. Horowitz committed malpractice in failing to accurately diagnose an emergency medical condition.

The appeals court agreed with other courts that have interpreted EMTALA that the statute was not intended to be used as a federal malpractice statute but, instead, was enacted to prevent "patient dumping," which is the practice of refusing to treat patients who are unable to pay.

Accordingly, an EMTALA "appropriate medical screening examination" is not judged by its proficiency in accurately diagnosing the patient's illness but, rather, by whether it was performed equitably in comparison to other patients with similar symptoms. If the hospital provided an appropriate medical screening examination, it is not liable under EMTALA even if the physician who performed the examination made a misdiagnosis that could subject him or her and his or her employer to liability in a medical malpractice action brought under state law. A hospital's failure to diagnose a patient's condition may be actionable under state medical malpractice law, but not under EMTALA. Questions regarding whether a physician or other hospital personnel failed to properly diagnose or treat a patient's condition are best resolved under existing and developing state negligence and medical malpractice theories of recovery. EMTALA does not impose any duty on a hospital requiring that the screening result in a correct diagnosis.

EMTALA is implicated only when individuals who are perceived to have the same medical condition receive disparate treatment. The essence of this requirement is that there be some screening procedure, and that it be administered evenhandedly. When a hospital does not follow its own standard procedures, the plaintiff(s) must prove that the hospital treated a patient differently from other patients. The Act is not intended to ensure that each emergency department patient obtains a correct diagnosis but, rather, to ensure that each is accorded the same level of treatment regularly provided to patients in similar medical circumstances. An appropriate medical screening is interpreted to mean a screening that the hospital would have offered to any paying patient. It is the plaintiff's burden to show that the hospital treated her differently from other patients; a hospital is not required to show that it had a uniform screening procedure.

The hospital's duty to stabilize the patient does not arise until the hospital first detects an emergency medical condition. Stabilization and transfer provisions of EMTALA "are triggered only after a hospital determines that an individual has an emergency medical condition." The hospital has no duty under EMTALA to stabilize a condition that was not ascertained in appropriate screening examination.

Discussion

1. Why was EMTALA not applicable in this case? Discuss your answer.
2. On what foundation should the plaintiff have brought this action? Discuss your answer.
3. Develop a root cause analysis and discuss in detail what actions hospitals might take to reduce the likelihood of similar occurrences in the future.

Screening and Assessment Under EMTALA

Citation: *Hazel I. Cruz-Vazquez, et al., Plaintiffs, v. Mennonite General Hospital, Inc.,* Civil No. 08-1236 (JAF/JP) (United States District Court, D. Puerto Rico, September 20, 2011)

Facts

In this case, the plaintiff Cruz arrived at the emergency room of Mennonite General Hospital around 10:15 p.m. on January 4, 2007 complaining of vaginal discharge and blood spotting and requesting medical services. She denied having pelvic pain or dysuria, did not have a fever, and was feeling fetal movements. At that time, Cruz was in her third trimester of pregnancy. Dr. Brenda M. Torres-Perez (Dr. Torres) performed a vaginal exam on her. Dr. Torres found that Cruz's cervix was not dilated. Thereafter, around 10:55 p.m., Dr. Torres called Cruz's obstetrician, Dr. Eduardo Gomez-Torres ("Dr. Gomez"), who advised that Dr. Torres should administer Bretine and Vistaryl so that Cruz could be discharged in a stable condition. Dr. Gomez also advised that Cruz should follow-up the next morning at Dr. Gomez's private office. The parties stipulate that these instructions were followed. Cruz was sent home at 12:15 a.m., less than two hours after her arrival at the emergency room.

The next morning, the record shows that Cruz was examined by Dr. Gomez at his office around 8:14 a.m. and was complaining of blood spotting, which had been occurring since the previous night. Upon examining Cruz, Dr. Gomez found a blood collection pool in Cruz's vagina, and found that Cruz was dilated 7 centimeters with bulging membranes. He also found that the baby was floating in the breach position and that the fetal cardiac rhythm was 142 beats per minute. Thereafter, Cruz was transferred to the San Juan City Hospital where a cesarean section was performed and Cruz's baby was born prematurely, with a weight of 2 pounds and 14 ounces. The baby died two days later.

The plaintiffs argued that Cruz was not given an appropriate medical screening because Dr. Torres should have conducted additional examinations and laboratory tests on Cruz before releasing her as per the hospital's protocol. The plaintiffs point to the existence of Mennonite hospital's "Gravid with 3rd Trimester Bleeding" protocol, requiring certain tests to be performed. According to Plaintiffs, because the additional tests were not performed, Cruz was given disparate treatment in violation of Emergency Medical Treatment and Active Labor Act (EMTALA), 42 U.S.C. § 1395dd. EMTALA is an anti-dumping statute that was enacted by Congress in response to concerns about the increasing number of reports that emergency rooms were refusing to accept or treat uninsured patients with emergency medical conditions

The statute imposes two categories of obligations upon hospitals. First, it requires that hospitals provide an appropriate medical screening to all individuals who come to the hospital's emergency room seeking assistance, 42 U.S.C. § 1395dd(a). Second, EMTALA requires that if an emergency medical condition exists, the hospital must render the services that are necessary to stabilize the patient's condition, unless transferring the patient to another facility is medically indicated and can be accomplished with relative safety.

On August 15, 2011, the Court entered an Opinion and Order denying defendants' motion for summary judgment (Docket No. 132). At the hearing held on August 16, 2011 and in their motion for summary judgment, the defendants argued that the plaintiffs did not present sufficient evidence to support a finding that the defendants failed to provide an appropriate screening to plaintiff Cruz upon her arrival to the defendant Mennonite General Hospital, Inc.'s emergency room as required by EMTALA.

The defendants argued that the Court should decline to exercise jurisdiction over plaintiffs' state law medical malpractice claims. After hearing the parties again on the issue of jurisdiction, the Court ordered the parties to file supplemental briefs on the issue of jurisdiction. The parties subsequently filed supplemental briefs (Docket Nos. 136, 139), and the defendants moved to dismiss the case for lack of federal jurisdiction (Docket No. 139).

Issue

Should Cruz's case be dismissed for lack of federal jurisdiction?

Holding

After considering the arguments presented by the parties at the hearing and the parties' supplemental briefs as to the issue of jurisdiction under EMTALA, the U.S. District Court vacated its previous decision and granted the defendants' motion to dismiss.

Reason

Dr. Torres made a medical judgment not to perform additional tests after performing the pelvic examination on Cruz, establishing that she was not experiencing any pain, and consulting Cruz's private physician. Dr. Torres's decision not to conduct additional tests had nothing to do with Cruz' ability to pay but rather with her assessment of Cruz's medical condition.

The Court determined that although Dr. Torres' diagnosis of Cruz's condition may have been incorrect it is not actionable under EMTALA. The purpose of EMTALA is not to guarantee that all patients are properly diagnosed. After examining Cruz, Dr. Torres consulted Cruz's private physician, Dr. Gomez, who advised administering certain medications to Cruz and that Cruz should visit Dr. Gomez's office the following morning. Even if Dr. Torres erroneously determined that further tests were unnecessary, her error amounts only to a faulty screening, which is appropriately dealt with under Puerto Rico's medical malpractice laws.

There is no question that Cruz had medical insurance, her own private physician, and that she was not denied admission or treatment when she arrived at the hospital. Indeed, upon her admission to the emergency room of the hospital, Dr. Torres examined Cruz in a timely manner. On reviewing the record of this case, the legislative purpose of EMTALA is to prevent the "dumping" of uninsured patients. EMTALA was designed to protect the uninsured. Neither EMTALA nor the First Circuit has ever stated that plaintiffs can use EMTALA as a jurisdictional door to bring to a federal court a case that is strictly a state court case.

Discussion

1. Should EMTALA require hospitals to establish appropriate protocols for screening patients? Discuss your answer.
2. Play the part of the judge here by describing how you would rule on the Cruz case based on the facts given. Remembering that not all Judges rule alike given the same fact pattern and their application of the law. Some Judges make decisions based on how they perceive the intent of the law as legislated by Congress. This is a slippery slope. What would the average person think if the hospital established a protocol for screening based on presenting complaints that are not consistently followed? Is it enough to say, "We screened the patient by taking their vital signs and sent them home to see their physician in the morning." Saying we screen every patient means nothing unless hospitals follow, at the very minimum, pre-established standards based on best practices, otherwise, antidumping legislation could be viewed merely as a sham legislated by Congress and enforced by the courts.
3. Do you think the hospital's screening of Cruz was adequate based on its own protocol described here? Discuss your answer.
4. Could the decision in the Cruz case be determined to be so egregious and lacking in justification that it amounted to a violation of EMTALA?
5. Describe why this case illustrates why physicians should not practice telephone medicine?

chapter five

Medical Diagnosis

When Your Doctor Doesn't Know

Patients who go for years without a diagnosis often are "medical disasters," says William Gahl, M.D., Ph.D., director of the NIH's Undiagnosed Diseases Program, which was launched in May 2008 to study some of the most difficult-to-diagnose medical cases. "They may be given diagnoses based on spurious test results that lead to treatments that are inappropriate or even harmful," he says. "And living for years without a diagnosis can accrue all sorts of complications."

Mary A. Fisher, AARP, *July/August 2011*

Medical diagnosis refers to the process of identifying a possible disease or disease process, thus providing the physician with treatment options. Screens, assessments, reassessments, and the results of medical diagnostic testing such as electroencephalography (EEG), electrocardiography (ECG), imaging, and laboratory findings are some of the tools of medicine that assists providers (e.g., physicians, osteopaths, dentists, podiatrists, nurse practitioners, physician's assistants) in diagnosing the possible causes of a patient's symptoms and medical problems from which a treatment plan is developed. The cases in this chapter describe some of the lawsuits that have occurred due to misdiagnoses and failure to properly treat the patient based on the results of diagnostic testing.

Five Commonly Misdiagnosed Diseases

The celebrity was John Ritter.

The actor died in 2003 of an aortic dissection—a tearing of the major artery that comes out of the heart. His widow later settled a wrongful death lawsuit against a California hospital, alleging his condition had been misdiagnosed "at least twice."

Experts who study malpractice cases and autopsy reports say certain diseases are misdiagnosed over and over again . . .

Elizabeth Cohen, CNN Health, *September 26, 2007*

Some of the more commonly misdiagnosed illnesses include aortic dissection, cancer, clogged arteries, heart attack, infection, lupus, Parkinsons disease, celiac disease, chronic fatigue syndrome, fibromyalgia, multiple sclerosis, stroke, and Lyme disease. The various autoimmune diseases, some of which have already been listed earlier, often go undiagnosed for years. In today's world, there are a variety of programs and websites that can assist physicians in making accurate diagnoses. "Computer-assisted diagnosis" programs are not new, but there has been reluctance in the past over their use. The purpose of such programs is not to replace the physician but to provide another tool to assist the physician in making an accurate diagnosis based on the patient's symptoms, diagnostic testing, and physician skills. Described next are some of the lawsuits that have occurred because of the failure of physician(s) to diagnose a patient's illness.

Failure to Diagnose and Treat

Citation: *Gerner v. Long Island Jewish Hillside Med. Ctr.*, 609 N.Y.S.2d 898 (N.Y. App. Div. 1994)

Facts

On March 8, 1971, the plaintiff gave birth to her infant son at the defendant medical center. Dr. Geller, a private physician, saw the infant 6 hours later as the attending pediatrician with resident privileges. On March 11, 1971, Dr. Geller ordered phototherapy, having noted and confirmed a slightly jaundiced condition. After 3 days of treatment and monitoring, the child's bilirubin count fell to a normal level, and Dr. Geller ordered the patient discharged. He continued to provide care for the child over the next 4 years. The child today is brain damaged, with permanent neurological dysfunction.

The plaintiff alleged medical malpractice on the part of both the medical center and the private attending physician for failing to diagnose and treat the jaundice in a timely manner. Following pre-trial examinations, the medical center's motion for summary judgment was granted. The plaintiff and Dr. Geller appealed.

Issue

Were there questions of fact regarding indications in the first 6 hours after the infant's birth (before the private attending pediatrician saw the patient) that should have alerted the hospital delivery and nursery staff of possible hyperbilirubinemia and, therefore, should have precluded summary judgment for the hospital?

Holding

The New York Supreme Court, Appellate Division, held that there were questions of fact precluding summary judgment for the hospital.

Reason

Two factual issues were left unresolved. The first is whether there were indications in the first 6 hours after birth that should have alerted the nursery staff of possible hyperbilirubinemia. According to the hospital's expert, one such overlooked indicator was a blood incompatibility between the mother and child. Because the hospital acted alone as the plaintiff's medical practitioner over those first 6 hours, it would have to bear sole responsibility for any malpractice committed during that period.

The second issue is whether the medical center should be exempt from sharing any responsibility for malpractice over the course of the next 6 days (until the infant's discharge) by reason of the fact that, for the balance of that period, the infant was technically under the care of a private attending physician. A number of allegations were raised as to negligence attributed solely to hospital staff during that period. For example, notes of attending nurses at the nursery failed to record any jaundiced condition, or any reference to color, until the third day after birth, despite the parents' complaints to hospital personnel about the baby's yellowish complexion. Additionally, Dr. Geller ordered a complete blood count and bilirubin test on the morning of March 11, as soon as he learned of the first recorded observation by a nurse of a jaundiced appearance. Test results showed a moderately elevated bilirubin, which was not reported by the laboratory until 10 hours after the blood sample was drawn, and it took another 3 hours before Dr. Geller's order for phototherapy was carried out. An issue is thus raised as to whether the 13-hour delay in commencement of the treatment had any permanent effect. Normally, a hospital is shielded from liability for the negligence of a private attending physician practicing at its facility; however, the hospital failed to dispel allegations of its own negligence. The hospital's motion should have been denied.

Discussion

1. If this case were tried in your state, would the statute of limitations time bar the lawsuit?
2. What is the importance of documentation as it relates to this case?
3. What is the importance of assessment and reassessment as it relates to patient care in general?
4. Why did the hospital bear sole responsibility for malpractice in this case?
5. What information management system(s) might the hospital design to help prevent such occurrences in the future?

Blaming the Victim

. . . Doctors had told the family he [Williams] had cirrhosis of the liver, internal bleeding, and ketoacidosis . . . from newly diagnosed diabetes. . . . When Williams family protested that they considered the 46-year-old electronics engineer . . . to be strictly a social drinker, the staff disagreed. "They can hide it really well," Janas said one nurse told her. . . . Williams slowly recovered, adjusting to life as an insulin-dependent diabetic. . . . Determined to find the cause of his health problems, he called his longtime friend Delbert Scott, pathologist . . . "we got out my Merck manual and looked up the possible causes of liver failure, and there it was," . . . a genetic disease that causes the body to absorb and store too much iron, causing organ damage. . . . Buried in his discharge summary. . . . Doctors had, in fact, tested his serum ferritin level and found it "markedly elevated.". . . Resta (hematologist) said he finds the decision not to pursue the abnormal findings baffling.

Sandra Boodman, The Washington Post, *June 14, 2011*

Misdiagnosis: Failure to Timely Review Lab Results

Citation: *Smith v. U.S. Dept. of Veterans Affairs*, 865 F. Supp. 433 (N.D. Ohio 1994)

Facts

Plaintiff, Mr. Smith, was first diagnosed as having schizophrenia in 1972. He had been admitted to the Veterans Affairs (VA) Hospital psychiatric ward 15 times since 1972. His admissions grew longer and more frequent as time passed. On March 17, 1990, he had been drinking in a bar, had gotten into a fight, and was eventually taken to the VA hospital. Dr. Rizk was assigned as Mr. Smith's attending physician.

On March 19, shortly after his arrival, Mr. Smith developed acute problems with his respiration and level of consciousness. It was determined that his psychiatric medications were responsible for his condition. Some medications were discontinued and others reduced, and a subsequent improvement in his condition was noted. However, by March 23, Mr. Smith began to complain of pain in his shoulders and neck. He attributed the pain to osteoarthritis and over 20 years' service as a letter carrier. His medical record indicated that he had had similar complaints in the past.

A rheumatology consultation was requested and carried out on March 29. The rheumatology resident conducted an examination and noted that Mr. Smith reported bilateral shoulder pain increasing with activity as an ongoing problem since 1979. Various tests were ordered, including an erythrocyte sedimentation rate (ESR).

On April 1, Mr. Smith became actively psychotic and was placed in four-point leather restraints. By April 3, Mr. Smith was incontinent and complained of shoulder pain, but that afternoon, he was out of restraints, walked to the shower, and bathed himself. Upon returning to his room, he claimed he could not get into bed. He was given a pillow and slept on the floor. By morning, Mr. Smith was lying on the floor in urine and complaining of numbness. His failure to move was attributed to his psychosis. That evening, it was noted that Mr. Smith could not lift himself and would not use his hands. On April 5, a medical student noted that Mr. Smith was having difficulty breathing and called for a pulmonary consultation. He was noted to be unwilling or unable to grasp a nurse's hand and continuing to complain that his legs would not hold him up.

By the morning of April 6, Mr. Smith was complaining that his neck and back hurt and that he had no feeling in his legs and feet. Later that day, a medical student noted that the results of Mr. Smith's ESR were more than twice the normal range, and his WBC was 18.1, well above the normal rate. There was a note on the medical record that Mr. Smith had been unable to move his extremities for about 5 days. A psychiatric resident noted that Mr. Smith had been incontinent for 3 days and had a fever of 101.1°.

On the morning of April 7, Mr. Smith was taken to University Hospital for magnetic resonance imaging of his neck. Imaging revealed a mass subsequently identified as a spinal epidural abscess. By the time it was excised, it had been pressing on his spinal cord too long for any spinal function below vertebra 4 or 5 to remain.

Issue

Was the physicians' failure to promptly review results of the plaintiff's erythrocyte sedimentation rate the proximate cause of his paralysis?

Holding

The District Court held that the negligent failure of physicians to promptly review laboratory tests results was the proximate cause of the plaintiff's quadriplegia.

Reason

Of primary importance was the plaintiff's ESR of 110, the result of which was available by April 2, but was not seen, or at least not noted in the record, until April 6. Although witnesses for both sides purported to disagree, there was little disagreement as to the nature and importance of this test. An elevated ESR generally accounts for one of three problems: infection, cancer, or a connective tissue disorder. Most experts agreed that, at the very least, a repeat ESR should have been ordered. The VA's care of the plaintiff fell below the reasonable standard of care in that nobody read the lab results, which were available on the patient care unit by April 2. The fact that the tests were ordered mandates the immediate review of their results.

In light of the absence of notes from Dr. Rizk in plaintiff's chart, it is impossible to know if he was aware of the plaintiff's symptoms. It appears that Dr. Rizk's care of the plaintiff was negligent because of the absence of Dr. Rizk's notes in the plaintiff's chart. The failure to review the results of the plaintiff's ESR constituted negligence under the relevant standard of care. That failure led to the failure to make an early diagnosis of the plaintiff's epidural abscess, and was itself the proximate cause of his eventual paralysis. Negligent conduct is the proximate cause of an injury if the injury is the natural and probable consequence of negligent conduct. An injury is the natural and probable consequence of negligent conduct if the injury might and should have been foreseen. An injury is foreseeable if a reasonably prudent person under the same or similar circumstances would have anticipated that injury to another was the likely result of his conduct. In light of the fact that a high ESR can manifest itself in a very serious illness, it was foreseeable that ignoring a high ESR would lead to serious injury.

Discussion

1. Discuss the importance of a computerized order entry and reporting system. How might the outcome of this case have been different if lab test panic values were immediately directed to the patient care unit and physician?
2. Discuss the importance of charting. How might the outcome of this case have been different if the plaintiff had been on an acute care medical/surgical unit?

Failure to Diagnose: Pap Smear

Citation: *Sander v. Geib, Elston, Frost Prof'l Ass'n*, 506 N.W.2d 107 (S.D. 1993)

Facts

As part of her regular care, the patient had several gynecological examinations, including Pap tests, in 1977, 1978, 1980, 1984, 1986, and 1987. All Pap tests were performed by her general practitioner, who then submitted them to the Geib Elston Frost Professional Association d.b.a. Clinical Laboratory of the Black Hills (Clinical Laboratory) for evaluation. The laboratory procedure consisted of a clerk assigning each specimen a number when it was received. A cytotechnologist would then screen the specimen, and if it were determined to be abnormal, a pathologist would mark it for review. Out of the Pap tests that were determined to be normal, only 1 in 10 was actually viewed by a pathologist. The pathologist made recommendations based on the classification of the Pap tests. A biopsy would be recommended if a Pap smear were determined to be Class IV.

Except for the Pap test in 1987, which showed premalignant cellular changes, all of the patient's other Pap tests were determined to be negative. In 1986, the laboratory made a notation to the patient's physician that "moderate inflammation" was present. The patient's physician, who was treating the patient with antibiotics for a foot inflammation, thought that the medication would also treat the other inflammation. In September 1987, the patient returned to her physician complaining of pain, erratic periods, and tiredness.

After completing a physical, her physician took a Pap test, which he sent to Clinical Laboratory. He also referred her to a gynecologist. A biopsy was recommended. Biopsies and further physical examinations revealed squamous cell carcinoma that had spread to her pelvic bones and to one-third of her vagina. Her Pap tests were reexamined by Clinical Laboratory, which reported that the 1986 smear showed malignancy was highly likely. The patient was referred to the University of Minnesota to determine whether she was a viable candidate for radiation treatment. However, the cancer had spread, and the patient was not considered a candidate for radiation treatment, as she had no chance of survival. When the University of Minnesota reviewed all of the available slides, they found cellular changes back to 1984.

The patient sued in 1988, alleging that Clinical Laboratory failed to detect and report cellular changes in her Pap tests in time to prevent the spread of the cancer. Before trial, the patient died. Her husband and sister were substituted as plaintiffs, and the complaint was amended to include a wrongful death action. After trial, a jury awarded $3.7 million in damages, which were reduced to $1 million by the circuit court. The jury found against Clinical Laboratory, and the laboratory appealed.

Issue

(1) Should the jury's award be restored to the $3.7 million damage award? (2) Was the damage award excessive in light of the evidence? (3) Does the statutory cap on awards apply to Clinical Laboratory as it is a medical corporation?

Holding

The Supreme Court of South Dakota upheld the jury verdict and restored the $3.7 million damage award. The court found that the damage award was not excessive in light of the evidence; the statutory cap on awards does not apply to Clinical Laboratory because it is a medical corporation.

Reason

The court determined that evidence relating to negligence claims pertaining to Pap tests taken more than 2 years before filing the action were admissible because the patient had a continuing relationship with Clinical Laboratory as a result of her physician's submitting her Pap tests to the laboratory over a period of time.

Discussion

1. What changes in procedure should Clinical Laboratory take to help ensure that Pap tests are properly classified?
2. How might continuous quality improvement activities improve the laboratory's operations?

Misdiagnosed with HIV

Citation: *Bramer v. Dotson*, 437 S.E.2d (W. Va. 1993)

Facts

On March 23 and 24, 1988, the plaintiff, Mr. Bramer, was seen by Dr. Dotson for a physical examination. Prior to his appointment, the patient had been suffering from diarrhea and weight loss. Following examination by Dr. Dotson, Mr. Bramer was diagnosed with Crohns disease. Dr. Dotson prescribed medications for the diarrhea.

On May 24, 1988, Mr. Bramer's diarrhea did not subside, so he returned to Dr. Dotson for further evaluation. A blood specimen was drawn and sent to SmithKline Laboratories for testing for human immunodeficiency virus (HIV). In early June, the laboratory informed Dr. Dotson that Mr. Bramer tested positive for HIV.

On June 13, 1988, Dr. Dotson informed the patient that he had acquired immune deficiency syndrome (AIDS). Mr. Bramer, not believing that his symptoms mimicked those of an individual with AIDS, was retested for HIV. On three separate occasions (July 1, 1988; July 15, 1988; and July 22, 1988) involving two separate laboratories, he tested negative for the virus. In September 1990, Mr. Bramer filed a lawsuit against Dr. Dotson and SmithKline for the negligent interpretation and reporting of his blood samples as being HIV-positive.

The circuit court, upon agreement of all parties to the lawsuit, agreed to the following certified question for review by the Supreme Court of Appeals of West Virginia: Did the plaintiff state a claim upon which relief could be granted in alleging that the defendants caused him to suffer major depression? The circuit court ruled yes.

Issue

Did the plaintiff state a claim upon which relief could be granted?

Holding

The Supreme Court of Appeals of West Virginia ruled that the plaintiff had stated a claim for the negligent infliction of emotional distress.

Reason

The Court found that, "Given the well known fact that AIDS had replaced cancer as the most feared disease in America and, as defendant SmithKline candidly acknowledges, a diagnosis of AIDS is a death sentence, conventional wisdom mandates that fear of AIDS triggers genuine—not spurious—claims of emotional distress. Accordingly, the first certified question was correctly answered by the circuit court . . . " Id. at 775.

Discussion

1. Based solely on the preceding facts, what provisions should the physician have made for reassessment of the patient's condition?
2. What instructions should the physician have provided to the patient for continuing care?

Negligent Barium Swallow: Perforation of Esophagus

Citation: *Fortney v. Al-Hajj*, 425 S.E.2d 264 (W. Va. 1992)

Facts

Mr. Fortney arrived at the emergency department of Thomas Memorial Hospital on November 23, 1987, believing that he had lodged a piece of chicken in his esophagus. Dr. Breland examined Mr. Fortney in the emergency department and ordered a barium swallow test, a procedure designed to identify foreign objects lodged in the upper gastrointestinal tract. The test is conducted by instructing a patient to drink a radiopaque liquid while X-rays are being taken. The presence of the liquid then delineates any irregularities of the gastrointestinal system. Dr. Breland ordered the test to determine whether the piece of chicken was still lodged in Mr. Fortney's esophagus. At the time Dr. Breland ordered the test, Mr. Fortney was not demonstrating any signs of breathing difficulty that could have indicated a perforation of his esophagus. Mr. Fortney was taken to the radiology department for the performance of the test. As Mr. Fortney's expert agreed, it was not the responsibility of Dr. Breland to actually perform the test. As Mr. Fortney attempted to drink the barium, his esophagus filled quickly, and the barium began coming back out of his mouth. The X-ray technician instructed the patient to continue drinking the barium, and the patient then began to gag. All of the witnesses at trial agreed that the gagging in the X-ray department caused a perforation in the patient's esophagus. When Mr. Fortney returned to the emergency department, he was in extreme pain. Dr. Breland contacted a consultant, Dr. Harper, a gastroenterologist. The barium swallow test had indicated the presence of a foreign object lodged where the esophagus joins the stomach and had also shown evidence of a perforation in the patient's esophagus. Dr. Harper suctioned out the barium in Mr. Fortney's esophagus but was unable to remove the chicken.

Dr. Figueroa, a cardiothoracic surgeon, was then consulted. He performed surgery, but no perforation in the esophagus was found. The physicians then concluded that the perforation had resealed itself after allowing the contents of the esophagus to escape into other areas of the body. During Mr. Forney's 6-week hospitalization in the intensive care unit, he was treated by Dr. Figueroa and Dr. Al-Hajj.

In December 1988, Mr. Fortney initiated a civil action alleging medical malpractice. Prior to the trial, the hospital settled for $47,000. During the trial, Dr. Breland's counsel attempted to establish the hospital's negligence, based on the difficulties encountered during the performance of the barium swallow. Dr. Breland now contends, however, that the trial court impermissibly limited argument regarding the hospital's negligence and failed to inform the jury of the hospital's settlement with Mr. Fortney. Dr. Breland also asserted on appeal that the trial court erred in permitting a general surgeon, Dr. John Wilson, to testify as an expert regarding the appropriate standard of care required in emergency medicine. Prior to opening statements, the trial court explained the following to the parties:

Don't get into this thing about pointing the finger at Thomas because they're not in this case. They're not in the case. And the only way I'm going to let them in the case is just by telling the jury that they were in the case and they settled. And the jury can make any inference they want from the evidence that comes in, but I don't want you all arguing that. Id. at 268.

During his opening statement, and without interruption by the lower court or opposing counsel, counsel for Dr. Breland stated:

In this case, Dr. Breland sent Mr. Fortney back there to radiology, and everyone is going to agree on everything up until that point. Dr. Breland sent him back there to have him take a couple sips of barium. Dr. Breland did not go back with him to do that.

Dr. Breland doesn't administer those tests, and he'll tell you that. He was out there caring for patients in the emergency room. He sent him back to radiology. And then Mr. Fortney can be the only one that can tell us about what happened back there in radiology, and he's going to tell you a horrible story.

People back at Thomas Memorial Hospital back in radiology gave him a sip of barium; kept having him sip more and more and more. He'll tell you that it was coming out of his mouth and going all over his clothes. He'll tell you that he was gagging, and he had a real problem back there in radiology; but remember, Dr. Breland is not giving that test back there. He decided that's the appropriate test, but he sent him back there to have it done by the radiology staff at Thomas Memorial Hospital, and Mr. Fortney is going to be the one that will tell you about what happened back there. Id. at 268.

Dr. Breland discussed the hospital's role when he questioned Mr. Fortney himself during cross-examination regarding his experience in the radiology department.

Question: Do you believe the standard of care was breached in administering the barium swallow itself, not in ordering?
Answer: I believe giving it, per se, was below the standard, which I've already stated.
Question: You already stated that?
Answer: Yes. The order is below the standard; to give it is below the standard . . . is below the standard. How meaningful it was, I don't know, but those are certainly bad things to do. Id. at 268.

Mr. Fortney contended that had Dr. Breland not ordered a barium swallow, no malpractice action would have been instituted. The proper procedure to identify any blockage would have been, according to Mr. Fortney, a bronchoscopy after a plain chest X-ray.

Issue

(1) Did the trial court impermissibly limit evidence regarding the hospital's negligence and the role such negligence might have played in the patient's injuries? (2) Was the general surgeon qualified to provide expert testimony on the issue of the standard of care of a physician rendering assistance to a patient suffering from impacted food blockage in the emergency department?

Holding

The Supreme Court of Appeals of West Virginia held that the trial court did not impermissibly limit evidence regarding the hospital's negligence and the role such negligence might have played in the patient's injuries. Furthermore, the general surgeon was qualified to provide expert testimony as to the standard of care required of a physician rendering assistance to a patient suffering from impacted food blockage.

Reason

Based on the Supreme Court's review of the record, all of the physicians were provided ample opportunity to explain the negligence of the hospital. The salient inquiry was to what extent Dr. Wilson was qualified under West Virginia Code § 55-7B-7 to testify as an expert on the issue of the standard of care required in treating a patient suffering an impacted food blockage. We conclude that Dr. Wilson was qualified to provide expert testimony on the issue of the standard of care of a physician rendering assistance to a patient suffering from an impacted food blockage. Any shortcomings that Dr. Breland believed existed in Dr. Wilson's credentials properly could have been the subject of cross-examination. With regard to whether Dr. Breland deviated from the normal standard of care in his treatment, the following dialogue during Dr. Wilson's testimony was relevant:

Question: Dr. Wilson, I guess maybe the best thing to do after all that is I will go back to my question. Do you have an opinion, based upon a reasonable degree of medical probability, through your experience and training, as you indicated, whether or not Dr. Breland deviated from the normal standard of care in his treatment of Mr. Fortney?

Answer: I have an opinion.

Question: What is your opinion?

Answer: I believe that he did. Id. at 271.

Discussion

1. What are the pros and cons of an emergency department physician overseeing the barium swallow procedure?
2. What are the competency issues described in this case?
3. What action should the organization take to reduce the likelihood of such occurrences?

Negligent Barium Enema: Perforation of Rectum

Citation: *Oberzan v. Smith*, 869 P.2d 682 (Kan. 1994)

Facts

Mr. Oberzan brought a medical malpractice action against a hospital radiologist for injuries allegedly incurred while being prepared by an X-ray technician for a barium enema. Mr. Oberzan admitted to the following nine facts:

1. The pretrial questionnaire prepared by the plaintiff alleges that Dr. Smith or his X-ray technician perforated plaintiff's rectum during the barium enema procedure.
2. The plaintiff was referred to Dr. Smith by Dr. Jones for the barium enema procedure.
3. The usual procedure for performing barium enemas is that the X-ray technician inserts the enema tip for the barium enema and then gets Dr. Smith to begin the examination. All patients are in the prone position with the tip in place when Dr. Smith walks into the room.
4. With respect to the plaintiff, when Dr. Smith walked into the room the plaintiff was already lying in the prone position with the tip already inserted by the technician.
5. In February 1988, Ms. Davis was employed by Maude Norton Hospital as an X-ray technician.
6. As an X-ray technician, Ms. Davis was trained to prep patients for examinations, which would include inserting enema tubes for barium enemas.
7. Ms. Davis inserted the enema tip into the rectum of the plaintiff for the barium enema before Dr. Smith entered the room for the procedure.
8. After Dr. Smith entered the room, the exam began. Immediately after Ms. Davis began injecting the barium, she noticed bleeding at the tip of the rectum.
9. After the procedure was halted, Dr. Smith immediately contacted Dr. Jones to inform him of the bleeding.

Mr. Oberzan claimed the physician was vicariously liable for the employee's negligent conduct.

Issue

(1) Was the radiologist vicariously liable for injuries allegedly sustained by the patient while being prepared by the technician for a barium enema? (2) Does administrative regulation providing for supervision of a hospital's radiology department by a designated medical staff physician create a legal duty for the medical staff physician to personally supervise all activities that occur in the radiology department?

Holding

The Supreme Court of Kansas held that the respondeat superior doctrine did not apply to the relationship between the technician employed by the hospital and the radiologist so as to impose vicarious liability on the radiologist. Administrative regulation did not impose a legal duty on the radiologist to personally supervise the enema procedure.

Reason

Ms. Davis was not an employee of Dr. Smith. She was not under his direct supervision and control at the time the injury occurred. Dr. Smith did not select Ms. Davis to perform the insertion of the enema tip; she was assigned by the hospital. Vicarious liability under respondeat superior did not impose liability on Dr. Smith. The master–servant relationship was not established, because Dr. Smith was not exercising personal control or supervision over Ms. Davis, a nonemployee, at the time of injury. Mr. Oberzan admitted that "[t]he usual procedure for performing barium enemas is that the X-ray technician inserts the enema tip for the barium enema and then gets Dr. Smith to begin the examination."

Mr. Oberzan argued that Kansas law K.A.R. 28-34-86(a) imposes a duty on radiologists to supervise patient services rendered in a hospital radiology department by requiring "the radiology department and all patient services rendered therein shall be under the supervision of a designated medical staff physician; wherever possible, this physician shall be attending or consulting radiologists." However, none of the K.A.R. 28-34-12 subsections require that the preparation of a patient for a barium enema be performed under a physician's direct supervision. The purpose of K.A.R. 28-34-12(c) is to establish an administrative head for the radiology department. Mr. Oberzan cited no authority in support of his position that K.A.R. 28-34-12(c) creates a legal duty for a designated medical staff physician to personally control and supervise all activities that occur in a radiology department. The construction suggested by Mr. Oberzan would create physician liability extending far beyond the intent of the regulation.

Discussion

1. Describe how the defendant attempted to apply Kansas law in this case.
2. Describe a scenario in which the radiologist might have shared liability with the hospital.
3. What is meant by vicarious liability?

Physician: Failure to Repeat Imaging Test

Citation: *Reed v. Weber*, 615 N.E.2d 253 (Ohio Ct. App. 1992)

Facts

On October 14, 1988, the patient was admitted to the hospital by his family physician for treatment of a severe headache and hypertension. On October 15, 1988, a computed tomography (CT) scan was performed. On October 17, 1988, Dr. Armitage, who served as consulting neurologist at the request of the decedent's family physician, ordered a cerebral angiogram, which was performed by Dr. Weber, a radiologist. In an affidavit submitted in support of Dr. Weber's motion for summary judgment, Dr. Armitage stated that he reviewed the angiogram with Dr. Weber and that he understood that Dr. Weber had performed only a "three-vessel study" because he "was technically unable to visualize the right vertebral artery after repeated attempts." Dr. Armitage testified that, "[a]s the consulting neurologist, and with the understanding that the right vertebral artery had not been visualized, it was [his] best medical judgment that the angiogram did not need to be repeated during [the decedent's] October 1988 hospitalization." Armitage further asserted that the decision of whether to "repeat" the angiogram was his and not Dr. Weber's and that, in his opinion, "Weber adhered to the standard of care applicable to radiologists under like or similar circumstances when he reviewed the angiogram films and reported the results to [Armitage] as the patient's consulting neurologist." Id. at 255.

On October 22, 1988, the patient was discharged by his family physician. On November 16, 1988, the patient died of a ruptured aneurysm of the right vertebral artery.

The trial court entered summary judgment for Dr. Weber upon its determination that Dr. Armitage's decisions and actions constituted a superseding/intervening cause, relieving Dr. Weber of any alleged liability for the incomplete nature of the angiogram study.

Issue

The question to be determined was whether a genuine issue of material fact existed as to the neurologist's failure to order a repeat of the incomplete angiogram, and did it constitute an intervening cause sufficient to break the causal connection between the radiologist's negligence in performing the angiogram and the patient's death from a cerebral aneurysm?

Holding

The Court of Appeals of Ohio held that a genuine issue of material fact existed as to whether the neurologist's failure to order a repeat angiogram was sufficient to break the causal connection.

Reason

There may be more than one proximate cause of an injury. The test is "whether the original and successive acts may be joined together as a whole, linking each of the actors as to the liability, or whether there is a new and independent act or cause which intervenes and thereby absolves the original negligent actor."

The determination of whether negligent conduct was the proximate cause of an injury or whether an intervening act operated to break the chain of causation presented a question of fact. The decedent's representative submitted in opposition to the motion for summary judgment two affidavits and the deposition of Dr. Grossman, a professor of radiology and section chief of neuroradiology at the Hospital of the University of Pennsylvania. Dr. Grossman therein expressed his opinion that (1) the aneurysm that caused the decedent's death was present on October 15, 1988, when Dr. Weber performed the angiogram; (2) in cases such as that of the decedent, a four-vessel study was essential; (3) Dr. Weber's performance of the angiogram fell below the requisite standard of care when he failed to visualize adequately all four cerebral vessels and then failed to "redo" the inadequate study; and (4) Dr. Weber's failure to visualize the right vertebral artery prevented detection of the aneurysm and precluded any possibility of remedial action.

Viewing the evidence presented, the court found that there remained a genuine issue of fact that was material to the dispositive issue of whether Dr. Armitage's conduct constituted an intervening cause. Accepting Dr. Grossman's statement of the breadth of Dr. Weber's duty to the decedent in performing the angiogram, the court was precluded from a determination as a matter of law that Dr. Armitage's conduct operated independently to break the causal connection between Dr. Weber's negligence and the decedent's death, when Dr. Weber must be said to share with Dr. Armitage responsibility for the inadequacy of the angiogram. Id. at 257.

Discussion

1. What is meant by intervening cause?
2. What discharge planning issues do you see in this case?

When Your Doctor Doesn't Know

Did you know? Ten percent of all hospital deaths involve a major diagnostic error. Legal claim payouts for diagnostic errors cost more than $2.5 billion a year.

Yale physician Sanders has identified three primary reasons behind the failure to diagnose: mistakes in how doctors think, overreliance on specialists and medical testing, and the human body itself, which can experience a multitude of ailments but has limited ways to communicate those ailments. . . .

Indeed, finding the right specialist—or even determining when to see one—is part of the challenge. "There are so many submedical specialties today, which can further fragment the complex diagnostic puzzle," says Marianne Genetti (Executive Director of In Need Of Diagnosis, a Florida patient–resource organization). Some hematologists, for instance, may do only chemotherapy, while some neurologists may focus only on the treatment of Alzheimers.

Mary A. Fisher, AARP, July/August 2011

Radiologist Misdiagnoses Spinal Mass

Citation: *Garrett v. L.P. McCuistion Commnity Hosp.*, 30 S.W.3d 653 (Tex. App. 2000)

Facts

Dorothy Garrett appealed a summary judgment granted in favor of L.P. McCuistion Community Hospital. Garrett sued the hospital, three physicians, including Dr. Schmidt, and their professional associations for medical malpractice. The hospital moved for summary judgment, which the trial court granted. Garrett later settled her claim with Dr. Schmidt, nonsuited the other physicians and their associations, and nonsuited the hospital with respect to all other claims.

Garrett's petition alleged that Dr. Schmidt misdiagnosed a spinal mass as a cancerous lesion instead of a spinal abscess. Dr. Schmidt, a radiologist, is a partner in Radiology Consultants, P.A., which contracted with the hospital to provide radiologists for the hospital's radiology department. Garrett alleged that the hospital was vicariously liable for the negligence of Dr. Schmidt under the theory of apparent or ostensible agency.

Issue

Was the hospital vicariously liable for the negligence of Dr. Schmidt under the theory of apparent or ostensible agency?

Holding

The court on appeal held that the summary judgment evidence fails to raise a fact issue on the second element of ostensible agency in that it failed to show that the hospital held out Dr. Schmidt as its agent or employee.

Reason

The hospital contended there was no evidence to support the second element of ostensible agency (e.g., that it affirmatively held out Dr. Schmidt as its agent or employee, or that it knowingly allowed Dr. Schmidt to hold himself out as its agent or employee).

A hospital may be vicariously liable for the negligence of its physicians under a theory of ostensible agency if the physician is negligent and proximately causes the injury, and if the plaintiff proves the elements of ostensible agency.

The elements of ostensible agency are

1. the patient had a reasonable belief that the physician was the agent or employee of the hospital;
2. such belief was generated by the hospital affirmatively holding out the physician as its agent or employee, or knowingly permitting the physician to hold himself out as the hospital's agent or employee; and
3. the patient justifiably relied on the representation of authority.

This case involves a radiologist who is not alleged to have directly met with, treated, or advised the patient. Thus, it cannot be contended that Dr. Schmidt's actions or omissions, or his mere presence as an authoritative medical specialist, held him out as the hospital's agent or employee.

Garrett testified in her deposition that the hospital did no affirmative act causing her to believe Dr. Schmidt was its employee. The court on appeal held that the summary judgment evidence fails to raise a fact issue on the second element of ostensible agency in that it failed to show that the hospital held out Dr. Schmidt as its agent or employee.

In a dissenting opinion, Justice Grant opined that no effort was made by the hospital to inform patients that on-sight radiologists chosen by the hospital were not hospital agents or employees. Therefore, the doctrine of apparent or ostensible agency should be applied to stop the hospital from disclaiming responsibility for the acts of the radiologists under the facts of this case. Further, providing facilities within the hospital premises and designating the specific radiologist to handle the care would be sufficient to establish a finding of apparent or ostensible agency.

Discussion

1. Discuss why the appeals court determined that the hospital was not responsible for the misdiagnosis of the patient's mass.
2. Why did Justice Grant give a dissenting opinion?
3. What precautions should hospitals take to protect themselves from the malpractice of ostensible agents?

Radiologists' Misdiagnosis of Brain Tumor

Citation: *Stone v. Radiology Servs., P.A. et al,,* 206 Ga. App. 851, 426 S.E.2d 663 (Ga. Ct. App. 1992)

Facts

The patient, Mr. Stone, and his wife filed malpractice and loss of consortium claims against radiologists and a neurologist, alleging that the physicians misdiagnosed and failed to treat his brain tumor. The defendant physicians and the professional associations that employed them had misdiagnosed Mr. Stone's condition by failing to recognize that a computed tomography (CT) scan of Mr. Stone's brain taken in September 1985 "showed a tumor on [Mr. Stone's] brain."

Mr. Stone had been experiencing severe headaches for many years, but a May 1983 brain scan had revealed no abnormalities. On September 30, 1985, Mr. Stone went to Radiology Services, at which time a CT scan of his brain was performed. Physician employees reviewed the CT film and signed a radiological report, which set forth that the scan had revealed no areas of abnormal density and concluded with the diagnostic impression that the described changes were consistent with cerebellar atrophy.

In early December 1988, an MRI scan of Mr. Stone's brain was taken. The MRI scan has advantages over other scans because it is more sensitive and reveals slightly different angles to physicians' view. The scan revealed that Mr. Stone was suffering from an astrocytoma (type of tumor) in his brain, rather than from changes consistent with cerebellar atrophy.

The superior court entered summary judgment for physician defendants based on a *statute of limitations defense*. The plaintiffs appealed as to when the statute of limitations began to toll.

Issue

Was the misdiagnosis of the brain tumor by radiologists time-barred because the statute of limitations had run?

Holding

The court of appeals held that the misdiagnosis of the brain tumor by radiologists was time-barred because the statute of limitations had run.

Reason

The critical issue is: When did Mr. Stone's injury occur? In most misdiagnosed cases, the injury begins immediately upon the misdiagnosis due to the pain, suffering, or economic loss sustained by the patient from the time of the misdiagnosis until the medical problem is properly diagnosed not the subsequent discovery of the proper diagnosis.

Here, Mr. Stone's injury began on September 30, 1985 when a CT scan was performed on him and he was diagnosed with cerebellar atrophy, not a brain tumor, which was later found with the more sensitive MRI scan in December 1988. Therefore, there was no error in the trial court's determination that Mr. Stone's suit filed in December 1990 was barred by the statute of limitations.

Discussion

1. Do you agree with the court's ruling that, from a statute of limitations point of view, the misdiagnosis itself is the injury and not the subsequent discovery of the proper diagnosis? Explain.
2. What is the importance of the statute of limitations from both the plaintiff and defendant perspectives?

Physician Misdiagnoses Massive Myocardial Infarction

Citation: *Roy v. Gupta,* 606 So.2d 940 (La. Ct. App. 1992)

Facts

On October 31, 1987, Mrs. Roy went to the emergency department of Humana Hospital–Marksville complaining of chest pains. At that time she was 42 years old. She had no prior history of heart disease but was taking medication for hypertension. The attending physician was Dr. Gupta, a physician on independent contract who was moonlighting on weekends for the hospital. Upon examination, Mrs. Roy exhibited normal vital signs. She showed no obvious physical abnormalities. Dr. Gupta performed an electrocardiogram that showed ischemic changes indicating a lack of oxygen to the heart tissue. He applied a transdermal nitroglycerin patch and gave her a prescription for nitroglycerin. After monitoring her progress, he sent her home. Several hours later, she returned to the emergency department experiencing more chest pains. She was admitted to the hospital, and it was determined that she was having a heart attack. Three days later, Mrs. Roy died of a massive myocardial infarction.

On October 29, 1990, a bench trial was held. The trial court found Dr. Gupta negligent in failing to hospitalize Mrs. Roy or failing to inform her of the serious nature of her situation so that she would agree to hospitalization. The trial court also found that had Mrs. Roy been hospitalized on her first visit, her chances of survival would have been greatly increased.

It was asserted that the trial court erred in finding that Dr. Gupta failed to advise Mrs. Roy that she should be hospitalized or point out the potential dangers of not being hospitalized.

Issue

(1) Did Dr. Gupta's discharge of the patient from the emergency department while she had chest pains constitute malpractice? (2) Did the trial court err in finding that the patient's chances of survival would have been greatly increased if she had been admitted to the hospital and given proper treatment?

Holding

The Court of Appeal of Louisiana held that Dr. Gupta was negligent in failing to advise Mrs. Roy that she should be hospitalized for chest pains or point out the potential dangers of not being hospitalized. Proper care would have increased Mrs. Roy's chances of survival.

Reason

Dr. Caskey and Dr. d'Autremont, two expert witnesses, testified that it is common practice to enter in a patient's record whether a recommendation of hospitalization was made. No such notation was made in Mrs. Roy's chart by Dr. Gupta. All of the medical expert witnesses, except Dr. Kilpatrick, a defense witness, testified that Mrs. Roy should have been admitted. Dr. Kilpatrick testified that such a decision varied greatly among physicians. "In any event the trial court disregarded his testimony because he was too hostile in his responses to be of any assistance." Id. at 943.

In his reasons for judgment, it was evident the trial judge was not convinced by Dr. Gupta's explanation of why Mrs. Roy was not hospitalized. He focused on Dr. Gupta's failure to have X-rays taken during the first visit, which might have allowed him to determine whether the ischemic changes were due to her hypertension medication or indicated the beginnings of a heart attack. The relative simplicity of the technique and its obvious availability lent credence to the trial judge's belief that the requisite attention was not paid to Mrs. Roy's complaints. Id. at 943–944.

The law does not require proof that proper treatment would have been the difference between Mrs. Roy's dying and living. It only requires proof that proper treatment would have increased her chances of survival. Even though the expert testimony of Dr. d'Autremont was guarded in this area, the inference can be drawn from her testimony that while nothing could ensure Mrs. Roy's survival, admittance on the first visit would have at least increased her chances. This is a difficult area in which to make factual determinations, and the degree of specialization requires the trier of fact to rely heavily on the testimony of the experts. The trial judge was present and able to determine the credibility and sincerity of all who testified. Our review of the record revealed the trial court's finding to be sound.

As the bench heard this case, determinations of possible breaches of the appropriate standard of care were left to the trial judge. He sat as the trier of fact and made his findings related to negligence based on the evidence and inferences therefrom. In order for the court to upset the factual findings of the trial court, there must exist manifest error.

Discussion

1. Why are emergency departments at high risk for lawsuits?
2. What can be done to reduce the risks?
3. What opportunities for improvement do you see in your emergency department?

Negligently Diagnosed HIV Positive

Citation: *Edgepeth v. Whitman Walker Clinic and Mary Fanning, MD*, No. 07-CV-158 Appellant CA-6244-05 (D.C. Ct. of App. 2011)

Facts

Hedgepeth, appellant, alleged that he suffered serious emotional distress after a doctor negligently diagnosed him as HIV positive when, in fact, he was not. He presented evidence that, as a result of the misdiagnosis, he was clinically depressed and suffered repercussions in his employment and personal life until, 5 years later, he was correctly diagnosed as not being afflicted with HIV. The Superior Court granted the appellees' motion for summary judgment on the grounds that the appellant had failed to establish the requisite facts for the tort of *negligent infliction of emotional distress* where there is no other harm. A division of the court affirmed, agreeing with the Superior Court that appellees' alleged negligence did not place appellant within a "zone of physical danger," as required for recovery of damages for emotional distress. A petition for rehearing was granted.

Issue

Should the "zone of physical danger test" be applied to preclude the appellant's claim that his doctor's negligent misdiagnosis caused him serious emotional injury?

Holding

After reviewing the development of the law on this issue, the court concluded that the appellant's claim should not be barred simply because he was not put at risk of physical injury.

Reason

The zone of physical danger requirement imposes an unnecessary limitation upon, and is not to be applied indiscriminately in all cases to, claims of emotional distress brought against a defendant who has a relationship with the plaintiff, or has undertaken an obligation to the plaintiff, and whose negligence causes serious emotional distress to the plaintiff.

The appeals court adopted a rule—itself a limited one—that supplements the zone of physical danger test, finding a duty to avoid negligent infliction of serious emotional distress will be recognized only where the defendant has an obligation to care for the plaintiff's emotional well-being or the plaintiff's emotional well-being is necessarily implicated by the nature of the defendant's undertaking to or relationship with the plaintiff, and serious emotional distress is especially likely to be caused by the defendant's negligence.

The appeals court concluded this is such a case: the appellees, in the context of a doctor–patient relationship, undertook to test and treat the appellant for HIV, an undertaking that would necessarily implicate the patient's emotional well-being and entail a specially likely risk of serious emotional distress.

Appellant has presented evidence supporting his allegations that appellees negligently misdiagnosed him as being HIV positive and that this misdiagnosis caused him to suffer serious emotional distress. The court reversed the grant of summary judgment for appellees and remanded the case for further proceedings consistent with the principles set out in this opinion.

Discussion

1. Discuss why the appeals court adopted a rule supplementing the "zone of physical danger test."
2. Discuss the pros and cons of such a ruling as it might apply in other cases (e.g., a patient claims he suffered emotional distress because the doctor told him he was stung by a wasp when indeed he was stung by a hornet).

Nurse Practitioner Misdiagnoses Patient's Condition
Citation: *Adams v. Krueger*, 856 P.2d 864 (Idaho 1993)

Facts

The plaintiff initially went to a physician's office for diagnosis and treatment. The plaintiff's initial assessment was performed by a nurse practitioner employed by the physician. The plaintiff was diagnosed by the nurse practitioner as having genital herpes. The physician prescribed an ointment to help relieve the patient's symptoms. The plaintiff eventually consulted with another physician who advised her that she had a yeast infection, not genital herpes.

The plaintiff and her husband then filed an action against the initial treating physician and his nurse practitioner for their failure to correctly diagnose and treat her condition. The action against the physician was based on his failure to review the nurse practitioner's diagnosis and treatment plan.

The court gave instructions to the jury that the plaintiff would recover nothing if the jury found the plaintiff more than 50% negligent. However, the plaintiff would recover if the plaintiff's negligence was less than 50% and the combined negligence of the defendants was greater than 50%. The jury found the plaintiff 49% negligent, the physician 10% negligent, and the nurse practitioner 41% negligent.

The trial court found in favor of the plaintiff, and the defendants appealed. The court of appeals affirmed, and further appeal was made.

Issue

Did the trial court err in imputing the nurse practitioner's negligence to the physician by applying the comparative negligence statute in effect at the time the present action arose?

Holding

The Supreme Court of Idaho held that the negligence of the nurse was properly imputed to the physician for purposes of determining comparative negligence.

Reason

The Supreme Court adhered to the reasoning of the Court of Appeals wherein the nurse practitioner and her employer/physician would "stand in relation as master and servant, whereby the negligent acts of the servant, or employee, are imputed to the master, or employer, under the doctrine of respondeat superior." *Smith v. Thompson*, 103 Idaho 909, 655 P.2d 116 (Idaho Ct. App. 1982). "Comparative negligence, in and of itself, has not changed these basic principles [of imputed negligence]. When negligence is apportioned in the presence of vicarious liability, the master bears the burden of his servant's negligence. If the master has been partially at fault, the percentage of negligence attributed to his servant is added to the percentage attributed to the master." *Schwartz Comparative Negligence* § 16.1 at 253 (2nd ed. 1986). In the present case, it was undisputed that the physician and nurse practitioner stood in a master–servant relationship and that the nurse acted within the scope of her employment. Consequently, her negligence was properly attributed to her employer/physician. Id. at 867.

Discussion

1. Do you agree with the court's decision? Explain.
2. What might the physician/employer do to limit his liability in the future for the negligent acts of his professional employees?
3. If the nurse practitioner has malpractice insurance, can the physician recover any of his losses from her insurance carrier?

Pathologist Misdiagnoses Tumor as Benign

Citation: *Suarez Matos v. Ashford Presbyterian Community Hosp.*, 4 F.3d 47 (1st Cir. 1993)

Facts

On October 30, 1989, Ms. Matos became ill while vacationing in Puerto Rico. She went to the Ashford Presbyterian Community Hospital emergency department for treatment. She was examined and admitted to the hospital by Dr. Lopez. Dr. Juncosa removed a uterine tumor from the patient. Dr. Carrasco, a pathologist on the hospital's medical staff, examined the tumor. He allegedly reported the tumor as being benign.

At the time of discharge, the patient was given instructions to obtain follow-up care upon her return to New York. For referral purposes, the patient was provided with the names of two physicians from whom she could seek such care. The patient visited a clinic upon her return to New York. Five months later, the patient experienced further pain and was diagnosed with incurable cancer. It was determined that the nature of her tumor was such that it could have become malignant and, therefore, should have been closely monitored. The patient had not been advised of this possibility. Dr. Carrasco admitted that he knew of the possibility of a malignancy. He testified that Dr. Juncosa was warned of this possibility. In addition, Dr. Carrasco testified that the nature of this tumor was also described on the face of his written pathology report. Contradicting Dr. Carrasco's testimony, Dr. Juncosa testified that he was told by Dr. Lopez that Dr. Carrasco told him, Dr. Lopez, the tumor was benign. A district court jury found the defendant guilty of malpractice, and the defendant appealed the finding.

Issue

Was there sufficient evidence to support a finding of negligence on the part of the pathologist, and if so, was the hospital chargeable with his conduct?

Holding

The United States Court of Appeals for the 1st Circuit held that the evidence was sufficient to support a finding of negligence on the part of the pathologist and the hospital was chargeable with his negligence.

Reason

Without reviewing further, it is enough to say—although difficult—that the jury could combine Dr. Carrasco's admission that he knew of the possibility of malignancy and Dr. Juncosa's statement that Dr. Carrasco told him the reverse and, thus, prevent an ordered judgment for defendants. In other words, the jury could find that Dr. Carrasco admittedly knew the tumor was dangerous but did not adequately convey this to the operating doctor so that the vital warning never reached the plaintiff. Id. at 50.

The hospital is chargeable due to the fact that Dr. Carrasco had been granted medical staff privileges and also shared in the hospital's profits.

Discussion

1. What mechanism should be in place for communication between the surgeon in an operating room and the pathologist who needs to report his findings on a frozen section to the operating surgeon? Face-to-face communications? A written report? Intercom? What are the pros and cons of these forms of communications?
2. Why was the hospital also liable for the physician's negligence?

Pathologist Misdiagnoses Breast Biopsy

Citation: *Hamilton v. Baystate Med. Educ. & Research Found.*, 866 F. Supp. 51 (D. Mass. 1994)

Facts

The defendants claim that Dr. Hamilton's performance as a pathologist began to deteriorate and became progressively worse. The first indication of Dr. Hamilton's slip in performance was when he incorrectly labeled a specimen in his pathology report in January 1986. A year later, in January 1987, a customary review of one of his cases revealed a misdiagnosis. In biopsies of a right and left breast, Dr. Hamilton incorrectly diagnosed a tumor in the right breast as benign rather than malignant and improperly classified the tumor in the left breast. Dr. Sullivan, chairperson of the pathology department, met with Dr. Hamilton. They discussed three more cases in which Dr. Hamilton erred in either the diagnosis from, or labeling of, a specimen. In November 1988, Dr. Hamilton misdiagnosed a sample of breast tissue and concluded that the patient had cancer of the right breast. As a result, the patient underwent an unnecessary mastectomy as well as chemotherapy and radiation treatment.

On January 19, 1989, Dr. Sullivan suggested to Dr. Hamilton that he take some vacation time to determine if he was ill. Dr. Sullivan also suggested to Dr. Hamilton that he should consider resigning. January 19, 1989, was the last day Dr. Hamilton performed his duties at the hospital. Near that time, Dr. Hamilton learned that he had been suffering from Graves disease for roughly the previous 3 years. Graves disease causes the body's immune system to attack the thyroid gland and can result in the impairment of a person's memory and ability to concentrate. Dr. Haag, Dr. Hamilton's treating physician, characterized his condition as severe and believed the Graves disease was most likely responsible for Dr. Hamilton's slip in performance as a pathologist. Dr. Hamilton then filed for long-term disability benefits.

By late spring of 1989, Dr. Hamilton's thyroid hormone levels were within normal limits and controlled by medication. He sent a letter to Dr. Sullivan indicating that he intended to return to work on September 1, 1989. In this same letter, he also stated that he did not view himself as being "cured." Dr. Sullivan denied Dr. Hamilton's request to return to work.

Dr. Sullivan, Dr. Hamilton, and other physicians met at the hospital on September 1, 1989. At this meeting, Dr. Hamilton reiterated his desire to return to work on a part-time basis. Dr. Sullivan once again denied his request, claiming that he was concerned about patient safety. Dr. Hamilton alleges that no one at this meeting told him he was formally discharged.

On September 7, 1989, Dr. Hamilton wrote Dr. Sullivan asking to return to work on September 11, 1989. The following day, Dr. Sullivan phoned Dr. Hamilton. Dr. Hamilton alleged that during this phone conversation Dr. Sullivan did not inform him that he was discharged. Defendants claim that by this time they had effectively discharged Dr. Hamilton.

In September 1989, Dr. Hamilton retained an attorney to negotiate a settlement on his claims against the hospital. Dr. Hamilton denies that he was ever told that he was terminated.

Issue

Was the employer's decision to terminate the plaintiff after he had committed serious medical errors reasonable, and did the termination constitute a breach of contract?

Holding

The District Court held that the employer's decision to terminate the plaintiff after he had committed serious medical errors was reasonable and did not constitute breach of contract.

Reason

For 3 years, Dr. Hamilton suffered from a disease that affected his mental faculties. He committed serious medical errors, made a gross misdiagnosis resulting in an unnecessary mastectomy, and subjected the patient to high levels of needless radiation therapy. It is undisputed that Dr. Hamilton himself told Dr. Sullivan that he did not regard himself as being cured. Although Dr. Hamilton asserts that he received medical clearance from expert medical personnel, he presented no evidence to support the claim that he was capable of returning to work.

All evidence before the court confirmed the reasonableness of the defendants' belief that Dr. Hamilton could not fulfill his obligations under the terms of the employment agreement. Whether Dr. Hamilton could have properly performed his obligations does not matter. Based on the undisputed facts, defendants' belief that Dr. Hamilton's illness substantially and adversely affected his ability to fulfill his obligations was reasonable.

Discussion

1. Discuss why physicians and hospitals seem to be reluctant to take disciplinary action on a timely basis.
2. How might this case have been handled differently?

Failure to Diagnose Extent of Breast Cancer

Citation: *Colbert v. Georgetown Univ.*, 623 A.2d 1244 (D.C. Ct. App. 1993)

Facts

In July 1982, Ms. Colbert felt a lump in her left breast. She went to see her gynecologist, who referred her to an oncologist, Dr. Kirson. Although a mammogram conducted on August 9 revealed no evidence of malignancy, a biopsy established that the lump was cancerous. Dr. Kirson urged Ms. Colbert to have the breast removed by a modified radical mastectomy. Because he was about to go out of town, Dr. Kirson gave her the names of two surgeons at Georgetown University Hospital who could perform the operation.

On August 13, Ms. Colbert and her husband met with Dr. Lee, one of the surgeons recommended by Dr. Kirson and employed full-time at Georgetown Hospital. At that meeting, Dr. Lee suggested a lumpectomy as an alternative treatment option. He told the Colberts that a lumpectomy was cosmetically more attractive than a mastectomy and that studies in Europe had shown it was as effective as a mastectomy at removing cancerous cells from the body when coupled with radiation treatments afterward. The Colberts agreed to the lumpectomy and scheduled the procedure with Dr. Lee. Six days later, Dr. Lee performed a lumpectomy on Ms. Colbert's left breast, and at the same time, he removed several of her left axillary lymph nodes. When one of the nodes tested positive for cancerous cells, he set up a program of systemic chemotherapy.

On September 7, 1982, Ms. Colbert began receiving chemotherapy treatments under the direction of Dr. Goldberg. Several weeks later, Ms. Colbert felt more lumps in her left breast. She tried at that time to get another appointment with Dr. Lee, but she was unsuccessful, so she brought the lumps to Dr. Goldberg's attention. At first, Dr. Goldberg did nothing in response to her concerns.

On September 28, 1982, at her last scheduled chemotherapy session, Dr. Goldberg asked Dr. Byrne to examine the lumps in Ms. Colbert's breast. Dr. Byrne arranged for two biopsies to be performed. The biopsies disclosed the continued presence of cancer in Ms. Colbert's left breast.

Mrs. Colbert was eventually able to schedule an appointment with Dr. Lee and he performed a mastectomy on Ms. Colbert's left breast. Ms. Colbert asked Dr. Lee if the delay in performing the mastectomy had caused any increased risk. According to her answer to an interrogatory, Dr. Lee replied, "the delay caused enhanced risk of a very high nature." Shortly after the mastectomy, Dr. Lee met with Mr. Colbert. At that meeting, according to Mr. Colbert's deposition, Dr. Lee stated "that it took him a long time to do the operation because in his entire career he had never seen so much tumor mass." Id. at 1247.

Dr. Lee also said that Ms. Colbert's chances of survival had decreased from 90% to 10%, and he admitted to Mr. Colbert that he had done "the wrong operation" in August when he performed the lumpectomy instead of the mastectomy recommended by Dr. Kirson. Mr. Colbert also stated in his deposition that Dr. Lee said he "had forgotten" that a lumpectomy was not the proper procedure for a patient such as Ms. Colbert with multicentric disease. Id. at 1247. On March 7, 1983, Ms. Colbert had a mastectomy performed on her right breast. In August 1986, Ms. Colbert consulted an internist because of low back pain. It was determined that Ms. Colbert's cancer had metastasized to her spine. The Colberts filed their malpractice action in August 1989. Ms. Colbert died in January 1992. Mr. Colbert was substituted for his wife as appellant. The court consequently ruled that Mrs. Colbert's claim and that of her husband were barred by the statute of limitations and granted the defendants' motion for summary judgment.

Issue

Did the statements of Dr. Lee that he should have performed a mastectomy instead of a lumpectomy demonstrate that the standard of care was breached?

Holding

The District of Columbia Court of Appeals held that an admission and other statements by the physician that he should have performed a mastectomy instead of a lumpectomy established a prima facie case of malpractice.

Reason

Dr. Lee's admission of negligence demonstrated that the standard of care was breached. His statement to Ms. Colbert in October 1982 that the delay in performing a mastectomy caused an "enhanced risk of a very high nature, but that only time would tell," provides evidence of causation. Id. at 1253. The admission and other statements of Dr. Lee establish a prima facie case of malpractice. They may not ultimately be enough to convince a jury that malpractice actually occurred, but there can be no doubt that they raise an issue that must be submitted to a jury. As with the evidence of the Colberts' state of mind in discovering the relevant injury, the Colberts' presentation of a prima facie case of malpractice necessitates reversal of the trial court's grant of summary judgment for the defendants.

Discussion

1. Do you agree with the court of appeals decision to reverse the trial court's finding? Explain.
2. What is meant by a prima facie case?
3. What are the case issues apparent in this case?

Delayed Diagnosis: Breast Cancer

Citation: *Tomcik v. Ohio Dept. of Rehabilitation and Correction,* 598 N.E.2d 900 (Ohio Ct. App. 1991)

Facts

This case arises from the events that transpired while the plaintiff was in the custody and control of the defendant, the Department of Rehabilitation and Correction (ORW). The plaintiff alleges that, because of certain acts and omissions, the defendant's employees failed to timely diagnose her breast cancer. The asserted result was that the cancer was allowed to progress to the point that the plaintiff was unable to utilize less drastic treatment procedures. Instead, the plaintiff was required to have her right breast removed.

The defendant denied any negligence on the part of its employees and claimed that the plaintiff's own negligence caused or contributed to whatever damages she may have sustained. The defendant contended that, even if its employees were negligent, the plaintiff's cancer was so far developed when discovered that it would have required the removal of her entire breast.

Pursuant to ORW's policy of medically evaluating all new inmates, Dr. Evans gave the plaintiff a medical examination on May 26, 1989. He testified that part of his required physical evaluation included an examination of the plaintiff's breasts. However, he stated that his examination was very cursory.

Issue

Did the delay in providing the plaintiff treatment fall below the medically accepted standard of care?

Holding

The Court of Appeals of Ohio held that the delay in providing the plaintiff treatment fell below the medically acceptable standard of care.

Reason

The court was "appalled" that the physician had characterized his evaluation as a medical examination or had implied that what he described as a "cursory breast examination" should be considered a medically sufficient breast examination. It seems incredible to the court that a physician would deliberately choose not to expend the additional few minutes (or seconds) to thoroughly palpate (to examine by touch) the sides of the breasts, which is a standard, minimally intrusive cancer detection technique. His admission that he merely "pressed" on plaintiff's breasts, coupled with the additional admission that such acts would not necessarily disclose lumps in the breasts, described substandard medical care. Id. at 902.

The day following her physical examination, the plaintiff examined her own breasts. At that time she discovered, in her right breast, a lump that she characterized as being about the size of a pea. The plaintiff then sought an additional medical evaluation at the defendant's medical clinic. Testimony indicated that less than half of the inmates who sign the clinic list are actually seen by medical personnel the next day. Also, those not examined on the day for which the list is signed are given no preference in being examined on the following day. In fact, their names are simply deleted from the daily list, and their only recourse is to sign the list repeatedly until they are examined.

The preponderance of the evidence indicated that, after May 27, 1989, the plaintiff signed the clinic list daily and listed the reason for the requested treatment. Medical personnel did not see her until June 21, 1989. The court concluded that such a delay in obtaining treatment was wholly unwarranted.

On June 21, 1989, Nurse Ardney examined the plaintiff and wrote in her nursing notes that the plaintiff had a "moderate large mass in right breast." Ms. Ardney recognized that the proper procedure was to measure such a mass, but she testified that this was impossible because no measuring device was available. The measuring device to which she alluded was a common ruler. The nurse concluded that Dr. Evans should examine the plaintiff again.

On June 28, 1989, Dr. Evans again examined the plaintiff. He recorded in the progress notes that the plaintiff had "a mass on her right wrist. Will send her to hospital and give her Benadryl for allergy she has." Id. at 904. Dr. Evans meant to write "breast" not "wrist." He again failed to measure the size of the mass on the plaintiff's breast.

The plaintiff was transferred to the Franklin County Prerelease Center (FPRC) on September 28, 1989. On September 30, 1989, a nurse at FCPR examined the plaintiff. The nurse recorded that the plaintiff had a "golf ball" size lump in her right breast.

On October 27, 1989, the plaintiff was transported to the hospital, where Dr. Walker treated her. The plaintiff received a mammogram, which indicated that the tumor was probably malignant. This diagnosis was confirmed by a biopsy performed on November 9, 1989. The plaintiff was released from confinement on November 13, 1989.

On November 16, 1989, a surgeon named Dr. Lidsky examined the plaintiff. Dr. Lidsky noted the existence of the lump in the plaintiff's breast and determined that the mass was approximately 4 to 5 cm and somewhat fixed. He performed a modified radical mastectomy of the plaintiff's right breast.

It was probable that an earlier procedure would have safely and reliably conserved a large part of the plaintiff's right breast. Through the inexcusable delays, the plaintiff lost this option, and instead, the breast had to be removed.

Discussion

1. What damages would you have awarded the plaintiff in this particular case?
2. Assuming for the moment that your particular state has a cap of $250,000 on pain and suffering, do you consider the plaintiff's total damages to be adequate compensation?
3. List the pros and cons of a cap on malpractice awards. Consider your list from the perspective of both the plaintiff and the defendant.
4. Do you think monetary awards are a deterrent to inferior medical care?

Pathologist Misdiagnosis: Treating Wrong Disease

Citation: *Winder v. Avet*, 613 So.2d 199 (La. Ct. App. 1992)

Facts

On February 2, 1982, Mr. Winder was admitted to a medical center for testing after experiencing symptoms of jaundice. Dr. Tedesco initially diagnosed Mr. Winder as having obstructive jaundice. Eight days later, Dr. Tedesco performed exploratory surgery after further testing indicated that Mr. Winder might have cancer of the pancreas. During the course of surgery, Dr. Tedesco sent several needle biopsies to Dr. Avet, a pathologist, in order to confirm his suspicions. Dr. Avet examined three frozen sections. Based on the third frozen section, he made a diagnosis of poorly differentiated malignancy. After examining the permanent section, Dr. Avet made a diagnosis of well-differentiated adenocarcinoma. Unfortunately, Mr. Winder's pancreas was too densely adhered to other vital structures, so it could not be removed surgically. Relying on the pathologist's positive identification of cancer, Dr. Tedesco bypassed the bile duct into the intestines to relieve the obstruction. Dr. Tedesco also had Dr. Weatherall, a radiologist, insert radioactive seeds into the pancreas.

Pancreatic cancer victims often die within 6 months of the diagnosis; Mr. Winder lived far beyond conventional expectations, although he was sick much of the time.

In November 1985, Dr. Henry, who began treating Mr. Winder's liver infections in 1983, asked Dr. Avet to review his original diagnosis in light of the fact that Mr. Winder had survived far beyond normal expectations. According to Dr. Henry, Dr. Avet examined the 1982 slides and admitted making a mistake. Specifically, Dr. Henry stated, "He said that. . . . [a]fter his re-review that his original diagnosis was a mistaken one and that this was—he said something to the effect—this is something that we taught in pathology, a mistake not to make." Id. at 200. At this point, Mr. Winder received treatment for chronic pancreatitis and other treatment, including more surgery, designed to counter the adverse effects of the radiation treatment. These attempts proved unsuccessful.

On January 14, 1986, Mr. Winder died. Although no autopsy was performed, it was presumed Mr. Winder died primarily from liver failure and infection. The defendants contended that the trial court erred, according to its own written reasons for judgment, in finding that the suit could proceed. The court's written reasons stated

---

The Court found as a fact that it was not until November 1985 (when Dr. Russell Henry and Dr. Phillip Avet had their discussion) that there was any basis upon which the plaintiffs could have had any knowledge to bring a claim. While the cited statute for medical malpractice has a 3-year limitation, the Court must grant a reasonable time to an innocent victim who has absolutely no knowledge nor any way of ascertaining the knowledge that there may have been a misdiagnosis by an expert, as is the case by a pathologist, that a person had cancer, and leaves that person as a victim. Id. at 201.

Because of Dr. Avet's erroneous diagnosis, Mr. Winder was subjected to continuous treatment for the wrong disease from February 10, 1982, until November 1985. Between November 2, 1982, and January 14, 1986, Mr. Winder was hospitalized 13 times for treatment of cancer of the pancreas and resultant complications. According to the testimony of Dr. Tedesco, more probably than not, the complications that caused Mr. Winder's death arose from the various treatments used to fight the cancer Mr. Winder did not have. Mr. Winder placed his trust and confidence in these physicians, and until November 1985, Mr. Winder did not possess knowledge, either actual or constructive, that he was the possible victim of medical malpractice.

The district court entered judgment in favor of the surviving spouse and children. The defendant appealed.

Issue

When did the 3-year prescriptive period for medical malpractice begin to run? Did the evidence establish that the pathologist misdiagnosed the patient's ailment?

Holding

> The Court of Appeal of Louisiana held that misdiagnosis was a continuing tort to which the 3-year prescriptive period did not begin to run at least until a correct diagnosis and evidence established the pathologist's malpractice in misdiagnosing chronic pancreatitis as pancreatic cancer.

Reason

> This is a case of a continuing tort. There was continuous action by Dr. Avet, as described earlier, that resulted in continuous damage to Mr. Winder—infection and liver failure brought about by the radiation treatment for cancer. The plaintiffs answered the appeal, seeking an increase in the trial court's award. The trial court had awarded the plaintiffs $500,000.
>
> Based on statements made by the trial court in its written reasons for judgment, the plaintiffs contended the trial court made a mistake in drafting the judgment. In essence, plaintiffs contended that the trial court erroneously believed that the total award based on medical malpractice could not exceed $500,000, including medical expenses.
>
> Based on the statements made by the trial court, it is clear the actual judgment did not reflect the trial court's intentions. The judgment of the trial court was revised to award past medical expenses in the amount stipulated by the parties, $154,750.73, in addition to the $500,000 awarded by the trial court.

Discussion

> 1. How did the court determine when the statute of limitations began to toll?
> 2. Do you agree with the court's decision? Explain.

Wrong Surgical Procedure: Multiple Mistakes

Citation: *Poulard v. Commissioner of Health*, 608 N.Y.S.2d 726 (N.Y. App. Div. 1994)

Facts

> A surgeon instituted an Article 78 proceeding to review a determination by the State Board for Professional Conduct that suspended the surgeon's license to practice medicine for 1 year.

On November 20, 1987, the record disclosed that a patient was admitted to the hospital and diagnosed as suffering from a Morgagni hernia, a condition in which part of the intestine protrudes into the chest cavity through a defect in the diaphragm. On November 27, the surgeon became involved in the patient's care and participated in the surgery to repair the hernia. During the course of the operation, it became apparent that the original diagnosis had been incorrect. The tissue previously thought to be a section of bowel penetrating the diaphragm was in fact a colonic interposition, which in this case was a segment of bowel that had been surgically substituted for the patient's esophagus some years earlier.

In January 1992, the Bureau of Professional Medical Conduct (BPMC) charged the surgeon with misconduct. Specifically, the surgeon was charged with practicing with gross negligence and failing to maintain adequate records. Those charges, which were supported by 25 separate allegations of misconduct, stemmed from the surgeon's care and treatment of the patient, a 28-year-old male with developmental disabilities. Following the surgeon's disciplinary hearing, the hearing committee imposed a 1-year suspension of petitioner's license to practice medicine, said suspension stayed indefinitely, and a fine of $10,000. The surgeon subsequently commenced a CPLR article 78 proceeding pursuant to Public Health Law § 230-c(5).

Issue

Did the evidence support a finding by the committee that the surgeon had practiced with gross negligence?

Holding

The New York Supreme Court, Appellate Division, held that the evidence supported a finding that the surgeon had practiced with gross negligence.

Reason

The hearing committee's determination of gross negligence was based on findings that the surgeon misinterpreted the patient's X-ray, failed to defer the patient's surgery after being informed of certain abnormal test results, failed to recognize the colonic interposition during the course of the patient's surgery, and rendered deficient postoperative care, as evidenced by the patient's severe weight loss. The appeals court was of the view that the testimony offered by an expert, Dr. Roome, a board-certified surgeon, together with other documentary evidence and, in some instances, the surgeon's admissions, provided the substantial evidence necessary to support the findings made as to each of the sustained allegations.

Discussion

1. What are the implications for healthcare organizations that fail to adequately conduct peer review activities?
2. Why are physicians often reluctant to take disciplinary action during the peer review process?

Delayed Diagnosis: Colon Cancer

Citation: *Sacks v. Mambu*, 632 A.2d 1333 (Pa. Super. Ct. 1993)

Facts

A medical malpractice action was brought by Mrs. Sacks against Dr. Mambu for failure to make a timely diagnosis of her husband's colon cancer. Mrs. Sacks alleged that Dr. Mambu was negligent in that he failed to properly screen Mr. Sacks for fecal occult blood. (A fecal occult blood test is utilized to determine if there is blood in the colon.) Dr. Mambu treated Mr. Sacks, who presented himself with a complaint of abdominal pains in March 1983. Dr. Mambu determined that Mr. Sacks was suffering from a urinary tract infection and prescribed an antibiotic. In August 1983, Mr. Sacks was hospitalized for removal of his gallbladder. The surgeon on the case did not detect any indication of cancer. Dr. Mambu saw the patient regularly following surgery. Because of complaints of fatigue by the patient, Dr. Mambu ordered blood tests that revealed normal hemoglobin, the results of which suggested that Mr. Sacks had not been losing blood. However, by late July 1984, Mr. Sacks experienced symptoms of jaundice. Dr. Mambu ordered an ultrasound test, and Mr. Sacks was subsequently diagnosed with a tumor of the liver. He was admitted to the hospital and diagnosed with having colon cancer. By the time the cancer was detected, it had invaded the wall of the bowel and had metastasized to the liver. The patient expired in March 1985, 7 months following his surgery. The court of common pleas entered judgment on a jury verdict for Dr. Mambu, and Mrs. Sacks appealed.

Issue

Was Dr. Mambu negligent in failing to order a fecal occult blood test, and if so, did that failure increase the risk of harm to Mr. Sacks by allowing the cancer to metastasize and, therefore, to become a substantial factor in causing the patient's death?

Holding

The Superior Court of Pennsylvania, holding for Dr. Mambu, upheld the decision of the trial court.

Reason

The possibility that Mr. Sacks would have died anyway was no defense if Dr. Mambu's negligence had been a substantial factor in reducing Mr. Sack's opportunity for survival because Dr. Mambu would have "effectively cut off any chance that [Sacks] had for survival." Id. at 1335. The jury had been instructed to address this concern. Had the jury found "the defendant physician negligent in failing to administer a fecal occult blood test, it was the jury's duty to determine whether the doctor's negligence was a proximate cause of the defendant's death." Id. at 1336. Mr. Sacks had an occult blood test administered by his primary care physician, Dr. Weiner, in October 1981. Dr. Mambu did not order a fecal occult blood test when he treated the patient in March 1993. The jury determined that the physician's failure to administer the test had not increased the risk of harm by allowing the cancer to metastasize to the liver before discovery and, therefore, was not a substantial factor in causing the patient's death. Although the presence of blood in the stool may be suggestive of polyps, cancer, and a variety of other diseases, not all polyps and cancers bleed. Physicians are therefore in disagreement as to the efficacy of the test.

 Discussion

Patient Assessment

1. Should the physician have performed a more thorough assessment?
2. What might the patient's record from previous providers have revealed?
3. Should the patient have provided a more definitive description of his ailment?
4. Were the data gathered regarding the patient's history adequate?
5. Were the screening processes sufficient, based on the patient's complaints?

6. Should the physician consider routine occult blood screening in future examinations? Explain.
7. What could the patient have done so the disease could have been diagnosed earlier?
8. What other actions might have been taken to avoid the outcome in this case?

Patient Reassessment

1. Was there a need for further physical assessment and follow-up?
2. Was follow-up conducted in a timely fashion?

Failure to Diagnose: Head Tumor

Citation: *In re Medical Review Panel of Cl. of Englert*, 605 So.2d 1349 (La. Sp. Ct. 1992)

Facts

Ms. Englert brought a malpractice action, individually and on behalf of her minor child, Kortnei, against Dr. Chin. The trial court, after a bench trial, found that the defendant physician breached the applicable standard of care in failing to timely diagnose a tumor in the child's head, and the court awarded damages totaling $225,000. On appeal by the defendant, the court of appeal in an unpublished opinion affirmed the finding of liability but reduced the amount of damages to $10,000, concluding that the only adverse effect of the failure to diagnose the tumor 6 months earlier was continued headaches and vomiting for the 6-month period—and perhaps some mental anguish.

The plaintiff argued that the evidence supported a finding that the child was taken to the physician with complaints of headaches more than a year and a half prior to the time that he referred her to a specialist who then diagnosed the tumor. The plaintiff further argued that the evidence supported a finding that, had surgery been performed sooner to remove the tumor, the entire tumor could have been removed, and the risk of future recurrence would have been reduced, thereby justifying the damage award made by the trial court.

The court of appeal summarized the facts and resolved the liability issue as follows: "In February 1986, when Kortnei was 7 years of age, the plaintiff took her to Dr. Chin, her pediatrician, with the complaint of headaches over a long period of time. He ordered a CT scan, which revealed a brain tumor.

On February 7, surgery was performed, and the tumor was removed except for a portion of it that was located on the brain stem. The tumor was benign and was described as a very slow growing tumor that took years to develop before causing symptoms. The possibility exists that the portion of the tumor at the brain stem will grow in the future, but there was no indication of growth at the time of the trial in August 1990." Id. at 1349–1350.

The child started vomiting with the headaches sometime before February 1986. The plaintiff testified that she regularly reported this to Dr. Chin. "Plaintiff's testimony was flatly contradicted by Dr. Chin's. He said he was never told about these headaches until February 1986. He said if she had complained, it would have been recorded in his records." The trial court resolved the conflict in favor of the plaintiff.

The court of appeal based its reduction in the amount of damages on the fact that nothing in the record suggests that Kortnei's condition was aggravated in any way by the delay in diagnosis, which is the only fault attributable to Dr. Chin. An award of $10,000 was the most that could be awarded. The plaintiff filed a writ application to the Supreme Court of Louisiana. The writ was granted to consider whether the substantial reduction in the amount of damages was warranted.

Issue

Was the plaintiff's writ application granted to consider whether the substantial reduction in the amount of damages was warranted?

Holding

The plaintiff's writ of application was granted and the Supreme Court amended the court of appeal's judgment to increase the award to $50,000.

Reason

The court concluded that it stands to reason that the new and additional growth of the tumor for 6 months increased the risk of future recurrence to some extent. The severity of the pain and suffering endured by the child during the 6-month period was somewhat understated by the court of appeal. The child is entitled to be compensated not only for the pain and suffering she endured during the 6-month period but also for the increased risk (although perhaps it is somewhat minimal) and 6-months of mental anxiety resulting from the delay in diagnosis and surgery. The court of appeal judgment was amended to increase the award from $10,000 to $50,000.

Discussion

1. Discuss the importance of detailed record-keeping and follow-up instructions.
2. What risks do defendants take when they appeal the amount of an award granted to the plaintiff?

Misdiagnosis of Cancer: Chemotherapy Not Necessary
Citation: *Hiers v. Lemley*, 834 S.W.2d 729 (Mo. 1992)

Facts

Mr. Hiers's survivors sued the oncologist for medical malpractice, alleging that he misdiagnosed the patient as having cancer, treated the patient with chemotherapy even though he knew the diagnosis of cancer was in doubt, and failed to promptly inform the patient upon learning that the diagnosis was in error.

On March 6, 1984, the patient was admitted to the hospital for tests to determine the cause of respiratory problems. Biopsies were performed. Three days later, Dr. Sheffield, a pathologist and director of the hospital's pathology laboratory, issued a report concluding that the patient had interstitial pneumonitis and bronchoalveolar carcinoma. Another pathologist, Dr. Boyce, also examined the biopsy slides with Dr. Sheffield. Dr. Boyce was uncertain of the diagnosis. As a result, a sample was sent to an expert in pulmonary diseases.

Dr. Lemley, an oncologist, also viewed the biopsy slides. He informed the patient that he had cancer and had only 3 weeks to live. Dr. Lemley recommended chemotherapy. Dr. Lemley's recommendation was based on the pathology report and his own examination of the tissue. Dr. Lemley was aware that a request had been made for an outside opinion. Extreme nausea, debilitation, loss of weight, loss of hair, and abnormal blood counts followed the treatment.

On March 23, 1984, a North Carolina pathologist issued his report that the tissue indicated only interstitial pneumonitis. On April 1, 1984, Dr. Lemley entered Mr. Hiers's hospital room. According to Mrs. Hiers, Dr. Lemley was very excited and reported, "We just received a report back stating your husband does not have cancer." Id. at 730. Approximately 2 years later Mr. Hiers died of interstitial pneumonitis.

Mrs. Hiers brought a survivor's action for medical malpractice against Dr. Lemley, submitting negligence in three respects:

1. Misdiagnosing Mr. Hiers as having cancer
2. Treating Mr. Hiers with chemotherapy even though he knew the cancer diagnosis was in doubt
3. Failing to promptly inform Mr. Hiers upon learning the diagnosis was in error

After the jury returned a verdict for Dr. Lemley, the circuit court granted the survivors' motion for a new trial.

Issue

Was there a submissible case of negligent treatment?

Holding

The Supreme Court of Missouri held that the survivors made a submissible case of negligent medical treatment.

Reason

The first theory of negligence was that Dr. Lemley made a misdiagnosis that Mr. Hiers had lung cancer. The defendant argued that he made no diagnosis or misdiagnosis of lung cancer. The hospital record includes the following entry dictated by Dr. Lemley:

Patient eventually underwent a right minithoracotomy at which time some confusion was initially encountered as to the etiology of his problem, being either desquamative interstitial pneumonitis vs. bronchoalveolar carcinoma; however, on review of pathology slide preparations, this definitely appears to be bronchoalveolar cell carcinoma.

Impression: On the basis of my interpretation of the pathology slide, I definitely feel this is broncho-alveolar cell type of lung carcinoma. Unfortunately, disease at this point is rather far advanced and the patient has a very poor prognosis. Id. at 732.

Dr. Lynch, a specialist in pathology, testified at trial that neither an oncologist nor a general pathologist would have had the expertise to make a proper diagnosis of the patient's condition. He also testified that Dr. Lemley's diagnosis and treatment did not measure up to the standard of care that a careful and reasonable physician would have exercised. Mrs. Hiers and a niece testified that Dr. Lemley told them that Mr. Hiers had cancer and would die in 3 weeks. Treating these facts as true, it could be said that there was evidence that Dr. Lemley negligently misdiagnosed the condition as being cancerous.

Discussion

1. In light of the patient's poor prognosis and apparent questionable diagnosis, was the physician's decision to prescribe chemotherapy premature? Explain.
2. In light of the record, discuss the regulatory agency standards, rules, and regulations that might apply.
3. Discuss the ethical issues in this case.
4. Should the patient have considered a second opinion as to his diagnosis and the advisability of undergoing chemotherapy? Discuss your answer.

Patient Refuses to Wait: Suffers Stroke

Citation: *Roberts v. Hunter*, 426 S.E.2d 797 (S.C. 1993)

Facts

On July 6, 1988, Mr. Roberts struck the left side of his neck when he fell from a scaffold. He went to the hospital emergency department at approximately 4:00 p.m., complaining of pain in his neck and shoulder. Dr. Hunter, the emergency department physician, examined him. Dr. Hunter found no apparent head injury but did find abrasions on Mr. Roberts's neck. A neurological check indicated that his condition was normal. Dr. Hunter then consulted Dr. Mincey, a vascular surgeon at the hospital. Dr. Hunter informed Dr. Mincey that, because of the location of the injury, he was concerned about the possibility of a carotid artery injury. After examining Mr. Roberts, Dr. Mincey concluded that a carotid artery injury was unlikely. Mr. Roberts was then sent to have his shoulder and neck X-rayed. When he returned, Mr. Roberts complained of blurred vision and seeing spots in front of his eyes. The neurological exam was repeated, but it indicated no abnormalities. Dr. Hunter again consulted with Dr. Mincey, who suggested a call to Dr. Hayes, a neurologist. Dr. Hunter then called Dr. Hayes, who was treating patients on another floor in the hospital. Dr. Hayes advised that he would examine

Mr. Roberts. However, Mr. Roberts left the hospital approximately 15 to 20 minutes later, before Dr. Hayes could examine him.

There was conflict in the testimony concerning Mr. Roberts's discharge from the hospital. Dr. Hunter testified that he emphasized to Mr. Roberts and his wife the serious nature of the injury, advising him that he should remain in the hospital for further evaluation. According to Dr. Hunter, Mr. Roberts refused to wait for Dr. Hayes. He did agree, however, to return to the hospital the following day. Mr. Roberts's wife testified that Dr. Hunter never advised them about the nature or possible severity of the injuries. Rather, they were given the option of remaining in the hospital or returning in the morning. In any event, Mr. Roberts was discharged from the hospital at approximately 7:30 p.m. At approximately 10:00 p.m., he returned to the emergency department with paralysis on the right side of his body. It was determined that he suffered a stroke after leaving the hospital emergency department. The neurologist was sued for medical malpractice. The circuit court directed a verdict for the neurologist, and the Robertses appealed.

Issue

Was a physician–patient relationship established?

Holding

The Supreme Court of Iowa held that no physician–patient relationship existed.

Reason

It is undisputed that Dr. Hayes neither examined Mr. Roberts nor reviewed his file. An examination was made impossible by Mr. Roberts's departure from the hospital. Based on these circumstances, it was held that no physician–patient relationship existed. Accordingly, a directed verdict in favor of Dr. Hayes was proper.

Discussion

1. In the emergency department setting, when does a physician–patient relationship begin?
2. At what point in the emergency department setting does the physician–patient relationship terminate?

Failure to Timely Diagnose AIDS

Citation: *Doe v. McNulty*, 630 So.2d 825 (La. Ct. App. 1993)

Facts

The plaintiff, Jane Doe, had been exposed to HIV as the result of sexual contact. The plaintiff consulted her defendant physicians, but they failed to diagnose her condition as being positive for either HIV or AIDS. The disease had weakened her immune system, and she had developed pneumocystis carinii pneumonia (PCP) and was admitted to a hospital.

The patient was eventually diagnosed with AIDS. The patient's infectious disease expert, Dr. Hill, claimed that proper diagnosis in August, prior to her acute episode, would have provided greater opportunity for improved long-term treatment. Dr. Hill stated that the patient would not have contracted PCP for another year and that this would have added another year to her life expectancy and ability to work. The defendants admitted that they negligently failed to timely diagnose the patient's condition.

The defendants' expert witness, Dr. Lutz, testified from his review of the patient's medical record that the patient's diagnosis could not have been determined based on the symptoms as described in the record. Dr. Lutz had never examined the patient and based his determination on the documentation contained in the medical record. Dr. Lutz did, however, agree that if the patient's immune system had not been totally destroyed, preventive treatment could have resulted in a longer life span.

The civil district court entered judgment on a jury verdict of $700,000 in general damages, which included pain and suffering, mental anguish, disability, and loss of the enjoyment of life, as well as $314,000 for medical and special damages.

The defendants appealed.

Issue

Did the defendants' failure to timely diagnose Doe's condition cause the plaintiff to lose 1 year of life? Did the jury commit obvious error in awarding $700,000 in general damages and $314,000 in medical damages?

Holding

The Court of Appeal of Louisiana held that the evidence supported the jury's finding of causation and the award of $700,000 was not excessive.

The medical expense award totaling $314,000 could, however, be reduced to $72,337.62.

Reason

The court found that it was unable to correlate from the evidence what expenses had accrued from September 1992 to the date of the trial as being caused by the defendants' negligence.

The medical defendants agreed that they negligently failed to timely diagnose the patient's condition. The plaintiff's expert witness testified repeatedly "that within the 'reasonable medical probability' standard and the 'more likely than not' standard, if the plaintiff had been properly diagnosed and treated no later than August 18, 1990, which was the date the medical defendants should have diagnosed and treated her, she would have not contracted pneumocystis carinii pneumonia." Id. at 826. She would have lived, as well as worked, for another year. As to the amount of the award, the Louisiana Supreme Court, in a number of cases (e.g., *Rossell v. ESCO*, 549 So.2d 840 [La. 1989]), established the standards for appellate review of general damages awards as follows: "The discretion vested in the trier of fact is 'great,' and even vast, so that an appellate court should rarely disturb an award of general damages." Id. at 827–828.

Discussion

1. On what basis should a physician determine the appropriateness of his or her patient's specific clinical needs (e.g., medical history)?
2. Discuss, from your experience, is medical misdiagnosis an all-too-frequent medical error?

chapter six

Treatment

When Your Doctor Doesn't Know

. . . Physicians spend less time with each patient than they used to, and they increasingly rely on tests to provide answers. When those tests are inconclusive or inaccurate, the patient and his or her physician may find themselves traveling down the wrong treatment path. "There are lots of diseases that can look like something else," explains Sanders [Yale physician] "And that's where clinical judgment and experience are essential. Doctors see test results as coming straight from God. But just because a test gives you a yes or no answer doesn't mean it's right."

Mary A. Fisher, AARP, July/August 2011

This chapter focuses on negligence cases that relate to *medical treatment*, which is the attempt to restore the patient to health following a diagnosis. It is the application of various remedies and medical techniques, including the use of medications for the purpose of treating an illness or trauma. Treatment can be: *active treatment*, directed immediately to the cure of the disease or injury; *causal treatment*, directed against the cause of a disease; *conservative treatment*, designed to avoid radical medical therapeutic measures or operative procedures; *expectant treatment*, directed toward relief of untoward symptoms but leaving cure of the disease to natural forces; *palliative treatment*, designed to relieve pain and distress with no attempt to cure; *preventive/prophylactic treatment*, aimed at the prevention of disease and illness; *specific treatment*, targeted specifically at the disease being treated; *supportive treatment*, directed mainly to sustaining the strength of the patient; or *symptomatic treatment*, meant to relieve symptoms without effecting a cure (i.e., intended to address the symptoms of an illness but not its underlying cause, as in scleroderma, lupus, or multiple sclerosis, for example).[1]

Medical Practice Guidelines are evidence-based best practices that are developed to assist physicians in the diagnosis and treatment of their patients. It should be remembered that best practices are not iron-clad rules. Skillful medical judgment demands that the physician determine how to use best practices and interpret the information.

Online Medical Treatment Advisor is a treatment program that uses medical specialists to accurately select the best and newest treatment for each patient, based on the individual patient's characteristics. Online Medical Treatment Advisor assesses each patient's symptoms with a knowledge base created by 1,500 specialist physicians. Online Medical Treatment Advisor includes treatments for 1,200 diseases.[2]

The cases that follow describe the failures of such attempts due to negligent treatment by provider/s.

Hospitals Are Not the Only Places Where Malpractice Can Injure Patients

Diagnostic errors were the No. 1 reason for adverse events that resulted in malpractice payouts in outpatient settings, according to the JAMA study, while surgical adverse events accounted for the biggest share of claims paid for in incidents that occurred in hospital settings. . . .

One of the biggest challenges is to improve diagnoses in the outpatient setting. After all, if someone is in the hospital, clinicians start from the perspective that the person is sick. In an outpatient setting, "You see a lot of people with chest pain, and the vast majority of the time it's nothing—a pulled muscle, a little heartburn," says Gandhi [Tejal Gandhi, the chief quality and safety officer for Tartners HealthCare in Massachusetts]. Identifying that one person whose chest pain signals a heart attack, "it's like finding a needle in a haystack."

Michelle Andrews, The Washington Post, *June 28, 2011*

Failure to Treat

Citation: *Reese v. Stroh*, 874 P.2d 200 (Wash. Ct. App. 1994)

Facts

In 1984, the plaintiff was being treating for asthma by Dr. April, who referred the plaintiff to Dr. Stroh, the defendant. Dr. Stroh diagnosed the plaintiff with asthma, chronic obstructive pulmonary disease, and alpha-1-anti-trypsin (AAT) deficiency. AAT prevents lung destruction, and an AAT deficiency can cause the development of emphysema. When the plaintiff was first diagnosed in 1985, the drug Prolastin was not available. He was prescribed antibiotics, steroids, and other medications and was told to stop smoking and to avoid environmental irritants.

In 1989, the plaintiff discovered that his brother, who also had an AAT deficiency, was starting on Prolastin therapy. Prolastin therapy had been introduced into the market in 1987. Expert testimony revealed that an injection of this drug into the blood raises the blood protein levels enough to prevent patients with an AAT deficiency from developing lung disease. The plaintiff went to see his brother's doctor, who started him on Prolastin in 1990.

The plaintiff then sued Dr. Stroh for failing to prescribe Prolastin, a failure that he claimed had worsened his lung function. A pulmonary specialist testified as an expert for the plaintiff, stating, among other things, that Prolastin was effective and was being used in 1992 to treat over 2,000 patients. He further testified that if it had been used on the plaintiff as soon as it became available, it would have reduced the patient's rate of physical decline by 50%. The trial court ruled that his testimony was inadmissible because it lacked the necessary foundation for admittance. The court granted a directed verdict in favor of the defendant, and the plaintiff appealed.

Issue

Was an adequate foundation laid for the expert's opinion that Prolastin would have improved the plaintiff's condition?

Holding

The Court of Appeals reversed the trial court's finding, ruling in favor of the plaintiff, noting that an adequate foundation was laid as to the expert's opinion on Prolastin.

Reason

For scientific testimony to be admissible at trial, it must assist the trier of fact to understand a fact that is in issue. Moreover, the expert's opinion must be based on scientific knowledge, not on speculation. In this case, the court found that the pulmonary specialist had extensive clinical experience with patients on Prolastin therapy and that numerous scientific tests had been completed with Prolastin before the Food and Drug Administration had approved it. Therefore, the court concluded, the expert's opinion was grounded in scientific knowledge and was reliable. Moreover, the court held, his testimony would assist the trier of fact in determining whether Dr. Stroh's failure to treat the emphysema with Prolastin was negligent. The court determined that it is not necessary to have statistical proof before expert testimony will be allowed and that even controversial theories are admissible so long as the expert's methodologies are sound.

Discussion

1. What are the conditions that must be met before a scientific expert will be allowed to testify about a fact in issue?
2. Is expert testimony required in every case involving malpractice? Explain.

ED: Physician's Preexisting Duty to Care

Citation: *Deal v. Kearney*, 851 P.2d 1353 (Alaska 1993)

Facts

On September 16, 1984, the plaintiff, Mr. Kearney, suffered a life-threatening injury and was taken by ambulance to the emergency department of Kodiak Island Hospital (KIH). Upon arrival at 3:45 p.m., he was examined Dr. Creelman, an on-call emergency department family practitioner. Dr. Creelman determined that a surgical consultation was necessary, and he called Dr. Deal, a surgeon with staff privileges at the hospital. After ordering certain tests, Dr. Deal was of the opinion that Mr. Kearney could not survive a transfer to Anchorage. Dr. Deal then performed emergency surgery that lasted 9 to 10 hours, ending the following morning.

The plaintiff was eventually transferred to Anchorage. His condition worsened, and he suffered loss of circulation and tissue death in both legs. The plaintiff alleged that KIH was negligent in failing to properly evacuate him to Anchorage.

On October 2, 1989, Lutheran Hospitals and Home Society of America (LHHS) and Mr. Kearney entered into a settlement agreement whereby LHHS paid $510,000 to Mr. Kearney. At the same time, LHHS and Mr. Kearney released Dr. Deal, and other healthcare providers from liability. In return, LHHS assigned to Mr. Kearney its rights to indemnity, equitable subrogation, and contribution against Dr. Deal.

Mr. Kearney, as assignee of the rights of LHHS, brought an action against Dr. Deal arising from his negligent acts or omissions in the care given Mr. Kearney. Dr. Deal moved for summary judgment, claiming in one instance that he was immune from suit under the Good Samaritan statute.

The trial court denied Dr. Deal's motion for summary judgment, ruling that the Good Samaritan statute was not applicable to Dr. Deal because he was acting under a preexisting duty to render the emergency care provided Mr. Kearney. Dr. Deal petitioned for review, and his petition was granted.

The superior court held that the immunity provided by the Good Samaritan statute is unavailable to physicians with a preexisting duty to respond to emergency situations. The court concluded that Dr. Deal was under a preexisting duty in the instant case by virtue of his contract with KIH, the duty being part of the consideration that Dr. Deal gave to KIH in exchange for staff privileges at the hospital. The court further found that the Good Samaritan statute did not apply to Dr. Deal in any event, because the actions allegedly constituting malpractice occurred during the follow-up care and treatment given Mr. Kearney after surgery. By then, the court reasoned, Dr. Deal had become Mr. Kearney's treating physician and was no longer responding to an emergency situation.

Issue

Does the Good Samaritan statute extend immunity to physicians who have a preexisting duty to render emergency care?

Holding

The Supreme Court of Alaska held that the Good Samaritan statute does not extend immunity to physicians who have preexisting duty to render emergency care.

Reason

Alaska Statute 09.65.090(a)

A person at a hospital or any other location who renders emergency care or counseling to an injured, ill, or emotionally distraught person who reasonably appears to be in immediate need of emergency aid in order to avoid serious harm or death is not liable for civil damages as a result of an act or omission in rendering emergency aid.

The legislature clearly intended this provision to encourage healthcare providers, including medical professionals, to administer emergency medical care, whether in a hospital or other setting, to persons who are not their patients by immunizing them from civil liability. The legislative history favors Mr. Kearney's position.

The statute does not cover those with a preexisting duty. Courts in other cases have held that a physician was entitled to claim immunity under a Good Samaritan statute when he or she provided emergency medical care in a hospital that was not part of the doctor's express or customary hospital function and therefore did not have a preexisting duty to treat the patients [e.g., *McKenna v. Cedars of Lebanon Hosp., Inc.*, 93 Cal.3d 282, 155 Cal. Rptr. 631 (Cal. 1979); *Matts v. Homsi*, 308 N.W.2d 284 (Mich. Ct. App. 1981); see generally 68 A.L.R. 4th 323-26].

In summary, the trial court was correct in holding that the Alaska Good Samaritan statute does not extend immunity to physicians who have a preexisting duty to render emergency care.

Discussion

1. Do you agree with the Alaska Statute 09.65.090(a), which provides that a person at a hospital or any other location who renders emergency care or emergency counseling to an injured, ill, or emotionally distraught person who reasonably appears to be in immediate need of emergency aid in order to avoid serious harm or death is not liable for civil damages as a result of an act or omission in rendering emergency aid?

2. What other options might have been available to care for this patient?

Reporting Failure to Treat: Public Policy Issue

Citation: *Kirk v. Mercy Hosp. Tri-County*, 851 S.W.2d 617 (Mo. Ct. App. 1993)

Facts

The plaintiff was an RN who, in 1983, was employed full time as a charge nurse with supervisory duties during her shifts. She reported directly to the hospital's director of nursing. A short time after one of her patients had been admitted to the hospital, the plaintiff diagnosed that the patient was suffering from toxic shock syndrome. Knowing that untreated toxic shock syndrome would result in death, the plaintiff believed that the physician would immediately order antibiotics. After a period of time had passed without her having received those orders from the physician, the plaintiff discussed the patient's situation with the director of nursing. The plaintiff was told by the director to "document, report the facts, and stay out of it." Id. at 618.

The plaintiff further discussed the patient's condition and the lack of orders with the medical chief of staff, who took the appropriate steps. However, the patient still died. After the director of nursing was informed by a member of the patient's family that the plaintiff offered to obtain the medical records for them, and after she was later told that the plaintiff had been heard to say that the physician was "paving her way to heaven" in reference to the patient and the delay in treatment, the director terminated the plaintiff.

After her termination, the plaintiff received a service letter from the hospital that directed her to refrain from making any further false statements about the hospital and its staff. The trial court entered a summary judgment for the defendant, stating that there were no triable issues of fact and there was no public policy exception to her at-will termination. Further, the court could not find any law or regulation prohibiting the hospital from discharging her as a nurse.

The plaintiff appealed, claiming there is a public policy exception to the Missouri employment-at-will doctrine.

Issue

Is there a public policy exception to the Missouri employment-at-will doctrine?

Holding

The Court of Appeals of Missouri reversed the granting of summary judgment and remanded the case for trial, holding that the Nursing Practice Act [§ 335.066.2(5),(6)] provided a clear mandate of public policy that the nurses had a duty to provide the best possible care to patients.

Reason

Public policy clearly mandates that a nurse has an obligation to serve the best interests of patients. Therefore, if the plaintiff refused to follow her supervisor's orders to stay out of a case in which the patient was dying from a lack of proper medical treatment, there would be no grounds for her discharge under the public policy exception to the employment-at-will doctrine. She then had a valid action for wrongful discharge. Pursuant to the Nursing Practice Act, the plaintiff risked discipline if she ignored improper treatment of the patient. Her persistence in attempting to get the proper treatment for the patient was her absolute duty. The hospital could not lawfully require that she stay out of a case that would have obvious injurious consequences to the patient. Public policy, as defined in case law, holds that "no one can lawfully do that which tends to be injurious to the public or against the public good." *Boyle v. Vista Eyewear, Inc.*, 700 S.W.2d 859 (Mo. Ct. App. 1985).

Discussion

1. Explain how a public policy would be analyzed and then determined to apply in an employment-at-will case.
2. What was the public policy mandate in this case?

Failure to Refer for Treatment

Citation: *Smith v. O'Neal*, 850 S.W.2d 797 (Tex. Ct. App. 1993)

Facts

On July 16, 1984, Dr. Smith, a general practice dentist, initially examined Ms. O'Neal. She testified that she informed Dr. Smith she had pain on her lower right side and wanted cosmetic work performed on her teeth. Dr. Smith and Ms. O'Neal discussed a plan for comprehensive treatment, including root canal and fillings.

On July 26, 1984, Dr. Smith told Ms. O'Neal that tooth number 14, an upper left molar, should be extracted. Ms. O'Neal advised Dr. Smith that another dentist had warned her in 1982 that tooth number 14 should not be pulled because it was embedded in the sinus. Dr. Smith responded that all of her top teeth were in the sinus and that extraction was no problem. Ms. O'Neal deferred to Dr. Smith's judgment, and tooth number 14 was extracted. Complications developed in the extraction process, resulting in an oral antral perforation of the sinus cavity wall. Dr. Smith began root canal work 4 days after the extraction, even though the antral opening wound was not healed. In performing these additional procedures, Dr. Smith used both high and low speed drills capable of flinging bacteria and other debris about the mouth. A tissue mass developed in the tooth socket 3 weeks after the extraction. The patient was referred to Dr. Herbert, an oral surgeon.

Dr. Herbert testified that the degree of infection inhibited proper healing and closure of the extraction site. After several more months, in January 1985, Ms. O'Neal was referred to Dr. Berman, an ear, nose, and throat specialist. Because of the continued deterioration, Dr. Berman performed an operation known as a Coldwell-Luc procedure. This surgical procedure sealed the extraction site. The surgery required hospitalization and a 4- to 6-week recuperation period.

Ms. O'Neal brought a malpractice action against the dentist. The trial court entered judgment in favor of Ms. O'Neal. The dentist appealed, arguing that the evidence was factually insufficient to support the judgment.

Dr. Miedzinski, an expert witness for the appellee, testified that Dr. Smith was negligent for not referring Ms. O'Neal to an oral surgeon for the necessary extraction, because of the known risks of roots embedded in the sinus floor. Dr. Smith was also negligent for not referring Ms. O'Neal to a specialist when the antral perforation first occurred and, later, by not referring her to a specialist when the oroantral fistula and the infection manifested itself. Dr. Smith's expert witness also testified that it is good medical practice to refer a patient to an oral surgeon or other specialist when complications arise from a sinus molar extraction.

Issue

Was the expert's testimony sufficient to support the verdict?

Holding

The Texas Court of Appeals held that the expert's testimony was sufficient to support the verdict.

Reason

The dentist's expert testimony was found sufficient to support a jury finding that the defendant was negligent in the treatment of his patient. The expert testified that the defendant was negligent by extracting the upper left molar without first attempting endodontic treatment to save the tooth. The patient was not experiencing pain on the left side of her mouth, and the tooth did not present an emergency.

Discussion

1. Was expert testimony necessary in order to establish the defendant's negligence? Explain.
2. What lessons are apparent as to the importance of a patient's prior physical and dental history?
3. What weight do you believe a practitioner should give to a consultant's opinion?

Negligent Collection of Blood Linked to HIV Infection

Citation: *J.K. & Susie L. Wadley Research Inst. v. Beeson*, 835 S.W.2d 689 (Tex. Ct. App. 1992)

Facts

In January 1983, a blood center knew that blood from homosexual or bisexual males should not be accepted under any circumstances. The blood center's written policy provided that donors who volunteer that they are gay should not be permitted to donate blood.

On April 22, 1983, Dr. Kraus, a cardiologist, discovered that Mr. Beeson, the patient, had severe blockage of two major arteries in his heart and recommended cardiac bypass surgery. During surgery, Mr. Beeson received seven units of blood by transfusion. In May 1987, Mr. Beeson had chest pain and trouble breathing. On June 5, 1987, Mr. Beeson was hospitalized. Dr. Kraus consulted with two specialists in pulmonary medicine about the unusual pneumonia evident in X-rays of Mr. Beeson's lungs. Because there was a possibility that the lung infection was secondary to acquired immune deficiency syndrome (AIDS), Mr. Beeson was tested for the human immunodeficiency virus (HIV). Although Mr. Beeson had not yet been formally diagnosed, physicians started him on therapy for AIDS.

Mr. Beeson was formally diagnosed as HIV-positive. His wife was then tested for HIV, and she learned that she was also HIV-positive. On July 2, 1987, Mr. Beeson expired. On April 21, 1989, the plaintiffs, Mrs. Beeson and her son, filed suit against the blood center alleging that her husband contracted HIV from the transfusion of a unit of blood donated at the blood center on April 19, 1983, by a donor identified at trial as John Doe. The parties stipulated at trial that Mr. Doe was a sexually active homosexual male with multiple sex partners.

The plaintiffs amended their original petition to contend that the blood center's negligence in testing and screening blood donors caused Mrs. Beeson's contraction of HIV. At trial, the jury awarded the plaintiffs $800,000 in damages. Following the trial court's denial of the blood center's motion for judgment notwithstanding the verdict, the blood center filed an appeal. The blood center argued that the trial court erred in denying its motion for judgment notwithstanding the verdict because the evidence of causation was legally insufficient to support the jury verdict.

Issue

Did the evidence support a finding that the blood center's negligence was the proximate cause of Mr. Beeson's contraction of HIV?

Holding

The Court of Appeals of Texas held that the evidence supported a finding that the blood center's negligence in the collection of blood was the proximate cause of Mr. Beeson's HIV infection.

Reason

If there is more than a scintilla of evidence to support the jury's answers to causation, the blood center's no evidence challenge must fail. The question of causation is a fact question for the jury. The issue of proximate cause includes two essential elements. The first is foreseeability, and the second is cause-in-fact. Both elements must be present, and both may be established by direct or circumstantial evidence.

Foreseeability is satisfied by showing that the actor, as a person of ordinary intelligence, should have anticipated the danger to others by his or her negligent act.

Cause-in-fact means that the act or omission was a substantial factor in bringing about the injury and that harm would not have occurred without the act or omission.

Mr. Doe testified that he did not know that he was at a high risk for AIDS and that he would never have given blood if he had known that he was at risk for AIDS. This evidence provided some indication that the blood center's screening procedure did not effectively educate donors. The jury could reasonably infer that the blood center's failure to effectively educate Mr. Doe and to ask Mr. Doe specific questions caused him to donate blood rather than to defer. There was more than a scintilla of evidence to support a finding that the blood center, despite its knowledge about the dangers of HIV-contaminated blood, failed to reject gay men, that the blood center's donor screening was inadequate, and that these omissions were substantial factors in causing Mr. and Mrs. Beeson's HIV infections.

The blood center's own technical director admitted that there was "strong evidence" that the blood accepted from Mr. Doe was contaminated with HIV. This statement was based on the fact that Mr. Doe's blood was broken into two components, with red blood cells given to another recipient 6 months later, and that both Mr. Beeson and the other recipient were subsequently diagnosed as HIV-positive less than 6 months apart from one another.

Discussion

1. What precautions should the blood center have taken to prevent this unfortunate event?

2. What is meant by foreseeability as it relates to this case?

3. What does cause-in-fact refer to as it relates to this case?

Shifting the Risk

. . . A 2008 study published in the *Journal of the American Medical Association* found that patients who suffered a heart attack in the hospital during off hours—were less likely to survive than those who had a cardiac arrest during normal business hours. Last year researchers at the University of Pennsylvania found that the quality of cardiopulmonary resuscitation at three urban teaching hospitals was poorer at night than during the day. And the president of New York's Beth Israel Medical Center decried the "stark discrepancy in quality between daytime and nighttime inpatient services" in a 2008 article in the *New England Journal of Medicine*.

Sandra G. Boodman, The Washington Post, *June 7, 2011*

Failure to Prescribe Antibiotics

Citation: *Pasquale v. Miller*, 599 N.Y.S.2d 58 (N.Y. App. Div. 1993)

Facts

The plaintiff, Ms. Pasquale, brought a suit against the defendant, Dr. Miller, for dental malpractice. On March 22, 1986, Dr. Miller treated the plaintiff for swollen gums. Dr. Miller removed tissue from her gums and used sutures to control the bleeding. Although it was common practice to prescribe antibiotics prior to or following gum surgery, Dr. Miller did not prescribe antibiotics in either case. The following May, after the plaintiff had experienced a persistent fever, she was diagnosed as having contracted subacute bacterial endocarditis. The plaintiff was treated in the hospital for nearly a month. Dr. Miller claimed that the bacterial infection could have resulted from a number of causes. The trial court, upon a jury verdict, found for the plaintiff.

Issue

Did the plaintiff offer sufficient proof to establish that Dr. Miller's failure to administer antibiotics was the cause of the plaintiff's subacute bacterial endocarditis?

Holding

The New York Supreme Court, Appellate Division, held that the evidence supported a finding of causation.

Reason

Sufficient proof was offered as to causation. "A plaintiff is required to offer sufficient proof from which a reasonable person may conclude that it is more probable than not that the injury was caused by the defendant, and the evidence need not eliminate every other possible cause." Id. at 59. The plaintiff's expert witnesses testified that her endocarditis was related to the dental surgery and that one of the risks of not prescribing an antibiotic is that bacteria can flow through the bloodstream to the heart. The jury could and did reject testimony from Dr. Miller that the endocarditis could have been caused by something other than the failure to administer antibiotics prior to or following gum surgery.

Discussion

1. What lessons can be learned from the Pasquale case?
2. What should the plan of care for a patient undergoing a surgical procedure include?
3. Could the postoperative complication of endocarditis have been avoided? If yes, how could the complication have been avoided? If no, why not?

Shifting the Risk

Linda Dembo knows firsthand what can happen to hospital patients at night. In May 2007, her 13-year-old son Jonathan was admitted to a St. Louis hospital for surgery to fix a blocked shunt that had been implanted in his head as part of successful treatment for brain cancer he had as a baby.

The neurosurgeon was at home, and Jonathan was being cared for by a resident, his mother said.

"It was a skeleton staff and very quiet," said Dembo, recalling that Sunday night. She said she insisted that a nurse summon a doctor when her son began complaining of a severe headache around 9 p.m. Dembo said that the resident on duty ordered a sedative by phone; she and her son fell asleep around 10:30, and Dembo said that records show no doctor saw him. At 5 a.m., Jonathan was found dead; an autopsy was not performed, but Demo said she was told he probably died from aspiration, essentially choking in his sleep.

Kathleen Parker, The Washington Post, *June 12, 2011*

Treatment: Untimely Care

Citation: *St. Paul Med. Ctr. v. Cecil*, 842 S.W.2d 808 (Tex. Ct. App. 1992)

Facts

On January 28, 1983, on or about 11:00 p.m., pregnant Mrs. Cecil believed that her water had broken. Mr. Cecil called the attending physician, Dr. Cook. Mr. Cecil was instructed to take his wife to the hospital.

The next day at 12:10 a.m., Mrs. Cecil was taken to the delivery room, and the nurse performed a pelvic examination and took vital signs. At approximately 1:30 a.m., at the request of the nurse, a resident was called and asked to perform a speculum examination. The resident determined that the membranes had ruptured and meconium was present. The nurse attached an external electronic fetal monitor to record the heart rate. Two hours later, the resident installed an internal electronic fetal monitor. The resident determined from a printout of the heart rate that the fetus showed severe fetal hypoxia, bradycardia (slow heart rate), and more meconium. The resident instructed the nurse to notify Dr. Cook and prepare Mrs. Cecil for an emergency Caesarean section. After arriving at the hospital, Dr. Cook further delayed the delivery because he wanted an anesthesiologist, even though a nurse anesthetist was on duty and present in the hospital. At 4:57 a.m., the infant was born with severe brain damage caused by prolonged hypoxia.

Dr. Cook settled with the plaintiffs before trial. The jury found that the defendants, the nurse and the hospital, proximately caused the infant's injuries, and the defendants appealed.

The hospital argued that there was insufficient evidence to support the jury's finding that the hospital was negligent independent of the negligent conduct of the other defendants, and no expert testimony was presented at trial as to the standard of care required of the hospital.

Issue

(1) Was expert testimony necessary to establish the standard of care required of the hospital? (2) Was there sufficient evidence presented to support the jury's findings? (3) Was the testimony of the plaintiffs and that of the defendants sufficiently inconsistent to establish that there was no evidence of negligence?

Holding

The Court of Appeals of Texas held that expert testimony was not necessary to establish that the hospital was negligent in assigning the nurse. There was sufficient evidence in the record to support the jury's finding of negligence. The court is not a fact finder, and cannot substitute its judgment for that of the jury.

Reason

As to the standard of care required, "the standard of nonmedical, administrative, ministerial, or routine care at a hospital need not be established by expert testimony because the jury is competent from its own experience to determine and apply such a reasonable-care standard." Id. at 812.

The evidence supports the allegations that the hospital had been independently negligent. The hospital was aware of the nurse's poor performance ratings. Three and one-half months before the negligent act occurred, the hospital rated the nurse's performance as unsatisfactory. She sometimes fell asleep on the job and was reluctant to seek guidance from her supervisors in matters concerning maternal and child health care, labor, and delivery. Despite these concerns, the hospital assigned her to the least supervised shift, the night shift. "Laymen, aided by these evaluations and guided by their common sense, could fairly determine whether the hospital was negligent in its supervision and assignment of the nurse." Id. at 813.

Discussion

1. Why was the hospital found negligent?
2. Do you agree that there was sufficient evidence to support the jury's findings?
3. Who is the fact finder at trial?

Negligent Injection: Permanent Hip Injuries

Citation: *Nueces v. Long Island College Hosp.*, 609 N.Y.S.2d 592 (N.Y. App. Div. 1994)

Facts

The plaintiff brought an action against the hospital seeking to recover damages resulting from a negligently administered injection and the resultant injury to the patient's left buttock. The supreme court entered judgment on a jury verdict for the patient, and the hospital appealed.

Issue

Was the hospital's agent negligent in administering an injection to the patient's left buttock, proximately causing permanent injuries, and was this supported by the evidence?

Holding

The New York Supreme Court, Appellate Division, held that the evidence supported a finding that the hospital's agent negligently administered the injection and is therefore liable for the damages suffered.

Reason

Contrary to the hospital's contention, a review of the evidence demonstrated that the jury's verdict was supported by sufficient evidence. There existed a rational basis for the jury's findings of negligence on the part of the hospital's agent in the administration of an injection to the plaintiff's left buttock proximately causing her permanent injuries. Because the parties' respective medical experts differed concerning the nature and cause of the plaintiff's injuries, the matter was properly left to the jury.

Discussion

1. What is the importance of assessing and reassessing the skills of professional staff?
2. Develop a skills checklist for new nurses.
3. What is the importance of continuing education?
4. What topics should be included in the orientation of a new employee? Consider employee orientation to both the hospital and the department.

Negligent Injection: Trigeminal Nerve

Citation: *Tesauro v. Perrige,* 650 A.2d 1079 (Pa. Super. 1994)

Facts

In 1984, Ms. Tesauro, appellee, saw Dr. Perrige, appellant, to have a lower left molar removed. A blood clot failed to form, and the appellant administered an injection of alcohol near the affected area. The appellee began to experience pain, burning, and numbness at the site of the injection—on the left side of her face. Several physicians diagnosed her as suffering from muscle spasms caused by a damaged trigeminal nerve. Over a 5-year period, the appellee was treated by a variety of specialists. In 1989, the plaintiff underwent radical experimental surgery. The surgery corrected the plaintiff's most oppressive symptoms. Although the most painful symptoms have been eliminated, the appellee continues to suffer numbness and burning on the left side of her face. A dental malpractice lawsuit was filed against Dr. Perrige alleging that he was negligent in administering the alcohol injection so close to the trigeminal nerve. The jury returned a verdict in favor of the plaintiffs in the amounts of $2,747,000 to Ms. Tesauro and $593,000 to Mr. Tesauro for loss of consortium. Dr. Perrige, the defendant/appellant, appealed.

Issue

Should a new trial be granted based on the excessiveness of the jury verdict?

Finding

The Superior Court held that the evidence supported the damage awards.

Reason

The decision to grant or not to grant a new trial based on the excessiveness of a jury verdict was found to be within the sound discretion of the trial court. In determining excessiveness, a court should consider: (1) the severity of the injury, (2) whether the injury is manifested by objective physical evidence or whether it is only revealed by the subjective testimony, (3) whether the injury is permanent, (4) whether the plaintiff can continue with his or her employment, (5) the size of out-of-pocket expenses, and (6) the amount of compensation demanded in the original complaint. Id. at 1081.

The Superior Court determined that the severity of the plaintiff's injury in itself would support the compensatory award. The plaintiff spent 5 years trying to find a cure for her pain. While much recovered, the plaintiff continues to suffer from numbness and burning. Her experience clearly falls into the category of severe injury. The severity of the injury had a huge effect on the marital relationship. The compensation awarded to Mr. Tesauro was, therefore, fair and just.

Discussion

1. If Dr. Perrige's practice were owned by a hospital, under what theory might liability be imputed to the hospital?
2. What are the obvious implications in this case for those hospitals considering the purchase of a professional practice?

Treatment: Negligent Supervision of Residents

Citation: *Mozingo v. Pitt County Mem'l Hosp.*, 415 S.E.2d 341 (N.C. 1992)

Facts

On December 5, 1984, the defendant, Dr. Kazior, began his assignment to provide on-call services for the obstetrics residents who were caring for patients. Dr. Kazior remained at his home, available to take telephone calls from the residents. That evening Dr. Kazior received a telephone call from Dr. Warren, a 2nd-year resident at the hospital, informing him that she had encountered a problem with a delivery. The baby was suffering shoulder dystocia, a condition in which a baby's shoulder becomes wedged in the mother's pelvic cavity during delivery. Dr. Kazior stated that he would be there immediately and left his home for the hospital, which was located approximately 2 miles away. When Dr. Kazior arrived at the hospital, the delivery of the infant had been completed.

On December 3, 1987, the plaintiffs filed an amended complaint alleging the negligent supervision of the obstetrics residents by Dr. Kazior. The plaintiffs alleged that the infant suffered severe and permanent injuries because of the shoulder dystocia and that Dr. Kazior's negligent supervision of the residents proximately caused these injuries.

In October 1989, the defendant filed a motion for summary judgment supported by four affidavits, the pleadings, and other material obtained during discovery. Three of the affidavits were given by the heads of the departments of obstetrics and gynecology of other teaching hospitals in North Carolina. The affidavits stated that the protocol of their respective medical schools "permitted the attending on-call physicians to afford coverage during the hours of their assignment by either being present in the hospital or, unless a problem is specifically anticipated, by being present at their residence or other specified place and immediately available to a telephone so as to come immediately to the hospital upon request." Id. at 343.

The plaintiffs responded with the sworn affidavit of Dr. Dillon, and the transcript of the deposition of Dr. Dillon, a board-certified obstetrician and an expert for th plaintiffs, "who stated that an on-call supervising physician should call in periodically during his coverage shift. Dr. Kazior had a "responsibility, when he came on call, to find out what obstetrical patients had been admitted to the hospital, their condition, and to formulate a plan of management." Id. at 343. According to Dr. Dillon, the mother "was a known gestation diabetic with extreme obesity and no established estimated fetal weight notwithstanding sonography. As such there was a known significant risk of an extremely large baby. Therefore, there were very significant known risk factors for this pregnancy which included a known significant risk factor of shoulder dystocia." Id. at 343.

In December 1989, the trial court granted summary judgment for Dr. Kazior, and the plaintiffs filed a notice of appeal. The plaintiffs again filed a notice of appeal with the court of appeals. A divided panel of the court of appeals reversed the trial court's entry of summary judgment. Dr. Kazior contended that the court of appeals erred in reversing the trial court's grant of summary judgment in his favor.

Issue

Did Dr. Kazior, who agreed to provide on-call supervision of obstetric residents at the hospital, owe the patient a duty of reasonable care in supervising residents who actually cared for the patient?

Holding

The Supreme Court of North Carolina held that Dr. Kazior owed patients a duty to reasonably supervise obstetrics residents who provided care. Whether Dr. Kazior breached a duty by merely being available for telephone calls was a fact question.

Reason

Uncontroverted evidence before the trial court tended to show that Dr. Kazior's first contact with the infant and his parents occurred when Dr. Kazior arrived at the hospital after the delivery of the infant on December 5, 1984, in response to the telephone call from Dr. Warren. In a stipulation dated March 28, 1988, Dr. Kazior stated he had responsibility for supervision of the OB/GYN residents and interns at the time of the birth of Mozingo. Based on this stipulation and the uncontested fact that Dr. Kazior knew the residents at the hospital were actually treating patients when he undertook the duty to supervise the residents as an on-call supervising physician, the court concluded that Dr. Kazior owed the patients a duty of reasonable care in supervising the residents. The court also concluded that Dr. Kazior's duty of reasonable care in supervising the residents was not diminished by the fact that his relationship with the plaintiffs did not fit traditional notions of the physician–patient relationship.

Dr. Kazior argued that the affidavits of the chairmen of the three teaching hospitals in North Carolina established that he did not breach the applicable standard of care for on-call supervising physicians. The court found that these affidavits are not as unequivocal as the defendant and the dissent suggest. In these affidavits, each chairman using nearly identical language stated that an on-call supervising physician may take calls at home "unless a problem is specifically anticipated." Id. at 346. "According to the defendant's own experts, simply remaining at home and available to take telephone calls is not always an acceptable standard of care for supervision of residents." Id.

The plaintiffs introduced the affidavit and deposition of Dr. Dillon, in which he stated that Dr. Kazior did not meet the accepted medical standard for an on-call supervising physician, given the known medical condition of the mother.

Discussion

1. What do you think would be an acceptable method of supervising residents?
2. What are the risks of supervising, diagnosing, and prescribing patient care over the telephone?

Failure to Transfer Patient Before Delivery

Citation: *Dent v. Perkins*, 629 So.2d 1354 (La. Ct. App. 1993)

Facts

The plaintiff notified Dr. Perkins's office that she was experiencing labor pains. She was instructed to go to the hospital. The plaintiff arrived at the hospital at 11:00 a.m. and, after examination by an obstetrical nurse, was found to be in labor. The nurse on duty, Ms. Patrick, notified Dr. Perkins at approximately 11:45 a.m. of the plaintiff's condition by telephone. Dr. Perkins was off-call beginning at 12:00 noon and his partner, Dr. Dean, was scheduled to attend to his patients. There was no available room for Ms. Dent in the obstetrical unit. The record indicated the patient was admitted to a nonobstetrical unit at approximately 2:30 p.m. At 3:40 p.m., the patient delivered a baby girl with the aid of an obstetrical nurse. No physician was present at the time of delivery. After delivery, the infant was transferred to the intensive care unit at another hospital and was listed in critical condition. The infant died 2 days later.

Based on the credibility of witnesses, it was concluded that Dr. Perkins acted below the required standard of care, and the jury properly found negligence on his part. The matter was referred to the trial court to determine the question of causation. The trial court determined that Dr. Perkins acted negligently in failing to limit the plaintiff's stay in a nonobstetrical unit to

15 minutes and in failing to advise Nurse Patrick that he was going off-call and that Dr. Dean would be attending to his patients. The jury apportioned responsibility to the extent of 35% on the part of Dr. Perkins and 65% on the part of the hospital.

The Patient's Compensation Fund appealed, claiming that the jury erred in apportioning fault to Dr. Perkins and that, if he was in fact negligent, the superseding and intervening negligence of the nurses and the hospital staff exonerated Dr. Perkins from liability.

Issue

Were Dr. Perkins's negligent acts and omissions a cause of the plaintiff's damages and suffering, and death of the plaintiff's infant child?

Holding

The Court of Appeals of Louisiana held that the physician's negligence in placing the plaintiff on a nonobstetrical unit for an unlimited period of time rendered him 35% at fault and the negligence of the hospital nurses and staff in observation and care of the patient, while rendering the hospital 65% at fault, did not supersede the physician's negligence.

Reason

In a medical malpractice claim against a physician, a plaintiff carries a two-fold burden of proof. The plaintiff must establish first, by a preponderance of the evidence, that the physician's treatment fell below the ordinary standard of care required of physicians in his or her medical specialty, and second, that a causal relationship was established between the alleged negligent treatment and the injury sustained.

Negligence is actionable only where both a cause in fact and a legal cause of the injury exist. Legal cause requires a proximate relation between the actions of a defendant and the harm that occurs, and such relation must be substantial in character. Based on the evidence, the court did not find that the jury erred in placing responsibility on Dr. Perkins and the hospital nurses and staff.

The physician's claim that the negligence of the hospital nurses and staff was an intervening and superseding cause of the infant's death was rejected. The record supported the findings. While Dr. Perkins was negligent in placing the plaintiff on a nonobstetrical unit for an unlimited period of time, the nurses were negligent in their observation and care of the plaintiff. However, this negligence did not supersede the physician's negligence. The nurses failed to adequately observe and monitor the plaintiff. The patient was left in the emergency department from 11:45 a.m., when she was first admitted to the hospital, until 2:30 p.m., when she was finally brought to the nonobstetrical unit of the hospital. Once the plaintiff was brought to this unit, the nurses on several occasions called the labor and delivery unit asking for an obstetrical nurse to respond to the plaintiff's complaints. When it appeared that the plaintiff was about to deliver, an obstetrical nurse assisted in the delivery. No physician was present at the child's birth. The plaintiff's expert testified that had the plaintiff been in the labor and delivery unit where a physician would have been present during delivery, the child would not have died.

Discussion

1. What changes would you make in hospital procedures?
2. Discuss the regulatory requirements that may apply in this case.

Failure to Prescribe

Citation: *Shelton v. United States*, 804 F. Supp. 1147 (E.D. Mo. 1992)

Facts

The plaintiff suffered an injury to the tip of his middle finger on his right hand. In spite of the fact that his finger was bleeding and painful, he walked six blocks to his home and called 911 for help. The plaintiff told the 911-dispatcher that he had been shot. On his way to the Veterans Affairs (VA) hospital in an ambulance, he told different versions regarding the nature of his injury. He claimed that he had been shot, and then claimed that he had been bitten. Although the plaintiff stated that he had told the admitting room nurse that he had been bitten, she had written on the admission form that he had suffered a "trauma" to his right middle finger.

The evening emergency department physician, a 2nd-year resident, examined the patient. During her training, the resident had seen and treated gunshot wounds and bites. The plaintiff told the resident he had been bitten, but would not tell the resident by whom and under what circumstances. At one point he changed his story and told the resident he had been shot. Again, he would not give any further information. The wound was irrigated and the plaintiff was sent for X-rays, which showed a fracture. When she again questioned the plaintiff about the cause of the injury, he again did not answer constructively. The resident explained to the plastic surgeon that the patient had given conflicting stories about the injury. She gave him the results of the X-rays and stated that her conclusion was that the laceration of the finger had been caused by a gunshot wound. The resident determined that, because it was a gunshot wound, there was no need to prescribe antibiotics. She told the plaintiff to use ice on his finger for the first 24 hours, then to keep the finger clean and dry. She further told him that he should check his finger and that, if he had any drainage or swelling, he should return immediately to the emergency department.

A nurse in the emergency department followed the physician's instructions and cleansed and dressed the finger. The patient was provided with written instructions. For 4 days, the patient had trouble eating and sleeping because of the pain. He put ice on the hand, but returned to the emergency department after he had taken the bandage off and discovered that his finger was discolored. He told a different emergency department physician that he had been struck on the finger. The physician examined his finger and discovered that it was grossly discolored, swollen, and full of pus. Tests indicated a massive infection and gangrene. His finger was amputated, after which the reports on the amputated portions indicated that the finger had suffered a human bite. He returned only twice for physical therapy, and was thereafter discharged from it. The plaintiff sued.

Issue

Was the 2nd-year resident negligent in not prescribing antibiotics, and was the plaintiff at fault for not following instructions with regard to care of the injury?

Holding

The 2nd-year resident was negligent in failing to prescribe antibiotics, the lack of which contributed to the seriousness of the infection, gangrene, and amputation. The plaintiff was 50% at fault for failing to follow instructions.

Reason

Medical testimony indicated that when a patient has a serious injury and tells conflicting stories about the origin of the injury, and the injury has a high potential for infection, the doctor should prescribe antibiotics. Moreover, no medical reason was found for not having had a culture done. Although the doctor indicated that she feared an allergic reaction to any antibiotic, there was nothing in the admission report that reflected an allergy to any antibiotic. Further, she never asked the patient if he had allergies. There was sufficient evidence of causation because it was shown that, if certain things had been properly done, the results that did occur would not have occurred.

The court addressed the issue of comparative negligence. There was evidence that the conduct of both the plaintiff and the defendant contributed to cause the damage. The plaintiff was given oral and written instructions that he failed to follow. In addition, if he had checked the wound earlier, he would have discovered the first signs of infection. He would have also minimized the risk of gangrene, which resulted in the amputation of his finger.

Discussion

1. When a patient comes to the emergency department, what treatment questions and steps should the staff, physician, and nurses take when the injury is of an unknown origin and the patient gives conflicting stories about it?
2. What routine instructions should emergency department patients be given regarding follow-up care?

Use of Unsterile Instruments

Citation: *Howard v. Alexandria Hosp.*, 429 S.E.2d 22 (Va. 1993)

Facts

A patient brought a medical malpractice action against a hospital, seeking damages arising out of an operation performed on her with unsterile instruments. The patient had entered the hospital for surgery to relieve her suffering from carpal tunnel syndrome. During her stay in the recovery room following surgery, the operating surgeon reported to the patient that she had been operated on with unsterile instruments. Allegedly, the nurse in charge of the autoclave that was used to sterilize the instruments did not properly monitor the sterilization process. Because of the patient's fear of a variety of diseases, she was administered several human immunodeficiency virus (HIV) tests, one of which was taken 6 months following her discharge from the hospital. The patient was evaluated by an infectious disease specialist and was administered antibiotics intravenously. Following her discharge, the patient was placed on several medications and, as a result, developed symptoms of pseudomembranous enterocolitis. Testimony was entered that described the patient's symptoms as resulting from the administration of the antibiotics. One expert testified that the patient had reason to be concerned for at least 6 months following the surgical procedure because of her risk of being infected with one of a variety of diseases. The hospital argued that the patient suffered no physical injury from the surgical procedure or the instruments utilized during the procedure.

The circuit court, entering summary judgment for the hospital, granted a motion by the hospital to strike the evidence on the grounds that no physical injury had been shown, and an appeal was taken.

Issue

Did the trial court err by sustaining the hospital's motion to strike the evidence and enter summary judgment for the hospital?

Holding

The Supreme Court of Virginia held that the patient had suffered injury resulting from measures taken to avoid infection following discovery of the use of unsterile instrumentation, even though the patient did not sustain any infection from use of the instruments. The case was reversed and remanded for a new trial on all issues.

Reason

Injury can be either physical or mental. It is clear that, because of the hospital's use of inadequately sterilized instruments, the plaintiff sustained positive physical and mental injury. As the direct result of the improper sterilization of the operating room instrumentation, dangerously unclean intravenous tubes, needles for administering pain shots, and instruments used to withdraw blood had invaded the plaintiff's body. She experienced the physical pain and discomfort of headache, nausea, vomiting, fever, chills, and unusual sweating. To argue that the plaintiff established mere emotional disturbance absent physical injury is to ignore the evidence in this case. "The plaintiff's evidence, at the very least, establishes a prima facie case of injury." Id. at 25.

Discussion

1. What is meant by summary judgment?
2. What are the educational issues evident in this case?

Improper Insertion of a Catheter

Citation: *Welte v. Bello*, 482 N.W.2d 437 (Iowa 1992)

Facts

On April 26, 1986, Ms. Welte was admitted to the hospital for surgery for the correction of a deviated septum. Approximately 3 hours before surgery, Ms. Welte conferred with her surgeon about the procedure. She then conferred with her anesthesiologist, Dr. Bello, who informed her that he would be administering sodium pentothal through an IV inserted into a vein in her arm. He told her about the potential risks associated with general anesthesia. Ms. Welte read and signed a written "consent to operate, administration of anesthetics, and rendering other medical services . . ." The consent form provided: "I consent to the administration of anesthesia to be applied by or under the direction and control of Dr. Bello." Also on the form was the statement that "anesthesia and its complications have been explained and accepted." Ms. Welte and Dr. Bello signed the consent form. After talking with the doctors, Ms. Welte was transferred to a presurgical room. While in this room, a nurse inserted a catheter into the vein of Ms. Welte's right arm. Ms. Welte complained of pain after the IV had been inserted. The nurse checked the IV and concluded that it was properly positioned inside the vein. Dr. Bello began injecting drugs through a port in the IV. Dr. Bello then rechecked the site of the IV and, for the first time, noticed swelling on Ms. Welte's arm near the point at which the IV had been inserted. As a consequence of the sodium pentothal infiltration of the tissues surrounding the vein, Ms. Welte sustained first-, second-, and third-degree burns resulting in a large permanent scar.

Ms. Welte and her husband commenced two separate malpractice actions, one against the hospital and another against Dr. Bello. The separate suits were consolidated for trial. Prior to trial, Dr. Bello filed a motion for summary judgment claiming Ms. Welte had failed to retain a qualified expert to testify against him and, therefore, the plaintiffs would be precluded from offering any expert testimony at trial. Ms. Welte argued that failure to obtain informed consent did not require expert testimony. The trial court concluded that any alleged negligence of the anesthesiologist was not so obvious as to be within the comprehension of a layperson.

Issue

Was expert testimony required to establish a claim against the anesthesiologist?

Holding

The Supreme Court of Iowa held that expert testimony was not required to establish a claim against Dr. Bello.

Reason

Citing *Donovan v. State*, 445 N.W.2d 763 (Iowa 1989), "If a doctor operates on the wrong limb or amputates the wrong limb, a plaintiff would not have to introduce expert testimony to establish that the doctor was negligent. On the other hand, highly technical questions of diagnoses and causation which lie beyond the understanding of a layperson require introduction of expert testimony." The chemical burn to Ms. Welte's arm was caused by sodium pentothal that the anesthesiologist injected into the patient's vein; the drug then infiltrated or escaped from the vein into the surrounding tissues. The Supreme Court of Iowa found that it was within the common experience of a layperson that such an occurrence in the ordinary course of things would not have occurred if reasonable care had been used. The insertion of a needle into a vein is a common medical procedure. It is a procedure that has become so common that laypersons know certain occurrences would not take place if ordinary care were used. Id. at 441.

The court concluded that the trial court erred in granting partial summary judgment on the general negligence claim against Dr. Bello. Even if expert evidence were required, the record was sufficient to defeat the summary judgment motion. Dr. Bello's expert, Dr. Maxwell, testified in his deposition that in the usual course of events, an IV instituted for purpose of anesthesia does not infiltrate the surrounding tissue. Id. at 442.

Discussion

1. What responsibility might an anesthesiologist have in supervising a nurse's negligence?
2. What mechanism might the hospital implement in order to help prevent such occurrences in the future?

Anesthesia Administered into Patient's Esophagus

Citation: *Denton Reg'l Med. Ctr. v. LaCroix*, 947 S.W.2d 941 (Tex. Ct. App. 1997)

Facts

In the early morning of January 25, 1991, appellees Mr. and Ms. LaCroix went to the Women's Pavilion of appellant hospital for the birth of their first child, Lawryn. Ms. LaCroix was admitted to the hospital under the care of her obstetrician, Dr. Dulemba. The Women's Pavilion, which opened in 1986, provided 24-hour anesthesia care.

Ms. LaCroix underwent a C-section. Mr. LaCroix was in the operating room for the C-section. Before the C-section began, Ms. LaCroix complained several times of breathing difficulty. When Dr. McGehee, the pediatrician who was going to treat the infant after she was delivered, arrived in the operating room, he noticed that Ms. LaCroix appeared to be in respiratory distress and heard her say, "I can't breathe." Dr. McGehee asked Ms. Blankenship, a nurse, if Ms. LaCroix was okay, and the nurse responded that Ms. LaCroix was just nervous. Mr. LaCroix testified that, soon thereafter, Ms. LaCroix's eyes "got big" and she whispered again to him that she could not breathe. Mr. LaCroix shouted, "She can't breathe! Somebody please help my wife!" Nurse Blankenship asked that Mr. LaCroix be removed from the operating room, because she believed Ms. LaCroix was having a seizure. Mr. LaCroix was escorted out of the operating room.

Nurse Blankenship could not establish an airway with an airbag and mask, because Ms. LaCroix's teeth were clenched shut from the seizure. She told one of the other nurses, "Get one of the anesthesiologists here now!" Dr. Green, who was in his car, was paged. When he received the page, he immediately drove to the Women's Pavilion. Dr. Dulemba was already making the C-section incision when the seizure occurred, and he told Ms. Blankenship that Ms. LaCroix's blood was dark (as opposed to oxygenated blood, which is bright red). When Lawryn was delivered, she was not breathing, and Dr. McGehee had to resuscitate her. Meanwhile, to intubate Ms. LaCroix to establish an airway for her, Ms. Blankenship had to paralyze her using the drug Anectine and put her to sleep using sodium pentothal, a general anesthetic. She was then able to intubate Ms. LaCroix, but it was an esophageal, rather than a tracheal, intubation. Dr. Dulemba, who was still working inside Ms. LaCroix's abdomen, pointed out that he thought the intubation was esophageal, so Ms. Blankenship removed the tube and then succeeded in a tracheal intubation.

While Dr. Dulemba was closing the C-section incisions, Ms. LaCroix's blood pressure and pulse dropped, and Ms. Blankenship gave her ephedrine to try to raise her blood pressure. Ms. LaCroix then became asystole—she went into full cardiac arrest and her heart stopped beating. A physician and nurse from the hospital's emergency department had responded to a code for assistance and came into the operating room. Dr. McGehee testified that the emergency department physician said that he did not know how to resuscitate pregnant women and left without providing any medical care. Dr. Dulemba and a nurse began cardiopulmonary resuscitation (CPR) on Ms. LaCroix, and Dr. McGehee, once he was finished treating Lawryn, took control of the code and directed nurses to give Ms. LaCroix atropine and epinephrine to resuscitate her. Ms. LaCroix's heart resumed beating after one dose of epinephrine.

Dr. Pourzan, who was doing a procedure in the hospital's main operating room, was told about the code, got someone to take over his case, and rushed to the Women's Pavilion. He arrived after Ms. LaCroix had been resuscitated and took over Ms. LaCroix's care from Dr. McGehee. Dr. Green also arrived after Ms. LaCroix had been resuscitated. Although Ms. LaCroix was resuscitated, she had suffered irreversible brain injury caused by hypoxia (deprivation of oxygen to the brain). She was comatose for 3 days and hospitalized for a total of 13 days. Ms. LaCroix was then transferred to Epic's Flow Rehab Hospital (Epic) for rehabilitation, where she stayed for 50 days. Because of her brain injury, Ms. LaCroix has a full scale IQ of 76, which places her on the borderline of intellectual functioning, and she is totally and permanently disabled from independent living.

Ms. Blankenship and Dr. Hafiz settled with the LaCroixes by paying $500,000 and $750,000, respectively, for a total settlement of $1.25 million. Dr. Hafiz was the Denton Anesthesiology Associates, PA (DAA) anesthesiologist on call for the Women's Pavilion on the day of Ms. LaCroix's incident.

The trial court entered a judgment against the hospital and for the LaCroixes, awarding the LaCroixes approximately $8.8 million in damages after applying the $1.25 million settlement credit.

Issue

Was the evidence legally and factually sufficient to hold the hospital liable for medical negligence under a theory of direct corporate liability notwithstanding the jury's failure to find that the treating physicians and nurse were negligent?

Holding

The evidence was legally and factually sufficient to hold the hospital liable for medical negligence under a theory of direct corporate liability notwithstanding the jury's failure to find that the treating physicians and nurse were negligent.

Reason

The evidence established that the hospital owed a duty to have an anesthesiologist provide or supervise all of her anesthesia medical care, including having an anesthesiologist personally present or immediately available in the operating suite, and that the hospital's breach of this duty had proximately caused her brain damage.

The responsible anesthesiologist must perform a preanesthetic evaluation and preparation in which the anesthesiologist:

1. Reviews the chart.
2. Interviews the patient to:
    a. Discuss medical history including anesthetic experiences and drug therapy.
    b. Perform any examinations that would provide information that might assist in decisions regarding risk and management.
3. Orders test and medications essential to the conduct of anesthesia.
4. Obtains consultations as necessary.
5. Records impressions on the preanesthesia summary along with brief discussion of planned anesthesia management, techniques, and ASA patient classification.
6. CRNAs will document the visit and discuss the evaluation of their patients with the supervising anesthesiologist or the operating physician; the discussion will be documented by the anesthesiologist or the operating physician by signing (with the nurse anesthetist) the preanesthetic summary.

Mr. LaCroix testified that, from the point the LaCroixes arrived at the hospital, they never were informed that a nurse anesthetist would administer Ms. LaCroix's anesthesia or that Ms. Hill or Ms. Blankenship was a nurse anesthetist. All along, Mr. LaCroix thought that Ms. Blankenship was a physician. Ms. Blankenship admitted that she never told the LaCroixes that she was a nurse anesthetist and was not a physician. It was undisputed that Ms. LaCroix was never seen by an anesthesiologist until she had suffered brain damage. It was also undisputed, and even agreed to by all the defendants, that the LaCroixes had a right to know that Ms. LaCroix was going to be receiving anesthesia care from a certified registered nurse anesthetist (CRNA) and not from an anesthesiologist. Finally, it was undisputed that no physician ever countersigned in Ms. LaCroix's medical chart any of the medical treatments that were signed by Ms. Blankenship. The hospital's policies and procedures required that the CRNA's supervising physician sign for the CRNA.

The evidence showed that the practice of anesthesia is a specialized practice of medicine by a physician—an anesthesiologist. An anesthesiologist is also trained in the practice of taking care of a patient just as any other physician is trained. An anesthesiologist is the most highly trained person who practices anesthesia. A CRNA is a registered nurse who has additionally completed a 2-year study in nurse anesthesia and has been certified by the American Association of Nurse Anesthetists. Nurse anesthetists may administer anesthesia, but only under the medical direction or supervision of a physician.

By virtue of a May 31, 1990, contract with the hospital, DAA was the exclusive anesthesia provider for the Women's Pavilion. The contract, which had a term of 3 years, was a renewal of DAA's prior exclusive contract with the hospital. The contract required DAA to provide "qualified coverage" (supervision and back-up of all CRNAs employed by DAA) in the Women's Pavilion 24 hours per day, 7 days per week, including weekends and holidays.

The hospital's anesthesia department had written policies and procedures governing anesthesia care at the hospital. The anesthesia department policies and procedures provided that a CRNA could provide "anesthetic patient care only under the direct and personal supervision of a physician."

When the LaCroixes arrived at the Women's Pavilion with Ms. LaCroix in labor, they were presented with—and signed—an anesthesia consent form that had the names of Dr. Green, Dr. Pourzan, and Dr. Hafiz preprinted on it. None of the physicians knew that the hospital was doing the anesthesia consent for patients at the Women's Pavilion in that manner. Ms. LaCroix never received a preanesthetic evaluation by an anesthesiologist, and no anesthesiologist ever explained the anesthesia consent to the LaCroixes.

The LaCroixes contended that the evidence was sufficient to establish that the hospital owed a duty to Ms. LaCroix to have an anesthesiologist provide or supervise all of Ms. LaCroix's anesthesia medical care, including having an anesthesiologist personally present or immediately available in the operating suite, and that the hospital's breach of this duty proximately caused Ms. LaCroix's brain damage.

The hospital, which opened the Women's Pavilion in 1986, initially entered into an exclusive contract with DAA to provide anesthesia care for the Women's Pavilion. The May 31, 1990, contract was a renewal of DAA's initial exclusive contract with the hospital. Mr. Ciulla, an employee of the hospital, was in charge of the DAA contract, which was drafted by Epic's legal department. According to Mr. Ciulla, he renewed the contract in conjunction with the hospital's medical staff.

Mr. Ciulla admitted that, before he renewed the contract with DAA, anesthesiologists who practiced at the hospital warned him that DAA's CRNAs were not being properly supervised in the Women's Pavilion. Both Dr. Mickey Via, chairman of the hospital's anesthesiology department in 1991, and Mr. Ciulla testified that Dr. Via and other anesthesiologists had complained to Mr. Ciulla about the lack of proper CRNA supervision in the Women's Pavilion. Dr. Via said that in renewing the contract with DAA, Mr. Ciulla did nothing to address the complaints that had been made.

According to Mr. Ciulla, he renewed the contract in conjunction with the hospital's medical staff. According to Dr. Via, the hospital's medical executive committee recommended to Mr. Ciulla that he not renew DAA's contract and that he seek another anesthesia group for the Women's Pavilion, but the hospital's board of directors renewed the contract anyway. Four months before the LaCroixes went to the hospital to have their baby, Dr. Via wrote a memo (dated September 10, 1990) to Mr. Ciulla complaining that DAA's anesthesiologists were still not supervising DAA's CRNAs in the Women's Pavilion.

Dr. Via wrote a memo describing the dissatisfaction of the staff anesthesiologists who voiced concern regarding the medical supervision, or lack thereof, of nurse anesthetists administering anesthetics at the hospital.

Administrators at the hospital not only have failed to heed these concerns but seemingly have promoted the practice by their inaction and the contractual arrangements in the Women's Pavilion. It has become apparent that the contracted anesthesiologists frequently are not present in that facility while nurse employees are providing anesthetics. This practice recently has been estimated to occur between 50 and 75% of the time. Additionally, nurse employees of Denton Anesthesia Associates on several occasions have provided anesthetics in the main operating room of the hospital without supervision by their employers.

After reviewing the entire record, the court of appeals held that the evidence was legally and factually sufficient to support a finding that the hospital owed a duty to Ms. LaCroix to have an anesthesiologist provide or supervise all of her anesthesia care and that its breach of this duty was the direct cause of her brain injury. As the testimony reflects, the issues of the duty the hospital owed to Ms. LaCroix and the medical cause of Ms. LaCroix's brain injury were at the center of a classic "battle of the experts," and the jury was free to accept or reject either side's theory, either of which is supported by sufficient evidence.

Discussion

1. Describe the many reasons why this outcome occurred and how similar events can be prevented in the future.
2. Discuss hospital policy issues as they relate to (a) contracts (e.g., approval of medical staff involvement, supervision of CRNAs); (b) competency (e.g., CRNAs, emergency department physicians); (c) anesthesia assessments (e.g., preanesthesia, preinduction, and post-anesthesia); (d) patient consent (e.g., informed consent); and (e) physician dissatisfaction with anesthesia services.
3. What other issues can you identify in this case?

Ambulance EMT Negligent

Citation: *Riffe v. Vereb Ambulance Serv., Inc.*, 650 A.2d 1076 (Pa. Super. 1994)

Facts

A complaint was filed against the defendant, Mr. Custozzo, who was employed by Vereb Ambulance Service as an emergency medical technician and, in that capacity, responded to an emergency call regarding Mr. Anderson. Mr. Custozzo began administering lidocaine to Mr. Anderson as ordered over the telephone by the medical command physician at the hospital. While en route to the hospital, Mr. Anderson was administered an amount of lidocaine 44 times the normal dosage. Consequently, normal heart function was not restored, and Mr. Anderson was pronounced dead at the hospital shortly thereafter.

Issue

Can the emergency medical technician's negligence be imputed to the hospital?

Holding

The Superior Court held that the liability of medical technicians could not be imputed to the hospital and action against the hospital based on the theory of vicarious liability was barred by earlier settlement by the Ambulance Company and technician.

Reason

The trial court noted the practical impossibility of the hospital carrying ultimate responsibility for the quality of care and treatment given patients by

Emergency Medical Services (EMS). This is propounded proportionately in relation to the density of the population, number of hospitals, and number of EMS services. It becomes obvious that the focus of training and monitoring of such services must lie with the EMS regional and local councils pursuant to and subject to regulations promulgated by the Department of Health. While hospitals, as facilities, participate in the overall operation of EMS services, the hospital command facility derives its function from the laws and regulations relating to the operation of EMS. The networking of EMS and command facilities is such that they have a common interrelated function that is apart from the administration of the hospitals to which they are attached. Because an EMS may be involved with several hospitals depending on specialization, and even allowing for patients' directions, a hospital's legal responsibility for the operation of any given EMS becomes too tenuous. The Superior Court found no error by the trial court in determining that no liability could be imputed on the part of St. Francis Hospital.

Discussion

1. Do you agree with the court's decision? Why?
2. What effect might a finding for the plaintiffs have on hospital-based EMS services?
3. What might the decision of the court have been if the ambulance was owned and operated by the hospital and the ambulance technicians were employees of the hospital?

Treatment of Patient Without Adequate Products

Citation: *Citron v. Northern Dutchess Hosp.*, 603 N.Y.S.2d 639 (N.Y. App. Div. 1993)

Facts

A deceased patient's husband instituted an action against the hospital for negligence, asserting that it failed to have blood products available for his wife, who suffered a ruptured uterus. The patient, 26-weeks pregnant, had complained to her obstetrician about back pain, cramps, and nausea. She was told to go to the hospital's emergency department. It was determined by personnel there that she was suffering from intra-abdominal bleeding. While undergoing surgery performed by her obstetrician, it was learned that her uterus had ruptured. Four hours following surgery, she died of anoxia due to loss of one-half of her total blood. Other than with her obstetrician, she had no physician–patient relationship with any of the emergency department physicians. The trial court jury found in favor of the plaintiff, and the hospital appealed.

Issue

Can a hospital be held vicariously liable for an independent physician's negligent acts if the patient enters the emergency department and seeks treatment from the hospital, not a specific physician?

Holding

The New York Supreme Court, Appellate Division, upheld the trial court's decision, finding that the hospital was vicariously liable for the acts of its emergency department physicians, including their treatment of the deceased without having the necessary blood products available.

Reason

Although neither the patient nor her husband asked for a specific physician once she was admitted to the emergency department, the court found that she "could properly assume that the treating doctors and staff of the hospital were acting on behalf of the hospital . . ." Id. at 641. Expert testimony had revealed that the failure to provide the decedent with proper blood products was a major factor in her death. The court further held that it was a deviation from accepted practice for the hospital not to have platelets on hand or "available within 1 hour." Id. at 639.

Discussion

1. What steps should the hospital take to prevent further incidents of this nature?
2. What issues do you see as to the assessment and reassessment of the patient's needs?

Failure to Treat

Citation: *Callahan v. Cardinal Glennon Hosp.*, 863 S.W.2d 852 (Mo. 1993)

Facts

A medical malpractice action was brought against the employer of a physician, alleging that the physician's failure to properly treat an abscess some

3 weeks after an infant received a live polio vaccine resulted in suppression of the infant's immune system and the infant's contraction of paralytic polio. The jury in the circuit court returned a $16 million verdict in favor of the plaintiffs, and the defendant appealed. The case was transferred from the court of appeals to the Missouri Supreme Court.

Issue

Was the $16 million verdict excessive, and did the trial court err in denying a new trial based on the alleged excessive verdict?

Holding

The Missouri Supreme Court held that there was no basis for a new trial on the grounds of excessiveness of the verdict.

Reason

There is no formula for determining the excessiveness of a verdict. Each case must be decided on its own facts to determine what is fair and reasonable. A jury is in the best position to make such a determination. The trial judge could have set aside the verdict if a determination was made that passion and prejudice brought about an excessive verdict. The size of the verdict alone does not establish passion and prejudice. The appellant failed to establish that the verdict was: (1) glaringly unwarranted and (2) based on prejudice and passion. Compensation of a plaintiff is based on such factors as the age of the patient, the nature and extent of injury, diminished earnings capacity, economic condition, and awards in comparable cases. "Furthermore, a jury is 'entitled to consider such intangibles' which 'do not lend themselves to precise calculation,' such as past and future pain, suffering, effect on lifestyle, embarrassment, humiliation, and economic loss." *Kenton v. Hyatt Hotels Corp.*, 693 S.W.2d 98 (Mo. 1985). The Supreme Court found no error that would substantiate passion or prejudice. Based on this issue, there was no basis for a new trial.

Discussion

1. Do you consider the verdict of $16 million to be excessive?
2. What factors should be taken into account when determining the amount of damages to be awarded a plaintiff?

Treatment: Independent Contractors Liable for Their Malpractice

Citation: *Sarivola v. Brookdale Hosp. and Med.* Ctr., 612 N.Y.S.2d 151 (N.Y. App. Div. 1994)

Facts

The plaintiff in this case seeks to impose liability on the defendant hospital for treatment provided by a radiologist who was not an employee of the hospital but maintained an office there. The plaintiff failed to submit an affidavit setting forth who she believed was responsible for her treatment. The evidence indicates a physician referred her to the radiologist. The radiologist alleged that he specifically advised the plaintiff that he was a private physician, unaffiliated with the hospital. There was no evidence of independent acts of malpractice committed by the hospital's technicians who operated the radiation equipment. There was no evidence or expert testimony that the physician's orders were so radically different from accepted practice that the technicians should have questioned them or not carried them out.

Issue

When treatment is rendered by a private attending physician, not an employee of the hospital, can the hospital, as a general rule, be liable for acts of malpractice that are committed in carrying out the independent physician's orders?

Holding

The New York Supreme Court, Appellate Division, held that the plaintiff could not recover from the hospital.

Reason

When treatment is rendered by a private attending physician not in the employ of a hospital, the general rule is that the hospital is free of liability for acts of malpractice that are committed in carrying out the independent physician's orders. However, a hospital may be held vicariously liable for the acts of an independent physician if the physician was provided by the hospital (or was otherwise acting on the hospital's behalf) and the patient reasonably believed that the physician was acting at the hospital's behest. Because the plaintiff did not seek treatment from the hospital directly and the hospital did not send the plaintiff to the radiologist, the plaintiff could not receive damages from the hospital. Furthermore, given the totality of the circumstances here, the plaintiff could not have reasonably believed that the physician was employed by the hospital, because it is quite common for independent physicians to utilize hospital office facilities.

Discussion

1. Under what circumstances are hospitals liable for the negligent acts of private practicing physicians?
2. From a contractual point of view, what are the differences between an employed physician and a private independent contractor?

Covering Physician and Duty to Treat

Citation: *West v. Adelmann*, 630 N.E.2d 846 (Ill. Ct. App. 1993)

Facts

On February 28, 1985, the plaintiff fell from a vehicle and was taken to the medical center; he was found to have fractured his left leg in three places. Dr. Woiteshek initially treated the plaintiff on February 28 by placing a pin in his lower leg, casting the lower portion, and placing the plaintiff in traction to align the fractured thighbone. Dr. Adelmann practiced with Dr. Woiteshek in Adelmann-Woiteshek Orthopedic Surgeons, SC, a medical partnership, and made hospital visits to the plaintiff, apparently in rotation with Dr. Woiteshek, on March 3, 5, 7, 10, 11, and 13. Dr. Adelmann also cared for the plaintiff from March 15 through 18 when Dr. Woiteshek was on vacation.

On March 15, 1985, Dr. Adelmann noticed a motor palsy (loss of nerve strength) in the plaintiff's left leg and padded the cast at the top to alleviate the problem. On March 17, 1985, the plaintiff complained of pain in his ankle, which Dr. Adelmann initially relieved by adjusting the plaintiff's foot inside the cast. On March 18, 1985, when pain persisted in the heel area, Dr. Adelmann found a blister there and treated it at 1:00 a.m. by cutting a "window" in the cast, repadding the area, and taping the cutout section into its original position.

On March 18, 1985, Dr. Adelmann discovered through new X-rays that there had been a shortening of the leg since the X-rays that were apparently taken 2 days earlier. There was a shortening of both the lower and upper portions of the leg by approximately 1 inch. That evening, Dr. Adelmann informed the plaintiff's parents what the X-rays revealed and urged them to allow him to recast the leg as soon as possible, including changing the pin, in order to avoid any further damage. The plaintiff's mother immediately consulted with physicians at another hospital, and the plaintiff was moved there that night without any further treatment being administered by Dr. Adelmann.

The plaintiff's expert witness, Dr. Yoslow, an orthopaedic surgeon, testified that the plaintiff's condition required a pin change and a cast change within 2 or 3 days of the initial treatment and that Dr. Woiteshek deviated from the accepted standards of orthopaedic surgery when he failed to take such action. Dr. Yoslow stated that the injuries caused by the failure to change the pin and cast included an infection under the cast, a blister on the left heel, shortening of the tibia and femur, and a peroneal nerve palsy. Dr. Yoslow initially had no criticism of Dr. Adelmann's care; however, his opinion was based on an assumption that Dr. Adelmann was covering (or "marking time") for Dr. Woiteshek when he saw the plaintiff on alternate days and supervised the plaintiff's treatment during Dr. Woiteshek's vacation.

The trial court, in granting summary judgment for Dr. Adelmann. The plaintiff contended that summary judgment was improperly granted by the trial court, because the court focused on whether Dr. Adelmann made a specific declaration that he had taken over the plaintiff's care from Dr. Woiteshek and not whether Dr. Adelmann's actions allowed a reasonable inference that Dr. Adelmann and the plaintiff enjoyed a physician–patient relationship, thus creating a duty of care for Dr. Adelmann. The plaintiff appealed.

Issue

Did an issue of material fact exist for purposes of a medical malpractice action as to whether the surgeon, who was a partner of the original treating surgeon, established a primary physician–patient relationship through his actions in treating and caring for the patient?

Holding

The Appellate Court of Illinois held that there was a genuine issue of material fact as to whether a primary physician–patient relationship existed, thus precluding summary judgment.

Reason

Whether a physician–patient relationship exists depends on the facts and circumstances of each case and is for the trier of fact to determine. A fair reading of Dr. Yoslow's deposition clearly establishes that he believed that if Dr. Adelmann did have a duty to treat the plaintiff after March 15, then he deviated from the applicable standard of care. The court found that the plaintiff clearly established evidence that raises a question as to whether Dr. Adelmann, through his actions in treating and caring for the plaintiff, established a primary physician–patient relationship. The evidence disclosed that Dr. Adelmann checked on the plaintiff every other day while he was in the hospital, approximately half of the time. The plaintiff sought Dr. Adelmann's assistance when he was in pain and accepted Dr. Adelmann's care of him.

The court expressed its curiosity about the varying responsibilities of a physician who is apparently in charge of a patient's treatment and a physician who "marks time" by checking in on another physician's patient on alternating days.

The court, while not sure of the meaning of "marking time," stated, "we certainly would not want our children or spouses to be under the care of a physician who is merely marking time." Id. at 850.

Discussion

1. What is necessary in order to establish a physician–patient relationship?
2. From a legal point of view, when does a physician–patient relationship end?
3. From both ethical and legal points of view, what steps would you take to terminate your professional relationship with a patient?

Negligent Treatment: Blood Vessels Severed

Citation: *Agustin v. Beth Israel Hosp.*, 586 N.Y.S.2d 252 (N.Y. App. Div. 1992)

Facts

The plaintiff brought a medical malpractice action to recover damages arising from the fatal injuries suffered by his wife as the result of surgery for a degenerative disc disorder in 1985. The evidence adduced at trial revealed that, during the surgery, the instrument used by the surgeon, Dr. Noh, severed three of the decedent's major blood vessels, causing internal bleeding from which she ultimately died. The evidence also revealed that, during the operation, the decedent suffered a precipitous drop in blood pressure, which, although potentially indicative of internal bleeding, was not reported to Dr. Noh by the primary anesthesiologist, Dr. Thiagarjah, or by his assistant.

Immediately following surgery, the decedent was taken to a recovery room while Dr. Noh went to a nearby room to write his postoperative report. The record is unclear as to when Dr. Noh was summoned and when he ultimately arrived in the recovery room, but he was recorded as present at 2:10 p.m. After Dr. Noh arrived, further tests were administered, but emergency surgery was not commenced until 3:00 p.m. The surgery was not successful, and the decedent died at 3:51 p.m. Expert testimony convincingly demonstrated that, had the surgery been commenced sooner, the chances of decedent's recovery would have been substantially enhanced. The jury found that Dr. Noh was not liable for malpractice, and the plaintiff appealed.

Issue

Was the jury's finding that Dr. Noh was not liable in cutting three of the decedent's major blood vessels during surgery against the weight of the evidence?

Holding

The New York Supreme Court, Appellate Division, held that the jury's finding was against the weight of the evidence.

Reason

The supreme court agreed with the trial court that the jury's finding that Dr. Noh was not liable was against the weight of the evidence and that a new trial was therefore required on the issue of whether Dr. Noh committed medical malpractice that was a proximate cause of the decedent's death. A court should find a verdict to be against the weight of the evidence and set it aside when it finds that "the jury could not have reached its verdict on any fair interpretation of the evidence" (*Yalkut v. City of New York*, 162 A.D.2d 185, 188, 557 N.Y.S.2d 3). The expert testimony overwhelmingly demonstrated that the surgery involved herein did not involve a legitimate risk of the disastrous outcome (the severance of the aorta, vena cava, and iliac artery).

Discussion

1. Based on the facts presented, what action should the hospital take in credentialing physicians who request surgical privileges?
2. Why did the supreme court agree with the trial court's finding?

Surgery and Wrong Sponge Count
Citation: *Holger v. Irish*, 851 P.2d 1122 (Or. 1993)

Facts

The decedent's estate sued a surgeon and the hospital that employed the nurses who assisted the surgeon during an operation performed upon the deceased. During the course of performing colon surgery, the surgeon placed laparotomy sponges in the decedent's abdomen. After he had removed the sponges at the end of surgery, the two nurses assisting him counted them and verified that they had all been removed. Two years later, a sponge was discovered in the patient's abdomen. It was removed, and the 92-year-old patient died. The decedent's estate settled with the hospital, and although the estate moved to exclude any mention of the settlement at the trial, the judge informed the jury about the settlement. The estate had also asked the judge to instruct the jury with regard to respondeat superior, but the judge would not give those instructions. The jury decided in favor of the defendants, and the decedent's estate appealed. The court of appeals reversed, and the Supreme Court of Oregon reviewed the case.

Issue

Were the operating room nurses agents or employees of the defendants, or were the facts sufficient to show that they were under the defendants' supervision and control, and were they negligent?

Holding

The Supreme Court of Oregon held that: (1) the surgeon was not vicariously liable, as a matter of law, for the negligence of the operating room nurses, (2) the decedent's estate was not entitled to a vicarious liability instruction, and (3) the trial judge should not have mentioned the settlement with the hospital. Thus, the case was remanded for trial.

Reason

There was no evidence presented that the nurses were the surgeon/defendant's employees or that they were under the supervision or control of the surgeon's regarding their counting of the sponges. It was their sole responsibility to count the sponges; the surgeon was responsible for concentrating on the patient. The nurses had been hired and trained by the hospital, which paid for their services.

The trial court should not have instructed the jury about the settlement with the hospital. The court asserted that it did so because the jury would wonder why the hospital was not mentioned throughout the trial. The supreme court found that the trial court had planted in the minds of the jurors that the decedent's estate had already been compensated for damages, therefore it may have seemed to jurors that nothing further should be given.

Discussion

1. What are the elements necessary to prove respondeat superior or vicarious liability?
2. Why was the surgeon not liable for the negligent acts of the nurses in the operating room?

Surgery: Needle Fragment Left in Patient

Citation: *Williams v. Kilgore,* 618 So.2d 51 (Miss. 1992)

Facts

A patient, Mrs. Williams, brought a medical malpractice suit against defendant physicians Dr. Kilgore and Dr. Berrong based on injuries she allegedly sustained from a biopsy needle fragment that had been left in her during surgery.

On March 31, 1964, Mrs. Williams had been admitted to the University Medical Center for treatment of metastatic malignant melanoma on her left groin. On April 6, 1964, an unknown resident performed a bone marrow biopsy. The needle broke during the procedure, and a fragment had lodged in the patient's lower back. She was told that the needle would be removed the following day when surgery was to be performed to remove a melanoma from her groin. The operating surgeons, Dr. Peede and Dr. Kilgore, were informed of the presence of the needle fragment prior to surgery. A notation by Dr. Peede stated that the needle fragment had been removed. Dr. Berrong, who was a radiology resident at the time of the surgery, was assigned the responsibility of studying the results of the surgery.

Although the needle fragment had not been removed, the patient remained asymptomatic until she was hospitalized for back pain in September 1985. During her hospitalization, the patient learned that the needle fragment was still in her lower back.

On October 7, 1985, the needle fragment was finally removed. The physician's discharge report suggested that there was a probable linkage between the needle fragment and recurrent strep infections that Mrs. Williams had been experiencing. Although the patient's treating physicians had known as early as 1972 that the needle fragment had not been removed, there was no evidence that Mrs. Williams was aware of this fact.

Summonses served on Dr. Kilgore and Dr. Berrong were returned. The whereabouts of Dr. Peede were unknown. The defendant physicians argued that the statute of limitations had tolled under Mississippi Code, thus barring the case from proceeding to trial. The circuit court entered a judgment for the physicians, and the plaintiff appealed.

Issue

Was the plaintiff's malpractice action time-barred?

Holding

The Supreme Court of Mississippi held that the plaintiff's action was not time-barred and was, therefore, remanded for trial.

Reason

A patient's cause for action begins to accrue, and the statute of limitations begins to run, when the patient can reasonably be held to have knowledge of the disease or injury. "In this instance, Mrs. Williams began to experience infections and back pain in 1985. Moreover, this is the date she discovered that the needle was causing her problems, never having been informed previously that the needle from the 1964 biopsy procedure remained lodged within her." Id. at 54. "As we [Mississippi Supreme Court] stated in *Gentry v. Wallace*, 606 So.2d 1117, 1122 (1992), '[t]his Court views statutes of repose with disfavor, and if the statute is ambiguous, we place upon it a construction which favors preservation of the plaintiff's cause of action.' We find therefore that Mrs. Williams properly filed her complaint in this case within 2 years of that time, thus conforming with the statute of limitations for medical malpractice . . ." Id. at 55.

Discussion

1. Under what circumstances would the plaintiff's action have been time-barred?
2. What is your impression of Dr. Peede's claim that the needle fragment had been removed?
3. What is the efficacy of X-rays following the alleged removal of the needle fragment?

Surgery: Sciatic Nerve Injury

Citation: *Lacombe v. Dr. Walter Olin Moss Reg'l Hosp.*, 617 So.2d 612 (La. Ct. App. 1993)

Facts

On May 31, 1988, the plaintiff, Mrs. Lacombe, was admitted to the hospital for surgery. Upon regaining consciousness in the recovery room, the plaintiff began complaining of severe, shooting pain from her right buttock down the back of her right leg. Mrs. Lacombe was eventually diagnosed with sciatic nerve injury. It is undisputed that the injury is permanent. Mrs. Lacombe filed a medical malpractice claim against the hospital and the surgeon. A medical review panel rendered a decision finding no breach of the standard of care.

Mrs. Lacombe then filed a medical malpractice suit against the hospital and physicians. By the time of trial, all defendants except the hospital had been dismissed from the litigation. After trial, the trial judge rendered judgment for the plaintiff.

The judge found that, applying the doctrine of res ipsa loquitur, the plaintiff had proven her case. He found the hospital responsible under the theory of respondeat superior for the negligent conduct of its agents (the personnel who prepared the plaintiff for surgery and the physicians who conducted the operation).

Negligence on the part of the defendant may be proved by circumstantial evidence alone when that evidence establishes, more probably than not, that

1.   the injury was of a kind which ordinarily does not occur in the absence of negligence,
2.   the conduct of the plaintiff or of a third person was sufficiently eliminated by the evidence as a more probable cause of the injury, and
3.   the indicated negligence was within the scope of the defendant's duty to the plaintiff.

Although the fact that an accident has occurred does not alone raise a presumption of the defendant's negligence, the doctrine of res ipsa loquitur permits the inference of negligence on the part of the defendant from the circumstances surrounding the injury.

The facts established by the plaintiff must also reasonably permit the jury to discount other possible causes and to conclude it was more likely than not that the defendant's negligence caused the injury.

The 14th Judicial District awarded damages to Mrs. Lacombe, and the hospital appealed.

Issue

Did the fact that the patient went into the hospital without sciatic nerve injury and came out with it warrant an inference of res ipsa loquitur?

Holding

The Court of Appeals of Louisiana held that the evidence warranted an inference of res ipsa loquitur.

Reason

Expert testimony established that the plaintiff was suffering from a sciatic nerve injury and that the injury was permanent. Experts on both sides agreed that sciatic nerve injury was not a known risk of the surgery. The testimony indicated that the plaintiff went into the hospital without the injury and came out with it.

The various experts expressed three theories as to the cause of the injury: (1) her position during surgery put pressure on the nerve, (2) the nerve was nicked or caught in a suture during surgery, or (3) either immediately prior to or after surgery, an injection of medication was made directly into the nerve. After reviewing the record, the court agreed with the trial court that the evidence warranted an inference that negligence on the part of the defendant caused the injury under the theory of res ipsa loquitur.

Discussion

1. Discuss the circumstances under which negligence may be proved by circumstantial evidence.
2. Describe the elements that must be established in order for a case to move forward on the basis of res ipsa loquitur.

Surgery: Improper Patient Positioning

Citation: *Wick v. Henderson*, 485 N.W.2d 645 (Iowa 1992)

Facts

The plaintiff, Ms. Wick, entered the defendant hospital for gallbladder surgery. Mr. Byrk, a nurse anesthetist employed by Medical Anesthesia

Associates (MAA), PC listed Dr. Henderson, an anesthesiologist also employed by the defendant MAA, on hospital documents as the anesthesiologist for Ms. Wick's surgery. There is no claim or showing that Dr. Henderson was personally present during the plaintiff's surgery.

Ms. Wick had no recollection of being in the operating room or the recovery room. She had pain in her left arm upon awakening. When Ms. Wick was discharged from the hospital on August 17, 1987, she was told that her arm was "stressed" during surgery. According to the plaintiff's evidence, she sustained a permanent injury to the ulnar nerve in her left upper arm.

Ms. Wick filed a malpractice action against the hospital and Dr. Henderson, seeking recovery for her injuries. The court directed a verdict for the hospital, and Ms. Wick appealed under the theory of res ipsa loquitur, claiming that testimony established that the main cause of her injury was the mechanical compression of her ulnar nerve as a result of improper positioning of her arm during surgery.

Issue

Does the doctrine of res ipsa loquitur apply in this case?

Holding

The Supreme Court of Iowa held that the res ipsa loquitur doctrine applies.

Reason

The trial court determined under the theory res ipsa loquitur (the thing speaks for itself) that the defendants' negligence can be inferred from the very nature of the accident, even without direct evidence of how any defendant acted.

The plaintiff must prove two foundational facts in order to invoke the doctrine of res ipsa loquitur. First, it must be proved that the defendants had exclusive control and management of the instrument that caused the plaintiff's injury and, second, that it was the type of injury that ordinarily would not occur if reasonable care had been used. As to control, it should be enough that the plaintiff can show an injury resulting from an external force applied while she lay unconscious in the hospital. Also, it is within the common knowledge and experience of a layperson to determine that an individual does not enter the hospital for gallbladder surgery and come out of surgery with an ulnar nerve injury to the left arm if reasonable care is given the individual.

Discussion

1. Describe three scenarios in which it would be considered common knowledge that a patient's injury was obviously caused by negligent care, so that res ipsa loquitur would apply.
2. What steps should the hospital take to prevent similar incidents?

Surgery: Injury from Leg Cast

Citation: *Graham v. Thompson*, 854 S.W.2d 797 (Mo. Ct. App. 1993)

Facts

This suit involves a claim for medical malpractice based on the doctrine of res ipsa loquitur. The trial court granted summary judgment in favor of Dr. Thompson, a plastic surgeon. Ms. Graham suffered a severe cut to the top of her right foot. She was taken to the hospital to receive an operation to repair nerve and tendon damage. Dr. Thompson performed the operation, during which the patient was unconscious. After the operation, Dr. Thompson put a plaster of Paris cast over a splint meant to immobilize the foot. The cast went almost to the top of her calf. When Ms. Graham woke up, she immediately began complaining of pain in her upper right calf in an area just under the cast. She had no problems with her calf prior to this surgery on her foot. Hospital personnel unwrapped the cast and, on Dr. Thompson's orders, washed off the surgical area with an antiseptic, then medicated the painful area (some 4 inches long and 3 inches wide), which showed blisters. The personnel applied a new splint and cast. Ms. Graham went home and, the next day, felt pain in the same spot. The blisters appeared larger, and Dr. Thompson's office personnel advised her to double her pain medication. A day or two later, she went to the doctor's office and was treated for burns, later diagnosed as third-degree burns, which created several spots of dead flesh on her calf. These burns formed the basis of her medical malpractice suit. The hospital was dismissed from the suit, leaving Dr. Thompson as the only defendant. No one seemed to know the cause of the burns.

The circuit court granted summary judgment for the plastic surgeon on the grounds that the plaintiff failed to provide expert medical testimony to support her claim and that the *res ipsa loquitur* doctrine did apply. An appeal was filed claiming the doctrine of *res ipsa loquitur* applied.

Issue

Can a layperson, as matter of common knowledge, conclude that third-degree burns were unusual and would not result if due care had been used in performing surgery?

Holding

The Missouri Court of Appeals held that a layperson, as matter of common knowledge, could conclude that injuries to the calf were so unusual and would not result if due care had been used in the operation, so as to bring the case within the *res ipsa loquitur* doctrine.

Reason

"Specifically, to invoke res ipsa loquitur, a party must show the occurrence resulting in injury ordinarily does not happen when due care is exercised by the party in control, the instrumentalities involved are under the care and management of the defendant, and the defendant possesses either superior knowledge or means of obtaining information about the cause of the occurrence." *Hasemeier v. Smith*, 361 S.W.2d 697, 799 (Mo. 1962). The plaintiff awoke from an operation with what turned out to be third-degree burns on the back of her calf. She was not negligent. She had no way of knowing whether the burns came from the operation itself or the application of the cast. What can be said is the injury was not a typical occurrence or was not the result of a necessary risk to the type of foot operation performed on her.

Laypersons, as a matter of common knowledge, could conclude the injuries were so unusual and would not result if due care had been used.

Discussion

1. What must a plaintiff show in order to move a case forward on the basis of res ipsa loquitur?
2. Why was expert testimony not necessary in this case?

Laceration of Child's Arm During Treatment

Citation: *Morris v. Children's Hosp. Med. Ctr.*, 597 N.E.2d 1110 (Ohio Ct. App. 1991)

Facts

The plaintiffs alleged in their complaint that Melissa Morris, while hospitalized at Children's Hospital Medical Center, suffered a laceration to her arm as
a result of treatment administered by the defendants and their agents that fell
below the accepted standard of care. Mrs. Morris alleged from personal observation that the laceration to her daughter's arm was caused by the jagged edges
of a plastic cup that had been split and placed on her arm to guard the intravenous site. In an affidavit, a nurse who stated her qualifications as an expert
expressed her opinion that the practice of placing a split plastic cup over an
intravenous site as a guard constituted a breach of the standard of nursing care.

Issue

Does the complaint state a claim in ordinary negligence under the doctrine of
respondeat superior, and was the registered nurse competent to give expert
testimony on liability issues?

Holding

The Court of Appeals of Ohio held that the complaint stated a claim in ordinary negligence on the theory of respondeat superior. The nurse was competent
to give expert testimony on liability issues. Melissa's injury was caused by the
negligence of the defendants and their agents. In the course of discovery, the
evidence supported an allegation of negligence on the part of the nursing staff.

Reason

Expert testimony is not essential to state a claim in ordinary negligence. Such
testimony is, however, admissible in evidence if the witness is qualified as
an expert and the expert's specialized knowledge will aid the trier of fact in
understanding the evidence. The registered nurse, by affidavit, attested to
her qualifications and her familiarity with the standards of nursing care and
expressed her opinion that the practice alleged to have caused the child's
injury was not in conformity with the accepted standards of nursing care.

Discussion

1. What are the criteria that a court utilizes to determine an individual's
   competency to testify as an expert?
2. What is the importance of competence assessments and skills checklists as they relate to this case?

Nurse's Suicide Highlights Twin Tragedies of Medical Errors

For registered nurse Kimberly Hiatt, the horror began last Sept. 14, the moment she realized she'd overdosed a fragile baby with 10 times too much medication.

Stunned, she told nearby staff at the Cardiac Intensive Care Unit at Seattle Children's Hospital what had happened. "It was in the line of, 'Oh my God, I have given too much calcium,'" recalled a fellow nurse, Michelle Asplin, in a statement to state investigators.

In Hiatt's 24-year career, all of it at Seattle Children's, dispensing 1.4 g of calcium chloride—instead of the correct dose of 140 mg—was the only serious medical mistake she'd ever made, public investigation records show.

"She was devastated, just devastated," said Lyn Hiatt, 49, of Seattle, Kim's partner and co-parent of their two children, Eli, 18, and Sydney, 16.

That mistake turned out to be the beginning of an unraveled life, contributing not only to the death of the child, 8-month-old Kaia Zautner, but also to Hiatt's firing, a state nursing commission investigation—and Hiatt's suicide on April 3 at age 50.

Hiatt's dismissal—and her death—raise larger questions about the impact of errors on providers, the so-called "second victims" of medical mistakes. That's a phrase coined a decade ago by Dr. Albert Wu, a professor of health policy and management at the Johns Hopkins Bloomberg School of Public Health.

JoNel Aleccia, Health Care on MSNBC, *June 27,2011*[3]

Drugs Misused at Nursing Homes

More than 5 years ago, the federal government warned that antipsychotic drugs often being prescribed to nursing homes residents posed serious, even deadly risks. But inappropriate use of these medications remains high, according to a recent report by *Consumer Reports Health Best Buy Drugs*.

Consumer Reports Health, The Washington Post, *May 24, 2011*

Citation: *Harrison v. Axelrod*, 599 N.Y.S.2d 96 (N.Y. App. Div. 1993)

Facts

A nurse was charged with patient neglect in that she administered the wrong dosage of the drug Haldol to a patient on seven occasions while she was employed at a nursing facility. The patient's physician had prescribed a 0.5 mg dosage of Haldol. The patient's medication record indicated that the nurse had been administering dosages of 5 mg that were being sent to the patient care unit by the pharmacy. A New York State Department of Health investigator testified that the nurse had admitted that she administered the wrong dosage and that she was aware of the nursing facility's medication administration policy, "which she breached by failing to check the dosage supplied by the pharmacy against the dosage ordered by the patient's doctor." Id. at 97. The nurse denied that she made these admissions to the investigator. The Commissioner of the Department of Health made a determination that the administration of the wrong dosage of Haldol on seven occasions constituted patient neglect. The nurse brought an Article 28 proceeding, requesting a review of the Commissioner's finding.

Issue

Was the evidence sufficient to establish that the nurse had been negligent in the administration of the drug Haldol?

Holding

The New York Supreme Court, Appellate Division, held that the evidence established that the nurse administered the wrong dosage of the prescribed drug Haldol to the nursing facility patient.

Reason

This was a breach of the nursing facility's medication administration policy and was sufficient to support the determination of patient neglect made by the Commissioner of Health.

Although the nurse had denied making the admissions to the investigator, "it is well settled that the duty of weighing the evidence and resolving conflicting testimony rests solely with the administrative agency, and that the courts may not weigh the evidence or reject the choice made by the agency . . ." Id. at 97.

Discussion

1. Prior to administering a medication, the nurse should check that she is administering the correct medication in the right dosage. What other protocol should a nurse follow in order to safely administer medication to a patient?
2. What steps can an organization take to reduce its medication error rate?
3. What culpability is there on the part of a pharmacist who delivers the wrong dosage of a medication?
4. What steps can pharmacists take to reduce an organization's medication error rate?

Negligent Administration of Medication

Citation: *Sullivan v. Sumrall by Ritchey*, 618 So.2d 1274 (Miss. 1993)

Facts

On April 26, 1988, the patient was admitted to the hospital suffering from a severe headache. Her physician ordered a CT scan for the following morning and prescribed Demerol and Dramamine to alleviate pain. Referring to the patient's medical chart, the nurse stated in her deposition that the patient had received injections of Demerol and Dramamine at 6:45 p.m. and 10:00 p.m. on April 26th. The nurse checked on the patient at 11:00 p.m. The patient's temperature and blood pressure were taken at midnight. Her blood pressure was recorded at 90/60, down from 160/80 at 8:00 p.m. At 12:25 a.m., 2 hours and 25 minutes after her last medication, the nurse administered another injection of Demerol and Dramamine because the patient was still complaining of pain. Although hospital rules require consultation with a patient's admitting physician when there is a question regarding the administration of medication, the nurse stated that she did not call the physician before administering another injection.

At 4:00 a.m., when the nurse made an hourly check of the patient, she discovered that the patient was not breathing. She issued a Code 99 (an emergency signal for a patient in acute distress). An emergency department physician responded and revived the patient. The patient was diagnosed as having suffered "respiratory arrest, with what appears to be hypoxic brain injury." Her CT scans revealed no bleeding, but other tests "revealed [a] grossly abnormal EEG with diffuse and severe slowing." Id. at 1275. The patient was transferred to a nursing facility where she apparently remained in a coma at the time of trial.

On October 21, 1988, the patient's daughter and husband filed a complaint against the hospital, alleging that the hospital had been negligent in monitoring and medicating the patient, in failing to notify a physician when her vital signs became irregular, in failing to properly assess her condition and intervene, and in failing to exercise reasonable care. Later, the complaint was amended to include the nurse.

On January 24, 1990, the defendant nurse filed a motion for summary judgment. She asserted that, as a matter of law, she was shielded from liability under the qualified immunity afforded public officials engaged in their performance of discretionary functions. The circuit court denied the motion, and the nurse appealed.

Issue

Is a nurse employed by a county hospital shielded by public official qualified immunity from a medical negligence action brought against her individually?

Holding

The Supreme Court of Mississippi held that an employee of a county hospital enjoys no qualified immunity.

Reason

There is no qualified immunity for any public hospital employees making treatment decisions. In a recent decision, the Supreme Court of Mississippi announced, "[W]e hold that common law qualified public official immunity will be restricted to its designed purpose. Accordingly, it will not be extended to decisions that involve only individual medical treatment. Those decisions will be judged on the same standards as if made by private providers." *Womble v. Singing River Hosp.*, 618 So.2d 1252, 1265 (Miss. 1993).

Discussion

1. Do you agree that the nurse should not be shielded from liability on the basis that she is a public official? Explain.
2. What assessment and reassessment issues do you see in this case?
3. Should the dramatic change in the patient's blood pressure have signaled a need to notify the attending physician of the patient's change in health status? Explain.
4. Was the nurse practicing medicine when she administered the second injection without contacting the attending physician?

Medication Overdose

Citation: *Harder v. Clinton, Inc.*, 948 P.2d 298 (Okla. 1997)

Facts

Ms. Kayser was admitted to the Heritage Care Center (nursing home) on July 14, 1992. On the evening of September 30, 1992, she was transferred to the Clinton Regional Hospital after ingesting an overdose of Tolbutamide, a diabetic medication. Then she was diagnosed as being in a hypoglycemic coma caused by the lowering of her blood sugar from ingestion of the medication. An intravenous device was inserted in the dorsum area of her right foot to treat the coma. Gangrene later developed in the same foot, and this eventually required an above-the-knee amputation.

Ms. Harder, Ms. Kayser's sister and guardian, brought a suit against the nursing home for harm caused to Ms. Kayser by an overdose of the wrong prescription administered to her while she was in the Center's care and custody. At the close of Ms. Harder's case, which followed a res ipsa loquitur pattern of proof, the trial court directed a verdict for the nursing home on Heritage's demurrer to the evidence,. The trial court ruled that Ms. Harder's evidence fell short of establishing a negligence claim because her proof failed to show all the requisite foundational elements for res ipsa loquitur.

Issue

Did the trial court err when it directed a verdict for the nursing home based on its ruling that Ms. Harder had not satisfied the requirements for a res ipsa loquitur submission?

Holding

By the evidence adduced at trial, Ms. Harder met the standards for submission of her claim based on the doctrine of res ipsa loquitur pattern of proof. The trial court's judgment on directed verdict was reversed, and the cause of action was remanded for further proceedings.

Reason

According to Ms. Harder, a directed verdict was inappropriate because she adduced reasonably supportive evidence to establish the foundation facts for application of the res ipsa loquitur pattern of proof. The nursing home counters that Ms. Harder cannot invoke the res ipsa loquitur evidentiary process because she failed to establish two foundation facts: (1) that the thing causing the injury (the Tolbutamide) was under its exclusive control and (2) that, but for the negligence in administering an overdose of the wrong medication, the harm of which plaintiff complains would not have occurred. In order to move the case forward on the basis of res ipsa loquitur application, Ms. Harder was required to show that

1. an overdose of the wrong prescription medication is not usually ingested in the course of administering prescription drugs to residents;

2. the nursing home had exclusive control and management of the instrumentality (prescription drugs) that caused the injury;
3. evidence shedding light on the harmful event is more accessible to the nursing home than to the plaintiff; and
4. the administration of the injurious overdose is the sort of occurrence which, in the ordinary course of events, would not have happened if one having control of the instrumentality exercised due care.

The foundation facts can be established by expert testimony or by demonstrating that the defendant's substandard conduct falls within the realm of common knowledge. If the showing of any foundation fact requires a degree of knowledge or skill not possessed by the average person, expert testimony must be adduced.

Foundation Fact I: The Injury Does Not Occur in the Ordinary Course of Operations

The first foundation fact requires a showing that the injury—an overdose of the wrong prescription—does not occur in the ordinary course of operations at the nursing home. Ms. Dixon, a licensed practicing nurse (and a medication clerk at the nursing home), testified that the residents' prescription drugs are stored at the nurses' station. She gave a detailed account of the method used for dispensing prescribed medication to the residents. The nursing home's residents have no access to prescription drugs except when they are administered to them by authorized personnel. When medication is to be administered, the correct dosage is removed from the storage site and placed in a cart that is pushed down the halls. The nurse (or certified medication aide) removes the medication from its container, places it in a cup, and then serves it to the resident. The cart is kept locked while the nurse or aide is administering the medication. Dr. Hays—Ms. Kayser's family physician since 1973 and medical director of the nursing home—testified that the administration of the wrong prescription drug in an amount that would cause harm is below the applicable standard of care.

The first res ipsa loquitur element is met by the evidence adduced because, under the applicable standard of care, the overdose of a wrong prescription drug would not occur in the ordinary course of operations at the defendant nursing home.

Foundation Fact II: The Nursing Home Has Exclusive Control of the Harm-Dealing Instrumentality

The second res ipsa loquitur element is satisfied by proof that the agency or instrumentality causing the injury was under the defendant's exclusive control or management at the time the negligence occurred. Exclusive control is a flexible concept that denotes no more than elimination, within reason, of all explanations for the genesis of the injurious event other than the defendant's negligence—a showing that defendant's negligence probably caused the accident. The nature and degree of control must be such that the reasonable probabilities point to the nursing home and support an inference that it was the negligent party.

The plaintiff established that (1) the offending drug was prescribed medicine, (2) the administration of prescription drugs to the residents is within the control of the defendant, and (3) at the time of the harmful event, the defendant, a nursing home resident, was at the nursing home and subject to the policies that govern there the distribution and administration of prescribed medicine. This constitutes a legally sufficient showing to satisfy the control-element requirement for the res ipsa loquitur pattern of proof.

Foundation Fact III: True Explanation for the Harm's Occurrence Is More Accessible to the Nursing Home

The third res ipsa loquitur element consists of evidence that the precise cause of the accident is more accessible to the defendant than to the plaintiff.

The nursing home is required to chart and keep in its records extensive data about each resident's health, medical history, physician orders, and overall medical treatment. Its records also contain information about the prescribed medication that is ordered, received, stored on its premises, and administered to its residents.

The evidence adduced clearly demonstrates that information about the circumstances surrounding the administration to Ms. Kayser of excessive dosage of the wrong prescription is more accessible to the nursing home than to Ms. Kayser.

Foundation Fact IV: The Defendant's Negligence

The fourth res ipsa loquitur element required Ms. Harder to present reasonably supportive evidence that an overdose of a wrong prescription would not ordinarily occur absent negligence on the part of someone who had the instrumentality in its exclusive control and management. It need not be shown that negligence is the only explanation for the injury but, merely, that it is the most probable one. This element is satisfied if, under the facts of the case, common experience indicates that the injury was more likely than not the result of the defendant's negligence.

In light of the circumstances that surround the injurious event, and disregarding the defendant's conflicting evidence, it seems reasonably clear that Ms. Kayser's ingestion of a Tolbutamide overdose would not have taken place in the absence of negligence by the nursing home's responsible staff. The record shows that Ms. Kayser had not been prescribed any diabetes medication while a resident at the nursing home and that she had never been prescribed that type of hypoglycemic drug. It is uncontradicted that Ms. Kayser was at the nursing home when she ingested the prescribed medication. There is no direct evidence that anyone else supplied to her the harm-dealing dosage or that the substance in question was kept in her room (or elsewhere within her control). Neither is there indication that any other cause contributed to the coma. According to Ms. Dixon, the nursing home is responsible for the administration of medication to its residents. As Dr. Hays testified, the administration of the wrong medication in an amount so excessive as to harm a resident would be below the applicable professional standard of care.

In sum, Ms. Harder's evidence laid before the trial court the requisite res ipsa loquitur foundation facts from which the trier may infer that the injury from an overdose of the wrong prescription was one that would not ordinarily occur in the course of controlled supervision and administration of prescribed medicine in the absence of negligence on the nursing home's part. Because nothing in the record irrefutably negates any of the critical elements for application of res ipsa loquitur, Ms. Harder clearly met her probative initiative by establishing the necessary components for invoking the rule. The responsibility for producing proof that would rebut the inferences favorable to Ms. Harder's legal position was thus shifted to the defendant.

Discussion

1. How would you have argued this case if you were the defendant nursing home?
2. What procedures would you consider implementing in order to reduce the likelihood of similar events from occurring in the future?

Wrong Prescriptions, Infant Deaths

Citation: *State Ex Rel. Stolfa v. Ely*, 875 S.W.2d 579 (Mo. Ct. App. 1994)

Facts

The plaintiffs were the parents of Amy and Ashley Stolfa, who died at birth on March 27, 1990. The plaintiffs claimed that the negligence of Kmart and its pharmacist in mistakenly filling a medication prescription caused the premature birth and the death of the two infants when Deborah, the mother, was 25-weeks pregnant.

The plaintiffs based their claim against Kmart on two separate grounds: (1) that the pharmacist was negligent in furnishing the wrong drug compound, Ritalin, instead of the ritodrine hydrochloride prescribed by the physician, and (2) that Kmart was negligent in failing to establish and maintain proper protocol and procedures to ensure that appropriate medications were dispensed to consumers.

The plaintiffs sought, by interrogatories, requests for the production of certain documents. By oral depositions, they sought to discover from Kmart information about earlier lawsuits involving allegations of professional liability, information about training of Kmart's pharmacy staff, and information relating to prior incidents involving negligence in the filling or dispensing of prescriptions in Kmart's pharmacies. The trial judge sustained Kmart's objections to such discovery.

Issue

(1) Did the discovery sought by the plaintiffs invade the attorney–client and work–product privilege? (2) Did an order compelling Kmart to respond to the subject discovery requests impose an extraordinary and unreasonable burden on Kmart?

Holding

The Court of Appeals of Missouri held that the information regarding other claims made against the Kmart pharmacy because of misfilled prescriptions was relevant and, hence, discoverable. Discovery of that information was not unreasonably oppressive and burdensome.

Reason

The plaintiffs in this case based their claim not only on the negligence of Kmart's pharmacist, for which Kmart would be liable under the doctrine of respondeat superior, but also on Kmart's personal corporate negligence, protocols, and procedures. These, according to the plaintiffs' postulation, were inadequate to prevent the kind of mischance that occurred. To prove notice to Kmart that its protocols and procedures were inadequate, it would be relevant that other claims had been made against Kmart because of misfilled prescriptions. The discovery sought by plaintiffs was a promising source of evidence that Kmart, from the claims made against it growing out of similar misfeasances by pharmacists in Kmart's employ, had actual or constructive notice of the inadequacy of its protocols and procedures.

Without the discovery of similar earlier claims against Kmart, plaintiffs would be hard put to prove notice to Kmart of the inadequacy of its protocols and procedures, if indeed they were inadequate. The necessity of the discovery for the plaintiffs outweighed the inconvenience to Kmart in supplying it.

Discussion

1. Do you agree with the court's finding? Explain your answer.
2. Can pharmacists be held individually liable for their negligent acts if their employers are held liable for the same negligent acts?

Wrongful Dispensing of Medications

Citation: *Caldwell v. Department of Prof'l Regulation*, 684 N.E.2d 913 (Ill. App. 1997)

Facts

The Illinois Department of Professional Regulation (Department) filed a 20-count complaint against the plaintiff, Dr. Caldwell. Counts XVII through XX alleged that, between 1984 and 1990, the plaintiff prescribed controlled substances to a patient, Ms. Barnes, for nontherapeutic purposes in violation of the Illinois Medical Practice Act, the Illinois Medical Practice Act of 1987, and the Illinois Controlled Substances Act. In each of these counts, the Department sought that plaintiff's medical license be suspended or revoked or that plaintiff be otherwise disciplined. The plaintiff testified on his own behalf. He stated that he first treated Ms. Barnes in 1984 and continues to treat her through the time of the hearing. Ms. Barnes has suffered from numerous ailments, including hypertension, arthritis, obesity, and a herniated disc in her back. The plaintiff treated Ms. Barnes by conducting physical examinations and prescribing medications. The Department introduced into evidence copies of at least 74 prescriptions plaintiff issued to Ms. Barnes for various painkillers and tranquilizers. The plaintiff identified each of these prescriptions, most of which authorized at least one refill.

The drugs prescribed by the plaintiff were Darvocet N-100, meprobamate, meprobamate, phenobarbital, and Tylenol 4. Darvocet and Tylenol 4 are analgesics used to relieve mild to moderate pain. Meprobamate is a tranquilizer that plaintiff testified can be used as a muscle relaxant. Phenobarbital is a sedative. All of these drugs are controlled substances and are capable of causing dependency.

The plaintiff testified that he believes his treatment of Ms. Barnes was consistent with accepted standards of medical care. The plaintiff never detected any signs that Ms. Barnes was becoming dependent on any of the medications he prescribed.

Dr. Singleton testified as an expert witness on the plaintiff's behalf. Dr. Singleton is board certified in neurology. Dr. Singleton testified that a proper course of treatment for a patient such as Ms. Barnes would include physical therapy and prescriptions for analgesics and muscle relaxants. It would not be improper to prescribe these medications again if the patient continued to experience pain. Under questioning from the hearing officer, Dr. Singleton testified that a patient who seeks numerous prescriptions for Darvocet and Tylenol 4, with refills, in the space of 2 months might be displaying signs of addiction.

Mr. Barnes stated that he contacted the plaintiff, complaining that his wife was addicted to pain pills. He asked the plaintiff to help her stop taking the pills, but the plaintiff continued to write these prescriptions. On April 12, 1990, Mr. Barnes found his wife on the bathroom floor unable to stand because she had taken too many pills. He called the paramedics, who took Ms. Barnes to St. Francis Hospital.

She remained there for 4 or 5 days. After her release from the hospital, she continued to see the plaintiff, and the plaintiff continued to prescribe the same drugs for her. Ms. Barnes was still seeing the plaintiff at the time of the hearing.

Dr. Koos testified that he was on duty at St. Francis Hospital when Ms. Barnes was admitted. He ordered tests, the results of which indicated that Ms. Barnes had suffered a drug overdose from ingesting a combination of phenobarbital, meprobamate, and Darvocet. Dr. Czarnecki, board certified in both cardiology and internal medicine testified as an expert witness for the Department. Prior to testifying, he reviewed insurance claim forms submitted by the plaintiff for the treatment of Ms. Barnes, the prescriptions plaintiff issued to Ms. Barnes, and some of plaintiff's progress notes concerning Ms. Barnes.

Dr. Czarnecki testified that the prescriptions did not conform to accepted medical standards in his opinion. He stated that the prescriptions were excessive in quantity and that many of them were inappropriate for Ms. Barnes's ailments. A treating physician should use these drugs to alleviate the patient's pain while other treatments are used to address the cause of the pain. Dr. Czarnecki testified that Darvocet and Tylenol 4 should be used very cautiously when taken with phenobarbital or meprobamate. He concluded that, in his opinion, the continued prescriptions of Darvocet, Tylenol 4, meprobamate, and phenobarbital served no therapeutic purpose.

The hearing officer found that the prescriptions were issued in a nontherapeutic manner with recklessness and disregard for the patient's well-being. He further specifically found that all of the witnesses who testified during the hearing, except plaintiff, were credible and that the Department had proved counts XVII through XX by clear and convincing evidence. As a result, he recommended that plaintiff's medical license be placed on probation for 5 years, that his controlled substances license be revoked, and that the plaintiff be fined $20,000.

The plaintiff filed an action for administrative review. The circuit court affirmed the Department Director's decision. The plaintiff filed a motion for reconsideration that the circuit court denied. Plaintiff filed a notice of appeal.

Issue

Was there ample evidence to support the Director's decision that the physician had recklessly prescribed controlled substances for nontherapeutic purposes without regard for the safety of his patient and in violation of the Medical Practice Act and the Controlled Substances Act?

Holding

There was ample evidence to support a decision that the physician had recklessly prescribed controlled substances for nontherapeutic purposes without regard for the safety of his patient and in violation of the Medical Practice Act and the Controlled Substances Act.

Reason

The prescriptions at issue in this case were written between 1984 and 1990. The Illinois Medical Practice Act was amended in 1987, and therefore, plaintiff was charged under the Act as it existed both before and after the amendment. Nonetheless, the relevant provisions are substantively the same.

The 1987 Statute

The Department may revoke, suspend, place on probationary status, or take any other disciplinary action as the Department may deem proper with regard to the license or visiting professor permit of any person issued under this Act to practice medicine, . . . upon any of the following grounds. . . .

    4. Gross negligence in practice under this Act. . . .

   17. Prescribing, selling, administering, distributing, giving, or self administering any drug classified as a controlled substance (designated product) or narcotic for other than medically accepted therapeutic purposes.

The hearing officer found the Department sustained its burden of proving by clear and convincing evidence that the plaintiff wrote prescriptions in a nontherapeutic manner in reckless disregard for Ms. Barnes's well-being. The Director adopted the hearing officer's finding and sanctioned plaintiff in a manner authorized by the Medical Practice Act.

The record in this case contains ample evidence to support the Director's decision that the plaintiff recklessly prescribed controlled substances for nontherapeutic purposes without regard for the safety of his patient and in violation of the Medical Practice Act and the Controlled Substances Act. Every witness who testified, including plaintiff and his own expert, provided such evidence. Plaintiff admitted that he issued these prescriptions. He allowed Ms. Barnes to receive narcotic painkillers, tranquilizers, and sedatives in sufficient quantity and with sufficient regularity that Ms. Barnes was almost never without these drugs for a period of 6 years. The plaintiff issued these prescriptions, most with at least one authorized refill, despite his admitted knowledge that Ms. Barnes was using the drugs too quickly.

According to Dr. Czarnecki, the plaintiff's treatment of Ms. Barnes failed to conform to accepted medical standards. Dr. Czarnecki testified that, under the circumstances, it should have been clear to the plaintiff that Ms. Barnes was developing a dependency on these drugs.

Discussion

1. Do you agree with the court's decision? Why or why not?
2. What are the implications for physicians who are attempting to control a patient's pain with the use of controlled substances?

Failure to Aggressively Treat the Patient

Citation: *Todd v. Sauls*, 647 So.2d 1366 (La. App. 1994)

Facts

Mr. Todd was admitted to Rapides General Hospital on October 3, 1988, and on October 4, 1988, Dr. Sauls performed heart bypass surgery. Postoperatively, Mr. Todd sustained a heart attack. During the following days, Mr. Todd did not ambulate well and suffered a weight loss of 19.5 pounds. The medical record indicated that Mr. Todd's sternotomy wound and the midlower left leg incision were reddened and his temperature was 99.6°.

Dr. Sauls admits he did not commonly read the nurses' notes but, instead, preferred to rely on his own observations of the patient. He indicated in his October 18 notes that there was no drainage. The nurse's notes, however, show that there was drainage at the chest tube site. Contrary to the medical records showing that Mr. Todd had a temperature of 101.2°, Dr. Sauls noted that the patient was afebrile.

On October 19, Dr. Sauls noted that Mr. Todd's wounds were improving and he did not have a fever. Nurses' notes indicated redness at the surgical wounds and a temperature of 100°. No white blood count (WBC) had been ordered. On October 20, nurses' notes again indicate wound redness and a temperature of 100.8°. No wound culture had yet been ordered. Dr. Kamil, one of Mr. Todd's treating physicians, noted that Mr. Todd's nutritional status needed to be seriously confronted and suggested that Dr. Sauls consider supplemental feeding. Despite this, no follow-up to his recommendation appears, and the record is void of any action by Dr. Sauls to obtain a nutritional consult. By October 21, Mr. Todd was transferred to the intensive care unit (ICU), because he was gravely ill with profoundly depressed ventricular function.

The nurses' notes on October 22 describe the chest tube site as draining foul smelling bloody purulence. The patient's temperature was recorded to have reached 100.6°. This is the first time that Dr. Sauls had the chest tube site cultured. The culture report from the laboratory indicated a staph infection, and Mr. Todd was started on antibiotics for treatment of the infection.

At the request of family, Mr. Todd was transferred to St. Luke's Hospital. Upon admission to St. Luke's, each of Mr. Todd's surgical wounds was infected. Dr. Leatherman, an internist and invasive cardiologist, treated Mr. Todd, and Dr. Zeluff, an infectious disease specialist, examined Mr. Todd's surgical wounds and prescribed antibiotic treatment. Despite Mr. Todd's care at St. Luke's, he died on November 2, 1988.

Issue

Did the surgeon breach his duty of care owed to the patient in failing to aggressively treat surgical wound infections, in not taking advantage of nurses' observations of infections, and in allowing the patient's body weight to steadily dwindle by failing to provide adequate nourishment to the patient following surgery?

Holding

The Court of Appeal of Louisiana held that Dr. Sauls committed medical malpractice when he breached the standard of care he owed to Mr. Todd.

Reason

Dr. Sauls's malpractice contributed to Mr. Todd's death because Mr. Todd was effectively ineligible for a heart transplant (his only chance of survival) after he'd suffered the infections and malnourishment under Dr. Sauls's substandard care. Dr. Sauls's testimony convinced the court that he failed to aggressively treat the surgical wound infections, that he chose not to take advantage of the nurses' observations of infection, and that he allowed Mr. Todd's body weight to dwindle, knowing firsthand that extreme vigilance was required because of Mr. Todd's already severely impaired heart. The awards of $4,975 for funeral expenses; $19,533.42 for medical expenses; $150,000 for Mrs. Todd; and $50,000 to each of his seven children for loss of love and affection were appropriate.

In cases where a patient has died, the plaintiff need not demonstrate "that the patient would have survived if properly treated." Rather, the plaintiff need only prove that the patient had a chance of survival and that his or her chance of survival was lost as a result of the defendant/physician's negligence. The defendant/physician's conduct "must increase the risk of a patient's harm to the extent of being a substantial factor in causing the result, but need not be the only cause." Dr. Sauls's medical malpractice exacerbated an already critical condition and deprived Mr. Todd of a chance of survival. Id. at 1379.

Dr. Leatherman stated that it was the responsibility of the surgeon and cardiologist to pay closer attention to Mr. Todd's nutritional status and to have better managed his weight. He emphasized that wounds cannot heal when a patient is malnourished. Dr. Leatherman opined that Dr. Sauls deviated from the required standard of care he owed to Mr. Todd.

Dr. Zeluff stated that impaired nutritional status depresses the body's immune system and adversely affects the body's ability to heal wounds. In response to a hypothetical fact situation based on Mr. Todd's medical records at Rapides General, Dr. Zeluff opined that Dr. Sauls further deviated from the standard of care by failing to initiate alimentation, parenterally or enterally, by at least October 20.

Dr. Pipkin, an expert cardiac surgeon, corroborated the testimony of Dr. Leatherman and Dr. Zeluff on the negative effect that malnourishment has on the healing process and the body's ability to fight infection. Dr. Pipkin stated that it was Dr. Sauls's responsibility to make certain that Mr. Todd received adequate calories and proteins. After reviewing the records of Mr. Todd, Dr. Pipkin found that there was a general wasting of Mr. Todd in the postoperative period as evidenced by his steady loss of weight. Dr. Pipkin opined that Dr. Sauls deviated from the standard of care owed Mr. Todd both with regard to wound infections and malnourishment.

Discussion

1. What liability might be imputed to the hospital if it had purchased Dr. Sauls's practice and hired him as an employee of the hospital?
2. Discuss how similar events can be prevented from occurring. Consider first why the event occurred, remembering that there may be more than one why.

Failure to Respond

Citation: *Ard v. East Jefferson Gen. Hosp.*, 636 So.2d 1042 (La. Ct. App. 1994)

Facts

On May 3, 1984, Mr. Ard, a patient, was admitted to the hospital. His admitting diagnosis was a past history of myocardial infarction, stroke, and unstable angina. On May 8, Mr. Ard subsequently underwent five-vessel coronary bypass surgery. He was transferred to the intensive care unit following his stay in the recovery room.

Mr. Ard was transferred from the intensive care unit on May 13. Two days later, Mr. Ard had respiratory failure and was transferred to the critical care unit. A bronchoscopy was performed to determine the cause of the respiratory problems.

Mr. Ard was transferred from the critical care unit on May 20. Mrs. Ard testified that the nursing staff did not respond timely to her calls for assistance from 5:30 p.m. to 6:45 p.m that day. At approximately 6:45 p.m., Mr. Ard stopped breathing, and a code was called. Mr. Ard never regained consciousness and died 2 days later from respiratory failure and cardiac arrest.

Mrs. Ard, who at the time of trial was 70 years old, testified that on the afternoon of May 20, 1984, she was with her husband. He began feeling nauseous and experiencing shortness of breath. She pressed the assistance buzzer for her husband several times and got no response. Finally, sometime in the evening, someone responded and brought him a tablet. However, his nausea worsened. He also vomited once or twice and was in terrible pain. Mrs. Ard described her husband as reeling from one side of the bed to the other. She was trying to hold him so he would not fall off the bed. As she continued to press the call button for a nurse, she noticed that Mr. Ard was having difficulty breathing. She called 10 or 12 times and was told a nurse was not there. She estimated she rang the bell for an hour and 15 minutes to an hour and a half. She told the nurse she rang that he was nauseous and vomiting and she could not hold him down. She also noted he was pale. The last time she called she noticed his eyes were rolled back. She reported he was dying and needed a nurse. Someone finally did respond and called a code.

The medical records indicated that, between 5:30 p.m. and 6:45 p.m. on May 20, 1984, there was no notation that any nurse or doctor checked on Mr. Ard. Therefore, Mrs. Ard's testimony regarding this time period was consistent with the medical records.

A wrongful death action was brought against the hospital. The district court granted judgment for Mrs. Ard and their only child. The hospital appealed.

Issue

(1) Was the testimony by the plaintiff consistent with notations in the medical record? (2) Was there sufficient evidence in the record to support the district court's conclusion that the nursing staff breached the standard of care in the community? (3) Did the negligence of the nurses lessen the patient's chance of survival? (4) Was the district court's award of general damages in the amount of $50,000 to the surviving spouse and $10,000 to the surviving only child an abuse of discretion?

Holding

The Court of Appeal of Louisiana held that the spouse's testimony that no one responded to her calls for assistance for 1 hour and 15 minutes was consistent with the medical records. There was ample evidence to support the district court's conclusion that the nursing staff breached its standard of care. There was evidence that the negligence of the nurses lessened the patient's chance of survival. Damages awarded were inadequate.

Reason

Ms. Krebs, an expert in general nursing, determined there were six breaches of the standard of care. She particularly stated that after May 15, 1984, it was obvious to the nurses from the doctors' progress notes that the patient was a high risk for aspiration. This problem was never addressed in the nurses' care plan or in the nurses' notes. It was something that should have been addressed. Id. at 1045.

On May 20, 1984, Mr. Ard's assigned nurse was Ms. Florscheim. Ms. Krebs stated that Ms. Florscheim did not do a full assessment of the patient's respiratory and lung status. There was nothing in the record indicating that she performed such an evaluation after he vomited. Ms. Krebs also testified that no nurse made a total swallowing assessment at any time. Although Ms. Florscheim testified that she checked on Mr. Ard around 6:00 p.m. on May 20, there was no documentation in the medical record.

Ms. Farris, an expert in intensive care nursing and a registered nurse, testified for the defense. She disagreed with Ms. Krebs that there was a breach of the standard of care. On cross-examination, she admitted that it would fall below the standard of care if a patient was in the type of distress described by Mrs. Ard and no nurse checked on him for an hour and 15 minutes.

Dr. Preis, a cardiologist; Dr. Iteld, a cardiologist; and Dr. Brach, a pulmonary expert, testified that, if Mr. Ard was in the type of distress described by his wife, someone should have responded.

The court concluded that there was ample evidence to support the trial judge's conclusion that the nursing staff breached the standard of care. Dr. Iteld testified that, with Mr. Ard's history and with reports of nausea, vomiting, rolling around in bed, and paleness, he would have wanted to be notified by the attending nurse had he been the treating physician. He indicated that he would have transferred Mr. Ard back to intensive care immediately, because it would have looked like he was going to have a respiratory and cardiac arrest. Possibly, had Mr. Ard been transferred to the cardiac unit, his chances of going into a code would have been averted. When asked whether this would be more probable than not, Dr. Iteld replied, "This is a very sick gentleman and already had two respiratory problems . . . I think he would have had a much better chance of survival in the intensive care unit" [emphasis added]. Id. at 1047.

There was sufficient evidence to show that the negligence of the nurses lessened Mr. Ard's chance of survival by his not being transferred to the intensive care unit prior to his being coded. In determining whether there had been an abuse of the discretion of the trial judge, we are guided by the following explanation given by the Louisiana Supreme Court in *Youn v. Maritime Overseas Corp.*, 623 So.2d 1257, 1261 (La. 1993):

---

the discretion vested in the trier of fact is "great," and even vast, so that an appellate court should rarely disturb an award of general damages. Reasonable persons frequently disagree about the measure of general damages in a particular case. It is only when the award is, in either direction, beyond that which a reasonable trier of fact could assess for the effects of the particular injury to the particular plaintiff under the particular circumstances that the appellate court should increase or decrease the award.

The court found an abuse of discretion and raised Mrs. Ard's general damages award from $50,000 to $150,000 and Ms. Bond's general damages award from $10,000 to $50,000.

Discussion

1. What should the reasonable standard of care be in responding to a call for assistance?
2. What are the nursing issues in this case?

Improper Placement of a Feeding Tube

Citation: *Minster v. Pohl*, 426 S.E.2d 204 (Ga. Ct. App. 1992)

Facts

Ms. Hattrich had been admitted to the hospital for surgery and later developed respiratory problems. It became necessary to insert a breathing tube and begin nasogastric feeding. She patient apparently pulled out the tubes, and Ms. Hines, a registered nurse, reinserted the feeding tube and asked Dr. Pohl, an emergency department physician, to view an X-ray to verify that she had properly replaced the tube. Dr. Pohl viewed the X-ray and observed that the tube was incorrectly placed in the decedent's right lung rather than in her stomach.

The tube was reinserted and Dr. Pohl made note of his findings in the patient's progress notes. A pneumothorax was later discovered in the patient's right lung, leading to her death.

Mr. Minster, executor of the estate, alleged that Ms. Hines was negligent in failing to properly restrain the patient to prevent her from extubating herself, and in improperly inserting and inadequately verifying the placement of the feeding tube. The hospital's liability was premised upon respondeat superior. Mr. Minster also alleged that although Dr. Pohl correctly noted that the feeding tube was improperly placed.

An affidavit of Dr. Fowler, proffered in opposition to the motion for summary judgment, provided evidence that a physician–patient relationship was established. Dr. Fowler was familiar with the practice of medicine in emergency departments. It was his opinion that, to a reasonable medical certainty, Dr. Pohl's entry on the patient's progress notes could be interpreted as a direction or instruction to replace the feeding tube. This action, as such, was an affirmative intervention into the patient's care. This would amount to treatment that created a limited physician–patient relationship.

The superior court denied the hospital and nurse's motions to dismiss the case and granted summary judgment to one physician. The hospital and nurse appealed.

Issue

Was there a physician–patient relationship because of Dr. Pohl's employment as an emergency department physician?

Holding

The Georgia Court of Appeals held that no physician–patient relationship existed between the patient and the physician, who viewed the patient's X-ray merely out of courtesy to the hospital staff and entered a note in the patient's records.

Reason

Although Dr. Pohl questionably took action with respect to the decedent, viewing the X-ray and making a notation on her chart, nothing in the record justified the inference that he was acting as her physician. Accordingly, the trial court properly found that no physician–patient relationship existed. In his affidavit proffered in support of the motion for summary judgment, Dr. Pohl claimed that he viewed the X-ray as a courtesy to the staff and not out of any obligation or duty.

The trial court found that creating an exception to the rule for the situation before the court would be detrimental to the healthcare delivery system, causing competent professionals who happen to be on the hospital premises but have no relationship to the patient to decline out of natural prudence to perform even minimal courtesies as a favor to hospital staff. The court of appeals found this danger to be greater than the risk suggested by the executrix of insulating such physicians from liability, particularly because applying the general rule did not leave the patient without a remedy should she prove negligence on the part of the hospital or its employees in any regard.

Discussion

1. What are the competency issues in this case?
2. What educational processes should an organization have in place for continuous competency improvement?

Multidisciplinary Approach to Patient Care and Treatment

Do patients believe that care is always well-coordinated? Are patients at times treated based on short "handwritten notes" by the prescribing physician? Are mistakes sometimes made because of illegible handwriting? Is it helpful to the radiologist if the ordering physician notes on the order sheet why a particular imaging study is required? Do nurses sometimes find it necessary to clarify medication orders? Do pharmacists find it necessary to contact the physician when there are dosing questions? Would it be helpful for the prescribing physician to discuss his patient's needs with the treating therapist? Would it be helpful if the physician reviewed the imaging studies of his or her patient with serious neck injuries prior to treatment by a therapist? Does understaffing affect the quality of care?

Jill recently visited a pain center where the medical director had integrated a pain therapist into the hospital's pain management program. After several visits to the hospital's pain management program, Jill complimented the staff as to their multidisciplinary approach to her care.

The medical director stated that the success of the hospital's pain management program was due to the multidisciplinary approach practice in the hospital. He stated that pain management is often poorly practiced because of the failure of the treating physician to become more involved in the patient's therapy. A patient's pain is often exacerbated because of a superficial treatment plan that fails to include the physician, and the failure to provide diagnostic images to the treating therapist. Both the physician and treating therapist, and most importantly the patient's care, are optimized when there is ongoing communications between caregivers. The medical director further stated that professionalism and satisfaction among caregivers improves when communications flow freely between caregivers.

Jill again complimented the staff and stated that she would not hesitate to recommend the hospital's pain management program to her family and friends.

The next time a patient is treated by a caregiver, the patient should ask, "What records have you seen? Have you discussed my treatment plan with my physician? What were my physician's specific orders? May I see them? What precautions have you been asked to follow with me? Have you seen my imaging studies; has anyone discussed them with you?"

My pledge as a patient, "I will ask myself, am I being treated in an assembly-line fashion, herded into a room like cattle without privacy in cramped corridors by a caregiver who, because of understaffing, is frantically moving from patient to patient, or am I truly getting individualized care and treatment in a style worthy of the words, 'I am receiving quality care.'"

Discussion

1. Regardless of your profession or healthcare setting, discuss how the multidisciplinary approach to patient care might be improved in your organization.
2. Consider and discuss what questions you might ask if you were the patient undergoing treatment.

Ineffective Drug Labeling Leads to Patient Injury

Citation: *Wyeth, v. Levine*, 129 S.Ct. 1187 (2009)

Facts

Phenergan is Wyeth's antihistamine used to treat nausea. The injectable form of Phenergan can be administered intramuscularly or intravenously, and it can be administered intravenously through either the "IV-push" method, whereby the drug is injected directly into a patient's vein, or the "IV-drip" method, whereby the drug is introduced into a saline solution in a hanging intravenous bag and slowly descends through a catheter inserted in a patient's vein. The drug is corrosive and causes irreversible gangrene if it enters a patient's artery.

Levine's injury resulted from an IV-push injection of Phenergan. On April 7, 2000, as on previous visits to her local clinic for treatment of a migraine headache, she received an intramuscular injection of Demerol for her headache and Phenergan for her nausea. Because the combination did not provide relief, she returned later that day and received a second injection of both drugs. This time, the physician assistant administered the drugs by the IV-push method, and Phenergan entered Levine's artery, either because the needle penetrated an artery directly or because the drug escaped from the vein into surrounding tissue where it came in contact with arterial blood. As a result, Levine developed gangrene, and doctors amputated first her right hand and then her entire forearm. In addition to her pain and suffering, Levine incurred substantial medical expenses and the loss of her livelihood as a professional musician.

After settling claims against the health center and clinician, Levine brought an action for damages against Wyeth, relying on common-law negligence and strict-liability theories. Although Phenergan's labeling warned of the danger of gangrene and amputation following inadvertent intra-arterial injection, Levine alleged that the labeling was defective because it failed to instruct clinicians to use the IV-drip method of intravenous administration instead of the higher risk IV-push method.

The jury found that petitioner Wyeth, the manufacturer of the drug, was negligent by failing to adequately provide a warning of Phenergan's risks, awarded damages to respondent Levine to compensate her for the amputation of her arm and the manufacturer appealed. The jury awarded total damages of $7,400,000, which the court reduced to account for Levine's earlier settlement with the health center and clinician. Declining to overturn the verdict, the trial court rejected Wyeth's argument that Levine's failure-to-warn claims were pre-empted by federal law because the federal Food and Drug Administration (FDA) had approved Phenergan's labeling. The Vermont Supreme Court affirmed. *Certiorari* was granted.

Issue

Does the FDA's approval provide Wyeth with a complete defense to Levine's tort claims?

Holding

The U.S. Supreme Court held that the FDA's approvals do not provide Wyeth with a complete defense to Levine's tort claims.

Reason

The trial record contains correspondence between Wyeth and the FDA discussing Phenergan's label. The FDA first approved injectable Phenergan in 1955. In 1973 and 1976, Wyeth submitted supplemental new drug applications, which the agency approved after proposing labeling changes. Wyeth submitted a third supplemental application in 1981 in response to a new

FDA rule governing drug labels. Over the next 17 years, Wyeth and the FDA intermittently corresponded about Phenergan's label. The most notable activity occurred in 1987, when the FDA suggested different warnings about the risk of arterial exposure, and in 1988, when Wyeth submitted revised labeling incorporating the proposed changes. The FDA did not respond. Instead, in 1996, it requested from Wyeth the labeling then in use and, without addressing Wyeth's 1988 submission, instructed it to retain the verbiage in current label regarding intra-arterial injection. After a few further changes to the labeling not related to intra-arterial injection, the FDA approved Wyeth's 1981 application in 1998, instructing that Phenergan's final printed label "must be identical" to the approved package insert.

Based on this regulatory history, the trial judge instructed the jury that it could consider evidence of Wyeth's compliance with FDA requirements but that such compliance did not establish that the warnings were adequate. He also instructed, without objection from Wyeth, that FDA regulations permit a drug manufacturer to change a product label to add or strengthen a warning about its product without prior FDA approval so long as it later submits the revised warning for review and approval.

On August 3, 2004, the trial court filed a comprehensive opinion denying Wyeth's motion for judgment as a matter of law. After making findings of fact based on the trial record, the court rejected Wyeth's pre-emption arguments. It determined that there was no direct conflict between FDA regulations and Levine's state-law claims because those regulations permit strengthened warnings without FDA approval on an interim basis and the record contained evidence of at least 20 reports of amputations similar to Levine's since the 1960's. The court also found that state tort liability in this case would not obstruct the FDA's work because the agency had paid no more than passing attention to the question whether to warn against IV-push administration of Phenergan. In addition, the court noted that state law serves a compensatory function distinct from federal regulation.

The Vermont Supreme Court affirmed. It held that the jury's verdict did not conflict with FDA's labeling requirements for Phenergan because Wyeth could have warned against IV-push administration without prior FDA approval, and because federal labeling requirements create a floor, not a ceiling, for state regulation.

The U.S. Supreme Court concluded that it is not impossible for Wyeth to comply with its state and federal law obligations. Accordingly, the judgment of the Vermont Supreme Court is affirmed.

Discussion

1. Discuss what is meant by "federal labeling requirements create a floor, not a ceiling, for state regulation?"
2. Discuss the moral obligations of drug companies to fully disclose drug risks.
3. Do you believe Wyeth, based on the information given, was sufficiently aggressive with the FDA to change the labeling of Phenergan? Discuss your answer.

NOTES

1. http://www.medical-dictionary.thefreedictionary.com/treatment
2. http://www.ccspublishing.com/online_medical_treatment.htm
3. http://www.msnbc.msn.com/id/43529641/ns/health-health_care/t/nurses-suicide-highlights-twin-tragedies-medical-errors/

chapter seven

Universal Protocols

The Pain of Wrong Site Surgery

When the president of the Joint Commission, the Chicago-based group that accredits the nation's hospitals, unveiled mandatory rules to prevent operations on the wrong patient or body part, he did not mince words.

"This is not quite 'Dick and Jane,' but it's pretty close," surgeon Dennis O'Leary declared in a 2004 interview about the "universal protocol" to prevent wrong site surgery. These rules require preoperative verification of important details, marking of the surgical site, and a timeout to confirm everything just before the procedure starts.

Mistakes such as amputating the wrong leg, performing the wrong operation, or removing a kidney from the wrong patient can often be prevented by what O'Leary called "very simple stuff": ensuring that an X-ray isn't flipped and that the right patient is on the table, for example. Such errors are considered so egregious and avoidable that they are classified as "never events," because they should never happen.

Sandra G. Boodman, Kaiser Health News, The Washington Post, *June 21, 2011*

A *Universal Protocol* is a guideline that has been developed and adopted by healthcare organizations to assist in preventing wrong patient, wrong procedure, and wrong site invasive procedures (e.g., surgical, cardiac catheterization). A Universal Protocol for invasive procedures is required by the Joint Commission (TJC) standards and is applicable wherever such procedures are performed. Various organizations (some accredited by TJC, others not), have adopted differing procedures in order to comply with a Universal Protocol, such as is required by the TJC.

The protocol adopted by an organization involves a verification process to ensure that the correct patient is on the procedure table, the correct procedure is scheduled to be performed, and the correct site has been identified. This process is accomplished, for example, by referencing and cross-referencing the patient's medical chart, wristband, imaging studies, and visual identification of the patient. The professional performing a procedure is expected to mark the correct bodily site with the patient's participation and, in some cases, with family participation.

Immediately prior to an invasive procedure, a final verification process, generally referred to as a "time-out," is conducted to be sure that the correct patient is undergoing the correct surgery at the correct site. To aid these goals, it is required that a verification mark be visible following the prep and draping of the patient and that the operative team members (immediately prior to surgery, with the patient on the table) unanimously agree that the correct patient is on the table, the correct procedure is scheduled to be performed, and the correct site has been identified. (If possible, the patient should take part in this final verification process.) If there is any disagreement during this process, the procedure must not advance until such disagreements are resolved. If imaging studies are to be utilized during the surgical process, verification must, again, be made that the imaging studies are being properly read to identify the correct patient, surgery, and surgical site. The cases that follow illustrate some of the failures of organizations either to implement Universal Protocol or to follow the adopted Universal Protocol.

Wrong-Sided Brain Surgery

TJC's Hospital Accreditation Standards 2011

See http://www.jointcommission.org/ to reference the Joint Commission's *Hospital Accreditation Standards 2011* (NPSG-18-NPSG-23) as they apply to the Universal Protocol and the recommended process for preventing wrong-sided surgery.

$20 Million Awarded for '04 Surgery Error—Jury Says Hospital Must Pay LR Family

Six years after a surgeon cut out the wrong part of their 15-year-old son's brain in an operation featured on the front page of the Arkansas Democrat-Gazette, Pamela and Kenny Metheny said their youngest child's healing really began Friday. That's when a Pulaski County jury awarded the family a $20 million judgment after finding that Arkansas Children's Hospital was negligent for the surgery.

"It is so apparent there's negligence that it boggles the mind we had to go through this," family attorney Grant Davis of Kansas City, Mo., told jurors in his closing arguments that capped 13 days of testimony.

John Lynch, Arkansas Democrat-Gazette, *September 25, 2010*

Medical Malpractice Cover-up Ends Up Costing Millions—Medical Negligence

Everything seemed procedurally correct. However, 4 hours into the surgery, surgeons realized they had been removing pieces from the wrong side of his brain, obvious medical negligence causing severe brain injury and associated symptoms. As soon as the surgical staff realized what they were doing, they immediately contacted the top four people connected to the hospital: the CEO, vice president, risk manager and nursing supervisor. At that time they performed a second operation on the correct side of the brain. They did not, at any time, contact Cody's parents. "All those people knew, but the family didn't know," said Grant Davis, attorney for the family.

Gary L. Lauber, Missouri Law Blog, *October 13, 2010*

Rhode Island Hospital Reprimanded for Wrong Site Surgeries

Imagine you are a patient in a hospital about to undergo surgery on your brain.

The anesthesiologist puts you out, you wake up to find out the surgeon operated on the wrong side of your head.

That is what happened Friday at the Rhode Island Hospital (RIH) to an unidentified 82-year-old patient.

Jane Akre, Injury Board, National News Desk, *12/14/2007*

42 CFR § 482.51 Condition of Participation: Surgical Services

(b) *Standard: Delivery of service.* Surgical services must be consistent with needs and resources. Policies governing surgical care must be designed to assure the achievement and maintenance of high standards of medical practice and patient care.

(2) A properly executed informed consent form for the operation must be in the patient's chart before surgery, except in emergencies.

Wrong Procedure

Citation: *Marsh v. Crawford Long Hosp.*, 44 S.E.2d 357 (Ga. App. 1994)

Facts

Ms. Marsh alleged that she requested and consented to an abdominal liposuction; however, Dr. Bostwick performed an abdominoplasty, a more invasive surgery, which left a scar across her entire abdomen. She also alleged that Dr. Bostwick and the hospital conspired to keep her from discovering their alleged mistake. The nursing assessment form, filled out upon Ms. Marsh's admission to the hospital, indicated that she was scheduled for bilateral mastectomy and liposuction. The intraoperative record indicated that the operative procedure to be performed was an abdominoplasty and a bilateral mastectomy. The intraoperative record also contained a checklist for the verification of the procedure location and acknowledgment of consent. This section of the intraoperative record was not completed.

Ms. Marsh maintains that she signed a form on which she handwrote her consent for liposuction because the consent form listed only the bilateral mastectomy procedure. No such consent form is contained in the record. The consent form contained in the record reflects that Ms. Marsh consented to a bilateral mastectomy and an abdominoplasty. She deposed that this consent form was presented to her after the surgery and that she was told to sign it by the physician's assistant.

The trial court granted the hospital's motion for summary judgment. Ms. Marsh appealed contending that the trial court erred in granting the hospital's motion for summary judgment "by determining the hospital's nurses had no duty as to Ms. Marsh and that such responsibility fell on the shoulders of Dr. Bostwick." Ms. Marsh's experts and several nurses from the hospital deposed that a patient's chart should be cross-referenced to determine that the appropriate procedure is being performed.

Ms. Marsh alleges that the hospital failed to discover the discrepancies in the documents contained in her chart with respect to the procedure to be performed. The hospital argued that the physician is in charge of the operating room and that the hospital's nursing staff is not responsible for mistakes made by the physician regarding what procedure is performed. Dr. Bostwick made the medical determination for an abdominoplasty. However, the hospital's nursing staff never discussed with Ms. Marsh or Dr. Bostwick the discrepancies in Ms. Marsh's records with regard to what procedure was to be performed.

Issue

Was there a material issue of fact as to whether the hospital's employees breached their duty of care to the patient by allegedly confusing the patient's records regarding which surgical procedure was to be performed on the patient, thus precluding summary judgment for the hospital?

Holding

The court of appeals held that there was a material issue of fact as to whether the hospital employees breached their duty of care to the patient by allegedly confusing the patient's records regarding which surgical procedure was to be performed on the patient, thus precluding summary judgment for the hospital.

Reason

The supreme court determined in *Hoffman v. Wells*, 260 Ga. 590, 397 S.E.2d 696 (1990) that "[t]here is no transfer of liability [to the physician] for the negligence of an employee in the performance of clerical or administrative tasks not requiring the exercise of medical judgment even though these tasks are related to the treatment of the patient." The trial court in the instant case, therefore, erred in determining that the hospital owed no duty to Ms. Marsh, and it is for the jury to determine whether the hospital breached its duty of reasonable care.

Discussion

1. Do you agree with the court's decision? Discuss your answer.
2. Discuss how the Joint Commission's *Universal Protocol for Preventing Wrong Site, Wrong Procedure, Wrong Person Surgery* is applicable in this case.

Wrong Site Surgery

Citation: *Bombagetti v. Amine*, 627 N.E.2d 230 (Ill. App. Ct. 1993)

Facts

The plaintiff, Mr. Bombagetti, injured his lower back after his 4-year-old daughter jumped on his back in the spring of 1982. On November 4, 1982, Mr. Bombagetti suffered severe pain and numbness in his legs and could not move his toes. He saw Dr. Amine and was diagnosed with a herniated disk at the L4-L5 space. Dr. Amine performed a laminectomy on the plaintiff on December 14, 1982.

On December 17, 1982, during a review of the plaintiff's postoperative X-rays, Dr. Amine noted that he had mistakenly removed the disk at L3-L4. The plaintiff testified that, after the surgery, his condition progressively worsened and he underwent a second surgical operation. Although the plaintiff's pain was relieved, he was unable to lift heavy objects and had limited ability to participate in recreational activities.

Six months following the surgery, in August 1983, the plaintiff noticed a snap in his back while lifting some pipe. A few days later the plaintiff awoke with his back kinked to the left. The plaintiff's expert, Dr. Lorenz, testified that removal of the healthy disk caused the space between L3-L4 to collapse and the vertebrae to shift and settle. Dr. Lorenz also testified that the plaintiff's condition is permanent. Even the defendant's expert witness testified that the removal of the healthy disk made the plaintiff more susceptible to future injuries.

The trial court directed a verdict against the defendant, based on the defendant's own admission and that of his expert, that he was negligent and that his negligence had caused at least some injury to the patient. The defendant appealed.

Issue

Was any of the plaintiff's pain and suffering proximately caused by the negligent removal of his healthy disk?

Holding

The Appellate Court of Illinois held that, based on the evidence presented at trial and the lack of any contradictory evidence, the trial court properly directed a verdict for the plaintiff.

Reason

Evidence was sufficient to support a determination that the defendant's negligence had caused the plaintiff's pain and suffering. The evidence was sufficient to establish that the pain and suffering experienced by the plaintiff was proximately caused by the defendant's removal of the plaintiff's healthy disk. "Both the plaintiff's expert and defendant's expert testified that the plaintiff's kinking episode was more probably than not caused by removal of the wrong disk . . ." Id. at 232. In addition, the "defendant admitted that the removal of the wrong disk predisposed the patient to future injury." Id. at 233. It is "well settled that a tortfeasor is liable for the injuries he causes, even though the injuries consist of the aggravation of a pre-existing condition." Id. at 233.

Discussion

1. What steps could the physician have taken to prevent this unfortunate incident?
2. What changes, if any, should be taken by the hospital in order to reduce the likelihood of such occurrences in the future?

The Pain of Wrong Site Surgery

"Health care has far too little accountability for results. . . . All the pressures are on the side of production; that's how you get paid," said Hopkins Pronovost (safety expert and medical director of the John Hopkins Center for Innovation and Quality), who adds that increased pressure to turn over operating rooms quickly has trumped patient safety, increasing the chance of error.

Sandra G. Boodman, Kaiser Health News, The Washington Post, *June 21, 2011*

Wrong Patient—Correct Procedure

Citation: *Meena v. Wilburn*, 603 So.2d 866 (Miss. 1992)

Facts

The plaintiff, a custodian, was cleaning when she bumped her right leg and injured it in 1987. The injury developed into an ulcer because of poor circulation. Due to the plaintiff's diabetic condition, the ulcer did not heal.

She visited her physician, who referred her to Dr. Maples, a vascular surgeon. Dr. Maples performed surgery. The surgery was a success and, according to Dr. Maples, the plaintiff was "doing acceptably well." Id. at 867.

Dr. Meena was at the hospital covering for one of his partners, Dr. Petro, who had asked him to remove the staples from one of his patients, 65-year-old Ms. Slaughter. Ms. Slaughter shared a semi-private room with another patient. Dr. Meena testified that he went and picked up Ms. Slaughter's chart at the nurse's desk and asked one of the nurses as to which bed she was in. Dr. Meena claimed that he was led to believe that she was in the bed next to the window. He picked up the chart and asked Ms. Greer, a nurse, to accompany him to the plaintiff's room.

Shortly thereafter, Dr. Meena received an emergency call at the nursing station. He later stated that, upon receiving the call, he asked Ms. Greer to take the staples out of Ms. Slaughter, because he had to respond to the emergency call at another hospital. Id. at 868. Ms. Greer "conceded during her testimony that, before removing staples from a patient, a nurse 'should read the chart, be familiar with the chart, look at the patient's arm band, and compare the arm band to the chart'—all of which she failed to do. Greer rationalized her failure: '[W]hen the doctor I work for is standing at the foot of a patient's bed, I would have no doubt—no reason to doubt what he tells me to do.'" Id.

Ms. Greer began to remove the plaintiff's staples. She soon realized that there was a problem. The plaintiff's "skin split wide open—revealing the scubcu, or layer of fat, under the skin." Id. Ms. Greer stopped the procedure and left the room to check the medical records maintained at the nursing station. She realized that she had removed staples from the wrong patient. At that point, she encountered Dr. Maples and explained to him what had happened. Dr. Maples immediately restapled the skin.

Following discharge, the plaintiff's health began to falter, and she developed a fever of 101°. The tissue where the staples had been removed became infected, and she was ultimately readmitted to the hospital for approximately 22 days, during which time she underwent more surgery and received intensive care for the infection. The plaintiff testified that she continued to experience pain upon being discharged from the hospital in May 1988. Her condition gradually improved and, presumably, she had recovered completely with the exception of some scarring and skin "indention."

In June 1988, a complaint was filed against Dr. Meena and Ms. Greer. After 4 days of trial, the jury returned a verdict against Dr. Meena and assessed damages in the amount of $125,000. The jury declined to hold the nurse liable for the plaintiff's injuries. Dr. Meena filed motions for a judgment notwithstanding the verdict, new trial, or remittitur—all of which the judge denied. Dr. Meena appealed in November 1990.

Issue

Was the jury's exoneration of Nurse Greer grounds for a new trial on the issue of physician's liability?

Holding

The Supreme Court of Mississippi held that the jury's exoneration of Ms. Greer was not grounds for a new trial on the issue of physician's liability.

Reason

Dr. Meena contends that the supreme court should reverse and remand the case for a new trial because "the jury was bound to return a verdict against both defendants, inasmuch as the defendants [were sued] as joint tortfeasors." Id. at 71. The plaintiff argued that the supreme court has often held that it would not reverse a case simply because one joint tortfeasor was deemed liable and the other was exonerated.

The supreme court rejected Dr. Meena's contention that the jury improperly returned a verdict against him but not the nurse.

Discussion

1. Do you agree with the court's decision? Explain.
2. Should liability have been apportioned between the nurse and physician?
3. What are the issues in this case that are applicable to all healthcare providers?

chapter *eight*

Discharge Planning and Follow-Up Care

When Discharge Fails

Follow-up is critical to ensure patients comply with post-hospital regimen.

A significant percentage of patients do not remember or understand the instructions they receive before leaving the hospital, according to a study in this month's *Journal of Hospital Medicine.*

"Anyone who's taken care of patients or put together a discharge plan only to have things not work out knows how frustrating that can be," says lead author Jonathan Flacker, MD (Assistant Professor of Medicine, Division of Geriatric Medicine and Gerontology, Emory University School of Medicine, Atlanta).

Norra MacReady, The Hospitalist, *October 2007*

Following the assessment, diagnostic testing, diagnosing, treatment, and in-hospital recovery process, the patient should be provided with discharge planning instructions for follow-up care after discharge from the hospital. These instructions should be in writing and signed by the patient to ensure that the patient understands the importance of follow-up care with their physician. The instruction sheet should provide a phone number for the patient care unit where the patient received in-hospital care so that he or she can call the hospital for clarification of any instructions that may be confusing.

It is also important that the patient understands the healthcare provider's accompanying spoken instructions before or after discharge. This can be done in a tactful way by asking the patient to repeat the instructions aloud. And, in some instances, a person other than the patient might need to accept and understand the follow-up instructions (e.g., a patient advocate, a family member, a nursing or rehab center nurse, or even a friend who can bridge a language barrier), but all of the foregoing provisions for wise follow-up care apply to these instances as well.

Discharge from a hospital is a process not an isolated event. It should involve the development and implementation of a plan to facilitate the transfer of an individual from a hospital to an appropriate setting. The individuals concerned and their caregiver(s) should be involved at all stages and kept fully informed by regular reviews and updates of the care plan.

Planning for hospital discharge is part of an ongoing process that should start prior to admission for planned admissions, and as soon as possible for all other admissions. This involves building on, or adding to, any assessments undertaken prior to admission.

Effective and timely discharge requires the availability of alternative and appropriate care options to ensure that any rehabilitation, recuperation, and continuing health and social care needs are identified and met.[1]

Title 42 of the Public Health Law, Chapter IV Centers for Medicare and Medicaid Services, Department of Health and Human Services under Part 482 Conditions of Participation for Hospitals requires that hospitals have a discharge planning and follow-up care process in place.

---

42 CFR § 482.43 Condition of Participation: Discharge Planning

The hospital must have in effect a discharge planning process that applies to all patients. The hospital's policies and procedures must be specified in writing.

(a) *Standard: Identification of patients in need of discharge planning.* The hospital must identify at an early stage of hospitalization all patients who are likely to suffer adverse health consequences upon discharge if there is no adequate discharge planning.

(b) *Standard: Discharge planning evaluation.* (1) The hospital must provide a discharge planning evaluation to the patients identified in paragraph (a) of this section, and to other patients upon the patient's request, the request of a person acting on the patient's behalf, or the request of the physician.

2.(B)(vii) Discharge summary with outcome of hospitalization, disposition of case, and provisions for follow-up care.

See Appendix A "U.S. Code of Federal Regulations" for further details regarding the conditions of participation for discharge planning.

The Joint Commission has in its standards a requirement that the hospital has in place a process that addresses each patient's need for continuing care, treatment, and services after discharge or transfer.

Hospital Accreditation Standards PC.04.01.01–PC.04.02.01

As noted in the cases presented next, legal problems associated with patient discharges include the fact that they often occur too soon, are delayed, are poorly managed from the patient and caregiver perspective, and/or result in the patient being transferred to an unsafe environment.[2]

The causes of the difficulties with discharge planning and resulting lawsuits can often be attributed to

- internal hospital factors (e.g., the timing of . . . rounds, the wait for diagnostic test results, the delay in referring for a home assessment and of this taking place, the organization and management of medication, and the availability of transport);
- coordination issues (e.g., the communication and organization of different health, social care, and other community-based services);
- capacity and resource issues (e.g., the limited availability of transitional and rehabilitation places, placement difficulties associated with care homes, and availability of a home care provider); and
- patient/caregiver involvement/choice (e.g., the lack of engagement with patients and caregiver in decisions about their care and the limited availability of choice of care options, the lack of involvement by independent sector providers in operational and strategic planning issues).[3]

LASIK Surgery and Follow-Up Treatment

Citation: *Wallace v. McGlothan*, 606 F. 3d 410 (Ct. of App., 7th Cir., 2010)

Facts

Tracey decided to undergo surgery so that she would no longer need to wear glasses or contact lenses, and she hired Dr. McGlothan to perform the procedure. On the patient history form that Tracey completed for Dr. McGlothan, she stated that she had trouble reading fine print and driving at night and in bright sunshine. On April 25, 2002, Dr. McGlothan performed LASIK surgery on Tracey's eyes to improve her vision. LASIK can correct a person's vision by changing the shape of the cornea.

Dr. McGlothan started with Tracey's right eye. After he cut the flap, he noticed a "buttonhole flap," a LASIK complication that occurs when the mechanical blade cuts the corneal flap too thin in one or more areas. Dr. McGlothan informed Tracey of the problem, checked his equipment, and replaced the blade. He then proceeded to the left eye. After he made the cut, he again noticed that a buttonhole flap complication had developed. He then stopped the surgery, replaced the flaps, put bandage contact lenses in Tracey's eyes, and sent her home.

Tracey returned to Dr. McGlothan's office for follow-up on April 26 and 29. During that time, Tracey stayed at home with the lights dimmed, shades drawn, and, occasionally, sunglasses on. Her eyes were very sensitive to light, and she described that they felt like they had sand thrown in them.

On April 29, after her visit with Dr. McGlothan, Tracey went to see another physician, Dr. Conner, O.D., an optometrist. Before meeting Dr. Conner, Tracey filled out a patient history form stating that she had been "bothered by glare or reflection, particularly when driving at night." Dr. Conner examined Tracey and saw "aberrations" in her corneas that were affecting her vision. He recommended that she see Dr. Price, M.D., an ophthalmologist and cornea specialist, whom Tracey visited the following day.

Dr. Price also examined Tracey's corneas and saw the complications caused by the surgery. He determined that her left eye was worse than her right, and the next day, Dr. Price performed a noninvasive, corrective procedure on Tracey's left eye.

Tracey continued to see Drs. Conner and Price regularly for some time. Both doctors saw improvement in Tracey's corneas and vision, but they also observed lingering problems. Tracey continually complained of defects in her vision, such as ghosting (a form of double vision), shadowing, and halos and glare around lights. By mid-2003, scarring had developed on Tracey's left cornea, so Dr. Price performed a corrective laser procedure to remove some of the scarring. After the treatment, he again observed improvement.

In 2002, the Wallaces filed a complaint with the Indiana Department of Insurance and appeared before a Medical Review Panel, pursuant to the Indiana Medical Malpractice Act. The Panel concluded that Dr. McGlothan did not act negligently when operating on Tracey's right eye but was negligent in operating on her left eye. In the Panel's view, Dr. McGlothan should not have proceeded to perform surgery on Tracey's left eye after the buttonhole flap complication arose on the right eye.

Tracey and Eric Wallace brought a suit against Dr. McGlothan for medical malpractice. At trial, the Wallaces argued that the LASIK complication injured Tracey's left eye and permanently impaired her vision. The jury heard testimony from several doctors, including Drs. Conner and Price.

After a trial on causation and damages, the jury returned a verdict for the Wallaces and awarded nearly $700,000 in damages. On appeal, Dr. McGlothan challenged the sufficiency of the evidence.

Issue

Was the evidence sufficient for the jury to return a verdict for the Wallaces?

Holding

The Court of Appeals affirmed the trial court's judgment, finding that there was sufficient evidence to return a verdict for the Wallaces.

Reason

Dr. McGlothan appealed; not disputing that he acted negligently in operating on Tracey's left eye, but argued that the evidence was insufficient for the jury to conclude his negligence was the proximate cause of a permanent injury.

To prove proximate cause, the plaintiff was required to show a reasonable connection between a defendant's conduct and the damages that the plaintiff has suffered. Dr. McGlothan argued that Indiana law requires expert testimony to prove causation in this case. In Indiana, expert testimony is usually required in medical malpractice cases involving issues of permanence and pre-existing injury. When the issue of cause is not within the understanding of a lay-person, testimony of an expert witness on the issue is necessary. To prove proximate cause, the plaintiff was required to show a reasonable connection between a defendant's conduct and the damages that the plaintiff suffered.

Dr. Conner stated that he could not foresee any further improvement in Tracey's vision, particularly in dim light or driving situations.

The jury also heard testimony from Dr. Price, via deposition transcript. Dr. Price explained that the best time to repair irregularities in a corneal flap is at the time of surgery, because the flap is easier to smooth out. Dr. Price recommended the "flap lift" procedure. On May 1, he performed this procedure on the left eye and discovered the cornea's condition was worse than he anticipated. He described it as one of the worst things he had ever seen.

On cross-examination, Dr. McGlothan's counsel asked Tracey about the patient history form she filled out in Dr. Conner's office. He asked whether her response on the form pertained to conditions that pre-existed the LASIK surgery, and she testified that she always had problems with it, and it's just been aggravated since the surgery.

The testimony of Drs. Price, Conner, and John was more than sufficient for the jury to find a permanent injury.

This expert testimony allowed the jury to conclude that the damage to Tracey's left cornea from the LASIK surgery never fully healed, and would never fully heal. Accordingly, the evidence was sufficient to show a permanent injury caused by Dr. McGlothan's negligence.

The evidence was sufficient to show that Dr. McGlothan's negligence was the proximate cause of the Wallaces' injuries, and Dr. McGlothan has not shown any perjury or discovery violations by the Wallaces that would warrant reversal.

Discussion

1. Do you agree with the court's decision? Explain.
2. In what way did Dr. McGlothan fail to provide the patient with adequate follow-up care?

Failure to Conduct Proper Discharge Planning

Citation: *Shields v. McLachlan*, 764 N.W.2d 239 (Mich. 2009)

Facts

Mr. Shields/patient/plaintiff was admitted to the hospital following a motorcycle accident in which he had sustained burns. He later developed osteomyelitis of his great left toe. At the time of admission, Shields reportedly suffered many medical conditions. Defendant Dr. McLachlan, an internist, was assigned to provide Shield's medical care. During his admission, Shields underwent an amputation of his left great toe. Following surgery, he remained at the hospital to recuperate and later discharged to his home, where he lived alone. Three days after his discharge, he fell and incurred a hip fracture that required an open reduction of the hip and subsequent inpatient care.

Shields filed a lawsuit claiming that the defendants failed to conduct proper discharge planning, which led to his fall and injury.

In support of his allegations, Shields forwarded a *Notice of Intent* (NOI) to sue the Hospital and filed a complaint with an *Affidavit of Merit* (AOM) to show that he had valid reasons to sue. The AOM, signed by a physician in the practice of internal medicine, provided that "the required standard of care for a medical doctor specializing in internal medicine and applicable hospital staff required careful discharge planning . . . and significant input by

McLachlan as well as the ancillary support staff." The AOM repeatedly referenced Dr. McLachlan and "ancillary support staff" of the hospital as failing to adequately address or evaluate his discharge planning needs, and the negligence of "the social services and therapy departments" in their assessment of his home environment and anticipation of problems.

The Hospital filed a motion for summary disposition asking the judge to make a ruling, without trial, asserting the NOI submitted by Shields was defective because it failed to identify any licensed medical professionals employed by the hospital that allegedly committed the malpractice claimed. The hospital further contended that the AOM was ineffective because it was signed only by a medical doctor and not by individuals licensed in the same areas of practice. Shields alleged that employees failed to follow the standard of care required. The trial court denied the hospital's motion for summary disposition, finding that the NOI and AOM complied with the relevant statutory provisions. The trial court also denied the hospital's subsequent motion for reconsideration, and the hospital appealed.

Issue

(1) Did the NOI identify the standard of care applicable to the Hospital? (2) Did the NOI adequately articulate how the alleged breach was the proximate cause of Shields's injuries? (3) Was the AOM signed by the physician adequate to show "ancillary support staff" breached the applicable standard of care?

Holding

The NOI clearly delineates the factual basis for Shields' claim. The AOM was sufficient to preclude the grant of summary disposition. The Court emphasized that, as presented, the existing claim is extremely narrow in scope, thus Shields was precluded (prevented), with the exception of Dr. McLachlan, from attempting to establish the vicarious liability of the hospital based on the negligence of any additional individuals or employees due to the failure of Shields to submit AOMs for other professions or disciplines.

Reason

The NOI delineated the factual basis for Shields' claim describing his health, reason for admission, medical procedures performed, his subsequent condition, and injuries incurred after discharge. The applicable standard of care was described in the NOI as necessitating "careful discharge planning" and "input" into such planning by his treating physicians and "ancillary support staff." The NOI alleged, the standard of care required that attention be paid to Shields's home physical environment prior to discharge. Implied in the NOI are statements indicating that the hospital and its staff were required to investigate Shields's home environment and needs prior discharge to determine the adequacy of the plan. This is sufficient to meet the requirements of MCL 600.2912b(4)(b) to identify the applicable standard of care. The NOI adequately addressed MCL 600.2912b(4)(c) in explaining how the applicable standard of care was breached, identifying the failure of staff to participate in discharge planning, the failure to devise a discharge plan that took into consideration Shields's needs and health concerns, and the absence of any investigation to evaluate his living environment or determine the deficiencies in that environment that could hinder Shields's recovery. The NOI also enumerates, pursuant to MCL 600.2912b(4)(d) the actions that should have been taken to achieve compliance with the standard of care as including (1) greater involvement by the physicians in discharge planning, (2) the identification and "voicing" of concerns or "objections" by staff with the discharge, (3) consideration of alternative settings for Shields's discharge, and impliedly, (4) the actual investigation of his home environment to determine its suitability and the availability of support to Shields following discharge.

The hospital did not dispute or challenge the content of the AOM; merely that it was insufficient by itself to impose liability on the hospital based on the alleged malpractice of nonphysician staff.

While the Court did not address the substantive merits of Shields's complaint, the Court found that the AOM was sufficient to preclude the grant of summary disposition at that stage of the proceedings and to permit the matter to proceed on a theory of vicarious liability against the hospital based solely on the alleged relationship between it and Dr. McLachlan. As such, the Court emphasize that, as presented, the existing claim is extremely narrow in scope and Shields is precluded from attempting to establish the vicarious liability of the hospital based on the negligence of any additional individuals or employees due to the failure to submit AOMs for other professions or disciplines.

Discussion

1. Discuss what steps a hospital should take to ensure that discharge planning is effective.
2. Discuss the importance of an interdisciplinary approach to discharge planning.

ED Discharge of Patient Considered Appropriate

Citation: *Holcomb v. Humana Med. Corp.*, 831 F. Supp. 829 (M.D. Ala. 1993)

Facts

The administratrix of the estate of a deceased patient, Mrs. Smith, sued the hospital, alleging a violation of the Emergency Medical Treatment and Active Labor Act (EMTALA). Mrs. Smith had entered the emergency department on May 4, 1990, a week after giving birth, with a complaint of a fever, aching, sore throat, and coughing. A physician's assistant and a physician examined Mrs. Smith. The examination revealed that Mrs. Smith had a temperature of 104.3°, a pulse of 146, respirations of 32, and a blood pressure of 112/64. Diagnostic tests ordered included a white blood cell count, urine analysis, and chest X-ray. After reviewing the results of Mrs. Smith's complaints and medical history, physical examination, and test results, the physician diagnosed the patient as having a viral infection. The physician ordered Tylenol and intravenous (IV) fluids as treatment. Mrs. Smith was maintained in the emergency department overnight. The physician conducted a second physical examination during the night. By morning, Mrs. Smith's vital signs had returned to normal. She was discharged with instructions for bed rest, fluids, and a request that she return to the hospital if her condition worsened. After returning home, Mrs. Smith reported that she was feeling better but then took a turn for the worse and was admitted to Jackson Hospital on May 6, 1990. She was diagnosed with endometritis, and she subsequently died on May 9, 1990.

Issue

Was the patient inappropriately discharged from the emergency department under the provisions of EMTALA?

Holding

The United States District Court for the Middle District of Alabama held that there was no violation of EMTALA.

Reason

The patient was appropriately examined and screened. The care rendered was standard for any patient based on the complaints given. In addition, the administratrix of Smith's estate failed to demonstrate that an emergency condition existed at the time the patient was discharged.

Discussion

1. What, if any, measures could have been routinely followed to reduce the likelihood of such occurrences in the future?
2. Generally speaking, describe how pressure from third-party payers, concerned with reducing the length of stay, could contribute to occurrences such as this.

ED Discharge and Transfer: Patient Not Stabilized First

Citation: *Huckaby v. East Ala. Med. Ctr.*, 830 F. Supp. 1399 (M.D. Ala. 1993)

Facts

The plaintiff brought an action against the hospital alleging that the deceased patient, Mrs. Wynn, was transferred from the hospital's emergency department before her condition was stabilized. Mrs. Wynn went to the hospital on September 19, 1990, suffering from a stroke. The complaint alleged that Mrs. Wynn's condition was critical and materially deteriorating. Dr. Wheat, the attending emergency department physician, informed Mrs. Wynn's family that she needed the services of a neurosurgeon but that the hospital "had problems in the past with getting neurosurgeons to accept patients from us." Id. at 1401. Upon the recommendation of Dr. Wheat, Mrs. Wynn was transferred to another hospital where she expired soon after arrival. The plaintiff alleged that Dr. Wheat did not inform the family regarding the risks of transfer and that the transfer of Mrs. Wynn in an unstable condition was the proximate cause of her death.

Issue

Did the plaintiff have a cause of action under EMTALA?

Holding

The United States District Court for the Middle District of Alabama held that the plaintiff stated a cause of action under EMTALA for which monetary relief could be granted.

Reason

In order for the plaintiff to overcome the defendant's motion to dismiss the case, the plaintiff had to demonstrate that, under EMTALA, Mrs. Wynn (1) went to the defendant's emergency department, (2) was diagnosed with an emergency medical condition, (3) was not provided with adequate screening, and (4) was discharged and transferred to another hospital before her emergency condition was stabilized. The plaintiff met this standard.

Discussion

1. Describe how the court decisions in the preceding EMTALA cases differ.
2. How might the comments of Dr. Wheat, the emergency department physician, affect the final outcome of this case?

Follow-Up Care by Telephone is Risky Business

Citation: *Stilloe v. Contini*, 599 N.Y.S.2d 194 (N.Y. App. Div. 1993)

Facts

The plaintiff suffered from a chronic skin condition for which he consulted the defendant, an internist. The defendant prescribed the steroid prednisone. The plaintiff sued for negligence, alleging that the defendant failed to properly monitor his dosage, as well as his condition. Further, the plaintiff complained that the defendant did not advise him of the risks or dangers associated with the medication. One of the recognized dangers was glaucoma, which the plaintiff contracted, causing him to become blind.

On October 15, 1982, the defendant began prescribing prednisone in 10-mg strength every other day for a month at a time. After receiving instructions to return in a year, the plaintiff saw the defendant on March 11, 1983, and January 17, 1984. Then, over the 5 years that followed, the defendant prescribed prednisone without actually seeing the plaintiff. The dosages increased beyond the prescriptions of 1982. The plaintiff sued within 18 months of the last prescription. The New York Supreme Court dismissed the complaint as being time-barred, and the plaintiff appealed claiming that renewal of a prescription by telephone constitutes continuous treatment.

Issue

When did the statute of limitations period for the suit begin to run?

Holding

The New York Supreme Court, Appellate Division, held that the statute of limitations period for the suit began to run on the date the prescription was last renewed by the physician over the telephone, rather than the earlier date when the physician last saw the patient.

Reason

Pursuant to the doctrine of continuous treatment, the time in which to bring a malpractice action is stayed when the course of treatment, including wrongful acts, has run continuously, and is related to the same original condition or complaint. The defendant admitted that the plaintiff was his patient for the time period, and he elected to treat plaintiff and prescribe medication without insisting on seeing the plaintiff-patient. The court held that there was a continuous relationship and treatment took place on every date that a prescription was renewed.

Discussion

1. Under what circumstances would continuous treatment not have applied?
2. What is the importance of patient education as it relates to medications?
3. What issues do you see as to the physician's assessment of the patient's medication needs?

Abortions and Substandard Aftercare

Citation: *Nehorayoff v. Fernandez*, 594 N.Y.S.2d 863 (N.Y. App. Div. 1993)

Facts

There were allegations that an obstetrician-gynecologist negligently and incompetently performed abortions on patients. The New York State Board of Professional Misconduct charged the physician with gross negligence on more than one occasion and with failure to maintain adequate records.

Evidence adduced at a 9-day hearing disclosed that the physician had performed several incomplete abortions that, coupled with substandard monitoring and "aftercare," resulted in two extensive emergency surgeries—one that resulted in a total abdominal hysterectomy and one that resulted in death. Expert testimony confirmed that the physician's records were sketchy at best and that he continually failed to follow established protocols (e.g., performing procedures in his office that should have been performed in the hospital because of their high risk factors).

Pursuant to Public Health Law, and upon notification of the charges, the physician's license to practice medicine was suspended for 3 years, 2 years of which were to be stayed if the physician entered into a qualified residency program. The Director of Public Health, acting on behalf of the Commissioner of Health, urged that the physician's license be revoked. A review committee of the New York State Board of Regents recommended a 3-year stayed suspension. The Board of Regents accepted the modified findings and, based on a "more serious view of the misconduct committed" (Id. at 864), revoked the petitioner's license to practice medicine. The physician commenced proceedings for review of the determination.

Issue

Did the physician's negligence in performing abortions and his failure to maintain adequate records justify revocation of his license to practice medicine?

Holding

The New York Supreme Court, Appellate Division, held that the physician's negligence in performing abortions and his failure to maintain adequate records justified revocation of his license to practice medicine.

Reason

Because of the serious and repeated nature of the physician's negligence and life-threatening consequences, the penalty imposed was not irrational or disproportionate to the offense "or to the harm or risk of harm . . . to the public." Id. at 865. The physician's petition was dismissed.

Discussion

1. What steps should a healthcare facility take in order to reduce the risks of harm to patients by incompetent healthcare professionals?
2. Describe a mechanism or process for handling questionable conduct.
3. What role should legal counsel play in the disciplinary process?
4. What is the value of obtaining counsel from an attorney who specializes in healthcare law?
5. Why can a decision not to take action be more costly than a decision to take action?

6. What is the potential liability of the administration, governing body, medical staff leadership, and other healthcare professionals who have the responsibility to act but fail to do so?
7. Is a hospital generally liable for the negligent act of a private independent practitioner that occurs in the practitioner's office? Explain.
8. Describe a scenario in which a hospital might be liable for the negligent act of a physician when the act occurred in an office practice.

Premature Discharge

Citation: *Somoza v. St. Vincent's Hosp.*, 192 A.D.2d 429, 596 N.Y.S.2d 789 (N.Y. App. Div. 1993)

Facts

The plaintiff was admitted to the hospital on December 12, 1982, in the 29th week of her pregnancy under the care of her private attending physician, Dr. Svesko. She presented herself to the hospital with complaints of severe abdominal pain. Upon admission to the hospital, the plaintiff was examined by hospital resident physician Dr. Gutwein who independently formed the impression that the plaintiff might be suffering from left pyelonephritis, premature labor, or polyhydramnios, according to the notations she made on the plaintiff's chart. Dr. Gutwein recorded a written plan and orders requiring that the plaintiff be hooked up to a fetal monitor. The plaintiff was also to undergo a number of diagnostic tests, including a renal pelvic sonogram. The results of the sonogram were abnormal, and the radiologist recommended a follow-up sonogram. Later on the same day, Dr. Svesko, the patient's physician conducted a second internal examination revealing that the cervix had become "very high" and "short." Despite the abnormal findings on the physical examinations and abnormal sonogram, Dr. Svesko decided to release the plaintiff from the hospital the next day because her pain had subsided. He orally conveyed this order to Dr. Gutwein before her rounds on December 15. According to Dr. Gutwein, she did not formulate an opinion as to the correctness of the decision to discharge because "[i]t wasn't my place to say one way or the other." Instead, on her early morning rounds, Dr. Gutwein simply signed an order discharging the plaintiff from the hospital pursuant to Dr. Svesko's instruction. Four days later, the plaintiff returned to the hospital suffering severe pain and, soon thereafter, delivered twin girls. The twins were diagnosed as suffering from cerebral palsy resulting from their premature birth. The plaintiff brought a medical malpractice action against the hospital and Dr. Svesko arising out of the premature birth of the twins.

The N.Y. Supreme Court, Appellate Division, denied the defendants' motion for summary judgment, and the defendants appealed.

Issue

Were there material issues of fact as to whether the mother's symptoms exhibited during her physical assessment contraindicated, by normal practice, her release from the hospital and ordinary prudence required further inquiry into the correctness of the discharge by the resident physician, Dr. Gutwein?

Holding

The Appellate Division of the New York Supreme Court held that there were sufficient material questions of fact as to whether the mother's symptoms exhibited during her physical assessments contraindicated her release from the hospital and that ordinary prudence required further inquiry by the resident physician, Dr. Gutwein.

Reason

The plaintiffs presented an affidavit by expert witness Dr. Sherman, who stated "the failure of the hospital staff to discharge without another physical examination, in my opinion, with a reasonable degree of medical certainty, is a departure from good and accepted medical practice. The resident clearly had an obligation to examine even a private patient in the face of a changing cervix and not just to discharge her pursuant to some attending physician's order." Id. at 791. It is well established that "[i]n the absence of an employment relationship, a hospital cannot be held legally responsible for the actions of a private physician attending his private patient so long as the hospital staff properly carries out the physician's orders" (*Hicks v. Ronald Fraser Clinic*, 169 A.D.2d 558, 559; 565 N.Y.S.2d 484). However, even when the action at issue has been ordered by a private physician, a hospital whose staff carries out that order may nevertheless be held responsible where the hospital staff knows, or should know, that a physician's orders are so clearly contraindicated by normal practice that ordinary prudence requires inquiry into the correctness of the orders. In this case, the plaintiff's release from the hospital was so clearly contraindicated by normal practice that ordinary prudence required further inquiry by Dr. Gutwein into the correctness of the discharge order.

Discussion

1. What further steps could the resident have taken to prevent the premature discharge of the patient?
2. What options do nurses have available to them when they are concerned about the premature discharge of a patient?
3. What process changes are needed in order to help prevent similar instances from occurring in the future?

Inappropriate Discharge Arrangements

Citation: *J.B. v. Sacred Heart Hosp. of Pensacola*, 635 So.2d 945 (Fla. 1994)

Facts

J.B., his wife, and their three minor children filed suit in Florida District Court against a hospital based on the following facts:

---

1. V. That on [or] about April 17, 1989, Sacred Heart hospital was requested by medical staff to arrange transportation for L.B., a diagnosed AIDS patient, to another treatment facility in Alabama.
2. VI. That the social services for the hospital were unable to arrange ambulance transport and, so, took it upon themselves to contact L.B.'s brother in Mississippi, namely J.B., requesting that he come to the hospital and provide the transportation.
3. VII. J.B., having visited L.B. at the hospital when he was first admitted, was under the impression that his brother's diagnosis was Lyme disease. He had not been notified that there was a change in diagnosis after his visit.
4. VIII. The patient, L.B., was released from the hospital with excessive fever and a heparin lock in his arm to the plaintiff, J.B., a layman providing a service without the benefit of training in the field of medical treatment and transport . . . .
5. X. The complainant could not provide adequate care for the transferee in an emergency situation, as he was the operator of the vehicle.
6. XI. That during the trip, L.B. began to thrash about and accidentally dislodged the dressing to his heparin lock, causing J.B. to reach over while driving in an attempt to prevent the lock from coming out of L.B.'s arm. In doing so, J.B. came in contact with fluid around the lock site. J.B.'s hand had multiple nicks and cuts due to a recent fishing trip. Id. at 947.

The complaint alleged that the hospital was negligent in arranging for J.B. to transport L.B. in that it knew of L.B.'s condition, the level of care that would be required in transporting him, and the risk involved. J.B.

alleged that, because he contracted the AIDS virus, his wife was exposed to it through him and his children have suffered a loss of relationship with him. The Florida District Court ruled that J.B.'s complaint stated a claim for medical malpractice and was thus subject to the presuit notice and screening procedures set out in Chapter 766, Florida Statutes (1989). Because J.B. did not follow those procedures, the court dismissed the complaint. On appeal, the Florida Circuit Court declined to rule on J.B.'s claim, concluding that the issues are appropriate for resolution by the Supreme Court of Florida.

Issue

Was this a claim for medical malpractice for purposes of the 2-year statute of limitations or pre-suit notice and screening requirements?

Holding

The Supreme Court of Florida answered that the claim was not a claim for medical malpractice for purposes of the 2-year statute of limitations or presuit notice and screening requirements.

Reason

Chapter 95, Florida Statutes (1989), sets a 2-year limitation period for medical malpractice actions. J.B.'s injury arose solely through the hospital's use of him as a transporter. Accordingly, this suit is not a medical malpractice action, and the 2-year statute of limitations is inapplicable. According to the allegations in J.B.'s complaint, the hospital was negligent in using J.B. as a transporter. The complaint does not allege that the hospital was negligent in any way in the rendering of, or the failure to render, medical care or services to J.B. Accordingly, the complaint does not state a medical malpractice claim for Chapter 766 purposes, and the notice and presuit screening requirements are inapplicable.

Discussion

1. Why was the claim made by the plaintiff not an action in malpractice?
2. What precautions should the hospital have taken to help prevent the patient's brother from contracting the virus?
3. What is the importance of patient-family education as it relates to this case?
4. What are the confidentiality issues in cases of this nature?
5. Were the transfer arrangements for the patient appropriate?

Need for Clear Discharge Instructions

Citation: *Blades v. Franklin Gen. Hosp.*, 604 N.Y.S.2d 590 (N.Y. App. Div. 1993)

Facts

The plaintiff had breast reduction surgery on September 9, 1986. Although she developed an infection, her physician did not discover it while she was in the hospital, causing it to go untreated. Upon her discharge from the hospital on September 13, the plaintiff was given antibiotics and was instructed to take them four times a day.

Five days later, her physician noted drainage from her right breast. He gave the patient more antibiotics and told her to wash the area with warm soapy water and to change the dressings. Two days later, the plaintiff was readmitted to the hospital through the emergency department, where it was noted that her right breast was tender and swollen. There was also evidence of a large amount of drainage. Once the plaintiff had been admitted, her dressing was changed. The hospital's admittance form contained information that she had begun oral antibiotics 2 days earlier. The infection caused scarring and deformity, and the patient sued. After trial, the jury found 75% fault by the physician, and 25% by the plaintiff. The court set aside the 25%, and the physician appealed.

Issue

Should the jury's finding of 25% contributory negligence by the plaintiff be set aside?

Holding

The New York Supreme Court, Appellate Division, upheld the trial court's decision to set aside the jury's finding of 25% contributory negligence by the plaintiff.

Reason

There was no evidence offered at trial that the plaintiff contributed to her injuries. In fact, it was the judge who first brought the subject up by asking if the physician wanted contributory negligence charged to the jury. Further, it was the court that asked the physician's expert if failure to take the prescribed antibiotics could have contributed to the breast injury. The expert stated that "[i]t's hard to say." Id. at 591. The physician's other expert, an infectious disease specialist, testified that it couldn't be determined if warm water soaks would help heal as deep an infection as the plaintiff had contracted. Moreover, there was no evidence presented that the plaintiff did not follow the instructions she had been given.

Discussion

1. What specifically would the physician have had to prove in order for the defense of contributory negligence to succeed against the plaintiff? Explain.
2. How could patient education have helped prevent this lawsuit?
3. Discuss the importance of the physician to provide clear discharge instructions.
4. Discuss how the following article might influence your decision as a juror in this case.

Failure to Timely Notify Patient of Test Results

Citation: *Turner v. Nama*, 689 N.E.2d 303 (Ill. App. 1997)

Facts

In 1982, Laura Nelson, plaintiff, began seeing Dr. Nama (OB/GYN), defendant. On September 18, 1990, the defendant performed a Pap test on Laura. Some time after September 25, 1990, the plaintiff's estate claims that the defendant received Laura's Pap test results, which indicated a Class IV carcinoma.

On December 14, 1993, after being diagnosed with cervical cancer by another physician, Laura returned to the defendant for a second opinion. The plaintiff alleges that it was at this visit that the defendant first told Laura of the results from the September 1990 test. The plaintiff alleges that Laura suffered a stroke on January 31, 1995, and that this caused Laura to be under legal disability from that date until she died from progressive metastatic cervical cancer on March 16, 1995.

Claiming that Laura was under the defendant's care from 1982 until December 1993, the plaintiff alleges that the defendant had a continuing duty to ensure that Laura was notified of the test results. According to the complaint, the defendant breached this duty by failing to notify Laura of the results from September 18, 1990, to December 1993 by telephone or by means that would confirm receipt, such as, but not limited to, registered letter or telegram with signature. The plaintiff attached to the complaint an unverified letter from an expert opining that such duty continued for at least a year and that the defendant's attempts to contact Laura and her relatives should have been carefully documented. The plaintiff claimed that the defendant's failure to notify Laura of the diagnosis was the proximate cause of her developing progressive metastatic cervical cancer, which ultimately caused her death.

The original complaint, filed on April 20, 1995, alleges survival and wrongful death claims based on medical malpractice. In 1982, decedent began seeing defendant, who specializes in obstetrics and gynecology. On September 18, 1990, defendant performed a Pap smear test. Some time after September 25, 1990, plaintiff avers that defendant received decedent's Pap smear results, which indicated a class four carcinoma . . . . Id. at 306.

According to the complaint, defendant was negligent in failing to follow up after the letter to ensure that Laura knew of the Pap test results; in failing to ensure that Laura was informed of the results from November 1, 1990, and continuing every month and a half until May 1991; and in failing to contact Laura when she did not return for either a 6-month or yearly check-up.

The estate filed a medical malpractice claim against the defendant alleging that the defendant failed to notify Laura that her Pap test was positive for carcinoma. The trial court granted defendant's motion to dismiss on the basis that plaintiff's complaint was not filed within the statute of repose period set forth in section 13-212(a) of the Limitations Act [735 ILCS 5/13-212(a) (West 1996)].

Issue

Was the Plaintiff's complaint time-barred?

Holding

On appeal, the appeals court affirmed the decision of the circuit court finding that the plaintiff's complaint is time-barred because the defendant's failure to notify the decedent of her diagnosis, which was the act or omission triggering the running of the statute of repose, occurred more than 4 years before the plaintiff's filing date.

Reason

Medical malpractice actions in Illinois must be filed within the statute of limitation periods mandated in section 13-212(a) of the Limitations Act [735 ILCS 5/13-212(a) (West 1996)].

Section 13-212(a) is bifurcated, providing both a statute of limitations and a statute of repose. Providing the statute of limitations and incorporating the "discovery rule," the first part of section 13-212(a) states that "no action for damages for injury or death against any [physician], . . . arising out of patient care shall be brought more than 2 years after the date on which the claimant knew, or through the use of reasonable diligence should have known, . . . of the existence of the injury or death for which damages are sought."

The focus in this case, however, is the repose period. The second part of section 13-212(a) provides that "in no event shall [a medical malpractice] action be brought more than 4 years after the date on which occurred the act or omission or occurrence alleged in such action to have been the cause of such injury or death." The distinction between the repose period and the limitations period is that the repose period is triggered by the defendant's wrongful act or omission that causes the injury, whereas the limitations period is triggered by the patient's discovery of the injury. The period of repose effectuates a different policy than the period of limitations; it is intended to terminate the possibility of liability after a defined period of time, regardless of a potential plaintiff's lack of knowledge of his cause of action. Although the statute of repose causes harsh consequences in some cases, the legislature intended to curtail the "long tail" exposure to medical malpractice claims brought about by the advent of the discovery rule by placing an outer time limit within which a malpractice action must be commenced.

Determining when the defendant's act or omission causing injury occurred triggers the statute of repose. The plaintiff alleges that the defendant's failure to notify began on November 1, 1990, and continued every month and a half until May 1991. In addition, plaintiff avers that defendant failed to notify Laura of the results when Laura returned for neither a 6-month check-up nor a yearly check-up. In its brief, the plaintiff argued that the obligation continued until the defendant successfully notified Laura of the results. Despite these assertions, the appeals court found as a matter of law that the defendant's failure to notify Laura triggered the statute of repose no later than late November 1990.

Once a healthcare provider receives unfavorable test results, it is obligated to timely inform the patient of the results. If the provider is a physician, the physician can delegate this task or do it directly. Nonetheless, the obligation is imposed and continues until the provider exhausts all reasonable means available, including, but not limited to, a letter, telephone call, or any other correspondence that would indicate receipt.

Considering the obligation that defendant is charged with, the defendant should and could have satisfied the obligation to notify within, at the very most, a 2-month period. When the defendant received the results in late September, defendant should have exhausted, as soon as possible, all reasonable means to notify Laura of the results. This could have included mailing one or two letters, phoning Laura and her relatives, and sending a letter by certified mail. The appeals court concluded that the defendant's omission giving rise to the injury occurred no later than at the end of a 2-month period in which defendant could have and should have, but failed to, notify Laura of the unfavorable results. Consequently, the plaintiff's filing date remains more than 4 months beyond the running of the statute of repose.

Although an obligation to notify might continue, to conclude that an omission of notification reoccurs into perpetuity would contravene the General Assembly's intent behind promulgating the statute of repose. Although the statute of repose creates harsh results in some cases, the court's role is to give effect to the statute in question—regardless of the result. The 4-year outer limit of the statute of repose was designed and enacted specifically to curtail the "long tail" exposure to medical malpractice claims brought about by the advent of the discovery rule and to terminate the possibility of liability after a defined period of time. The statute of repose is only excepted by fraudulent concealment and postponed by an ongoing course of continuous negligent medical treatment. Finding that neither of these applied to the allegations in this case, the appeals court concluded that the trial court properly dismissed the plaintiff's action for being barred by the statute of repose.

Discussion

1. In what way does the "statute of limitations" and "statute of repose" differ?
2. Do you agree that the cause of action in this case should have been time-barred? Discuss your answer.
3. If this case had not been time-barred due to the tolling of the statute of limitations, discuss what the outcome of the suit might have been.

Court Does Not Buy Rationalization of Questionable Discharge

Citation: *Moses v. Providence Hospital and Medical Centers, Inc. and Lessem*, M.D., 561 F.3d 573 (2009)

Facts

On December 13, 2002, Moses-Irons took Howard to the emergency room of Providence Hospital because Howard was exhibiting signs of illness. Howard's physical symptoms included severe headaches, muscle soreness, high blood pressure and vomiting. Howard was also experiencing slurred speech, disorientation, hallucinations and delusions. Moses-Irons reported these symptoms to the emergency room staff, and also informed them that Howard had "demonstrated threatening behavior, which made her fearful for her safety." The emergency room physicians decided to admit Howard to conduct more tests. Among the physicians who evaluated Howard during his stay at the hospital were Dr. Silverman, a neurologist; Dr. Lessem, a psychiatrist; and Dr. Mitchell, an internist.

Dr. Silverman examined Howard on December 14, 2002. Dr. Silverman determined that Howard "was acting inappropriately." In addition to informing Dr. Silverman of Howard's symptoms, Moses-Irons also told him that Howard had told her that he "had bought caskets." Dr. Silverman "felt that a psychiatric evaluation would be warranted. "His notes from the evaluation indicate his belief that "an acute psychotic episode must be ruled out."

Dr. Lessem examined Howard several times during Howard's stay at the hospital. On December 17, 2002, Dr. Lessem determined that Howard was not "medically stable from a psychiatric standpoint," and decided that Howard should be transferred to the hospital's psychiatric unit called "4 East" to "reassess him." According to Dr. Lessem, 4 East is intended for patients "who are expected to be hospitalized and stabilized and who are acutely mentally ill." Dr. Lessem felt Howard could be more closely observed at 4 East, and planned to conduct "reality testing" of Howard there to determine the extent of Howard's delusions. Dr. Lessem's order notes from December 17, 2002 state, "will accept patient to 4 East if patient's insurance will accept criteria" and "please observe carefully for any indications of suicidal ideation or behavior." Under the heading "orders for 4 East," Dr. Lessem wrote, "suicide precautions." The notes also indicate that Dr. Lessem believed Howard had an atypical psychosis and depression.

Howard was never transferred to the psychiatric unit, and instead was informed on December 18, 2002 that he would be released. A hospital clinical progress report signed by Dr. Mitchell that day states that "patient declines 4 East, wants to go home. His affect is brighter. No physical symptoms now. Patient wishes to go home, wife fears him. Denies any suicidality." Howard stated in a deposition that he never declined going to 4 East.

In Howard's discharge summary form filled out on December 18, 2002, the hospital's "final diagnosis" of Howard, written by a resident, was that he had a "migraine headache" and an "atypical psychosis with delusional disorder." A report dated December 19, 2002, signed by Dr. Mitchell, indicated that Howard would be "discharged home today . . . cannot stay as he is medically stable and now does not need 4E." Howard was released on December 19, 2002, and on December 29, 2002, Howard murdered Moses-Irons.

Plaintiff Johnella Moses a representative of the Estate of Marie Moses-Irons filed a lawsuit against Providence Hospital and Medical Centers, Inc. and Dr. Lessem to the United States Court of Appeals, Sixth Circuit pursuant to the Emergency Medical Treatment and Active Labor Act ("EMTALA"), 42 U.S.C. § 1395dd, and common law negligence.

The plaintiff alleged the defendants violated EMTALA by releasing Moses-Irons' husband from the hospital ten days before he murdered Moses-Irons. The plaintiff appealed the district court's decision to grant defendants' motion for summary judgment and dismiss plaintiff's claims.

Issue

Will the summary judgment be upheld? Does the plaintiff have standing to sue the hospital and physicians pursuant to EMTALA?

Holding

The United States Court of Appeals, Sixth Circuit, concluded that the plaintiff has standing to sue pursuant to EMTALA, reversing the district court's decision and remanding the case for further proceedings with respect to the hospital. The court did affirm summary judgment for the physicians.

Reason

The plaintiff's expert report Dr. Bursztajn, a professor of psychiatry at Harvard Medical School concluded that Howard did have an emergency medical condition upon arriving at the hospital, and had not stabilized by the time he was discharged. Dr. Bursztajn based his conclusion on Dr. Lessem's own notes from December 17, 2002, in which Dr. Lessem had diagnosed Howard as having an atypical psychosis and possibly suicidal behavior. Dr. Bursztajn concluded that "the symptoms and mental state described by Dr. Lessem could not be resolved in one to two days, yet the decision to discharge Mr. Howard was made one day later."

For all hospitals that participate in Medicare and have an emergency department, EMTALA sets forth two requirements. First, for any individual who "comes to the emergency department" and requests treatment, the hospital must "provide for an appropriate medical screening examination . . . to determine whether or not an emergency medical condition . . . exists." 42 U.S.C. § 1395dd(a). Second, if "the hospital determines that the individual has an emergency medical condition, the hospital must provide either (A) within the staff and facilities available at the hospital, for such further medical examination and such treatment as may be required to stabilize the medical condition, or (B) for transfer of the individual to another medical facility[.]" § 1395dd(b). Thus, for any individual who seeks treatment in a hospital, the hospital must determine whether an "emergency medical condition" exists, and if the hospital believes such a condition exists, it must provide treatment to "stabilize" the patient.

The statute defines "emergency medical condition" as "a medical condition manifesting itself by acute symptoms of sufficient severity (including severe pain) such that the absence of immediate medical attention could reasonably be expected to result in . . . placing the health of the individual . . . in serious jeopardy." § 1395dd(e)(1)(A)(i). "To stabilize" a patient with such a condition means "to assure, within reasonable medical probability, that no material deterioration of the condition is likely to result from or occur during the transfer of the individual from a facility." § 1395dd(e)(3)(A). "Transfer" is defined in the statute to include moving the patient to an outside facility or discharging him. § 1395dd(e)(4).

Contrary to Defendants' interpretation, EMTALA imposes an obligation on a hospital beyond admitting a patient with an emergency medical condition to an inpatient care unit. The statute requires "such treatment as may be required to stabilize the medical condition," § 1395dd(b), and forbids the patient's release unless his condition has "been stabilized," § 1395dd(c)(1). A patient with an emergency medical condition is "stabilized" when "no material deterioration of the condition is likely, within reasonable medical probability, to result from or occur during" the patient's release from the hospital. § 1395dd(e)(3)(B). Thus, EMTALA requires a hospital to treat a patient with an emergency condition in such a way that, upon the patient's release, no further deterioration of the condition is likely.

Emergency care does not always stop when a patient is wheeled from the emergency room into the main hospital. The defendants argued that, to the extent that Howard had an emergency medical condition at the time of his admission, the hospital physicians no longer believed that he had such a condition when they released him. The hospital attempted to construe information in the medical record as showing signs that Howard was ready for discharge.

The plaintiff introduced evidence that challenged whether any of these signs of stability noted existed with respect to Howard. First, the "final diagnosis" of Howard upon discharge of an "atypical psychosis [with] delusional disorder" was substantially the same as Dr. Lessem's diagnosis on December 17, 2002, which included "atypical psychosis." Moreover, Dr. Bursztajn's report concludes that "the symptoms and mental state described by Dr. Lessem could not be resolved in one to two days, yet the decision to discharge Mr. Howard was made one day later." The doctors were aware on the day they released Howard that Howard's wife did not think he had improved, and in fact still "feared him." Finally, Dr. Lessem's note dated December 17, 2002, in which he writes "will accept Howard to 4 east if Howard's insurance will accept criteria," creates at the very least a credibility issue with respect to whether the hospital physicians actually believed that no emergency condition existed upon Howard's release.

The United States Court of Appeals, Sixth Circuit held that although the question of whether EMTALA allows a private right of action against an individual physician is one of first impression for this Court, other circuits to have considered the issue have held or opined that EMTALA does not authorize an action against an individual physician. The Appeals Court agreed.

Discussion

1. Should the plaintiff have sued the physicians under a pure malpractice theory? Discuss your answer.
2. Describe and discuss any ethical issues you see in this case.

NOTES

1. http://www.dh.gov.uk/prod_consum_dh/groups/dh_digitalassets/@dh/@en/documents/digi-talasset/dh_4116525.pdf
2. Id.
3. Id.

chapter nine

Employee and Patient Safety

This chapter reviews a variety of safety concerns faced by employees and patients in the hospital setting. Although this chapter is not exhaustive of the hazards, it represents a broad overview of the extensiveness of safety issues.

EMPLOYEE SAFETY

Although much attention is paid to employee safety in healthcare organizations, the injuries that affect employees often go unnoticed (e.g., back and needlestick injuries). The Occupational Safety and Health Administration (OSHA) discusses many of these risks at their website, which includes the following:

There are numerous health and safety issues associated with healthcare facilities. They include bloodborne pathogens and biological hazards, potential chemical and drug exposures, waste anesthetic gas exposures, respiratory hazards, ergonomic hazards from lifting and repetitive tasks, laser hazards, hazards associated with laboratories, and radioactive material and X-ray hazards. Some of the potential chemical exposures include formaldehyde used for preservation of specimens for pathology; ethylene oxide, glutaraldehyde, and paracetic acid used for sterilization; and numerous other chemicals used in healthcare laboratories.[1]

Healthcare facilities also employ a wide variety of trades that have health and safety hazards associated with them. These include mechanical maintenance, medical equipment maintenance, housekeeping, food service, building and grounds maintenance, laundry, and administrative staff.

As noted in the following article, employee safety has apparently "slipped off the radar screen." More attention needs to be paid to the toll taken on healthcare workers in the environment within which they work.

Employee Safety: As Critical as Patient Safety

Many hospitals are focusing on patient safety while employee safety slips off the radar. But improving employee safety and health boosts patient safety as well as the bottom line.

According to the Bureau of Labor Statistics, more healthcare workers become ill or injured than in any other industry sector with at least 100,000 employees. In fact, more than 250,000 healthcare workers are injured on the job each year. The healthcare industry spends $20 billion annually in workers' compensation and related costs due to employee injuries and illnesses. Clearly, elevating employee safety and health to the same level as patient safety is overdue.

Linda Chaff, Hospitals & Health Networks, *April 7, 2009*

Many hospitals provide programs for improving a safe workplace for employees. One such hospital is Valley View Hospital. An excerpt from their safety program follows. See their website for additional information.

Providing a safe workplace is a priority for Valley View Hospital. All employees receive safety training and education during the new-hire orientation process. This training is reinforced on a continual basis with both general and job-specific education and by education, required annually. The goal is that all employees have education and training in all aspects of their jobs and have a thorough understanding of how to maintain and promote a safe work environment.

The hospital supports employee safety through specific committees and through Employee Health. These groups provide a collaborative process for employees and management to maintain a safe work environment. Representatives from all areas are given the opportunity to serve on these committees. The employee health nurse reviews, analyzes, and investigates employee accident reports; identifies the root causes of accidents; and makes recommendations for safety improvements.[2]

PATIENT SAFETY

Massachusetts Workers' Rights Board Releases Report on Nurse Staffing

Crisis at Tufts Medical Center as Nurses Prepare for 1-Day Strike
Finds Patient Safety Compromised by Falling Staffing Numbers

Members of the Massachusetts Workers' Rights Board hand-delivered a report today to Tufts Medical Center CEO Ellen Zane that documents serious concerns the board has about the quality and safety of patient care at the hospital, as well as the treatment of registered nurses who are attempting to convince management to improve inadequate staffing conditions. The delegation included political, faith, and community leaders who are concerned over the actions taken in recent days regarding nurses at the medical center.

PRNewswire-US Newswire, *May 3, 2011*[3]

Medical Mistake: Surgeon Operates on the Wrong Eye of a 4-Year-Old Boy

Jesse Matlock went to a doctor today to find out if he suffered any permanent damage when a surgeon performed corrective surgery on the wrong eye and then, without consulting the boy's parents, quickly operated on the correct eye.

"Right now we're in the dark about what this will be like in the future," Tasha Gaul, mother of 4-year-old Jesse, told ABC news. The doctor they saw today told her they will have to wait 5 weeks for his eyes to completely heal before they can determine if there has been any permanent damage.

"No parent, no child, nobody should have to live through the torture of that day," Gaul said.

Michael Murray, ABC World News, *April 19, 2011*

Medical errors are one of the leading causes of death and injury to patients. It has been estimated that over 100,000 patients die annually in the United States due to medical mistakes. If one considers medication errors, hospital-acquired infections, surgical errors, and so on, some estimates of deaths due to such errors climb to as many as 250,000 per year. There are a plethora of cases relating to employee and patient safety. Some of those are presented next. Whatever the number, it is most likely underestimated. The Institute of Medicine of the National Academies reports that medication errors are among the most common medical errors, harming at least 1.5 million people every year. "The extra medical costs of treating drug-related injuries occurring in hospitals alone conservatively amount to $3.5 billion a year, and this estimate does not take into account lost wages and productivity or additional healthcare costs," the report says.[4]

Deaths from Avoidable Medical Error More than Double in Past Decade, Investigation Shows

Preventable medical mistakes and infections are responsible for about 200,000 deaths in the U.S. each year, according to an investigation by the Hearst media corporation. The report comes 10 years after the Institute of Medicine's "To Err is Human" analysis, which found that 44,000 to 98,000 people were dying annually due to these errors and called for the medical community and government to cut that number in half by 2004.

Katherine Harmon, Scientific American, *August 10, 2009*

The Agency for Healthcare Research and Quality (AHRQ) is the health services research arm of the U.S. Department of Health and Human Services (HHS). The Agency for Healthcare Research and Quality has identified various patient safety tips for hospitals. Ten of those tips are listed next. For detailed information, see the AHRQ website: http://www.ahrq.gov/qual/10tips.htm.

The cases that follow are a sampling of those involving both employee and patient safety.

Employees Exposed to Ambulance Fumes

On July 4, 2012, pharmacy technicians at Community Medical Center were observed by a health department inspector working in an enclosed IV admixture room mixing various IV bags for patients. It was summer, and it was hot. The windows to the room were open, and ambulances were backed up to those windows with their engines running and their exhaust pipes located within a few feet of the open windows, so clouds of carbon monoxide permeated the IV Admixture Room. The employees were asked how long they had been working under these conditions. They claimed that this had been going on for years, as this was where many of the city's ambulances parked. Unfortunately, these employees had already been exposed to the carbon monoxide, at the very least, for several years by that time. When the employees were asked if they had reported this health risk, their answers

Table 9–1 Patient Safety Tips for Hospitals*

Medical errors may occur in different healthcare settings, and those that happen in hospitals can have serious consequences. The Agency for Healthcare Research and Quality, which has sponsored hundreds of patient safety research and implementation projects, offers these 10 evidence-based tips to prevent adverse events from occurring in your hospital.

1. Prevent central line-associated blood stream infections. Be vigilant and prevent central line-associated blood stream infections by taking five steps every time a central venous catheter is inserted: wash your hands, use full-barrier precautions, clean the skin with chlorhexidine, avoid femoral lines, and remove unnecessary lines. Taking these steps consistently reduced this type of deadly healthcare-associated infection to zero in a study at more than 100 large and small hospitals.[1] Additional AHRQ resources on preventing healthcare-associated infections are available at http://www.ahrq.gov/qual/hais.htm.

2. Re-engineer hospital discharges. Reduce potentially preventable readmissions by assigning a staff member to work closely with patients and other staff to reconcile medications and schedule necessary follow-up medical appointments. Create a simple, easy-to-understand discharge plan for each patient that contains a medication schedule, a record of all upcoming medical appointments, and names and phone numbers of whom to call if a problem arises. AHRQ-funded research shows that taking these steps can help reduce potentially preventable readmissions by 30%.[2] An online toolkit is available at http://www.bu.edu/fammed/projectred/.

3. Prevent venous thromboembolism. Eliminate hospital-acquired venous thromboembolism (VTE), the most common cause of preventable hospital deaths, by using an evidence-based guide to create a VTE protocol. This free guide explains how to take essential first steps, lay out the evidence and identify best practices, analyze care delivery, track performance with metrics, layer interventions, and continue to improve. Ordering information for *Preventing Hospital-Acquired Venous Thromboembolism: A Guide for Effective Quality Improvement* (AHRQ Publication No. 08-0075) is available at http://www.ahrq.gov/qual/vtguide/.

4. Educate patients about using blood thinners safely. Patients who have had surgery often leave the hospital with a new prescription for a blood thinner, such as warfarin (brand name: Coumadin®), to keep them from developing dangerous blood clots. However, if used incorrectly, blood thinners can cause uncontrollable bleeding and are among the top causes of adverse drug events. A free, 10-minute patient education video and companion 24-page booklet, in both English and Spanish, help patients understand what to expect when taking these medicines. Ordering information for *Staying Active and Healthy with Blood Thinners* (AHRQ Publication No. 09-0086-DVD) and *Blood Thinner Pills: Your Guide to Using Them Safely* (AHRQ Publication No. 09-0086-C) is available at http://www.ahrq.gov/consumer/btpills.htm.

(Continues)

Table 9–1 Patient Safety Tips for Hospitals*

5. Limit shift durations for medical residents and other hospital staff if possible. Evidence shows that acute and chronically fatigued medical residents are more likely to make mistakes. Ensure that residents get ample sleep and adhere to 80-hour workweek limits. Residents who work 30-hour shifts should only treat patients for up to 16 hours and should have a 5-hour protected sleep period between 10 p.m. and 8 a.m.[3] *Resident Duty Hours: Enhancing Sleep, Supervision, and Safety* is available at http://books.nap.edu/openbook.php?record_id=12508&page=R1.
6. Consider working with a Patient Safety Organization. Report and share patient safety information with Patient Safety Organizations (PSOs) to help others avoid preventable errors. By providing both privilege and confidentiality, PSOs create a secure environment in which clinicians and healthcare organizations can use common formats to collect, aggregate, and analyze data that can improve quality by identifying and reducing the risks and hazards associated with patient care. Information on PSOs and Common Formats is available at http://www.pso.ahrq.gov/.
7. Use good hospital design principles. Follow evidence-based principles for hospital design to improve patient safety and quality. Prevent patient falls by providing well-designed patient rooms and bathrooms and creating decentralized nurses' stations that allow easy access to patients. Reduce infections by offering single-bed rooms, improving air filtration systems, and providing multiple convenient locations for hand washing. Prevent medication errors by offering pharmacists well-lit, quiet, private spaces so they can fill prescriptions without distractions. Ordering information for a free, 50-minute DVD, *Transforming Hospitals: Designing for Safety and Quality* (AHRQ Publication No. 07-0076-DVD), is available at http://www.ahrq.gov/qual/transform.htm.
8. Measure your hospital's patient safety culture. Survey hospital staff to assess your facility's patient safety culture. AHRQ's free *Hospital Survey on Patient Safety Culture* and related materials are designed to provide tools for improving the patient safety culture, evaluating the impact of interventions, and tracking changes over time. If your health system includes nursing homes or ambulatory care medical groups, share culture surveys customized for those settings. Free patient safety culture surveys for hospitals (AHRQ Publication No. 04-0041), nursing homes (AHRQ Publication No. 08-0060), and medical offices (AHRQ Publication No. 08(09)-0059) are available at http://www.ahrq.gov/qual/patientsafetyculture/.
9. Build better teams and rapid response systems. Train hospital staff to communicate effectively as a team. A free, customizable toolkit called TeamSTEPPS™, which stands for Team Strategies and Tools to Enhance Performance and Patient Safety, provides evidence-based techniques for promoting effective communication and other teamwork skills among staff in various units or as part of rapid response teams. Materials can be tailored to any healthcare setting, from emergency departments to ambulatory clinics. A free, 2.5-day train-the-trainer course is currently being offered in five locations nationwide. Ordering information for the TeamSTEPPS Multimedia Resource Kit (AHRQ Publication No. 06-0020-3) and information on the training sessions are available at http://teamstepps.ahrq.gov.

(Continues)

Table 9–1 Patient Safety Tips for Hospitals* (Continued)

10. Insert chest tubes safely. Remember UWET when inserting chest tubes. The easy-to-remember mnemonic is based on a universal protocol from the Joint Commission and stands for: Universal Precautions (achieved by using sterile cap, mask, gown, and gloves); **W**ider skin prep; **E**xtensive draping; and **T**ray positioning. A free, 11-minute DVD provides video excerpts of 50 actual chest tube insertions to illustrate problems that can occur during the procedure. Ordering information for *Problems and Prevention: Chest Tube Insertion* (AHRQ Publication No. 06-0069-DVD) is available at http://www.ahrq.gov/qual/chesttubes.htm.
* *10 Patient Safety Tips for Hospitals.* AHRQ Publication No. 08-P003. Revised December 2009. Rockville, MD, Agency for Healthcare Research and Quality. http://www.ahrq.gov/qual/10tips.htm

were blurry at best, as though they were fearful to provide an answer. When pressed for more direct answers, they spoke up to say they'd been well aware of the working conditions, and the inspector pointed out there was no exhaust vent in the room.

Out of concern as to the effect these conditions might have on employee health, the situation was reported to management. The following day it was observed that the ambulance zone was permanently relocated to a safer area, an architect presented drawings to add an exhaust system in the room, and a construction team completed the system installation over night. Management was asked to follow-up on the health of the employees who were exposed under these conditions.

Discussion

1. Do you believe that the organization followed up as to the health of the employees working in the pharmacy? Discuss your answer.
2. Discuss why you believe management did not address this safety issue on a timelier basis but permitted it to persist for years.

Child Abuse: Immunity for Reporting

Citation: *Michaels v. Gordon*, 439 S.E.2d 722 (Ga. Ct. App. 1993)

Facts

As part of an investigation of a report of possible child molestation, the Gwinnett County Department of Family and Children Services placed two children in the temporary custody of a foster family and referred one child, C.J.M., to Dr. Gordon, a licensed psychologist, for evaluation. After two interviews that included a psychological evaluation, Dr. Gordon formed the professional opinion that C.J.M. had been sexually molested. Based in part on statements made by the child, Dr. Gordon further believed that the perpetrator of the suspected molestation was C.J.M.'s father. At a hearing before the juvenile court, the court determined that the evidence adduced did not support a finding that C.J.M. had been abused by his father or that he was at risk at home. Custody was returned to the parents.

C.J.M.'s parents subsequently initiated an action for medical malpractice on behalf of themselves and the two minors. After extensive discovery, Dr. Gordon moved for summary judgment, based in part on a claim of immunity from liability as provided by the child abuse reporting statute, OCGA § 19-7-5. The trial court granted this motion, and the parents appealed, arguing that the immunity provisions of OCGA § 19-7-5 do not apply to Dr. Gordon, because she was not a "mandatory reporter" under that statute.

OCGA § 19-7-5(f)

Any person . . . participating in the making of a report . . . or participating in any judicial proceeding or any other proceeding resulting [from such a report of suspected child abuse] shall in so doing be immune from any civil or criminal liability that might otherwise be incurred or imposed, provided such participation pursuant to this Code section . . . is made in good faith. Any person making a report, whether required by this Code section or not, shall be immune from liability as provided in this subsection [emphasis added].

Issue

(1) Was the psychologist immune from liability under the child abuse reporting statute? (2) Did the evidence establish that the psychologist acted in bad faith, therefore depriving her of immunity under the child abuse statute?

Holding

The Court of Appeals of Georgia held that the child abuse reporting statute's grant of immunity from liability extended to the psychologist. The evidence did not establish bad faith on the part of the psychologist so as to deprive her of such immunity.

Reason

The statutory language "participating in the making of a report" presupposes the involvement of more than one person and so includes acts beyond the initial communication of suspected child abuse because of a visual inspection of the child, or observed behavior, or the child's statement. The grant of qualified immunity covers every person who, in good faith, participates over time in the making of a report to a child welfare agency.

The parents' evidence of alleged unprofessional acts and omissions committed by Dr. Gordon would authorize a finding that she was negligent or exercised bad judgment in formulating her professional opinion that the child had been sexually abused. However, this proof of mere negligence or bad judgment is not proof that Dr. Gordon refused to fulfill her professional duties out of some harmful motive or that she consciously acted for some dishonest purpose. There was no competent evidence that Dr. Gordon acted in bad faith.

Discussion

1. What is immunity?
2. Should immunity extend to the general public?

Improper Maintenance: Chair Lift

Citation: *Thibodeaux v. Century Mfg. Co.*, 625 So.2d 351 (La. Ct. App. 1993)

Facts

The plaintiff, Ms. Thibodeaux, a nurse's aide at the Rosewood nursing facility, sued Century Manufacturing Company (Century) after she was injured while operating a Saf-Kary chair lift manufactured by Century. The Saf-Kary chair fell and smashed the plaintiff's finger when the chair's lifting arm failed. The failure occurred as a patient was being lifted from a whirlpool bath. The plaintiff alleged that Century manufactured a defective chair lift that was the cause of her injuries.

Century argued that the chair lift was not defective in design and that the failure of the chair was caused by air in the Saf-Lift hydraulic system, resulting from the nursing facility's lack of maintenance. The plaintiff's expert witness testified that, after inspecting the equipment, he found that the accident was caused by the safety lock failing to prevent the chair from disconnecting from the lift. Century "theorized that this want of maintenance caused the whole lift apparatus, including the chair still connected to the lifting arm of the lift column, to rapidly descend on Irene's finger." Id. at 353. Approximately 4 months before the accident, a Century-licensed service technician, Deryl Bryant, performed an inspection of the equipment. He found leaks of hydraulic fluid, deteriorating seals and rings, a corroded lift base, and an air-contaminated lifting column. He took the chair lift out of service and recommended that Rosewood not use it until repairs were made to restore it to safe operation. These findings were communicated to Rosewood in writing. Rosewood did not make the repairs. Id. at 353. The court, on a jury verdict, found that the sole cause of the accident was poor maintenance on the part of the nursing facility. The plaintiff appealed.

Issue

Did the evidence support a finding that Century was negligent in its design of the lifting chair and the failure of its safety lock?

Holding

The Court of Appeal of Louisiana held that the evidence supported the conclusion that the accident was caused by the nursing home's failure to properly maintain the equipment and that the injury was not the result of poor design.

Reason

Virtually all products are subject to wear and tear and therefore need periodic maintenance. The nursing facility had been warned by the manufacturer of the need for repairs on the chair lift. The nursing facility failed to heed that warning.

Discussion

1. What procedures should an organization adopt for the safe and effective use of its medical equipment?
2. Should nonmedical equipment be included in an organization's preventive maintenance program? Explain your answer.

Improper Use of Patient Bed

Citation: *Parris v. Uni Med, Inc.*, 861 S.W.2d 694 (Mo. Ct. App. 1993)

Facts

In January 1987, the plaintiff was admitted to St. Francis Hospital for a urinary tract infection. While there, he used a Mediscus (a hospital bed marketer and distributor) bed that was designed with 21 separate air pockets to prevent decubitus ulcers. In May 1987, the plaintiff was again admitted for what turned out to be a decubitus ulcer. He was put in a Mediscus bed that was set up by a Uni Med Imaging, Inc. employee. It took the employee one and a half hours to set up the bed and make adjustments. Upon discharge on May 31, 1987, the pressure ulcer was only barely apparent.

On June 15, 1987, the plaintiff was readmitted. A Mediscus bed (a low air loss bed system that can be used in the treatment of burn and bedsore patients) was set up for him in only 5 minutes, and he was placed in it. At the time of the June admission, the plaintiff's pressure ulcer was healing. Four days later, a nurse noted that the ulcer condition had worsened and a new pressure ulcer had formed. The nurse noticed that the dressing on the first site was touching the metal frame on the bed, thus putting pressure on the plaintiff's sacral area every time he sat. The nurse called Uni Med, and a company employee made adjustments to the bed. In spite of observed improvement in the pressure ulcers at the time of discharge, the patient deteriorated to such an extent that surgery was required. Evidence showed that the beds were not monitored regularly and that the nurses were not trained to turn the patients or adjust or regulate the beds.

The plaintiff, a 37-year-old paraplegic, brought an action against Uni Med, Inc. for pressure ulcers he sustained during his hospital stay. The jury found that the inadequate pressure setting on the bed was caused by its being improperly set up, thus exacerbating the ulcers and necessitating surgery.

Issue

Did the company employee fail to set up the Mediscus bed properly, thus causing the patient's pressure ulcers and subsequent surgery needed to correct his condition?

Holding

The Court of Appeals of Missouri found that (1) the hospital bed was not set up properly, (2) the failure to set it up properly caused the patient's pressure ulcers and subsequent surgery, and (3) nurses were properly qualified as testimonial experts regarding pressure ulcers.

Reason

Evidence demonstrated that the bed had been hastily set up; continuous pressure of 2 hours on one area of skin can cause pressure ulcers; and nurses did not change the pressure gauges because they had not been trained properly. The court also found that Uni Med had no monitoring system and that the patient's original pressure ulcer had been healing prior to the hospital visit and then worsened after coming into contact with the bed frame. Further, the court found that the patient developed more ulcers on the sacral area, which were present upon discharge.

Discussion

1. What safeguards should Uni Med have implemented to help prevent this unfortunate event?
2. What is the importance of continuing education programs for individuals operating medical equipment?

Failure to Follow Policy: Causes Patient Injury

Citation: *Bowe v. Charleston Area Med. Ctr.*, 428 S.E.2d 773 (W. Va. 1993)

Facts

The plaintiff, a nurse's aide, brought an action against a medical center for retaliatory discharge and breach of contract. The nurse's aide had assisted a patient to the bathroom and placed him on the commode. She left him unattended for about 10 minutes. When she returned, the patient was found lying on the floor in a pool of blood. The patient had apparently hit his head on the sink when he fell.

Following an investigation of the incident, the hospital found that the nurse had been grossly negligent, and it terminated her employment. The personnel director had authorized the employee's termination because of a provision in the employee handbook that makes gross negligence a dischargeable offense. The nurse's aide claimed she had been terminated in retaliation because of complaints she had made about the lack of patient care on the oncology unit to which she had been assigned. Her manager and the patient complaint representative could not substantiate evidence of her complaints. In addition, there was no evidence in the employee's personnel file that would indicate that she had filed a grievance over patient care.

Upon jury verdict, the circuit court entered judgment for the plaintiff. The plaintiff was awarded $36,238.17 in lost wages and $15,000 for mental suffering. The circuit court added an additional $5,218.30 in interest.

Issue

The medical center appealed, raising the following questions: (1) Did the evidence establish that the nurse's aide was discharged because of patient neglect? (2) Did the employee handbook give rise to a contractual relationship between the aide and the medical center?

Holding

The Supreme Court of Appeals of West Virginia held that (1) the evidence established that patient neglect by the plaintiff prompted an investigation that led to her subsequent discharge, and (2) the disclaimer in the employee handbook adequately shielded the employer from any contractual liability based on the employee handbook.

Reason

The evidence showed that the nurse's aide, contrary to the medical center's policy, had assisted a patient in getting on a commode and then left him unattended, resulting in a fall and his subsequent death. Leaving the patient unattended for 10 minutes on the commode was clearly against hospital policy. The nurse's aide failed to establish that her discharge was a retaliatory act or that it contravened some public policy. The evidence presented during the development of the present case substantially cast doubt as to whether the plaintiff had ever actually made any complaints about patient care. Id. at 777.

The hospital's disclaimer specifically stated that the employee handbook was not intended to create any contractual rights. Employment was subject to termination at any time by either the employee or employer. The disclaimer in the employee handbook read,

---

Because of court decisions in some states, it has become necessary for us to make it clear that this handbook is not part of a contract, and no employee of the Medical Center has any contractual right to the matters set forth in this handbook. In addition, your employment is subject to termination at any time by either you or by the Medical Center. Id. at 779.

Discussion

1. What value is there in placing a disclaimer in an employee handbook?
2. Will failure to place a disclaimer in an employee handbook result in the handbook being construed as an unconditional contract with employees?

Failure to Have Proper Equipment Available

Citation: *Jenkins County Hosp. Auth. v. Landrum*, 426 S.E.2d 572 (Ga. Ct. App. 1992)

The parents of a minor child brought a medical malpractice action against a physician and hospital on behalf of their child, who suffered injuries during a Caesarean delivery. The parents alleged that the attending physician was negligent in performing a premature Caesarean section without having a proper mechanical ventilator available. The equipment was necessary to alleviate the child's respiratory distress. The parents alleged that the hospital was negligent by not having the necessary equipment available. As required by statute (OCGA § 9-1-9.1), the parents filed, with their complaint, an affidavit addressing the specific allegations made against the physician. The hospital filed a motion to dismiss on the grounds that the parents failed to comply with the statute, claiming that the affidavit did not address any of the allegations of negligence attributed to the hospital. The superior court denied the hospital's motion to dismiss, and an interlocutory appeal was granted as to whether or not an affidavit was required.

The court of appeals held that the affidavit, under the statute requiring an affidavit of a competent expert to accompany charges of professional malpractice, was not required as to allegations of negligence against the hospital. This case was controlled by *Lamb v. Candler Gen. Hosp.*, 262 Ga. 70, 413 S.E.2d 720 (1992), therefore, an affidavit under OCGA § 9-1-9.1 is not necessary, and the trial court did not err in denying the hospital's motion to dismiss.

Discussion

1. What safety issues are relevant to this case and similar cases?
2. What are the differences between ordinary negligence and malpractice in relation to this case?

Fall from Nursing Facility Window

Citation: *Waters Ex Rel. Walton v. Del-Ky, Inc.*, 844 S.W.2d 250 (Tex. Ct. App. 1992)

Facts

Mr. Walton was a patient at the Sunnyvale nursing facility who required constant attention. On October 4, 1987, he fell from a second-floor window of the nursing facility. Mr. Walton was discharged from the nursing facility on October 5, 1987. On October 6, the nursing facility called Ms. Waters, Mr. Walton's sister, and informed her of the incident. On October 10, Mr. Walton expired from his injuries. Mr. Walton's death certificate indicated that he died as the result of multiple blunt force injuries from an accident that occurred at the nursing facility.

Katherine Bates, the executive director of United People for Better Nursing Facilities, said that Ms. Waters did not know that her brother had died or that he had been in a nursing facility.

On October 9, 1989, Ms. Waters sent a notice letter to the nursing facility claiming damages for the negligent care of her brother. Ms. Waters's claim against the nursing facility was later filed based on negligence and negligence per se under the survivorship statute. Ms. Waters claimed damages on behalf of her brother's estate for medical and funeral expenses, physical pain, suffering, mental anguish, and all other damages sustained by her brother before his death.

The nursing facility moved for summary judgment on all of Ms. Waters's claims based on the 2-year statute of limitations. The trial court granted the motion, and the plaintiff appealed.

Texas statute (Tex. Civ. Prac. & Rem. Code Ann. § 71.021 [Vernon 1986]) provides that a decedent's action survives his death. The survivor prosecutes the action on his behalf. The survivorship action is wholly derivative of the decedent's rights. The actionable wrong is that which the decedent suffered before his death.

Ms. Waters alleged she could recover for her brother's estate for medical and funeral expenses, physical pain, suffering, mental anguish, and all other damages he sustained before his death.

Issue

The question arises as to when the 2-year statute of limitations begins to run?

Holding

The Court of Appeals of Texas held that the survivorship action against the nursing facility accrued, for purposes of the 2-year statute of limitations for medical liability claims, on the date the patient fell from the second floor of the nursing facility resulting in his death several days later.

Reason

The statute of limitations in § 10.01 of article 4590i provides that, except as otherwise provided in the section, it applies to all persons regardless of minority or other legal disability. When the precise date of the tort is known, the statutory 2-year period begins on that date. Ms. Waters's negligence claim for her brother's personal injuries resulting from the nursing facility's negligence was a derivative action. Because the negligence action is derivative, Ms. Waters had no more rights than her brother would have had if he had lived. Therefore, after October 4, 1989, Section 10.01 barred her cause of action for personal injuries suffered because of the facility's negligence on October 4, 1987. The 2-year limitations applied unless Ms. Waters had a viable legal reason for tolling the statute.

Ms. Waters contended that the nursing facility fraudulently concealed its negligence and the cause in fact of her brother's injuries. The record did not support Ms. Waters's assertion that the facility had a fixed purpose to conceal the wrong. The summary judgment rule did not provide for a trial by deposition or affidavit. The rule provided a method of summarily ending a case that involved only a question of law and no genuine issue of material fact. The trial court's duty was to determine if there were any fact issues to try, not to weigh the evidence or determine its credibility and try the case on affidavits. The summary judgment evidence showed that if Ms. Waters did not know of Mr. Walton's injuries and their causes on October 11, 1987, she did know about them at least by November 16, 1987, the date when Ms. Bates talked to her about her brother's injuries and the causes of those injuries. Ms. Waters did not give notice until October 9, 1989. Her survivorship action is derivative of her brother's common law action. She discovered his injuries while there was still a reasonable time to sue. She had more than 22 months within which to file suit under the survivorship statute.

Discussion

1. Do you think that a statute of limitations of 2 years is reasonable in this case? Explain.
2. How would you describe the ethical issues in this case?

Patient Falls from a Gurney

Citation: *Hussey v. Montgomery Mem'l Hosp.*, 441 S.E.2d 577 (N.C. Ct. App. 1994)

Facts

On June 14, 1986, Mr. Hussey suffered permanent brain damage when he fell from a gurney at the defendant hospital. He had been ill and was taken to the hospital by his wife. Upon arrival, he was seated on a gurney in the emergency department. The gurney had no side rails. Shortly thereafter, Mr. Hussey fell from the gurney and was rendered unconscious. As a result of the fall, Mr. Hussey suffered severe head injury and was comatose and unresponsive. He experienced continuous seizures. After being treated by a physician in the hospital's emergency department, the physician advised Mrs. Hussey that her husband's condition was caused by swelling in the brain, which was the result of his head striking the floor. Mr. Hussey was moved by ambulance to another hospital, where he was diagnosed with a dislocated clavicle, laceration of the skin, and two fractures of the lateral wall of the right orbit. He underwent surgery for the dislocated clavicle.

On June 23, 1986, Mr. Hussey was discharged from the hospital. At the time of discharge, he had significant memory loss and was nervous and depressed.

The plaintiffs alleged that during the 10-day period after the fall and again on July 10, 1986, they questioned Dr. Andrews, the attending physician, as to whether there was any permanent brain damage or injury. On each occasion, Dr. Andrews answered that there was not, and would not be, any brain damage. Two months after the fall, the plaintiffs consulted with an attorney concerning a possible claim against the defendant hospital, but the plaintiffs decided not to pursue a lawsuit at that time, because they feared doing so might impair the plaintiff husband's ability to receive medical treatment.

For the next 3 1/2 years, Mr. Hussey continued to see his medical providers. He was kept on medication for his nerves. No physicians had ever disclosed to the plaintiffs that Mr. Hussey had suffered a brain injury or that he may suffer permanent brain impairment.

By April 1990, Mr. Hussey's behavior became so severely erratic and unpredictable that Mrs. Hussey took him to Sandhills Center for Mental Health. Mr. Hussey was examined and transferred to the Dartmouth Clinic where Dr. Lee informed the plaintiffs that test results indicated "permanent and residual brain impairment." On June 12, 1990, the plaintiffs filed a complaint alleging negligence against the hospital. The hospital filed a motion to dismiss on the grounds that the action was barred by the 3-year statute of limitations.

On December 22, 1992, the hospital filed a motion for summary judgment seeking dismissal of the complaint on the grounds that the statute of limitations had tolled. The trial judge granted the hospital's motion for summary judgment, and the plaintiffs filed an appeal as to whether or not the action was time-barred.

Issue

Did the statute of limitations bar the action from going forward?

Holding

The Court of Appeals held that the action was time-barred, noting that, where the injury is latent, the claim is held not to accrue until the plaintiff discovers the injury. Where causation of an injury is unknown, the action accrues when both the injury and its cause have been (or should have been) discovered.

Reason

The statute of limitations accrued on June 14, 1986, the date of Mr. Hussey's fall. The head injury was not latent. The court acknowledged that the plaintiffs questioned hospital personnel on occasions immediately after the fall to attempt to ascertain the extent of the plaintiff husband's injuries, and that on those occasions, the plaintiffs were told by hospital personnel that there was not, and would not be, any brain damage or injury. Nonetheless, Mr. Hussey had a cause of action on the date he fell from the gurney. Upon falling from the gurney, he suffered a severe head injury and was rendered unconscious. A treating physician in the emergency department advised Mr. Hussey's wife that swelling in the brain caused her husband's condition. The probable cause of the accident was the hospital's negligence. On the date of the fall, it was apparent that there had been wrongdoing, most likely attributable to the hospital. The ultimate injuries sustained by Mr. Hussey were a direct result of the fall on June 14, 1986, caused by the hospital's wrongdoing that occurred on that date.

Discussion

1. What steps might the hospital take in order to help prevent the likelihood of such occurrences?
2. Do you agree that this action should be time-barred? Explain.

Fire—Wrongful Death

Citation: *Stacy v. Truman Med. Ctr.*, 836 S.W.2d 911 (Mo. 1992)

Facts

The patients' families brought wrongful death actions against a medical center and one of its nurses. The wrongful death actions resulted from a fire in the decedents' room at the medical center. On the day of the fire, Ms. Stacy visited her brother Mr. Stacy, a patient at the hospital who suffered from head injuries and was not supposed to walk around, in his shared room, Room 327. When Ms. Stacy arrived, Mr. Stacy was seated in a chair and was smoking a cigarette with the permission of one of the nurses. No one told Ms. Stacy not to let her brother smoke. Because Ms. Stacy did not see an ashtray in the room, she got a juice cup and a plastic soup tray for the ashes.

At approximately 5:00 p.m., a nurse came in and restrained Mr. Stacy in his chair with ties to prevent him from sliding out of the chair. Before Ms. Stacy left, she lit a cigarette, held it for Mr. Stacy to puff, and then extinguished it in the soup tray. When Ms. Stacy left, she believed there were one or two cigarette butts in the soup container. Ms. Stacy testified that she did not think she dumped the soup tray into the wastebasket but that she could have. Shortly after 5:00 p.m., a fire started in a wastebasket in Room 327, a room with no smoke detector. A Mr. Wheeler was in the bed next to the windows. When Ms. Schreiner, the nurse in charge, discovered the fire, she did not think Mr. Wheeler was in immediate danger. She unsuccessfully tried to untie Mr. Stacy from his restraints. Then she attempted to put out the fire by smothering it with a sheet. When her attempts to extinguish the fire failed, she ran to the door of the room and yelled for help, which alerted nurses Ms. Cominos and Ms. Rodriguez. After calling for help, Ms. Schreiner resumed her attempts to smother the flames with bed linens. Subsequently, she and others grabbed Mr. Stacy by the legs and pulled him and his chair toward the hallway. In the process, Mr. Stacy's restraints burned through, and he slid from the chair to the floor. Ms. Schreiner and her assistants pulled him the remaining few feet out of the room and into the hallway. Ms. Schreiner tried to get back into the room but was prevented by the intense smoke, flames, and heat.

After initially entering Room 327, both Ms. Rodriguez and Ms. Cominos returned to the nurse's station to sound alarms and to call security. Neither attempted to remove Mr. Wheeler from the room. Both ran directly past a fire extinguisher, but neither grabbed it before returning to the room. After Mr. Stacy was removed from the room, Ms. Cominos entered the room with a fire extinguisher and tried to rescue Mr. Wheeler. Because of the intense smoke and heat, however, she was unable to reach Mr. Wheeler. Mr. Wheeler died in the room from smoke inhalation. Mr. Stacy survived for several weeks, then he died as a result of complications from infections secondary to burns.

The medical center's policy on December 30, 1986, in case of fire, called for the removal of a patient from the room and out of immediate danger first.

In its fire-training programs, the medical center used the acronym "RACE" to supply a chronology of steps to take in case of a fire.

R—Rescue or remove the patient first.
A—An alarm should be sounded second.
C—The fire should be contained third.
E—Extinguish the fire last.

The medical center also had a training movie depicting a trash can fire (started by cigarettes) that showed how to pull a patient out of bed by the sheets and drag the patient across the floor at the first recognition of a fire.

The medical center's written smoking policy at the time of the fire stated, "No smoking shall be permitted in the Truman Medical Center Health Care Facility except those areas specifically designated and posted as smoking areas . . . ." Room 327 was not posted as a designated smoking area on the date of the fire. The smoking policy further stated, "In the event violations of this policy are observed, the person violating the policy must be requested to discontinue such violation. This shall be the responsibility of all employees and particularly supervisory and security employees." Ms. Cominos admitted that she was a supervisor and that she violated this portion of the smoking policy on the date of the fire by allowing smoking and the use of a juice cup as an ashtray in Room 327.

The circuit court entered judgment in favor of the patients' families. The circuit court later entered judgment notwithstanding the verdict based on the doctrine of sovereign immunity. The court of appeals reversed on the same doctrine.

Issue

Did the evidence sufficiently establish a causal connection between the medical center's negligence and the patients' death?

Holding

The Supreme Court of Missouri held that a causal connection between the medical center's negligence and the patients' death was sufficiently established. The medical center owed a duty of reasonable care to all its patients. A hospital's duty is proportionate to the needs of the patient, meaning that the hospital must exercise such care and attention as the patient's condition requires.

Reason

The medical center argued that there was no evidence to causally link the alleged negligence in allowing smoking without an approved ashtray to the death of Mr. Wheeler. On the date of the fire, Ms. Stacy was also smoking in Room 327 and was using a juice container and soup container for her ashes. Ms. Cominos knew Ms. Stacy was smoking and that she did not have an ashtray. The medical center's policy concerning ashtrays stated that the ashtrays must be of noncombustible material, safe design, and approved by the hospital. When Ms. Cominos made rounds on the date of the fire, she did not see any ashtray in the room. There was evidence that the fire started in the trash can from discarded smoking materials. The jury was free to believe from the evidence presented that had Ms. Stacy been given a hospital-approved ashtray, she would have discarded her cigarette in a proper ashtray and that the fire would not have occurred.

Fire Chief Lehman testified that a smoke detector would have given an earlier warning in this fire and that the fire was burning 1 to 3 minutes before Ms. Schreiner initially discovered it. The individual in charge of fire safety training at the medical center, Lieutenant Campbell, testified that he did not use the medical center's fire safety manual in his orientation and training of the nurses. He testified that the hospital policy was to first remove a patient from the room and out of immediate danger in case of fire. Chief Lehman testified that the particular training received by the medical center nurses was below the standard of care and that attempting to put the fire out with linens would also be indicative of a lack of training. The medical center's expert, Fire Captain Gibson, testified that throwing dry sheets on the fire would have added to the problem by fueling the fire. The jury could have found that if the medical center's nurses had been properly trained, they would have followed their training and prevented Mr. Wheeler's death by removing him from the room, in accordance with their training acronym RACE.

Discussion

1. Do you agree with the court's finding? Explain.
2. What is the importance of continuing education in fire safety?
3. What topics should be covered when designing a continuing education program for an organization's staff?

Patient Burned by Lamp

Citation: *Rice v. Vandenebossche*, 586 N.Y.S.2d 303 (N.Y. App. Div. 1992)

Facts

> The plaintiff alleged that while she was being treated for a laceration to her fore-head, Dr. Bhargava negligently placed a lamp dangerously close to her, causing burns to her forehead. The complaint contained one general ad damnum clause specifying damages against Dr. Bhargava and the hospital without allocating particular amounts as to each cause of action. Dr. Bhargava and the hospital each moved to dismiss the complaint on the ground that the plaintiff failed to attach a certificate of merit to her complaint. The court denied the motion, reasoning that the cause of action sounded in negligence rather than malpractice.

Issue

> Does this case raise an issue of malpractice or negligence?

Holding

> The New York Supreme Court, Appellate Division, held that the complaint alleging the patient was injured by a lamp being used by the physician while he was treating her sounded in medical malpractice.

Reason

> The critical question in determining whether an action sounds in medical malpractice or negligence is the nature of the duty to the plaintiff that the defendant is alleged to have breached. When the duty owing to the plaintiff by the defendant arises from the physician–patient relationship or is substantially related to medical treatment, the breach thereof gives rise to an action sounding in medical malpractice as opposed to simple negligence. However, if the conduct complained of may be readily assessed on the basis of common, everyday experience of the trier of facts, and expert testimony is unnecessary for such a review, then the cause of action sounds in negligence. In the instant case, the cause of action against Dr. Bhargava and the hospital clearly alleged that the plaintiff was burned on the forehead by a lamp that was being used while the physician was treating her for a forehead laceration. Because the conduct complained of was substantially related to the medical treatment, the cause of action sounded in medical malpractice.

Discussion

1. Do you agree with the court's reasoning? Explain.
2. Why is expert testimony generally not required in cases involving simple negligence?

County to Pay $150,000 to Claustrophobic Ex-Employee Who Worked in Cubicle

Jayne Feshold was a data technician hired by the county-run hospital in 1999. Her suit says she "worked without incident" until May 2007. Then the hospital's medical records department was moved to a new building, and she was assigned to work in an area "consisting of a small cubicle workspace instead of a more open environment."

Soon after, she began to exhibit "symptoms of severe anxiety, making it impossible for her to work efficiently." Her symptoms were later diagnosed as the result of claustrophobia . . . . Her supervisor was sympathetic and let her work in an open area.

A new supervisor a few months later, the lawsuit says, forced her to work in a cubicle. Her anxiety grew to such a degree that she sought help at UMC's emergency room in July 2007. When she found she would not be allowed to work in an open environment, she found a new job as a guard in UMC's Labor and Delivery Unit.

Then in February 2008, she filed a request to be accommodated under guidelines of the Americans with Disabilities Act—she wanted to work in more open space.

Joe Schoenmann, Las Vegas Sun, *July 5, 2011*

Patient Fall in X-Ray Room

Citation: *Cockerton v. Mercy Hosp. Med. Ctr.*, 490 N.W.2d 856 (Iowa Ct. App. 1992)

Facts

On June 23, 1987, the plaintiff, Ms. Cockerton, was admitted to the hospital for the purpose of surgery to correct a problem with her open bite. Dr. Maletta, her physician, ordered postsurgical X-rays for her head and face to be taken the next day. The next morning, between 8:00 a.m. and 8:15 a.m., a hospital employee took the plaintiff from her room to the X-ray department by wheelchair. A nurse had assessed her condition as slightly "oozy" and drowsy. She was wearing a urinary catheter. An IV and a nasogastric tube were still in place.

Ms. Alexander, an X-ray technician, took charge of the plaintiff in the X-ray room. It was her 3rd day on the job. After the plaintiff was taken inside the X-ray room, she was transferred from a wheelchair to a portable chair for the X-rays. Upon being moved, the plaintiff complained of nausea, and Ms. Alexander observed that the plaintiff's pupils were dilated. She did not use the restraint straps to secure the plaintiff to the chair when the X-rays were taken. At some point during the X-ray procedure, the plaintiff had a fainting seizure, and Ms. Alexander called for help. When Ms. Hewitt, another hospital employee, entered the room, Ms. Alexander was holding the plaintiff, who appeared nonresponsive, in an upright position. The plaintiff only remembered having been stood up and having a lead jacket across her back and shoulders. Ms. Alexander maintains that the plaintiff did not fall.

At the time the plaintiff left the X-ray room, her level of consciousness was poor. She was brought back to the ward, and the nasogastric tube was removed. Dr. Maletta noticed a deflection of the plaintiff's nose but had difficulty assessing it because of the surgical procedure from the day before. Because the plaintiff had fainted in the X-ray room, Dr. Maletta requested an incident report from the radiology department. The following day, the deflection of the plaintiff's nose was much more evident. Dr. Maletta consulted Dr. Ericson, a specialist, who attempted to correct the deformity. Dr. Ericson observed that it would require a substantial injury to the nose to deflect it to that severity.

The plaintiff instituted proceedings against the hospital, alleging that the negligence of the nurses or X-ray technicians allowed her to fall during the X-ray procedure and subsequently caused injury to her nose. The trial court did not require expert testimony concerning the standard of care by the X-ray technician. The jury concluded that the hospital was negligent in leaving the plaintiff unattended or failing to restrain her, which proximately caused her to fall and to be injured. The jury rendered a verdict of $48,370, and the hospital appealed.

Issue

Is expert testimony required whenever the health provider's lack of care is so obvious as to be within the comprehension of a layman and to require only common knowledge and experience to understand?

Holding

The Court of Appeals of Iowa held that the patient was not required to present expert testimony on the issue of the hospital's negligence.

Reason

Ordinarily, evidence of negligence in a medical malpractice action must be proven by expert testimony. The court rejected the hospital's argument that the X-ray procedure could not be categorized as routine or ministerial care. The conduct in question was simply the way the X-ray technician handled the plaintiff during the X-ray examination. In arguing for a professional standard, the hospital pointed to the elaborate training requirements for an X-ray technician, as required by the Iowa Administrative Code. However, the fact that an X-ray technician must meet certain requirements under the Iowa Administrative Code does not make all of the technician's conduct professional in nature. The applicable standard requires that of reasonable care.

The X-ray technician testified that during the X-ray, the plaintiff appeared to have a "seizure episode." She also testified that she left the plaintiff unattended for a brief period of time and that she did not use the restraint straps that were attached to the portable X-ray chair. Use of the restraint straps would have secured the plaintiff to the portable chair during the X-ray examination.

Dr. Maletta testified that there had been no problems with the septum during surgery, and that he had never had a complication such as the plaintiff's injury occur during surgery. While the plaintiff was in recovery immediately following surgery, Dr. Maletta observed no injuries to her nose. She did not leave her bed until she was taken to the X-ray room that next morning. The plaintiff had a syncopal episode (similar to a seizure) while she was in the X-ray room. Following the X-ray examination, her nose appeared "grotesque" and injured. The court found substantial evidence existed to establish a causal connection between the hospital's conduct and the plaintiff's injury.

Discussion

1. Should the radiologist share responsibility for the negligence of the X-ray technician? Explain.
2. What is the difference between ministerial and professional care?

Food Poisoning

Citation: *Connerwood Healthcare, Inc. v. Estate of Herron*, 683 N.E.2d 1322 (Ind. App. 1997)

Facts

In June 1995, approximately 70 people at the Connerwood residential nursing facility developed symptoms of food poisoning. Thirty-four residents tested positive for salmonella, and 3 died during the outbreak. The estate of one of the residents who died from the alleged salmonella infection filed suit against Connerwood and requested that the case be maintained as a class action.

The complaint alleged that Connerwood's negligence caused injury to the residents.

The trial court issued findings that (1) in June 1995, there occurred an outbreak of salmonella poisoning at the facility, as evidenced by the Indiana State Health Report; (2) up to 70 residents and employees were affected; (3) the poisoning resulted in physical illness and several deaths; and (4) given the older age and infirm physical condition of many of the residents, certification of this case as a class action would be appropriate in order to fairly and adequately protect the interests of this class.

The court concluded that the plaintiffs had satisfied Indiana Trial Rule 23 and conditionally certified the matter as a class action. Connerwood appealed and argued that the claim failed to meet the requirements of class action certification.

Issue

Did the trial court abuse its discretion when it conditionally certified the case as a class action?

Holding

The court of appeals held that the trial court did not abuse its discretion when it conditionally certified the case as a class action.

Reason

The court found that, given the age and physical condition of the residents affected by the food poisoning, certification was appropriate and not impractical in order to fairly and adequately protect the interests of this class. Although the number of class members is small, they would have been unable to protect their interests and pursue remedies on an individual basis.

The commonality requirement is satisfied if the individual claims are derived from a common course of conduct. The plaintiff claimed that the negligent use and preparation of nonpasteurized egg products caused the food poisoning. The court concluded that this constitutes a common course of conduct and therefore satisfies the commonality requirement.

The court also determined that class action treatment is a superior method of adjudication in this case. The potential class members are elderly, medically compromised, and may be incapable of exercising their own rights. Both state and federal courts have determined that class action treatment is appropriate for a mass tort such as food poisoning.

Discussion

1. Why did the appeals court uphold the findings of the trial court?
2. Do you agree with the court's holding? Explain.
3. Discuss the safety precautions that should be followed to prevent food contamination (e.g., required hand-washing in bathrooms and upon entering the kitchen; use of hair nets, sterile gloves, and face masks where appropriate).

CFR Title 42 § 482.27 Condition of Participation: Laboratory Services

(c) *General blood safety issues.* For lookback activities only related to new blood safety issues that are identified after August 24, 2007, hospitals must comply with FDA regulations as they pertain to blood safety issues in the following areas:

   (1) Appropriate testing and quarantining of infectious blood and blood components.
   (2) Notification and counseling of recipients that may have received infectious blood and blood components.

[57 FR 7136, Feb. 28, 1992, as amended at 61 FR 47433, Sept. 9, 1996; 72 FR 48573, Aug. 24, 2007]

Blood Collection and the Transmission of Hepatitis

Citation: *Raskin v. Community Blood Ctrs. of S. Florida, Inc.*, 699 So.2d 1014 (1997)

Facts

Appellant, Betty Raskin, was hospitalized at Boca Raton Community Hospital in December 1991. While at the hospital, she was transfused with five units of whole blood supplied by appellee, Community Blood Centers of South Florida, Inc. In April 1992, the appellant was readmitted to the hospital, where it was determined she had contracted viral hepatitis B. The treating physicians made entries in the hospital records indicating the transfused blood was the source of the virus. Appellants alleged breach of implied warranty under section 672.316(5), Florida Statutes (1989), which provided

(5) The procurement, processing, storage, distribution, or use of whole blood, plasma, blood products, and blood derivatives for the purpose of injecting or transfusing the same, or any of them, into the human body for any purpose whatsoever is declared to be the rendering of a service by any person participating therein and

does not constitute a sale, whether or not any consideration is given therefor; and the implied warranties of merchantability and fitness for a particular purpose are not applicable as to a defect that cannot be detected or removed by a reasonable use of scientific procedures or techniques. Fla. Stat. § 672.316(5) (1989).

It was appellants' position that their obligation was to show the defect could "be detected or removed by a reasonable use of scientific procedures or techniques." The record plainly showed this to be an issue of fact. The appellants introduced evidence-supporting causation.

Issue

Was it necessary for the appellants to show the appellee was negligent in its testing?

Holding

The appeals court held that it was not necessary for the appellants to show the appellee was negligent in its testing.

Reason

On remand, the trial court was directed to permit the appellants to amend their cause of action for implied warranty. The Florida Supreme Court has held that Florida law prior to the enactment of § 672.316(5) was that blood suppliers were strictly liable for defects in blood, under breach of implied warranties, even when the defect was undetectable.

Section 672.316(5) was clearly an effort by the legislature to limit implied warranty actions against blood suppliers.

Application of § 672.316(5), Florida Statutes, provides that a plaintiff may maintain an action for damages on the grounds of breach of implied warranty of fitness or merchantability only if he alleges and proves that the defect of which he complains is detectable or removable by the use of reasonable scientific procedures or techniques.

Discussion

1. Why must a defect be detectable in order for a suit to be filed on the basis of implied warranty?
2. If the appellants could show that the appellee was negligent in its testing of blood for hepatitis, could liability be established for negligent conduct? Discuss.

Wrong Blood Administered

Citation: *Dodson v. Community Blood Ctr.*, 633 So.2d 252 (La. Ct. App. 1993)

Facts

The Patients' Compensation Fund (PCF) appealed from an order of the trial court, which awarded damages to a patient who contracted hepatitis following blood transfusion.

Mr. Dodson was scheduled to undergo surgery at a medical center. In anticipation of the surgery and out of fear of contracting AIDS through blood transfusions from unknown donors, he arranged to have three known donors donate blood earmarked for his use should transfusion be required.

After surgery, Mr. Dodson was transfused with two pints of blood. However, the blood used was not the blood obtained from Mr. Dodson's voluntary donors. The blood had been taken from the hospital's general inventory, which had been obtained from the Community Blood Center. Mr. Dodson subsequently learned that as a result of the transfusions, he had been infected with what at the time was called non-A non-B hepatitis. It is now referred to as hepatitis C.

Issue

Was the award of $325,000 in general damages excessive?

Holding

The Court of Appeal of Louisiana held that the award of damages was not excessive.

Reason

The PCF contended the trial court erred in assessing general damages. PCF alleges that the sum of $150,000 in general damages is the maximum to which the plaintiffs are entitled, thus quantum should be reduced accordingly. A review of the record revealed that Mr. Dodson contracted non-A and non-B hepatitis through the blood transfusions received. Based on tests prior to trial, the chronic hepatitis was either resolved or quiescent. The plaintiff had a good prognosis; however, this prognosis was not guaranteed. There remained a chance that the chronic hepatitis may become active in the future.

In reasons for judgment, the trial court found that Mr. Dodson was a credible witness. He did not exaggerate his symptoms, fears, or worries about his condition. The court believed Mr. Dodson when he said he felt like a leper and feared infecting his wife, child, and friends with the disease. The trial court arrived at what it determined to be an appropriate award for general damages. After careful review of the record and in light of the vast discretion of the trial court to assess general damages, the court found that there was no abuse of discretion.

Discussion

1. Under what circumstances will an appellate court overturn the decision of a lower court?
2. What are the proper procedures for handling blood and blood products in this case?

NOTES

1. http://www.osha.gov/SLTC/healthcarefacilities/index.html
2. http://www.vvh.org/pages/p-qoc-safety-employee-7.php
3. http://www.prnewswire.com/news-releases/massachusetts-workers-rights-board-releases-report-on-nurse-staffing-crisis-at-tufts-medical-center-as-nurses-prepare-for-one-day-strike-121192264.html
4. http://www8.nationalacademies.org/onpinews/newsitem.aspx?RecordID=11623

chapter ten

Human Resources

Shifting the Risk

Being in a hospital at night or over a weekend can be hazardous to your health, and even has a name: "the weekend effect." A raft of studies has documented higher rates of death, complications, and medical errors affecting patients treated at night or on weekends. . . . There's less nursing care, less access to a doctor and more demands on doctors. . . . To bridge the chasm between the day and night shifts, hospitals from Syracuse to Seattle are hiring a new breed of subspecialist called a "nocturnist"—an experienced doctor who works overnight taking care of patients outside the emergency room.

Sandra B. Boodman, The Washington Post, *June 7, 2011*

Human Resources, as used herein, is a term used to describe the individuals who make up the workforce of healthcare organizations. *Human Resources* is also the term used to describe the department charged with the overall responsibility for developing and implementing personnel policies and procedures; overseeing the development of staffing patterns; developing job descriptions in corroboration with the various department managers; assisting in determining the hiring criteria for each category of employee; advertising position openings; screening and interviewing prospective employment candidates; selecting, training, and administering employee benefits; overseeing the performance evaluation process; conducting exit interviews; and so on. The purpose of the employment process is to ensure that each position filled helps the organization carry out its stated mission. The human resources department is also responsible for ensuring that federal, state, and local labor laws and regulations are implemented and adhered to. Finally, the human resources department is also responsible for promoting ethical employee business practices and protecting the rights of the employer and employee.

A variety of legal cases as they relate to human resources and hospital staff are presented next.

Hospital Nurse Staffing and Quality of Care

Hospitals with low nurse staffing levels tend to have higher rates of poor patient outcomes such as pneumonia, shock, cardiac arrest, and urinary tract infections, according to research funded by the Agency for Healthcare Research and Quality (AHRQ) and others. . . .

The largest of the studies discussed here found significant associations between lower levels of nurse staffing and higher rates of pneumonia, upper gastrointestinal bleeding, shock/cardiac arrest, urinary tract infections, and failure to rescue. Other studies found associations between lower staffing levels and pneumonia, lung collapse, falls, pressure ulcers, thrombosis after major surgery, pulmonary compromise after surgery, longer hospital stays, and 30-day mortality. However, researchers stress that, at present, such "nursing-sensitive" adverse outcomes should be viewed more as indicators or sentinel outcomes than as measures of the full impact of nurse staffing on patient outcomes.

Mark W. Stanton, Research in Action, Issue 14, Agency for Healthcare Research and Quality of Care, *March, 2004*[1]

Discharge and Employment Discrimination

Citation: *Staub v. Proctor Hospital,* (No. 09-400) 560 F. 3d 647, reversed and remanded, (2011)

Facts

The petitioner Vincent Staub worked as an angiography technician for the respondent Proctor Hospital until 2004, when he was fired. Staub and Proctor hotly disputed the facts surrounding the firing.

While employed by Proctor, Staub was a member of the Army Reserve, which required him to attend a drill 1 weekend per month and to train full time for 2 to 3 weeks a year. Both Mulally, Staub's immediate supervisor, and Korenchuk, Mulally's supervisor, were hostile to Staub's military obligations. Staub's supervisor scheduled him for additional shifts without notice so that he could pay back to the department for everyone else having to cover his schedule for the Reserves. Staub's supervisor also informed Staub's co-worker, Leslie Sweborg, that Staub's military duty had been a strain on the department and asked Sweborg to help her get rid of him.

In January 2004, Staub's supervisor issued a "Corrective Action" disciplinary warning for his having purportedly violated a company rule requiring him to stay in his work area whenever he was not working with a patient. The Corrective Action included a directive requiring Staub to report to Mulally or Korenchuk whenever he had no patients waiting and the angio cases were completed.

A co-worker of Staub's named Day complained to Ms. Buck, Proctor's VP of Human Resources (HR), and Mr. McGowan, Proctor's Chief Operating Officer (COO), about Staub's frequent unavailability and abruptness. The COO directed Korenchuk and HR to create a plan that would solve Staub's availability problems. But 3 weeks later, before they had time to do so, Korenchuk informed HR that Staub had left his desk without informing a supervisor, in violation of the January Corrective Action. Staub now contends this accusation was false: he had left Korenchuk a voicemail notification that he was leaving his desk. HR relied on Korenchuk's accusation, however, and after reviewing Staub's personnel file, HR decided to fire him. The termination notice stated that Staub had ignored the directive issued in the January 2004 Corrective Action.

Staub challenged his firing through Proctor's grievance process, claiming that his supervisor had fabricated the allegation underlying the Corrective Action out of hostility toward his military obligations. HR did not follow up with Staub's supervisor about his claim.

Staub sued Proctor under the Uniformed Services Employment and Reemployment Rights Act of 1994, 38 U.S.C. §4301 et seq., claiming that his discharge was motivated by hostility to his obligations as a military reservist. His contention was not that HR had any such hostility but that his supervisor and Korenchuk did, and that their actions influenced HR's ultimate employment decision. A jury found that Staub's "military status was a motivating factor in Proctor's decision to discharge him," and awarded $57,640 in damages.

The U.S. Court of Appeals 7th Circuit reversed the trial court's decision, holding that Proctor was entitled to judgment as a matter of law. The 7th Circuit observed that Staub had sought to hold his employer liable for the animus of a supervisor who was not charged with making the ultimate employment decision. The 7th Circuit explained that a case could not succeed unless the non-decision-maker exercised such singular influence over the decision-maker that the decision to terminate was the product of *blind reliance*. It then noted that "HR looked beyond what Mulally and Korenchuk said," relying in part on her conversation with Day and her review of Staub's personnel file. The court admitted that HR's investigation could have been more robust, because it "failed to pursue Staub's theory that his supervisor fabricated the write-up. It was established that the HR director was not wholly dependent on the advice of Korenchuk and Mulally. Staub then filed a petition for writ of certiorari with the Supreme Court asking the Supreme Court to review the decision of the 7th Circuit.

Issue

The Supreme Court considered the circumstances under which an employer may be held liable for employment discrimination based on the discriminatory animus of an employee who influenced, but did not make, the ultimate employment decision.

Holding

The Supreme Court granted certiorari, and Justice Scalia delivered the opinion on March 1, 2011, reversing and remanding the case back to the 7th Circuit.

Reason

USERRA

The Uniformed Services Employment and Reemployment Rights Act (USERRA) provides in relevant part

A person who is a member of . . . or has an obligation to perform service in a uniformed service shall not be denied initial employment, reemployment, retention in employment, promotion, or any benefit of employment by an employer on the basis of that membership, . . . or obligation. 38 U. S. C. §4311(a).

Elaboration in §4311(c)

An employer shall be considered to have engaged in actions prohibited . . . under subsection (a), if the person's membership . . . is a motivating factor in the employer's action, unless the employer can prove that the action would have been taken in the absence of such membership. §4311(c).

The statute is very similar to Title VII, which prohibits employment discrimination because of race, color, religion, sex, or national origin and states that such discrimination is established when one of those factors was a *motivating factor* for any employment practice, even though other factors also motivated the practice.

If a company official makes the decision to take an adverse employment action, personally acting out of hostility to the employee's membership in or obligation to a uniformed service, a motivating factor exists. The problem the Supreme Court confronted arose when that official has no discriminatory animus but is influenced by previous company action that is the product of a like animus in someone else.

Even if dismissal was not the object of Mulally's and Korenchuk's reports, it may have been their result, or even their foreseeable consequence, but that was not enough to render Mulally or Korenchuk responsible. Staub, however, was seeking to hold Proctor liable, not Mulally and Korenchuk.

If the employer's investigation results in an adverse action for reasons unrelated to the supervisor's original biased action, then the employer will not be liable. The supervisor's biased report may remain a causal factor if the independent investigation takes it into account without determining if the adverse action was entirely justified. The independent investigation does not somehow relieve the employer of *fault*. The employer is at fault because one of its agents committed an action based on discriminatory animus that was intended to cause, and did in fact cause, an adverse employment decision.

The biased supervisor and the ultimate decision-maker, however, acted as agents of Proctor that the plaintiff seeks to hold liable; each of them possessed supervisory authority delegated by Proctor and exercised it in the interest of their employer.

The Supreme Court therefore held that if a supervisor performs an act motivated by antimilitary animus that is intended by the supervisor to cause an adverse employment action, and if that act is a proximate cause of the ultimate employment action, then the employer is liable under the Uniformed Services Employment and Reemployment Rights Act USERRA.

Applying analysis to the facts of this case, it is clear that the 7th Circuit's judgment must be reversed. Both Mulally and Korenchuk were acting within the scope of their employment when they took the actions that allegedly caused HR to fire Staub. As the 7th Circuit recognized, there was evidence that Mulally's and Korenchuk's actions were motivated by hostility toward Staub's military obligations. There was also evidence that Mulally's and Korenchuk's actions were causal factors underlying HR's decision to fire Staub.

HR's termination notice expressly stated that Staub was terminated because he had "ignored" the directive in the Corrective Action. Finally, there was evidence that both Mulally and Korenchuk had the specific intent to cause Staub to be terminated. Mulally stated she was trying to get rid of Staub, and Korenchuk was aware that Mulally was out to get Staub. Moreover, Korenchuk informed HR, Proctor's personnel officer responsible for terminating employees, of Staub's alleged noncompliance with Mulally's Corrective Action, and HR fired Staub immediately thereafter; a reasonable jury could infer that Korenchuk intended that Staub be fired. The 7th Circuit therefore erred in holding that Proctor was entitled to judgment as a matter of law.

It is less clear whether the jury's verdict should be reinstated or whether Proctor is entitled to a new trial. The jury instruction did not hew precisely to the rule the Supreme Court adopted; it required only that the jury find that "military status was a motivating factor in Proctor's decision to discharge him." Whether the variance between the instruction and the Supreme Court's rule was harmless error or should mandate a new trial is a matter the 7th Circuit may consider.

Discussion

1. Should an employer, if it knew or should have known, be liable for damages suffered by an employee who as a result of a supervisor's bias is terminated by the employer?
2. Discuss what issues the HR director should take into consideration when reviewing a manger's decision to terminate an employee (e.g., why the company is taking the adverse action, what has led to the decision, who provided input into the decision, and whether any input from a supervisor was "rubber-stamped" or whether Human Resources conducted an independent investigation).

Unfair Labor Practices

Citation: *NLRB v. Shelby Mem'l Hosp. Ass'n*, 1 F.3d 550 (7th Cir. 1993)

Facts

The National Labor Relations Board (NLRB) brought an action to enforce its unfair labor practices orders against a nursing facility.

In the early summer of 1990, nurses at the facility began a union drive. The facility unsuccessfully opposed the union. The first case heard by the board arose when Ms. Sands, an affiliate of the International Brotherhood of Teamsters and a licensed practical nurse employed by the facility, filed charges of unfair labor practices against the facility in July 1990. The National Labor Relations Act, 29 U.S.C. § 158(a)(1) makes it an unfair labor practice for an employer "to interfere with, restrain, or coerce employees in the exercise of the rights guaranteed in" § 157.

Ms. Welton worked in the facility's dietary department. She attended a union organization meeting on July 5 and signed a union authorization card. At a hearing before the administrative law judge (ALJ), she testified that her dietary supervisor, Ms. Fisher, took her aside at work on the day after the meeting and asked whether she or anyone from the dietary department had attended that meeting. Ms. Welton denied any knowledge of the meeting. Before the ALJ, Ms. Fisher denied having any conversation with Ms. Welton about the union meeting. The board found that the questioning of Ms. Welton constituted unlawful interrogation in violation of § 158(a)(1). The board credited Ms. Welton's testimony over that of Ms. Fisher because Ms. Welton was no longer employed by the facility at the time of the hearing and had nothing to gain by testifying falsely about the incident.

Mr. Hopkins worked as a janitor for the facility. In April 1990, he was laid off as a result of the financial problems the facility was then experiencing. He was rehired in late June. Following his return, Mr. Hopkins attended the aforementioned meeting on July 5, and he also signed an authorization card. He testified before the ALJ that, on July 15, 5 days after the Teamsters Union had filed an election petition, Mr. Carlson, the facility's maintenance supervisor, approached him at work and said, "I've got to ask you this question. You can tell me if it's none of my business it you want to. Has [sic] any of the nurses or aides harassed you about the union?" Id. at 559. Mr. Hopkins said no. The board credited Mr. Hopkins's version of the events, noting that he, like Ms. Welton, was not employed by the facility at the time and had nothing to gain by fabricating his testimony.

On July 18, the facility circulated a memorandum to all employees that stated, "This is to advise that the NLRB has tentatively set a hearing on Wednesday, July 25th, to decide who can vote in a union election. Our position is supervisors, RNs, and LPNs cannot vote. We will keep you advised." Id. at 560.

On July 19, the facility held a mandatory meeting for all registered nurses (RNs), licensed practical nurses (LPNs), and supervisors. Facility administrator Mr. Wimer, facility attorney Mr. Yocum, and chief executive officer Mr. Colby (of the facility's affiliated hospital) conducted the meeting. Mr. Yocum told the nurses that, in the facility's opinion, all RNs and LPNs were supervisors who could not vote in the upcoming election but must remain loyal to the facility. When asked by union supporter Ms. Sands what he meant by loyalty, Mr. Yocum replied that all RNs and LPNs were prohibited from engaging in union activities. When asked by Ms. Sands why the facility opposed the union, Mr. Yocum responded, "Well, for one thing, they cost too . . . much money . . . [D]o you think those dues come out of thin air?" Id. at 560.

The board concluded that the facility, through Mr. Yocum, violated § 158(a)(1) by telling the LPNs present at the meeting that they could not vote in the upcoming union election or participate in union activities. The LPNs were told that engaging in such activities could subject them to dismissal.

Issues

Did the questioning by supervisors of their subordinates regarding a union meeting constitute an unfair labor practice?

Holding

The questioning by supervisors of their subordinates regarding a union meeting constituted an unfair labor practice.

Reason

The United States Court of Appeals for the 7th Circuit held that the employer's interrogation of nursing facility employees about a union meeting constituted an unfair labor practice. On the record as a whole, substantial evidence supported the board's conclusions that the questioning of Ms. Welton and Mr. Hopkins amounted to unlawful interrogation in violation of § 158(a)(1).

Discussion

1. What should be the proper conduct of an organization during an attempt by employees to seek union representation?
2. Do you consider the supervisors' questioning of the employees an unfair labor practice? Explain your answer.

Employment-At-Will: Termination without Cause

Citation: *Yambor v. St. Vincent Med. Ctr.*, 631 N.E.2d 187 (Ohio Com. Pl. 1993)

Facts

Mr. Yambor, a family counselor, brought a wrongful termination action against St. Vincent Medical Center, its program manager, and its program coordinator. Mr. Yambor was hired by St. Vincent as a family counselor in 1984 under an oral agreement. Mr. Yambor understood that so long as he was employed by the medical center, he was to be compensated. He believed he could quit at any time and also assumed that St. Vincent could terminate him at any time. Mr. Yambor acknowledged that, in a letter dated March 29, 1991, the medical center advised him that any further failure to perform to standards; any carelessness in areas of documentation or charting; any unscheduled, unexcused, or unauthorized absences; any communication problems or insubordination; or any careless performance would result in his termination. The record showed copies of reports of employee conferences, employee coaching forms, and memoranda reciting his history of discipline at the medical center. He was terminated from employment on July 2, 1991.

Under Ohio law, it is presumed that every employment relationship is "at-will," meaning either party may terminate the relationship at any time for any reason not contrary to law. This presumption of at-will employment can be rebutted if the parties agree that an employee will be discharged only for cause. Mr. Yambor contended that the medical center, by expressing reasons for his termination and by implementing a grievance procedure, represented to him that he could be terminated only for just cause. To this end, he relied on his own assumptions that his termination had to be based on a logical reason. Mr. Yambor argued that disciplinary letters containing complaints over his performance set forth issues of fact that prevented summary judgment.

Issue

Could the counselor, an employee at-will, be terminated without just cause?

Holding

The Court of Common Pleas held that the counselor was an employee at-will who could be terminated without just cause.

Reason

Mr. Yambor did not come forward with any evidence that the medical center had agreed he would be terminated only for just cause or that he had any basis for this belief. The basis of his claim for breach of oral agreement was the simple fact that he was terminated. Mr. Yambor was not able to specify any policies that were violated. Subjective understandings are insufficient to create material issues of fact.

Discussion

1. Describe the terminology employee-at-will.
2. Why was Mr. Yambor considered an at-will employee?

Discharge Arbitrary

Citation: *Ward v. Brown*, 22 F.3d 516 (2nd Cir. 1994)

Facts

The plaintiff was a nurse at a Veterans Affairs (VA) Medical Center for 9 years. In 1990, he was accused of verbally abusing three patients. It was a matter of record that the nurse was a labor organizer who had filed a number of grievances against his supervisor. He was discharged after a panel conducted an investigation and decided that all three of the charges were substantiated.

After the nurse received a letter of discharge, he requested and was granted a hearing before the department's disciplinary board. The board sustained only one of the charges, but still recommended the plaintiff's discharge for intentionally teasing, speaking harshly to, threatening, and intimidating a patient.

The plaintiff brought a suit against the VA, the Secretary of Veterans Affairs, and the director of VA Medical Center. Although the court found that the nurse's conduct constituted patient abuse, it ruled that the medical center's imposition of the penalty of discharge was arbitrary and capricious in light of their policy that was outlined in their manual. Their own policy mandated that the department treat similar offenses with similar penalties, and that they must punish the employees in proportion to the offense committed. The government appealed.

Issue

Was the discharge penalty arbitrary and capricious considering the policy manual and the offense committed?

Holding

The United States Court of Appeals for the 2nd Circuit held that the penalty of discharge was arbitrary and capricious and, thus, had to be vacated.

Reason

Applicable statutes mandated that the board consider punishments that were within the prescribed limitations set by the Secretary of Labor. The penalties varied from a reprimand, to a suspension, to a reduction of pay, and finally to discharge. Further, the board had to recommend a penalty that was appropriate for the offense that was committed. The necessary principle to apply was "like penalties for like offenses." The board was found by the court not to have applied that principle. Therefore, it was held that it was arbitrary and capricious for the board not to have considered the applicable statutes. The punishment was inconsistent with that which was imposed on other employees who had committed patient abuse. The policy was required to be considered before recommending a penalty.

Discussion

1. Do you agree with the court of appeals decision? Explain your answer.
2. What was the court referring to when it stated that the board failed to apply the principle "like penalties for like offenses"?

Breach of Contract

Citation: *Chapman v. University of Mass. Med. Ctr.*, 628 N.E.2d 8 (Mass. 1994)

Facts

The plaintiff, Ms. Chapman, had brought an action against the state university medical center for wrongful discharge in breach of her employment contract. Ms. Chapman was hired as a supervisor of her department in 1978. In 1984, she became the assistant hospital director. She reported directly to Mr. Scarbeau, the chief executive officer. Ms. Chapman was one of four employees who reported directly to Mr. Scarbeau, none of whom had been employed longer than she had. Ms. Chapman had trained one of the three other associates who reported to Mr. Scarbeau, and she substituted for the two associates she had not trained. She received regular merit raises and had never been criticized. Ms. Chapman's last written contract, which was for the 5-year period covering December 10, 1985, through December 9, 1990, provided that the appointments to the professional staff were contingent on the availability of funds. Ms. Chapman was the only person in her job category, and Mr. Scarbeau determined that her position was expendable, although he could have saved it by choosing to lay off other employees. Two months prior to the layoffs, Ms. Chapman had complained to Mr. Scarbeau about the high cost of purchasing radiation equipment. He told her to "mind her own business and she would be spared in the upcoming layoffs." Id. at 11. Of the 138 employees laid off, 70 to 80 employees were rehired within a year. Ms. Chapman was not one of them. The superior court held for the plaintiff finding that Mr. Scarbeau violated the medical center's employment contract with the plaintiff by acting in bad faith when he terminated her position.

Issue

Did Mr. Scarbeau act in bad faith by selectively eliminating the plaintiff's position during layoffs, rather than allowing her to bump others in her department?

Holding

The Supreme Judicial Court of Massachusetts affirmed the trial court's decision by finding that Mr. Scarbeau had acted in bad faith.

Reason

The court held that the judge could infer from the proffered testimony that Mr. Scarbeau threatened the plaintiff when she had complained to him about improper equipment bidding and purchasing procedures. He carried out his threat by firing her during layoffs for reasons other than unavailability of funds. The evidence supported the plaintiff's argument that her position was substantially the same as those held by the three associate directors. The plaintiff was qualified to bump others in her department.

Discussion

1. Could the employment-at-will doctrine have been an effective defense for the defendant?
2. Is it possible that the outcome in this case might have been different in another state? What about a different court or a different jury?

Retaliatory Discharge

Citation: *Dalby v. Sisters of Providence*, 865 P.2d 391 (Or. Ct. App. 1993)

Facts

The plaintiff, Ms. Dalby, a pharmacy technician, brought an action against her former employer for retaliatory discharge and the infliction of emotional distress. Ms. Dalby alleged that in 1989 she was retaliated against for reporting to her supervisor on several occasions that there were inaccuracies in the drug inventory and that record keeping regarding these inaccuracies was in violation of Oregon administrative rules. Ms. Dalby alleged that, rather than comply with the regulations, her supervisor retaliated against her because of her insistence that her employer comply with the rules.

Retaliatory actions against Ms. Dalby included accusations of her stealing cocaine from the hospital's drug inventory in 1990. In 1991, Ms. Dalby learned that the sheriff's department had been asked to arrest her for stealing cocaine from the inventory but that the department had refused to make the arrest. Ms. Dalby also alleged that her supervisor refused to talk to her except for job-related purposes and that hospital attendance policies were rigidly applied against her. As a result of the defendant's actions, Ms. Dalby resigned her position.

Ms. Dalby's former employer argued that the allegations did not demonstrate constructive discharge, which include "(1) that the employer deliberately created or deliberately maintained the working condition(s), (2) with the intention of forcing the employee to leave the employment, and (3) that the employee left the employment because of the working conditions" [*Bratcher v. Sky Chiefs, Inc.*, 308 Or. 501, 506, 738 P.2d 4 (1989)].

The circuit court dismissed Ms. Dalby's claim, and she appealed claiming a cause of action for wrongful discharge and emotional distress.

Issue

Can the plaintiff's allegation be assumed to be true?

Holding

The Court of Appeals of Oregon, assuming the plaintiff's allegation to be true, reversed and remanded the case, holding that the pharmacy technician had stated a cause of action for wrongful discharge and the intentional infliction of emotional distress.

Reason

Ms. Dalby made a good faith report as to the hospital's noncompliance with drug inventory and record-keeping requirements required under Oregon regulations. Her report fulfilled an important "societal obligation." An employer may not discharge an employee for making such reports. The conduct of the employer, including false accusations that she had stolen cocaine, gave rise to an action for the infliction of emotional distress.

Discussion

1. Regardless of the final disposition of this case by the trial court, what issues remain open for review by management and the governing body?
2. What control mechanisms should be in place to ensure oversight in the drug inventory?

Nurse's Discharge Extraordinarily Severe

Citation: *Ward v. Derwinski*, 837 F. Supp. 517 (W.D. N.Y. 1992)

Facts

The plaintiff, a nurse, was discharged from the Veterans Affairs Medical Center in Canandaigua, New York (VACNY), for verbally abusing a psychiatric patient under his care. The plaintiff had been assigned to a nursing unit with 50 male patients who were hospitalized for chronic conditions, many of which were psychiatric in nature. During the morning of March 31, 1989, the plaintiff spoke with W.J., one of the patients on his floor. The patient had a history of hallucinations and unprovoked attacks on others. W.J. was leaning his head down in front of him. W.J. was giggling and talking to himself. The plaintiff, believing that the patient was hallucinating, called his name twice, but W.J. did not respond. The plaintiff patted W.J. on the shoulder and asked how he was feeling. W.J. responded, "Not good." The plaintiff then asked W.J. "if he felt like fighting." W.J. smiled and said, "Yes." Apparently it was common for the staff to question W.J. about fighting. W.J. was then asked if he would like medication, to which he replied, "Yes." The plaintiff administered Haladol, which was administered to W.J. on an as-needed basis.

Approximately 2 weeks later, two nurses filed written incident reports alleging that the plaintiff had abused W.J. The nurses claimed that the plaintiff had taunted W.J. and threatened to put him in restraints and "let the other patients at him." Id. at 519. The incident was reported to the plaintiff's supervisor, who suggested that they write memos to the medical director to initiate patient abuse charges against the plaintiff. An investigation of the incident by a three-member panel included interviews of nine employees, whose statements were recorded. Upon completion of the investigation, the panel recommended that the plaintiff be discharged. The medical director approved the panel's findings and the proposed discharge. The plaintiff appealed the medical director's decision to a disciplinary board. The board sustained the medical director's decision to discharge the plaintiff for charges of abuse against W.J. The plaintiff appealed to the Secretary of Veterans Affairs, who sustained the medical director's decision. The plaintiff then sought judicial review, alleging that the decision of the board was arbitrary and capricious and not supported by substantial evidence. The plaintiff claimed that "other nurses received less severe penalties for conduct which was much more egregious than the conduct for which he was terminated." Id. at 520.

Issue

(1) Was the finding that the plaintiff verbally abused the patient arbitrary and capricious? (2) Was the discharge penalty for the plaintiff arbitrary and capricious when compared to penalties in other disciplinary cases?

Holding

The United States District Court for the Western District of New York held that the finding by the Secretary of Veterans Affairs (that the plaintiff verbally abused the patient) was not arbitrary and capricious; however, it held that the discharge penalty for the plaintiff was arbitrary and capricious when compared to penalties imposed in other disciplinary cases. The case was remanded for reconsideration of a penalty consistent with the court's decision.

Reason

The record indicated that the charge of verbal abuse was properly investigated. Nine employees were interviewed under oath. The fact that the board accepted some testimony against the plaintiff was not subject to review by the district court. The district court found that it could not overrule a credibility termination made by those who actually heard the testimony. As to the second issue, the choice of the penalty was largely within the agency's discretion. Although the discharge is permissible, the Veterans Affairs manual recommended that penalties administered be progressively severe before discharge action is initiated, "unless the offense is so serious that it warrants removal action." Id. at 523–524. There was no evidence in the record "so serious" as to warrant the plaintiff's discharge. The record contained numerous instances of conduct that were much more severe in nature but did not result in the penalty of discharge. For example:

- A nurse threw a milkshake in a 75-year-old patient's face after he spat medication at her. The nurse was suspended for 1 day.
- A nurse held down a patient while two other nursing assistants beat him for attempting to leave his area of confinement. The nurse received a 14-day suspension.
- A nurse inflated the retaining balloon and an abdominal feeding tube of a patient in order to facilitate its removal. This was against the hospital policy and procedure. No disciplinary action was taken.

Even more troubling is the indication in the record that plaintiff is the only professional nurse disciplined for patient abuse who received the penalty of discharge in the 30-year history of VACNY. On this record it is clear that, when compared to the penalties imposed for other instances of verbal and physical patient abuse, plaintiff's penalty is not consistent with VA policy, is extraordinarily severe, and is, therefore, arbitrary and capricious. On this record, the determination of an experienced nurse, found to have committed only one instance of verbal patient abuse, is unjustified in fact. Id. at 524.

Discussion

1. What alternative disciplinary actions could have been taken?
2. What was the U.S. District Court's reasoning for determining that the discharge penalty was arbitrary and capricious?

Nursing Supervisors Not Entitled to NLRB Protection

Citation: *Health Care & Retirement Corp. v. NLRB*, 987 F.2d 1256 (6th Cir. 1993)

Facts

The petitioner, *Health Care & Retirement Corp. (HCR)* operates a nursing facility in Urbana, Ohio. A director of nursing, an assistant director, 15 RNs and LPNs, and 50 aides staffed the nursing department. The aides reported directly to the LPNs. From 1988 to 1989, there were continuing disputes between management and employees. After the nursing home administrator refused to meet with three nurses to discuss their complaints, they met instead with the director and vice president of the Health Care and Retirement Corporation, who promised to conduct an investigation. At the completion of the investigation, the three nurses were fired for participating in concerted protective conduct for the purpose of collective conduct and more aides were hired at increased salaries. The nurses, who were also supervisors, filed a complaint with the NLRB for unfair labor practices. After a hearing, the NLRB (National Labor Relations Board) found that the nurses were not supervisors, according to the National Labor Relations Act (NLRA), and ordered their reinstatement. An administrative law judge (ALJ) initially found the nurses to be "employees" within the meaning of the NLRA and, therefore, protected by the Act. HCR filed a petition to review the Board's decision.

Issue

Were the LPNs supervisors and, therefore, entitled to the NLRA's protection?

Holding

The U.S. Court of Appeals, however, found that they were supervisors and not entitled to the NLRA's protection.

Reason

The Court of Appeals for the 6th Circuit found that the nurses were supervisors and not covered under the NLRA. Therefore, the court did not have to address the unfair labor practice claims.

. . . it is up to Congress to carve out an exception for the health care field, including nurses, should Congress not wish for such nurses to be considered supervisors. It is the responsibility of this Court to interpret the law as written by Congress and promulgated through case decisions. Although the Board has maintained it will not yield this point, when the facts so warrant, as in the case at bar, this court must reverse the decision of the Board. Since the staff nurses are supervisors and not covered under the Act, this court need not review the merits of the unfair labor practice claims. Id. at 1261.

NLRA 29 U.S.C. 152 (11)

29 U.S.C. 152 (11) of the NLRA defines a supervisor as

any individual having authority, in the interest of the employer, to hire, transfer, suspend, lay off, recall, promote, discharge, assign, reward, or discipline other employees, or responsibly direct them, or to adjust their grievances, or effectively to recommend such action, if in connection with the foregoing the exercise of such authority is not of a merely routine or clerical nature, but requires the use of independent judgment.

The nurses failed to establish, by substantive evidence, that they did not serve in a supervisory capacity. Nurse aides reported directly to them, and they had the authority to assign them. It was the LPNs' responsibility to find replacements for the aides if they did not report to work or were late. The LPNs were also responsible for approving lunches and breaks for the aides. An employee was considered a supervisor if any one of the enumerated tasks was performed and if the authority was exercised in the interests of the employer and required independent judgment.

Discussion

1. What would make a nurse a supervisor under the NLRA, resulting in no protection for the nurse under the act?
2. Why did the court determine that the nurses were supervisors?

Employee Handbook: Termination–at-Will

Citation: *Frank v. South Suburban Hosp. Found.*, 628 N.E.2d 953 (Ill. App. Ct. 1993)

Facts

The plaintiff, who was hired as a nurse by the South Suburban Hospital Foundation, became the nursing supervisor of the oncology unit when it opened. When she was hired in 1984, she had to attend an orientation meeting and was told to bring her employee handbook with her. There were other versions of that handbook produced during her employment. In addition, she kept personnel policies and procedures that were distributed. The various sections of the handbook, such as the welcome and foreword, described the purpose of the handbook as providing guidelines about the employees' rights and responsibilities. It was also referred to as a "general manual." All units had additional specific operating manuals, policies, procedures, and rules.

The discipline section of the handbook outlined five types of disciplinary action that could be taken under certain circumstances. The type of action was dependent on the severity of the offense.

The "Progressive Discipline Operational Practice Standard Procedure" mandated that the supervisor or manager was required to review the facts of the case and the action to be taken with the employee. The employee had to sign the disciplinary action form.

On March 17, 1987, a patient on the plaintiff's unit was experiencing an erratic and accelerated heart rate (170–180 beats per minute). After the completion of a series of tests, Dr. Fanaipour, the patient's physician, ordered intravenous digoxin. The plaintiff, noting from the patient's chart that the patient had been given digoxin in the past, was concerned that the patient might be "digtoxic." She decided to order a digoxin test to determine the level of digoxin in the patient's blood. While awaiting the results of the blood tests, the hospital noted that a staff nurse was preparing to give the patient another injection of digoxin as ordered by Dr. Mehta, one of the patient's other physicians. The hospital ordered the staff nurse not to follow the physician's order until the laboratory results were completed. Instead, she massaged the patient to lower his heart rate, which was not to have been done unless the patient was being monitored; in this case, he was not. When Dr. Mehta arrived and discovered that his orders had not been followed, the nurse supervisor was suspended for 3 days until an investigation could be conducted. At the end of the 3 days, she was placed on paid sick leave and then terminated.

The plaintiff filed suit claiming that the hospital's employee handbook created contractual rights giving her employment status that could not be terminated at the will of the hospital. The circuit court granted the hospital's motion for summary judgment based on a finding that the employee handbook did not constitute a clear promise to form an employee contract. The plaintiff appealed to the Illinois Appellate Court.

Issue

Did the employee handbook and policies provided to the plaintiff at the time of employment create contractual rights so that she could not be terminated at-will by the hospital?

Holding

The Appellate Court of Illinois held that the handbook did not create contractual rights giving the employee employment status that could not be terminated at the will of the hospital.

Reason

The handbook clearly stated that the type of discipline imposed on an employee would depend on the circumstances and severity of the infraction. It was clear that the employer had the discretion to use progressive discipline or not. The only contract found to exist in this case was that the hospital would abide by the policies and procedures distributed to the employees. The court found that there was no material issue of fact, and thus the employer was entitled to summary judgment.

In order for an employee handbook to constitute a contract, thereby giving enforceable rights to the employee, the following elements must be present:

- The policy must be expressed in language that clearly sets forth a promise that the employee can construe to be an offer.
- The statement must be distributed to the employee, making him or her aware of it as an offer.
- After the employee learns about the offer, he or she must begin or continue to work.

Even if it was determined that a contract existed between the hospital and the plaintiff, the hospital had complete discretion in implementing its progressive disciplinary procedure. The hospital followed its policies and procedures in this case in that it discharged the plaintiff for a serious breach of hospital practice.

Discussion

1. What are the benefits of an employment contract?
2. Why should employment disclaimers be included in employee handbooks?
3. Is the employment-at-will concept appropriate in today's society?
4. What are the pros and cons of the employment-at-will doctrine?
5. Describe the elements that are necessary for an employee handbook to form a valid contract that grants enforceable rights to an employee.

Physician's Loss of Title Challenged

Citation: *Hanna v. Board of Trustees of N.Y. Univ. Hosp.*, 663 N.Y.S.2d 180 (N.Y. App. Div. 1997)

Facts

The plaintiff physician commenced this action for a mandatory injunction to restore his title of Chief of Pediatric Urology and his blocked operating room time, claiming that his professional privileges at the defendant hospital were improperly withdrawn in violation of Public Health Law 2801-b, which provides that "[i]t shall be an improper practice for the governing body of a hospital to . . . curtail, terminate, or diminish in any way a physician's . . . professional privileges in a hospital, without stating the reasons therefore." Professional privileges, also known as hospital privileges or clinical privileges, "are defined as 'permission to provide medical or other patient care services in the granting institution, within well defined limits, based on the individual's professional license and his/her experience, competence, ability, and judgment.' [Joint Commission on Accreditation of Healthcare Organizations, The Accreditation Manual for Hospitals 53 (1993)]. . . . Physicians must have such privileges in order to use the beds, equipment, and support staff within the facility."

Issue

Was the plaintiff's removal from his position as Chief of the Division of Pediatric Urology and the termination of his blocked time in the operating room subject to judicial review under Public Health Law 2801-b?

Holding

The plaintiff's removal from his position as Chief of the Division of Pediatric Urology and the termination of his blocked time in the operating room was not subject to review under Public Health Law 2801-b.

Reason

Because professional privileges in this context are understood to be the ability to admit and treat patients—and this understanding was the reason given by the Public Health Council (the administrative body with expertise regarding staff privileges) for declining to investigate plaintiff's complaint—the plaintiff did not suffer a termination or diminishment of his professional privileges in the hospital, and the complaint should have been found legally insufficient on defendant's pre-answer motion to dismiss. It is well settled that for statutes and regulations requiring special expertise and a knowledge of underlying operational practices, the construction given by the agency responsible for their administration, if not irrational or unreasonable, should be upheld. The Public Health Council's construction of the statute should be accorded due deference and, accordingly, plaintiff's removal from his position as Chief of the Division of Pediatric Urology and the termination of his blocked time in the operating room are not subject to judicial review under Public Health Law 2801-b.

Discussion

1. Discuss a scenario under which the Public Health Council might have agreed to investigate this case.
2. Discuss why clinical privileges are important to physicians.

Credentialing Physicians

Citation: *Candler Gen. Hosp., Inc. v. Persaud*, 442 S.E.2d 775 (Ga. Ct. App. 1994)

Facts

On or about February 15, 1990, Ms. Persaud was referred to Dr. Freeman for consultation and treatment of infected gallstones. Dr. Freeman recommended that Ms. Persaud undergo a laparoscopic laser cholecystectomy.

On February 16, 1990, Dr. Freeman requested and was granted temporary privileges to perform the procedure. He submitted a certificate of completion of a laparoscopic laser cholecystectomy workshop, which he had taken on February 10, 1990. Dr. Freeman performed the cholecystectomy on February 20, 1990, assisted by Dr. Thomas.

A complaint by the administrator of the patient's estate, supported by an expert's affidavit, alleged that the cholecystectomy was negligently performed, causing the patient to bleed to death. The complaint charged the hospital with negligence in permitting Dr. Freeman, assisted by Dr. Thomas, to perform the procedure on the decedent without having instituted any standards, training requirements, protocols, or otherwise instituting any method for judging the qualifications of a surgeon to perform the procedure. The complaint also alleged that the hospital knew or reasonably should have known that it did not have a credentialing process that could have assured the hospital of the physicians' education, training, and ability to perform the procedure.

The trial court denied the hospital's motion for summary judgment on the ground that the plaintiffs' evidence was sufficient to raise a question of fact regarding whether a surgical permit should have been issued by the hospital to Dr. Freeman. The hospital appealed.

Issue

Was there a material issue of fact as to whether the hospital was negligent in granting the specific privileges requested by Dr. Freeman?

Holding

The Court of Appeals held that there was a material issue of fact as to whether the hospital was negligent in granting the specific privileges requested, thus precluding summary judgment.

Reason

The hospital argued that there is no cause of action against a hospital based solely on the issuance of a surgical permit for a specific procedure to an independent surgeon already duly and properly appointed to its active surgical staff. The plaintiff in *Joiner v. Mitchell County Hosp. Auth.*, 125 Ga. Ct. App. 1, 2(1), 186 S.E.2d 307 (1971), aff'd, 229 Ga. 140, 189 S.E.2d 412 (1972), "who had brought her husband into the hospital for emergency treatment, alleged that the negligence of the treating physician who was on the staff of the hospital resulted in her husband's death. She also sought to hold the hospital liable, not under the doctrine of respondeat superior or principal and agent, but rather upon the doctrine of independent negligence in permitting the alleged negligent physician to practice his profession in the hospital when his incompetency was known." 229 Ga. at 141, 189 S.E.2d 412. "Joiner identified negligence as failing to investigate and require satisfactory proof of the physician's qualifications and as failing to exercise care in determining his professional competency." Id. at 777.

The Court of Appeals found that the question "in this case is whether this authority recognized by the Supreme Court in Joiner gives rise to a duty which the hospital owes to a patient when: (1) the patient rather than the hospital selected the independent staff surgeon to perform the procedure at issue, and (2) the hospital was allegedly negligent, not in its appointment or retention of the surgeon on its staff, but rather in its grant to him of privileges to practice a procedure which he allegedly was not qualified to perform." Id. at 777.

The court interpreted Joiner as authority to support the proposition that a hospital has a direct and independent responsibility to its patients to take reasonable steps to ensure that staff physicians using hospital facilities are qualified for privileges granted. The hospital owed a duty to the plaintiffs' decedent to act in good faith and with reasonable care to ensure that the surgeon was qualified to practice the procedure that he was granted privileges to perform. While there was no evidence of Dr. Freeman's curtailment or denial of staff privileges at other hospitals, the hospital did not dispute that there was a material issue of fact on the question of whether it was negligent in its granting of the staff privileges requested.

Discussion

1. Do you agree that the hospital was negligent in the granting of the privileges requested by Dr. Freeman?
2. If the patient had suffered no injuries, do you think the plaintiffs could have recovered any monetary damages?
3. What credentialing issues are evident in this case?

Employee Claims Defamation on Performance Appraisal

Citation: *Schauer v. Memorial Care Sys.*, 856 S.W.2d 437 (Tex. Ct. App. 1993)

Facts

On January 9, 1989, the plaintiff, Ms. Schauer, had applied for and was given a supervisory position at Memorial Hospital's new catheterization laboratory. In March 1989, she received an employment appraisal for the period June 1988 through December 1988. At that time, her supervisor rated Ms. Schauer's performance as commendable in two categories and fair in eight categories with an overall rating of "fair." Although Ms. Schauer had not lost her job as a result of the appraisal, she brought an action against the hospital and her former supervisor for libel and emotional distress as a result of the appraisal. The hospital moved for summary judgment on the grounds that the employment appraisal was not defamatory as a matter of law; the hospital had qualified privilege to write the performance appraisal; and the claim for emotional distress did not reach the level of severity required for a claim for intentional infliction of emotional distress. The trial court granted the hospital's motion for summary judgment, and Ms. Schauer appealed claiming for defamation and the intentional infliction of emotional distress.

To sustain her claim of defamation, Ms. Schauer had to show that the hospital published her appraisal in a defamatory manner that injured her reputation in some way. A statement can be unpleasant and objectionable to the plaintiff without being defamatory. The hospital argued that the statements contained in the appraisal were truthful, permissible expressions of opinion, and not capable of a defamatory meaning. Ms. Schauer's supervisor prepared the performance appraisal as part of her supervisory duties. The appraisal was not published outside the hospital and was prepared in compliance with the hospital policy for all employees.

Issue

Was Ms. Schauer's overall appraisal libelous and did the hospital intentionally inflict emotion distress?

Holding

The Court of Appeals of Texas held that the statements contained in the performance appraisal were not libelous and the appraisal was subject to qualified privilege. Moreover, the hospital's conduct and the statements contained in the appraisal did not support the claim for intentional infliction of emotional distress.

Reason

"Clearly, this is a statement of her supervisor's opinion and is not defamatory as a matter of law." Id. at 447. In her performance appraisal, Ms. Schauer objected to the statement, "Ms. Schauer was not sensitive to employee relations." Id. at 447. Ms. Schauer conceded in her deposition that there were a number of interpersonal problems in the catheterization laboratory and that she did not get along with everyone. The court found that given these admissions the statement was not defamatory.

As to the plaintiff's claim of emotional distress, the plaintiff failed to show that the hospital acted intentionally and recklessly.

The Restatement of Torts, Second, § 46 (1977)

The Restatement of Torts, Second, § 46 (1977) provides that

[l]iability has been found only where the conduct has been so outrageous in character, and so extreme in degree, as to go beyond all possible bounds of decency, and to be regarded as atrocious, and utterly intolerable in a civilized community. . . . The liability

clearly does not extend to mere insults, indignities, threats, annoyances, petty oppressions, or other trivialities. Complete emotional tranquility is seldom attainable in this world, and some degree of transient and trivial emotional distress is part of the price of living among people. The law intervenes only where the distress is so severe that no reasonable man could be expected to endure it . . .

Discussion

1. Under what circumstances might the trial court have denied the defendant's motion for summary judgment?
2. Why do supervisors often find it difficult to prepare written performance appraisals?
3. What should be included in a management-training program to assist managers in preparing fair and objective performance appraisals?
4. What steps can an organization take to ensure the competence of its staff?
5. What measures can an organization take to improve the competence of its staff?
6. Why is it important that the qualifications of a particular position be commensurate with defined job responsibilities?
7. Should there be a correlation between the job description and performance evaluation? Explain.
8. What mechanisms should the governing body have in place for ensuring that performance evaluations are conducted on a timely basis?
9. What summary information should be included in competency reports to the organization's governing body?

Public Policy and the Whistleblower

Doctor's Suit Faults Care at 2 Clinics

Catholic Charities disputes claims by fired employee, Charles Briggs.

. . . Briggs, 66, says he was fired in retaliation for raising concerns about patient care with supervisors who did little to address them. He was told by Catholic Charities that "he interfered with the smooth running of the Clinic," He wants his job back and $2 million in damages.

• • •

The whistleblower lawsuit, filed Thursday in D.C. Superior Court, identifies the plaintiff, Charles Briggs, as the sole staff doctor at the clinic from March 2008 until October 1, 2010, when he was fired.

For those patients, "Catholic Charities was the place they trusted to go for quality health care," said Alexis Ronickher, a lawyer with Katz, Marshall & Banks, which is representing Briggs. ". . . Instead of addressing the problems, Catholic Charities took the all too common approach of shooting the messenger."

Lena H. Sun, The Washington Post, *April 8, 2011*

A whistleblower is a person who reports to the public or someone in authority about an alleged dishonest or illegal conduct observed, for example, in a government or hospital setting. The alleged misconduct may be classified in many ways, including a violation of a law, rule, and/or regulation. When such occurs, it can be considered a direct threat to public safety as noted in the previous news clipping.

Whistleblowers often make their allegations internally (e.g., to an organization's compliance officer) or externally (e.g., to regulatory agencies). Whistleblower lawsuits are filed under the False Claims Act.

Nurse Alleges Equal Pay Violation

Citation: *Stevens v. St. Louis Univ. Med. Ctr.*, 83 F. Supp. 737 (E.D. Mo. 1993)

Facts

The plaintiff, a clinical nurse, alleged that she was paid less than a male employee who held a similar position and that she was wrongfully discharged in November 1990 after lodging complaints about such unequal pay. The plaintiff had brought her complaint to the Equal Employment Opportunity Commission (EEOC). The EEOC found that there was no reasonable cause to believe that she had been discriminated against on the basis of sex. The basis on which the medical center assigned various pay levels for clinical nurses included skill, effort, general job responsibilities, working conditions, scope of supervisory responsibilities, complexity of the position, size of the budget managed, and volume of procedures performed. The plaintiff had supervisory responsibility for three employees. Her male counterpart, Mr. Roth, had responsibility for 14 employees in the laboratory. The plaintiff periodically worked in the laboratory. Mr. Roth supervised her work during the times she worked in the laboratory.

Issue

Was the plaintiff discriminated against on the basis of sex, and was she wrongfully discharged in retaliation for reporting her complaints to regulatory agencies?

Holding

The United States District Court for the Eastern District of Missouri granted the medical center's motion for summary judgment, dismissing the case.

Reason

The plaintiff's position was not comparable or substantially equal to the position held by the male employee. The Equal Pay Act does not mandate that jobs be identical, rather that they be substantially equal [29 U.S.C.G. § 206(d)]. Employers may differentiate between the sexes based on a seniority system, merit system, a system that measures earnings by quantity or quality of production, or a differential based on any other factor other than sex [29 U.S.C.G. §§ 206(d), (d)(1)].

In the absence of a specific nonretaliation law, a claim for wrongful discharge may be stated only where an employee is terminated for refusal to perform an illegal act or where the employee reported the employer's illegal act. No such allegations were made in this case.

Discussion

1. On what bases are employers prohibited from discharging an employee?
2. What is the employment-at-will doctrine?
3. Do you believe that the employment-at-will common law doctrine is applicable in today's society? Explain your answer.

NOTES

1. http://www.ahrq.gov/research/nursestaffing/nursestaff.htm

chapter eleven

Criminal Conduct in the Healthcare Industry

This chapter describes a variety of legal cases involving criminal conduct in healthcare settings (e.g., fraud, physical and sexual abuse, and murder).

To Save on Health Care, First Crack Down on Fraud

According to some estimates, health care fraud is a $250 billion-a-year industry, and about $100 billion of that is stolen from Medicare, the health care program for the elderly, and Medicaid, the insurance program for the poor and disabled.

Kathleen Sharp, The New York Times, *September 26, 2011*

Healthcare fraud involves nearly every aspect of health care. The chapter presents a variety of the more common fraud cases that plague the healthcare industry. The Code of Federal Regulations under Title 42, Subchapter 7, Part A § 1320a-1-15 describes those individuals and entities who have mandatory exclusion from participation in Medicare healthcare programs:

1. Conviction of program-related crimes
2. Conviction relating to patient abuse
3. Felony conviction relating to healthcare fraud
4. Felony conviction relating to controlled substance
5. Exclusion or suspension under Federal or State healthcare program

6. Claims for excessive charges or unnecessary services and failure of certain organizations to furnish medically necessary services
7. Fraud, kickbacks, and other prohibited activities
8. Entities controlled by a sanctioned individual
9. Failure to disclose required information
10. Failure to supply requested information on subcontractors and suppliers
11. Failure to supply payment information
12. Failure to grant immediate access
13. Failure to take corrective action
14. Default on health education loan or scholarship obligations
15. Individuals controlling a sanctioned entity

When a healthcare fraud is perpetrated, the healthcare provider passes the costs along to its customers. Because of the pervasiveness of healthcare fraud, statistics now show that 10 cents of every dollar spent on health care goes toward paying for fraudulent healthcare claims.[2]

False Medicaid Claims by Dentist

Citation: *People v. Williamson,* 517 N.W.2d 846 (Mich. Ct. App. 1994)

Facts

The defendant, a dentist, was convicted before the circuit court for falsely certifying and filing Medicaid claims. Seven of the defendant's convictions arose from instances in which he billed the Medicaid program for taking a full set of X-rays, although he actually took less. The defendant contended that § 7 of the Medicaid False Claim Act is unconstitutionally vague because the definition of what constitutes a false Medicaid claim is found in the Medicaid provider manual, the contents of which were not promulgated as rules in accordance with the Administrative Procedures Act. There was also evidence that the defendant was billing the patient's private insurer in addition to Medicaid.

Issue

(1) Was § 7 of the Medicaid False Claim Act unconstitutionally vague? (2) Was evidence of instances wherein the defendant submitted such claims admissible? (3) Did the trial court err when it allowed evidence of double billing by the defendant?

Holding

The Supreme Court of Michigan held that § 7 of the Medicaid False Claim Act was not unconstitutionally vague. Evidence that the defendant had submitted Medicaid claims for full sets of X-rays, when only partial sets were taken, was admissible. However, evidence that the defendant billed both Medicaid and a patient's private insurer for the same procedure was inadmissible.

Reason

The defendant conceded that he had constructive knowledge of guidelines setting forth the appropriate method of billing the Medicaid program for procedures he performed. The provider manual seized from his dental office stated that billing for a full set of X-rays is only appropriate for a minimum of 16 films. This guideline is unambiguous and put the defendant on notice that taking less than 16 films should not be billed as a full series of dental films. The defendant was on notice that he must conform with the guidelines set forth in the Medicaid provider's manual and that deviation from the billing practices set forth in the manual would constitute a false claim.

As to similar instances of submitting false claims, the argument is without merit. The evidence was offered for the purpose of showing absence of mistake regarding what had been considered a full series of X-rays. Such evidence was relevant and had probative value. Evidence that the defendant billed both Medicaid and the patient's private insurer for the same procedure was inadmissible because the defendant was charged with filing a false claim. As a general rule, evidence that tends to show the commission of other criminal acts by a defendant is not admissible to prove guilt of the charged offense. Evidence of double billing in this case was not "so blended or connected with the crime of which the defendant is accused that proof of one incidentally involves the other or explains the circumstances of the crime." *People v. Delgado*, 404 Mich. 76-83, 273 N.W.2d 395 (1978).

Discussion

1. Why was the evidence of double billing entered in error?
2. Was the evidence of doubling billing so prejudicial to the defendant that it could have affected the outcome of the case?

Filing False Instruments

Citation: *People v. Evans*, 605 N.Y.S.2d 287 (N.Y. App. Div. 1993)

Facts

Between 1985 and 1990, the defendant, Evans, and a partner engaged in a complicated and sophisticated scheme to defraud the Medicaid system in excess of $500,000. In essence, they used various fictitious corporations and payees to bill Medicaid for services, such as the reading of sonograms by a specialist, although they knew such services had not been provided. The defendant argued that she misunderstood the Medicaid regulations. When claims were rejected under one code, she would merely resubmit the claim under another code.

The Bronx County Supreme Court jury found the defendant guilty of grand larceny in the second and third degrees, and 20 counts of offering a false instrument for filing in the first degree. The defendant appealed.

Issue

(1) Did the filing of false Medicaid claims for services not provided constitute a false instrument for filing? (2) Was evidence of billing Medicaid twice for the same service, forging physicians' signatures, billing for services never performed, and billing for readings of sonograms by specialists who had never read them admissible in the prosecution for conspiracy to commit grand larceny?

Holding

The New York Supreme Court, Appellate Division, upheld the convictions.

Reason

The New York Supreme Court determined that the filing of documents to support fraudulent Medicaid claims with regard to services not provided constitutes the offering of a false instrument for filing. The court further found the other fraudulent acts were admissible as evidence to prove the conspiracy to commit grand larceny. The court rejected the defendant's argument that, at trial, the government offered evidence of alleged additional crimes, such as double billings and forgeries. The court found that the evidence was merely further evidence of the crimes charged.

In view of the long term, systematic and sophisticated nature of defendant's offense, involving the theft of money from a critical service provided by the Government to people in need, and in view of the fraudulent and deceitful nature of her conduct and the harm done to the Medicaid system thereby (*see*, Matter of *Manyam v. Sobol, 183 AD2d 1022, 1023*), defendant's sentence and the order requiring her to make restitution were neither harsh nor excessive. Id. at 192.

Discussion

1. Is healthcare fraud of significant concern to regulatory agencies? Explain.
2. What steps should organizations take to reduce the frequency of healthcare fraud?
3. What role should healthcare compliance officers play in reducing the frequency of healthcare fraud?

Federal Regulations

U.S.Code

TITLE 42 CHAPTER 7 SUBCHAPTER XI Part A § 1320a-7

Exclusion of certain individuals and entities from participation in Medicare and State healthcare programs

1. when a judgment of conviction has been entered against [an] individual or entity by a Federal, State, or local court, regardless of whether there is an appeal pending or whether the judgment of conviction or other record relating to criminal conduct has been expunged;
2. when there has been a finding of guilt against [an] individual or entity by a Federal, State, or local court;
3. when a plea of guilty or nolo contendere by [an] individual or entity has been accepted by a Federal, State, or local court; or
4. when [an] individual or entity has entered into participation in a first offender, deferred adjudication, or other arrangement or program where judgment of conviction has been withheld.

False Medicaid Claims

Citation: *Travers v. Shalala*, 20 F.3d 993 (9th Cir. 1994)

Facts

Dr. Travers was accused of filing a false Medicaid claim that resulted in overpayment for services in violation of Utah Code. The physician pled "no contest" to the charge. He agreed to pay restitution, investigation costs, and a penalty. The plea provided that if Dr. Travers failed to make payment within 60 days, the Utah court would accept his no contest plea and proceed with prosecution. If payment were properly received, the court would allow him to withdraw his no contest plea and dismiss the charges with prejudice.

Dr. Travers made timely payment as required under the agreement, and the criminal charges were dismissed. The Secretary of Health and Human Services determined that Dr. Travers had been convicted of a criminal offense under the Medicaid and Medicare programs, requiring a mandatory exclusion from participation in the Medicaid program for a period of 5 years. Dr. Travers brought an action against the Secretary of Health and Human Services for her decision to exclude him from participation in the Medicare and Medicaid programs. An administrative judge of a Health and Human Services Appeals Board, and the United States District Court, upheld the 5-year exclusion, and Dr. Travers appealed.

Issue

Was Dr. Travers properly excluded from participation in the Medicare and Medicaid programs?

Holding

The United States Court of Appeals for the 10th Circuit held that there was substantial evidence in the record to support the Appeals Board determination that the state criminal proceeding against Dr. Travers resulted in a "conviction" of a program-related offense mandating exclusion of his participation in the Medicare and Medicaid programs for a period of 5 years.

Reason

The Social Security Act mandates that the Inspector General of the Department of Health and Human Services exclude providers from participation in the Medicare and Medicaid programs for a period of 5 years when they have been convicted of a criminal offense related to the delivery of care or service under the Medicare or Medicaid programs. Congress broadened the definition of "conviction" to include first offender, deferred adjudication, or other programs where judgment of conviction has been withheld. [42 U.S.C. § 1320a-7(I).]

Dr. Travers argued that his conviction, which was withheld under state law, had no bearing on what constituted a "conviction" under federal law. Dr. Travers's participation in a first offender, deferred adjudication, or other arrangement or program where judgment of conviction has been withheld falls within the meaning of "conviction" as described earlier. "Travers was not at liberty to withdraw his plea and proceed to trial upon his failure to comply with the plea agreement. On the contrary, had he failed to comply, the court would have accepted his no contest plea and proceeded to set the matter for imposition of sentence." Id. at 997.

Discussion

1. Does a state agreement not to prosecute a case bar federal action?
2. What is a no contest plea?

Fraudulent Billing Practices: License Revocation

Citation: *Llewellyn v. Board of Chiropractic Exam'rs*, 850 P.2d 411 (Or. Ct. App. 1993)

Facts

The State Board of Chiropractic Examiners revoked a chiropractor's license based on findings of insurance fraud and unethical conduct. The chiropractor sent bills to insurance companies for chiropractic services that he purportedly provided to insured patients. In fact, he did not provide any service to those patients, because they failed to keep their appointments. The chiropractor instructed his staff to bill for a service that would likely have been provided if the patients had kept their appointments. In response to the insurance companies' requests for documentation to support those bills, he produced chart notes indicating the patient had received treatment when, in fact, there was no treatment rendered. The chiropractor repeatedly engaged in conduct with intent to deceive the insurance companies and to induce them to make payments that they would not otherwise have made.

The board revoked the chiropractor's license on two independent grounds, either one of which it said would warrant revocation of his license. After the board determined that the chiropractor obtained fees through fraud, the chiropractor sought review as to whether or not the board's finding of fraud was supported by substantial evidence.

Issue

Was there substantial evidence that supported the board's order?

Holding

The Court of Appeals of Oregon held that substantial evidence supported the board's order.

Reason

The chiropractor's argument does not merit extended discussion. The evidence against him was extensive and persuasive.

Discussion

1. Do you agree that there was sufficient evidence to support the board's decision to revoke the chiropractor's license? Explain.
2. Do you think the licenses of health professionals who commit insurance frauds should be permanently revoked? Explain.

Illegal Distribution of Drugs

Citation: *United States v. Neighbors*, 23 F.3d 306 (10th Cir. 1994)

Facts

The defendant pharmacist, Mr. Neighbors, was convicted in the United States District Court of various drug offenses, and he appealed. He was charged with knowingly and intentionally possessing, with the intent to distribute and illegally dispense, Dilaudid, a Schedule II controlled substance, in violation of 21 U.S.C. § 841 (a)(1) (1988). A jury convicted the defendant on a 45-count indictment, and he was sentenced to 78 months imprisonment on each of the first 15 counts, as well as on counts 44 and 45, and 28 months imprisonment on counts 16 through 43, all to be served concurrently. The defendant appealed his conviction and sentence.

Morton Comprehensive Health Services, Inc. (Morton) of Tulsa, Oklahoma, is a charitable, tax-exempt community health organization that receives funding in the form of grants from the federal government. Morton is composed of a medical clinic, a pharmacy located therein, and a homeless clinic. For 10 years the defendant was the chief pharmacist at Morton clinic pharmacy, continuing until he resigned in March 1991.

The government's theory of the case was that for a number of years the defendant ordered various drugs, including Dilaudid and Valium, from Bergen-Brunswig, a drug supplier, and that thereafter the defendant possessed and converted the Valium and Dilaudid for his own purposes. The government's evidence was largely circumstantial (e.g., there were no eyewitnesses; the defendant, when questioned by FBI agents, did not confess to any criminal act). The FBI went through all of the prescriptions filled at the pharmacy from December 29, 1989, to April 2, 1991, a total of some

24,900 prescriptions. Agent Josh Nixon of the FBI testified that, because the prescriptions were numbered sequentially, he and his assistants were able to physically locate and account for all but four prescriptions during that time. The audits revealed that no prescriptions were filled by Morton pharmacy for Dilaudid tablets during the relevant time period and that, although a few prescriptions were found for Valium tablets, those prescriptions contained a pharmacy notation indicating that they had been filled with the generic equivalent of Valium-Diazepam. The audits also revealed that, during this same time period, January 1, 1990, to March 31, 1991, Morton pharmacy had ordered and received some 6,500 4-mg tablets of Dilaudid and over 135,000 5- and 10-mg Valium tablets from Bergen-Brunswig.

Other than the defendant, who was the only full-time pharmacist, there were three part-time pharmacists working at Morton. According to their testimony, Morton pharmacy never kept a stock supply of either Valium tablets or Dilaudid tablets during the relevant time period. The government introduced inventory documents that supported the part-time pharmacists' assertion that Dilaudid and Valium tablets were not stocked at Morton. Under Oklahoma state law, Morton pharmacy was required to submit a yearly inventory of controlled substances to state authorities. One such inventory dated July 12, 1990, which was signed by the defendant, indicated that Morton pharmacy did not have any Dilaudid in stock. The defendant cosigned an inventory when he left Morton that also indicated that Morton had no stock supply of Valium tablets or Dilaudid. Additionally, Ms. Myers, who took over as chief pharmacist when the defendant resigned, performed an inventory of Morton's stock medications. She found no Dilaudid and no Valium tablets.

Issue

Was there sufficient evidence presented to support a conviction of the defendant?

Holding

The United States Court of Appeals for the 10th Circuit held that the evidence was sufficient to support a conviction.

Reason

There was evidence that showed rather conclusively Bergen-Brunswig delivered Valium and Dilaudid to Morton pharmacy that greatly exceeded the

Valium or Dilaudid dispensed by the pharmacy. The record was convincing that the verdicts of the jury on all 45 counts were amply supported. The government's evidence, though basically circumstantial in nature, was, to the court, most convincing.

Discussion

1. What circumstantial evidence was used against the defendant at trial?
2. What is the difference between direct and circumstantial evidence?

False Medicaid Claims: Grand Larceny

Citation: *Surpris v. State of N.Y. Admin. Review Bd.*, 610 N.Y.S.2d 373 (N.Y. App. Div. 1994)

Facts

A psychiatrist was convicted of grand larceny in the third degree upon a plea of guilty and his admission that between February 1, 1988, and September 12, 1988, he submitted false Medicaid claims for which he was reimbursed $39,320. The psychiatrist was charged with professional misconduct. Following a hearing before a committee of the State Board for Professional Conduct, his license to practice medicine was revoked. The psychiatrist sought review of the revocation of his license, contending that the penalty was excessive. He also claimed that the hearing committee was arbitrary and capricious for not allowing him to present 34 New York City Human Resources Administration referral forms as evidence of the economic condition of patients who had come to him and the type of treatment they had received.

Issue

(1) Were the referral forms improperly withheld from the hearing committee? (2) Was the revocation of the psychiatrist's license to practice medicine excessive?

Holding

The Supreme Court of New York, Appellate Division, held that the referral forms were properly excluded from the hearing before the committee of the State Board for Professional Medical Conduct. Moreover, the psychiatrist's submission of false Medicaid claims warranted revocation of his license to practice medicine.

Reason

The court agreed with the state that the referral forms had little relevance to the issue of the mitigation of the penalty revoking the psychiatrist's license. As to the issue of the penalty imposed for the psychiatrist's submission of over 1,600 claims for psychiatric services that were never rendered, the evidence provided ample justification for revocation of the psychiatrist's license to practice medicine.

Discussion

1. Was the revocation of the psychiatrist's license excessive?
2. What is meant by "professional misconduct"?

Earl Bradley, Predator Doctor, Convicted on 24 Child Sex Counts, Could Get Life

(CBS/AP) Georgetown, Del. - Former Delaware pediatrician Earl Bradley was found guilty Thursday of sexually assaulting scores of young patients at his office, which was decked out with a merry-go-round and a small Ferris wheel.

Prosecutors said Bradley, 58, made videos of the abuse. He was found guilty on all 24 counts, including 14 counts of rape, and could be sentenced to life in prison on each of those counts.

Barry Leibowitz, CBS NEWS, June 23, 2011, 5:24 PM

Physician's Sexual Abuse

Citation: *Nghiem v. State*, 73 Wn App. 405, 869 P.2d 1086 (1994)

Facts

On October 26, 1989, the Washington State Medical Disciplinary Board charged a physician with unprofessional conduct. The board alleged that the physician had asked inappropriate sexual questions of four of his patients. It also alleged that the physician had inappropriate sexual contact with three of the patients. On December 15 and 16, 1989, the board held a hearing regarding these allegations, at which time three patients described their allegations of sexual abuse by the physician. Prior to the hearing, the physician was evaluated by a psychologist who concluded in a prehearing report that the physician was at a significant risk for similar conduct with other patients. The physician presented a number of witnesses who testified as to his good character and reputation in the community. Among the witnesses was a psychologist who testified that the physician admitted to asking sexually oriented questions but denied any sexual contact. As a result of the physician's admission to asking sexually oriented questions, the psychologist testified that the physician "did not exercise good judgment" and that if the inappropriate sexual contact allegations were true and the physician's denial false, then "he's not fit to practice" medicine. Id. at 1089.

RCW 18.130.180(1) and (24)

Following the hearing, the board concluded that the physician had engaged in professional misconduct as described within the meaning of RCW 18.130.180(1) and (24), which provide in part

The following conduct, acts or conditions constitute unprofessional conduct for any license holder or applicant under the jurisdiction of this chapter: (1) The commission of any act involving moral turpitude. . . . (24) Abuse of a client or patient or sexual conduct with a client or patient.

The board revoked the physician's license to practice medicine for 10 years. Reinstatement of his license after that period of time was contingent upon his successful completion of a rehabilitation program.

An appeal was taken to the superior court, and the board's findings were upheld. A further appeal was then taken to the court of appeals.

Issue

Did the evidence support the board's findings that the physician had engaged in inappropriate sexual behavior toward patients?

Holding

The Court of Appeals of Washington held that the evidence supported the board's findings that the physician had engaged in inappropriate sexual behavior toward patients. The board did not exceed its authority by ordering that revocation of the physician's license last at least 10 years or by conditioning reinstatement on proof of rehabilitation.

Reason

Substantial evidence is "evidence in sufficient quantum to persuade a fair-minded person of the truth of the declared premises." *Olmstead v.*

Department of Health, 61 Wash. App. 888, 893; 812 P.2d 527 (1986). Id. at 1090. The board's findings were based on substantial evidence that the physician engaged in sexually inappropriate physical examinations and inappropriate sexual questioning of his patients.

The 10-year revocation of the physician's license and its return contingent upon the physician's successful completion of a rehabilitation program were permissible based on state statute.

RCW 18.130.160

RCW 18.130.160 states in part

Upon a finding that a license holder or applicant has committed unprofessional conduct ... the disciplining authority may issue an order providing for one or any combination of the following:

(1) Revocation of the license; ....

RCW 18.130.150 states in part:

A person whose license has been suspended or revoked under this chapter may petition the disciplining authority for reinstatement *after an interval as determined by the disciplining authority in the order.* Id. 413–414

Discussion

1. Assuming you were the plaintiff's attorney in a similar case, how would you defend your client?
2. Do you agree that sexually oriented questions by a practitioner to a patient are sufficient reason to remove the practitioner's license?

Nurse's Physical Abuse

Citation: *State v. Houle*, 642 A.2d 1178 (Vt. 1994)

Facts

The defendant, a licensed practical nurse, had criminal charges brought against her stemming from her treatment of a stroke patient. It was alleged that she had slapped the patient's legs repeatedly and shackled him to his bed at the wrists and ankles. By the time of trial, the patient had died of causes unrelated to the charged conduct. During the trial, the state presented the testimony of eyewitnesses including the patient's wife, hospital employees, and an investigator from the Office of the Attorney General. The defendant did not deny that she had restrained the patient but claimed that her actions were necessary for the patient's protection, as well as her own, and that her actions were neither assaultive nor cruel. The defendant produced the testimony of another nurse who was familiar with the patient's medical condition and his need for restraint. This nurse was also used to impeach the credibility of one of the state's witnesses.

The defendant's first claim was that the trial court improperly admitted, over objection, evidence that the patient gave consistent accounts of the incidents underlying the charges to Ms. Herrick, a hospital employee. The defendant contended that the testimony was not relevant.

Issue

Was the evidence that the victim gave relevant and admissible?

Holding

The Supreme Court of Vermont held that the evidence that the victim gave was relevant and admissible.

Reason

The patient's awareness of what happened to him was relevant to the state's case because the trial court, in its instruction to the jury, defined cruelty as "intentional and malicious infliction of physical or emotional pain or suffering upon a person." By showing that the patient was aware of what had happened to him, the state allowed the jury to infer that he had suffered physical or emotional pain. The state presented a witness who was present when the incident occurred and who was able to describe the acts of abuse in detail. The credibility of this eyewitness testimony, and not what the patient's testimony would have been, was the focus of the trial.

Discussion

1. Why was the evidence admissible at trial?
2. At what point does the application of restraints become a cruelty?

Nurse's Sexual Abuse

Citation: *Gilpin v. Board of Nursing*, 254 Mont., 308, 837 P.2d 1342 (Mont. 1992)

Facts

From 1980 through 1990, the defendant was a registered nurse. His license lapsed at the end of 1990 and was, thereafter, revoked by the Montana Board of Nursing. In 1987, he was convicted of two counts of sexual assault on an 11- and 12-year-old girl. After having been sentenced to consecutive terms of 4 years in prison on each count, the Montana Board of Nursing began a disciplinary proceeding against him involving his license.

As a result of his criminal conviction, the Board initiated a license disciplinary proceeding against him. The disciplinary proceeding was delayed while Gilpin appealed his criminal conviction and pursued an action in federal court.

A hearing examiner heard the case, which was presented on an agreed statement of facts. His license was revoked when the board affirmed the hearing examiner's findings. The defendant then appealed to the district court, which, after hearing both parties' arguments, affirmed the board's decision to revoke the nurse's license. Thereafter, the nurse appealed to the Supreme Court of Montana.

Issue

(1) Does the licensing Board have jurisdiction over a lapsed nursing license? (2) Was the nurse provided a proper and fair hearing? (3) Can the licensing Board consider the licensure of criminals in revoking a nursing license?

Holding

(1) The court determined that the Board retains jurisdiction over a lapsed nursing license. (2) The nurse was provided a proper and fair hearing. (3) The licensing Board can consider the licensure of criminals in revoking a nursing license.

Reason

The decision of the board and district court was affirmed, and the license was revoked, although not on a permanent basis. The statute that regulates the licensing provisions for nurses in Montana (S 37-8-431(3) MCA) gives the board the power to reinstate a license for 3 years after it lapses. Therefore, the court determined that the Board retained jurisdiction over the lapsed nursing license for 3 years after the nurse failed to renew it.

On the issue of whether the nurse had a fair hearing, the material facts of the case were stipulated to, and the nurse gave his arguments against the findings of the examiner at the hearing itself. Thus, the court found the nurse was not entitled to any further hearings.

Finally, regarding the issue surrounding whether the board properly considered the criteria for the licensure of criminals in revoking the nursing license, the court found that the policy of the state and the intent of the legislature are to protect the public health, safety, and welfare of its citizens. Although a license may not be revoked solely on the basis of a prior criminal conviction, when the conviction is one that relates to the public health, welfare, and safety as it applies to the occupation for which the license is sought, the licensing agency may deny or revoke the license if the agency finds that the applicant has not been rehabilitated to the point that would warrant public trust. Here, the crimes of sexual assault upon young girls were sufficient to revoke the license. Because the practice of nursing brings the nurse into close physical contact with patients, the conviction of sexual assault makes a person unfit to practice nursing. The board properly considered the criteria for licensing criminal defendants.

Discussion

1. What criteria should a board of nursing take into consideration when deciding whether to revoke the license of a nurse convicted of a crime?
2. What procedures should healthcare organizations take in order to prevent similar offenses from occurring in their facilities?

Accusations of Child Abuse Unfounded

Citation: *Heinrich v. Conemaugh Valley Mem'l Hosp.*, 648 A.2d 53 (Pa. Super. 1994)

Facts

Molly, a young child born February 17, 1991, was involved in an accident, on or about September 25, whereby her walker tipped over, causing her to strike the back of her head on the kitchen floor. Jean Heinrich, Molly's mother, noticed that Molly was experiencing some discomfort associated in and around the area of her ears and scheduled an appointment on September 27 with Dr. Caroff. Dr. Caroff examined Molly, diagnosed her as possibly beginning an ear infection, and prescribed an antibiotic. The next day, Ms. Heinrich noticed swelling on and around Molly's left temple, ear, and eye. Because the swelling persisted, she brought Molly to the emergency department of Conemaugh Valley Memorial Hospital. The triage coordinator classified Molly's injury as "non-urgent." Dr. George examined Molly and then left. Dr. George returned with Dr. Opila, who also examined Molly. According to the complaint, Dr. George and Dr. Opila observed a non–life-threatening swelling on the left side of the child's head that exhibited no scrapes or abrasions of the skin and arbitrarily concluded that the child suffered a hematoma or bruises to that area of the child's head.

Dr. Opila returned and asked Ms. Heinrich to consent to X-rays of Molly's head, and she consented. Molly was taken for X-rays and was brought back to the emergency department. Ms. Heinrich claims that she could clearly hear a number of nurses at the emergency department desk loudly discussing Molly's condition and treatment, as well as allegations of abuse and neglect, in front of a busy emergency department waiting room. Furthermore, X-rays were taken of Molly's entire body and were not limited to the X-rays of the child's head that Ms. Heinrich had consented to.

Dr. George told Ms. Heinrich that the X-rays were negative and that he would attempt to contact Dr. Caroff to confirm the results of his examination. Shortly thereafter, Dr. Opila returned and once again began questioning Ms. Heinrich (and Molly's grandparents, who were also there) as to the source of Molly's injury. During this questioning, Dr. Opila gave the opinion that the swelling observed was most consistent with having had a blow to that area of the head. Ms. Heinrich and the grandparents were introduced to Ms. Stock, who identified herself as an employee of the hospital's Department of Social Services. Ms. Stock stated that she had been contacted by Dr. Opila and asked to ascertain how Molly was injured or the source or cause of the swelling. Ms. Stock questioned Ms. Heinrich and the grandparents, who were also present, for approximately 20 minutes. During this time, Dr. George informed Ms. Heinrich and the grandparents that he had spoken with Dr. Caroff, who reported that there had been no swelling on Molly's head when he examined her the day before. Ms. Heinrich responded angrily that she had told him earlier that she had not noticed any swelling prior to the morning of September 28, 1991.

Ms. Stock left and returned shortly thereafter to inform Ms. Heinrich and the grandparents that the physicians wanted to admit Molly in order to observe the head injury for 24 hours. Shortly thereafter, she again began to question Ms. Heinrich and the grandparents. Dr. George entered and informed Ms. Heinrich that he wanted to admit Molly for observation. Ms. Heinrich responded that she wanted Dr. Caroff to examine Molly, or she wanted to take Molly to another hospital, because the child had not received any treatment for her swelling since arrival.

Dr. Cole and Dr. Devellen entered the examining room and introduced themselves as family practitioners. They then proceeded to examine Molly. During this time, Dr. Devellen cleaned Molly's ears and observed that her eardrums were slightly red and stated that the swelling was not consistent with a blow to the head because there was no bruising. Ms. Heinrich spoke by telephone with Ms. Stouffer, who introduced herself as a representative of Cambria County Children and Youth Services (CYS). She informed Ms. Heinrich that if she did not admit Molly, CYS would come to the hospital and take custody of the child. Ms. Heinrich informed Ms. Stouffer that she had never refused to admit the child, but had only objected to the fact that the child was not receiving any treatment for the swelling.

Dr. Green, who was covering for Dr. Caroff, examined Molly. He stated that the physicians had diagnosed the swelling as cellulitis from an inner ear infection. On September 30, 1991, Dr. Caroff examined Molly. He informed Ms. Heinrich that he had already contacted CYS in an attempt to resolve any misunderstanding and to correct any misinformation. Dr. Caroff further stated that Dr. Sheridan of Johnstown Pediatrics Association would examine Molly later that day. At approximately 10:00 a.m., a pediatric resident of Johnstown Pediatrics Association examined Molly and reviewed the medical case history with Ms. Heinrich.

On October 1, 1991, Dr. Sheridan and two of his associates examined Molly and further questioned Ms. Heinrich and the grandparents. Dr. Sheridan stated that the fall on her head was the cause of the swelling and diagnosed the child's condition as a subaponeurotic hematoma, caused by a broken blood vessel from Molly's fall in the walker. At this time, he directed that Molly was not suffering from an infection. He notified Ms. Heinrich that he was contacting Dr. Caroff concerning Molly's discharge from the hospital. At 5:30 p.m., Ms. Ott, a social worker, spoke with Ms. Heinrich and informed her that she was still under investigation for suspected child abuse. At approximately 6:00 p.m., Molly was discharged from the hospital by authorization of Dr. Caroff. On October 3, 1991, Ms. Stouffer informed Ms. Heinrich that the report of suspected child abuse was held to be unfounded, and that she promised to destroy the paperwork as soon as possible.

Ms. Heinrich asserted in her complaint that she had been confronted by friends, family members, and neighbors who had learned of the incident and the investigation of suspected child abuse. Ms. Heinrich also asserted that she has suffered from physical manifestations of stress resulting from this incident. She asserted that the actions of the hospital, by and through its employees, representatives, and agents during their dealings and conversations with her, were insulting, outrageous, and taken in bad faith, with bad motive, due to their preconceived suspicions, biases, and prejudice based on her economic situation.

A four-count complaint was filed in which causes of action against the hospital for corporate negligence and defamation were alleged, as were causes of action for intentional and negligent infliction of emotional distress. The hospital filed preliminary objections in which they raised, among other things, immunity from suit under Section 6318 of the Child Protective Services Law. After hearing the argument, the trial court issued an order in which it (1) dismissed Dr. Cole, Dr. Devellen, and Ms. Ott from the lawsuit, because they executed their duties in good faith and because the second amended complaint failed to provide specific material facts that would indicate bad faith in order to overcome the statutory presumption of good faith; (2) dismissed the claim of corporate negligence on the basis that the facts alleged in the second complaint were insufficient to constitute a breach of duty, a legal injury, or legal causation; (3) allowed the appellants 20 days to plead more specifically their defamation claim; (4) dismissed the claim for intentional and negligent infliction of emotional distress for failing to state facts that would support extreme and outrageous conduct that rose to and beyond all bounds of decency, and for failing to set forth evidence of any physical or bodily injury; (5) dismissed the claims for punitive damages for failing to state facts that show outrageous behavior; and (6) dismissed as defendants the hospital and Dr. Opila, Dr. George, and Ms. Stock under the protection of immunity.

Issue

Should the Appellees' preliminary objections have been granted because the question of whether the Appellees acted in good faith is a question of fact for the jury, and their complaint makes sufficient, specific allegations of bad faith.

Holding

The Pennsylvania Superior Court held that the appellants failed to overcome statutory presumption of good faith, and thus, the hospital and its agents were immune from liability.

Reason

The purpose of the law is to bring about quick and effective reporting of suspected child abuse so as to serve as a means for providing protective services competently and to prevent further abuse of the children while providing rehabilitative services for them and the parents. To this end, the law requires, under threat of criminal penalty, that healthcare professionals and others report suspected abuse.

23 Pa. C.S. §§ 6311(a) and (b)

These persons are required to report suspected child abuse.

(a) General rule—Persons who, in the course of their employment, occupation or practice of their profession, come into contact with children shall report or cause a report to be made in accordance with section 6313 (relating to reporting procedure) when they have reason to believe, on the basis of their medical, professional or other training and experience, that a child coming before them in their professional or official capacity is an abused child. The privileged communication between any professional person required to report and the patient or client of that person shall not apply to situations involving child abuse and shall not constitute grounds for failure to report as required by this chapter.

(b) Enumeration of persons required to report—Persons required to report under subsection (a) include, but are not limited to, any licensed physician, osteopath, medical examiner, coroner, funeral director, dentist, optometrist, chiropractor, podiatrist, intern, registered nurse, licensed practical nurse, hospital personnel engaged in the admission, examination, care or treatment of persons, a Christian Science practitioner, school administrator, school teacher, school nurse, social services worker, day-care center worker or any other child-care or foster-care worker, mental health professional, peace officer or law enforcement official. 23 Pa. C.S. §§ 6311(a) and (b).

23 Pa. C.S. § 6318 on Immunity from Liability

Immunity is clearly provided to those who report under the law.

(a) General rule—A person, hospital, institution, school, facility, or agency participating in good faith in the making of a report, cooperating with an investigation, or testifying in a proceeding arising out of an instance of suspected child abuse, the taking of photographs, or the removal or keeping of a child pursuant to section 6315 (relating to taking child into protective custody) shall have immunity from any civil or criminal liability that might otherwise result by reason of those actions.

(b) Presumption of good faith—For the purpose of any civil or criminal proceeding, the good faith of a person required to report pursuant to section 6311 (relating to persons required to report suspected child abuse) shall be presumed. 23 Pa. C.S. § 6318.

There is no dispute that all appellees fall within the protection provided under the law. The appellants were afforded three opportunities to amend their complaint so as to assert sufficient specific facts tending to show that the appellees acted in bad faith and thus overcame the statutory presumption. The trial court concluded that the appellants had failed to do so on each occasion. The superior court agreed.

The urgency of prompt reporting is stressed throughout the law's provisions. The law does not envision any prereporting investigation, and in light of the mandatory reporting procedure and the law's presumption of good faith, the court was unwilling to presume that the failure to conduct such an investigation was in bad faith.

Discussion

1. Do you think the hospital overreacted as to the number of individuals involved in this case? Why?
2. What privacy and confidentiality issues can you identify in this case?

Serial Murder by Healthcare Professionals

The prosecution of Charles Cullen, a nurse who killed at least 40 patients over a 16-year period, highlights the need to better understand the phenomenon of serial murder by healthcare professionals. The authors conducted a LexisNexis search which yielded 90 criminal prosecutions of healthcare providers that met inclusion criteria for serial murder of patients. . . .

The number of patient deaths that resulted in a murder conviction is 317, and the number of suspicious patient deaths attributed to the 54 convicted caregivers is 2113. These numbers are disturbing and demand that systemic changes in tracking adverse patient incidents associated with presence of a specific healthcare provider be implemented. Hiring practices must shift away from preventing wrongful discharge or denial of employment lawsuits to protecting patients from employees who kill.

Yorker BC, Kizer KW, Lampe P, Forrest AR, Lannan JM, Russell DA, Journal of Forensic Science, *November 2006*[3]

The question of serial killers (e.g., Cullen, Shipman, Harvey, Angelo) opens up numerous questions in terms of the ongoing provision of superficial references that allows questionable individuals, including serial killers, to float from one healthcare organization to the next. It is clear that patients, at the most vulnerable period of their lives, are dependent on hospitals, nursing facilities, and so on to be aware of the red flags that help identify those individuals likely to cause harm and to take appropriate action to help prevent the stream of neutral references (e.g., merely providing position and dates of employment). Hospitals have been accused of allowing suspected criminals to drift from one healthcare facility to the next, fired under a cloud of suspicion. Individuals are rarely brought to justice until a long trail of evidence has unraveled a pattern of criminal conduct. Hospitals need to be aware that, depending on the attendant circumstances, providing neutral references could lead to such charges as being an accessory to a crime.

Ex-Delaware Pediatrician Guilty of Child Sex Abuse

Georgetown, Del. (AP)—A former Delaware pediatrician was found guilty Thursday, June 23, of sexually assaulting scores of young patients at his office, which was decked out with a merry-go-round and a small Ferris wheel.

Prosecutors said Earl Bradley, 58, took homemade videos of the abuse. He was found guilty of all 24 counts, including 14 counts of rape. He will be sentenced Aug. 26 and could be sentenced to life in prison on each of those counts. . . .

Bradley's arrest followed previous police investigations and years of suspicions among parents. His colleagues also questioned his strange behavior.

Since his arrest, reviews have found that state medical society officials, individual doctors, and the Delaware Department of Justice violated state law by not reporting possible unprofessional behavior to the medical licensing board. The board itself was criticized for failing to act on information it did receive about Bradley.

Gov. Jack Markell signed nine bills about a year ago prompted by the Bradley case that tightened regulation of doctors and clarified the obligations of the medical and law-enforcement communities to report and communicate about suspected physician misconduct and child abuse.

Randall Chase, Associated Press, *June 23,2011*[4]

Though Rare, the Possibility of Serial Murders in Healthcare Settings Demands Vigilance

By the time a mortician in the northeast British town of Hyde, Greater Manchester, United Kingdom, noticed Dr. Harold Shipman's patients were dying at an exorbitant rate, the doctor had probably killed close to 300 of them, according to Kenneth V. Iserson, MD, MBA, professor of emergency medicine at the University of Arizona College of Medicine, and author of "Demon Doctors: Physicians as Serial Killers."

Shipman, labeled "the most prolific serial killer in the history of the United Kingdom—and probably the world," was officially convicted of killing 15 patients in

2000 and sentenced to 15 consecutive life sentences. In January 2004 he was found hanged in his prison cell. . . .

An investigation revealed that Cullen had a history of reported incidents at hospitals in Pennsylvania and New Jersey, but there were no tracking or disclosure systems in place as he moved from one hospital to another. His employment history included termination from several hospitals because of misconduct, hospitalizations for mental illness, and a criminal investigation regarding improper medication administration. . . .

Cullen had been investigated by three hospitals, a nursing home, and two prosecutors for suspicious patient deaths. He was fired by five hospitals and one nursing home for suspected wrongdoing. But Cullen continued to find employment and kill patients.

Andrea Sattinger, The Hospitalist, *August 2007*

Lethal Dose of Anesthesia

Citation: *People v. Protopappas*, 246 Cal. Rptr. 915 (Cal. Ct. App. 1988).

Facts

A licensed dentist and an oral surgeon were convicted in the superior court of second-degree murder for the deaths of three patients who died after receiving general anesthesia. The record revealed that the three patients received massive doses of drugs, which resulted in their deaths. The dosages had not been tailored to the patients' individual conditions. The dentist had also improperly instructed surrogate dentists, who were neither licensed nor qualified to administer general anesthesia, to administer preset dosages for an extended time with little or no personal supervision. In addition, the dentist had been habitually slow in reacting to resulting overdoses. In one case, the patient's general physician informed the defendant that the 24-year-old, 88-pound patient suffered from lupus, total kidney failure, high blood pressure, anemia, heart murmur, and chronic seizure disorder and should not be placed under anesthesia even for a short time. The defendant consciously elected to ignore that medical opinion.

Issue

Was there sufficient evidence of implied malice to support the jury's findings that the dentist and the oral surgeon were guilty of second-degree murder?

Holding

On appeal, the court of appeals found that there was sufficient evidence of implied malice to support the jury's findings that the dentist and the oral surgeon were guilty of second-degree murder.

Reason

This is more than gross negligence. These are the acts of a person who knows that his conduct endangers the life of another and who acts with conscious disregard for life. . . . Many murders are committed to satisfy a feeling of a hatred or grudge, it is true, but this crime may be perpetrated without the slightest trace of personal ill will.

Discussion

1. Do you agree with the court's decision? Discuss your answer.
2. Discuss the price to be paid when an individual is wrongfully accused of a crime (e.g., mental anguish).

Judge Rejects Plea Deal for Former Fugitive Surgeon

For five years, former patients of Chicago surgeon Mark Weinberger's feared that the man they claim maimed them with unnecessary surgeries had made a clean getaway.

In 2004, with hundreds of malpractice lawsuits piling up and federal investigators probing his northwest Indiana medical practice, Weinberger disappeared from his 80-foot yacht docked off the Greek island of Mykonos. He left behind his wife and $6 million in debts, an escape he apparently had been plotting for months.

Weinberger was arrested five years later when Italian authorities found him camped in the snow in the foothills of the Alps. He was extradited to face insurance fraud charges in the U.S. and more than 300 civil lawsuits claiming he performed useless operations and overbilled patients to fund an extravagantly lavish lifestyle.

Andy Grimm, Chicago Tribune, *April 27, 2011*

Fugitive Surgeon with Criminal Charges and 300 Claims of Malpractice

Citation: *Medical Insurance Company, Inc. v. Hellman, et al.*, 610 F.3d 371 (2010)

Facts

Dr. Weinberger maintained a prosperous ear, nose, and throat practice in Merrillville, Indiana. He supplemented his income by using his practice to defraud numerous insurance companies of millions of dollars. In September 2004, while vacationing with his wife in Greece, Weinberger "went for a run" and did not come back. At the time, it seemed that Weinberger had no intention of returning to the United States, in all likelihood because he was facing $5.7 million in creditor claims and 22 criminal counts of billing fraud upon his return. The U.S. government took various steps, including having an international arrest warrant issued, to locate Weinberger. Weinberger was arrested in Italy in December 2009, he has since been extradited to the United States, and is now facing healthcare fraud charges in the Northern District of Indiana.

Criminal charges are not the only allegations pending against Weinberger. He is also facing more than 350 medical malpractice claims, most of which were filed after his disappearance. These claims have been proceeding through Indiana's medical malpractice process.

Weinberger's medical malpractice insurance carrier, the Medical Assurance Company, Inc. (Medical Assurance), has been conducting his defense, but Weinberger's disappearance prompted it to file this suit. The insurance contracts between Medical Assurance and Weinberger include a typical cooperation clause, which requires Weinberger to participate in his defense. Needless to say, Weinberger was not cooperating during his extensive European "vacation."

Medical Assurance brought a declaratory judgment action in federal court in Indiana asking the court to declare that Weinberger breached his responsibilities under the contract and therefore Medical Assurance no longer has a duty to defend or indemnify him.

The U.S. District Court was concerned that such a declaration would intrude too severely on the state's medical malpractice actions. It thought that Medical Assurance could not show that Weinberger's lack of cooperation was prejudicing the company without improperly interfering with the state cases. It therefore decided to refrain from going forward pending the resolution of the state court proceedings, and it issued a stay of the federal proceedings.

Medical Assurance had appealed by arguing that the court erred in doing so and that it should have proceeded to resolve the merits of the declaratory judgment action.

Issue

Did the U.S. District Court err by "not" proceeding to resolve the merits of the declaratory judgment action?

Finding

The United States Court of Appeals, Seventh Circuit concluded that although district courts enjoy some discretion over requests for declaratory judgments, that discretion is not unlimited and remanded the case to the district court with instructions to lift the stay and to proceed to the merits. In so doing, the court will be able to take into account Weinberger's return to Indiana and any other pertinent developments.

Reason

Between 1996 and 2004, Medical Assurance provided professional liability insurance coverage to Weinberger and his businesses under various policies. The contractual provisions provide that Medical Assurance has a duty to defend and indemnify Weinberger, but Medical Assurance is relieved of those duties if Weinberger violates the policy's cooperation clause, which is found in Paragraph 5 of the General Conditions and Requirements for each policy and reads as follows in relevant part:

The insured must fully cooperate with Medical Assurance and defense counsel in the investigation, handling, and defense of the legal proceeding. The insured's duty to cooperate includes, but is not limited to:

- When requested, attendance at and preparation for meetings, hearings, depositions, and trials;
- Securing and providing evidence and assisting in obtaining the attendance of witnesses;
- Truthfully and completely informing Medical Assurance about the facts and circumstances that surround any professional incident or legal proceeding and, specifically, the nature of [the insured's] acts or omissions, so that Medical Assurance may correctly assess liability;
- Supplementing the information previously provided to Medical Assurance or defense counsel as additional information becomes known to [the insured].

Medical Assurance's amended complaint asked the court to issue the following declaratory judgment:

1. That Weinberger has failed and refused to assist and/or cooperate with the defense of the Claims, meaning the individual malpractice claims;
2. That Weinberger's failure to assist and cooperate in the defense of the Claims constitutes a material breach of the contracts of insurance between the Weinberger Defendants and Medical Assurance...;

3. That Medical Assurance has been prejudiced by Weinberger's failure and refusal to assist and/or cooperate with the defense of the Claims;

4. That Medical Assurance is under no obligation to defend the Claims on behalf of any of the Weinberger Defendants;

5. That Medical Assurance is under no obligation to pay any judgments, damages, costs or expenses that are associated with or arise out of the Claims, or to indemnify the Weinberger Defendants for any such amounts;

6. Medical Assurance owes no defense or coverage under the Policies in connection with the claims alleged by [one of two named claimants], or any other Claimants who have asserted "fraud-based" claims, pursuant to the coverage exclusion contained in the Policies for such fraud-based claims.

With these principles in mind, Indiana law provided the basis for the underlying litigation against Weinberger. The state cases were proceeding under the familiar framework for a medical-malpractice claim: the plaintiff must show that the defendant owed a duty to the plaintiff, that he breached his duty by conduct falling below the standard of care, and that the breach proximately caused a compensable injury.

Medical Assurance wanted a declaratory judgment to get it off the hook altogether on the policies it wrote for Weinberger. It argued that the court can and should declare that its obligations to Weinberger were over because of his failure to comply with the policies' cooperation clauses. In Indiana, however, an insurer cannot prevail on that theory unless it can show that the breach resulted in actual prejudice. Indiana law also has something to say about proving actual prejudice. The insured's absence alone is not enough to establish prejudice; to prove actual prejudice, the insurer must show somehow that the outcome of the underlying case would have been altered by the insured's cooperation. "The requirement that the insurer must prove at least a reasonable probability of actual prejudice caused by the insured's failure to appear is in harmony with the more general Indiana holdings that the insurer must prove prejudice, and that prejudice requires proof that the insured's failure to cooperate actually produced a judgment less favorable in the underlying tort action."

Medical Assurance has not had the opportunity to develop its position or even to discover the facts that would support it. The court was not willing to assume that the only way Medical Assurance could prove its case was by an excursion into factual questions that the state courts have been, or would be, asked to address.

The purpose of the Declaratory Judgment Act is to facilitate efficient outcomes. Here, that purpose is best effected by allowing Medical Assurance to go forward with its challenge to its duty to defend. An insurer that believes it has no duty to defend a tendered claim can avoid liability if it either defends under a reservation of rights or seeks a declaratory judgment that it has no obligation to defend.

That question is sufficiently distinct from the issues that have arisen in state proceedings, and the value of having a single ruling about the effect of Weinberger's behavior on his contractual relations with Medical Assurance is sufficient for the court to conclude that it was an abuse of discretion to stay this action.

For these reasons, the United States Court of Appeals, Seventh Circuit vacated the stay and remanded the case for further proceedings consistent with this opinion.

Discussion

1. Do you agree with the Court's decision? Discuss your answer.
2. Discuss how you would rule on this case.

NOTES

1. http://topics.law.cornell.edu/wex/healthcare_fraud
2. http://www.ncbi.nlm.nih.gov/pubmed/17199622
3. http://de.newszapforums.com/forum41/102074.html

chapter twelve

Summary Case—Star Chamber

"There is nothing," says Plato, "so delightful as the hearing or the speaking of truth"–
for this reason there is no conversation so agreeable as that of the man of integrity,
who hears without any intention to betray, and speaks without any intention to
deceive.

Thomas Sherlock (1678–1761)

I am part of all I have met.

Alfred Tennyson (1809–1892)

The following *closet drama* has been placed here to help the reader better understand human conflict and the real world of working relationships.
This drama is intriguing in that it arises out of the complex and diversified
affairs of humanity.

It is anticipated that legal and ethical issues will be applied here. Many
professionals, regardless of their field of training, will undoubtedly face similar issues during their career. This drama ends with a variety of thought-
provoking questions.

CODE OF SILENCE

LIST OF CHARACTERS

Marcus: Administrative Reviewer
Magistrate: Hearing Officer
Counselor: Representing Marcus
Mr. Damon Antonio: Nurse reviewer
Luke: Counsel representing the defendants
Dr. Machiavelli: Physician reviewer
Margaret: Nurse trainee
Ophelia: Guide
Dr. Caesar: Patient's physician
Bruce: Marcus's manager
Carol: Bruce's manager

SETTINGS

Rome: Marcus's home town
Health Review Council: An entity responsible for evaluating the quality of care in health centers from Rome to Athens
Courtroom of the Chief Magistrate: Site of the hearing in Athens
Athens Health Center: A local medical facility in Athens that Marcus was assigned to review
Pelopidas Street Inn: Hotel where the reviewers lodged

Marcus worked for the Health Review Council whose mission was to visit health centers from Rome, Maine to Athens, California and review the quality of patient care. He traveled much of the time, writing, consulting, educating, and reviewing the quality of care rendered to the people. His travels took him to hundreds of health centers in villages and cities. In order to have some semblance of family life, he stayed at various inns during his travels. He sacrificed family life to serve a call and a mission to help improve the quality of patient care throughout the United States. Marcus encouraged each health center to set higher standards, and to practice state of the art medicine, to fly with the eagles. He encouraged caregivers to dare to dream, to become possibility optimists and not impossibility pessimists.

Marcus collected numerous best practices from the centers he visited, sharing them with others throughout his travels. He spent thousands of hours on the road, at work, and at his home in Rome, Maine organizing the information that he had gathered.

He shared that information with the Health Review Council leadership as well as the health centers he visited. He encouraged the brightest and best to freely share best practices for improving the health of the people. He challenged many not to merely collect and sell healthcare information but to provide it freely to all healthcare centers, for he knew some had been collecting the information, reformatting it, and selling to all takers willing to pay for it.

As politics began to change in Rome, Maine and Athens, California with the appointment of new and inexperienced members to the Health Review Council, Marcus saw leadership make unfortunate and thoughtless decisions. This planted a seed in his soul to consider resigning and pursuing his passion for publishing updates to his published books. Marcus describes here the defining moments that caused him to reluctantly leave his position for a higher calling, a most fortuitous decision for him.

These defining moments for Marcus followed a long and mysterious cascade of events that were revealed during a hearing before the Chief Magistrate in Athens, California.

WHAT HAPPENED SUNDAY, OCTOBER 2 AT THE PELOPIDAS STREET INN?

If a thousand old beliefs were wrong in our march to truth we must still march on.

Stopford A. Brooke (1832–1916)

A Mind is a Terrible Thing to Change

A politician may be able to survive cavorting with prostitutes, sexting with coeds and comingling with interns, but heaven forbid he should change his mind—the transgression that trumps all compassion.

Or thinking.

After all, thinking can lead to that most dangerous territory for a politician—doubt—and, inevitably, the implication that dare not be expressed, "I could be wrong."

Kathleen Parker, The Washington Post, *June 12, 2011*

[Counselor prepares to question Mr. Antonio regarding his October 2 arrival at the Pelopidas Street Inn in Athens.]

Magistrate: Counselor, you may proceed with your questioning.
Counselor: Magistrate, for the record, this complaint was filed on behalf of Marcus, who was abruptly removed, without provocation, from his review of the Athens Health Center on Pelopidas Street in Athens.
Magistrate: Counselor, you may proceed.
Counselor: I would like to call Mr. Antonio to the stand.
Magistrate: So granted.

[Counselor calling Mr. Antonio to the witness box.]

Counselor: Could you please state your full name?
Mr. Antonio: Mr. Antonio.
Counselor: Who is your employer?
Mr. Antonio: The Hospital Review Council.
Counselor: Where is the Council located?
Mr. Antonio: In Washington, DC.
Counselor: Could you tell the Magistrate what your position is with the Council?
Mr. Antonio: I am a nurse reviewer.
Counselor: Could you describe what you do as a nurse reviewer for the Council?
Mr. Antonio: I review a health center's level of care provided to the citizens of Rome, Maine and Athens, California.
Counselor: Mr. Antonio, could you describe for the Magistrate what can happen to a center if it fails to meet care standards?
Mr. Antonio: It can lose its funding status from Medicare.
Counselor: Do you review centers in a particular region of the U.S.?
Mr. Antonio: No, I am not assigned to any particular region of the country.
Counselor: How long have you been reviewing health centers with the Hospital Review Council?
Mr. Antonio: Approximately 7 years.
Counselor: Did there come a time when you were assigned to review the Athens Health Center?
Mr. Antonio: Yes.
Counselor: Do you recall the dates of your review in Athens?

Mr. Antonio: No.

Counselor: Would an itinerary from that trip refresh your recollection?

Mr. Antonio: Yes.

Counselor: Magistrate, I would like to approach Mr. Antonio with what has been labeled Exhibit A, the October assignment sheet for Marcus.

Magistrate: You may proceed.

[Counselor handing Exhibit A to Mr. Antonio.]

Counselor: Do you recognize this document?

Mr. Antonio: Yes.

Counselor: What do you recognize Exhibit A to be?

Mr. Antonio: The October assignment sheet for Marcus.

Counselor: Is Exhibit A a fair and accurate representation of the health center to which you were assigned to work?

Mr. Antonio: Yes.

Counselor: Does this refresh your recollection as to your work assignment?

Mr. Antonio: Yes, it does.

Counselor: What were the dates of your assignment in Athens, California?

Mr. Antonio: October 3–7.

Counselor: What health center were you assigned to review?

Mr. Antonio: Athens Health Center on Pelopidas Street.

Counselor: Does Marcus's itinerary reflect what health reviewers were assigned to review the Athens Health Center on Pelopidas Street?

Mr. Antonio: Yes.

Counselor: Could you read the names and titles of those health reviewers listed on the assignment sheet?

Mr. Antonio: Yes, Marcus was the administrative reviewer; Dr. Machiavelli was the physician reviewer; Mr. Antonio was the nurse reviewer; and Margaret was a nurse trainee.

Counselor: Were the individuals listed on Marcus's assignment sheet present during the week that you reviewed patient care at the Athens Health Center in Athens, California?

Mr. Antonio: Yes.

Counselor: Can you tell the Magistrate where you stayed in Athens?

Mr. Antonio: Yes, the Pelopidas Street Inn.

Counselor: Is that on the same street as the Athens Health Center?

Mr. Antonio: Yes, it is.

Counselor: When did you arrive at the inn?

Mr. Antonio: On Sunday, October 2.

Counselor: Do you recall what time of day you arrived?

Mr. Antonio: I don't recall the time. I know it was in the afternoon.

Counselor: Was it two o'clock or three o'clock?

Luke: I object. Mr. Antonio has already answered this question. He doesn't know what time he arrived.

Magistrate: Objection sustained.

Counselor: Upon your arrival at the inn, did you observe Marcus in the lobby area?

Mr. Antonio: Yes, I did. I had just gotten off an elevator and he was sitting at a table.

Counselor: What was he doing at the table?

Mr. Antonio: He was having lunch.

Counselor: Did you have a conversation with him?

Mr. Antonio: Yes, I walked past the registration desk to greet him.

Counselor: Do you recall that conversation?

Mr. Antonio: Yes.

Counselor: Could you describe your conversation with Marcus?

Mr. Antonio: I said, "Marcus, I haven't seen you in a long time. How are you doing?"

Counselor: And what, if anything, was his response?

Mr. Antonio: He said he was doing well and asked how I was.

Counselor: Was there any further conversation?

Mr. Antonio: Yes. I asked about how his wife was doing.

Counselor: Why did you ask about his wife?

Mr. Antonio: She had some medical problems.

Counselor: And what was his response?

Mr. Antonio: As I recall, he said she was doing fine.

Counselor: Did there come a time during your conversation with Marcus when you asked him if he knew or had ever reviewed health centers with Dr. Machiavelli?

Mr. Antonio: Yes, I asked him if he knew or ever worked with Dr. Machiavelli.

Counselor: Had you ever worked with Marcus before?

Mr. Antonio: Yes.

Counselor: Did you enjoy working with Marcus?

Luke: I object to the question, Your Honor. I see no relevance in this question.

[The Magistrate hesitating for a moment.]

Gossip May Put an Evil Eye on People

"Gossip changes the way we view people, but it also changes the way we literally see a person," said Lisa Barrett . . . a psychology professor at Northeastern University, in an interview. "Gossip reaches all the way down into our visual system."

Christian Torres, The Washington Post, June 7, 2011

Magistrate: Counselor?

Counselor: Your Honor, I will establish the relevance of that question as I continue my questioning.

Magistrate: I will allow the question. Mr. Antonio, you may respond.

Mr. Antonio: Yes, I enjoyed working with him.

Counselor: What if anything else did you say?

Mr. Antonio: I don't recall.

Counselor: Let me refresh your recollection. Do you recall saying that Dr. Machiavelli was a physician health reviewer?

Mr. Antonio: Yes, I did say that.

Counselor: Do you recall saying he was a retired military commander?

Mr. Antonio: Yes, I did say that.

Counselor: Since you were rushing to check in, why was this information so important?

Mr. Antonio: Well, I was trying to establish if Marcus knew Dr. Machiavelli.

Counselor: What was Marcus's response?

Mr. Antonio: Excuse me, what is the question?

Counselor: What was Marcus's response to your question as to whether or not he knew Dr. Machiavelli?

Mr. Antonio: He said that he did not know him.

Counselor: Did he say anything else?

Mr. Antonio: Yes, Marcus asked me why I had asked that question.

Counselor: Did you answer his question?

Mr. Antonio: No.

Counselor: And why did you not answer his question?

Mr. Antonio: I told Marcus that I had just worked with Dr. Machiavelli the previous week and that I would like to know his impression of him at the end of the Athens Health Center review.

Counselor: What role did you play in your previous health center review with Dr. Machiavelli?

Mr. Antonio: I was the lead nurse in charge of the overall review.

Counselor: You stated that you had just worked with Dr. Machiavelli, is that correct?

Mr. Antonio: Yes.

Counselor: And you are referring to the week prior to the Athens Health Center review?

Mr. Antonio: Yes.

Counselor: Was there any other conversation that you recall from this brief encounter with Marcus?

Mr. Antonio: No, not to my recollection.

Counselor: So your conversation was somewhat short, is that correct?

Mr. Antonio: Yes, it was.

Counselor: So was it less than, or more than, 5 minutes in length?

Luke: I object, Your Honor. That question has already been answered.

Magistrate: I will allow the question? You may answer the question Mr. Antonio.

Mr. Antonio: Less than 5 minutes.

Counselor: Was it less than 4 minutes?

Luke: I object, Your Honor. Mr. Antonio has already answered that question.

Magistrate: Objection sustained.

Counselor: So, Mr. Antonio. We have established that you spoke to Mr. Marcus for less than 5 minutes. You asked how he and his wife were, and then you asked Marcus if he would give you his impression of Dr. Machiavelli at the end of the Pelopidas Street review. Is that correct?

Mr. Antonio: Yes.

Counselor: Why was your conversation so short? Especially since you had not seen Marcus in such a long time?

Luke: I object, Your Honor. That question has already been answered.

Magistrate: Objection overruled. I will allow the witness to answer.

Mr. Antonio: I was just checking into the hotel. I wanted to get my things to my room.

Counselor: So you were happy to see that Marcus was on the review?

Mr. Antonio: Yes.

Counselor: And why was that?

Mr. Antonio: I worked with Marcus before. He has always been pleasant to work with, and I enjoyed his professional stature, wisdom, and sense of humor.

Counselor: Did you meet up with Marcus later that day to discuss old times, anything?

Mr. Antonio: No, I did not.

Counselor: So you had not seen Marcus in some time, you always enjoyed reviewing with him, and you did not meet with him later in the day. Yet, your third question was to ascertain his impression of Dr. Machiavelli at the end of the review. Is that correct?

Mr. Antonio: Yes, I guess about the third question.

Counselor: Did you have any other questions at that time?

Mr. Antonio: No, I just told him I had to check in.

Counselor: What was so important about asking that question that you were willing to wait 5 days for an answer?

Luke: I object, Your Honor. That question has already been answered.

Magistrate: I will allow the question. You may answer the question Mr. Antonio.

Mr. Antonio: Well, I felt he had sort of a military style of reviewing. He seemed as though he thought he had some sort of right to be in charge of the review that I was in charge of the previous week. I think he resented that.

Counselor: And why do you believe he resented that?

Mr. Antonio: Partially because I was at a lower rank and in a different branch of the military. Also, I was thinking that he was having difficulty in adapting to a civilian role.

Counselor: So on the week we are talking about here, he is now in charge? Is that correct?

Mr. Antonio: Yes.

Counselor: So were you concerned about Dr. Machiavelli being in charge?

Mr. Antonio: Yes, sort of.

Counselor: So Marcus was a friend?

Mr. Antonio: Yes.

Counselor: A good friend.

Luke: Magistrate, I object. The question has been asked and answered.

Magistrate: I will allow the question. Counselor, you may proceed.

Counselor: So you considered Marcus a trusted colleague with whom you enjoyed working.

Mr. Antonio: Yes, I did.

Counselor: And, to your knowledge, he thought the same of you?

Mr. Antonio: Yes, I believe so.

Counselor: Yet you foresaw there might be problems on this review?

Luke: Magistrate, I object to the form of the question.

Magistrate: Are you sure you would not like to just object to the question in any form? Your objection is overruled! Counselor, you may proceed with your questioning.

Counselor: Mr. Antonio, you stated that you and Marcus were good working colleagues, yet you failed to warn your friend of possible problems ahead during this review. Is that correct?

Luke: Magistrate, I object.

Magistrate: I will allow the question.

Mr. Antonio: Could you repeat the question?

Counselor: In summary, did you leave your friend out to dry?

Luke: Magistrate, I object.

Magistrate: Objection sustained. Counselor, do you wish to reword that question?

Counselor: No, I have no further questions at this time but reserve the right to recall Mr. Antonio to the witness box.

Magistrate: Granted. We will take a short recess.

EVENTS OF WEDNESDAY, OCTOBER 5

[Counselor questions Marcus regarding Day 3 of the Athens Health Center review.]

Counselor: Before we proceed, could you please verify if the testimony previously provided by Mr. Antonio is, to your recollection, fair and accurate?

Marcus: Yes, it was.

Counselor: Thank you. Could you please describe for the Magistrate what occurred on the afternoon of Wednesday, October 5.

Marcus: Yes, I can. I would like to refer to my notes.

Counselor: Magistrate, I would like to place into evidence the notes that Marcus is going to refer to as he describes what occurred on the afternoon of Wednesday, October 5.

Magistrate: You may proceed.

Counselor: Marcus, how long have you been working for the Hospital Review Council.

Marcus: Approximately 10 years.

Counselor: Could you please describe for the Magistrate what occurred on the afternoon of Wednesday, October 5.

Marcus: Yes, I can. At approximately 12:50 P.M., Dr. Machiavelli asked what I planned to review for the afternoon.

Counselor: And what did you say?

Marcus: I said, since none of the reviewers had asked for a complex medical case, I was planning to ask the Atnens Health Center's staff for such a case to review.

Counselor: What, if anything else, did you say to Dr. Machiavelli at that time?

Marcus: I asked if that was okay with him.

Counselor: And what did he say?

Marcus: He said, "That sounds like a good idea."

Counselor: Then what happened?

Marcus: Ophelia, my Athens Health Center guide, opened the door to the room where I had just finished eating lunch with my colleagues. She entered the room and inquired if I had a particular case in mind that I would like to review.

Counselor: And what did you say?

Marcus: I said yes and suggested a complex medical case.

Counselor: What is the responsibility of the Athen's Health Center guide?

Marcus: That person is responsible for leading me to each patient care area where I plan to review a case. Ophelia also had a scribe with her who was assigned to take notes on all our conversations.

Counselor: So, Ophelia located the type of case you requested?

Marcus: Yes, Ophelia said that she had such a case, and she escorted me to the patient care unit where the patient had been admitted.

Counselor: Did you review the patient's record?

Marcus: Yes, the charge nurse searched for the patient's record that I planned to review and brought it to me.

Counselor: Is that part of the patient care review process?

Marcus: Yes, it is.

Counselor: Then what happened?

Marcus: I was introduced to the staff nurse assigned to care for the patient.

Counselor: Then what happened?

Marcus: The staff nurse reviewed the record with me in a conference room on the patient care unit.

Counselor: What questions, if any, did you ask her?

Marcus: I asked her for some preliminary information about the patient, which included the patient's age and diagnosis.

Counselor: How did the nurse respond?

Marcus: She answered my questions, providing me with the patient's admitting information and medical problems.

Counselor: Did you ask any other questions?

Marcus: Yes, after reviewing the patient's record I asked whether any of the patient's lab results helped to identify the patient's medical problems.

Counselor: So that is part of the Hospital Review Council's expectations of you?

Marcus: Yes, it is.

Counselor: What was the nurse's response?

Marcus: She said that she could not answer the question. A nurse manager in the room where I was reviewing the patient's record asked if I would like to speak to Dr. Caesar, the patient's physician.

Counselor: What was your response?

Marcus: I said that would be fine, provided he was available and not busy with other patients.

Counselor: Then what happened?

Marcus: Dr. Caesar was summoned. Upon entering the room, he stood inside the doorway, at which time I introduced myself. He appeared somewhat disturbed that he had been summoned.

Counselor: In your opinion, why do you believe Dr. Caesar was disturbed?

Luke: Objection, Magistrate. I see no relevance to this question. It is mere speculation as to why the physician was disturbed.

Magistrate: I will allow the question. Marcus, you may proceed with your response.

Marcus: It is normal, in general, for physicians to be anxious when questioned by a reviewer from the Hospital Review Council. Reviewers are not always the highlight of a physician's or any other caregiver's day. To be questioned about a patient's care can be intimidating.

Counselor: Then what happened?

Marcus: Well, he introduced himself, asked what questions I had and what kind of physician I was.

Counselor: What was your response?

Counselor: I stated that I was not a physician and that I just had a few questions for him.

Counselor: What questions did you ask?

Marcus: I asked Dr. Caesar if any of the patient's lab results identified any of the patient's ailments.

Counselor: What was his response?

Marcus: He said that he was only there to treat the patient's immediate needs and not all of the patient's complex issues.

Counselor: Then what happened?

Marcus: I let the remaining questions pass and asked if it would be okay if I visited with the patient.

Counselor: What did he say?

Marcus: He said that would be fine and started to leave the room.

Counselor: Then what happened?

Marcus: I asked Dr. Caesar if he would ask the patient if it would be okay for me to interview him.

Counselor: And how did Dr. Caesar respond?

Marcus: He said, "That's not necessary."

Counselor: Then what happened?

Marcus: He left the conference room room and walked down the hallway to the patient's room.

Counselor: Did you follow Dr. Caesar down the hallway?

Marcus: Yes, I and the scribe did.

Counselor: Did you follow Dr. Caesar into the patient's room?

Marcus: No, I waited for him to return to the hallway.

Counselor: Then what happened?

Marcus: Dr. Caesar returned and said, "I had to awaken the patient. He is willing to speak to you."

Counselor: Then what happened?

Marcus: I entered the patient's room and walked towards his bedside. Dr. Caesar stood with his back to the wall facing the patient's bed. The scribe had also followed me into the room and stood by the physician taking notes.

Counselor: Then what happened?

Marcus: Dr. Caesar asked me if I wanted him to leave. I said he was welcome to stay if he wished.

Counselor: Did he remain in the room?

Marcus: Yes, and I began to introduce myself to the patient. As I began to introduce myself, the patient interrupted, "I know who you are." I asked, "How do you know?" He said with a smile, "My wife is a nurse. She works here. She told me you might be coming."

Counselor: Then what happened?

Marcus: I said that I had only a few questions that I would like to ask him. He said okay. I asked about his care at the Athens Health Center. He stated that he was receiving excellent care. After some discussion about his care, the patient repeated that he was getting very good care.

Counselor: Then what happened?

Marcus: I thanked him for his time and speaking to me. I began to leave the patient's room when Dr. Caesar said he would like to say something.

Counselor: And what did you reply?

Marcus: I said that would be fine.

Counselor: What did Dr. Caesar say?

Marcus: He began to describe to the patient his disease process and described how he could die from his disease. I was bewildered. I looked at the patient, observed his emotions of sadness, and said, "You will be okay."

Counselor: Why were you bewildered?

Marcus: The patient had already been under Dr. Caesar's care in the hospital for 2 weeks. I could not think of why he would say that. The timing of that statement was inappropriate and added nothing to the interview but more stress for the patient.

Counselor: Were you telling the patient that he would be okay clinically?

Marcus: No, I was not referring to his clinical condition but was responding to his emotional status at the time, resulting from Dr. Caesar's description as to how his disease could progress. I thanked the patient again and left the room.

Counselor: Then what happened?

Marcus: Dr. Caesar quickly followed me to the doorway, somewhat agitated, said, "Don't you ever tell my patients they will be okay."

Counselor: Then what happened?

Marcus: A nurse asked if we could move the conversation down the hall, away from the patient's doorway, at which time, Dr. Caesar asked me again, "What kind of physician are you?"

Counselor: So he had asked you this question twice: "What kind of physician are you?"

Marcus: Yes, and I restated that I was not a physician. I attempted to calm him down, I extended my hand, and I thanked him for his time.

Counselor: Did he shake your hand?

Marcus: Yes, he did.

Counselor: Then what happened?

Marcus: He turned and walked away.

Counselor: Were any nurses listening to you during the time you were in the hallway with the physician?

Marcus: Yes, the scribe was taking notes, and the nurse manager was present. The nurse stated that this was unusual behavior by the physician.

Counselor: Then what happened?

Marcus: At that point, Ophelia had arrived and led me back up the hallway with the scribe following closely behind. As we walked down the hallway, Ophelia asked what had happened. I then described what happened during the patient interview to her. Ophelia then asked the scribe, "Why didn't you intervene? I knew from the minute he entered the chart review room he was going to be a problem. I should have stayed with you, Marcus. I would never have let him get away with that. But, while you were reviewing the chart, I was called to another unit, where he had a problem with a staff nurse."

Counselor: Did the scribe respond to Ophelia?

Marcus: Yes, she said that she didn't think she needed to get involved.

Counselor: Did the scribe say anything else to you?

Marcus: Yes, she later asked me if I thought she should have intervened.

Counselor: And what did you say to her?

Marcus: I told her no and that if she intervened it might have inflamed the situation. She had to work at the Arhens Health Center after I left, and I didn't think she needed a poor working relationship with Dr. Caesar.

Counselor: Do you now regret, in retrospect, her not intervening?

Luke: Magistrate, I strongly object. We are talking about what happened, not what Marcus wishes had happened.

Magistrate: Objection sustained. Counselor, do you have any further questions at this time?

Counselor: Not at this time but I will most likely recall Marcus to the witness box.

Magistrate: I understand. We will take a short break at this time. Luke and Counselor, I would like to see you in my chambers.

The most striking contradiction of our civilization is the fundamental reverence for truth, which we profess, and the thorough–going disregard for it, which we practice.

Vilhjalmur Stefansson (1879–1962)

THURSDAY AM, OCTOBER 6

[Magistrate hearing continues with Counselor questioning Mr. Antonio.]

Counselor: Are you aware if Marcus had ever previously reviewed the Athens Health Center?

Mr. Antonio: To my knowledge, he had not.

Counselor: Did Marcus ever say to you that he knew any employee on the staff of the Athens Health Center?

Mr. Antonio: No, he did not.

Counselor: Did you and your colleagues brief each morning your previous day's findings with the Athens Health Center's leadership?

Mr. Antonio: Yes, we did.

Counselor: What is the purpose of briefings?

Mr. Antonio: The reviewers describe to the Athens Health Center's leadership the previous day's observations as opportunities for improving patient care.

Counselor: Do you recall the substance of Marcus's report on Wednesday of the review?

Mr. Antonio: I don't recall.

Counselor: Do you recall if he was complimentary of his observations on the previous day's activities?

Mr. Antonio: I am sure he did, yes. But I don't recall the specifics. As on all the reviews that I worked with Marcus, he was sensitive to recognize the good things he observed. We all did that.

Counselor: How much time is generally allotted to each health reviewer to present at the morning briefings?

Mr. Antonio: Generally 10 minutes.

Counselor: Is that time set in stone?

Mr. Antonio: No, it is not.

Counselor: Did the reviewers stick to the time allotted?

Mr. Antonio: No.

Counselor: Did you stick to your time limit?

Mr. Antonio: Not always.

Counselor: Did Dr. Machiavelli stick to his time limit?

Mr. Antonio: Not always.

Counselor: So there were days that you stuck to your schedule, and there were days that you did not. Is that correct?

Mr. Antonio: Yes, that is correct.

Counselor: And why didn't you always stick to your time allotment?

Mr. Antonio: It depended on the number of observations I had.

Counselor: Were there any other factors as to why a reviewer may have gone over his or her allotted time to present his or her report?

Mr. Antonio: Yes, it depended on how many times Dr. Machiavelli interrupted to add something in an attempt to clarify or relate a personal experience to emphasize what a reviewer was saying.

Counselor: In your experience, have you ever observed a health reviewer say "I pass" and say nothing more?

Mr. Antonio: No.

Counselor: Most reviewers say something?

Mr. Antonio: Yes, most health reviewers have something to say.

Counselor: Do you recall Marcus reporting on a physician's disruptive behavior on Wednesday?

Mr. Antonio: Yes, that I do remember.

Counselor: Could you summarize what Marcus reported?

Mr. Antonio: He talked about Dr. Caesar, the patient's physician. He described Dr. Caesar's approach to him following the interview and how he was unprofessional to him and the patient.

Counselor: In what way was Dr. Caesar unprofessional to Marcus?

Mr. Antonio: Following Marcus's interview with the patient, Dr. Caesar told him not to ever tell any of his patients that they would be okay.

Counselor: In order to save time here, have you read Marcus's transcript?

Mr. Antonio: Yes.

Counselor: Is Marcus's description of what occurred on Wednesday afternoon in the patient's room a fair and accurate representation of what he reported on Thursday morning to the Athens Health Center leadership?

Mr. Antonio: Yes, it is accurate to my recollection.

Counselor: When this incident began to unfold, do you recall who Marcus reported was in the patient's room with him?

Mr. Antonio: Yes, there was Marcus, Dr. Caesar, the patient, and the scribe.

Counselor: Why did Marcus report the incident with Dr. Caesar on Thursday morning?

Mr. Antonio: He was concerned this might be a pattern with Dr. Caesar or perhaps he'd just had a bad day or been very busy. If there was a pattern of bad behavior in his record, it needed to be addressed.

Counselor: Did you see Ophelia, at the Wednesday morning briefing, lean toward Marcus and whisper something to him?

Mr. Antonio: Yes.

Counselor: Did you ever learn what Ophelia said?

Mr. Antonio. Yes, at Thursday's luncheon. Marcus told the nurse trainee and myself.

Counselor: And what did he say?

Mr. Antonio: He said she whispered, "Good job. Your presentation was fair and well-balanced."

Counselor: And what did you think of her comments?

Mr. Antonio: I just told Marcus she was right.

Counselor: Meaning?

Mr. Antonio: That Marcus was very diplomatic in his approach to a delicate matter. He really left it up to the Athens Health Center's leadership to determine how to handle the matter. He could have reported the incident to the Health Review Council but chose a more diplomatic route.

Counselor: If Marcus had reported the incident to a Council manager, what do you think the manager would have said to Marcus?

Mr. Antonio: Good job, Marcus. I am pleased that you presented this incident at the leadership meeting. This way it cannot be swept under a rug.

Counselor: Interesting comment, Mr. Antonio, do you think certain leaders in an organization would do such a thing?

Luke: Objection, Counselor is asking an opinion about organizations in general.

Magistrate: Objection sustained. Counselor, please stick to the facts of this case before me.

[Counselor acknowledges the magistrate's admonition.]

Counselor: Do you believe, in general, that one often gets an answer to a question by the way he or she words or asks a question?

Mr. Antonio: Yes, I do.

Counselor: Do you believe that the tone in one's voice and the way a question is presented will influence the listener?

Mr. Antonio: Yes.

Counselor: So the listener could draw the conclusion he or she wanted or thought was intended?

Mr. Antonio: Yes.

Counselor: So if Dr. Machiavelli had reported Marcus's incident with Dr. Caesar to the Health Review Council, the response he received from the Council might have been different than if Marcus reported this incident?

Mr. Antonio: Yes, of course.

Counselor: If you had reported Marcus's encounter with Dr. Caesar to the Council, based on your previous reviews with Dr. Machiavelli, do you think you might have presented the incident differently than he would have?

[Mr. Antonio hesitates for what seems like forever, while the Magistrate waits patiently for an answer.]

Mr. Antonio: Yes, I do. Everyone is different.

Counselor: So Mr. Antonio, getting back to your remark at lunch to Marcus that you did not want to be placed in the middle. You know that you placed yourself squarely in the middle of really what was your problem and relationship with Dr. Machiavelli from a previous survey. Is that correct?

Luke: Magistrate, I object.

Magistrate: Objection sustained.

Counselor: Do you recall if Marcus spent an inordinate amount of time reporting on his encounter with Dr. Caesar?

Mr. Antonio: No, he had a long report but presented it within a reasonable amount of time.

Counselor: Do you think Dr. Machiavelli would agree with you?

Mr. Antonio: No.

Counselor: And why is that?

Mr. Antonio: It was just an observation. Well, he did comment later that the morning briefings had to be shortened.

Counselor: As the reviewers presented their reports that morning, were there ever interruptions by Dr. Machiavelli?

Mr. Antonio: Yes, he generally had a few of his own personal stories that he added to the conversation.

Counselor: Had he interrupted your report and made further comments?

Mr. Antonio: Yes, on several occasions that morning.

Counselor: Did he interrupt Marcus on Thursday morning?

Mr. Antonio: Not as I recall.

Counselor: Do you recall Dr. Machiavelli being uneasy and fidgeting around in his chair as Marcus presented his report?

[Mr. Antonio again hesitates. The Magistrate appears uneasy and ready for a break.]

Magistrate: Mr. Antonio, could you please answer the question?

Mr. Antonio: Yes, I do recall that Dr. Machiavelli was uneasy, actually a bit rude in his facial expressions.

Counselor: Where were you sitting at the time Marcus presented his report?

Mr. Antonio: I was sitting at the head of the table with Margaret and other members of the organization's leadership.

Counselor: So you could actually see Dr. Machiavelli's facial expressions, let's say, in a face-to-face manner?

Mr. Antonio: That is correct.

Counselor: Are you aware if anyone else in the Athens Health Center's leadership observed Dr. Machiavelli's mannerisms?

Mr. Antonio: Yes. The table was oval in shape and I could easily see that the leadership must have been wondering why Dr. Machiavelli seemed so disengaged with Marcus.

Counselor: So you were actually sitting where the organization's leadership could observe Dr. Caesar's behavior?

Luke: Objection, this question has already been answered.

Magistrate: Motion overruled. Mr. Antonio, you may proceed with your answer.

Mr. Antonio: Yes, I was.

Counselor: Did Margaret also note his behavior?

Mr. Antonio: Yes.

Counselor: Are you aware as to whether or not Marcus was distracted by Dr. Machiavelli's behavior?

Mr. Antonio: I believe so, but I noticed he tried not to look at Dr. Machiavelli's body language. Actually, I'm sure it was distracting to him.

Counselor: Did Marcus mention to you whether or not the Athen's Health Center's leadership had noted Dr. Machiavelli's behavior?

Mr. Antonio: Yes, according to Marcus, Ophelia said, "Dr. Machiavelli appeared to be somewhat disengaged with you. He hadn't done this with any of the other reviewers."

Counselor: So Marcus pretty much felt the same way?

Mr. Antonio: Yes, he remarked that he had never met Dr. Machiavelli and could not understand his behavior.

Counselor: Do you agree that the Dr. Machiavelli's behavior was out of line in that setting?

Mr. Antonio: Yes, without question.

Counselor: Magistrate, I have no further questions at this time.

THURSDAY LUNCHEON, OCTOBER 6

[After a short recess, Counselor recalls Mr. Antonio to the witness box.]

Counselor: Returning to that afternoon luncheon on Thursday, where did you have lunch?

Mr. Antonio: In the Athens Health Center's library.

Counselor: Did there come a time at lunch that Marcus again asked why you had asked him for his impression of Dr. Machiavelli at the end of the survey?

Mr. Antonio: Yes.

Counselor: Was Dr. Machiavelli in the room when this conversation took place?

Mr. Antonio: No.

Counselor: Do you know where he was?

Mr. Antonio: I am not sure. He had left the room. I think he went to speak to the CEO.

Counselor: Did you answer Marcus's question?

Mr. Antonio: I told Marcus I did not want to get in the middle of this.

Counselor: Mr. Antonio, reflecting back to Sunday in the Pelopidas Street Inn, don't you think you already placed yourself in the middle?

Luke: Objection.

Magistrate: I will allow the question. You can answer the question, Mr. Antonio.

Mr. Antonio: Well uh, well, I didn't think this would happen.

Counselor: What did you expect to happen? Watch Dr. Machiavelli give Marcus a hard time?

Mr. Antonio: Well, I didn't expect it to go this far.

Counselor: Far? What do you mean?

Mr. Antonio: Well, Dr. Machiavelli had a bit of uh, uh—

Counselor: Uh, uh, what?

Mr. Antonio: I just didn't think Dr. Machiavelli would be so hard on Marcus.

Counselor: I see. So, it sounds like he gave you some problems during a previous review?

[Mr. Antonio hesitates as the Magistrate stares at him. Even the magistrate guards seem mesmerized by the hearing. Counselor, growing impatient, restates the question.]

Counselor: Mr. Antonio, could you please answer the question?

Mr. Antonio: Could you please repeat the question?

Counselor: Did you have a previous encounter with Dr. Machiavelli at a previous health center review?

Mr. Antonio: Well, yes I did.

Counselor: And you are referring to the health center review that took place the week prior to the one that was being conducted at the Athens Health Center?

Mr. Antonio: Yes, I am.

Counselor: Were you happy or unhappy with Dr. Machiavelli's behavior at that review, that is, the review prior to the Athens review?

Mr. Antonio: I was not totally happy.

Counselor: So, again, you chose to allow Marcus to walk into the minefield?

Luke: I object to this line of questioning.

Magistrate: Objection—

[Before the magistrate can say "sustained" or "overruled," Counselor breaks in . . .]

Counselor: I withdraw my question.

Magistrate: Withdrawal noted. You may proceed.

Counselor: And now that Dr. Machiavelli was in charge of the review at the Athens Health Center, you thought his style would match his name and that he might have met his match in Marcus. Is that right?

Luke: Objection, he is leading the witness.

Magistrate: Objection sustained.

Counselor: What, if anything else, did Marcus say to you about you being placed in the middle of something?

Mr. Antonio: He just kept asking me, in the middle of what? He was trying to prod an answer out of me.

Counselor: And you refused to give an answer. Is that correct?

Mr. Antonio: Yes.

Counselor: Did he say anything else that you recall?

Mr. Antonio: Uh no, uh, I mean I don't recall.

Counselor: Did he refresh your memory?

Mr. Antonio: What do you mean?

Counselor: Going back to your conversation with Marcus on the first day in the inn lobby, did he ask again at lunch on Thursday why you wanted to know what he thought of Dr. Machiavelli on the last day of the Athens review?

Mr. Antonio: Yes, he did.

Counselor: And you replied you would tell him on Friday at the end of the Athens review. Is that correct?

Mr. Antonio: Yes.

Counselor: So, previously on the record, Marcus said he never met Dr. Machiavelli. Is that correct?

Mr. Antonio: Yes.

Counselor: So you knew that there was something Marcus should know, but you sort of let him walk into the middle of a minefield and find out for himself. And you call yourself his friend. Is that correct?

Luke: Magistrate, I have already objected to this question!

Magistrate: I will allow the question. I believe I see where Counselor is leading, and we need to hear it. You may answer the question, Mr. Antonio.

Mr. Antonio: Well, I wouldn't put it that way.

Counselor: How would you put it?

Luke: I object.

Magistrate: Objection overruled. You may answer the question.

Mr. Antonio: I just did not want to get involved. I did not expect Dr. Machiavelli would be so rude to Marcus.

Counselor: What else did Marcus say during that luncheon?

Mr. Antonio: He said Dr. Machiavelli was not responsive to him except that Dr. Machiavelli shifted around in his chair with inappropriate body language at the morning sessions when Marcus presented his daily report to the Athens leadership. He said, "I don't even know him. Why is he doing that?"

Counselor: Do you recall anything else that Marcus might have said regarding Dr. Machiavelli's body language?

Mr. Antonio: No.

Counselor: Let me refresh your memory. Do you recall Marcus saying to you and Margaret that the Athens staff sensed that Dr. Machiavelli appeared to be disengaged with him each morning he made his reports and that Dr. Machiavelli did not do this with any of the other health reviewers?

Mr. Antonio: Yes, I believe I answered that before. I recall that.

Counselor: Do you recall if anyone else was present in the room during this conversation?

Mr. Antonio: Yes, as you just said, Margaret, the nurse trainee.

Counselor: Did she participate in this conversation?

Mr. Antonio: No.

Counselor: Magistrate, I may wish to call Margaret to the witness box at a later date.

Magistrate: Understood.

Counselor: Before we proceed, do you recall if, earlier during the Thursday luncheon, Marcus gave you some sort of CD?

Mr. Antonio: Yes, he did.

Counselor: In general, do you recall what was contained on that disc?

Mr. Antonio: Yes, Marcus had collected thousands of pages of best practices over the years that he shared with reviewers and the health centers he reviewed.

Counselor: Could you describe for the Magistrate why Marcus collected and distributed those practices?

Mr. Antonio: Yes, I think so. It was sort of a mission with him to share best practices so that healthcare organizations did not have to waste valuable time "reinventing the wheel." He believed that human resources should be used wisely, and if organizations were willing to share with one another, everyone benefited.

Counselor: Are you aware of anyone else in your career that has embarked on such a project?

Mr. Antonio: No, I am not. Marcus is the only reviewer that I am aware of.

Counselor: Since, as you well know, Marcus is no longer with the Hospital Review Council, has it come to your attention that the Council is now sharing such or similar information freely, sort of borrowing the idea from Marcus?

Mr. Antonio: Yes, I am aware that this has occurred.

Counselor: About this disc, did Marcus provide you with any specific instructions as to with whom it should or should not be shared?

Mr. Antonio: Yes.

Counselor: What was his request?

Mr. Antonio: He requested that we use these disc files for personal reference. He asked that they not be shared with others at this time. He was in the process of editing them and wanted to share a copy with us.

Counselor: Did you agree to his request?

Mr. Antonio: Yes, I did.

Counselor: Are you aware that Margaret received a copy of the disc?

Mr. Antonio: Yes, she did.

Counselor: Did she agree to Marcus's request?

Mr. Antonio: Yes, she did. We both agreed.

Counselor: Do you recall shortly after the Athens Health Center review that a member of the Hospital Review Council used certain files from that disc during a conference call with all of your colleagues in Rome to improve the quality of the conference call?

Mr. Antonio: Yes, I recall that, however, I did not provide a copy to anyone at the Council.

Counselor: Was Marcus credited with providing that information in any way?

Mr. Antonio: No, he was not.

Counselor: Do you know who provided the disc to the leadership at the Hospital Review Council?

Mr. Antonio: No, I am not aware of how the Council obtained a copy of the disc.

Counselor: Did the information on this disc serve to improve your approach in conducting health center reviews?

Mr. Antonio: Yes, definitely.

Counselor: Mr. Antonio, do you recall anything else that Marcus asked you at the Thursday lunch?

Mr. Antonio: No.

Counselor: Let me refresh your memory. Did Marcus ask you again, and I quote: "Mr. Antonio, You asked for my impression of Dr. Machiavelli on Sunday, before I ever met him, and now you don't want to answer as to why you asked that question?"

Luke: I object, this question has been asked and answered many times over.

Counselor: I am setting the background for my next question.

Magistrate: Objection overruled. Mr. Antonio, you may proceed.

Mr. Antonio: Yes, he did say that.

Counselor: And how did you respond?

Mr. Antonio: I said I didn't want to get in the middle of it. I suggested that he sit down with Dr. Machiavelli and talk to him.

Counselor: And what did Marcus say?

Mr. Antonio: He said, the middle of what? He said he'd tried on several occasions to speak to Dr. Machiavelli but he was nonresponsive.

Counselor: Did Marcus relate to you his attempts at conversation with Dr. Machiavelli in an elevator at the Pelopidas Street Inn?

Mr. Antonio: Yes, he said that his last attempt to have a casual conversation with Dr. Machiavelli was on the elevator on Tuesday evening at the Inn after that day's review.

Counselor: And did Marcus describe how Dr. Machiavelli's responded?

Mr. Antonio: He said that Dr. Machiavelli failed to respond and that he got off on a floor just below his, walked away, never said good night, never acknowledged that he, Marcus, was in the elevator. He said that Dr. Machiavelli just got off the elevator and walked away with the elevator doors closing behind him.

Counselor: In other words, he ignored Marcus's attempt at any conversation?

Luke: Objection, Your Honor. He is leading the witness.

Magistrate: Objection sustained.

Counselor: Does Dr. Machiavelli appear to have a hearing problem that you are aware of?

Mr. Antonio: Oh no, quite the opposite.

Counselor: Could you describe the size of that elevator?

Luke: I object, Your Honor. I see no relevance to this line of questioning.

Magistrate: Let us see where this is going. Overruled. Mr. Antonio, you may answer the question.

Mr. Antonio: It was small. Six people, and it would have been crowded.

Counselor: So, even if Dr. Machiavelli was hard of hearing, he most likely heard Marcus's comment.

Mr. Antonio: Yes.

The withholding of truth is sometimes a worse deception then a direct misstatement. There is an idiom in truth which falsehood never can imitate.

Lord Napier (1819–1898)

LATE THURSDAY AFTERNOON, OCTOBER 6

[Counselor recalls Mr. Antonio to the witness box to testify regarding events of late afternoon Thursday, October 6. Counselor's first questions of Mr. Antonio at this time have to do with Marcus having just finished the 4th day of his 5-day review in Athens and returning to the conference room assigned by the Athens Health Center as home base for the health reviewers. Not only the morning briefings with the Athens Health Center leadership but also the afternoon debriefings with the reviewers were being held there. But, as Marcus headed back to the conference room shortly before time for that evening's debriefing, he observed his colleagues Mr. Antonio and Margaret scurry past him, avoiding eye contact, as if they just wanted to get out of the Athens Health Center. Marcus thought that strange, and he supposed that there must not be an afternoon debriefing after all.]

Counselor: Mr. Antonio, following lunch on Thursday, did you again see Marcus before leaving the Athen's health center?

Mr. Antonio: Yes.

Counselor: And when was that?

Mr. Antonio: I saw him at the end of the day.

Counselor: And where were you when you saw him?

Mr. Antonio: I was leaving the review for the day and was headed back to the inn.

Counselor: And who was with you?

Mr. Antonio: Margaret.

Counselor: Did you and Margaret leave separately from Marcus?

Mr. Antonio: Yes.

Counselor: With whom did you leave at the end of the day to return to the Pelopidas Street Inn on Monday, Tuesday, and Wednesday?

Mr. Antonio: We all left together.

Counselor: Who are "we"?

Mr. Antonio: The nurse trainee, Marcus, Dr. Machiavelli, and myself.

Counselor: So you and Margaret left on Thursday without Marcus and Dr. Machiavelli?

Mr. Antonio: Yes.

Counselor: And why was that?

Luke: Magistrate, I object. I fail to see any relevance to this question.

Magistrate: Overruled. You may answer the question.

Mr. Antonio: Dr. Machiavelli said he talked to Bruce and they planned a conference call with Marcus.

Marcus: Who is Bruce?

Mr. Antonio: He is Marcus's manager at the Council office.

Counselor: So you generally meet as a team at the end of each day to debrief and review the team's findings?

Mr. Antonio: Yes.

Counselor: On Thursday, October 6th you did not have such a meeting?

Mr. Antonio: No.

Counselor: So you walked past Marcus on Thursday with Margaret, and you saw Marcus coming toward the two of you. Is that correct?

Mr. Antonio: Yes.

Counselor: So were you in the hallway when you spotted him, or someplace else?

Mr. Antonio: We were in an office area when we passed him in a small aisle between desks.

Counselor: Did he ask where you were going?

Mr. Antonio: I don't recall.

Counselor: So you never acknowledged that you saw him. Is that correct?

Mr. Antonio: Well, what could I say?

Counselor: I am asking the questions. You are to answer them. Magistrate, could you please instruct the witness as to protocol?

Magistrate: Mr. Antonio, answer the questions. I don't want a cat and mouse game before me.

Mr. Antonio: I did not acknowledge him.

Counselor: How far apart were you when you walked by him?

Mr. Antonio: A few feet.

Counselor: Did you make eye contact with him?

Mr. Antonio: No, I did not.

Counselor: So you knew that a confrontation was awaiting Marcus, when he met up with Dr. Machiavelli?

Luke: Objection.

Magistrate: Overruled.

Counselor: So you knew Marcus was about to be ambushed when he walked into the conference room?

Mr. Antonio: Ugh—

Luke: Objection, Your Honor.

Magistrate: Objection sustained. Counselor, please tone down your question a few notches.

Counselor: Were you aware that Dr. Machiavelli was waiting for Marcus to return from his day's activities?

Mr. Antonio: Yes, I was.

Counselor: And what else did you know?

Mr. Antonio: That Bruce maneuvered to have Marcus removed from the review.

Counselor: Maneuvered?

Mr. Antonio: Oh uh, I mean, planned.

Counselor: So you knew that your "friend" was going to be facing an early removal from the review. Is that correct?

Mr. Antonio: Yes, I did.

Counselor: You considered Marcus your friend earlier in the week. Are you still friends?

Mr. Antonio: I assume so.

Counselor: Do you think your assumption is accurate?

Luke: Objection, the question has been asked and answered.

Magistrate: Objection sustained.

Counselor: Mr. Antonio, I understand you were a military officer. Is that correct?

Mr. Antonio: Yes, I am retired.

Counselor: So who held the highest rank, you or Dr. Machiavelli?

Mr. Antonio: Dr. Machiavelli.

Counselor: Mr. Antonio, were you intimidated by Dr. Machiavelli because of his rank?

[Mr. Antonio was in fact intimidated, but he does not wish to reveal that to the Magistrate.]

Mr. Antonio: No.

Counselor: Let me reword that question. Because of Dr. Machiavelli's military rank, do you believe you held back from responding to Marcus when he kept asking you why you wanted his opinion of Dr. Machiavelli? Did you feel like you were in the middle, like you were between a rock and a hard place?

Luke: Objection.

Magistrate: What is the basis for your objection?

Luke: Objection withdrawn.

Magistrate: Mr. Antonio, you may answer the question.

Mr. Antonio: Well yes, he had a higher rank—substantially higher rank.

Counselor: I have no more questions at this time.

THURSDAY EVENING, OCTOBER 6

[Marcus is recalled to the witness box.]

Counselor: When you arrived back at the conference room, how did Dr. Machiavelli greet you?

Marcus: There was no greeting, really. He just said, "Follow me. We have to go to another room for a conference call with Bruce. We can't make a conference call from the phone in this room."

Counselor: Then what happened?

Marcus: I asked, "What conference call?"

Counselor: How did Dr. Machiavelli respond to your question?

Marcus: He disregarded the question.

Counselor: Then what happened?

Marcus: He walked away and I followed him, like a sheep to slaughter, into a small conference room, probably 9 feet by 11 feet, that had a small circular conference table with four chairs around it and a telephone in the middle.

Counselor: Then what happened?

Marcus: Dr. Machiavelli placed a phone call to Bruce, who was sitting in his office waiting.

Counselor: Who is Bruce?

Marcus: He is my supervisor at the Council office?

Counselor: You may continue.

Marcus: Bruce stated that he was removing me from the Athens Health Center review until he conducted an investigation.

Counselor: Did he ever explain to you what he was investigating?

Marcus: No, he did not. I asked if it had something to do with me reporting Dr. Caesar's behavior.

Counselor: What was his response?

Marcus: He just reiterated that he had to conduct some sort of investigation. I assumed it had to do with my reporting Dr. Caesar at the Thursday morning briefing with the Athens leadership.

Counselor: So he did not answer your question?

Marcus: No, he did not give an answer. Basically, he said he was my manager, end of story. I think he needed time to make up something from whole cloth.

Counselor: What do you mean by "whole cloth"?

Marcus: He had to fabricate an answer; he did not have a clear answer. He had to come up with something.

Counselor: Do you know if Bruce was an officer in the military?

Marcus: Yes, he was.

Counselor: Did he have a higher rank than Dr. Machiavelli?

Marcus: No, he did not.

Counselor: Did you ask any other questions as to why you were being removed from this review?

Marcus: Yes, I asked Bruce why I would be removed from a review at the end of the 4th day of a 5-day survey, especially in light of the fact the 5th day was truly only a half-day of reviewing and one half-day having lunch and preparing the final report.

Counselor: And what did he say?

Marcus: He said he is the supervisor and that it was his decision.

Counselor: Did Bruce describe how he was going to go about his investigation?

Marcus: He said that he wanted to talk to the CEO but that she went on vacation after the review. He said that, after her return from vacation, he would get back to me within 2 weeks.

Counselor: Did Bruce get back to you?

Marcus: No, he did not. As a matter of fact, I learned later from Ophelia that the CEO of the Athens Health Center had resigned her position as CEO. I assume that is one of the reasons she was said to be on vacation.

Counselor: Do you doubt that Bruce actually ever spoke to the CEO?

Marcus: Yes, I have my doubts. But then, I don't know. There is no written record of any discussion.

Counselor: Did he tell you why he wanted to talk to the CEO?

Marcus: No, he did not.

Counselor: How did you learn that the CEO resigned?

Marcus: Ophelia, my guide at the Athens Health Center related this information to me after I had returned home.

Counselor: Did Ophelia contact you, or did you contact her?

Marcus: She e-mailed me on my corporate e-mail and asked that I call her. She said that she preferred not to communicate through e-mails.

Counselor: Did she include a telephone number in the email?

Marcus: Yes, she provided me with her direct line at the Athens Health Center, as well as her cell phone number.

Counselor: Do you have any notes of that telephone conversation?

Marcus: Yes.

[Counselor speaks to the Magistrate.]

Counselor: Magistrate, I would like to show these papers to the witness.

Magistrate: Request granted.

Counselor: Do you recognize these papers?

Marcus: Yes.

Counselor: What do you recognize them to be?

Marcus: These are the notes I took during the phone conversation I had with Ophelia.

Counselor: Magistrate, I would like to have these notes marked as Exhibit B and have Marcus read them into the record.

[The following notes are entered into the record and read by Marcus]

Notes by Ophelia

Marcus, first of all, I want to thank you. I want you to know it was a pleasure to work with you. You have a wonderful way of putting people at ease and of politely gleaning information from them. You were able to determine from your questions the quality of care we offer here at the Athens Health Center. When I think of the book *If Disney Ran Your Health Center* and the fact that you went over and beyond in customer service . . . I saw that in you. I have a report somewhere here on my desk from staff feedback and how well you related to them—you should see it. I am off to a meeting right now, but I will share it with you later.

As for Dr. Caesar, he was definitely wrong. Any person has a right to give a patient hope. Just like our Chaplain, you are a layperson. You would be expected to say things like "You will be okay." You were not making a clinical statement, and I would expect that you would not say anything less encouraging.

As I told you before, this physician has a bit of history.

Your presentation regarding Dr. Caesar was fair and well balanced during the Thursday AM session.

The team leader was less than polite to you. He was disengaged from you, but he did not do this with the other health reviewers. Other staff members commented on this.

On Friday morning I was told you would not be back. Dr. Machiavelli never mentioned a thing about you or why you were not there. Health reviewers were coming and going all week, so I don't think anyone thought anything about it. I was very disturbed about the whole thing.

If anybody asks me, you will get a good report.

A Mind is a Terrible Thing to Change

A politician may be able to survive cavorting with prostitutes, sexting with coeds, and comingling with interns, but heaven forbid he should change his mind—the transgression that trumps all compassion.

Or thinking.

After all, thinking can lead to that most dangerous territory for a politician—doubt—and, inevitably, the implication that dare not be expressed, "I could be wrong."

Kathleen Parker, The Washington Post, *June 12, 2011*

FORWARD CLOSET DRAMA TO DECEMBER 27–29 EDUCATIONAL CONFERENCE

[The Counselor continued to question Marcus regarding his early dismissal from participating in the review at the Athens Health Center by Bruce, who claimed he wanted to investigate Marcus's encounter with Dr. Caesar. This was a typical shoot-the-messenger investigation.]

Counselor: Did there come a time when you approached Bruce and asked him for the results of his investigation?

Marcus: Yes, I did at noon during the first day of the annual training conference, December 27.

Counselor: Up until that time, did you have any feedback from Bruce as to the results of his investigation?

Marcus: No, I did not. That's why I decided to contact him at the conference.

Counselor: Did you ever provide information as to what occurred at the Athens Health Center to Bruce prior to the conference?

Marcus: Yes I did.

Counselor: In what form did you relate that information?

Marcus: I relayed the information in the form of several memorandums to Bruce on the date of my encounter with Dr. Caesar.

Counselor: Could you explain to the Magistrate why you wrote memorandums to Bruce the day of and the day after you were removed from the Athens Health center review?

Marcus: I wanted to get across the facts of my experience with Dr. Caesar and not depend on recollection at a later date, which turned out to be *much* later. I simply did not wish to be accused of making up a story.

Counselor: During the investigation did you ever meet your accusers in the same room, in the presence of Bruce or any other leadership member, to ask them questions?

Marcus: No.

Counselor: How would you describe the investigation?

Marcus: It was somewhat amorphous.

Counselor: So you would suggest that it was trumped up?

Luke: Objection, Counselor is leading Marcus.

Magistrate: Objection sustained.

Counselor: So when you saw Bruce at the December educational conference, what was the essence of your conversation?

Marcus: I told Bruce that his mysterious investigation had gone on for several months and that I would like to sit down with him and learn what was going on.

Counselor: And what did he say?

Marcus: He said, "You're right, I should have gotten back to you sooner."

Counselor: What else did he say?

Marcus: Well, let's see—I've got a half-hour slot for you on the 29th, 3:00 to 3:30 before you fly home at 6:00 PM, at least that's what our travel agent tells me.

Counselor: How did you respond?

Marcus: I asked for more time and an earlier meeting, but he said he was too busy and didn't have another time for me.

Counselor: So, repeat for the record, please, on what day of the conference was this that you spoke with Bruce about wanting to meet with him concerning the investigation?

Marcus: It was on December 27th, at noon, the first day of the conference.

Counselor: So you eventually did meet with Bruce.

Marcus: Yes.

Counselor: Where did he meet with you?

Marcus: He met me in a small conference room at the hotel.

Counselor: Was he alone?

Marcus: No, his manager, Michelle, was also there.

Counselor: Why was she there?

Marcus: I am not sure, other than to provide Bruce support. She added nothing to the discussion.

Counselor: What happened at this half-hour meeting?

Marcus: Bruce provided me with a 5-page document that appeared to have been hastily written at the conference that he wanted me to sign.

Counselor: So he gave you 30 minutes to sign a 5-page document. Is that correct?

Marcus: Yes.

Counselor: [Handing the document to Marcus.] Is this the document he wanted you to read, digest, and sign in less than 30 minutes?

Marcus: Yes.

Counselor: Magistrate, I would like to mark this document into evidence as Exhibit C.

Magistrate: So ordered.

Counselor: Marcus, could you read the contents of Exhibit C?

Marcus: Yes.

[Marcus read Exhibit C into the record.]

Counselor: You read from Exhibit C, "Marcus, you recommended that the hospital purchase a car wash to help pay for a dental clinic." What is that about?

Marcus: Some physicians, nurses, and myself were brainstorming some ideas on how to save the Pediatric Dental clinic at the Athens Health Center.

Counselor: So these 5-pages sound as though someone was pulling snippets of communications out of context and placing his or her spin on the communications that you were having with staff at the hospital, is that correct?

Luke: Objection, he is leading the witness.

Magistrate: I will allow the question. Marcus, You may answer the question.

Marcus: Yes, that is correct. He said that I had to sign the document before returning to work. I said, "This was supposed to have been a review of your investigation, but instead, I am handed a 5-page document and told I have to sign it here and now."

Counselor: Then what happened?

Marcus: I said, "I need more time to review what you have written here." He then asked how much time I needed, and I said 21 days to prepare a response.

Counselor: Then what happened?

Marcus: I noticed that his supervisor, Carol, who had claimed she was there just to observe, nodded no at Bruce. He then said to me, "Can you get this back by Friday?"

Counselor: Then what happened?

Marcus: I said it was already Wednesday afternoon and that I needed at least the weekend. He looked over at Michelle again, and she gave him a reluctant nod okay.

Counselor: Going back to the car wash for clarification purposes. Could you explain in more detail why you suggested a car wash?

Luke: Objection, this has nothing to do with this hearing.

Magistrate: Objection overruled, since it was important enough to place in the 5-page report, it is important enough to discuss. You may continue Marcus.

Marcus: We were talking about fundraising in one of the Athens Health Center's clinics as I recall. They were concerned that they might have to close it due to lack of funds, and we got into a discussion of how to save the clinic. I said that, in life, there is something everybody can do in order to fund healthcare projects. When I reviewed health centers, I would often say that all age groups and people from all walks of life have something to offer. For example, kids could do car washes, you could even buy a car wash, nursing home patients can knit sweaters for selling in gift shops, and there are so many other things people can do to raise funds. It was an example of what can be done when you're considering closing programs that benefit the community. The statement was taken out of context and, honestly, Dr. Machiavelli and friends didn't understand that.

Counselor: I have no more questions for Marcus at this time. I would like to call Dr. Caesar to the witness stand at this time.

Magistrate: We will take a 15-minute break at this time. Counselors, I would like to speak with you in my chambers.

[The magistrate and counselors return to the hearing.]

Magistrate: Counselor, you may continue.

Counselor: At some point, were you told that Marcus was reviewing a case of yours?

Dr. Caesar: Yes, I was.

Counselor: Do you recall who told you?

Dr. Caesar: One of the staff nurses.

Counselor: Were you invited by the nurse to attend the review?

Dr. Caesar. Yes I was.

Counselor: Did you go to the conference room?

Dr. Caesar: Yes, I did.

Counselor: Did Marcus at any time introduce himself to you as a physician?

Dr. Caesar: No, he did not.

Counselor: Did there come a time when Marcus asked about the care of one of your patients?

Dr. Caesar: Yes, he did.

Counselor: Did you object to his questions?

Dr. Caesar: No, I did not.

Counselor: Were you aware that such questions are part of the process of reviewing the quality of health care at the Athens Health Center?

Dr. Caesar: Yes, I was aware but not of the protocol as to how the reviewers could go about the process in only 5 days.

Counselor: So are you more understanding now of what Marcus's role was in this process?

Dr. Caesar: Yes, I am.

Counselor: Did there come a time when Marcus asked to speak to the patient?

Dr. Caesar: Yes.

Counselor: So Marcus talked to your patient?

Dr. Caesar: Yes he did.

Counselor: What happened after he spoke to your patient?

Dr. Caesar: I asked if I could say something.

Counselor: What did you say to the patient?

Dr. Caesar: I was blunt with the patient as to the serious nature of his prognosis.

Counselor: How did the patient react?

Dr. Caesar: He started to break down.

Counselor: Then what happened?

Dr. Caesar: Marcus told the patient that he would be okay.

Counselor: Then what happened?

Dr. Caesar: I followed closely behind Marcus and stopped him in the doorway telling him never tell a patient of mine that he would be okay.

Counselor: Did there come a time when the nurse asked you and Marcus to step away from the entrance to the patient's room?

Dr. Caesar: Yes, she did not want to upset the patient.

Counselor: Why were you disturbed with Marcus?

Dr. Caesar: Well, I was upset that Marcus had said to my patient that he would be okay. But that was only because I thought he was speaking clinically about my patient.

Counselor: So you now understand that Marcus was not speaking as to your clinical skills or competence?

Dr. Caesar: That is correct.

Counselor: So his departing words were?

Dr. Caesar: He thanked me for my time.

Counselor: Did he extend his hand and say thank you?

Dr. Caesar: Yes, he did.

Counselor: Did the nurses ever explain to you that Marcus was not a physician?

Dr. Caesar: Yes, they explained that to me the following day. Honestly, I can't believe that this was taken to such an extreme. I thought it was over. I had no clue this was a continuing saga. I don't understand why no one ever spoke to me. After all, it was just the two of us that spoke to one another.

Counselor: Let's back-up a minute. Let me paraphrase here: you said that you were never aware that Marcus was being investigated because of this incident?

Dr. Caesar: I never knew there was an investigation. No one ever asked me any questions about our interactions, and I have since apologized to Marcus for my failure to recognize that he was not a physician and was merely getting a general picture of the patient's satisfaction with his care.

Counselor: Are you aware that Marcus resigned his position as a result of this incident, because of the wall of silence surrounding this mystery investigation?

Dr. Caesar: No, I was never aware that there was an investigation. I thought our interaction was over the day I left that unit. No one ever spoke to me.

Counselor: Did Marcus ever contact you regarding the incident?
Dr. Caesar: Yes, he did.
Counselor: Did you ever receive an email from Marcus?
Dr. Caesar: Yes I did.
Counselor: Were there several e-mails back forth between you and Marcus?
Dr. Caesar: Yes, there were several e-mails.
Counselor: [Handing the e-mails to Dr. Caesar.] Are these the e-mails that took place between you and Marcus?
Dr. Caesar: Yes, they are.
Counselor: Magistrate, I would like to mark these e-mails into evidence as Exhibits D, E, and F.
Magistrate: So ordered. You may proceed.
Counselor: The e-mails by date and time are as follows:

EXHIBIT D

December 19 (8:24 A.M.)
Dear Dr. Caesar:

As you may or may not know, as a result of your response to me during my survey at your hospital, I never again worked for the Health Review Council. Isn't it sad how you found it necessary to be so rude to me? I hope each time you look in the mirror that you always remember that day. I was never anything but polite towards you and compassionate towards your patient. Hopefully someday you will find the strength to apologize. And as I said, I was not a doctor and was not judging your clinical skills. Why you kept asking if I was a doctor was a mystery to me. Maybe you had me mixed up with the Health Review Council team leader who was a physician. Even though I found you rude on that one occasion, I do wish you much success.

Sincerely,
Marcus

EXHIBIT E

December 19 (10:15 A.M.)
Dear Marcus,

Thank you for contacting me. We have so many interactions in life, good and bad; although this case was obviously the latter, it is a rare opportunity to try to clear the air and, perhaps, for me to apologize. Based on what you wrote, that may not be possible, but I would like to try. If you would be willing to send me a phone number, I would like to talk to you about it. I will be watching my e-mail all day, and I offer to telephone you at any time you prefer.

Even though it has been a year, I remember you, that day, and my patient's case very well. My patient struggled with a potentially life-threatening condition that baffled many of my colleagues, and to add to it, he was the husband of a colleague of mine. At that time, we were uncertain if he would improve or not (the condition frequently leads to long-term disability and is associated with high mortality). The comment that I remember most clearly was to the effect "Don't worry, he will be okay." (I am paraphrasing, of course).

That's a completely understandable and considerate thing to say to a sick person in the hospital. However, it would not be an appropriate comment coming from a physician (which I was told by a nurse on the floor that you were). That, along with your confident demeanor (an attribute) and your probing me with questions regarding different possible diagnoses (asked in a manner similar to my old attending physicians), increased my anxiety to the point that I assumed you were criticizing me as a physician. That's when I snapped at you not to tell my patients they would be okay. To be honest, I would snap at any medical student or resident who made a remark like yours, and it would be justified, but what I said to you was certainly not.

Regardless of all that, I'm sorry, and if you would be so kind as to send a contact number, I will call you promptly.

Take care, and like your comment to me, I do wish you the best,
Dr. Caesar

EXHIBIT F

December 19 (11:28 A.M.)
Dear Dr. Caesar,

I truly was happy to see your quick response. It was important for me to let you know that I was never for a moment judging your clinical skills. I have always taken pride in working well with physicians. When I left my hospital as Administrator in _____, both my physicians and nurses wore black armbands wanting me to stay. I have read about your successful career and just wanted you to know a little more about me and that I was not a "gotcha" type administrator reviewer. I have always been an out-of-the-box type guy seeing the tough world in which physicians must practice.

Would be eager to speak with you on a happier note. My home number is ___-___-___.

Again and again, I appreciate your nice comments.
Sincerely,
Marcus

Counselor: So, Dr. Caesar, did there come a time that you called Marcus?

Dr. Caesar: Yes, the same day the emails were written.

Counselor: Do you recall the substance of that conversation?

Dr. Caesar: Yes, I do.

Counselor: Could you summarize it for the Magistrate?

Dr. Caesar: Yes, I can. On the same day that Marcus and I had corresponded through emails, I called Marcus and said, "You can have an interaction with someone for 10 minutes, and there are high stakes in those 10 minutes. I must tell you that 36 hours after you left, I never heard anything about our conversation regarding my patient. I am so sorry you went through all of this. Actually, we need people like you working in our medical societies. Our conversation just shows what can happen in a high stakes environment. There are occasions, there are times, when I have interactions that are antithetical to why I went into medicine. If I learned anything in medicine, it is that life is short. Marcus, if you ever need a letter or anything else to clear this up, I will happy to do anything I can." That is close to what I told him, and like I said, I just can't believe this has gone on for so long. No one ever talked to me. I can't for the life of me believe that a reviewer was removed from a survey from doing his job. You know, I teach ethics, and I find this behavior totally unethical.

Counselor: Did there come a time during your telephone conversation that you asked Marcus if he wanted you to send a letter on his behalf?

Dr. Caesar: Yes, I did.

Counselor: How did Marcus respond to your suggestion?

Dr. Caesar: He said that is not necessary. He thanked me for the offer.

Counselor: Thank you, Dr. Caesar. Thank you. Magistrate, I would like to summarize at this point.

Magistrate: You may proceed.

Counselor: In summary, there was no investigation that included Marcus, or Ophelia, or Dr. Caesar. The notes of the scribe were never forthcoming and were apparently misplaced or destroyed. The positive feedback about Marcus from the staff at the Athens Health Center to Ophelia can no longer be located. There is no evidence of a written conversation between the CEO and Bruce. The memo that was once offered to Marcus by Bruce and was supposedly written by the CEO, was never provided. In fact, Michelle claims that it never existed. The investigation, in my opinion, was made of whole cloth, and a snowball started to roll downhill at the Health Review Council. The new leadership apparently was brought into an incident that they were not willing to understand. They relied on staff managers who wished that Marcus would just disappear. They had to cover themselves. They made an unfortunate decision cloaked in a "code of silence." The truth was so convoluted by the old leadership that the new leadership had no clue what to do and could only rely on what was being regurgitated to them. It is unfortunate that the Health Review Council's leadership never admitted to their wrongdoing. (Pause) Magistrate, this is a case of don't confuse me with facts. I have no more questions.

Magistrate: Counselor Luke, do you have any witnesses or documents to bring forth?

Luke: No, I do not.

Magistrate: Counselor, you may sum up your thoughts.

Counselor: I will be brief. I suggest that what we have here is a *Star Chamber* in the Council's handling of this case. The Health Review Council's practice of strict arbitrary rulings and secretive proceedings reminds me of the English Court Star Chamber of the 1600s. As you know, Magistrate, this is a pejorative term intended to cast doubt on the legitimacy of the proceedings. I find in this case no good faith attempt by the Health Review Council to clear Marcus's worthy name. It is a sad day when an organization fails to live up to its own ethical standards.

Magistrate: Having listened to the testimony as to what occurred during this review, I need no time for further consideration, for I have heard enough. And I find this an appalling account. I strongly reprimand the leadership of the Council for failing to ferret out the truth. Based on what I have heard, I do not believe the full truth will ever be heard, because they've dug themselves in so deeply that they do not know what the truth is. This session is dismissed.*

To seek for the truth, for the sake of knowing the truth, is one of the noblest objects a man can live for.

William Ralph Inge (1860–1954)

---

* The playwright who wrote this closet drama remains anonymous and retains the rights of ownership of the information contained herein.

Discussion

When responding to the discussion questions, apply the virtues and values presented in the *Pillars of Moral Strength* (Figure 12-1) presented next.

1. Describe the ethical and legal issues in this closet drama as it relates to the various characters.
2. Describe the virtues and values at play.
3. Describe why you think there was a breakdown in communications between Dr. Caesar and Marcus.
4. In light of the fact that 70% of diagnoses are made as the result of labs tests, would you expect Marcus to inquire what the lab results had revealed about the patient's state of health?
5. Describe your overall impression of this case, and how you would have handled it if you were Marcus.
6. After considering yourself in the position of each character in this closet drama, describe which role you would have chosen to play? Explain that choice of character.
7. How would you describe the culture of the Health Review Council?

PILLARS OF MORAL STRENGTH

The *Pillars of Moral Strength* Figure 12-1 shown next lists various virtues and values that make up each individual's moral character. What sets each

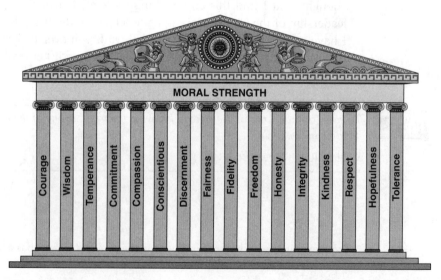

Figure 12–1   Pillars of Moral Strength

individual apart from the crowd? In the final analysis, it is the degree and worth a person assigns to each virtue and value and the price he or she is willing to pay to be the person he or she wants to be. Believing requires practicing what you believe. Is the dollar, for example, more important than integrity? Are you willing to sacrifice the one(s) you love because of the one(s) you fear? If we do not possess the courage to do what is right, all other virtues begin to crumble, and our lives become meaningless and in disarray. The virtues and values listed on the pillars are not just words. They require action. Compassion is more than a virtue, it must be pursued. Compassion is not simply giving lip service or some sort of ceremony; it requires action, a trait in our lives revealing who we are. Ask yourself, "Do I know the meaning of each virtue and value listed in the *Pillars of Moral Strength*?" "Do I apply them to my life?" "Do I know their value?" "In what way are they part of me?" Each person must evaluate for him or herself who he or she is. Both the *Pillars of Moral Strength* Figure 12-1 and the *Process of Communication* Figure 2-1 (the latter is located within Communications and Information Management) will assist the reader in defining who he or she is.

chapter thirteen

Too Big to Fail

How far you go in life depends on your being tender with the young, compassionate with the aged, sympathetic with the striving, and tolerant of the weak and strong. Because someday in life you will have been all of these.

George Washington Carver (1864–1943)

Are healthcare systems becoming a mirror image of the big banks, too big to manage and too easy to fail? The question arises, "Is the nation coming close to the point that history will repeat itself and health systems will have to be bailed out because they are *too big to allow them to fail?*"

As you read the following newspaper articles, you will likely grow concerned that the future does not look so bright for quality health care. Reading these articles and the case that follows them should give you some perspective about the obstacles patients continue to face with the healthcare and insurance systems, and about the havoc that lies ahead.

Healing the Hospitals

Hospitals are the latest casualties of the economic crisis. As their investment incomes tumble, hospitals' already stretched operating budgets are being squeezed even further. At the same time, they must treat an increasing number of patients who are uninsured or cannot pay their medical bills; recent Obama administration estimates reveal that crushing healthcare costs trigger a personal bankruptcy every 30 seconds.

So it's not surprising that more than half of the nation's hospitals are operating in the red, according to a recent Thomson Reuters study. Credit rating agencies are downgrading hospitals. Moody's and Fitch recently changed the outlook for the not-for-profit hospital sector from stable to negative. And across the country, hospitals are cutting staff and services; many are being forced to close their doors.

Michael Jhin, The Baltimore Sun, *June 23, 2009*

Hospitals Courting Primary Care Doctors

In one of the first concrete steps to remake the way medical care is delivered, hospitals are competing to hire primary-care physicians, trying to lure them from their private practices to work as salaried employees alongside specialists.

The push is forcing doctors to make decisions about how to deliver care to patients, many of whom have relied on long-standing relationships with trusted independent neighborhood physicians and wonder what lies ahead.

It also spotlights benefits and drawbacks for patients and doctors alike in one of the healthcare overhaul's much-touted initiatives, set to begin next year. As frontline doctors, primary-care physicians are key to this effort. . . .

In 2008, about half of physician practices were hospital-owned, according to an industry group. A survey last fall by another industry group found that 74% of hospital leaders planned to hire more doctors in the next 12 to 36 months. Most want primary-care doctors.

Locally, all the major hospital systems have ramped up efforts. In Northern Virginia, Inova Health plans to hire 200 primary-care doctors over the next 5 to 8 years. . . .

Hospital-employed primary-care doctors are a way for hospitals to direct referrals to their own specialists. If healthcare rules change to pay hospitals one lump sum for taking care of someone the entire year, instead of payment for each service or procedure, a huge incentive exists for hospitals to own as many pieces of health care as possible.

Experts are concerned, too, that if one hospital system becomes too large, it will result in less competition and higher prices, a charge that hospital executives deny.

Lena A Sun, The Washington Post, *July 19, 2011*

In addition to hospitals that compete by acquiring physician practices, major insurance carriers are now actively pursuing the purchase of physician-owned practices.

Managed Care Enters the Exam Room

Even if UnitedHealth Group isn't your insurance company, there's a good chance it touches you in some way. The $100 billion behemoth sells technology to hospitals and other insurers, distributes drugs, manages clinical trials, and offers continuing medical education, among other things, through the growing web of firms it owns.

Now, that touch could get a lot more personal. United health services wing is quietly gaining control of doctors who treat patients covered by United plans—buying medical groups and launching physician management companies, for example.

It's the latest sign that the barrier between companies that provide health coverage and those that provide care is crumbling. . . .

Many patients insured by these companies are going to see much tighter management of their care. . . .

"The doctors, at the end of the day, control the patients, and currently they're financially incentivized to do more tests, more procedures," said Chris Rigg, a Wall Street analyst for Susquehanna Financial Group. "But, if they're employed by a managed care company, they're financially incentivized" to do less.

That thought unnerves consumer advocate Anthony Wright of Health Access in Sacramento, who worries that profit pressure could affect care. But Wright also said there may be upsides to more tightly managed care: "No patient wants to get more procedures than they actually need.". . .

Some observers watching the developments say the health law, which was sold as a way to rein in insurers, has had the opposite result, opening the door for the companies to take control of even more parts of the healthcare system.

"There's a gigantic Murphy's Law emerging here," said Ian Morrison, a California-based healthcare consultant who does work for United, as well as most of its competitors. "The very people who were the demons in all this, that the public can't stand"—managed-care firms—"are the big winners."

Christopher Weaver, Kaiser Health News, The Washington Post, *July 3, 2011*

Insuring Your Health

Hospitals Are Not The Only Places Where Malpractice Can Injure Patients

The focus of patient safety efforts in recent years has been on problems in hospitals rather than in outpatient settings such as doctor's offices and urgent care centers. Hospitals have come under scrutiny for everything from medication errors and hospital-acquired infections to wrong-site surgeries. But a recent study found that serious errors that resulted in malpractice awards also occur frequently in outpatient settings, suggesting that more attention needs to be paid to the mistakes that happen outside the hospital.

The study, published June 15 in the Journal of the American Medical Association, found that of 10,739 malpractice claims paid on behalf of physicians in 2009, 48% were in the inpatient setting, while 43% were in the outpatient setting. . . .

Sherril Ismay went to an urgent care center in Grand Junction, Colo., one night in January 2009 to have her right foot examined. She didn't think she had a serious problem but it was swollen and sore, and red around the joint of her big toe. The physician assistant who examined her gave her a diagnosis of gout, prescribed pain pills and a gout medication. . . .

It turned out that Ismay had necrotizing fasciitis, commonly referred to as flesh-eating bacteria, a potentially life–threatening infection that destroys soft tissue. Over the months that followed, doctors amputated more and more as they struggled to contain the infection. Her leg now ends an inch before the knee. . . .

Ismay's lawyer, who filed a malpractice lawsuit in January, says that by not taking proper steps to diagnose Ismay's condition, whose symptoms were consistent with both gout and infection, the physician assistant breached the standard of care.

Michelle Andrews, The Washington Post, *June 28, 2011*

Hospitals Liable for Physician Negligence

Citation: *Mejia v. Community Hosp. of San Bernardino*, 122 Cal.Rptr.2d 233, 99 Cal.App.4th 1448 (2002)

Facts

Maria heard something pop in her neck when she bent over to move some boxes. Her neck immediately became stiff, and she suffered neck pain and stiffness off and on for a few weeks. Maria was using acetaminophen to control her pain when, on May 3, she awoke with severe neck pain, and her head was twisted to one side. That night, Maria's mother convinced her to go to the hospital emergency room.

A neighbor took Maria, her mother, and her cousin to the ER at respondent hospital and dropped them off. Around 3:00 A.M., an ER physician examined Maria. The ER physician prescribed hydrocodone and acetaminophen for the pain and a tranquilizer to relax her muscles, and ordered X-rays of Maria's neck. The ER physician sent at least one X-ray to the on-call radiologist for an evaluation. The radiologist reported that he saw a congenital fusion, but nothing else. Based in part on the radiologist's report, the ER physician discharged Maria, telling her that she had a twisted neck, but was otherwise all right.

When a nurse came in to escort Maria and her family out, Maria began to feel nauseous from the medication and vomited several times. The last time she vomited, her family had to lift her head out of the toilet and put her in a wheelchair. When they left respondent hospital, Maria tried to get into her sister's car, but was unable, so her family lifted her into the car. After taking Maria home, her family put her in bed. Maria slept all day and all night. When she awoke the next morning, she could feel the pain in her neck again but could not move her arms or legs and felt numb throughout her body. She was taken by an ambulance to another hospital, where it was determined that her neck was actually broken and she was paralyzed.

Maria filed a medical malpractice suit against respondent, the ER physician, the radiologist, Emergency Physicians Medical Group (the company that contracted to run the ER for respondent and employed the ER physician), and MSB Radiology Medical Group (the company that contracted to run the radiology department for respondent and employed the radiologist).

The case proceeded to trial, where the hospital successfully moved for a nonsuit immediately after the close of plaintiff's case. As to the remaining defendants, the jury found that the radiologist and his employer, MSB Radiology, were negligent but the ER physician and his employer, Emergency Physicians Medical Group, were not.

Issue

On appeal, plaintiff argues that the hospital was not entitled to a nonsuit, because there was a triable issue as to whether the negligent radiologist was the ostensible agent of the hospital.

Holding

The appeals court agreed.

Reason

Present-day hospitals, as their manner of operation plainly demonstrates, do far more than furnish facilities for treatment. They regularly employ on a salary basis a large staff of physicians, nurses, interns, and others, and they charge patients for medical care, collecting for such services, if necessary, by legal action. The person who avails himself of hospital facilities expects that the hospital will attempt to cure him or her. In light of this modern reality, the overwhelming majority of jurisdictions employ ostensible or apparent agency to impose liability on hospitals for the negligence of independent contractor physicians.

Although the cases discussing ostensible agency use various linguistic formulations to describe the elements of the doctrine, in essence, they require the same two elements of (1) conduct by the hospital that would cause a reasonable person to believe that the physician was an agent of the hospital, and (2) reliance on that apparent agency relationship by the plaintiff.

Public policy dictates that the public has every right to assume and expect that the hospital is the medical provider it purports to be. Because it is commonly believed that hospitals are the actual providers of care, ostensible agency can be readily inferred whenever someone seeks treatment at a hospital.

In California, ostensible agency is defined by statute. Civil Code section 2300 provides, "An agency is ostensible when the principal intentionally, or by want of ordinary care, causes a third person to believe another to be his agent who is not really employed by him."

Ostensible agency is based on appearances. Thus, the fact that a hospital actually contracts with an intermediary to hire and schedule physicians is only relevant if the patient had some reason to know about that arrangement. In this case, it is beyond dispute that plaintiff had no idea the radiologist was actually employed and scheduled by MSB Radiology.

In conclusion, absent evidence that plaintiff should have known that the radiologist was not an agent of respondent hospital, plaintiff has alleged sufficient evidence to get to the jury merely by claiming that she sought treatment at the hospital.

The judgment was reversed and the plaintiff could recover court costs.

Discussion

1. In light of the newspaper articles summarized earlier, discuss why it is getting increasingly difficult for patients to distinguish hospital employees from independent contractors.
2. With hospitals hiring primary care physician practices, is it likely or less likely that hospitals will face an increasing number of malpractice suits?

Insuring Your Health

New Law Gives Consumers More Power to Fight Plans That Refuse to Pay Claims

Under the 2010 health law, the situation should improve. Health plans will be required to inform members that they can appeal disputed claims internally within the health plan, as well as to an independent review organization not affiliated with the health plan. The new rules become effective in July.

Michelle Andrews, The Washington Post, *June 21, 2011*

The following letter illustrates the continuing battle that patients and their families have with health insurance companies.

I AM BARRED FROM FEEDING MY BABY

Dear Sir or Madam:

We received a letter from you denying my claim for coverage for Neocate Infant formula. I am appealing your decision and requesting insurance coverage and reimbursement for my daughter, Marie, for whom the use of Neocate Infant formula was prescribed by her doctor. You denied insurance coverage on the grounds that "charges for food supplements were not covered." I want to clarify that Neocate Infant formula is not a food supplement, it is her sole source of nutrition and it is life-sustaining and medically necessary. Marie does not have any other source of nutrition.

Neocate is specifically designed to meet the nutritional needs of infants with severe cow milk protein or multiple food protein allergies who are unable to ingest a normal diet. My daughter has failed to tolerate breast milk, cow's milk and protein hydrolysate infant formulas. Neocate Infant formula is medically necessary for my daughter, and will provide the proper nutrition management for her. Without the use of an elemental formula, she will experience more complications, which can result in hospitalization and/or costly parenteral nutrition.

Based on the foregoing, I believe the use of Neocate Infant formula should qualify for coverage and reimbursement under our policy. Please review this appeal and contact me or Marie's doctor directly with any questions or concerns.

Sincerely,

Kathryn

Discussion

1. Discuss Kathryn's appeal letter, considering the impact of managed care companies acquiring primary care physician practices.
2. Discuss your thoughts as to why Americans are frustrated by the health insurance system and how that frustration is likely to grow in the future.

TOO BIG AND TOO SMALL TO FAIL?

The total number of hospitals and inpatient days is dwindling in part due to: mergers; new technology; improved surgical techniques; use of computer-based diagnosis and treatment; the implementation of best practices; holistic medicine; preventative care lifestyles encouraged by TV shows such as Dr. Oz; financial incentives by managed care companies that encourage physicians to scrutinize tests and procedures more carefully that often lead, rightfully or wrongfully, to the denial of coverage for provider services; reimbursement constraints by Medicare and Medicaid; and a push to provide care in outpatient settings. All of these have resulted in shorter hospital stays and the perceived need for fewer hospitals. With approximately 5,900 community hospitals in 1975 and less than 5,000 in 2005, the impact of hospital closures can be financially devastating to the employees and community economies. More importantly, such closures often lead to poor care due to the inability to access hospitals for emergency care and treatment. Hospitals large or small can fail, as noted in a few of the hundreds of newspaper articles noted next.

Hawaii Medical Center to close hospitals in Liliha and Ewa

Judge Robert Faris, who has been presiding over the Hawaii Medical Center bankruptcy, says he's saddened by the closure of the West and East hospitals and he says despite the disaster he believes all parties involved did what they could to avoid this outcome.

Tim Sakahara, Hawaii News Now, *December 16, 2011*[1]

The bankrupt Hawaii Medical Center hospitals in Liliha and Ewa will put nearly 1,000 people out of work and eliminate more than 340 hospital beds.

Caring for Poor, Hospitals Reach Brink of Closure

Two charity hospitals in Illinois are facing a life-or-death decision. There's not much left of either of them—one in Chicago's south suburbs, the other in impoverished East St. Louis—aside from emergency rooms crowded with patients seeking free care. Now they would like the state's permission to shut down.

Carla K. Johnson (AP Medical Writer), Associated Press, Chicago, *May 9, 2011* (AP)[2]

"Two" Big to Fail in Health Care

If we all work together, I know with strong leadership and the talent in the medical and health care delivery systems, we can get it right for all our communities and citizens. It will just take cooperation, humility, and caring more for the community our ultimate customer. Let's leave our medical and health care system better than we inherited it. Are you up to the challenge?

John D. Laslavic (President, ThistleSea Business Development, LLC), Western Pennsylvania Hospital News[3]

NOTES

1. http://www.hawaiinewsnow.com/story/16342241/breaking-news-hawaii-medical-center-to-close-hospitals
2. http://abcnews.go.com/US/wireStory?id=13563500#.TwHG0BzUo3U
3. http://www.wphospitalnews.com/two-big-to-fail-in-health-care/

summary notes

Nurses and the Law

NEGLIGENCE

Negligence is a tort, a civil or personal wrong. It is the unintentional omission or commission of an act that a reasonably prudent person would or would not do under given circumstances. Negligence is a form of conduct caused by heedlessness or carelessness that constitutes a departure from the standard of care generally imposed on reasonable members of society. It can occur when, after considering the consequences of an act: (1) a person does not exercise the best possible judgment; (2) when one fails to guard against a risk that should be appreciated; or (3) when one engages in behavior expected to involve unreasonable danger to others.

MALPRACTICE

Malpractice merely refers to negligence of a professional person (e.g., nurse practitioner, pharmacist, physician, physician's assistant). It is the unintentional *omission* or *commission* of an act that a reasonably prudent person would or would not do under given circumstances.

Commission of an act would include the following:

- Administering the wrong medication
- Administering the wrong dosage of a medication

- Administering medication to the wrong patient
- Performing a surgical procedure without patient consent
- Performing a surgical procedure on the wrong patient or body part (e.g., wrong site surgery, such as removal of the healthy left kidney instead of the diseased right kidney)
- Performing the wrong surgical procedure

Omission of an act would include the following:

- Failure to conduct a thorough history and physical examination
- Failure to assess and reassess a patient's nutritional needs
- Failure to administer medications
- Failure to order diagnostic tests
- Failure to follow up on abnormal or critical test results

Forms of Negligence

1. *Malfeasance:* performance of an unlawful or improper act (e.g., performing an abortion in the third trimester where such is prohibited by state law).
2. *Misfeasance:* improper performance of an act, resulting in injury to another (e.g., wrong-sided surgery, such as removal of a healthy left kidney instead of the diseased right kidney; mistakenly administering a lethal dose of a medication).
3. *Nonfeasance:* failure to act, when there is a duty to act as a reasonably prudent person would in similar circumstances (e.g., failing to order diagnostic tests or prescribe medications that should have been ordered or prescribed under the circumstances).

Degrees of Negligence

1. *Ordinary negligence:* failure to do, under the circumstances, what a reasonably prudent person would or would not do.
2. *Gross negligence:* intentional or wanton omission of care that would be proper to provide, or the doing of that which would be improper to do.

Elements of Negligence

The plaintiff must establish the following elements in order to prove liability:

1. Duty to care
   a. There must be an obligation to conform to a recognized standard of care.
   b. Standard of care is based on
      i. regulations—legislative enactments (e.g., Good Samaritan acts, licensing laws),
      ii. judicial decisions,
      iii. absence of a legal definition—based on age, knowledge, education, training, mental capacity, expert testimony (required when there is a need to explain the customary standard of behavior that is claimed to have been violated), and so on
2. Breach of duty
   a. There must be a deviation from the recognized standard of care.
   b. There must be a failure to adhere to an obligation.
3. Injury
   a. Actual damages must be established.
   b. If there are no injuries, no monetary damages are due to the plaintiff(s).
4. Causation
   a. The departure from the standard of care must be the cause of the plaintiff's injury.
   b. The injury must be *foreseeable*.

Damages

1. *Nominal damages* are awarded as a mere token in recognition that wrong has been committed when the actual amount of compensation is insignificant.
2. *Compensatory damages* are estimated reparation in money for detriment or injury sustained (including loss of earnings, medical costs, and loss of financial support).
3. *Punitive damages* are additional money awards authorized when an injury is caused by gross carelessness or complete disregard for the safety of others.

Respondeat Superior

- Legal doctrine holding an employer liable for the negligence of its employees (also referred to as vicarious liability).
- Purpose of the Doctrine—encourage employer to control the acts and job performance of employees.
- In order to transfer liability to the employer, a plaintiff must establish
  ○ negligence occurred,
  ○ the tortfeasor/wrongdoer is the agent or servant of the employer, and
  ○ the tort was committed within the scope of employment.

NEGLIGENT ACTS

Failure to Follow Instructions

- physician's instructions
  ○ failure to question instructions when in doubt

Failure to Recognize

- changes in patient's condition
- erroneous orders

Inappropriate Discharge

- harm to patient likely
- need to report
- failure to follow hospital policy and/or discharge procedures

Failure to Report

- changes in patient's condition
- professional misconduct

Telephone Orders from Physician

- verify with physician confusing orders
- repeat orders to physician
- date and sign the order
- have physician date and sign all verbal orders

Burns

- food/drinks
- heating pads
- hot water bottles
- showers
- baths
- surgical instruments
- chemicals
- medical equipment

Falls

- patients walking in the hallway post-surgery
- bathroom
- beds
- wheelchairs
- examination tables
- spills/wet floors
- medication related
- stairwells
- stretchers
- chairs
- transfers

Preventing Falls

- identify patients at risk
- assess need for restraints (time-limited signed orders)
- follow orders
- conduct frequent rounds and make observations
- utilize bed alarms
- display wet floor signs
- clean spills promptly
- report hazards promptly
- make repairs promptly

Nursing Procedures Challenges

- failure to follow procedures
- failure to track vital signs

- improper performance of a procedure
- failure to provide adequate inservice training
- failure to document

Infections

Causes

- failure to follow approved policies and procedures
  - preventing cross-contamination between patients
  - improper isolation technique
- poor aseptic technique during dressing changes
- needlesticks

Reducing the Risks of Infection

- adhere to policies and procedures
  - adopt CDC guidelines
  - follow approved aseptic techniques
  - wear proper attire (e.g., gowns, gloves, boots, and masks)
- require periodic employee physical

Emergency Department Challenges

- failure to assess and reassess patient needs
- improper triage
- delay in treatment
- leaving patient unattended
- failure to monitor, record, and recognize changes in a patient's vital signs
- failure to recognize and report signs of abuse

Operating Room (O.R.) Challenges

Issues

- confirm patient has signed the appropriate consent forms
- make and verify accurate sponge/instrument counts
- O.R. suite not adequately cleaned
- avoid cross contamination
- participate in universal protocol and time-out requirements
  - confirm correct patient
  - confirm patient is about to undergo the correct procedure

- confirm that the patient has been properly prepped for surgery
- confirm patient is properly draped with the correct operative site exposed
- confirm patient has not eaten within the prescribed time period
- confirm patient is not wearing dentures
- document time-out in the patient's record
- practice aseptic technique and maintain sterile environment
- properly prep patient
- ensure appropriate instrumentation is present and sterile
- ensure appropriate meds, blood, and blood products are available to complete procedure/s
- protect patient from injury by correctly positioning patient and securing limbs

Medical Equipment Challenges

- lack of training
- improper use
- defective/faulty equipment and alarms
- failure to monitor
- failure to have backup
- prompt reporting of equipment failures
- check dated equipment stickers to ensure preventative maintenance is timely

Maintain Safe Environment

- frayed electrical cords
- spills
- wet floors
- clutter
- improper placement of equipment

Medication Errors

- wrong patient
- wrong drug
- wrong dosage
- wrong route (e.g., given intramuscularly v. orally)
- wrong frequency
- failure to administer

- negligent injection
- failure to discontinue
- repeated dosage
- lack of consent for use of experimental drugs
- no prescription
- transcription errors
- untimely administration

Minimizing Medication Errors

- check chart and verify written orders, correct medication, route, dosage, and patient allergies
- check the label—do not administer unlabeled medications
- identify patient by checking wristband and talking to the patient
- question concerns with physician or pharmacist
- monitor, report, and chart adverse reactions
- communicate untoward reactions
- follow procedures for preparation, labeling, storage, and record keeping
- use PDR as necessary
- follow proper procedures in administering investigational drugs
- document medications administered, including dosage, route, and time, and initial it
- maintain current policies and procedures on each patient care unit
- maintain patient profile on patient unit
- computerize record keeping

Nutrition

- conduct screens
- ensure correct diet
- request nutritional assessments and reassessments as necessary by a dietitian

Medical Records

Purpose

- communication across disciplines
- documentation of patient care
- protection of legal interests of both patient and healthcare facility
- provision of information for education and research

Problems

- failure to record or make entries
- incomplete records
- inaccurate records
- inconsistent/intermittent charting
- correcting
- distorting
- falsifying
- making fraudulent entries for insurance, reimbursement, and legal purposes
- unauthorized entries
- failure to retain records
- ambiguous abbreviations
- failure to date, time, or sign records
- illegible handwriting

Charting Reminders

- be accurate
- be complete
- date all entries
- be legible
- make relevant entries
- write with clarity
- be concise
- do not make defamatory entries
- when making corrections, do not make erasures
- do not use correction fluids
- line out mistaken entries
- write in correct information
- use different-colored ink when making corrections (blue or black)
- initial and date corrections
- do not tamper with the chart
- do not make entries in a patient's chart without advice of legal counsel if a suit has been threatened
- authenticate student entries
- report normal and abnormal findings
- report patient complaints
- protect records from unauthorized access and entries
- release records only to authorized persons

REPORTING REQUIREMENTS

- professional (e.g., National Practitioner Data Bank)
- child abuse
- elder abuse
- criminal (e.g., suspicious deaths, rape)

Informed Consent

- duty of physician to disclose information necessary to enable patient to understand a procedure before consenting to it
- should be dated, signed, and witnessed
- generally implied in emergency situations

Special Consent

- investigational drugs and procedures
- invasive procedures (e.g., surgery)

Substituted Judgment

- confirm surrogate rights

Refusal of Treatment

- obtain written release
- if refused: note refusal on release form, date it, sign it (both physician and other caregiver), and file with medical record

PATIENT RIGHTS

- participate in care decisions
- confidentiality
- privacy
- refuse treatment
- advance directives
- appointment of surrogate decision-maker

PATIENT RESPONSIBILITIES

- provide staff with accurate and complete information
- abide by rules and regulations of organization
- treat others with respect and dignity
- make it known whether one comprehends proposed course of action and what is expected of oneself

NEGLIGENCE/MALPRACTICE DEFENSES

Ignorance of Fact and Unintentional Wrongs

- Ignorance of the law is not a legal defense.

Assumption of a Risk

- The plaintiff voluntarily and knowingly assumed the risks associated with the inherent dangers of, for example, smoking or drinking.

Contributory Negligence

- This defense might be applied whenever a person has contributed to his or her own injury.

Good Samaritan Statutes

- Provisions that can relieve a caregiver from liability in certain situations in which emergency care was given.

Borrowed Servant Doctrine

- Applies when an employer lends an employee to another for a particular employment.

Captain of the Ship Doctrine

- Although not always easily applied, this defense can direct responsibility to the person in command (e.g., a surgeon in the O.R.).

Comparative Negligence

- The healthcare provider must prove, with respect to the plaintiff's conduct after medical treatment is initiated, that the plaintiff owed himself a duty of care, the plaintiff breached that duty, and the breach was a proximate cause of the damages the plaintiff sustained.

Statute of Limitations

- The time period within which a lawsuit must be brought forward in order for a suit to be valid under the law. The time period is established by statute in the different states and often varies based on when a negligent act occurred and when the plaintiff (the party instituting the suit) knew, or should have known, when the alleged negligence occurred. Once this is established, the time begins to toll. If, for example the statute of limitations is 2 years, and if the suit is not filed for 2 years and 1 day, the suit can be "time-barred" from moving forward based on the wording of the law.

Sovereign Immunity

- This doctrine holds that government cannot commit a legal wrong and is immune from a civil or criminal case.

Intervening Cause

- A defense called upon when the act of a third party, independent of the defendant's original negligent conduct, is the proximate cause of an injury.

TIPS

- avoid criticizing caregivers
- be a good listener
- be empathetic
- be respect and maintain patient privacy
- keep patient and family informed
- be responsive to patient needs
- be observant of changes in patient's condition
- maintain timely, complete, and accurate records
- provide sufficient time and care to each patient (explain treatments and follow-up care to the patient, family, and other caregivers)
- prior to rendering care:
  - check patient's chart and note changes in physician orders
  - if orders seem vague or questionable, clarify with physician
  - ask patient's name and verify/check patient wristband
- be observant of changes in patient's condition, vital signs, IVs, etc.
- be observant of medical equipment connected to the patient, including signs of possible malfunctioning

© *Nurses and the Law, Summary Notes* by Gp Health Care Consulting are copyright pending. The preeminent guide to law in healthcare management entitled *Legal Aspects of Health Care Administration, 11th Edition*, as well as *Legal and Ethical Issues for Health Care Professionals, 3rd Edition*, both by George D. Pozgar, are available from Jones & Bartlett Learning, 5 Wall St, Burlington, MA 01803. Telephone: 1-800-832-0034. Website: http://www.jblearning.com.

summary notes

Pharmacists and the Law

NEGLIGENCE

Negligence is a tort, a civil or personal wrong. It is the unintentional omission or commission of an act that a reasonably prudent person would or would not do under given circumstances. Negligence is a form of conduct caused by heedlessness or carelessness that constitutes a departure from the standard of care generally imposed on reasonable members of society. It can occur when, after considering the consequences of an act, a person does not exercise the best possible judgment; when one fails to guard against a risk that should be appreciated; or when one engages in behavior expected to involve unreasonable danger to others.

MALPRACTICE

Malpractice merely refers to negligence of a professional person (e.g., nurse practitioner, pharmacist, physician, physician's assistant). It is the unintentional *omission* or *commission* of an act that a reasonably prudent person would or would not do under given circumstances.

Commission of an act would include the following:

- Administering the wrong medication
- Administering the wrong dosage of a medication

- Administering medication to the wrong patient
- Performing a surgical procedure without patient consent
- Performing a surgical procedure on the wrong patient or body part (e.g., wrong site surgery, such as removal of the healthy left kidney instead of the diseased right kidney)
- Performing the wrong surgical procedure

Omission of an act would include the following:

- Failure to conduct a thorough history and physical examination
- Failure to assess and reassess a patient's nutritional needs
- Failure to administer medications
- Failure to order diagnostic tests
- Failure to follow up on abnormal or critical test results

Forms of Negligence

1. *Malfeasance:* performance of an unlawful or improper act (e.g., performing an abortion in the third trimester where such is prohibited by state law).
2. *Misfeasance:* improper performance of an act, resulting in injury to another (e.g., wrong-sided surgery, such as removal of a healthy left kidney instead of the diseased right kidney; mistakenly administering a lethal dose of a medication).
3. *Nonfeasance:* failure to act, when there is a duty to act as a reasonably prudent person would in similar circumstances (e.g., failing to order diagnostic tests or prescribe medications that should have been ordered or prescribed under the circumstances).

Degrees of Negligence

1. *Ordinary negligence*: failure to do, under the circumstances, what a reasonably prudent person would or would not do.
2. *Gross negligence*: intentional or wanton omission of care that would be proper to provide, or the doing of that which would be improper to do.

Elements of Negligence

The plaintiff must establish the following elements in order to prove liability:

1. Duty to care
   a. There must be an obligation to conform to a recognized standard of care.
   b. Standard of care is based on
      i. regulations—legislative enactments (e.g., Good Samaritan acts, licensing laws),
      ii. judicial decisions,
      iii. absence of a legal definition—based on age, knowledge, education, training, mental capacity, expert testimony (required when there is a need to explain the customary standard of behavior that is claimed to have been violated), and so on
2. Breach of duty
   a. There must be a deviation from the recognized standard of care.
   b. There must be a failure to adhere to an obligation.
3. Injury
   a. Actual damages must be established.
   b. If there are no injuries, no monetary damages are due to the plaintiff(s).
4. Causation
   a. The departure from the standard of care must be the cause of the plaintiff's injury.
   b. The injury must be foreseeable.

Damages

1. *Nominal damages* are awarded as a mere token in recognition that wrong has been committed when the actual amount of compensation is insignificant.
2. *Compensatory damages* are estimated reparation in money for detriment or injury sustained (including loss of earnings, medical costs, and loss of financial support).
3. *Punitive damages* are additional money awards authorized when an injury is caused by gross carelessness or complete disregard for the safety of others.

Respondeat Superior

- Legal doctrine holding an employer liable for the negligence of its employees (also referred to as vicarious liability).
- Purpose of the Doctrine—encourage employer to control the acts and job performance of employees.
- In order to transfer liability to the employer, a plaintiff must establish
  - negligence occurred,
  - the tortfeasor/wrongdoer is the agent or servant of the employer, and
  - the tort was committed within the scope of employment.

NEGLIGENT ACTS

Pharmacy Checklist

Documents

- policies and procedures
  - expanding role of the pharmacist, not merely to dispense drugs
    - attendance at, and participation in, cardiac events
    - expertise from neonates to adults
    - consultative role
    - member of the treatment team
      - pain management (e.g., expertise for complex patient pain management issues)
  - oversight and stocking of crash carts
    - ensuring the correct dilutions for various age groups
  - oversight of pharmacy technicians
    - verify correct dilutions of drugs (e.g., neonate intensive care unit)
    - training of staff (e.g., observation and recording of each patient's reactions to drugs administered)
- patient medication profiles
- patient events reporting and tracking system

Tour

- locked pharmacy entrance door
- pharmacy licenses are posted
- unit dosing implemented to prevent mislabeling
- watch for mislabeling by manufacturer

- process in place to spot expired drugs on pharmacy shelves
- security of drugs
- laminar flow hoods (inspection, cleaning)
- computerization
- intake and exhausts
- open windows

Interview

- scope of service
- hours of operation
- staffing (evening, night, weekend, and on-call coverage)
- satellite pharmacies (emergency stock within and outside the pharmacy)
- emergency drugs—how obtained
- department orientation
- skills checklists
- in-service education
- continuing education
- competency reviews
- are patient care needs assessed
- how is uniform quality assured

Ordering/Prescribing

- credentialing
- who can prescribe: physicians, nurse practitioners, physician assistants
- mechanism to control
- identification of limitations per practitioner
- what happens to an order from the time it is initiated
- computer/order entry
- verbal orders (misheard, misunderstood, mistranscribed)

Patient Medication Profiles

- age
- weight
- height
- diagnoses
- allergies
- medications list for each patient

Medication Errors

- failure to interpret order correctly
- drugs mislabeled
- wrong drug dispensed
  - wrong dosage dispensed
  - wrong route
  - wrong frequency
  - outdated drugs dispensed
- failure to remove outdated drugs from stock

Minimizing Medication Errors

- education (initial orientation and continuing education)
- confirm correct medication, and dosage dispensed
- when filling drug orders question concerns with physician/nurse or 2nd pharmacist as appropriate
- monitor adverse drug reactions reported by nursing
- follow procedures for preparation, labeling, storage, and record keeping
- follow proper procedures in dispensing investigational drugs
- maintain patient profile (e.g., age, weight, allergies, current medication profile)
- review patient profiles to determine potential for
  - drug-drug interactions
  - drug-food interactions
  - correct dosage for special needs patients (neonates, cancer)

Delivery of Written Orders

- computer order entry
- FAX machines
- pneumatic tubes secure

Care Decisions

- appropriateness of medications ordered
- multi-disciplinary treatment plan
- ethical issues
- determining goals
- evaluation of effectiveness of medications ordered
- recommendations for alternative medications

Emergency Department

- responding to emergency department calls for drug information
  - patients on multiple medications
  - identification of drugs
  - patients on investigational drugs

Competency

- screening process (e.g., application)
- physical and mental status
- consent for release of information
- insurance
- licensure
- national practitioner data bank
- references
- interview process
- interview
- board action
- clinical privileges
- continuing education
- appeal process
- peer review and reappointment
- renewal
- limiting, suspension, and removal of privileges

Infection Control

- comply with regulatory requirements (e.g., CDC)
- comply with hospital policy
  (e.g., http://www.hosp.uky.edu/pharmacy/departpolicy/PH17-01.pdf)

Causes

- cross-contamination
- poor aseptic technique
- needlesticks
- air filtering equipment malfunction

Reducing Risks

- require periodic employee physicals
- practice proper technique

- follow policies and procedures
- utilize proper attire (e.g., gowns, gloves, boots, and masks)

Pharmacy Equipment

- training
- proper use
- equipment maintenance and alarms
- failure to monitor
- failure to maintain
- computerize record keeping

Formulary

- development (who has input, who approves, how published, how updated)
- maintenance (additions, deletions, and substitutions)
- mechanism for additions and deletions
- nonformulary drugs (how obtained)

Adverse Drug Reactions

- unexpected reaction to a drug
- mechanism for reporting
- tracing/monitoring effect on patient

Investigational Drugs

- policy and procedure
- obtain informed consent
- criteria for study
- Institutional Review Board
  - purpose
    - provides oversight for experimental mediations and various procedures (e.g., invasive)
    - recommends privileging requirements for use of experimental medications and new medical procedures adopted by the hospital

Reporting Requirements

- adverse drug reactions
- controlled substances

Informed Consent

- legal concept predicated on the duty to disclose information necessary to enable the patient to evaluate a proposed medical or surgical procedure or an investigational drug before consenting to it

Forms

- written: completed, dated, signed, and witnessed
- oral
- implied

Special Consent Required

- investigational drugs and procedures
- invasive procedures (e.g., surgery)

Dispensing

- authorization for dispensing
- orders for drugs (handling)

Sample Drugs

- controlling
- tracking (e.g., register lot numbers with pharmacy)
- recalls
- on formulary prior to use
- maintain lot numbers
  - which patient receives which lot

Patients on Multiple Drugs

- protocol for handling
- contraindications

Patient/Family Education

- access to community resources on drugs
- investigational drugs (informed consent)
  - potential side-effects
- role in discharge planning
- food–drug interactions

- food–food interactions
- determine whether patient understands instructions

Administration

- confirm identity of patient
  - medical record
  - wristband
- ensure appropriate consent forms have been signed

Controlling

- policy and procedure
- dispensing, waste, and returns

Monitoring

- how information is obtained

Emergency Medications

- availability
- dispensing when pharmacy is closed (procedures)
- generic substitution
- accuracy
- mixing IVs after hours

Crash Cart Stocking

- security
- system for control/process monitoring
- check laryngoscope batteries
- check for expired medications

Cost Reduction

- appropriateness of therapy
  - selection of drugs that are efficacious
  - selection of cost-effective antibiotics
- thrombolics: TPA v. streptokinase

Pharmacy and Therapeutics Committee

- composition (dietitian, lab tech, physician, and pharmacist)
- approves formulary
  - addition and deletion of drugs

Performance Improvement

- interdisciplinary meetings
- national and local benchmarking—comparing with the best external databases, literature review, site visits, experts
- kinds of aggregate data available
- area of focus (e.g., high-risk drugs)
- success over time

Medical Records

Purpose

- communications across disciplines
- documentation of patient care (e.g., medication administration record)
- protect legal interests of both patient and healthcare facility
- provide information for education and research

Problems

- failure to record or make entries
- incomplete records
- inaccurate records
- inconsistent/intermittent charting
- correcting
- distorting
- falsifying
- fraudulent entries for insurance, reimbursement, and legal purposes
- failure to retain records
- ambiguous abbreviations
- failure to date, time, or sign records
- illegible handwriting
- unauthorized entries

Charting Reminders

- be accurate
- be complete
- date all entries
- be legible
- make relevant entries
- write with clarity
- be concise
- when making corrections, do not make erasures
- do not use correction fluids
- line out mistaken entries
- write in correct information
- use different-colored ink when making corrections (blue or black)
- initial and date corrections
- do not tamper with the chart
- protect records from unauthorized access and entries
- release records only to authorized persons
- obtain appropriate authorization for release of records

Patient Rights

- admission/emergency care
- participation in care decisions
- complaint resolution process
- confidentiality
- privacy
- discharge
- transfer
- advance directives/self-determination
- refuse treatment
- appointment of surrogate decision maker

Patient Responsibilities

- provide physician with accurate and complete information
- abide by rules and regulations of organization
- treat others with respect and dignity
- ask questions

NEGLIGENCE/MALPRACTICE DEFENSES

Ignorance of Fact and Unintentional Wrongs

Ignorance of the law is not a legal defense in a lawsuit.

Assumption of a Risk

The plaintiff voluntarily and knowingly assumed the risks associated with the inherent dangers of, for example, smoking or drinking.

Contributory Negligence

This defense might be applied whenever a person has contributed to his or her own injury.

Good Samaritan Statutes

Provisions that can relieve a caregiver from liability in certain situations in which emergency care was given.

Borrowed Servant Doctrine

Applies when an employer lends an employee to another for a particular employment.

Captain of the Ship Doctrine

Although not always easily applied, this defense can direct responsibility to the person in command (e.g., a surgeon in the O.R.).

Comparative Negligence

The healthcare provider must prove, with respect to the plaintiff's conduct after medical treatment is initiated, that the plaintiff owed himself a duty of care, the plaintiff breached that duty, and the breach was a proximate cause of the damages the plaintiff sustained.

Statute of Limitations

This refers to the time period/time frame within which a lawsuit must be brought forward in order for a suit to be valid under the law. The time frame is established by statute in the different states and often varies based on when a negligent act occurred and when the plaintiff (the party instituting the suit) knew, or should have known, when the alleged negligence occurred. Once this is established, the time begins to toll. If, for example the statute of limitations is 2 years, and if the suit is not filed for 2 years and 1 day, the suit can be "time-barred" from moving forward based on the wording of the law.

Sovereign Immunity

This doctrine holds that government cannot commit a legal wrong and is immune from a civil or criminal case.

Intervening Cause

A defense called upon when the act of a third party, independent of the defendant's original negligent conduct, is the proximate cause of an injury.

TIPS

- avoid criticizing caregivers
- check patient's chart and note recordings by other caregivers
- maintain confidentiality standards
- be a good listener
- be empathetic
- respect patient privacy
- be observant of changes in patient's condition
- be observant of medical equipment functioning (e.g., pain pumps)
- provide patient/family education
- maintain timely, complete, and accurate records

© *Pharmacists and Malpractice, Summary Notes* by Gp Health Care Consulting are copyright pending. The preeminent guide to law in health-care management entitled *Legal Aspects of Health Care Administration, 11th Edition*, as well as *Legal and Ethical Issues for Health Care Professionals, 3rd Edition*, both by George D. Pozgar, are available from Jones & Bartlett Learning, 5 Wall St, Burlington, MA 01803. Telephone: 1-800-832-0034. Website: http://www.jblearning.com.

summary notes

Physicians and the Law

NEGLIGENCE

Negligence is a tort, a civil or personal wrong. It is the unintentional omission or commission of an act that a reasonably prudent person would or would not do under given circumstances. Negligence is a form of conduct caused by heedlessness or carelessness that constitutes a departure from the standard of care generally imposed on reasonable members of society. It can occur when, after considering the consequences of an act, a person does not exercise the best possible judgment; when one fails to guard against a risk that should be appreciated; or when one engages in behavior expected to involve unreasonable danger to others.

MALPRACTICE

Malpractice merely refers to negligence of a professional person (e.g., nurse practitioner, pharmacist, physician, physician's assistant). It is the unintentional *omission* or *commission* of an act that a reasonably prudent person would or would not do under given circumstances.

Commission of an act would include the following:

- Administering the wrong medication
- Administering the wrong dosage of a medication

- Administering medication to the wrong patient
- Performing a surgical procedure without patient consent
- Performing a surgical procedure on the wrong patient or body part (e.g., wrong site surgery, such as removal of the healthy left kidney instead of the diseased right kidney)
- Performing the wrong surgical procedure

Omission of an act would include the following:

- Failure to conduct a thorough history and physical examination
- Failure to assess and reassess a patient's nutritional needs
- Failure to administer medications
- Failure to order diagnostic tests
- Failure to follow up on abnormal or critical test results

Forms of Negligence

1. *Malfeasance:* performance of an unlawful or improper act (e.g., performing an abortion in the third trimester where such is prohibited by state law).
2. *Misfeasance:* improper performance of an act, resulting in injury to another (e.g., wrong-sided surgery, such as removal of a healthy left kidney instead of the diseased right kidney; mistakenly administering a lethal dose of a medication).
3. *Nonfeasance:* failure to act, when there is a duty to act as a reasonably prudent person would in similar circumstances (e.g., failing to order diagnostic tests or prescribe medications that should have been ordered or prescribed under the circumstances).

Degrees of Negligence

1. *Ordinary negligence:* failure to do, under the circumstances, what a reasonably prudent person would or would not do.
2. *Gross negligence:* intentional or wanton omission of care that would be proper to provide, or the doing of that which would be improper to do.

Elements of Negligence

The plaintiff must establish the following elements in order to prove liability:

1. Duty to care
   a. There must be an obligation to conform to a recognized standard of care.
   b. Standard of care is based on
      i. regulations—legislative enactments (e.g., Good Samaritan acts, licensing laws),
      ii. judicial decisions,
      iii. absence of a legal definition—based on age, knowledge, education, training, mental capacity, expert testimony (required when there is a need to explain the customary standard of behavior that is claimed to have been violated), and so on
2. Breach of duty
   a. There must be a deviation from the recognized standard of care.
   b. There must be a failure to adhere to an obligation.
3. Injury
   a. Actual damages must be established.
   b. If there are no injuries, no monetary damages are due to the plaintiff(s).
4. Causation
   a. The departure from the standard of care must be the cause of the plaintiff's injury.
   b. The injury must be foreseeable.

Damages

1. *Nominal damages* are awarded as a mere token in recognition that wrong has been committed when the actual amount of compensation is insignificant.
2. *Compensatory damages* are estimated reparation in money for detriment or injury sustained (including loss of earnings, medical costs, and loss of financial support).
3. *Punitive damages* are additional money awards authorized when an injury is caused by gross carelessness or complete disregard for the safety of others.

Respondeat Superior

- Legal doctrine holding an employer liable for the negligence of its employees (also referred to as vicarious liability).
- Purpose of the Doctrine—encourage employer to control the acts and job performance of employees.
- In order to transfer liability to the employer, a plaintiff must establish
  ○ negligence occurred,
  ○ the tortfeasor/wrongdoer is the agent or servant of the employer, and
  ○ the tort was committed within the scope of employment.

NEGLIGENT ACTS

Emergency Services

- failure to respond to an emergency department call
- failure to triage, assess, and reassess patient needs
- delay in treatment
- leaving patient unattended
- failure to monitor, record, and recognize changes in patient's vital signs
- failure to recognize and report signs of abuse or neglect of patient
- telephonic medicine can be risky
- avoid telephone medicine

Patient Assessments

- inadequate history and physical exams
  ○ must be thorough and complete
  ○ utilize to develop treatment plan

Abandonment of Patient

To prove abandonment, the plaintiff (injured party) must show all these:

1. Medical care was unreasonably discontinued.
2. Discontinuance was against patient's will.
3. Physician failed to arrange for patient's future care.
4. Foresight indicated discontinuance might result in physical harm to the patient.
5. Actual harm was suffered.

Delay in Treatment

Choice of Treatment

- determine treatment options with the patient
- review the options with the patient
- select an agreed upon treatment choice

Failure to Order Diagnostic Tests

A plaintiff claiming a physician failed to order proper diagnostic tests must show all of these to be true:

1. It is standard practice to use a certain diagnostic test under the circumstances of the case.
2. The physician failed to use the test and, therefore, failed to diagnose the patient's illness.
3. The patient suffered injury as a result.

Failure to Promptly Review Test Results

Aggravation of Pre-Exisiting Condition

- aggravation through negligence may result in liability for malpractice
- liability will be imposed only for additional harm suffered by aggravation

Anesthesiology

- plan for care
- failure to conduct thorough pre-anesthesia assessment
  - patient must be an active participant and address concerns with the anesthesiologist
  - discuss prior problems with anesthesia
    - process including intubation problems (e.g., size of intubation tubes)
- failure to obtain informed consent (risks, benefits, and alternatives)
- administration of anesthetics
- safety issues
  - improper placement of tube(s) into the esophagus
  - integrity of equipment

- care of the patient during administration of anesthesia (e.g., physiological monitoring)
- failure to maintain airway
- charting
- providing sterile environment
- maintaining sterile techniques
- failure to perform post-procedure assessment and monitoring

Blood Transfusions

- assess need, risks, benefits, and alternatives
  - fully document on informed consent form
  - have order note if patient has planned ahead for use of his/her own blood

Care Decisions

- coordination of care/multidisciplinary treatment plan
- include the patient and family involvement
- determining goals
- implementation
- evaluate and revise as necessary

Discharge and Follow-Up Care

- patient-family instructions upon discharge
- referrals for continuum of care

Education

- patient and family
- community resources
- diet
- medications
- follow-up care
- medical equipment

Infections

- cross-contamination
- improper isolation

- hand hygiene
- poor aseptic technique
  - dressing changes
  - needle sticks
  - reducing the risk of infection
    - follow CDC guidelines (e.g., hand hygiene)
    - require periodic employee physical
    - proper sterilization of instruments and equipment
    - follow policies and procedures
    - utilize proper attire (e.g., gowns, gloves, boots, and masks

Diagnostic Imaging Services

- failure to order appropriate studies
- inadequate imaging examination
- misinterpretation of imaging studies
- failure to consult with radiologist
- failure to read imaging studies
- delay in conveying imaging results
- failure to communicate imaging results

Failure to Make a Timely Diagnosis

Failure to Obtain Second Opinion

Failure to Refer

Practicing Outside Field of Competence and Expertise

Misdiagnosis

- pathologist misdiagnoses breast cancer
  - diabetic acidosis
  - heart failure
  - perforated bowel
  - autoimmune diseases
  - severity of concussions

Failure to Form a Differential Diagnosis

Failure to Stay Thoroughly Informed
- medical record entries (consultants and other professional staff)
- test results (e.g., lab, imaging)

Failure to Use Patient Data Gathered
- assume nothing

Medication Errors
- availability
- ordering
- preparation
- administration
  - wrong patient
  - wrong drug
  - wrong dosage
  - wrong route
  - wrong frequency
  - failure to administer
  - negligent injection
  - failure to discontinue
  - repeated dosage
  - no prescription
  - transcription errors
  - consent for use of experimental drugs
  - mislabeled
  - untimely administration
  - order change
  - outdated
  - administering recalled drug
  - failure to monitor patient
- abuse in prescribing

Minimizing Medication Errors
- check chart and verify written orders—correct medication, route, dosage, patient allergies

- check the label—do not administer unlabeled medications
- identify patient by checking wristband and by talking to the patient
- question concerns with nurse or pharmacist
- monitor, report, and chart adverse reactions
- communicate untoward reactions
- follow procedures for preparation, labeling, storage, and record keeping
- use PDR as necessary
- follow proper procedures in administering investigational drugs
- document medications administered (e.g., dosage, route, and time) and initial the report
- maintain correct policies and procedures on each patient care unit
- maintain patient profile on patient unit
- computerize record keeping

Failure to Obtain Informed Consent

- invasive procedures (e.g., cardiac catheter, surgery)
- investigational drugs and procedures
- substituted judgment
- confirm surrogate rights

Surgery

- presurgery confirmations
  - operating room suite is adequately cleaned
  - equipment, instruments, and supplies are prepared and ready for the correct procedure
  - required staff is present to conduct the surgical procedure
  - the patient
    - has been properly screened for surgery (with documentation in the patient's record)
    - has not eaten within the prescribed time period
  - informed consent has been obtained on forms that indicate patient, procedure, surgical site, surgeon(s), etc.
    - dated, signed, and witnessed
    - implied in emergency
  - Universal Protocol confirmations
    - the correct patient is on the O.R. table
    - the surgical site has been marked

- the operating surgeon(s), anesthesiologist and other staff, as required, are in the O.R. suite
- the patient has been properly draped
- the correct operative site is exposed
- a final time-out is conducted to confirm the previously listed checks prior to proceeding with surgery
  - all staff present must unanimously agree
- postsurgery confirmations
  - sponge/instrument counts are accurate and double-checked
- prevent infections
  - follow sterile technique procedures (e.g., recommended hand hygiene protocol)
  - practice aseptic technique and maintain sterile environment
  - ensure patient has not eaten
  - properly prep patient
  - ensure appropriate instrumentation is present and sterile
  - ensure appropriate meds, blood, and blood products are available to complete procedure
- postoperative care
  - closely monitor patient's vital signs, surgical site, etc.

Improper Performance of a Procedure

Refusal of Treatment

- obtain written release
- if signature refused, note patient's refusal on release form, date it, sign it (both physician and other caregiver), and file it with medical record

Obstetrics

- highly vulnerable medical specialty
- failure to monitor baby and/or mother
- delay in C-section can lead to injury to both baby and mother
- failure to perform a C-section
- failure to perform delivery
- injury to brachial plexus nerves
- emergency assistance
- nurse assessment
- wrongful death of a viable unborn fetus

Psychiatry

- major areas of concern
  - failure to provide proper evaluation
  - commitment
  - release
  - electroshock therapy
  - duty to warn of released patient's propensity to cause harm
  - suicidal patients

Restraints

- assess need for restraints
- time limit and sign orders

Premature Discharge

- harm to patient likely
- need to report

Failure to Follow-Up

Medical Records

- Purpose
  - communications across disciplines
  - documentation of patient care
  - protect legal interests of both patient and healthcare facility
  - provide information for education and research
- Problems
  - lack of documentation
  - failure to record or make entries
  - incomplete records
  - inaccurate records
  - inconsistent/intermittent charting
  - correcting
  - distorting
  - falsifying
  - fraudulent entries for insurance, reimbursement, and legal purposes
  - failure to retain records
  - ambiguous abbreviations

- ○ failure to date, time, or sign records
- ○ illegible handwriting
- ○ unauthorized entries
- Charting Reminders
  - ○ be accurate
  - ○ be complete
  - ○ date all entries
  - ○ be legible
  - ○ make relevant entries
  - ○ write with clarity
  - ○ be concise
  - ○ do not make defamatory entries
  - ○ when making corrections do not make erasures
  - ○ do not use correction fluids
  - ○ line out mistaken entries
  - ○ write in correct information
  - ○ use different-colored ink when making corrections (blue or black)
  - ○ initial and date corrections
  - ○ do not tamper with the chart
  - ○ do not make entries in patient's chart without advice of legal counsel if a suit has been threatened
  - ○ countersign entries by residents
  - ○ protect records from unauthorized access and entries
  - ○ release records only to authorized persons
  - ○ obtain appropriate authorization for release of records

Patient Rights

- admission/emergency care
- participation in care decisions
- complaint resolution process
- confidentiality
- privacy
- discharge
- transfer
- advance directives/self-determination
- refuse treatment
- appointment of surrogate decision maker
- do not resuscitate orders

Patient Responsibilities

- provide physician with accurate and complete information
- abide by rules and regulations of organization
- treat others with respect and dignity
- make it known whether one comprehends proposed course of action and what is expected of oneself

NEGLIGENCE/MALPRACTICE DEFENSES

Ignorance of Fact and Unintentional Wrongs

Ignorance of the law is not a legal defense in a lawsuit.

Assumption of a Risk

The plaintiff voluntarily and knowingly assumed the risks associated with the inherent dangers of, for example, smoking or drinking.

Contributory Negligence

This defense might be applied whenever a person has contributed to his or her own injury.

Good Samaritan Statutes

Provisions that can relieve a caregiver from liability in certain situations in which emergency care was given.

Borrowed Servant Doctrine

Applies when an employer lends an employee to another for a particular employment.

Captain of the Ship Doctrine

Although not always easily applied, this defense can direct responsibility to the person in command (e.g., a surgeon in the O.R.).

Comparative Negligence

The healthcare provider must prove, with respect to the plaintiff's conduct after medical treatment is initiated, that the plaintiff owed himself a duty of care, the plaintiff breached that duty, and the breach was a proximate cause of the damages the plaintiff sustained.

Statute of Limitations

This refers to the time period/time frame within which a lawsuit must be brought forward in order for a suit to be valid under the law. The time frame is established by statute in the different states and often varies based on when a negligent act occurred and when the plaintiff (the party instituting the suit) knew, or should have known, when the alleged negligence occurred. Once this is established, the time begins to toll. If, for example the statute of limitations is 2 years, and if the suit is not filed for 2 years and 1 day, the suit can be "time-barred" from moving forward based on the wording of the law.

Sovereign Immunity

This doctrine holds that government cannot commit a legal wrong and is immune from a civil or criminal case.

Intervening Cause

A defense called upon when the act of a third party, independent of the defendant's original negligent conduct, is the proximate cause of an injury.

TIPS

- avoid criticizing caregivers
- prior to rendering care, check patient's chart and note recordings by other caregivers
- obtain consultations when needed
- maintain confidentiality standards
- be a good listener
- be empathetic
- respect patient privacy
- keep patient and family informed
- be responsive to patient needs
- be observant of changes in patient's condition
- be observant of medical equipment connected to the patient, including signs of possible malfunctioning
- provide patient/family education

- do not guarantee treatment outcome
- provide for cross-coverage during days off
- maintain timely, complete, and accurate records
- do not make erasures in records
- personalize your treatment
- do not overextend your practice
- provide sufficient time and care to each patient (explain treatment plans and follow-up care to the patient, family, and other caregivers)
- avoid telephone-based examinations and prescriptions
- do not become careless because you know the patient
- request consultations when indicated and refer if necessary
- seek advice of counsel should you suspect the possibility of a malpractice claim
- perform patient examinations in the presence of another caregiver

© *Physicians and Malpractice, Summary Notes* by Gp Health Care Consulting are copyright pending. The preeminent guide to law in health-care management entitled *Legal Aspects of Health Care Administration, 11th Edition*, as well as *Legal and Ethical Issues for Health Care Professionals, 3rd Edition*, both by George D. Pozgar, are available from Jones & Bartlett Learning, 5 Wall St, Burlington, MA 01803. Telephone: 1-800-832-0034. Website: http://www.jblearning.com.

Plaintiffs and Medical Malpractice

FILE A COMPLAINT ABOUT PATIENT CARE

Centers for Medicare and Medicaid Services (CMS)

1. A complaint can be against a Medicare or Medicaid provider (e.g., hospitals, home health agencies, hospices, nursing homes) for improper care or treatment.

2. CMS is the Federal agency that runs the Medicare program, the State Medicaid Agency, and the State survey agency (usually part of your state's health department). These agencies work together to make sure providers meet Federal standards. The State survey agency can help you with the following types of complaints:
   a. Claims of abuse to a person in a nursing home;
   b. A mistake in giving out or prescribing medication;
   c. Poor quality of care in a hospital (including psychiatric and rehabilitation hospitals), nursing home, dialysis facility, ambulatory surgery center, home health agency, hospice, intermediate care facility for the mentally retarded, and others;
   d. Unsafe conditions, like water damage or electrical or fire safety concerns; and
   e. Laboratory results that were wrong and lead to improper care.

For more information, call: 1-800-MEDICARE (1-800-633-4227), or
visit:
    http://www.medicare.gov/Publications/Pubs/pdf/11313.pdf.
    TTY users should call 1-877-486-2048.

The Joint Commission (TJC)

1. TJC is a not-for-profit organization that accredits and certifies healthcare organizations. TJC accreditation and certification is recognized
nationwide as a symbol of quality that reflects an organization's commitment to meeting certain performance standards.

2. Steps to filing a patient complaint with the JC can be found at this
website:
    a. http://jcwebnoc.jcaho.org/QMSInternet/IncidentEntry.aspx

FILE A MALPRACTICE CASE

What Is Medical Malpractice?

Medical malpractice is the unintentional *omission* or *commission* of an act
that a reasonably professionally (e.g., physician, nurse practitioner, physician's assistant) prudent person would or would not do under given circumstances. Malpractice can occur, for example, when a professional: (1) fails to
guard against a risk that should have been recognized; (2) engages in behavior expected to involve unreasonable danger to others; or (3) when a professional has considered the consequences of an act and exercised his/her best
possible judgment.

Why File a Malpractice Case?

1. Preservation of peace between individuals by providing a substitute
for retaliation
2. To find fault for wrongdoing
3. Deterrence, by discouraging the wrongdoer from committing future
wrongful acts
4. Compensation (to indemnify the person(s) injured)

Do I Have a Medical Malpractice Case?

1. If you believe your healthcare provider (hospital, nursing facility, doctor, nurse, or other caregiver) made a careless mistake by doing something, or not doing something, while treating you, and if the mistake resulted in an injury to your health, you *could* file a malpractice lawsuit against the caregiver(s) for the damages suffered.
2. Not every injury can result in an action for malpractice, due to the fact that many injuries are a *known risk* and the patient consented to and accepted the risk.
    a. For example, a patient could accept the risk of suffering a fatal stroke during a cardiac catherization. A lawsuit filed in such cases would most likely be dismissed, unless the patient could establish that the caregiver failed to adhere to the standard of care required in performing the catherization.
3. So-called *frivolous lawsuits* are frowned upon by the courts and could, in rare instances, lead to a countersuit for a wrongful action.

Legal Costs to the Plaintiff(s)

Most lawyers take medical malpractice cases based on a *contingency fee,* meaning that attorneys will pay most, if not all, of the costs of the case up front and won't charge attorney's fees unless the case is won. If the plaintiff wins, the plaintiff's attorney will take a percentage of the amount of money awarded as his/her fees and reimbursement for the costs associated with the case.

NEGLIGENCE

1. *Negligence* is defined as the unintentional omission (failure to act) or commission of an act that a reasonably prudent person would or would not do under given circumstances.

Elements of Negligence

The Patient/Plaintiff/Injured Party must show/prove that all of the following elements of negligence occurred in order to establish that the professional was negligent:

1. Duty to care requires one to care and safeguard the rights of another.

2. Breach of duty
   a. The patient/plaintiff must establish that the defendant failed to comply with, or adhere to, the prevailing standard of care.
   b. The standard of care is based on the expected conduct of accepted practice of other professionals that treat similar patients with the same or similar ailment or injury. Most jurisdictions recognize not merely a local standard but a national standard of care.
   c. Standard of care is based on
      i. expert testimony that is often necessary to help establish the expected standard of care, for it is important that the jury understand what was expected of the professional and whether the standard of care expected was delivered or deviated from;
      ii. regulations, or legislative enactments, such as the Good Samaritan acts and licensing laws;
      iii. judicial decisions; and
      iv. absence of legal definition, based on age, knowledge, education, training, mental capacity, and expert testimony (these required when there is a need to explain the customary standard of behavior that is claimed to have been violated).
3. Injury
   a. It is not enough to show that one's doctor made some sort of mistake. Before a lawsuit can be filed, it must also be shown that the mistake caused the patient damage or further harm (e.g., amputation of the wrong limb, brain damage after an operation, a medical condition or disease got worse after treatment, or even death), for unless harm has been suffered there are no grounds for a medical malpractice case.
   b. Damages include
      i. economic damages (e.g., medical expenses and wages);
      ii. noneconomic damages (e.g., pain and suffering); or
      iii. punitive damages.
4. Causation
   a. There must be a close and causal connection between the defendant's conduct and the resulting damages suffered by the plaintiff. In other words, the injury must have been connected to, and caused by, the professional's mistake. Often times a medical expert is needed to establish that the injury was the result of the breach of the standard of care.

      b.   Foreseeability—it must be established as to whether someone of ordinary prudence and intelligence should have anticipated that harm or injury would have resulted from an act or an omission to act. Liability is limited if the injury is not foreseeable.

Forms of Negligence

1. *Malfeasance*—execution of an unlawful or improper act.
2. *Misfeasance*—improper peformance of an act.
3. *Nonfeasance*—failure to act, when there is a duty to act, as a reasonably prudent person would under similar circumstances.

Respondeat Superior

1. A legal doctrine holding that the liability of an employee's negligence can be imputed to the employer (also referred to as *vicarious liability*). The purpose of the doctrine is to encourage employers to control the acts and job performance of its employees.
2. In order to transfer liability to the employer, a plaintiff must establish that
   a. negligence occurred,
   b. the tortfeasor/wrongdoer is the agent or servant of the employer, and
   c. the tort was committed within the scope of employment.

MISTAKES MADE

The topics that follow describe areas where patient care mistakes often occur, ranging from misdiagnoses to treatment, and including steps hospitals take to help reduce the number of mistakes and resulting lawsuits.

Burns

- food/drinks
- heating pads
- hot water bottles
- showers
- baths
- surgical instruments
- chemical
- medical equipment

Emergency Department

- failure to assess and reassess patient needs
- improper triage
- delay in treatment
- leaving patient unattended
- failure to monitor, record, and recognize changes in a patient's vital signs
- failure to recognize and report signs of abuse

Inappropriate Discharge

- harm to patient likely
- need to report

Failure to Follow Instructions

- policies and procedures of hospital and department
- supervisor's
- physician's

Failure to Recognize

- changes in patient's condition
- obvious incorrect orders

Failure to Report

- changes in patient's condition
- professional misconduct

Falls

Examples

- bathroom
- beds
- wheelchairs
- examination tables
- spills/wet floors
- medications

- stairwells
- stretchers
- chairs
- transfers

Preventing Falls

- assess need for restraints (time-limited signed orders)
- follow orders
- conduct frequent rounds and make observations
- utilize bed alarms
- display wet floor signs
- clean spills promptly
- report hazards promptly
- make repairs promptly

Nursing Procedures

- failure to follow procedures
- failure to track vital signs
- improper performance of a procedure
- failure to provide adequate in-service education
- failure to document

Infections

Hospital Acquired Conditions

Hospital Acquired Conditions (HACs) are serious conditions that patients may acquire during an inpatient hospital stay. If hospitals follow proper procedures using evidence-based guidelines to treat and care for patients, patients are less likely to get an HAC.

Causes

- cross-contamination
- improper isolation technique
- poor aseptic technique during dressing changes
- needlesticks

Reducing the Risks of Infection

- require periodic employee physical
- practice proper technique
- follow policies and procedures
- utilize proper attire (e.g., gowns, gloves, boots, and masks)

Medical Records

Purpose

- communication across disciplines
- documentation of patient care
- protection of legal interests of both patient and healthcare facility
- provision of information for education and research

Problems

- failure to record or make entries
- incomplete records
- inaccurate records
- inconsistent/intermittent charting
- correcting
- distorting
- falsifying
- making fraudulent entries for insurance, reimbursement, and legal purposes
- unauthorized entries
- failure to retain records
- ambiguous abbreviations
- failure to date, time, or sign records
- illegible handwriting

Charting Reminders

- be accurate
- be complete
- date entries
- be legible
- make relevant entries
- write with clarity
- be concise

- do not make defamatory entries
- when making corrections, do not make erasures
- do not use correction fluids
- line out mistaken entries
- write in correct information
- use different-colored ink when making corrections (blue or black)
- initial and date corrections
- do not tamper with the chart
- do not make entries in a patient's chart without advice of legal counsel if a suit has been threatened
- authenticate student entries
- report normal and abnormal findings
- report patient complaints
- protect records from unauthorized access and entries
- release records only to authorized persons

Operating Room

Issues

- sponge/instrument miscounts
- O.R. suite not adequately cleaned
- cross-contamination
- confirm that the patient on the O.R. table has been properly identified for surgery (with documentation in the patient's record)
- confirm correct patient
- confirm patient is about to undergo the correct procedure
- confirm patient is properly draped with the correct operative site exposed
- confirm patient has not eaten within the prescribed time period
- confirm patient has signed the appropriate consent forms
- confirm patient is not wearing dentures

Preventing O.R. Lawsuits

- practice aseptic technique and maintain sterile environment
- ensure patient has not eaten
- properly prep patient
- ensure appropriate instrumentation is present and sterile
- ensure appropriate meds, blood, and blood products are available to complete procedure

- protect patient from injury by correctly positioning patient and securing limbs

Telephone Orders

- verify physician orders with staff on second phone line
- repeat orders to physician

Medical Equipment

- lack of training
- improper use
- defective/faulty equipment and alarms
- failure to monitor
- failure to have backup

Preventing Medical Equipment Malfunction

- prompt reporting
- preventive maintenance program for all equipment

Medication Errors

- wrong patient
- wrong drug
- wrong dosage
- wrong route (e.g., given intramuscularly v. orally)
- wrong frequency
- failure to administer
- negligent injection
- failure to discontinue
- repeated dosage
- lack of consent for use of experimental drugs
- no prescription
- transcription errors
- untimely administration

Minimizing Medication Errors

- check chart and verify written orders, correct medication, route, dosage, and patient allergies
- check the label—do not administer unlabeled medications

- identify patient by checking wristband and by talking to the patient
- question concerns with physician or pharmacist
- monitor, report, and chart adverse reactions
- communicate untoward reactions
- follow procedures for preparation, labeling, storage, and record keeping
- use PDR as necessary
- follow proper procedures in administering investigational drugs
- document medications administered (including dosage, route, and time), and initial it
- maintain current policies and procedures on each patient care unit
- maintain patient profile on patient unit
- computerize record keeping

Unsafe Environment

- frayed electrical cords
- spills
- wet floors
- clutter
- improper placement of equipment

Dietary

- incorrect diet

Obstetrics

- one of the most vulnerable medical specialties

TIPS

- avoid criticizing caregivers
- prior to rendering care:
  - check patient's chart and note changes in physician orders
  - if orders seem vague or questionable, clarify with physician
  - ask patient's name
  - verify/check patient wristband
- follow a risk management program:
  - report and investigate incidents promptly
  - establish prevention programs
  - identify potential hazardous occurrences and take preemptive action

- develop a quality improvement program that includes:
  - ○ planning and designing
  - ○ measuring
  - ○ assessing with internal and external databases
  - ○ improving and redesigning processes
- keep patient and family informed within hospital policy and medical, legal, and ethical guidelines
- disseminate information:
  - ○ poison control
  - ○ hospital formulary
  - ○ hospital-sponsored educational programs
- be observant of changes in patient's condition, vital signs, IVs, etc.
- be observant of medical equipment connected to the patient, including signs of possible malfunctioning
- provide patient/family education

Reporting Requirements

- professional (e.g., National Practitioner Data Bank)
- child abuse
- elder abuse
- rape

Informed Consent

- a legal concept predicated on the duty of the physician to disclose the information necessary to enable the patient to evaluate a proposed medical or surgical procedure before consenting to it.

Forms

- written: completed, dated, signed, and witnessed
- oral
- implied

Refusal of Treatment

- obtain written release
- if signature refused
  - ○ note patient's refusal on release form
  - ○ date it

- sign it (both physician and other caregiver)
- file it with medical record

Special Consent

- investigational drugs and procedures
- invasive procedures (e.g., surgery)

Substituted Judgment

- confirm surrogate rights

Patient Rights

- admission/emergency care
- participation in care decisions
- complaint resolution process
  - confidentiality
  - privacy
  - discharge
- transfer
- advance directives/self-determination
- refuse treatment
- appointment of surrogate decision maker
- do not resuscitate orders

Patient Responsibilities

- provide physician with accurate and complete information
- abide by rules and regulations of organization
- treat others with respect and dignity
- make it known whether one comprehends proposed course of action and what is expected of oneself

© *Medical Malpractice, Summary Notes* by Gp Health Care Consulting are copyright pending. The preeminent guide to law in healthcare management entitled *Legal Aspects of Health Care Administration, 11th Edition*, as well as *Legal and Ethical Issues for Health Care Professionals, 3rd Edition*, both by George D. Pozgar, are available from Jones & Bartlett Learning, 5 Wall St, Burlington, MA 01803. Telephone: 1-800-832-0034. Website: http://www.jblearning.com.

Appendix A

U.S. Code of Federal Regulations

Data is current as of July 14, 2011

Title 42: Public Health

PART 482—CONDITIONS OF PARTICIPATION FOR HOSPITALS

Section Contents

Subpart A—General Provisions

Subpart B—Administration

Subpart C—Basic Hospital Functions

Subpart D—Optional Hospital Services

Subpart E—Requirements for Specialty Hospitals

General Requirements for Transplant Centers

Transplant Center Data Submission, Clinical Experience, and Outcome Requirements

§ 482.80   Condition of participation: Data submission, clinical experience, and outcome requirements for initial approval of transplant centers.

§ 482.82   Condition of participation: Data submission, clinical experience, and outcome requirements for re-approval of transplant centers.

Transplant Center Process Requirements

§ 482.90   Condition of participation: Patient and living donor selection.

§ 482.92   Condition of participation: Organ recovery and receipt.

§ 482.94   Condition of participation: Patient and living donor management.

§ 482.96   Condition of participation: Quality assessment and performance improvement (QAPI).

§ 482.98   Condition of participation: Human resources.

§ 482.100   Condition of participation: Organ procurement.

§ 482.102   Condition of participation: Patient and living donor rights.

§ 482.104   Condition of participation: Additional requirements for kidney transplant centers.

Authority: Secs. 1102, 1871 and 1881 of the Social Security Act (42 U.S.C. 1302, 1395hh, and 1395rr), unless otherwise noted.

Source: 51 FR 22042, June 17, 1986, unless otherwise noted.

Subpart A—General Provisions

§ 482.1   Basis and scope.

(a) *Statutory basis.*

   (1) Section 1861(e) of the Act provides that—

     (i)   Hospitals participating in Medicare must meet certain specified requirements; and

     (ii) The Secretary may impose additional requirements if they are found necessary in the interest of the health and safety of the individuals who are furnished services in hospitals.

   (2) Section 1861(f) of the Act provides that an institution participating in Medicare as a psychiatric hospital must meet certain specified requirements imposed on hospitals under section 1861(e), must be primarily engaged in providing, by or under the supervision of a physician,

psychiatric services for the diagnosis and treatment of mentally ill persons, must maintain clinical records and other records that the Secretary finds necessary, and must meet staffing requirements that the Secretary finds necessary to carry out an active program of treatment for individuals who are furnished services in the hospital. A distinct part of an institution can participate as a psychiatric hospital if the institution meets the specified 1861(e) requirements and is primarily engaged in providing psychiatric services, and if the distinct part meets the records and staffing requirements that the Secretary finds necessary.

(3) Sections 1861(k) and 1902(a)(30) of the Act provide that hospitals participating in Medicare and Medicaid must have a utilization review plan that meets specified requirements.

(4) Section 1883 of the Act sets forth the requirements for hospitals that provide long term care under an agreement with the Secretary.

(5) Section 1905(a) of the Act provides that "medical assistance" (Medicaid) payments may be applied to various hospital services. Regulations interpreting those provisions specify that hospitals receiving payment under Medicaid must meet the requirements for participation in Medicare (except in the case of medical supervision of nurse-midwife services. See §§440.10 and 440.165 of this chapter.).

(b) *Scope.* Except as provided in subpart A of part 488 of this chapter, the provisions of this part serve as the basis of survey activities for the purpose of determining whether a hospital qualifies for a provider agreement under Medicare and Medicaid.

[51 FR 22042, June 17, 1986, as amended at 60 FR 50442, Sept. 29, 1995]

§ 482.2 *Provision of emergency services by nonparticipating hospitals.*

(a) The services of an institution that does not have an agreement to participate in the Medicare program may, nevertheless, be reimbursed under the program if—

(1) The services are emergency services; and

(2) The institution meets the requirements of section 1861(e) (1) through (5) and (7) of the Act. Rules applicable to emergency services furnished by nonparticipating hospitals are set forth in subpart G of part 424 of this chapter.

(b) Section 440.170(e) of this chapter defines emergency hospital services for purposes of Medicaid reimbursement.

[51 FR 22042, June 17, 1986, as amended at 53 FR 6648, Mar. 2, 1988]

Subpart B—Administration

§ 482.11 Condition of participation: Compliance with Federal, State and local laws.

(a) The hospital must be in compliance with applicable Federal laws related to the health and safety of patients.

(b) The hospital must be—
  (1) Licensed; or
  (2) Approved as meeting standards for licensing established by the agency of the State or locality responsible for licensing hospitals.

(c) The hospital must assure that personnel are licensed or meet other applicable standards that are required by State or local laws.

§ 482.12 Condition of participation: Governing body.

The hospital must have an effective governing body legally responsible for the conduct of the hospital as an institution. If a hospital does not have an organized governing body, the persons legally responsible for the conduct of the hospital must carry out the functions specified in this part that pertain to the governing body.

(a) *Standard: Medical staff.* The governing body must:
  (1) Determine, in accordance with State law, which categories of practitioners are eligible candidates for appointment to the medical staff;
  (2) Appoint members of the medical staff after considering the recommendations of the existing members of the medical staff;
  (3) Assure that the medical staff has bylaws;
  (4) Approve medical staff bylaws and other medical staff rules and regulations;
  (5) Ensure that the medical staff is accountable to the governing body for the quality of care provided to patients;
  (6) Ensure the criteria for selection are individual character, competence, training, experience, and judgment; and
  (7) Ensure that under no circumstances is the accordance of staff membership or professional privileges in the hospital dependent solely upon certification, fellowship, or membership in a specialty body or society.
  (8) Ensure that, when telemedicine services are furnished to the hospital's patients through an agreement with a distant-site hospital, the agreement is written and that it specifies that it is the responsibility of the governing body of the distant-site hospital to meet the

requirements in paragraphs (a)(1) through (a)(7) of this section with regard to the distant-site hospital's physicians and practitioners providing telemedicine services. The governing body of the hospital whose patients are receiving the telemedicine services may, in accordance with §482.22(a)(3) of this part, grant privileges based on its medical staff recommendations that rely on information provided by the distant-site hospital.

(9) Ensure that when telemedicine services are furnished to the hospital's patients through an agreement with a distant-site telemedicine entity, the written agreement specifies that the distant-site telemedicine entity is a contractor of services to the hospital and as such, in accordance with §482.12(e), furnishes the contracted services in a manner that permits the hospital to comply with all applicable conditions of participation for the contracted services, including, but not limited to, the requirements in paragraphs (a)(1) through (a)(7) of this section with regard to the distant-site telemedicine entity's physicians and practitioners providing telemedicine services. The governing body of the hospital whose patients are receiving the telemedicine services may, in accordance with §482.22(a)(4) of this part, grant privileges to physicians and practitioners employed by the distant-site telemedicine entity based on such hospital's medical staff recommendations; such staff recommendations may rely on information provided by the distant-site telemedicine entity.

(b) *Standard: Chief executive officer.* The governing body must appoint a chief executive officer who is responsible for managing the hospital.

(c) *Standard: Care of patients.* In accordance with hospital policy, the governing body must ensure that the following requirements are met:

(1) Every Medicare patient is under the care of:

(i) A doctor of medicine or osteopathy (This provision is not to be construed to limit the authority of a doctor of medicine or osteopathy to delegate tasks to other qualified health care personnel to the extent recognized under State law or a State's regulatory mechanism.);

(ii) A doctor of dental surgery or dental medicine who is legally authorized to practice dentistry by the State and who is acting within the scope of his or her license;

(iii) A doctor of podiatric medicine, but only with respect to functions which he or she is legally authorized by the State to perform;

> (iv) A doctor of optometry who is legally authorized to practice optometry by the State in which he or she practices;
>
> (v) A chiropractor who is licensed by the State or legally authorized to perform the services of a chiropractor, but only with respect to treatment by means of manual manipulation of the spine to correct a subluxation demonstrated by x-ray to exist; and
>
> (vi) A clinical psychologist as defined in §410.71 of this chapter, but only with respect to clinical psychologist services as defined in §410.71 of this chapter and only to the extent permitted by State law.

(2) Patients are admitted to the hospital only on the recommendation of a licensed practitioner permitted by the State to admit patients to a hospital. If a Medicare patient is admitted by a practitioner not specified in paragraph (c)(1) of this section, that patient is under the care of a doctor of medicine or osteopathy.

(3) A doctor of medicine or osteopathy is on duty or on call at all times.

(4) A doctor of medicine or osteopathy is responsible for the care of each Medicare patient with respect to any medical or psychiatric problem that—

> (i) is present on admission or develops during hospitalization; and
>
> (ii) Is not specifically within the scope of practice of a doctor of dental surgery, dental medicine, podiatric medicine, or optometry; a chiropractor; or clinical psychologist, as that scope is—
>
> > (A) Defined by the medical staff;
> >
> > (B) Permitted by State law; and
> >
> > (C) Limited, under paragraph (c)(1)(v) of this section, with respect to chiropractors.

(d) *Standard: Institutional plan and budget.* The institution must have an overall institutional plan that meets the following conditions:

(1) The plan must include an annual operating budget that is prepared according to generally accepted accounting principles.

(2) The budget must include all anticipated income and expenses. This provision does not require that the budget identify item by item the components of each anticipated income or expense.

(3) The plan must provide for capital expenditures for at least a 3-year period, including the year in which the operating budget specified in paragraph (d)(2) of this section is applicable.

(4) The plan must include and identify in detail the objective of, and the anticipated sources of financing for, each anticipated capital

expenditure in excess of $600,000 (or a lesser amount that is established, in accordance with section 1122(g)(1) of the Act, by the State in which the hospital is located) that relates to any of the following:

(i)   Acquisition of land;

(ii) Improvement of land, buildings, and equipment; or

(iii) The replacement, modernization, and expansion of buildings and equipment.

(5) The plan must be submitted for review to the planning agency designated in accordance with section 1122(b) of the Act, or if an agency is not designated, to the appropriate health planning agency in the State. (See part 100 of this title.) A capital expenditure is not subject to section 1122 review if 75 percent of the health care facility's patients who are expected to use the service for which the capital expenditure is made are individuals enrolled in a health maintenance organization (HMO) or competitive medical plan (CMP) that meets the requirements of section 1876(b) of the Act, and if the Department determines that the capital expenditure is for services and facilities that are needed by the HMO or CMP in order to operate efficiently and economically and that are not otherwise readily accessible to the HMO or CMP because—

(i)   The facilities do not provide common services at the same site;

(ii) The facilities are not available under a contract of reasonable duration;

(iii) Full and equal medical staff privileges in the facilities are not available;

(iv) Arrangements with these facilities are not administratively feasible; or

(v)   The purchase of these services is more costly than if the HMO or CMP provided the services directly.

(6) The plan must be reviewed and updated annually.

(7) The plan must be prepared—

(i)   Under the direction of the governing body; and

(ii) By a committee consisting of representatives of the governing body, the administrative staff, and the medical staff of the institution.

(e) *Standard: Contracted services.* The governing body must be responsible for services furnished in the hospital whether or not they are furnished under contracts. The governing body must ensure that a contractor of services (including one for shared services and joint ventures) furnishes services that permit the hospital to comply with all applicable conditions of participation and standards for the contracted services.

    (1) The governing body must ensure that the services performed under a contract are provided in a safe and effective manner.

    (2) The hospital must maintain a list of all contracted services, including the scope and nature of the services provided.

(f) *Standard: Emergency services.*

    (1) If emergency services are provided at the hospital, the hospital must comply with the requirements of §482.55.

    (2) If emergency services are not provided at the hospital, the governing body must assure that the medical staff has written policies and procedures for appraisal of emergencies, initial treatment, and referral when appropriate.

    (3) If emergency services are provided at the hospital but are not provided at one or more off-campus departments of the hospital, the governing body of the hospital must assure that the medical staff has written policies and procedures in effect with respect to the off-campus department(s) for appraisal of emergencies and referral when appropriate.

[51 FR 22042, June 17, 1986; 51 FR 27847, Aug. 4, 1986, as amended at 53 FR 6549, Mar. 1, 1988; 53 FR 18987, May 26, 1988; 56 FR 8852, Mar. 1, 1991; 56 FR 23022, May 20, 1991; 59 FR 46514, Sept. 8, 1994; 63 FR 20130, Apr. 23, 1998; 63 FR 33874, June 22, 1998; 68 FR 53262, Sept. 9, 2003; 76 FR 25562, May 5, 2011]

§ 482.13   Condition of participation: Patient's rights.

A hospital must protect and promote each patient's rights.

(a) *Standard: Notice of rights —*

    (1) A hospital must inform each patient, or when appropriate, the patient's representative (as allowed under State law), of the patient's rights, in advance of furnishing or discontinuing patient care whenever possible.

    (2) The hospital must establish a process for prompt resolution of patient grievances and must inform each patient whom to contact to file a grievance. The hospital's governing body must approve and be responsible for the effective operation of the grievance process and must review and resolve grievances, unless it delegates the

responsibility in writing to a grievance committee. The grievance process must include a mechanism for timely referral of patient concerns regarding quality of care or premature discharge to the appropriate Utilization and Quality Control Quality Improvement Organization. At a minimum:

    (i)   The hospital must establish a clearly explained procedure for the submission of a patient's written or verbal grievance to the hospital.

    (ii) The grievance process must specify time frames for review of the grievance and the provision of a response.

    (iii) In its resolution of the grievance, the hospital must provide the patient with written notice of its decision that contains the name of the hospital contact person, the steps taken on behalf of the patient to investigate the grievance, the results of the grievance process, and the date of completion.

(b) *Standard: Exercise of rights.*

(1) The patient has the right to participate in the development and implementation of his or her plan of care.

(2) The patient or his or her representative (as allowed under State law) has the right to make informed decisions regarding his or her care. The patient's rights include being informed of his or her health status, being involved in care planning and treatment, and being able to request or refuse treatment. This right must not be construed as a mechanism to demand the provision of treatment or services deemed medically unnecessary or inappropriate.

(3) The patient has the right to formulate advance directives and to have hospital staff and practitioners who provide care in the hospital comply with these directives, in accordance with §489.100 of this part (Definition), §489.102 of this part (Requirements for providers), and §489.104 of this part (Effective dates).

(4) The patient has the right to have a family member or representative of his or her choice and his or her own physician notified promptly of his or her admission to the hospital.

(c) *Standard: Privacy and safety.*

(1) The patient has the right to personal privacy.

(2) The patient has the right to receive care in a safe setting.

(3) The patient has the right to be free from all forms of abuse or harassment.

(d) *Standard: Confidentiality of patient records.*
   (1) The patient has the right to the confidentiality of his or her clinical records.
   (2) The patient has the right to access information contained in his or her clinical records within a reasonable time frame. The hospital must not frustrate the legitimate efforts of individuals to gain access to their own medical records and must actively seek to meet these requests as quickly as its record keeping system permits.

(e) *Standard: Restraint or seclusion.* All patients have the right to be free from physical or mental abuse, and corporal punishment. All patients have the right to be free from restraint or seclusion, of any form, imposed as a means of coercion, discipline, convenience, or retaliation by staff. Restraint or seclusion may only be imposed to ensure the immediate physical safety of the patient, a staff member, or others and must be discontinued at the earliest possible time.
   (1) *Definitions.*
      (i) A *restraint* is—
         (A) Any manual method, physical or mechanical device, material, or equipment that immobilizes or reduces the ability of a patient to move his or her arms, legs, body, or head freely; or
         (B) A drug or medication when it is used as a restriction to manage the patient's behavior or restrict the patient's freedom of movement and is not a standard treatment or dosage for the patient's condition.
         (C) A restraint does not include devices, such as orthopedically prescribed devices, surgical dressings or bandages, protective helmets, or other methods that involve the physical holding of a patient for the purpose of conducting routine physical examinations or tests, or to protect the patient from falling out of bed, or to permit the patient to participate in activities without the risk of physical harm (this does not include a physical escort).
      (ii) *Seclusion* is the involuntary confinement of a patient alone in a room or area from which the patient is physically prevented from leaving. Seclusion may only be used for the management of violent or self-destructive behavior.

(2) Restraint or seclusion may only be used when less restrictive interventions have been determined to be ineffective to protect the patient a staff member or others from harm.

(3) The type or technique of restraint or seclusion used must be the least restrictive intervention that will be effective to protect the patient, a staff member, or others from harm.

(4) The use of restraint or seclusion must be—

  (i) In accordance with a written modification to the patient's plan of care; and

  (ii) Implemented in accordance with safe and appropriate restraint and seclusion techniques as determined by hospital policy in accordance with State law.

(5) The use of restraint or seclusion must be in accordance with the order of a physician or other licensed independent practitioner who is responsible for the care of the patient as specified under §482.12(c) and authorized to order restraint or seclusion by hospital policy in accordance with State law.

(6) Orders for the use of restraint or seclusion must never be written as a standing order or on an as needed basis (PRN).

(7) The attending physician must be consulted as soon as possible if the attending physician did not order the restraint or seclusion.

(8) Unless superseded by State law that is more restrictive—

  (i) Each order for restraint or seclusion used for the management of violent or self-destructive behavior that jeopardizes the immediate physical safety of the patient, a staff member, or others may only be renewed in accordance with the following limits for up to a total of 24 hours:

    (A) 4 hours for adults 18 years of age or older;

    (B) 2 hours for children and adolescents 9 to 17 years of age; or

    (C) 1 hour for children under 9 years of age; and

  (ii) After 24 hours, before writing a new order for the use of restraint or seclusion for the management of violent or self-destructive behavior, a physician or other licensed independent practitioner who is responsible for the care of the patient as specified under §482.12(c) of this part and authorized to order restraint or seclusion by hospital policy in accordance with State law must see and assess the patient.

  (iii) Each order for restraint used to ensure the physical safety of the non-violent or non-self-destructive patient may be renewed as authorized by hospital policy.

(9) Restraint or seclusion must be discontinued at the earliest possible time, regardless of the length of time identified in the order.

(10) The condition of the patient who is restrained or secluded must be monitored by a physician, other licensed independent practitioner or trained staff that have completed the training criteria specified in paragraph (f) of this section at an interval determined by hospital policy.

(11) Physician and other licensed independent practitioner training requirements must be specified in hospital policy. At a minimum, physicians and other licensed independent practitioners authorized to order restraint or seclusion by hospital policy in accordance with State law must have a working knowledge of hospital policy regarding the use of restraint or seclusion.

(12) When restraint or seclusion is used for the management of violent or self-destructive behavior that jeopardizes the immediate physical safety of the patient, a staff member, or others, the patient must be seen face-to-face within 1 hour after the initiation of the intervention—

  (i) By a—
   (A) Physician or other licensed independent practitioner; or
   (B) Registered nurse or physician assistant who has been trained in accordance with the requirements specified in paragraph (f) of this section.

  (ii) To evaluate—
   (A) The patient's immediate situation;
   (B) The patient's reaction to the intervention;
   (C) The patient's medical and behavioral condition; and
   (D) The need to continue or terminate the restraint or seclusion.

(13) States are free to have requirements by statute or regulation that are more restrictive than those contained in paragraph (e)(12)(i) of this section.

(14) If the face-to-face evaluation specified in paragraph (e)(12) of this section is conducted by a trained registered nurse or physician assistant, the trained registered nurse or physician assistant must consult the attending physician or other licensed independent practitioner who is responsible for the care of the patient as specified under §482.12(c) as soon as possible after the completion of the 1-hour face-to-face evaluation.

(15) All requirements specified under this paragraph are applicable to the simultaneous use of restraint and seclusion. Simultaneous restraint

and seclusion use is only permitted if the patient is continually monitored—

   (i) Face-to-face by an assigned, trained staff member; or
   (ii) By trained staff using both video and audio equipment. This monitoring must be in close proximity to the patient.

(16) When restraint or seclusion is used, there must be documentation in the patient's medical record of the following:

   (i) The 1-hour face-to-face medical and behavioral evaluation if restraint or seclusion is used to manage violent or self-destructive behavior;
   (ii) A description of the patient's behavior and the intervention used;
   (iii) Alternatives or other less restrictive interventions attempted (as applicable);
   (iv) The patient's condition or symptom(s) that warranted the use of the restraint or seclusion; and
   (v) The patient's response to the intervention(s) used, including the rationale for continued use of the intervention.

(f) *Standard: Restraint or seclusion: Staff training requirements.* The patient has the right to safe implementation of restraint or seclusion by trained staff.

(1) *Training intervals.* Staff must be trained and able to demonstrate competency in the application of restraints, implementation of seclusion, monitoring, assessment, and providing care for a patient in restraint or seclusion—

   (i) Before performing any of the actions specified in this paragraph;
   (ii) As part of orientation; and
   (iii) Subsequently on a periodic basis consistent with hospital policy.

(2) *Training content.* The hospital must require appropriate staff to have education, training, and demonstrated knowledge based on the specific needs of the patient population in at least the following:

   (i) Techniques to identify staff and patient behaviors, events, and environmental factors that may trigger circumstances that require the use of a restraint or seclusion.
   (ii) The use of nonphysical intervention skills.
   (iii) Choosing the least restrictive intervention based on an individualized assessment of the patient's medical, or behavioral status or condition.

(iv) The safe application and use of all types of restraint or seclusion used in the hospital, including training in how to recognize and respond to signs of physical and psychological distress (for example, positional asphyxia);

(v) Clinical identification of specific behavioral changes that indicate that restraint or seclusion is no longer necessary.

(vi) Monitoring the physical and psychological well-being of the patient who is restrained or secluded, including but not limited to, respiratory and circulatory status, skin integrity, vital signs, and any special requirements specified by hospital policy associated with the 1-hour face-to-face evaluation.

(vii) The use of first aid techniques and certification in the use of cardiopulmonary resuscitation, including required periodic recertification.

(3) *Trainer requirements.* Individuals providing staff training must be qualified as evidenced by education, training, and experience in techniques used to address patients' behaviors.

(4) *Training documentation.* The hospital must document in the staff personnel records that the training and demonstration of competency were successfully completed.

(g) *Standard: Death reporting requirements:* Hospitals must report deaths associated with the use of seclusion or restraint.

(1) The hospital must report the following information to CMS:

(i) Each death that occurs while a patient is in restraint or seclusion.

(ii) Each death that occurs within 24 hours after the patient has been removed from restraint or seclusion.

(iii) Each death known to the hospital that occurs within 1 week after restraint or seclusion where it is reasonable to assume that use of restraint or placement in seclusion contributed directly or indirectly to a patient's death. "Reasonable to assume" in this context includes, but is not limited to, deaths related to restrictions of movement for prolonged periods of time, or death related to chest compression, restriction of breathing or asphyxiation.

(2) Each death referenced in this paragraph must be reported to CMS by telephone no later than the close of business the next business day following knowledge of the patient's death.

(3) Staff must document in the patient's medical record the date and time the death was reported to CMS.

(h) *Standard: Patient visitation rights.* A hospital must have written policies and procedures regarding the visitation rights of patients, including those setting forth any clinically necessary or reasonable restriction or limitation that the hospital may need to place on such rights and the reasons for the clinical restriction or limitation. A hospital must meet the following requirements:

(1) Inform each patient (or support person, where appropriate) of his or her visitation rights, including any clinical restriction or limitation on such rights, when he or she is informed of his or her other rights under this section.

(2) Inform each patient (or support person, where appropriate) of the right, subject to his or her consent, to receive the visitors whom he or she designates, including, but not limited to, a spouse, a domestic partner (including a same-sex domestic partner), another family member, or a friend, and his or her right to withdraw or deny such consent at any time.

(3) Not restrict, limit, or otherwise deny visitation privileges on the basis of race, color, national origin, religion, sex, gender identity, sexual orientation, or disability.

(4) Ensure that all visitors enjoy full and equal visitation privileges consistent with patient preferences.

[71 FR 71426, Dec. 8, 2006, as amended at 75 FR 70844, Nov. 19, 2010]

Subpart C—Basic Hospital Functions

§ 482.21 Condition of participation: Quality assessment and performance improvement program.

The hospital must develop, implement, and maintain an effective, ongoing, hospital-wide, data-driven quality assessment and performance improvement program. The hospital's governing body must ensure that the program reflects the complexity of the hospital's organization and services; involves all hospital departments and services (including those services furnished under contract or arrangement); and focuses on indicators related to improved health outcomes and the prevention and reduction of medical errors. The hospital must maintain and demonstrate evidence of its QAPI program for review by CMS.

(a) *Standard: Program scope.*

(1) The program must include, but not be limited to, an ongoing program that shows measurable improvement in indicators for which

there is evidence that it will improve health outcomes and identify and reduce medical errors.

(2) The hospital must measure, analyze, and track quality indicators, including adverse patient events, and other aspects of performance that assess processes of care, hospital service and operations.

(b) *Standard: Program data.*

(1) The program must incorporate quality indicator data including patient care data, and other relevant data, for example, information submitted to, or received from, the hospital's Quality Improvement Organization.

(2) The hospital must use the data collected to—

(i) Monitor the effectiveness and safety of services and quality of care; and

(ii) Identify opportunities for improvement and changes that will lead to improvement.

(3) The frequency and detail of data collection must be specified by the hospital's governing body.

(c) *Standard: Program activities.*

(1) The hospital must set priorities for its performance improvement activities that—

(i) Focus on high-risk, high-volume, or problem-prone areas;

(ii) Consider the incidence, prevalence, and severity of problems in those areas; and

(iii) Affect health outcomes, patient safety, and quality of care.

(2) Performance improvement activities must track medical errors and adverse patient events, analyze their causes, and implement preventive actions and mechanisms that include feedback and learning throughout the hospital.

(3) The hospital must take actions aimed at performance improvement and, after implementing those actions, the hospital must measure its success, and track performance to ensure that improvements are sustained.

(d) *Standard: Performance improvement projects.* As part of its quality assessment and performance improvement program, the hospital must conduct performance improvement projects.

(1) The number and scope of distinct improvement projects conducted annually must be proportional to the scope and complexity of the hospital's services and operations.

    (2) A hospital may, as one of its projects, develop and implement an information technology system explicitly designed to improve patient safety and quality of care. This project, in its initial stage of development, does not need to demonstrate measurable improvement in indicators related to health outcomes.

    (3) The hospital must document what quality improvement projects are being conducted, the reasons for conducting these projects, and the measurable progress achieved on these projects.

    (4) A hospital is not required to participate in a QIO cooperative project, but its own projects are required to be of comparable effort.

(e) *Standard: Executive responsibilities.* The hospital's governing body (or organized group or individual who assumes full legal authority and responsibility for operations of the hospital), medical staff, and administrative officials are responsible and accountable for ensuring the following:

    (1) That an ongoing program for quality improvement and patient safety, including the reduction of medical errors, is defined, implemented, and maintained.

    (2) That the hospital-wide quality assessment and performance improvement efforts address priorities for improved quality of care and patient safety; and that all improvement actions are evaluated.

    (3) That clear expectations for safety are established.

    (4) That adequate resources are allocated for measuring, assessing, improving, and sustaining the hospital's performance and reducing risk to patients.

    (5) That the determination of the number of distinct improvement projects is conducted annually.

[68 FR 3454, Jan. 24, 2003]

§ 482.22 Condition of participation: Medical staff.

The hospital must have an organized medical staff that operates under bylaws approved by the governing body and is responsible for the quality of medical care provided to patients by the hospital.

(a) *Standard: Composition of the medical staff.* The medical staff must be composed of doctors of medicine or osteopathy and, in accordance with State law, may also be composed of other practitioners appointed by the governing body.

(1) The medical staff must periodically conduct appraisals of its members.

(2) The medical staff must examine credentials of candidates for medical staff membership and make recommendations to the governing body on the appointment of the candidates.

(3) When telemedicine services are furnished to the hospital's patients through an agreement with a distant-site hospital, the governing body of the hospital whose patients are receiving the telemedicine services may choose, in lieu of the requirements in paragraphs (a)(1) and (a)(2) of this section, to have its medical staff rely upon the credentialing and privileging decisions made by the distant-site hospital when making recommendations on privileges for the individual distant-site physicians and practitioners providing such services, if the hospital's governing body ensures, through its written agreement with the distant-site hospital, that all of the following provisions are met:

(i) The distant-site hospital providing the telemedicine services is a Medicare-participating hospital.

(ii) The individual distant-site physician or practitioner is privileged at the distant-site hospital providing the telemedicine services, which provides a current list of the distant-site physician's or practitioner's privileges at the distant-site hospital.

(iii) The individual distant-site physician or practitioner holds a license issued or recognized by the State in which the hospital whose patients are receiving the telemedicine services is located.

(iv) With respect to a distant-site physician or practitioner, who holds current privileges at the hospital whose patients are receiving the telemedicine services, the hospital has evidence of an internal review of the distant-site physician's or practitioner's performance of these privileges and sends the distant-site hospital such performance information for use in the periodic appraisal of the distant-site physician or practitioner. At a minimum, this information must include all adverse events that result from the telemedicine services provided by the distant-site physician or practitioner to the hospital's patients and all complaints the hospital has received about the distant-site physician or practitioner.

(4) When telemedicine services are furnished to the hospital's patients through an agreement with a distant-site telemedicine entity, the governing body of the hospital whose patients are receiving the telemedicine services may choose, in lieu of the requirements in paragraphs (a)(1) and (a)(2) of this section, to have its medical staff rely upon the credentialing and privileging decisions made by the distant-site telemedicine entity when making recommendations on privileges for the individual distant-site physicians and practitioners providing such services, if the hospital's governing body ensures, through its written agreement with the distant-site telemedicine entity, that the distant-site telemedicine entity furnishes services that, in accordance with §482.12(e), permit the hospital to comply with all applicable conditions of participation for the contracted services. The hospital's governing body must also ensure, through its written agreement with the distant-site telemedicine entity, that all of the following provisions are met:

(i) The distant-site telemedicine entity's medical staff credentialing and privileging process and standards at least meet the standards at §482.12(a)(1) through (a)(7) and §482.22(a)(1) through (a)(2).

(ii) The individual distant-site physician or practitioner is privileged at the distant-site telemedicine entity providing the telemedicine services, which provides the hospital with a current list of the distant-site physician's or practitioner's privileges at the distant-site telemedicine entity.

(iii) The individual distant-site physician or practitioner holds a license issued or recognized by the State in which the hospital whose patients are receiving such telemedicine services is located.

(iv) With respect to a distant-site physician or practitioner, who holds current privileges at the hospital whose patients are receiving the telemedicine services, the hospital has evidence of an internal review of the distant-site physician's or practitioner's performance of these privileges and sends the distant-site telemedicine entity such performance information for use in the periodic appraisal of the distant-site physician or practitioner. At a minimum, this information must include all adverse events that result from the telemedicine services provided by the distant-site physician or practitioner to the hospital's patients and all complaints the hospital has received about the distant-site physician or practitioner.

(b) *Standard: Medical staff organization and accountability.* The medical staff must be well organized and accountable to the governing body for the quality of the medical care provided to patients.

    (1) The medical staff must be organized in a manner approved by the governing body.

    (2) If the medical staff has an executive committee, a majority of the members of the committee must be doctors of medicine or osteopathy.

    (3) The responsibility for organization and conduct of the medical staff must be assigned only to an individual doctor of medicine or osteopathy or, when permitted by State law of the State in which the hospital is located, a doctor of dental surgery or dental medicine.

(c) *Standard: Medical staff bylaws.* The medical staff must adopt and enforce bylaws to carry out its responsibilities. The bylaws must:

    (1) Be approved by the governing body.

    (2) Include a statement of the duties and privileges of each category of medical staff (e.g., active, courtesy, etc.)

    (3) Describe the organization of the medical staff.

    (4) Describe the qualifications to be met by a candidate in order for the medical staff to recommend that the candidate be appointed by the governing body.

    (5) Include a requirement that—

        (i) A medical history and physical examination be completed and documented for each patient no more than 30 days before or 24 hours after admission or registration, but prior to surgery or a procedure requiring anesthesia services. The medical history and physical examination must be completed and documented by a physician (as defined in section 1861(r) of the Act), an oromaxillofacial surgeon, or other qualified licensed individual in accordance with State law and hospital policy.

        (ii) An updated examination of the patient, including any changes in the patient's condition, be completed and documented within 24 hours after admission or registration but prior to surgery or a procedure requiring anesthesia services, when the medical history and physical examination are completed within 30 days before admission or registration. The updated examination of the patient, including any changes in the patient's condition, must be completed and documented by a physician (as defined in section 1861(r) of the Act), an oromaxillofacial surgeon, or other qualified licensed individual in accordance with State law and hospital policy.

(6) Include criteria for determining the privileges to be granted to individual practitioners and a procedure for applying the criteria to individuals requesting privileges. For distant-site physicians and practitioners requesting privileges to furnish telemedicine services under an agreement with the hospital, the criteria for determining privileges and the procedure for applying the criteria are also subject to the requirements in §482.12(a)(8) and (a)(9), and §482.22(a)(3) and (a)(4).

(d) *Standard: Autopsies.* The medical staff should attempt to secure autopsies in all cases of unusual deaths and of medical-legal and educational interest. The mechanism for documenting permission to perform an autopsy must be defined. There must be a system for notifying the medical staff, and specifically the attending practitioner, when an autopsy is being performed.

[51 FR 22042, June 17, 1986, as amended at 59 FR 64152, Dec. 13, 1994; 71 FR 68694, Nov. 27, 2006; 72 FR 66933, Nov. 27, 2007; 76 FR 25563, May 5, 2011]

§ 482.23   Condition of participation: Nursing services.

The hospital must have an organized nursing service that provides 24-hour nursing services. The nursing services must be furnished or supervised by a registered nurse.

(a) *Standard: Organization.* The hospital must have a well-organized service with a plan of administrative authority and delineation of responsibilities for patient care. The director of the nursing service must be a licensed registered nurse. He or she is responsible for the operation of the service, including determining the types and numbers of nursing personnel and staff necessary to provide nursing care for all areas of the hospital.

(b) *Standard: Staffing and delivery of care.* The nursing service must have adequate numbers of licensed registered nurses, licensed practical (vocational) nurses, and other personnel to provide nursing care to all patients as needed. There must be supervisory and staff personnel for each department or nursing unit to ensure, when needed, the immediate availability of a registered nurse for bedside care of any patient.

(1) The hospital must provide 24-hour nursing services furnished or supervised by a registered nurse, and have a licensed practical nurse or registered nurse on duty at all times, except for rural hospitals that have in effect a 24-hour nursing waiver granted under §488.54(c) of this chapter.

(2) The nursing service must have a procedure to ensure that hospital nursing personnel for whom licensure is required have valid and current licensure.

(3) A registered nurse must supervise and evaluate the nursing care for each patient.

(4) The hospital must ensure that the nursing staff develops, and keeps current, a nursing care plan for each patient.

(5) A registered nurse must assign the nursing care of each patient to other nursing personnel in accordance with the patient's needs and the specialized qualifications and competence of the nursing staff available.

(6) Non-employee licensed nurses who are working in the hospital must adhere to the policies and procedures of the hospital. The director of nursing service must provide for the adequate supervision and evaluation of the clinical activities of non-employee nursing personnel which occur within the responsibility of the nursing service.

(c) *Standard: Preparation and administration of drugs.* Drugs and biologicals must be prepared and administered in accordance with Federal and State laws, the orders of the practitioner or practitioners responsible for the patient's care as specified under §482.12(c), and accepted standards of practice.

(1) All drugs and biologicals must be administered by, or under supervision of, nursing or other personnel in accordance with Federal and State laws and regulations, including applicable licensing requirements, and in accordance with the approved medical staff policies and procedures.

(2) With the exception of influenza and pneumococcal polysaccharide vaccines, which may be administered per physician-approved hospital policy after an assessment of contraindications, orders for drugs and biologicals must be documented and signed by a practitioner who is authorized to write orders by hospital policy and in accordance with State law, and who is responsible for the care of the patient as specified under §482.12(c).

    (i) If verbal orders are used, they are to be used infrequently.

    (ii) When verbal orders are used, they must only be accepted by persons who are authorized to do so by hospital policy and procedures consistent with Federal and State law.

(3) Blood transfusions and intravenous medications must be administered in accordance with State law and approved medical staff policies and procedures. If blood transfusions and intravenous

medications are administered by personnel other than doctors of medicine or osteopathy, the personnel must have special training for this duty.

(4) There must be a hospital procedure for reporting transfusion reactions, adverse drug reactions, and errors in administration of drugs.

[51 FR 22042, June 17, 1986, as amended at 67 FR 61814, Oct. 2, 2002; 71 FR 68694, Nov. 27, 2006; 72 FR 66933, Nov. 27, 2007]

§ 482.24 Condition of participation: Medical record services.

The hospital must have a medical record service that has administrative responsibility for medical records. A medical record must be maintained for every individual evaluated or treated in the hospital.

(a) *Standard: Organization and staffing.* The organization of the medical record service must be appropriate to the scope and complexity of the services performed. The hospital must employ adequate personnel to ensure prompt completion, filing, and retrieval of records.

(b) *Standard: Form and retention of record.* The hospital must maintain a medical record for each inpatient and outpatient. Medical records must be accurately written, promptly completed, properly filed and retained, and accessible. The hospital must use a system of author identification and record maintenance that ensures the integrity of the authentification and protects the security of all record entries.

(1) Medical records must be retained in their original or legally reproduced form for a period of at least 5 years.

(2) The hospital must have a system of coding and indexing medical records. The system must allow for timely retrieval by diagnosis and procedure, in order to support medical care evaluation studies.

(3) The hospital must have a procedure for ensuring the confidentiality of patient records. In-formation from or copies of records may be released only to authorized individuals, and the hospital must ensure that unauthorized individuals cannot gain access to or alter patient records. Original medical records must be released by the hospital only in accordance with Federal or State laws, court orders, or subpoenas.

(c) *Standard: Content of record.* The medical record must contain information to justify admission and continued hospitalization, support the diagnosis, and describe the patient's progress and response to medications and services.

(1) All patient medical record entries must be legible, complete, dated, timed, and authenticated in written or electronic form by the person responsible for providing or evaluating the service provided, consistent with hospital policies and procedures.

  (i) All orders, including verbal orders, must be dated, timed, and authenticated promptly by the ordering practitioner, except as noted in paragraph (c)(1)(ii) of this section.

  (ii) For the 5 year period following January 26, 2007, all orders, including verbal orders, must be dated, timed, and authenticated by the ordering practitioner or another practitioner who is responsible for the care of the patient as specified under §482.12(c) and authorized to write orders by hospital policy in accordance with State law.

  (iii) All verbal orders must be authenticated based upon Federal and State law. If there is no State law that designates a specific timeframe for the authentication of verbal orders, verbal orders must be authenticated within 48 hours.

(2) All records must document the following, as appropriate:

  (i) Evidence of—

    (A) A medical history and physical examination completed and documented no more than 30 days before or 24 hours after admission or registration, but prior to surgery or a procedure requiring anesthesia services. The medical history and physical examination must be placed in the patient's medical record within 24 hours after admission or registration, but prior to surgery or a procedure requiring anesthesia services.

    (B) An updated examination of the patient, including any changes in the patient's condition, when the medical history and physical examination are completed within 30 days before admission or registration. Documentation of the updated examination must be placed in the patient's medical record within 24 hours after admission or registration, but prior to surgery or a procedure requiring anesthesia services.

  (ii) Admitting diagnosis.

  (iii) Results of all consultative evaluations of the patient and appropriate findings by clinical and other staff involved in the care of the patient.

    (iv) Documentation of complications, hospital acquired infections, and unfavorable reactions to drugs and anesthesia.

    (v) Properly executed informed consent forms for procedures and treatments specified by the medical staff, or by Federal or State law if applicable, to require written patient consent.

    (vi) All practitioners' orders, nursing notes, reports of treatment, medication records, radiology, and laboratory reports, and vital signs and other information necessary to monitor the patient's condition.

    (vii) Discharge summary with outcome of hospitalization, disposition of case, and provisions for follow-up care.

    (viii) Final diagnosis with completion of medical records within 30 days following discharge.

[51 FR 22042, June 17, 1986, as amended at 71 FR 68694, Nov. 27, 2006; 72 FR 66933, Nov. 27, 2007]

§ 482.25 Condition of participation: Pharmaceutical services.

The hospital must have pharmaceutical services that meet the needs of the patients. The institution must have a pharmacy directed by a registered pharmacist or a drug storage area under competent supervision. The medical staff is responsible for developing policies and procedures that minimize drug errors. This function may be delegated to the hospital's organized pharmaceutical service.

(a) *Standard: Pharmacy management and administration.* The pharmacy or drug storage area must be administered in accordance with accepted professional principles.

    (1) A full-time, part-time, or consulting pharmacist must be responsible for developing, supervising, and coordinating all the activities of the pharmacy services.

    (2) The pharmaceutical service must have an adequate number of personnel to ensure quality pharmaceutical services, including emergency services.

    (3) Current and accurate records must be kept of the receipt and disposition of all scheduled drugs.

(b) *Standard: Delivery of services.* In order to provide patient safety, drugs and biologicals must be controlled and distributed in accordance with applicable standards of practice, consistent with Federal and State law.

(1) All compounding, packaging, and dispensing of drugs and biologicals must be under the supervision of a pharmacist and performed consistent with State and Federal laws.

(2) (i) All drugs and biologicals must be kept in a secure area, and locked when appropriate.

    (ii) Drugs listed in Schedules II, III, IV, and V of the Comprehensive Drug Abuse Prevention and Control Act of 1970 must be kept locked within a secure area.

    (iii) Only authorized personnel may have access to locked areas.

(3) Outdated, mislabeled, or otherwise unusable drugs and biologicals must not be available for patient use.

(4) When a pharmacist is not available, drugs and biologicals must be removed from the pharmacy or storage area only by personnel designated in the policies of the medical staff and pharmaceutical service, in accordance with Federal and State law.

(5) Drugs and biologicals not specifically prescribed as to time or number of doses must automatically be stopped after a reasonable time that is predetermined by the medical staff.

(6) Drug administration errors, adverse drug reactions, and incompatibilities must be immediately reported to the attending physician and, if appropriate, to the hospital-wide quality assurance program.

(7) Abuses and losses of controlled substances must be reported, in accordance with applicable Federal and State laws, to the individual responsible for the pharmaceutical service, and to the chief executive officer, as appropriate.

(8) Information relating to drug interactions and information of drug therapy, side effects, toxicology, dosage, indications for use, and routes of administration must be available to the professional staff.

(9) A formulary system must be established by the medical staff to assure quality pharmaceuticals at reasonable costs.

[51 FR 22042, June 17, 1986; 51 FR 27848, Aug. 4, 1986; 71 FR 68694, Nov. 27, 2006]

§ 482.26 *Condition of participation: Radiologic services.*

The hospital must maintain, or have available, diagnostic radiologic services. If therapeutic services are also provided, they, as well as the diagnostic services, must meet professionally approved standards for safety and personnel qualifications.

(a) *Standard: Radiologic services.* The hospital must maintain, or have available, radiologic services according to needs of the patients.

(b) *Standard: Safety for patients and personnel.* The radiologic services, particularly ionizing radiology procedures, must be free from hazards for patients and personnel.

    (1) Proper safety precutions must be maintained against radiation hazards. This includes adequate shielding for patients, personnel, and facilities, as well as appropriate storage, use, and disposal of radioactive materials.

    (2) Periodic inspection of equipment must be made and hazards identified must be promptly corrected.

    (3) Radiation workers must be checked periodically, by the use of exposure meters or badge tests, for amount of radiation exposure.

    (4) Radiologic services must be provided only on the order of practitioners with clinical privileges or, consistent with State law, of other practitioners authorized by the medical staff and the governing body to order the services.

(c) *Standard: Personnel.*

    (1) A qualified full-time, part-time, or consulting radiologist must supervise the ionizing radiology services and must interpret only those radiologic tests that are determined by the medical staff to require a radiologist's specialized knowledge. For purposes of this section, a radiologist is a doctor of medicine or osteopathy who is qualified by education and experience in radiology.

    (2) Only personnel designated as qualified by the medical staff may use the radiologic equipment and administer procedures.

(d) *Standard: Records.* Records of radiologic services must be maintained.

    (1) The radiologist or other practitioner who performs radiology services must sign reports of his or her interpretations.

    (2) The hospital must maintain the following for at least 5 years:

        (i) Copies of reports and printouts.

        (ii) Films, scans, and other image records, as appropriate.

[51 FR 22042, June 17, 1986; 51 FR 27848, Aug. 4, 1986]

§ 482.27 Condition of participation: Laboratory services.

The hospital must maintain, or have available, adequate laboratory services to meet the needs of its patients. The hospital must ensure that all laboratory services provided to its patients are performed in a facility certified in accordance with part 493 of this chapter.

(a) *Standard: Adequacy of laboratory services.* The hospital must have laboratory services available, either directly or through a contractual agreement with a certified laboratory that meets requirements of part 493 of this chapter.

    (1) Emergency laboratory services must be available 24 hours a day.

    (2) A written description of services provided must be available to the medical staff.

    (3) The laboratory must make provision for proper receipt and reporting of tissue specimens.

    (4) The medical staff and a pathologist must determine which tissue specimens require a macroscopic (gross) examination and which require both macroscopic and microscopic examinations.

(b) *Standard: Potentially infectious blood and blood components —*

    (1) *Potentially human immunodeficiency virus (HIV) infectious blood and blood components.* Potentially HIV infectious blood and blood components are prior collections from a donor—

        (i) Who tested negative at the time of donation but tests reactive for evidence of HIV infection on a later donation;

        (ii) Who tests positive on the supplemental (additional, more specific) test or other follow-up testing required by FDA; and

        (iii) For whom the timing of seroconversion cannot be precisely estimated.

    (2) *Potentially hepatitis C virus (HCV) infectious blood and blood components.* Potentially HCV infectious blood and blood components are the blood and blood components identified in 21 CFR 610.47.

    (3) *Services furnished by an outside blood collecting establishment.* If a hospital regularly uses the services of an outside blood collecting establishment, it must have an agreement with the blood collecting establishment that governs the procurement, transfer, and availability of blood and blood components. The agreement must require that the blood collecting establishment notify the hospital—

        (i) Within 3 calendar days if the blood collecting establishment supplied blood and blood components collected from a donor who tested negative at the time of donation but tests reactive for evidence of HIV or HCV infection on a later donation or who is determined to be at increased risk for transmitting HIV or HCV infection;

(ii) Within 45 days of the test, of the results of the supplemental (additional, more specific) test for HIV or HCV, as relevant, or other follow-up testing required by FDA; and

(iii) Within 3 calendar days after the blood collecting establishment supplied blood and blood components collected from an infectious donor, whenever records are available, as set forth at 21 CFR 610.48(b)(3).

(4) *Quarantine and disposition of blood and blood components pending completion of testing.* If the blood collecting establishment (either internal or under an agreement) notifies the hospital of the reactive HIV or HCV screening test results, the hospital must determine the disposition of the blood or blood product and quarantine all blood and blood components from previous donations in inventory.

(i) If the blood collecting establishment notifies the hospital that the result of the supplemental (additional, more specific) test or other follow-up testing required by FDA is negative, absent other informative test results, the hospital may release the blood and blood components from quarantine.

(ii) If the blood collecting establishment notifies the hospital that the result of the supplemental, (additional, more specific) test or other follow-up testing required by FDA is positive, the hospital must—

(A) Dispose of the blood and blood components; and

(B) Notify the transfusion recipients as set forth in paragraph (b)(6) of this section.

(iii) If the blood collecting establishment notifies the hospital that the result of the supplemental,(additional, more specific) test or other follow-up testing required by FDA is indeterminate, the hospital must destroy or label prior collections of blood or blood components held in quarantine as set forth at 21 CFR 610.46(b)(2), 610.47(b)(2), and 610.48(c)(2).

(5) *Recordkeeping by the hospital.* The hospital must maintain—

(i) Records of the source and disposition of all units of blood and blood components for at least 10 years from the date of disposition in a manner that permits prompt retrieval; and

(ii) A fully funded plan to transfer these records to another hospital or other entity if such hospital ceases operation for any reason.

(6) *Patient notification.* If the hospital has administered potentially HIV or HCV infectious blood or blood components (either directly through its own blood collecting establishment or under an agreement) or released such blood or blood components to another entity or individual, the hospital must take the following actions:

   (i)   Make reasonable attempts to notify the patient, or to notify the attending physician or the physician who ordered the blood or blood component and ask the physician to notify the patient, or other individual as permitted under paragraph (b)(10) of this section, that potentially HIV or HCV infectious blood or blood components were transfused to the patient and that there may be a need for HIV or HCV testing and counseling.

   (ii)   If the physician is unavailable or declines to make the notification, make reasonable attempts to give this notification to the patient, legal guardian, or relative.

   (iii)   Document in the patient's medical record the notification or attempts to give the required notification.

(7) *Timeframe for notification* —

   (i)   *For donors tested on or after February 20, 2008.* For notifications resulting from donors tested on or after February 20, 2008 as set forth at 21 CFR 610.46 and 21 CFR 610.47, the notification effort begins when the blood collecting establishment notifies the hospital that it received potentially HIV or HCV infectious blood and blood components. The hospital must make reasonable attempts to give notification over a period of 12 weeks unless—

      (A)   The patient is located and notified; or

      (B)   The hospital is unable to locate the patient and documents in the patient's medical record the extenuating circumstances beyond the hospital's control that caused the notification timeframe to exceed 12 weeks.

   (ii)   For donors tested before February 20, 2008. For notifications resulting from donors tested before February 20, 2008 as set forth at 21 CFR 610.48(b) and (c), the notification effort begins when the blood collecting establishment notifies the hospital that it received potentially HCV infectious blood and blood components. The hospital must make reasonable attempts to give notification and must complete the actions within 1 year of the date on which the hospital received notification from the outside blood collecting establishment.

(8) *Content of notification.* The notification must include the following information:

(i) A basic explanation of the need for HIV or HCV testing and counseling;

(ii) Enough oral or written information so that an informed decision can be made about whether to obtain HIV or HCV testing and counseling; and

(iii) A list of programs or places where the person can obtain HIV or HCV testing and counseling, including any requirements or restrictions the program may impose.

(9) *Policies and procedures.* The hospital must establish policies and procedures for notification and documentation that conform to Federal, State, and local laws, including requirements for the confidentiality of medical records and other patient information.

(10) *Notification to legal representative or relative.* If the patient has been adjudged incompetent by a State court, the physician or hospital must notify a legal representative designated in accordance with State law. If the patient is competent, but State law permits a legal representative or relative to receive the information on the patient's behalf, the physician or hospital must notify the patient or his or her legal representative or relative. For possible HIV infectious transfusion recipients that are deceased, the physician or hospital must inform the deceased patient's legal representative or relative. If the patient is a minor, the parents or legal guardian must be notified.

(11) *Applicability.* HCV notification requirements resulting from donors tested before February 20, 2008 as set forth at 21 CFR 610.48 will expire on August 24, 2015.

(c) *General blood safety issues.* For lookback activities only related to new blood safety issues that are identified after August 24, 2007, hospitals must comply with FDA regulations as they pertain to blood safety issues in the following areas:

(1) Appropriate testing and quarantining of infectious blood and blood components.

(2) Notification and counseling of recipients that may have received infectious blood and blood components.

[57 FR 7136, Feb. 28, 1992, as amended at 61 FR 47433, Sept. 9, 1996; 72 FR 48573, Aug. 24, 2007]

§ 482.28 Condition of participation: Food and dietetic services.

The hospital must have organized dietary services that are directed and staffed by adequate qualified personnel. However, a hospital that has a contract with an outside food management company may be found to meet this Condition of participation if the company has a dietitian who serves the hospital on a full-time, part-time, or consultant basis and if the company maintains at least the minimum standards specified in this section and provides for constant liaison with the hospital medical staff for recommendations on dietetic policies affecting patient treatment.

(a) *Standard: Organization.*
    (1) The hospital must have a full-time employee who—
        (i) Serves as director of the food and dietetic service;
        (ii) Is responsible for the daily management of the dietary services; and
        (iii) Is qualified by experience or training.
    (2) There must be a qualified dietitian, full-time, part-time, or on a consultant basis.
    (3) There must be administrative and technical personnel competent in their respective duties.

(b) *Standard: Diets.* Menus must meet the needs of the patients.
    (1) Therapeutic diets must be prescribed by the practitioner or practitioners responsible for the care of the patients.
    (2) Nutritional needs must be met in accordance with recognized dietary practices and in accordance with orders of the practitioner or practitioners responsible for the care of the patients.
    (3) A current therapeutic diet manual approved by the dietitian and medical staff must be readily available to all medical, nursing, and food service personnel.

§ 482.30 Condition of participation: Utilization review.

The hospital must have in effect a utilization review (UR) plan that provides for review of services furnished by the institution and by members of the medical staff to patients entitled to benefits under the Medicare and Medicaid programs.

(a) *Applicability.* The provisions of this section apply except in either of the following circumstances:
    (1) A Utilization and Quality Control Quality Improvement Organization (QIO) has assumed binding review for the hospital.

(2) CMS has determined that the UR procedures established by the State under title XIX of the Act are superior to the procedures required in this section, and has required hospitals in that State to meet the UR plan requirements under §§456.50 through 456.245 of this chapter.

(b) *Standard: Composition of utilization review committee.* A UR committee consisting of two or more practitioners must carry out the UR function. At least two of the members of the committee must be doctors of medicine or osteopathy. The other members may be any of the other types of practitioners specified in §482.12(c)(1).

(1) Except as specified in paragraphs (b) (2) and (3) of this section, the UR committee must be one of the following:

   (i) A staff committee of the institution;

   (ii) A group outside the institution—

       (A) Established by the local medical society and some or all of the hospitals in the locality; or

       (B) Established in a manner approved by CMS.

(2) If, because of the small size of the institution, it is impracticable to have a properly functioning staff committee, the UR committee must be established as specified in paragraph (b)(1)(ii) of this section.

(3) The committee's or group's reviews may not be conducted by any individual who—

   (i) Has a direct financial interest (for example, an ownership interest) in that hospital; or

   (ii) Was professionally involved in the care of the patient whose case is being reviewed.

(c) *Standard: Scope and frequency of review.*

(1) The UR plan must provide for review for Medicare and Medicaid patients with respect to the medical necessity of—

   (i)   Admissions to the institution;

   (ii) The duration of stays; and

   (iii) Professional services furnished, including drugs and biologicals.

(2) Review of admissions may be performed before, at, or after hospital admission.

(3) Except as specified in paragraph (e) of this section, reviews may be conducted on a sample basis.

(4) Hospitals that are paid for inpatient hospital services under the prospective payment system set forth in Part 412 of this chapter must conduct review of duration of stays and review of professional services as follows:

   (i) For duration of stays, these hospitals need review only cases that they reasonably assume to be outlier cases based on extended length of stay, as described in §412.80(a)(1)(i) of this chapter; and

   (ii) For professional services, these hospitals need review only cases that they reasonably assume to be outlier cases based on extraordinarily high costs, as described in §412.80(a)(1)(ii) of this chapter.

(d) *Standard: Determination regarding admissions or continued stays.*

   (1) The determination that an admission or continued stay is not medically necessary—

      (i) May be made by one member of the UR committee if the practitioner or practitioners responsible for the care of the patient, as specified of §482.12(c), concur with the determination or fail to present their views when afforded the opportunity; and

      (ii) Must be made by at least two members of the UR committee in all other cases.

   (2) Before making a determination that an admission or continued stay is not medically necessary, the UR committee must consult the practitioner or practitioners responsible for the care of the patient, as specified in §482.12(c), and afford the practitioner or practitioners the opportunity to present their views.

   (3) If the committee decides that admission to or continued stay in the hospital is not medically necessary, written notification must be given, no later than 2 days after the determination, to the hospital, the patient, and the practitioner or practitioners responsible for the care of the patient, as specified in §482.12(c);

(e) *Standard: Extended stay review.*

   (1) In hospitals that are not paid under the prospective payment system, the UR committee must make a periodic review, as specified in the UR plan, of each current inpatient receiving hospital services during a continuous period of extended duration. The scheduling of the periodic reviews may—

      (i) Be the same for all cases; or

      (ii) Differ for different classes of cases.

(2) In hospitals paid under the prospective payment system, the UR committee must review all cases reasonably assumed by the hospital to be outlier cases because the extended length of stay exceeds the threshold criteria for the diagnosis, as described in §412.80(a)(1)(i). The hospital is not required to review an extended stay that does not exceed the outlier threshold for the diagnosis.

(3) The UR committee must make the periodic review no later than 7 days after the day required in the UR plan.

(f) *Standard: Review of professional services.* The committee must review professional services provided, to determine medical necessity and to promote the most efficient use of available health facilities and services.

§ 482.41   Condition of participation: Physical environment.

The hospital must be constructed, arranged, and maintained to ensure the safety of the patient and to provide facilities for diagnosis and treatment and for special hospital services appropriate to the needs of the community.

(a) *Standard: Buildings.* The condition of the physical plant and the overall hospital environment must be developed and maintained in such a manner that the safety and well-being of patients are assured.

(1) There must be emergency power and lighting in at least the operating, recovery, intensive care, and emergency rooms, and stairwells. In all other areas not serviced by the emergency supply source, battery lamps and flashlights must be available.

(2) There must be facilities for emergency gas and water supply.

(b) *Standard: Life safety from fire.*

(1) Except as otherwise provided in this section—

(i) The hospital must meet the applicable provisions of the 2000 edition of the Life Safety Code of the National Fire Protection Association. The Director of the Office of the Federal Register has approved the NFPA 101®2000 edition of the Life Safety Code, issued January 14, 2000, for incorporation by reference in accordance with 5 U.S.C. 552(a) and 1 CFR part 51. A copy of the Code is available for inspection at the CMS Information Resource Center, 7500 Security Boulevard, Baltimore, MD or at the National Archives and Records Administration (NARA). For information on the availability of this material at NARA, call 202–741–6030, or go to: *http://www.archives.gov/federal_ register/code_of_federal_regulations/ibr_locations.html.* Copies may be obtained from the National Fire Protection Association, 1 Batterymarch Park, Quincy, MA 02269. If any changes in this edition of the Code are incorporated by reference, CMS will publish notice in the Federal Register to announce the changes.

 (ii) Chapter 19.3.6.3.2, exception number 2 of the adopted edition of the LSC does not apply to hospitals.

(2) After consideration of State survey agency findings, CMS may waive specific provisions of the Life Safety Code which, if rigidly applied, would result in unreasonable hardship upon the facility, but only if the waiver does not adversely affect the health and safety of the patients.

(3) The provisions of the Life Safety Code do not apply in a State where CMS finds that a fire and safety code imposed by State law adequately protects patients in hospitals.

(4) Beginning March 13, 2006, a hospital must be in compliance with Chapter 19.2.9, Emergency Lighting.

(5) Beginning March 13, 2006, Chapter 19.3.6.3.2, exception number 2 does not apply to hospitals.

(6) The hospital must have procedures for the proper routine storage and prompt disposal of trash.

(7) The hospital must have written fire control plans that contain provisions for prompt reporting of fires; extinguishing fires; protection of patients, personnel and guests; evacuation; and cooperation with fire fighting authorities.

(8) The hospital must maintain written evidence of regular inspection and approval by State or local fire control agencies.

(9) Notwithstanding any provisions of the 2000 edition of the Life Safety Code to the contrary, a hospital may install alcohol-based hand rub dispensers in its facility if—

 (i) Use of alcohol-based hand rub dispensers does not conflict with any State or local codes that prohibit or otherwise restrict the placement of alcohol-based hand rub dispensers in health care facilities;

 (ii) The dispensers are installed in a manner that minimizes leaks and spills that could lead to falls;

 (iii) The dispensers are installed in a manner that adequately protects against inappropriate access;

 (iv) The dispensers are installed in accordance with chapter 18.3.2.7 or chapter 19.3.2.7 of the 2000 edition of the Life Safety Code, as amended by NFPA Temporary Interim Amendment

00–1(101), issued by the Standards Council of the National Fire Protection Association on April 15, 2004. The Director of the Office of the Federal Register has approved NFPA Temporary Interim Amendment 00–1(101) for incorporation by reference in accordance with 5 U.S.C. 552(a) and 1 CFR part 51. A copy of the amendment is available for inspection at the CMS Information Resource Center, 7500 Security Boulevard, Baltimore, MD and at the Office of the Federal Register, 800 North Capitol Street NW., Suite 700, Washington, DC. Copies may be obtained from the National Fire Protection Association, 1 Batterymarch Park, Quincy, MA 02269; and

(v) The dispensers are maintained in accordance with dispenser manufacturer guidelines.

(c) *Standard: Facilities.* The hospital must maintain adequate facilities for its services.

(1) Diagnostic and therapeutic facilities must be located for the safety of patients.

(2) Facilities, supplies, and equipment must be maintained to ensure an acceptable level of safety and quality.

(3) The extent and complexity of facilities must be determined by the services offered.

(4) There must be proper ventilation, light, and temperature controls in pharmaceutical, food preparation, and other appropriate areas.

[51 FR 22042, June 17, 1986, as amended at 53 FR 11509, Apr. 7, 1988; 68 FR 1386, Jan. 10, 2003; 69 FR 49267, Aug. 11, 2004; 70 FR 15238, Mar. 25, 2005; 71 FR 55340, Sept. 22, 2006]

§ 482.42 Condition of participation: Infection control.

The hospital must provide a sanitary environment to avoid sources and transmission of infections and communicable diseases. There must be an active program for the prevention, control, and investigation of infections and communicable diseases.

(a) *Standard: Organization and policies.* A person or persons must be designated as infection control officer or officers to develop and implement policies governing control of infections and communicable diseases.

(1) The infection control officer or officers must develop a system for identifying, reporting, investigating, and controlling infections and communicable diseases of patients and personnel.

(2) The infection control officer or officers must maintain a log of incidents related to infections and communicable diseases.

(b) *Standard: Responsibilities of chief executive officer, medical staff, and director of nursing services.* The chief executive officer, the medical staff, and the director of nursing services must—

    (1) Ensure that the hospital-wide quality assurance program and training programs address problems identified by the infection control officer or officers; and

    (2) Be responsible for the implementation of successful corrective action plans in affected problem areas.

§ 482.43 Condition of participation: Discharge planning.

The hospital must have in effect a discharge planning process that applies to all patients. The hospital's policies and procedures must be specified in writing.

(a) *Standard: Identification of patients in need of discharge planning.* The hospital must identify at an early stage of hospitalization all patients who are likely to suffer adverse health consequences upon discharge if there is no adequate discharge planning.

(b) *Standard: Discharge planning evaluation.*

    (1) The hospital must provide a discharge planning evaluation to the patients identified in paragraph (a) of this section, and to other patients upon the patient's request, the request of a person acting on the patient's behalf, or the request of the physician.

    (2) A registered nurse, social worker, or other appropriately qualified personnel must develop, or supervise the development of, the evaluation.

    (3) The discharge planning evaluation must include an evaluation of the likelihood of a patient needing post- hospital services and of the availability of the services.

    (4) The discharge planning evaluation must include an evaluation of the likelihood of a patient's capacity for self-care or of the possibility of the patient being cared for in the environment from which he or she entered the hospital.

    (5) The hospital personnel must complete the evaluation on a timely basis so that appropriate arrangements for post-hospital care are made before discharge, and to avoid unnecessary delays in discharge.

    (6) The hospital must include the discharge planning evaluation in the patient's medical record for use in establishing an appropriate discharge plan and must discuss the results of the evaluation with the patient or individual acting on his or her behalf.

(c) *Standard: Discharge plan.*

    (1) A registered nurse, social worker, or other appropriately qualified personnel must develop, or supervise the development of, a discharge plan if the discharge planning evaluation indicates a need for a discharge plan.

    (2) In the absence of a finding by the hospital that a patient needs a discharge plan, the patient's physician may request a discharge plan. In such a case, the hospital must develop a discharge plan for the patient.

    (3) The hospital must arrange for the initial implementation of the patient's discharge plan.

    (4) The hospital must reassess the patient's discharge plan if there are factors that may affect continuing care needs or the appropriateness of the discharge plan.

    (5) As needed, the patient and family members or interested persons must be counseled to prepare them for post-hospital care.

    (6) The hospital must include in the discharge plan a list of HHAs or SNFs that are available to the patient, that are participating in the Medicare program, and that serve the geographic area (as defined by the HHA) in which the patient resides, or in the case of a SNF, in the geographic area requested by the patient. HHAs must request to be listed by the hospital as available.

        (i) This list must only be presented to patients for whom home health care or post-hospital extended care services are indicated and appropriate as determined by the discharge planning evaluation.

        (ii) For patients enrolled in managed care organizations, the hospital must indicate the availability of home health and posthospital extended care services through individuals and entities that have a contract with the managed care organizations.

        (iii) The hospital must document in the patient's medical record that the list was presented to the patient or to the individual acting on the patient's behalf.

    (7) The hospital, as part of the discharge planning process, must inform the patient or the patient's family of their freedom to choose among

participating Medicare providers of posthospital care services and must, when possible, respect patient and family preferences when they are expressed. The hospital must not specify or otherwise limit the qualified providers that are available to the patient.

(8) The discharge plan must identify any HHA or SNF to which the patient is referred in which the hospital has a disclosable financial interest, as specified by the Secretary, and any HHA or SNF that has a disclosable financial interest in a hospital under Medicare. Financial interests that are disclosable under Medicare are determined in accordance with the provisions of Part 420, Subpart C, of this chapter.

(d) *Standard: Transfer or referral.* The hospital must transfer or refer patients, along with necessary medical information, to appropriate facilities, agencies, or outpatient services, as needed, for followup or ancillary care.

(e) *Standard: Reassessment.* The hospital must reassess its discharge planning process on an on-going basis. The reassessment must include a review of discharge plans to ensure that they are responsive to discharge needs.

[59 FR 64152, Dec. 13, 1994, as amended at 69 FR 49268, Aug. 11, 2004]

§ 482.45 *Condition of participation: Organ, tissue, and eye procurement.*

(a) *Standard: Organ procurement responsibilities.* The hospital must have and implement written protocols that:

(1) Incorporate an agreement with an OPO designated under part 486 of this chapter, under which it must notify, in a timely manner, the OPO or a third party designated by the OPO of individuals whose death is imminent or who have died in the hospital. The OPO determines medical suitability for organ donation and, in the absence of alternative arrangements by the hospital, the OPO determines medical suitability for tissue and eye donation, using the definition of potential tissue and eye donor and the notification protocol developed in consultation with the tissue and eye banks identified by the hospital for this purpose;

(2) Incorporate an agreement with at least one tissue bank and at least one eye bank to cooperate in the retrieval, processing, preservation, storage and distribution of tissues and eyes, as may be appropriate to assure that all usable tissues and eyes are obtained from potential

donors, insofar as such an agreement does not interfere with organ procurement;

(3) Ensure, in collaboration with the designated OPO, that the family of each potential donor is informed of its options to donate organs, tissues, or eyes or to decline to donate. The individual designated by the hospital to initiate the request to the family must be an organ procurement representative or a designated requestor. A designated requestor is an individual who has completed a course offered or approved by the OPO and designed in conjunction with the tissue and eye bank community in the methodology for approaching potential donor families and requesting organ or tissue donation;

(4) Encourage discretion and sensitivity with respect to the circumstances, views, and beliefs of the families of potential donors;

(5) Ensure that the hospital works cooperatively with the designated OPO, tissue bank and eye bank in educating staff on donation issues, reviewing death records to improve identification of potential donors, and maintaining potential donors while necessary testing and placement of potential donated organs, tissues, and eyes take place.

(b) *Standard: Organ transplantation responsibilities.*

(1) A hospital in which organ transplants are performed must be a member of the Organ Procurement and Transplantation Network (OPTN) established and operated in accordance with section 372 of the Public Health Service (PHS) Act (42 U.S.C. 274) and abide by its rules. The term "rules of the OPTN" means those rules provided for in regulations issued by the Secretary in accordance with section 372 of the PHS Act which are enforceable under 42 CFR 121.10. No hospital is considered to be out of compliance with section 1138(a)(1)(B) of the Act, or with the requirements of this paragraph, unless the Secretary has given the OPTN formal notice that he or she approves the decision to exclude the hospital from the OPTN and has notified the hospital in writing.

(2) For purposes of these standards, the term "organ" means a human kidney, liver, heart, lung, or pancreas.

(3) If a hospital performs any type of transplants, it must provide organ-transplant-related data, as requested by the OPTN, the Scientific Registry, and the OPOs. The hospital must also provide such data directly to the Department when requested by the Secretary.

[63 FR 33875, June 22, 1998]

Subpart D—Optional Hospital Services

§ 482.51   Condition of participation: Surgical services.

If the hospital provides surgical services, the services must be well organized and provided in accordance with acceptable standards of practice. If outpatient surgical services are offered the services must be consistent in quality with inpatient care in accordance with the complexity of services offered.

(a) *Standard: Organization and staffing.* The organization of the surgical services must be appropriate to the scope of the services offered.

    (1) The operating rooms must be supervised by an experienced registered nurse or a doctor of medicine or osteopathy.

    (2) Licensed practical nurses (LPNs) and surgical technologists (operating room technicians) may serve as "scrub nurses" under the supervision of a registered nurse.

    (3) Qualified registered nurses may perform circulating duties in the operating room. In accordance with applicable State laws and approved medical staff policies and procedures, LPNs and surgical technologists may assist in circulatory duties under the surpervision of a qualified registered nurse who is immediately available to respond to emergencies.

    (4) Surgical privileges must be delineated for all practitioners performing surgery in accordance with the competencies of each practitioner. The surgical service must maintain a roster of practitioners specifying the surgical privileges of each practitioner.

(b) *Standard: Delivery of service.* Surgical services must be consistent with needs and resources. Policies governing surgical care must be designed to assure the achievement and maintenance of high standards of medical practice and patient care.

    (1) Prior to surgery or a procedure requiring anesthesia services and except in the case of emergencies:

        (i) A medical history and physical examination must be completed and documented no more than 30 days before or 24 hours after admission or registration.

        (ii) An updated examination of the patient, including any changes in the patient's condition, must be completed and documented within 24 hours after admission or registration when the medical history and physical examination are completed within 30 days before admission or registration.

(2) A properly executed informed consent form for the operation must be in the patient's chart before surgery, except in emergencies.

(3) The following equipment must be available to the operating room suites: call-in-system, cardiac monitor, resuscitator, defibrillator, aspirator, and tracheotomy set.

(4) There must be adequate provisions for immediate post-operative care.

(5) The operating room register must be complete and up-to-date.

(6) An operative report describing techniques, findings, and tissues removed or altered must be written or dictated immediately following surgery and signed by the surgeon.

[51 FR 22042, June 17, 1986, as amended at 72 FR 66933, Nov. 27, 2007]

§ 482.52   Condition of participation: Anesthesia services.

If the hospital furnishes anesthesia services, they must be provided in a well-organized manner under the direction of a qualified doctor of medicine or osteopathy. The service is responsible for all anesthesia administered in the hospital.

(a) *Standard: Organization and staffing.* The organization of anesthesia services must be appropriate to the scope of the services offered. Anesthesia must be administered only by—

(1) A qualified anesthesiologist;

(2) A doctor of medicine or osteopathy (other than an anesthesiologist);

(3) A dentist, oral surgeon, or podiatrist who is qualified to administer anesthesia under State law;

(4) A certified registered nurse anesthetist (CRNA), as defined in §410.69(b) of this chapter, who, unless exempted in accordance with paragraph (c) of this section, is under the supervision of the operating practitioner or of an anesthesiologist who is immediately available if needed; or

(5) An anesthesiologist's assistant, as defined in §410.69(b) of this chapter, who is under the supervision of an anesthesiologist who is immediately available if needed.

(b) *Standard: Delivery of services.* Anesthesia services must be consistent with needs and resources. Policies on anesthesia procedures must include the delineation of preanesthesia and post anesthesia responsibilities.

The policies must ensure that the following are provided for each patient:

(1) A preanesthesia evaluation completed and documented by an individual qualified to administer anesthesia, as specified in paragraph (a) of this section, performed within 48 hours prior to surgery or a procedure requiring anesthesia services.

(2) An intraoperative anesthesia record.

(3) A postanesthesia evaluation completed and documented by an individual qualified to administer anesthesia, as specified in paragraph (a) of this section, no later than 48 hours after surgery or a procedure requiring anesthesia services. The postanesthesia evaluation for anesthesia recovery must be completed in accordance with State law and with hospital policies and procedures that have been approved by the medical staff and that reflect current standards of anesthesia care.

(c) *Standard: State exemption.*

(1) A hospital may be exempted from the requirement for physician supervision of CRNAs as described in paragraph (a)(4) of this section, if the State in which the hospital is located submits a letter to CMS signed by the Governor, following consultation with the State's Boards of Medicine and Nursing, requesting exemption from physician supervision of CRNAs. The letter from the Governor must attest that he or she has consulted with State Boards of Medicine and Nursing about issues related to access to and the quality of anesthesia services in the State and has concluded that it is in the best interests of the State's citizens to opt-out of the current physician supervision requirement, and that the opt-out is consistent with State law.

(2) The request for exemption and recognition of State laws, and the withdrawal of the request may be submitted at any time, and are effective upon submission.

[51 FR 22042, June 17, 1986 as amended at 57 FR 33900, July 31, 1992; 66 FR 56769, Nov. 13, 2001; 71 FR 68694, Nov. 27, 2006; 72 FR 66934, Nov. 27, 2007]

§ 482.53 Condition of participation: Nuclear medicine services.

If the hospital provides nuclear medicine services, those services must meet the needs of the patients in accordance with acceptable standards of practice.

(a) *Standard: Organization and staffing.* The organization of the nuclear medicine service must be appropriate to the scope and complexity of the services offered.

    (1) There must be a director who is a doctor of medicine or osteopathy qualified in nuclear medicine.

    (2) The qualifications, training, functions, and responsibilities of nuclear medicine personnel must be specified by the service director and approved by the medical staff.

(b) *Standard: Delivery of service.* Radioactive materials must be prepared, labeled, used, transported, stored, and disposed of in accordance with acceptable standards of practice.

    (1) In-house preparation of radiopharmaceuticals is by, or under, the direct supervision of an appropriately trained registered pharmacist or a doctor of medicine or osteopathy.

    (2) There is proper storage and disposal of radioactive material.

    (3) If laboratory tests are performed in the nuclear medicine service, the service must meet the applicable requirement for laboratory services specified in §482.27.

(c) *Standard: Facilities.* Equipment and supplies must be appropriate for the types of nuclear medicine services offered and must be maintained for safe and efficient performance. The equipment must be—

    (1) Maintained in safe operating condition; and

    (2) Inspected, tested, and calibrated at least annually by qualified personnel.

(d) *Standard: Records.* The hospital must maintain signed and dated reports of nuclear medicine interpretations, consultations, and procedures.

    (1) The hospital must maintain copies of nuclear medicine reports for at least 5 years.

    (2) The practitioner approved by the medical staff to interpret diagnostic procedures must sign and date the interpretation of these tests.

    (3) The hospital must maintain records of the receipt and disposition of radiopharmaceuticals.

    (4) Nuclear medicine services must be ordered only by practitioner whose scope of Federal or State licensure and whose defined staff privileges allow such referrals.

[51 FR 22042, June 17, 1986, as amended at 57 FR 7136, Feb. 28, 1992]

§ 482.54 Condition of participation: Outpatient services.

If the hospital provides outpatient services, the services must meet the needs of the patients in accordance with acceptable standards of practice.

(a) *Standard: Organization.* Outpatient services must be appropriately organized and integrated with inpatient services.

(b) *Standard: Personnel.* The hospitals must—

    (1) Assign an individual to be responsible for outpatient services; and

    (2) Have appropriate professional and nonprofessional personnel available.

§ 482.55 Condition of participation: Emergency services.

The hospital must meet the emergency needs of patients in accordance with acceptable standards of practice.

(a) *Standard: Organization and direction.* If emergency services are provided at the hospital—

    (1) The services must be organized under the direction of a qualified member of the medical staff;

    (2) The services must be integrated with other departments of the hospital;

    (3) The policies and procedures governing medical care provided in the emergency service or department are established by and are a continuing responsibility of the medical staff.

(b) *Standard: Personnel.*

    (1) The emergency services must be supervised by a qualified member of the medical staff.

    (2) There must be adequate medical and nursing personnel qualified in emergency care to meet the written emergency procedures and needs anticipated by the facility.

§ 482.56 Condition of participation: Rehabilitation services.

If the hospital provides rehabilitation, physical therapy, occupational therapy, audiology, or speech pathology services, the services must be organized and staffed to ensure the health and safety of patients.

(a) *Standard: Organization and staffing.* The organization of the service must be appropriate to the scope of the services offered.

(1) The director of the services must have the necessary knowledge, experience, and capabilities to properly supervise and administer the services.

(2) Physical therapy, occupational therapy, speech-language pathology or audiology services, if provided, must be provided by qualified physical therapists, physical therapist assistants, occupational therapists, occupational therapy assistants, speech-language pathologists, or audiologists as defined in part 484 of this chapter.

(b) *Standard: Delivery of services.* Services must only be provided under the orders of a qualified and licensed practitioner who is responsible for the care of the patient, acting within his or her scope of practice under State law, and who is authorized by the hospital's medical staff to order the services in accordance with hospital policies and procedures and State laws.

(1) All rehabilitation services orders must be documented in the patient's medical record in accordance with the requirements at §482.24.

(2) The provision of care and the personnel qualifications must be in accordance with national acceptable standards of practice and must also meet the requirements of §409.17 of this chapter.

[51 FR 22042, June 17, 1986, as amended at 72 FR 66406, Nov. 27, 2007; 75 FR 50418, Aug. 16, 2010]

§ 482.57   Condition of participation: Respiratory care services.

The hospital must meet the needs of the patients in accordance with acceptable standards of practice. The following requirements apply if the hospital provides respiratory care service.

(a) *Standard: Organization and Staffing.* The organization of the respiratory care services must be appropriate to the scope and complexity of the services offered.

(1) There must be a director of respiratory care services who is a doctor of medicine or osteopathy with the knowledge experience, and capabilities to supervise and administer the service properly. The director may serve on either a full-time or part-time basis.

(2) There must be adequate numbers of respiratory therapists, respiratory therapy technicians, and other personnel who meet the qualifications specified by the medical staff, consistent with State law.

(b) *Standard: Delivery of Services.* Services must be delivered in accordance with medical staff directives.

   (1) Personnel qualified to perform specific procedures and the amount of supervision required for personnel to carry out specific procedures must be designated in writing.

   (2) If blood gases or other laboratory tests are performed in the respiratory care unit, the unit must meet the applicable requirements for laboratory services specified in §482.27.

   (3) Services must only be provided under the orders of a qualified and licensed practitioner who is responsible for the care of the patient, acting within his or her scope of practice under State law, and who is authorized by the hospital's medical staff to order the services in accordance with hospital policies and procedures and State laws.

   (4) All respiratory care services orders must be documented in the patient's medical record in accordance with the requirements at §482.24.

[51 FR 22042, June 17, 1986; 51 FR 27848, Aug. 4, 1986, as amended at 57 FR 7136, Feb. 28, 1992; 75 FR 50418, Aug. 16, 2010]

Subpart E—Requirements for Specialty Hospitals

Source: 72 FR 15273, Mar. 30, 2007, unless otherwise noted.

§ 482.60 Special provisions applying to psychiatric hospitals.

Psychiatric hospital must—

(a) Be primarily engaged in providing, by or under the supervision of a doctor of medicine or osteopathy, psychiatric services for the diagnosis and treatment of mentally ill persons;

(b) Meet the conditions of participation specified in §§482.1 through 482.23 and §§482.25 through 482.57;

(c) Maintain clinical records on all patients, including records sufficient to permit CMS to determine the degree and intensity of treatment furnished to Medicare beneficiaries, as specified in §482.61; and

(d) Meet the staffing requirements specified in §482.62.

[72 FR 60788, Oct. 26, 2007]

§ 482.61 Condition of participation: Special medical record requirements for psychiatric hospitals.

The medical records maintained by a psychiatric hospital must permit determination of the degree and intensity of the treatment provided to individuals who are furnished services in the institution.

(a) *Standard: Development of assessment/diagnostic data.* Medical records must stress the psychiatric components of the record, including history of findings and treatment provided for the psychiatric condition for which the patient is hospitalized.

    (1) The identification data must include the patient's legal status.

    (2) A provisional or admitting diagnosis must be made on every patient at the time of admission, and must include the diagnoses of inter-current diseases as well as the psychiatric diagnoses.

    (3) The reasons for admission must be clearly documented as stated by the patient and/or others significantly involved.

    (4) The social service records, including reports of interviews with patients, family members, and others, must provide an assessment of home plans and family attitudes, and community resource contacts as well as a social history.

    (5) When indicated, a complete neurological examination must be recorded at the time of the admission physical examination.

(b) *Standard: Psychiatric evaluation.* Each patient must receive a psychiatric evaluation that must—

    (1) Be completed within 60 hours of admission;

    (2) Include a medical history;

    (3) Contain a record of mental status;

    (4) Note the onset of illness and the circumstances leading to admission;

    (5) Describe attitudes and behavior;

    (6) Estimate intellectual functioning, memory functioning, and orientation; and

    (7) Include an inventory of the patient's assets in descriptive, not interpretative, fashion.

(c) *Standard: Treatment plan.*

    (1) Each patient must have an individual comprehensive treatment plan that must be based on an inventory of the patient's strengths and disabilities. The written plan must include—

        (i) A substantiated diagnosis;

        (ii) Short-term and long-range goals;

(iii) The specific treatment modalities utilized;

(iv) The responsibilities of each member of the treatment team; and

(v) Adequate documentation to justify the diagnosis and the treatment and rehabilitation activities carried out.

(2) The treatment received by the patient must be documented in such a way to assure that all active therapeutic efforts are included.

(d) *Standard: Recording progress.* Progress notes must be recorded by the doctor of medicine or osteopathy responsible for the care of the patient as specified in §482.12(c), nurse, social worker and, when appropriate, others significantly involved in active treatment modalities. The frequency of progress notes is determined by the condition of the patient but must be recorded at least weekly for the first 2 months and at least once a month thereafter and must contain recommendations for revisions in the treatment plan as indicated as well as precise assessment of the patient's progress in accordance with the original or revised treatment plan.

(e) *Standard: Discharge planning and discharge summary.* The record of each patient who has been discharged must have a discharge summary that includes a recapitulation of the patient's hospitalization and recommendations from appropriate services concerning follow-up or aftercare as well as a brief summary of the patient's condition on discharge.

[72 FR 60788, Oct. 26, 2007]

§ 482.62 Condition of participation: Special staff requirements for psychiatric hospitals.

The hospital must have adequate numbers of qualified professional and supportive staff to evaluate patients, formulate written, individualized comprehensive treatment plans, provide active treatment measures, and engage in discharge planning.

(a) *Standard: Personnel.* The hospital must employ or undertake to provide adequate numbers of qualified professional, technical, and consultative personnel to:

(1) Evaluate patients;

(2) Formulate written individualized, comprehensive treatment plans;

(3) Provide active treatment measures; and

(4) Engage in discharge planning.

(b) *Standard: Director of inpatient psychiatric services; medical staff.* Inpatient psychiatric services must be under the supervision of a clinical director, service chief, or equivalent who is qualified to provide the leadership required for an intensive treatment program. The number and qualifications of doctors of medicine and osteopathy must be adequate to provide essential psychiatric services.

  (1) The clinical director, service chief, or equivalent must meet the training and experience requirements for examination by the American Board of Psychiatry and Neurology or the American Osteopathic Board of Neurology and Psychiatry.

  (2) The director must monitor and evaluate the quality and appropriateness of services and treatment provided by the medical staff.

(c) *Standard: Availability of medical personnel.* Doctors of medicine or osteopathy and other appropriate professional personnel must be available to provide necessary medical and surgical diagnostic and treatment services. If medical and surgical diagnostic and treatment services are not available within the institution, the institution must have an agreement with an outside source of these services to ensure that they are immediately available or a satisfactory agreement must be established for transferring patients to a general hospital that participates in the Medicare program.

(d) *Standard: Nursing services.* The hospital must have a qualified director of psychiatric nursing services. In addition to the director of nursing, there must be adequate numbers of registered nurses, licensed practical nurses, and mental health workers to provide nursing care necessary under each patient's active treatment program and to maintain progress notes on each patient.

  (1) The director of psychiatric nursing services must be a registered nurse who has a master's degree in psychiatric or mental health nursing, or its equivalent from a school of nursing accredited by the National League for Nursing, or be qualified by education and experience in the care of the mentally ill. The director must demonstrate competence to participate in interdisciplinary formulation of individual treatment plans; to give skilled nursing care and therapy; and to direct, monitor, and evaluate the nursing care furnished.

  (2) The staffing pattern must insure the availability of a registered professional nurse 24 hours each day. There must be adequate numbers of registered nurses, licensed practical nurses, and mental health workers to provide the nursing care necessary under each patient's active treatment program.

(e) *Standard: Psychological services.* The hospital must provide or have available psychological services to meet the needs of the patients.

(f) *Standard: Social services.* There must be a director of social services who monitors and evaluates the quality and appropriateness of social services furnished. The services must be furnished in accordance with accepted standards of practice and established policies and procedures.

    (1) The director of the social work department or service must have a master's degree from an accredited school of social work or must be qualified by education and experience in the social services needs of the mentally ill. If the director does not hold a masters degree in social work, at least one staff member must have this qualification.

    (2) Social service staff responsibilities must include, but are not limited to, participating in discharge planning, arranging for follow-up care, and developing mechanisms for exchange of appropriate, information with sources outside the hospital.

(g) *Standard: Therapeutic activities.* The hospital must provide a therapeutic activities program.

    (1) The program must be appropriate to the needs and interests of patients and be directed toward restoring and maintaining optimal levels of physical and psychosocial functioning.

    (2) The number of qualified therapists, support personnel, and consultants must be adequate to provide comprehensive therapeutic activities consistent with each patient's active treatment program.

[72 FR 60788, Oct. 26, 2007]

§ 482.66 Special requirements for hospital providers of long-term care services ("swing-beds").

A hospital that has a Medicare provider agreement must meet the following requirements in order to be granted an approval from CMS to provide posthospital extended care services, as specified in §409.30 of this chapter, and be reimbursed as a swing-bed hospital as specified in §413.114 of this chapter:

(a) *Eligibility.* A hospital must meet the following eligibility requirements:

    (1) The facility has fewer than 100 hospital beds, excluding beds for newborns and beds in intensive care type inpatient units (for eligibility of hospitals with distinct parts electing the optional reimbursement method, see §413.24(d)(5) of this chapter).

(2) The hospital is located in a rural area. This includes all areas not delineated as "urbanized" areas by the Census Bureau, based on the most recent census.

(3) The hospital does not have in effect a 24-hour nursing waiver granted under §488.54(c) of this chapter.

(4) The hospital has not had a swing-bed approval terminated within the two years previous to application.

(b) *Skilled nursing facility services* . The facility is substantially in compliance with the following skilled nursing facility requirements contained in subpart B of part 483 of this chapter.

(1) Resident rights (§483.10 (b)(3), (b)(4), (b)(5), (b)(6), (d), (e), (h), (i), (j)(1)(vii), (j)(1)(viii), (l), and (m)).

(2) Admission, transfer, and discharge rights (§483.12 (a)(1), (a)(2), (a)(3), (a)(4), (a)(5), (a)(6), and (a)(7)).

(3) Resident behavior and facility practices (§483.13).

(4) Patient activities (§483.15(f)).

(5) Social services (§483.15(g)).

(6) Discharge planning (§483.20(e)).

(7) Specialized rehabilitative services (§483.45).

(8) Dental services (§483.55).

[72 FR 60788, Oct. 26, 2007]

§ 482.68 Special requirements for transplant centers.

A transplant center located within a hospital that has a Medicare provider agreement must meet the conditions of participation specified in §§482.72 through 482.104 in order to be granted approval from CMS to provide transplant services.

(a) Unless specified otherwise, the conditions of participation at §§482.72 through 482.104 apply to heart, heart-lung, intestine, kidney, liver, lung, and pancreas centers.

(b) In addition to meeting the conditions of participation specified in §§482.72 through 482.104, a transplant center must also meet the conditions of participation specified in §§482.1 through 482.57.

§ 482.70 Definitions.

As used in this subpart, the following definitions apply:

Adverse event means an untoward, undesirable, and usually unanticipated event that causes death or serious injury, or the risk thereof. As applied to transplant centers, examples of adverse events include (but are not limited to) serious medical complications or death caused by living donation; unintentional transplantation of organs of mismatched blood types; transplantation of organs to unintended recipients; and unintended transmission of infectious disease to a recipient.

End-Stage Renal Disease (ESRD) means that stage of renal impairment that appears irreversible and permanent, and requires a regular course of dialysis or kidney transplantation to maintain life.

ESRD Network means all Medicare-approved ESRD facilities in a designated geographic area specified by CMS.

Heart-Lung transplant center means a transplant center that is located in a hospital with an existing Medicare-approved heart transplant center and an existing Medicare-approved lung center that performs combined heart-lung transplants.

Intestine transplant center means a Medicare-approved liver transplant center that performs intestine transplants, combined liver-intestine transplants, or multivisceral transplants.

Network organization means the administrative governing body to the network and liaison to the Federal government.

Pancreas transplant center means a Medicare-approved kidney transplant center that performs pancreas transplants alone or subsequent to a kidney transplant as well as kidney-pancreas transplants.

Transplant center means an organ-specific transplant program (as defined in this rule) within a transplant hospital (for example, a hospital's lung transplant program may also be referred to as the hospital's lung transplant center).

Transplant hospital means a hospital that furnishes organ transplants and other medical and surgical specialty services required for the care of transplant patients.

Transplant program means a component within a transplant hospital (as defined in this rule) that provides transplantation of a particular type of organ.

General Requirements for Transplant Centers

§ 482.72   Condition of participation: OPTN membership.

A transplant center must be located in a transplant hospital that is a member of and abides by the rules and requirements of the Organ Procurement and Transplantation Network (OPTN) established and operated in accordance with section 372 of the Public Health Service (PHS) Act (42 U.S.C. 274).

The term "rules and requirements of the OPTN" means those rules and requirements approved by the Secretary pursuant to §121.4 of this title. No hospital that provides transplantation services shall be deemed to be out of compliance with section 1138(a)(1)(B) of the Act or this section unless the Secretary has given the OPTN formal notice that he or she approves the decision to exclude the transplant hospital from the OPTN and also has notified the transplant hospital in writing.

§ 482.74 Condition of participation: Notification to CMS.

(a) A transplant center must notify CMS immediately of any significant changes related to the center's transplant program or changes that could affect its compliance with the conditions of participation. Instances in which CMS should receive information for follow up, as appropriate, include, but are not limited to:

 (1) Change in key staff members of the transplant team, such as a change in the individual the transplant center designated to the OPTN as the center's "primary transplant surgeon" or "primary transplant physician;"

 (2) A decrease in the center's number of transplants or survival rates that could result in the center being out of compliance with §482.82;

 (3) Termination of an agreement between the hospital in which the transplant center is located and an OPO for the recovery and receipt of organs as required by section 482.100; and

 (4) Inactivation of the transplant center.

(b) Upon receiving notification of significant changes, CMS will follow up with the transplant center as appropriate, including (but not limited to):

 (1) Requesting additional information;

 (2) Analyzing the information; or

 (3) Conducting an on-site review.

§ 482.76 Condition of participation: Pediatric Transplants.

A transplant center that seeks Medicare approval to provide transplantation services to pediatric patients must submit to CMS a request specifically for Medicare approval to perform pediatric transplants using the procedures described at §488.61 of this chapter.

(a) Except as specified in paragraph (d) of this section, a center requesting Medicare approval to perform pediatric transplants must meet all the conditions of participation at §§482.72 through 482.74 and §§482.80 through 482.104 with respect to its pediatric patients.

(b) A center that performs 50 percent or more of its transplants in a 12-month period on adult patients must be approved to perform adult transplants in order to be approved to perform pediatric transplants.

    (1) Loss of Medicare approval to perform adult transplants, whether voluntary or involuntary, will result in loss of the center's approval to perform pediatric transplants.

    (2) Loss of Medicare approval to perform pediatric transplants, whether voluntary or involuntary, may trigger a review of the center's Medicare approval to perform adult transplants.

(c) A center that performs 50 percent or more of its transplants in a 12-month period on pediatric patients must be approved to perform pediatric transplants in order to be approved to perform adult transplants.

    (1) Loss of Medicare approval to perform pediatric transplants, whether voluntary or involuntary, will result in loss of the center's approval to perform adult transplants.

    (2) Loss of Medicare approval to perform adult transplants, whether voluntary or involuntary, may trigger a review of the center's Medicare approval to perform pediatric transplants.

    (3) A center that performs 50 percent or more of its transplants on pediatric patients in a 12-month period is not required to meet the clinical experience requirements prior to its request for approval as a pediatric transplant center.

(d) Instead of meeting all conditions of participation at §§482.72 through 482.74 and §§482.80 through 482.104, a heart transplant center that wishes to provide transplantation services to pediatric heart patients may be approved to perform pediatric heart transplants by meeting the Omnibus Budget Reconciliation Act of 1987 criteria in section 4009(b) (Pub. L. 100–203), as follows:

    (1) The center's pediatric transplant program must be operated jointly by the hospital and another facility that is Medicare-approved;

    (2) The unified program shares the same transplant surgeons and quality improvement program (including oversight committee, patient protocol, and patient selection criteria); and

    (3) The center demonstrates to the satisfaction of the Secretary that it is able to provide the specialized facilities, services, and personnel that are required by pediatric heart transplant patients.

Transplant Center Data Submission, Clinical Experience, and Outcome Requirements

§ 482.80   Condition of participation: Data submission, clinical experience, and outcome requirements for initial approval of transplant centers.

Except as specified in paragraph (d) of this section, and §488.61 of this chapter, transplant centers must meet all data submission, clinical experience, and outcome requirements to be granted initial approval by CMS.

(a) *Standard: Data submission.* No later than 90 days after the due date established by the OPTN, a transplant center must submit to the OPTN at least 95 percent of required data on all transplants (deceased and living donor) it has performed. Required data submissions include, but are not limited to, submission of the appropriate OPTN forms for transplant candidate registration, transplant recipient registration and follow-up, and living donor registration and follow-up.

(b) *Standard: Clinical experience.* To be considered for initial approval, an organ-specific transplant center must generally perform 10 transplants over a 12-month period.

(c) *Standard: Outcome requirements.* CMS will review outcomes for all transplants performed at a center, including outcomes for living donor transplants, if applicable. Except for lung transplants, CMS will review adult and pediatric outcomes separately when a center requests Medicare approval to perform both adult and pediatric transplants.

    (1) CMS will compare each transplant center's observed number of patient deaths and graft failures 1-year post-transplant to the center's expected number of patient deaths and graft failures 1-year post-transplant using the data contained in the most recent Scientific Registry of Transplant Recipients (SRTR) center-specific report.

    (2) The required number of transplants must have been performed during the time frame reported in the most recent SRTR center-specific report.

    (3) CMS will not consider a center's patient and graft survival rates to be acceptable if:

        (i) A center's observed patient survival rate or observed graft survival rate is lower than its expected patient survival rate or expected graft survival rate; and

        (ii) All three of the following thresholds are crossed over:

            (A) The one-sided p-value is less than 0.05,

(B) The number of observed events (patient deaths or graft failures) minus the number of expected events is greater than 3, and

(C) The number of observed events divided by the number of expected events is greater than 1.5.

(d) *Exceptions.*

(1) A heart-lung transplant center is not required to comply with the clinical experience requirements in paragraph (b) of this section or the outcome requirements in paragraph (c) of this section for heart-lung transplants performed at the center.

(2) An intestine transplant center is not required to comply with the outcome performance requirements in paragraph (c) of this section for intestine, combined liver-intestine or multivisceral transplants performed at the center.

(3) A pancreas transplant center is not required to comply with the clinical experience requirements in paragraph (b) of this section or the outcome requirements in paragraph (c) of this section for pancreas transplants performed at the center.

(4) A center that is requesting initial Medicare approval to perform pediatric transplants is not required to comply with the clinical experience requirements in paragraph (b) of this section prior to its request for approval as a pediatric transplant center.

(5) A kidney transplant center that is not Medicare-approved on the effective date of this rule is required to perform at least 3 transplants over a 12-month period prior to its request for initial approval.

§ 482.82 Condition of participation: Data submission, clinical experience, and outcome requirements for re-approval of transplant centers.

Except as specified in paragraph (d) of this section, and §488.61 of this chapter, transplant centers must meet all data submission, clinical experience, and outcome requirements in order to be re-approved.

(a) *Standard: Data submission.* No later than 90 days after the due date established by the OPTN, a transplant center must submit to the OPTN at least 95 percent of the required data submissions on all transplants (deceased and living donor) it has performed over the 3-year approval period. Required data submissions include, but are not limited to, submission of the appropriate OPTN forms for transplant candidate registration, transplant recipient registration and follow-up, and living donor registration and follow-up.

(b) *Standard: Clinical experience.* To be considered for re-approval, an organ-specific transplant center must generally perform an average of 10 transplants per year during the re-approval period.

(c) *Standard: Outcome requirements.* CMS will review outcomes for all transplants performed at a center, including outcomes for living donor transplants if applicable. Except for lung transplants, CMS will review adult and pediatric outcomes separately when a center requests Medicare approval to perform both adult and pediatric transplants.

    (1) CMS will compare each transplant center's observed number of patient deaths and graft failures 1-year post-transplant to the center's expected number of patient deaths and graft failures 1-year post-transplant using data contained in the most recent SRTR center-specific report.

    (2) The required number of transplants must have been performed during the time frame reported in the most recent SRTR center-specific report.

    (3) CMS will not consider a center's patient and graft survival rates to be acceptable if:

        (i) A center's observed patient survival rate or observed graft survival rate is lower than its expected patient survival rate and graft survival rate; and

        (ii) All three of the following thresholds are crossed over:

            (A) The one-sided p-value is less than 0.05,

            (B) The number of observed events (patient deaths or graft failures) minus the number of expected events is greater than 3, and

            (C) The number of observed events divided by the number of expected events is greater than 1.5.

(d) *Exceptions.*

    (1) A heart-lung transplant center is not required to comply with the clinical experience requirements in paragraph (b) of this section or the outcome requirements in paragraph (c) of this section for heart-lung transplants performed at the center.

    (2) An intestine transplant center is not required to comply with the outcome requirements in paragraph (c) of this section for intestine, combined liver-intestine, and multivisceral transplants performed at the center.

    (3) A pancreas transplant center is not required to comply with the clinical experience requirements in paragraph (b) of this section or the

outcome requirements in paragraph (c) of this section for pancreas transplants performed at the center.

(4) A center that is approved to perform pediatric transplants is not required to comply with the clinical experience requirements in paragraph (b) of this section to be re-approved.

Transplant Center Process Requirements

§ 482.90 Condition of participation: Patient and living donor selection.

The transplant center must use written patient selection criteria in determining a patient's suitability for placement on the waiting list or a patient's suitability for transplantation. If a center performs living donor transplants, the center also must use written donor selection criteria in determining the suitability of candidates for donation.

(a) *Standard: Patient selection.* Patient selection criteria must ensure fair and non-discriminatory distribution of organs.
  (1) Prior to placement on the center's waiting list, a prospective transplant candidate must receive a psychosocial evaluation, if possible.
  (2) Before a transplant center places a transplant candidate on its waiting list, the candidate's medical record must contain documentation that the candidate's blood type has been determined.
  (3) When a patient is placed on a center's waiting list or is selected to receive a transplant, the center must document in the patient's medical record the patient selection criteria used.
  (4) A transplant center must provide a copy of its patient selection criteria to a transplant patient, or a dialysis facility, as requested by a patient or a dialysis facility.
(b) *Standard: Living donor selection.* The living donor selection criteria must be consistent with the general principles of medical ethics. Transplant centers must:
  (1) Ensure that a prospective living donor receives a medical and psychosocial evaluation prior to donation,
  (2) Document in the living donor's medical records the living donor's suitability for donation, and
  (3) Document that the living donor has given informed consent, as required under §482.102.

§ 482.92 Condition of participation: Organ recovery and receipt.

Transplant centers must have written protocols for validation of donor-recipient blood type and other vital data for the deceased organ recovery, organ receipt, and living donor organ transplantation processes. The transplanting surgeon at the transplant center is responsible for ensuring the medical suitability of donor organs for transplantation into the intended recipient.

(a) *Standard: Organ recovery.* When the identity of an intended transplant recipient is known and the transplant center sends a team to recover the organ(s), the transplant center's recovery team must review and compare the donor data with the recipient blood type and other vital data before organ recovery takes place.

(b) *Standard: Organ receipt.* After an organ arrives at a transplant center, prior to transplantation, the transplanting surgeon and another licensed health care professional must verify that the donor's blood type and other vital data are compatible with transplantation of the intended recipient

(c) *Standard: Living donor transplantation.* If a center performs living donor transplants, the transplanting surgeon and another licensed health care professional at the center must verify that the living donor's blood type and other vital data are compatible with transplantation of the intended recipient immediately before the removal of the donor organ(s) and, if applicable, prior to the removal of the recipient's organ(s).

§ 482.94 Condition of participation: Patient and living donor management.

Transplant centers must have written patient management policies for the transplant and discharge phases of transplantation. If a transplant center performs living donor transplants, the center also must have written donor management policies for the donor evaluation, donation, and discharge phases of living organ donation.

(a) *Standard: Patient and living donor care.* The transplant center's patient and donor management policies must ensure that:

   (1) Each transplant patient is under the care of a multidisciplinary patient care team coordinated by a physician throughout the transplant and discharge phases of transplantation; and

   (2) If a center performs living donor transplants, each living donor is under the care of a multidisciplinary patient care team coordinated by a physician throughout the donor evaluation, donation, and discharge phases of donation.

(b) *Standard: Waiting list management.* Transplant centers must keep their waiting lists up to date on an ongoing basis, including:

   (1) Updating of waiting list patients' clinical information;

   (2) Removing patients from the center's waiting list if a patient receives a transplant or dies, or if there is any other reason the patient should no longer be on a center's waiting list; and

   (3) Notifying the OPTN no later than 24 hours after a patient's removal from the center's waiting list.

(c) *Standard: Patient records.* Transplant centers must maintain up-to-date and accurate patient management records for each patient who receives an evaluation for placement on a center's waiting list and who is admitted for organ transplantation.

   (1) For each patient who receives an evaluation for placement on a center's waiting list, the center must document in the patient's record that the patient (and in the case of a kidney patient, the patient's usual dialysis facility) has been informed of his or her transplant status, including notification of:

     (i) The patient's placement on the center's waiting list;

     (ii) The center's decision not to place the patient on its waiting list; or

     (iii) The center's inability to make a determination regarding the patient's placement on its waiting list because further clinical testing or documentation is needed.

   (2) If a patient on the waiting list is removed from the waiting list for any reason other than death or transplantation, the transplant center must document in the patient's record that the patient (and in the case of a kidney patient, the patient's usual dialysis facility) was notified no later than 10 days after the date the patient was removed from the waiting list.

   (3) In the case of patients admitted for organ transplants, transplant centers must maintain written records of:

     (i) Multidisciplinary patient care planning during the transplant period; and

     (ii) Multidisciplinary discharge planning for post-transplant care.

(d) *Standard: Social services.* The transplant center must make social services available, furnished by qualified social workers, to transplant patients, living donors, and their families. A qualified social worker is an individual who meets licensing requirements in the State in which he or she practices; and

(1) Completed a course of study with specialization in clinical practice and holds a master's degree from a graduate school of social work accredited by the Council on Social Work Education; or

(2) Is working as a social worker in a transplant center as of the effective date of this final rule and has served for at least 2 years as a social worker, 1 year of which was in a transplantation program, and has established a consultative relationship with a social worker who is qualified under (d)(1) of this paragraph.

(e) *Standard: Nutritional services.* Transplant centers must make nutritional assessments and diet counseling services, furnished by a qualified dietitian, available to all transplant patients and living donors. A qualified dietitian is an individual who meets practice requirements in the State in which he or she practices and is a registered dietitian with the Commission on Dietetic Registration.

§ 482.96   Condition of participation: Quality assessment and performance improvement (QAPI).

Transplant centers must develop, implement, and maintain a written, comprehensive, data-driven QAPI program designed to monitor and evaluate performance of all transplantation services, including services provided under contract or arrangement.

(a) *Standard: Components of a QAPI program.* The transplant center's QAPI program must use objective measures to evaluate the center's performance with regard to transplantation activities and outcomes. Outcome measures may include, but are not limited to, patient and donor selection criteria, accuracy of the waiting list in accordance with the OPTN waiting list requirements, accuracy of donor and recipient matching, patient and donor management, techniques for organ recovery, consent practices, patient education, patient satisfaction, and patient rights. The transplant center must take actions that result in performance improvements and track performance to ensure that improvements are sustained.

(b) *Standard: Adverse events.* A transplant center must establish and implement written policies to address and document adverse events that occur during any phase of an organ transplantation case.

(1) The policies must address, at a minimum, the process for the identification, reporting, analysis, and prevention of adverse events.

(2) The transplant center must conduct a thorough analysis of and document any adverse event and must utilize the analysis to effect changes in the transplant center's policies and practices to prevent repeat incidents.

§ 482.98   Condition of participation: Human resources.

The transplant center must ensure that all individuals who provide services and/or supervise services at the center, including individuals furnishing services under contract or arrangement, are qualified to provide or supervise such services.

(a) *Standard: Director of a transplant center.* The transplant center must be under the general supervision of a qualified transplant surgeon or a qualified physician-director. The director of a transplant center need not serve full-time and may also serve as a center's primary transplant surgeon or transplant physician in accordance with §482.98(b). The director is responsible for planning, organizing, conducting, and directing the transplant center and must devote sufficient time to carry out these responsibilities, which include but are not limited to the following:

    (1) Coordinating with the hospital in which the transplant center is located to ensure adequate training of nursing staff and clinical transplant coordinators in the care of transplant patients and living donors.

    (2) Ensuring that tissue typing and organ procurement services are available.

    (3) Ensuring that transplantation surgery is performed by, or under the direct supervision of, a qualified transplant surgeon in accordance with §482.98(b).

(b) *Standard: Transplant surgeon and physician.* The transplant center must identify to the OPTN a primary transplant surgeon and a transplant physician with the appropriate training and experience to provide transplantation services, who are immediately available to provide transplantation services when an organ is offered for transplantation.

    (1) The transplant surgeon is responsible for providing surgical services related to transplantation.

    (2) The transplant physician is responsible for providing and coordinating transplantation care.

(c) *Standard: Clinical transplant coordinator.* The transplant center must have a clinical transplant coordinator to ensure the continuity of care of patients and living donors during the pre-transplant, transplant, and discharge phases of transplantation and the donor evaluation, donation, and discharge phases of donation. The clinical transplant coordinator must be a registered nurse or clinician licensed by the State in which the clinical transplant coordinator practices, who has experience and knowledge of transplantation and living donation issues. The clinical transplant coordinator's responsibilities must include, but are not limited to, the following:

(1) Ensuring the coordination of the clinical aspects of transplant patient and living donor care; and

(2) Acting as a liaison between a kidney transplant center and dialysis facilities, as applicable.

(d) *Standard: Independent living donor advocate or living donor advocate team.* The transplant center that performs living donor transplantation must identify either an independent living donor advocate or an independent living donor advocate team to ensure protection of the rights of living donors and prospective living donors.

(1) The living donor advocate or living donor advocate team must not be involved in transplantation activities on a routine basis.

(2) The independent living donor advocate or living donor advocate team must demonstrate:

   (i) Knowledge of living organ donation, transplantation, medical ethics, and informed consent; and

   (ii) Understanding of the potential impact of family and other external pressures on the prospective living donor's decision whether to donate and the ability to discuss these issues with the donor.

(3) The independent living donor advocate or living donor advocate team is responsible for:

   (i) Representing and advising the donor;

   (ii) Protecting and promoting the interests of the donor; and

   (iii) Respecting the donor's decision and ensuring that the donor's decision is informed and free from coercion.

(e) *Standard: Transplant team.* The transplant center must identify a multidisciplinary transplant team and describe the responsibilities of each member of the team. The team must be composed of individuals with the appropriate qualifications, training, and experience in the relevant areas of medicine, nursing, nutrition, social services, transplant coordination, and pharmacology.

(f) *Standard: Resource commitment.* The transplant center must demonstrate availability of expertise in internal medicine, surgery, anesthesiology, immunology, infectious disease control, pathology, radiology, blood banking, and patient education as related to the provision of transplantation services.

§ 482.100 Condition of participation: Organ procurement.

The transplant center must ensure that the hospital in which it operates has a written agreement for the receipt of organs with an OPO designated by the Secretary that identifies specific responsibilities for the hospital and for the OPO with respect to organ recovery and organ allocation.

§ 482.102 Condition of participation: Patient and living donor rights.

In addition to meeting the condition of participation "Patient's rights" requirements at §482.13, the transplant center must protect and promote each transplant patient's and living donor's rights.

(a) *Standard: Informed consent for transplant patients.* Transplant centers must implement written transplant patient informed consent policies that inform each patient of:
(1) The evaluation process;
(2) The surgical procedure;
(3) Alternative treatments;
(4) Potential medical or psychosocial risks;
(5) National and transplant center-specific outcomes, from the most recent SRTR center-specific report, including (but not limited to) the transplant center's observed and expected 1-year patient and graft survival, national 1-year patient and graft survival, and notification about all Medicare outcome requirements not being met by the transplant center;
(6) Organ donor risk factors that could affect the success of the graft or the health of the patient, including, but not limited to, the donor's history, condition or age of the organs used, or the patient's potential risk of contracting the human immunodeficiency virus and other infectious diseases if the disease cannot be detected in an infected donor;
(7) His or her right to refuse transplantation; and
(8) The fact that if his or her transplant is not provided in a Medicare-approved transplant center it could affect the transplant recipient's ability to have his or her immunosuppressive drugs paid for under Medicare Part B.

(b) *Standard: Informed consent for living donors.* Transplant centers must implement written living donor informed consent policies that inform the prospective living donor of all aspects of, and potential outcomes from, living donation. Transplant centers must ensure that the prospective living donor is fully informed about the following:

(1) The fact that communication between the donor and the transplant center will remain confidential, in accordance with the requirements at 45 CFR parts 160 and 164.

(2) The evaluation process;

(3) The surgical procedure, including post-operative treatment;

(4) The availability of alternative treatments for the transplant recipient;

(5) The potential medical or psychosocial risks to the donor;

(6) The national and transplant center-specific outcomes for recipients, and the national and center-specific outcomes for living donors, as data are available;

(7) The possibility that future health problems related to the donation may not be covered by the donor's insurance and that the donor's ability to obtain health, disability, or life insurance may be affected;

(8) The donor's right to opt out of donation at any time during the donation process; and

(9) The fact that if a transplant is not provided in a Medicare-approved transplant center it could affect the transplant recipient's ability to have his or her immunosuppressive drugs paid for under Medicare Part B.

(c) *Standard: Notification to patients.* Transplant centers must notify patients placed on the center's waiting list of information about the center that could impact the patient's ability to receive a transplant should an organ become available, and what procedures are in place to ensure the availability of a transplant team.

(1) A transplant center served by a single transplant surgeon or physician must inform patients placed on the center's waiting list of:

(i) The potential unavailability of the transplant surgeon or physician; and

(ii) Whether the center has a mechanism to provide an alternate transplant surgeon or transplant physician.

(2) At least 30 days before a center's Medicare approval is terminated, whether voluntarily or involuntarily, the center must:

(i) Inform patients on the center's waiting list and provide assistance to waiting list patients who choose to transfer to the waiting list of another Medicare-approved transplant center without loss of time accrued on the waiting list; and

(ii) Inform Medicare beneficiaries on the center's waiting list that Medicare will no longer pay for transplants performed at the center after the effective date of the center's termination of approval.

(3) As soon as possible prior to a transplant center's voluntary inactivation, the center must inform patients on the center's waiting list and, as directed by the Secretary, provide assistance to waiting list patients who choose to transfer to the waiting list of another Medicare-approved transplant center without loss of time accrued on the waiting list.

§ 482.104 Condition of participation: Additional requirements for kidney transplant centers.

(a) *Standard: End stage renal disease (ESRD) services.* Kidney transplant centers must directly furnish transplantation and other medical and surgical specialty services required for the care of ESRD patients. A kidney transplant center must have written policies and procedures for ongoing communications with dialysis patients' local dialysis facilities.

(b) *Standard: Dialysis services.* Kidney transplant centers must furnish inpatient dialysis services directly or under arrangement.

(c) *Standard: Participation in network activities.* Kidney transplant centers must cooperate with the ESRD Network designated for their geographic area, in fulfilling the terms of the Network's current statement of work.

Appendix B

Centers for Medicare and Medicaid Services Certification Process[1]

HOSPITALS

The following provides basic information about being certified as a Medicare and/or Medicaid hospital provider and includes links to applicable laws, regulations, and compliance information.

A hospital is an institution primarily engaged in providing, by or under the supervision of physicians, inpatient diagnostic and therapeutic services or rehabilitation services.

The State Survey Agency evaluates each general hospital as a whole for compliance with the Medicare requirements and certifies it as a single provider institution including all components:

- Under the legal control of the hospital governing body and part of the same corporation or governmental administrative entity; and
- Subject to the direction of the hospital administrator and medical staff organization.

The State Survey Agency evaluates and certifies the whole hospital even when the components are separately housed.

It is not permissible to certify only part of a general hospital. However, the following are not considered parts of the hospital and are not to be included in the evaluation of the hospital's compliance:

- Components appropriately certified as other kinds of providers or suppliers. (i.e., a distinct part Skilled Nursing Facility and/or distinct part Nursing Facility, Home Health Agency, Rural Health Clinic, or Hospice); and
- Excluded residential, custodial, and non-service units not meeting certain definitions in the Social Security Act.

Accredited Hospitals

A hospital accredited by the Joint Commission or AOA is deemed to meet all Medicare requirements for hospitals (except the requirements for Utilization Review, the special conditions for psychiatric hospitals, the Skilled Nursing Facility Requirements for swing-bed designation, and any higher-than-national standards approved by the Secretary).

When notified that a participating hospital has been accredited, the State Survey Agency verifies the accreditation, removes the hospital from future resurvey schedules, and discontinues any follow-up on deficiencies. If Condition-level deficiencies still exist, the State refers the matter to the CMS Regional Office.

Surveyors assess the hospital's compliance with the Medicare Conditions of Participation (CoPs) for all services, areas, and locations in which the provider receives reimbursement for patient care services billed under its provider number.

Although the survey generally occurs during daytime working hours (Monday through Friday), surveyors may conduct the survey at other times. This may include weekends and times outside of normal daytime (Monday through Friday) working hours. When the survey begins at times outside of normal work times, the survey team modifies the survey, if needed, in recognition of patients' activities and the staff available.

All hospital surveys are unannounced.

- Should an individual or entity (hospital) refuse to allow immediate access upon reasonable request to either a State Agency or CMS surveyor, the Office of the Inspector General (OIG) may exclude the hospital from participation in all Federal healthcare programs.
- The CMS State Operations Manual (SOM) provides CMS policy regarding survey and certification activities.

Death Reporting Requirements

Previously, hospitals were required to report to CMS only those patient deaths that occurred while the patient was restrained or in seclusion for behavior management or where it was reasonable to assume that a patient's death was the result of restraint or seclusion used for behavior management. Now, key reporting provisions at 42 CFR 482.13(g) of the Patients' Rights Final Rule, published December 8, 2006, (71 FR 71378) specify that:

1. Hospitals must report the following information to CMS:
   - Each death that occurs while a patient is in restraint or seclusion.
   - Each death that occurs within 24 hours after the patient has been removed from restraint or seclusion.
   - Each death known to the hospital that occurs within one week after restraint or seclusion where it is reasonable to assume that use of restraint or placement in seclusion contributed directly or indirectly to a patient's death. "Reasonable to assume" in this context includes (but is not limited to) deaths related to restrictions of movement for prolonged periods of time or death related to chest compression, restriction of breathing, or asphyxiation.
2. Each death must be reported to CMS by telephone no later than the close of business the next CMS business day following knowledge of the patient's death.
3. Hospital staff must document in the patient's medical record the date and time the death was reported to CMS.

See the **downloads** section next for the Patient's Rights Final Rule that includes more information on the hospital death reporting requirements related to restraint and seclusion.

Downloads

EMTALA (PDF, 23 KB)
Patient's Rights Regulation published 12/8/2006 (PDF, 335 KB)

Related Links Inside CMS

State Operations Manual Chapter 2, Section 2020–2040
Guidance For Laws and Regulations for Hospitals
Survey and Certification General Enforcement Information
CMS' EMTALA Home Page

Related Links Outside CMS

Section 1861(e) and (j)(1) of the Social Security Act
Section 1867 of the Social Security Act
42 CFR Part 482
42 CFR 489.20(l), (m), (q), (r) and 489.24

NOTES

1. https://www.cms.gov/CertificationandComplianc/08_Hospitals.asp

Appendix C

Assessing the Quality of Health Care

Self-Evaluation Questionnaire

The healthcare industry must reduce the number of human errors that are often the "root cause" of the numerous injuries and deaths that occur each year in the delivery of patient care. Outcomes need to be predictable. This can occur more frequently if redundant (backup) systems, procedures, and processes are in place for safe and effective patient care. Carefully designed systems and processes, if adhered to, will reduce the likelihood of human error.

The National Aeronautics and Space Administration (NASA) had numerous redundant (backup) systems in place prior to launch of the first shuttle as well as during each step of the flight. These steps were improved and followed each time a shuttle was flown into space for the safety of the astronauts. A successful launch requires collaboration among many professionals. Although mishaps do occur, being vigilant, following established procedures, and applying common sense can reduce their numbers.

As with NASA's evolving backup systems to protect shuttle astronauts, hospitals continue to design redundant systems and processes for patient safety. For example, a patient about to undergo surgery has a variety of clinical tests (e.g., electrocardiogram) and assessments prior to the surgical procedure. These tests and assessments are then reviewed to be sure that the patient is a candidate for surgery. This requires that all assessments are timely and thoroughly reviewed prior to the start of surgery, and then vital signs are closely monitored throughout the procedure. A protocol must be followed to verify that the correct patient is in the correct surgical suite at the correct time and is about to undergo the correct procedure on the correct body part. What is more, identification and marking of the surgical site prior to surgery is to include participation by the patient whenever possible, and a final time-out process must be conducted (again including the patient if possible) for verification prior to the administration of anesthesia and the surgical incision.

It is important to review sentinel events occurring in healthcare organizations and to conduct root cause analyses, seeking answers as to why an unfortunate outcome occurred and how to prevent similar events from repeating themselves. The "how to prevent" an undesirable outcome is as valuable as the "why" an unintended outcome occurred in the first place. Organizations need to focus on "how" to deliver the right care at the right time to the right person in order to lessen the likelihood of having to ask "why" things went wrong in the first place..

Redundant systems can improve diagnosis and effective treatment. The questions that follow, although far from exhaustive, are meant to be thought-provoking and should lead to deeper inquiry into designing meaningful redundancy in systems.

LEADERSHIP

- What are the organization's mission, vision, and values?
- How have the organization's mission, vision, and values changed over time?
- How does the planning process relate to the organization's mission, vision, and values?
- Is there a strategy that charts the direction of the organization's response to community need?
- Does the planning process identify the organization's strengths and opportunities for improvement?
- Has a process for setting priorities been established?
- How are the organization's mission, vision, values, and long-range plans communicated throughout the organization and community?
- What is the scope of services provided by the organization?
- How is the scope of services determined?
- How does the leadership effectuate collaboration among the organization's leaders?

- How does the organization plan services for specific patient populations (e.g., indigent patients, seniors)?
- What are the characteristics of the governing body?
- What is the composition (community representation) of the governing body?
- What is the size of the board?
- What is the organization's process for orienting and educating new board members?
- What is the organization's process for ongoing education?
- How does one become a member?
- Is there a systems board, single board, or both?
- Is there a community advisory board, and if so, how does one become a member?
- What is the purpose of the community advisory board?
- Is patient input solicited to improve services through, for example, patient satisfaction surveys and patient focus groups?
- What are the mechanisms used to educate the organization's leadership?
- Does the leadership conduct annual retreats?
- Are there internal and external continuing education programs for the board?
- How does the organization's leadership know if clinical outcomes are improving?
- What is the organization's mechanism for addressing conflict?
- Has the governing body adopted a conflict-of-interest policy?
- How does the organization assure itself that the same level of care is being delivered across the organization?
- What redundant systems does the organization have in place to improve patient outcomes?
- How does the organization assure itself that the appropriateness of therapy is not based on costs alone?
- Does the organization have a corporate compliance program in place for the prevention of fraud and abuse?
- How do the organization's leaders address performance improvement issues (e.g., directing and staffing services, coordinating and integrating services)?
- How does the governing body assure itself that the organization is delivering quality care?
- How does the governing body assure itself that patient care and clinical outcomes are improving?

- How does the governing body assure (and reassure itself) that it is doing the right thing?
- Does the governing body monitor the effectiveness of its leadership?
- Does the governing body conduct a self-assessment?
- What is the governing body's process for evaluating, reviewing, and improving its effectiveness?

Planning

- What is the organization's planning process, its "plan for planning"?
- Is planning conducted on a collaborative basis?
- What is the organization's plan for identifying and addressing community needs?
- How do the organization's leadership and community leadership collaborate to design and prioritize the need for new services?
- Does prioritizing include administration, trustees, nursing, and medical staff?
- Are power brokers driving their own agenda(s) in prioritizing organizational needs?
- How do services relate to the organization's mission, vision, and values?
- How does the organization ensure that services are relative to community need?
- Does the organization have a strategic plan that charts the course and direction of the organization in response to the ever-looming financial crisis?
- Does the organization obtain patient and family input as to how the organization is meeting the needs of patients?
- What is the organization's mechanism for obtaining community feedback (e.g., satisfaction surveys)?
- Are satisfaction surveys used in the planning process?

Resource Allocation

- What processes are in place for the organization to position itself for economic survival?
- What is the mechanism for leadership participation in resource allocation for human resources, new and expanded services, and capital acquisitions?
- How are priorities set for allocation of financial resources?
- Who has input into setting resource allocation priorities?

- What is the process for defining and approving new services?
- How do department directors participate in the organization's ongoing decision-making processes for planning and budgeting?
- What are the organization's parameters for feedback on variance reporting?
- How are funds allocated for orientation, training, and education of staff, patient, and family education?
- What is the relationship of patient care services to patient care needs?
- What financial data does the organization provide to its managers?
- What is the organization's process for developing budgets (e.g., capital, human resource, and expense)?
- What is the organization's process for approving expenditures?
- What information is made available to the organization's leadership and managers to support decision-making processes, operations, and performance improvement activities?
- What services does the organization contract out?
- How does the organization ensure effective communications in the delivery of patient care as it relates to language barriers, age-specific barriers, cultural, and religious barriers?

CREDENTIALING PROFESSIONALS

- Is there a process for credentialing licensed healthcare practitioners?
- Is the National Practitioner Data Bank utilized in the credentialing process?
- Is there an ongoing evaluation of each professional?
- Does the delineation of clinical privileges include: a description of the privileges requested; relevant education, training, and experience; limitations on privileges requested; evidence of competency in performing requested privileges; verification of current licensure; relevant references; and evaluation of current competency?

PATIENT RIGHTS

- How are advance directives addressed?
- Are patients queried to determine if they have an advance directive?
- What happens if the patient has an advance directive?
  - Is a copy placed on the patient's individual record?
- What happens if the patient has no advance directive?
  - Is the patient given information and an opportunity to execute an advance directive?

- How does the organization address ethical issues?
- Does the organization have a code of ethical behavior?
  - Does the code address admissions, discharge, transfer, and billing practices?

ETHICS COMMITTEE

- Does the organization have an ethics committee?
- What are the functions of the ethics committee?
- Does committee membership include significant representation from both community and providers?
- How are the patient and staff educated as to the existence and functions of the ethics committee?
- Are patients provided a statement as to their rights and responsibilities upon admission?
- Do patients have a right to review their medical records?
- How are complaints handled?
- What are the organization's policies and procedures for asking patients and families about organ donations?

INFECTION CONTROL

- Are hand hygiene protocols adhered to?
- Are temperature and humidity levels maintained?
- Are patients, when appropriate, assessed for the possibility of developing pressure ulcers?
- Are protocols to prevent development of pressure ulcers followed?
- Are food products labeled as to contents and expiration dates?
- Do infection-control policies and procedures include gown, mask, and glove changes between patients?
- Are furniture, equipment, and toys disinfected with appropriate germicidal solutions?

SPIRITUAL CARE SERVICES

- How are the religious and spiritual needs of patients addressed?
- How do patients know such services are available?

- Do organizational policies and procedures address the psychosocial, spiritual, and cultural variables that influence one's understanding and perception of illness?
- How do caregivers make referrals for spiritual assessment, reassessment, and follow-up?
- What evidence and documentation is placed in a patient's record to indicate that a patient's spiritual needs have been addressed?

PATIENT COMPLAINT PROCESS

- What is the organization's patient complaint process?
- How does the patient know about the process?
- How are complaints addressed in the organization, both internally and externally?
- Is the patient informed after his or her complaint is addressed?

HUMAN RESOURCES

- Have the technical skills of each position been identified?
- Is the position applied for a part of the applicant's career path or "just another job"?
- Does the applicant appear motivated?
- Does the applicant exhibit a sense of excitement about the position?
- Are the applicant's communications skills appropriate for the position applied for?
- How does the organization know that it is adequately staffed?
- What data does the organization collect that indicates the organization is appropriately staffed?
- Has the organization identified the mix, numbers of, and competencies of each position?
- Are there programs in place to promote, recruit, retain, develop, and give recognition to staff?
- What is the organization's process for verification of licensure?
- Are job descriptions reflective of each staff member's duties and responsibilities?
- What effect has reengineering of positions had on staff?
- How does the governing body know that the competency review process is effective?

- How does the governing body ensure that annual competency evaluations are being performed?
- Do competency reports to the governing body include contracted and agency staff?
- What mechanisms does the organization have in place to monitor the competency of individuals whose jobs have been reengineered?
- How is the performance of senior management staff evaluated?
- How does the organization assess the effectiveness and appropriateness of training and education programs?
- How are employees oriented to the culture of the organization?
- How does the organization assess competency?
- How does the competency evaluation relate to the job description?
- Are performance evaluations criteria-based?
- How are agency and contracted staff oriented to the organization?
- How are age-specific competencies evaluated?
- Does the organization utilize a self-testing module (e.g., Erickson's Growth and Development)?
- Are age-specific criteria applicable to the job classification?
- Describe the organization's general orientation program.
  - Does the orientation program provide education relative to mission, vision, and values?
  - Is there a review of organizational and department policies and procedures?
  - Are safety issues discussed?
  - Do topics such as equipment management receive attention?
  - What is the organization's performance improvement process?
- Is there a department-specific orientation program for employees, agency and contracted staff, and volunteers?
- What mechanisms are in place to promote job-related education and advancement goals of staff members?
- How does the organization assess the education and training needs of staff?
- Are volunteers oriented to the organization?
- Are volunteers oriented to the volunteer service?
- Are organized volunteer services provided under the direction of a designated hospital employee or by the establishment of a self-governing auxiliary?

PATIENT ASSESSMENT

- Is there a process for assessing patient care needs?
- Does the organization have a policy for conducting screenings and assessments?
- Are second opinions obtained as necessary; literature searched; and other resources used to provide current, timely, and accurate diagnoses and treatment of patients?
- Have criteria for nutritional screens been developed and approved?
- Are nutritional screens and assessments performed by a dietitian or appropriately trained nurse?
- Are patients on special diets monitored to ensure that they have the appropriate food tray?
- Have functional screens been developed and implemented?
- Is a functional assessment consult requested if the screen triggers the need for a consultation by an appropriate rehabilitation person (e.g., physical therapist, speech therapist, audiologist, occupational therapist)?

EMERGENCY DEPARTMENT

- Are patients triaged, assessed, and treated within a reasonable period of time?
- Are all patients assessed and treated by a physician prior to discharge?
- Is the response time by on-call physicians timely?
- What is the organization's mechanism for obtaining consultations?
- What is the definitive ECG to needle time for the administration of thrombolytics?
- Does the emergency department have an "express care" treatment area?
- Have criteria for admission and discharge been established?
- If an admission is necessary, how is an attending physician selected to be responsible for the patient's care?
- What are the specific competencies required of staff working in the emergency department?
- Is there sufficient staff by discipline, available to care for patients?
- Are medical records maintained for each patient treated in the emergency department?
- Are medical records maintained for each patient who meets his or her private physician in the emergency department?
- Are copies of the medical records of patients seen in the emergency department sent to each patient's attending physician?

- If a patient has been treated in other settings within the organization (e.g., ambulatory care settings), how are records from those settings accessed?
- What is the process for providing patient education in the emergency department prior to discharge?
- Is there a procedure in place for reading X-rays and other imaging studies when there is no radiologist readily available?
- How are ED patients notified of abnormal lab results after discharge?
- Who is responsible for follow-up with patients who have abnormal diagnostic tests?
- What documentation is maintained regarding notification of patients as to test results?
- What are the issues and perceptions identified by patients as to the care being rendered in the emergency department?
- What transfer agreements does the organization have in place to effectuate a timely transfer of a patient in need of an alternate level of care?
- What evaluation tools does the organization utilize to improve the care rendered in the emergency department?

INFORMATION MANAGEMENT

- How does the organization address its information systems needs?
- Does the organization have an interdisciplinary committee structure for assessing and reassessing needs?
  - Does the committee address satisfaction?
  - Does the committee address timeliness of information?
  - Does the committee address clinical needs?
- Is there an ongoing process for assessment and reassessment of information needs in the organization?
- What is the methodology for prioritizing needs?
- Has the organization committed appropriate funds for upgrading systems?
- How does the organization maintain systems security and confidentiality?

MEDICAL STAFF

- What are the organization's processes for credentialing physicians and other healthcare practitioners (e.g., physician's assistant, nurse practitioner)?
- Is information collected from the National Practitioner Data Bank utilized in the credentialing process?

- How does the organization review and evaluate the competency of the members of the medical staff?
- What mechanism does the organization have in place for ongoing evaluation and reevaluation?

MEDICATION USE

- What is the organization's process for evaluating high-risk, high-volume, and high-cost medications?
- Who is responsible for overseeing the storage and control of medications maintained on patient care units?
- What risk reduction activities does the organization have in place to reduce the likelihood of adverse drug reactions and medication errors?
- What disciplines have been credentialed to prescribe medications (physician's assistants and nurse practitioners)?
- How are controlled substances monitored, inventoried, and wasted, and is wasting witnessed and documented?
- What is the organization's mechanism for monitoring the effect of medications on patients?
- Is consent obtained for the use of investigational drugs and high-risk medications?
- Are look-alike medications repackaged or relabeled, as necessary, in the pharmacy?
- How are causes and trends of medication errors tracked?
- What educational processes have been implemented to reduce the likelihood of medication errors?
- What is the organization's process for monitoring, tracking, and trending medication errors?
- Are medication errors tracked and trended by profession (nurse, pharmacist, and physician)?
  - How is the information gathered utilized to reduce the likelihood of medication errors?
- What are the common causes, trends, and patterns for medication errors?
  - Are errors trended by patient unit?
- What processes does the organization have in place to reduce the likelihood of transcription errors?
- What is the frequency of
  - transcription errors?
  - dosing errors (including age-related dosing for neonates, infants, adolescents, adult, and geriatric populations)?

- ○ administration errors?
- ○ double dosing?
- ○ administering medications not ordered?
- ○ untimely administration of medications?
- ○ administering a medication to the wrong patient?
- ○ packaging errors by pharmacy staff?
- ○ packaging errors by drug manufacturers?
- ○ errors due to illegible or ambiguous handwriting?
- What is the frequency of "missed" doses?
- How do reported adverse drug reactions compare with like organizations?
- Is there a mechanism in place for monitoring side effects?
- Is there a mechanism in place for reducing the frequency of adverse drug reations?
- How are emergency medications obtained when the pharmacy is closed?
- How are medications obtained that are not included in the hospital's formulary?
- Is informed consent obtained from patients prior to the use of investigational drugs?
- Describe the organization's procedure for reviewing and approving research protocols?
- Does the organization have a mechanism in place for approving and overseeing the use of investigational drugs?
- How are protocols and criteria developed and approved for the use of investigational drugs?
- Does the organization permit the dispensing of sample medications?
- What information is maintained in patient records in the event a sample drug is recalled?
- Does the organization maintain a medication log for tracking the dispensing of sample drugs?
- Does the log include the following pertinent information: medication dispensed; date medication was dispensed; patient name; patient record number; dosage and amounts given; medication control/lot numbers for purposes of recall; expiration date; and physician signature?
- Are patients permitted to self-administer medications (e.g., insulin)?
- Where are the medications stored?
- How is monitoring conducted?
- Who is responsible for stocking medications in crash carts?
- Who is responsible for checking laryngoscope batteries?
- Who is responsible for ensuring that medications have not expired?

- Who is responsible for ensuring the integrity of crash carts (e.g., appropriate medications, equipment, and supplies are available when needed)?
- Are logs maintained?
- Does the organization maintain the appropriate equipment on crash carts for treating both children and adults?
- Are staff members appropriately trained in the testing and use of equipment contained in or on the crash cart?
- How are staff members who participate in codes evaluated?
- Do pharmacists attend codes?
  - What value might be added if pharmacists attended codes?
- Is there a collaborative approach to reviewing the organization's procedures after a code?
- What mechanisms are in place for reviewing medications administered during a code?
- Is patient education conducted in all settings (e.g., inpatient, ambulatory, emergency department, home care) on a collaborative basis?
- How is information on medication monitoring obtained?
- What are the organization's cost reduction activities, and how have those activities affected patient care (e.g., Zantac v. Tagamet; antibiotics; thrombolytics Activase v. streptokinase)?
- What is the correlation between knowledge, research, and appropriateness?
- What kinds of aggregate data are available for performance improvement activities?
- What systems does the organization have in place to minimize the likelihood of drug–drug interactions?
- What is the protocol for handling patients on multiple medications?
- What stat lab tests does the organization have in place for patients who have overdosed?
- Is the organization's mechanism for ordering, preparing, dispensing, administering, and monitoring of parenteral nutrition defined by the medical staff?

Medication Safety Tips

- Drugs are safely stored, ordered, and distributed.
- Potentially dangerous look-alike drugs are separated in the pharmacy to prevent mix-ups.
- All medications are labeled including the drug, dosage, and expiration date.

- A process is implemented for obtaining and documenting a complete listing of a patient's current medications upon admission to the organization.
- The medications to be continued during the patient's stay are determined by the attending physician.
- Upon discharge, the attending physician instructs the patient as to which drugs should be continued or discontinued.
- A complete list of drugs is made available to the next provider when the patient is transferred to another setting, service, practitioner, or level of care within or outside the organization.
- Risk-reduction activities are in place to reduce the likelihood of adverse drug reactions and medication errors.
- There is a mechanism for monitoring the effect of medications on patients.
- Responsibility for ensuring the integrity of crash carts has been assigned.
- The organization maintains the appropriate medications and equipment on crash carts for treating both children and adults.
- Staff members are appropriately trained in the testing and use of equipment contained in or on the crash cart.
- Staff members who participate in codes are periodically tested for competency.
- High-risk drugs are easily identified and standardized when feasible.
- There is a mechanism in place for approving and overseeing the use of investigational drugs.
- Investigational drug protocols and criteria have been developed and approved.

LABORATORY

- Does the laboratory staff participate in activities of the pharmacy and therapeutics committee?
- Describe the importance of having laboratory representation on the pharmacy and therapeutics committee (e.g., the laboratory provides end data, panic values; monitors therapeutic ranges; checks blood levels for toxicity; determines therapeutic levels; provides lab data vital to evaluating the nutritional status of patients, drugs in–data out information, organism–drug interactions, culture and sensitivity studies, consultative role; evaluates physician ordering practices).
- Does the laboratory look at test results to discern, review, and evaluate results with clinical presentation and history?
- If test results do not fit the clinical picture or expected outcomes, what happens?

- Are laboratory personnel reviewing test results for drug interactions through testing procedures (e.g., patients can produce antibodies to drugs that can cross-react with laboratory tests)?
- Are critical lab values promptly reported?
  - Is data collected to measure and assess the success of timely reporting?
  - Is action is taken, when necessary, to improve the reporting process?
- Are therapeutic ranges closely monitored?
- Are blood levels for toxicity closely followed?
- Does communication between the laboratory and pharmacy facilitate the production of more useful data from laboratory tests and allow better utilization of laboratory resources to improve patient care and decrease direct costs to the patient and provider (e.g., documentation of draw times on specimens for therapeutic drug monitoring so that the drug level determined at a known point in time can be related to the specific dose given at a specific time—without such a relationship in time, interpretation of serum drug levels to drug dosage would be questionable)?
- How do the pharmacy, laboratory, and dietary work collaboratively to improve patient care?
- How is monitoring of the various shifts conducted?
- Why should patient assessment include questions of what medications are being administered?
- Are second reads conducted, as appropriate, prior to radical surgeries (e.g., breast removal)?
- Are procedures implemented to reduce the risk of surgical specimen mix-ups?
- Are specimens properly jarred and labeled at the surgical table?
- Are all specimens labeled before leaving one's possession?
- Is there a strict chain of custody for each specimen?
- Are preoperative and postoperative pathology report discrepancies addressed?

NUTRITIONAL CARE

- How is the diet manual developed and approved?
- How are the criteria for nutritional screens developed and approved?
  - Who participates in determining criteria?
  - Who performs nutritional screens?
- What is the organization's process for screening and assessing patients at nutritional risk?
  - Is every patient's nutritional status screened?

- Is a physician's order necessary to conduct a full assessment?
- How is the potential for food–drug interactions monitored?
- Who is responsible for modified diet counseling?
- What criteria has the organization established for determining high-risk patients?
- How are diet changes monitored?
- Are nutritional assessments conducted on a timely basis?
- How is the appropriateness of diet prescriptions monitored?
- How is the appropriateness and effectiveness of nutritional care monitored?
- How is competency to screen patients assessed?
- Is the patient consulted as part of the screening?

PERFORMANCE IMPROVEMENT (PI)

- What is the organization's process for PI?
- Does the organization have a PI improvement coordinating committee?
- Describe the membership of the committee.
  - Is membership interdisciplinary?
- What is done to educate staff in PI processes?
- What is the organization's methodology for establishing priorities for PI (i.e., how are priorities set)?
- How does the organization go about chartering PI teams?
- How has PI improved the health of the community?
- Do PI teams periodically review and revisit the results of their activities?
- How do PI teams go about outcomes measurement?
- What is the organization's methodology for PI?
- How is training and education provided to the staff?
- What organizational successes have come about as a result of PI activities?
- What measurement systems does the organization participate in?
- How does the organization integrate the ambulatory care and other outpatient sites into the organization's PI process?
- What is the organization doing to evaluate the effectiveness and appropriateness of its PI program?
- Is the leadership committed to PI?
  - Has commitment and buy-in to PI flowed throughout the organization?
- Are measurement and assessment major components of the PI process?
- Is the organization's leadership committed to the PI process?

- Is consideration given to involving patients and family in the PI process (e.g., focus groups)?
- How does the organization know it is doing well clinically?
- Describe the organization's success in integrating evening and weekend shifts into the PI process?
- What evidence and documentation does the organization have to demonstrate that internal processes are continuously and systematically assessed and improved?
- What is the organization's process for setting priorities?
- How does the organization decide what to review and improve (high-risk, high-volume, problem-prone activities)?
- What is the organization's process for involvement across disciplines?
- Does the organization have collaborative practice teams?
- How does the organization ensure that all staff members participate in PI processes?
- How does the organization identify opportunities for improvement?
- What data does the organization trend for PI activities?
- How does the organization collect data?
- How does the organization measure or validate its successes?
- What clinical databases does the organization have in place for benchmarking?
- What internal and external databases does the organization use for benchmarking?
- What happens when measurement data suggest opportunities for improvement?
- Is intensive assessment conducted when variables of measurement are unacceptable?
- How are data assessed?
- How does the organization assess its success with critical pathways?
- How are PI processes improved?
- What effect has PI had on teamwork?

STERILE SUPPLY

- What is the mandated dress code for decontamination?
- Is decontamination performed elsewhere in the organization (e.g., labor and delivery and emergency departments)?
- Are staff members cross-trained for each area?
- How does the organization handle implants?

- Describe the monitoring process of the sterilizers.
- Describe the flow of activities when contaminated instruments are received.
- Is biological testing being conducted, and are records being maintained?

SURGICAL AND INVASIVE PROCEDURES

- Have physicians had the appropriate training and experience in the specialty for which privileges are being sought?
- Is there a listing of which procedures each physician can perform?
- What is the process for credentialing surgeons as to what procedures they can perform?
- Are the credentials of physicians and other professional staff both current and organization-specific?
- Who ensures that all appropriate assessments have been completed prior to surgery (e.g., history, physical, and anesthesia)?
- Are pertinent and thorough history and physical examinations completed and reviewed prior to surgery?
- Does the organization have assessment criteria for emergent and non-emergent surgical cases?
- What patient education is in place prior to surgery?
  - Are patients educated about medical equipment that may be used?
- What is the organization's procedure for ensuring that patients have been informed of the risks, benefits, and alternatives of anesthesia, surgical procedures, and administration of blood or blood products?
- Who is responsible for informing the patient of the risks, benefits, and alternatives to anesthesia, surgical procedures, and the administration of blood or blood products?
- Who verifies that consent forms (e.g., anesthesia, surgical, blood) have been completed and placed in the patient's record)?
- Does the organization have a process by which there is correlation of pathology and imaging findings?
- What is the organization's process for ensuring that it selected the right site and right surgical procedure for the right patient?
- Who is responsible for ensuring that the appropriate equipment, supplies, and staffing are available prior to induction (administration of anesthesia)?
  - Is surgical equipment properly cleaned and stored following each procedure?

- ○ Is blood stored in the operating room suite?
- ○ Is blood stored at appropriate temperatures?
- ○ How are temperatures monitored?
- ○ Is there an alarm system on refrigerators to warn if temperatures fall too low or rise too high?
- Who is responsible for ensuring that each operating room has been properly cleaned prior to the next procedure?

Universal Protocol: Ensuring Correct Patient, Correct Site, and Correct Surgery

- Have the following procedures been implemented?
  - ○ A process has been implemented to clearly mark the correct surgical site.
  - ○ Both the operating physician and patient are involved in the preoperative marking process.
  - ○ The patient's medical record is available to help determine the correct site prior to the start of surgery.
  - ○ Imaging studies are available for review prior to surgery to help determine the correct surgical site.
  - ○ There is verbal verification of the correct site by each member of the team in the operating room prior to induction of anesthesia.
  - ○ Observation confirms that the correct site has been marked, with the patient's participation.
  - ○ Anesthesia is not administered until the operating surgeon is in the operating suite.
  - ○ The surgical team (all disciplines) conducts a "time out" prior to the start of surgery to confirm the correct patient, correct site, and correct procedure.
- Do anesthesiologists cover all anesthetizing locations for all procedures?
- Who is responsible for developing and updating the organization's conscious sedation policy?
- Do nurse anesthetists administer conscious sedation and/or general anesthesia?
- What is the process for credentialing nurse anesthetists?
- How is competency reviewed?
- Who monitors their work?
- Is backup coverage readily available from an anesthesiologist?
- Are there any limitations as to what forms of anesthesia can be administered?

- Are surgical nurses ACLS certified?
- How are patients monitored?
- Is monitoring the same at all locations?
- Are vital signs, airway, and surgical site assessments continuously monitored?
- Has a procedure for instrument and sponge counts prior to closing the surgical site been implemented?
- Does the organization have a mechanism in place for reviewing and monitoring unplanned returns to the operating suite?
- What are the criteria for discharge from the postanesthesia recovery unit?
- What redundant systems does the organization have in place for electrical failures, equipment breakdown, backup staffing, etc.?
- What processes does the organization have in place to follow up with patients who have postoperative infections?
  - How does the organization identify postoperative infections in day-surgery patients?
  - What are the organization's procedures for follow-up on patients who have developed postoperative infections?
  - Is there routine consultative care by an infectious disease specialist when a patient develops a nosocomial infection?
  - How does the organization's infection rate compare with other organizations?
- Does the organization have an ongoing process for improving the outcome of surgical procedures?
- Is there appropriate separation of clean and soiled instrumentation?
- Does the organization perform surgical case reviews 100% of the time?
  - When sampling for case review, how are cases selected for review?

REHABILITATION SERVICES

- How are functional screens conducted?
- Is a physician's order necessary for a full assessment?
- If it is determined that a full assessment is necessary, within what time frame must it be completed?
- Who provides patient–family education?
- Does the organization provide for weekend coverage to ensure continuity of care?
- Who conducts the assessment and treatment of occupational performance?
- What skills does the occupational therapist evaluate (e.g., work adjustment, educational, social skills, neuromuscular, cognitive, psychosocial, treatment goals established)?

PATIENT SAFETY

- Does the organization have a designated smoking area?
- Do fire-rated doors
  - have a self-closing device?
  - have a positive latching mechanism?
- Are fire-rated doors smoke tight, provided with vertical gaps no greater than $\frac{1}{8}$ inch and undercuts no greater than $\frac{3}{4}$ inch?
- Are designated smoking areas appropriately ventilated?
  - Is air exhausted to the outside?
- Are through-the-wall penetrations appropriately sealed to prevent the spread of smoke?
- Is there a clear space 18 inches below sprinkler heads?
- Are exit signs
  - clear as to direction of egress?
  - illuminated?
- Do linen and trash chutes have positive latching?
  - Do linen chutes have a sprinkler system on alternating floors?
  - Does the outlet storage room have a sprinkler system?
  - How are the air handling systems monitored for replacement of air filters?
  - Is there both visual and mechanical monitoring?
  - Is there gown and glove change between patients?
  - Are chairs disinfected with germicidal solutions between patients?
- What is the organization's process for disposing of hazardous wastes?
- Are electrical panels secure/locked, labeled, and provided with preventive maintenance?
- Are primary and secondary shutoff valves for utility systems labeled?
- Is medical gas vacuum safely achieved?
  - How is air gas filtered prior to exhaust (e.g., air wash)?
  - Is the air intake a minimum of 10 feet from nearest air exhaust?
- Are exit corridors blocked with storage?
- Is there a safety committee?
  - Are safety reports submitted to the governing body?
- Are fire drills conducted?
- Are disaster drills conducted?
- Are fire circuits tested?
- Are portable fire extinguishers maintained according to appropriate safety codes?
- What precautions are taken for the storage of flammable gases and liquids?

- Have security and safety issues been addressed throughout the organization (e.g., nursery and operating suites)?
- Are hazardous wastes stored in a safe and secure environment?
- Are hazardous materials inventoried by location?
- Is there a hazardous materials (HAZMAT) response team?
- What hazardous materials and wastes does the organization handle?
- What precautions are taken in handling and storing hazardous materials and wastes?
- How would hazardous spills be handled?
- Are reports of incidents related to spills maintained?
- Does the organization maintain written criteria as to the selection of medical equipment?
- Is equipment tested prior to use?
- Who is responsible for training the "end user"?
- How is equipment testing documented?
  - How are user errors reported?
  - How are programs evaluated?
  - Are there any trends?
  - Are actions taken as appropriate?
  - Are outside maintenance contracts monitored?
- Do medical equipment policies and procedures provide for
  - selecting and acquiring equipment?
  - written criteria to identify, evaluate, and inventory medical equipment?
  - Assessing and minimizing clinical and physical risks associated with medical equipment by providing preventive and corrective maintenance services?
  - monitoring and acting on medical equipment hazardous notices and recalls?
  - monitoring and reporting incidents that may have caused or contributed to an injury?
  - reporting and investigating equipment management problems?
- Is there is a reliable, adequate emergency power system to provide electricity to all critical areas?
- Are there current safety policies and procedures for each department?
- How are equipment failures reported?
- How are patients monitored during a total power failure?
- What procedures does the organization follow in the event of loss of water, power, medical gas, heat, and cooling?

RESOURCE CENTER

- What resources are available to the staff (e.g., Medline)?
- How are needs assessed?
- Are resources available to patients and families?
- In what PI activities does the medical librarian participate?

PATIENT UNIT

- What is the role of the unit and its size, special characteristics, census data, staffing patterns, results of patient satisfaction surveys, etc?
- How are medications stored?
- Where and what hazardous materials are stored, handled, and disposed of?
- What happens if there is a power failure?
- What is the smoking policy?
- Are bathrooms safe (e.g., provided with handrails, call buttons)?
- How is patient assessment integrated into the patient's record by the various disciplines?
- How are formulary updates communicated to the staff?
- How are patient records documented, having to do with admission records, history and physicals, anesthesia reports, operative reports, consent, medication records, patient–family education records, physician's orders, progress notes, rehabilitative service records, respiratory therapy, test result reporting records (e.g., laboratory, ECG, EEG, imaging reports), nurses' notes, advance directives, restraints, discharge planning, etc.?
- Are there unique safety concerns specific to the unit (e.g., special isolation procedures)?
- Are there age-specific requirements of the unit?
- Describe how patient rights are addressed.
- How are confidentiality issues addressed?
- Are the results of tests available in a timely manner (e.g., laboratory reports, including routine, stat, panic values)?
- Is there evidence of patient–family education?
  - Is there an assessment of a patient's readiness, willingness, ability, and need to learn?
  - Are patients provided information as to allergies, blood type, etc.?
- What are the security issues specific to the unit?
- What PI activities are conducted on the unit?

- Which of the following are features of specialty units such as the intensive care unit and the coronary care unit?
  - Are there monitors in all patient rooms?
  - Is there visual observation of patients at all times?
  - Are there admission criteria to the unit by diagnosis?
  - Are there discharge criteria?
  - Is there a consultation policy?
  - Are there specific triggers to generate a consultation (e.g., infection)?
  - What are the age groups of patients treated on the unit?
  - Are there age-specific criteria in job descriptions or on skills and competency checklists?

PATIENT VISIT (SAMPLE QUESTIONS ONE MIGHT ASK THE PATIENT)

- Greeting: Hello, I'm from the _____. In our process for continuously improving patient care, may I ask you a few questions as to your understanding of the care you are receiving?
  - How are you today?
  - What brought you to the hospital?
  - Sounds like you had a (bad/good) day—is that right?
  - Who is your physician?
  - Have your care and treatment been explained to you?
  - Have you had an opportunity to ask questions about your care?
  - Did you understand the explanation given?
  - Do you believe that the staff has been responsive to your needs?
  - Do you feel comfortable asking questions?
  - Are you comfortable with your care?
  - Are there any questions about your care that remain unanswered?
  - Have you been to physical therapy?
  - What activities do you participate in?
- Will patient education be properly addressed?
  - Will the patient receive clear medication instructions?
  - Will the patient receive any needed diet education?
  - Will the patient be provided any necessary equipment?
  - Will the patient and family be involved in treatment planning and education?
- Will adequate and clear discharge instructions be forthcoming?

PATIENT–FAMILY EDUCATION

- Does a patient's first contact with a staff member involve establishment of trust emanating from that patient's recognition of the caregiver's confidence, knowledge, and competence?
- How are the learning needs of patients and families addressed?
- How is patient education provided?
- What is the organization's mechanism for documentation on the patient record?
- How will the organization address the issue of
  - medication use?
  - medical equipment use?
  - drug–food interactions?
  - access to community resources?
  - how to obtain further care, if necessary?
  - responsibilities of patient and family?
  - resources available for patient–family education?
- Is the teaching reaching the patient?
  - Does the patient understand the message?
  - What is the likelihood that the patient and family will comply with instructions?
  - How is reinforcement of education conducted?
- Is there an interdisciplinary approach to patient and family education?
- What is the physician's role in patient and family education?
- What are the key factors to assessment and readiness to learn?
- How do you evaluate the effectiveness of patient education resources?
- What resources are available for patient and family education?
- What are your options or opportunities for follow-up and reinforcement of education?

PATIENT IDENTIFICATION

- Will the patient's wristband be checked for identification prior to rendering treatment?
- Are at least two identifiers (i.e., patient's name, birth date, medical record number, etc.) to be noted prior to treatment and matched to the patient's wristband and medical chart?
- Is it clear to staff that a patient's room number or bed location within a room are never to be used as patient identifiers?

SECURITY

- Have security issues been addressed throughout the organization?
- Have sensitive areas been identified?
- Are newborns foot-printed?
- Has the organization approved an identification band that is to be attached to mothers and infants?
- Do identification badges for mother and infant match?
- Do staff members have current color photo identification badges?
- Are staff and parents educated as to security procedures?
- Are infant abduction drills conducted?
- Does the organization have an electronic security alarm system installed?
- Are security cameras and monitors installed?

EMERGENCY PREPAREDNESS

- Does the organization have an emergency preparedness plan for both internal and external disasters?
- Was the plan developed in cooperation with local and national emergency preparedness disaster programs?
- Does the organization identify its vulnerabilities (e.g., equipment, supplies, staff, communications) and implement improvements?
- Are there disaster drills conducted to determine an organization's readiness for a variety of disasters (e.g., earthquake, hurricane, act of terrorism)?

Appendix D

Websites

Hope is the last thing that dies in man; and though it be exceedingly deceitful, yet it is of this good use to us, that while we are traveling through life, it conducts us in an easier and more pleasant way to our journey's end.

Francois de La Rochefoucauld (1613–1680)

This appendix is designed to assist the reader in conducting a search of standards, rules, and regulations that apply to hospitals and other healthcare organizations. Many of the more commonly referenced legal, ethics, and health-related websites are included in this listing. Each website includes a short description of what can be found on the website, saving time in the research process. Every attempt has been made to choose those websites and addresses that are trustworthy over time. However, it should be noted that websites periodically change their addresses and that a topic may need to be searched in order to locate an updated website.

Website information in this chapter is organized under nine headings.

- Evaluating Websites
- Government Websites
- Ethics Websites
- Legal Websites
- Best Practices
- Healthcare Resources
- Hospital and Physician Finders
- International Medical Websites
- References

EVALUATING WEBSITES

Health On the Net: www.hon.ch

When evaluating healthcare websites on the Internet, look for the symbol of the Health On the Net Foundation (HON) code of conduct for health care at the bottom of web pages. HON is the leading organization promoting and guiding the deployment of useful and reliable online medical and health information and its appropriate and efficient use. Created in 1995, HON is a nonprofit, nongovernmental organization, accredited by the Economic and Social Council of the United Nations.

Quackwatch: www.quackwatch.com

A website guide to avoiding healthcare fraud and quackery and to making intelligent decisions. It discusses questionable products, services, advertisements, and theories. It also covers education, consumer protection, research, additional links to other websites, and legal and political activities, as well as sources not recommended for health advice.

GOVERNMENT WEBSITES

Centers for Disease Control: http://www.cdc.gov/

This is the CDC's primary online communication channel. Annually, there are close to 500 million page views to the site, averaging 41 million page views per month. The website provides users with credible, reliable health information on data and statistics, diseases and conditions, emergencies and disasters, environmental health, healthy living, injury, violence and safety, life stages and populations, travelers' health, and workplace safety and health.

Centers for Medicare and Medicaid Services (CMS): www.cms.gov

The CMS web pages ensure effective, up-to-date healthcare coverage and promote quality care for beneficiaries. The website provides information on Medicaid, Medicare, Children's Health Insurance Programs, Regulations and Guidance, and other relevant information. CMS central and regional offices share a common vision and mission as well as a shared commitment to the five key objectives: skilled, committed, and highly motivated workforce;

affordable healthcare system; high-value health care; confident, informed consumers; and collaborative partnerships. This website includes, for example, links to: About CMS; Regulations and Guidance; Research, Statistics, Data and Systems; Outreach and Education; Search Tool; Questions; Newsroom; Contact CMS and Search Link

CMS Survey and Certification Home Page: www.cms.hhs.gov/ SurveyCertificationGenInfo

This page provides general information regarding the activities of CMS Survey and Certification. The Interpretive Guidelines and S&C letters may also be accessed from this page.

Interpretative Guidelines: http://www.cms.gov/manuals/downloads/ som107ap_a_hospitals.pdf

The Interpretive Guidelines and Survey Procedures for various providers or suppliers are located in the appendices to the State Operations Manual (SOM). For example, hospitals in Appendix A, psychiatric hospitals in Appendix AA, EMTALA in Appendix V, and critical access hospitals in Appendix W. There are many other appendices, but there is also a table of contents web page that lists all the appendices in the SOM. On the table of contents web page, one need only 'click' on the appendix to be referenced.

Survey and Certification Letters: www.cms.hhs.gov/SurveyCertificationGenInfo/ PMSR/list.asp

CMS Survey and Certification (S&C) releases information related to survey and certification guidance for various providers and suppliers to its Regional Offices and the State Survey Agencies through communications called Survey and Certification Letters. The letters are released on an ongoing basis. Once a letter is released, it is posted on the CMS website. The letters are organized by Federal fiscal years. For example, the first letter released for fiscal year 2009 would be labeled "S&C 09-01."

Social Security Act: http://www.ssa.gov/OP_Home/ssact/ssact-toc.htm

The laws that apply Medicare, Medicaid, and other CMS programs are located in the Social Security Act (SSA, or The Act). The Act is divided up into *Titles*. Medicare is *Title XVIII* and Medicare is *Title XIX*.

Social Security Act: http://www.ssa.gov/OP_Home/ssact/ssact-toc.htm

The laws that apply Medicare, Medicaid, and other CMS programs are located in the Social Security Act (SSA, or The Act). The Act is divided up into *Titles*. Medicare is *Title XVIII* and Medicare is *Title XIX*.

Code of Federal Regulations (Electronic Version): http://ecfr.gpoaccess.gov

The Electronic Code of Federal Regulations (e-CFR) is an electronic version of the Code of Federal Regulations (CFR). Note that, although e-CFR is a daily updated version of the CFR, it is not an official, legal edition of it. The e-CFR is an editorial compilation of CFR material and Federal Register amendments produced by the National Archives and Records Administration's Office of the Federal Register (OFR) and the Government Printing Office. The OFR updates the material in the e-CFR on a daily basis, and the current update status appears at the top of all e-CFR web pages. The CFR is divided into "Titles", with "Title 42 Public Health", containing CMS regulations. The Federal Register within the Government Printing Office publishes the CFR on an annual basis.

Hospital Compare: http://www.hospitalcompare.hhs.gov/

Medicare publishes patient-satisfaction ratings on this site, and will begin to adjust payment to hospitals based on those scores. Quality of care concerns and complaints can be reported via the Hospital Compare database, and information on hospital-acquired conditions can be downloaded.

Central Intelligence Agency/The World Factbook: https://www.cia.gov/library/publications/the-world-factbook/

The World Factbook provides information on the history, people, government, economy, geography, communications, transportation, military, and transnational issues for 266 world entities. Reference tabs include maps of the major world regions, as well as flags of the world, physical map of the world, political map of the world, standard time zones, guide to country comparisons, and much more.

ClinicalTrials.gov: www.clinicaltrials.gov

The joint National Library of Medicine (NLM) and National Institutes of Health (NIH) database about clinical research trials provides information to the public about studies in which new treatments, drugs, diagnostic procedures, vaccines, and other therapies are tested in people to see if they are safe and effective. A clinical trial can be searched by the name of the disease, the location, type of treatments, or sponsoring institution. The results will show what studies are being conducted, whether a trial is recruiting, the purpose of the study, where and when it will take place, whom to contact, and sources for more information. This website includes, for example, links to: Search for Clinical Trials; Investigator Instructions; Background Information; List Studies by Condition; List Studies by Drug Intervention; List Studies by Sponsor; List Studies by Location; and Search Tool.

Congress: www.congress.org

This nonpartisan news and information website is devoted to encouraging civic participation and to providing information about public policy issues of the day, along with tips on effective advocacy, so that citizens can make their voices heard. At the heart of the website is an award-winning software program that makes it easy for citizens to write their elected officials. This software assures that your letter will be delivered directly to the decision makers whose opinions you hope to influence.

Congressional Directory: www.congress.org/congressorg/directory/congdir.tt

An easy-to-use directory finds state representatives, demographics, committees, and offices.

Department of Health and Human Services: www.hhs.gov

The Department of Health and Human Services (HHS) is the U.S. Government's principal agency for protecting the health of all Americans and providing essential human services, especially for those who are least able to help themselves. The work of HHS is conducted by the Office of the Secretary and by 11 agencies. The agencies perform a wide variety of tasks and services, including research, public health, food and drug safety, grants and other funding, health insurance, and many others. The subdivisions of the Office of the Secretary provide direct support for the Secretary's initiatives. This website includes, for example, links to: About Us; HHS Secretary; News; Jobs; Grants/Funding, Diseases, Regulations, Preparedness; and Search Tool.

Department of Justice: www.justice.gov

The Department of Justice (DOJ) enforces the law, ensures public safety, seeks just punishment, and ensures fair and impartial administration of justice for all Americans. Its website provides information related to the DOJ mission, including forms, publications, news, grants, and an overview of the American Recovery and Reinvestment Act of 2009.

Department of Labor: www.dol.gov

The Department of Labor fosters and promotes the welfare of the job seekers, wage earners, and retirees of the United States by improving their working conditions, advancing their opportunities for profitable employment, protecting their retirement and healthcare benefits, helping employers find workers, strengthening free collective bargaining, and tracking changes in employment, prices, and other national economic measurements. In carrying out this mission, the department administers a variety of federal labor laws, including those that guarantee workers' rights to safe and healthful working conditions, a minimum hourly wage and overtime pay, freedom from employment discrimination, unemployment insurance, and other income support.

FedLaw: http://www.thecre.com/fedlaw/default.htm

FedLaw was developed to see if legal resources on the Internet could be a useful and cost-effective research tool for Federal lawyers and other Federal employees. Fedlaw has assembled references of use to people doing Federal legal research, and the reference can be accessed directly through "point and click" hypertext connections.

- Topical and title index
  - Alphabetical index of subjects in FedLaw—go directly to a specific subject or law
- Federal statutes and regulations
  - This will likely be the section used most—many different categories
- Federal judiciary
  - Supreme Court; Circuit, District, Bankruptcy, and other Courts
- Legislative branch
  - General Accounting Office; Congress; legislation
- Arbitration and mediation
  - Federal laws; arbitration and mediation rules; alternate dispute resolution

- General research and reference
  - Legal and business research sites; finding people, places, and things; Federal Government information; publications and news sources; directions, maps, and travel; weather; currency
- Professional associations and organizations
- "How-to" legal-relates sites
- Tips for lawyers and about writing

Food and Drug Administration (FDA): www.fda.gov

The FDA is responsible for protecting and advancing public health. Its website offers research and regulatory information on food, drugs, medical devices, vaccines, veterinary drugs, cosmetics, radiation-emitting products, and tobacco products. There is also news, help on reporting problems, and recalls and alerts.

Government Manual: www.gpoaccess.gov/gmanual

The U.S. Government Manual provides comprehensive information on the agencies of the legislative, judicial, and executive branches. It also includes information on quasi-official agencies, international organizations in which the United States participates, and boards, commissions, and committees.

Healthfinder: www.healthfinder.gov

Healthfinder.gov provides current and reliable health information and tools, including a health topic index, services and information, personal health tools, and the Freedom of Information Act.

Health Insurance Portability and Accountability Act (HIPAA): www.hhs.gov/ocr/privacy

HIPAA provides various protections for personal health information. The Department of Health and Human Services provides a wealth of information on HIPAA including summaries of both the Privacy Rule and the Security Rule, directions in filing complaints, simplification statues and rules, and enforcement actions and results.

Health Insurance Portability and Accountability Act—Forms: http://hipaa.ucsf.edu/documentation/default.html

Forms for patients, staff, data sharing, and more are provided by the University of California, San Francisco. Most forms may be found on state websites.

Health Privacy Project: www.cdt.org/issue/health-privacy

Part of the Center for Democracy and Technology, the Health Privacy page gives links to HIPAA, Health Information Technology for Economic and Clinical Health, American Recovery and Reinvestment Act, and more privacy protections. Included in the resources are archives, research, and analysis reports.

Health Resources and Services Administration: www.hrsa.gov

The Health Resources and Services Administration, an agency of the U.S. Department of Health and Human Services, is the primary federal agency for improving access to healthcare services for people who are uninsured, isolated, or medically vulnerable. Their goals are to improve access to quality care and services, strengthen the health workforce, build healthy communities, and improve health equity. The website also includes information about grants, statistics, National Health Services Corps, the Health Professions Workforce, and more.

MedlinePlus: www.medlineplus.gov

MedlinePlus will direct you to information to help answer health questions. MedlinePlus brings together authoritative information from NLM, NIH, and other government agencies and health-related organizations. Preformulated MEDLINE searches are included in MedlinePlus and give easy access to medical journal articles. MedlinePlus also has extensive information about drugs, an illustrated medical encyclopedia, interactive patient tutorials, and the latest health news.

Museum of Medical Research: www.nlm.nih.gov/hmd/medtour/nih.html

Founded in 1868 as a part of the NIH, the museum exhibits seek to educate the public about the process of biomedical research, generally focusing on the research of NIH investigators. The museum collects, preserves, and interprets biomedical research instruments and memorabilia, especially those related to the NIH.

National Cancer Institute: www.cancer.gov

The National Cancer Institute, part of the NIH, is the Federal Government's principal agency for cancer research and training. Cancer.gov is comprised of resources such as dictionaries of terms and drugs, funding opportunities, free publications, cancer statistics, and news.

National Center for Health Statistics: www.cdc.gov/nchs

As the nation's principal health statistics agency, the National Center for Health Statistics compiles statistical information to guide actions and policies to improve the health of our people. Information found on the website includes statistics systems, publications, and data access tools about health statistics.

National Guideline Clearinghouse: www.guideline.gov

A public resource for evidence-based clinical practice guidelines, National Guideline Clearinghouse provides useful resources such as annotated bibliographies, hospital-acquired conditions, patient resources, and more.

NICHSR: www.nlm.nih.gov/nichsr

The National Information Center on Health Services Research and Health Care Technology (NICHSR) was created to improve the ". . . collection, storage, analysis, retrieval, and dissemination of information on health services research, clinical practice guidelines, and healthcare technology."

National Institute on Aging: http://www.nih.gov/nia

NIA, one of the 27 Institutes and Centers of NIH, leads a broad scientific effort to understand the nature of aging and to extend the healthy, active years of life. In 1974, Congress granted authority to form NIA to provide leadership in aging research, training, health information dissemination, and other programs relevant to aging and older people. Subsequent amendments to this legislation designated the NIA as the primary Federal agency on Alzheimers disease research.

National Institute of Medicine: www.iom.edu

The Institute of Medicine is an independent, nonprofit organization that works outside of government to provide unbiased and authoritative advice to decision makers and the public. IOM.edu has an extensive database of medicinal reports that provides objective and straightforward advice and also undertakes many different types of activities, all aimed at improving health.

National Institutes of Health (NIH): www.nih.gov

Helping to lead the way toward important medical discoveries that improve health and save lives, NIH scientists investigate ways to prevent disease and to discover the causes, treatments, and even cures for common and rare diseases. Composed of 27 institutes and centers, the NIH provides leadership and financial support to researchers in every state and throughout the world. NIH.gov gives links to the various institutes and centers, the NIH Almanac, recoveries and reinvestments, and updated news and legislation regarding health.

National Labor Relations Board: www.nlrb.gov/

The National Labor Relations Board is an independent federal agency created by Congress in 1935 to administer the National Labor Relations Act, the primary law governing relations between unions and employers in the private sector. The statute guarantees the right of employees to organize and to bargain collectively with their employers and to engage in other protected concerted activity with or without a union, or to refrain from all such activity.

National Library of Medicine (NLM): www.nlm.nih.gov

The NLM, on the campus of the NIH in Bethesda, Maryland, is the world's largest medical library. The NLM collects materials and provides information and research services in all areas of biomedicine and health care. Widespread resources in the human genome, biomedicine, and environmental health can be found on the website, as well as online exhibitions, training and outreach, and health news and publications.

National Network of Libraries of Medicine: www.nnlm.gov

The mission of the National Network of Libraries of Medicine is to advance the progress of medicine and improve the public health by providing all U.S. health professionals with equal access to biomedical information and improving the public's access to information to enable them to make informed decisions about their health. Not only does this website provide member services, but it also provides electronic journal access, document delivery plans, and resource sharing.

National Practitioner Data Bank (NPDB): www.npdb-hipdb.hrsa.gov/

The legislation that led to the creation of the NPDB was enacted because the U.S. Congress believed that the increasing occurrence of medical malpractice litigation and the need to improve the quality of medical care had become nationwide problems that warranted greater efforts than any individual state could undertake. The intent is to improve the quality of health care by encouraging state licensing boards, hospitals and other healthcare entities, and professional societies to identify and discipline those who engage in unprofessional behavior and to restrict the ability of incompetent physicians, dentists, and other healthcare practitioners to move from state to state without disclosure or discovery of previous medical malpractice payment and adverse action history. Adverse actions can involve licensure, clinical privileges, professional society membership, and exclusions from Medicare and Medicaid.

Occupational Safety and Health Administration: www.osha.gov/

The purpose of the Occupational Safety and Health Administration is to ensure safe and healthful working conditions for working men and women by authorizing enforcement of the standards developed under the act, by assisting and encouraging the states in their efforts to ensure safe and healthful working conditions, and by providing for research, information, education, and training in the field of occupational safety and health.

Office of History, NIH: www.history.nih.gov

The Office of History of the NIH exists to advance historical understanding of biomedical research within the NIH and around the world. Through innovative exhibits, educational programs, preserving records of significant NIH achievements, and training researchers from multiple disciplines, the Office of History explores the past to enhance present understanding of the health sciences and the NIH.

Oregon's Death with Dignity Act: http://www.leg.state.or.us/ors/127.html

This link provides information regarding *Oregon's Death with Dignity Act* regulations and includes: Powers of Attorney; Advance Directives for Health Care; Physician Orders for Life-Sustaining Treatment Registry; Declarations for Mental Health Treatment; and Death with Dignity.

PubMed.gov: http://www.ncbi.nlm.nih.gov/sites/entrez

PubMed comprises more than 19 million citations for biomedical literature from MEDLINE, life science journals, and online books. Citations may include links to full-text content from PubMed Central and publisher websites.

United States Courts: www.uscourts.gov

United States Courts is the government website for all things related to the U.S. courts, including links to the federal courts, judges, court reporters, and more.

United States Government: http://www.gov.com

Provides ability to access every publicly accessible official government information channel. 94 million pages currently available.

ETHICS WEBSITES

Advance Directives: www.mindspring.com/~scottr/will.html

An organized set of links to living will (advance directive) web pages

Agency for Healthcare Policy and Research: http://www.ahcpr.gov/clinic/cpgsix.htm

National Guideline clearing house

American Association of Tissue Banks: www.aatb.org

The American Association of Tissue Banks (AATB) is a professional, non-profit, scientific, and educational organization. It is the only national tissue banking organization in the United States, and its membership totals more than 100 accredited tissue banks and 1000 individual members. Among other benefits, the AATB website offers information on the certification of tissue bank personnel, as well as accreditation processes.

American Health Lawyers Association: http://www.healthlawyers.org/Pages/Default.aspx

With more than 10,000 members, the American Health Lawyers Association is the nation's largest, nonpartisan, 501(c)(3) educational organization devoted to legal issues in the healthcare field.

American Society of Law, Medicine and Ethics (ASLME): www.aslme.org

With roots extending back to 1911, ASLME is a nonprofit educational organization. Its mission is to provide high-quality scholarship, debate, and critical thought for professionals at the intersection of law, medicine, and ethics.

Members come together to examine big health questions with far-reaching social ramifications like genetic testing and research, medical record privacy, end-of-life decisions, and the dynamics of informed consent.

American Society of Transplantation: www.a-s-t.org

The American Society of Transplantation is an international organization of transplant professionals dedicated to advancing the field of transplantation through the promotion of research, education, advocacy, and organ donation to improve patient care. A-S-T.org offers education and research related to transplantation.

Association of Organ Procurement Organizations (AOPO): www.aopo.org

AOPO represents and serves organ procurement organizations through advocacy, support, and development of activities that will maximize the availability of organs and tissues and enhance the quality, effectiveness, and integrity of the donation process. The AOPO website provides information on committees, councils, and taskforces, as well as a calendar of AOPO events.

Bioethics.net: www.bioethics.net

A leading website on medical ethics, it contains articles, journals, news, jobs, events, and more related to bioethics.

Biotech & Health Care Ethics: http://www.scu.edu/ethics/practicing/focusareas/medical

The site has articles, cases, and links on medical ethics, biotechnology and ethics, clinical ethics, end-of-life decision making, culturally competent health care, and public health policy from the Markkula Center for Applied Ethics at Santa Clara University. Center staff and scholars work with hospitals, public health departments, and other agencies to analyze real-world ethical issues in medicine and biotechnology and to develop innovative tools and programs to address them.

Center for Bioethics and Human Dignity: www.cbhd.org/

The center exists to equip thought leaders to engage the issues of bioethics using the tools of rigorous research, conceptual analysis, charitable critique, leading-edge publication, and effective teaching.

Center for the Study of Ethics in the Professions: http://ethics.iit.edu/

In June 1996, the Center received a grant from the National Science Foundation to put its extensive collection of codes of ethics on the web. This included those codes of ethics of professional societies, corporations, government, and academic institutions of the over 850 codes in the paper archive. Earlier versions of codes of ethics of some organizations represented are available to allow researchers to study the development of codes. A literature review, an introduction to the codes, and a user's guide are included.

Cornell University Law School: www.law.cornell.edu/uscode/

Find U.S. Code materials.

Donate Life America: www.shareyourlife.org

Donate Life America assists in mobilizing the transplantation community to educate the American public on the need for organ, eye, and tissue donation and motivating the public to make an actionable donor designation. The organization publishes brochures, program kits, and other materials; provides technical assistance and referral services; coordinates the national campaign for organ, eye, and tissue donation; identifies measurable best practices; and leads the Donor Designation Collaborative.

Emerald: http://emerald7tfb.wordpress.com/2011/05/22/legal-aspects-of-reproductive-rights/

Articles and Discussion on Women's Reproductive Rights

National Association of Emergency Medical Technicians: EMT Oath and Code of Ethics: http://www.naemt.org/about_us/emtoath.aspx

EMT Oath

Be it pledged as an Emergency Medical Technician, I will honor the physical and judicial laws of God and man. I will follow that regimen which, according to my ability and judgment, I consider for the benefit of patients and abstain from whatever is deleterious and mischievous, nor shall I suggest any such counsel. Into whatever homes I enter, I will go into them for the benefit of only the sick and injured, never revealing what I see or hear in the lives of men unless required by law.

I shall also share my medical knowledge with those who may benefit from what I have learned. I will serve unselfishly and continuously in order to help make a better world for all mankind.

While I continue to keep this oath unviolated, may it be granted to me to enjoy life, and the practice of the art, respected by all men, in all times. Should I trespass or violate this oath, may the reverse be my lot.

So help me God.

Written by: Charles B. Gillespie, M.D.
Adopted by the National Association of Emergency Medical Technicians, 1978

EthicsWeb.ca: www.ethicsweb.ca/resources/bioethics/

EthicsWeb.ca is a collection of ethics-related websites run by philosopher–ethicist Chris MacDonald. Chris has been administering respected ethics-related websites since 1994. The style and function of the various EthicsWeb.ca websites vary, but each strives to present a selected range of high-quality, ethics-related resources on a particular topic. Most of the EthicsWeb.ca sites have a Canadian "slant," while providing many links to U.S. top healthcare ethics websites providing information that is of interest to international visitors.

Eye Bank Association of America (EBAA): www.restoresight.org

The EBAA champions the restoration of sight through core services to its members, who advance donation, transplantation, and research in their communities and throughout the world. EBAA online has information about donations, awards and grants, and accreditations and certifications.

Index of Ethics Codes: http://ethics.iit.edu/indexOfCodes.php?cat_id=31

Listed by profession

Kantian Ethics: http://ethics.sandiego.edu/theories/Kant/index.asp

Immanuel Kant and Kantian ethics website

Kennedy Institute of Ethics: http://kennedyinstitute.georgetown.edu/

The Kennedy Institute of Ethics is one of the world's premier bioethics institutes. Founded at Georgetown University in 1971, its faculty includes founders of the field as well as next-generation leaders. With a top-ranked graduate program, the world's most comprehensive bioethics library, a highly praised intensive summer course for health care practitioners, and faculty expertise on issues such as health care reform, death and dying, clinical research ethics, abortion, and environmental ethics, the Institute is a renowned resource for the University, the policy world, and the global bioethics community.

Living Wills/Advance Directives: http://www.mindspring.com/~scottr/will.html

An organized set of links to living will (advance directive) web pages

Markkula Center for Applied Ethics: www.scu.edu/ethics/practicing/focusareas/medical

This website contains articles, cases, and links on medical ethics, biotechnology ethics, clinical ethics, end-of-life decision making, culturally competent health care, and public health policy from the Markkula Center for Applied Ethics at Santa Clara University. Center staff and scholars work with hospitals, public health departments, and other agencies to analyze real-world ethical issues in medicine and biotechnology and to develop innovative tools and programs to address them.

MedlinePlus: www.nlm.nih.gov/medlineplus/endoflifeissues.html

Comprehensive review of "end-of-life" issues

National Advisory Board on Social Welfare and Health Care Ethics: www.etene.fi/en

The National Advisory Board on Social Welfare and Health Care Ethics deals with ethical issues related to health care and the status and rights of patients from the point of view of principle.

National Center for Biotechnology Information: www.ncbi.nlm.nih.gov/

The National Center for Biotechnology Information advances science and health by providing access to biomedical and genomic information.

National Marrow Donor Program: www.marrow.org

The National Marrow Donor Program and the Be the Match Foundation are nonprofit organizations dedicated to creating an opportunity for all patients to receive the bone marrow or umbilical cord blood transplantation they need, when they need it.

Provider & Patient Rights: http://www.nahc.org/Consumer/wamraap.html

A model patient bill of rights the National Association for Home Care (NAHC) has developed, based on the patient rights currently enforced by law.

Questia: http://www.questia.com/

Online library of books, with over 77,000 full-text books; 4 million journal, magazine, and newspaper articles; and encyclopedia entries. A subscription to the Questia academic library also includes digital productivity tools for highlighting text, taking notes, and generating footnotes and bibliographies in seven different styles.

Scientific Registry of Transplant Recipients: www.ustransplant.org/

The Scientific Registry of Transplant Recipients is a national database of statistics related to solid organ transplantation—kidney, liver, pancreas, intestine, heart, and lung. The registry covers the full range of transplantation activity, from organ donation and waiting list candidates to transplant recipients and survival statistics.

TransWeb.org: www.transweb.org

TransWeb.org provides information about donation and transplantation to the general public in order to improve organ and tissue procurement efforts worldwide and to provide transplant patients and families worldwide with information specifically dealing with transplantation-related issues and concerns.

United Network for Organ Sharing (UNOS): www.unos.org

UNOS is a nonprofit, scientific and educational organization that administers the nation's only Organ Procurement and Transplantation Network (OPTN), established by the U.S. Congress in 1984. Through the OPTN, the UNOS collects and manages data about every transplantation event occurring in the United States, facilitates the organ matching and placement process using UNOS-developed data technology and the UNOS Organ Center, and brings together medical professionals, transplant recipients, and donor families to develop organ transplantation policy.

LEGAL WEBSITES

American Bar Association (ABA): www.abanet.org

The ABA is the largest voluntary professional association in the world. With more than 400,000 members, the ABA provides law school accreditation, continuing legal education, information about the law, programs to assist lawyers and judges in their work, and initiatives to improve the legal system for the public.

American Health Lawyers Association (AHLA): www.healthlawyers.org

With more than 10,000 members, the AHLA is the nation's largest, non-partisan, 501(c)(3) educational organization devoted to legal issues in the healthcare field. AHLA provides resources to address the issues facing its active members who practice in law firms, government, in-house settings, and academia and who represent the entire spectrum of the health industry. Members of this association have benefits including webinars, publications, and help for continuing law education.

American Society of Law, Medicine & Ethics (ASLME): www.aslme.org

The ASLME is a community of colleagues across three major disciplines. The ASLME publishes two nationally acclaimed peer-reviewed journals: *The Journal of Law, Medicine & Ethics* and *The American Journal of Law & Medicine*; the society also sponsors conferences and webinars, as well as research and grants.

Black's Law Dictionary: http://www.blackslawdictionary.com/Home/Mobile.aspx

Black's Law Dictionary includes thousands of new terms and definitions.

Court Reporters: www.courtreporters.com

The website provides legal professionals immediate Internet access to the highest caliber and most reliable court reporters nationwide. It also was created as an Internet community for the court reporting professionals and other individuals wishing to receive information on valuable resources such as career opportunities, education, and other resources.

Courtroom Sciences: www.courtroomsciences.com

Courtroom Sciences provides litigation solutions to corporations and law firms through a complete set of tools and services. Each Courtroom Sciences service can be used independently or together, with experts in each respective area of litigation support.

FindLaw: www.findlaw.com

FindLaw, a Thomson Reuters business, is the world's leading provider of online legal information and Internet marketing solutions for law firms. The company has the largest team of online experts in the industry, a national network of sales consultants, and a proven ability to get results for its clients.

Free Employment Law and HR Reference Center: http://ppspublishers.com/ articles/resources/?c15payperclick&source5google_ads&kw5employees

Extensive employment law articles and information

Google Scholar: http://en.wikipedia.org/wiki/Google_Scholar

Google Scholar is a freely accessible web search engine that indexes the full text of scholarly literature across an array of publishing formats and disciplines.

Guide to Law Online: www.loc.gov/law/guide

The Guide to Law Online, prepared by the Law Library of Congress Public Services Division, is an annotated guide to sources of information on government and law available online. It includes selected links to useful and reliable sites for legal information.

Healthcare Law Net: http://www.healthcarelawnet.com

Health Insurance for students, professionals, and the public

Health Law Resource: www.netreach.net/~wmanning

Primarily, this page is intended as a resource for healthcare practitioners, professionals, or anyone interested in learning more about the dynamic field of healthcare law and, more specifically, the regulatory and transactional aspects of healthcare law practice.

HGExperts.com: www.hgexperts.com

HGExperts.com is a legal experts dictionary with an expert witness directory, litigation support, publications for expert witnesses, forensic science, and more.

InjuryBoard: www.injuryboard.com

InjuryBoard is a growing community of attorneys, medical professionals, safety industry experts, and local activists committed to making a difference by helping families stay safe and avoid injury and helping those who are injured get the assistance they need.

Jury Verdict Review & Analysis: http://www.jvra.com/

State and national monthly publications, providing an excellent resource for regular review and analysis of civil jury verdicts throughout the United States since 1980

Law.com: www.law.com

Through Law.com's linked information sites, legal professionals can track developments in their practice specialties within the practice centers, research legal technology purchases, participate in accredited online training, access VerdictSearch.com (the nation's most current verdict and settlement database), use LawJobs.com to conduct national job searches, identify expert witnesses at ALMExperts.com, and purchase books, newsletters, and other publications at LawCatalog.com.

Law Dictionary: http://dictionary.law.com/

Simply enter a term or phrase to conduct a search of this legal dictionary on law.com.

LawGuru.com: www.lawguru.com

LawGuru.com is a law database, available to both students and professionals, from which individuals may receive answers to questions, search past answers, and find a local attorney.

Lawyers: www.lawyers.com

Lawyers.com is the most complete, trusted source for identifying qualified legal counsel. Resources on the site include legal forms, panel discussions, lawyer selection, and legal issue explanations and discussions.

Legal Information Institute (LII): www.law.cornell.edu

LII is a not-for-profit group that believes everyone should be able to read and understand the laws that govern them, without cost. LII carries out this vision by publishing law online for free, creating materials that help people understand law, and exploring new technologies that make it easier for people to find the law.

LexisNexis: www.lexisnexis.com

LexisNexis is a leading global provider of content-enabled workflow solutions to professionals in law firms, corporations, government, law enforcement, taxes, accounting, academic institutions, and risk/compliance assessment.

National Medical Malpractice—Review and Analysis: http://www.jvra.com/ sample_edition/mmra.pdf:

The site samples a monthly national review of state and federal civil jury medical malpractice verdicts with professional analysis and commentary. The cases summarized in detail are obtained from an ongoing monthly survey of the state and federal courts throughout the United States.

NoLo: www.nolo.com

NoLo aims to help Americans understand the legal rules and procedures that affect their lives so they can handle legal matters themselves or seek expert help armed with the knowledge they need. Not only is free law information provided, but the site also includes articles discussing various law issues including taxes, employment laws, immigration, and more.

Resources for Attorneys: www.resourcesforattorneys.com

Despite its name, this directory is actually useful for the general Internet community as well, and it includes legal resources, law practice listings, and even lifestyle management information.

State Resources (legal links): www.alllaw.com/state_resources

AllLaw.com provides state legal links on a range of topics from attorneys to law schools to forms to the state bar. The easy-to-use site is particularly helpful for researching state-by-state information.

Supreme Court Collection: www.law.cornell.edu/supct

This database of all Supreme Court decisions can be explored by case name, topic, or the individual justices.

United States Code: http://www.law.cornell.edu/uscode/

This version of the U.S. Code is generated from the most recent official version made available by the U.S. House of Representatives. The House server provides exact, current information.

United States Courts.gov: www.uscourts.gov

United States Courts is the government website for all things related to the U.S. courts, including links to the federal courts, judges, court reporters, and more.

United States Court: http://www.uscourts.gov/court_locator.aspx#7th

Tabs for federal courts, rules and policies, judges and judgeships, statistics, forms and fees, court records, educational resources and news

VersusLaw: www.versuslaw.com

VersusLaw is a web-based research site that provides three different law research plans, each containing both federal and state appellate case law opinions.

WashLaw: www.washlaw.edu

This legal research website divides legal topics nationally, internationally, and statewide.

Westlaw: www.westlaw.com

Although subscription is required, Westlaw has up-to-date legal products and services.

Wrong Diagnosis: www.wrongdiagnosis.com/

WrongDiagnosis.com provides a free health information service to help people understand their health better, offering crucial and factual health information that is otherwise difficult to find. The objective of the site is to encourage consumers to be informed and interested in managing their health and to know what questions to ask their doctors to help ensure they are getting the best health care possible.

BEST PRACTICES

Advisory Board Company (ABC): www.advisoryboardcompany.com

ABC serves nearly 3000 progressive organizations worldwide—healthcare, health benefits, and educational organizations alike—and provides innovative solutions to their most pressing challenges so they can "hardwire" best-practice performance.

American Cancer Society (ACS): www.cancer.org

The goal of ACS is to prevent cancer, save lives, and diminish suffering from cancer through research, cancer information services, advocacy, community service, and international programs.

Association of Cancer Online Resources (ACOR): www.acor.org

At the heart of ACOR is a large collection of cancer-related Internet mailing lists serving subscribers around the globe through informative email messages. In addition to supporting the mailing lists, ACOR develops and hosts state-of-the-art Internet-based knowledge systems that allow the public to find and use credible information relevant to their illness.

CancerLinks: www.cancerlinks.org

With this search engine, visitors can locate relevant websites with answers to questions and concerns about anything cancer-related. This website includes, for example, links to: Search A-Z Cancer Links; and Cancers Supportive Care.

Careplans.com: www.careplans.com

Careplans.com provides resources for nursing assessment, planning, implementation, and evaluation. The site includes articles, links, and libraries to assist caregivers in the care planning process.

Centre for Evidence Based Medicine (CEBM): www.cebm.net

Established in Oxford, CEBM provides free support and resources to doctors, clinicians, teachers, and others interested in learning more about evidence-based medicine through resources such as research and development, training of students and clinicians, and training of the trainers.

Clinical Pathways: www.openclinical.org/clinicalpathways.html

The website provides explanation of clinical pathways and their benefits. The website's host OpenClinical.org is designed to be a "one-stop shop" for anyone interested in learning about and/or tracking developments on advanced knowledge management technologies for health care such as point-of-care decision support systems, "intelligent" guidelines, and clinical workflow.

Clinical Practice Guidelines: www.ahcpr.gov/clinic/cpgsix.htm

This website is under the Agency for Healthcare Research and Quality and provides links to archives and the National Guideline Clearinghouse. This website includes, for example, links to: Evidence Based Practice; Outcomes and Effectiveness; Technology Assessments; Preventative Services; Funding Opportunities; and, National Guideline Clearinghouse.

Clinical Trials Listing Service of CenterWatch: www.centerwatch.com

CenterWatch is committed to providing patients and their advocates information on clinical trials, specific drugs, and other essential health and educational resources. CenterWatch's Clinical Trials Listing Service offers several resources including site promotion and identification services, grant opportunities, and a variety of educational books and publications; they also offer a wide range of tools and resources to help clinical trial sponsors remain current and strong.

Institute for Safe Medication Practices (ISMP): www.ismp.org/

The ISMP, based in suburban Philadelphia, is the nation's only 501(c)(3) nonprofit organization devoted entirely to medication error prevention and safe medication use. ISMP represents over 30 years of experience in helping healthcare practitioners keep patients safe and continues to lead efforts to improve the medication use process.

MD Consult: www.mdconsult.com

MD Consult offers instant access to more than 80 medical journals and clinics, 50 leading medical references across a wide range of specialties, clinically relevant drug information, and 10,000 patient handouts.

National Cancer Institute (NCI) Clinical Trials: www.cancer.gov/clinicaltrials

NCI's Clinical Trials web page is a collection of clinical trials, results, and educational materials about the trials.

National Council of State Boards of Nursing: http://www.ncsbn.org

The National Council of State Boards of Nursing (NCSBN) provides education, service, and research through collaborative leadership to promote evidence-based regulatory excellence for patient safety and public protection.

National Organization for Rare Diseases (NORD): www.rarediseases.org

NORD provides information about diseases, referrals to patient organizations, research grants and fellowships, advocacy for the rare disease community, and medication assistance programs that help needy patients obtain certain drugs they could not otherwise afford.

HEALTHCARE RESOURCES

Alternative Medicine: www.askdrweil.com

Dr. Andrew Weil, MD, answers questions on health care, aging, vitamins, health plans, and more.

American Academy of Pain Management: www.painmed.org

Founded in 1983 as the American Academy of Algology, the American Academy of Pain Medicine has evolved as the primary organization for physicians practicing the specialty of pain medicine in the United States.

American Hospital Association (AHA): www.aha.org

AHA is a society of healthy communities where all individuals reach their highest potential for health through advocacy, issues, research and trends, and a news, member, and resource center.

American Library Association: www.ala.org

The American Library Association is the oldest and largest library association in the world, with more than 65,000 members. This is a subscription based website.

American Medical Association (AMA): www.ama-assn.org/

AMA promotes the art and science of medicine and the betterment of public health through physician resources, education and careers, advocacy, and medical journals. This is a subscription based website.

American Pain Foundation: www.painfoundation.org

Founded in 1997, the American Pain Foundation is an independent nonprofit 501(c)(3) organization that seeks to help people with pain through information, advocacy, and support. Their mission is to improve the quality of life of people with pain by raising public awareness, providing practical information, promoting research, and advocating to remove barriers and increase access to effective pain management. This is a subscription based website.

Directory of Open Access Journals: www.doaj.org/

This service covers free, full-text, quality-controlled scientific and scholarly journals, covering all subjects and languages. There are now 3231 journals in the directory. Currently 1036 journals are searchable at article level.

Dr. Oz: http://www.doctoroz.com/

Dr. Oz, world-renowned thoracic surgeon, hosts an informative TV health show. This website includes links to, for example: Home, Ask Oz, Oz's Transformation Nation, Recent Shows, and Search link.

FamilyDoctor.org: www.familydoctor.org/online/famdocen/home.html

Health information for the whole family from the American Academy of Family Practitioners

Guide to Internet Resources for Cancer: http://www.cancerindex.org/clinks1.htm

The Guide to Internet Resources for Cancer is a gateway to cancer information on the Internet established in 1996. This nonprofit guide contains over 100 pages and more than 4,000 links to cancer-related information. It is regularly updated, and links are periodically verified using a link-checker.

HealthWorld Online: www.healthy.net

HealthWorld Online offers natural solutions to all health-related questions while providing a community for the health conscious.

InteliHealth: www.intelihealth.com

InteliHealth is one of the nation's leading diversified healthcare benefits companies, serving approximately 37.2 million people with information and resources to help them make better informed decisions about their health care. InteliHealth offers a broad range of traditional and consumer-directed health insurance products and related services, including medical, pharmacy, dental, behavioral health, group life and disability plans, and medical management capabilities and healthcare management services for Medicaid plans.

Library Spot: www.libraryspot.com

Library Spot is a free virtual library resource center for educators and students, librarians and their patrons, families, businesses, and just about anyone exploring the web for valuable research information.

Life Extension Foundation: www.lef.org

The Life Extension Foundation is the world's largest organization dedicated to finding scientific methods for addressing disease, aging, and death. The Life Extension Foundation is a nonprofit group that funds pioneering scientific research aimed at achieving an indefinitely extended healthy human life span. The fruits of this research are used to develop novel disease prevention and treatment protocols.

MayoClinic.com: www.mayoclinic.com/

One of the nation's finest clinics provides online information on diseases and conditions, drugs and supplements, treatment decisions, and healthy living.

MD's Choice: www.mdschoice.com

MD's Choice is a scientifically based company dedicated to health and understanding of individual nutritional needs. Information and education are the primary goals. This site contains more than 800 printed pages of vitamin, mineral, herbal, and nutritional information.

Medscape: www.medscape.com

Medscape from WebMD offers robust and integrated medical information and educational tools from specialists, primary care physicians, and other health professionals. Key features consist of selected daily professional medical news for specialties from Reuters, Medscape Medical News, and medical news journal publishers, as well as business, financial, managed care, and medical practice information.

Medscape: http://search.medscape.com/reference-search

Physician site for discovering state of the art treatments, trends, and technologies by speciality

National Health Museum (NHM): www.accessexcellence.com

NHM is a national educational program that provides health, biology, and life science teachers online access to their colleagues, scientists, and other critical sources of new scientific information.

Orchid: http://www.orchidrecoverycenter.com/

"Where Women Heal" healthcare centers and treatment

Telemedicine: www.amdtelemedicine.com/

AMD Global Telemedicine is a supplier of medical technology for telemedicine with over 5700 installations in 79 countries. This includes medical devices, complete telemedicine encounter management solutions, and application software for telemedicine.

Virtual Hospital: www.uihealthcare.com/vh/

From the University of Iowa (UI), Virtual Hospital provides health content, prepared and reviewed by health professionals, and continues to serve the UI healthcare mission of educating patients and families about their health and informing them about the expert services available at UI hospitals and clinics for maintaining their health and well-being.

Virtual Library Pharmacy: www.pharmacy.org

Virtual Library Pharmacy includes all pharmacy-related Internet resources compiled by David Bourne, PhD, Professor of Pharmaceutics at the University of Oklahoma.

HOSPITAL AND PHYSICIAN FINDERS

American Board of Medical Specialties (ABMS): www.abms.org

The primary function of ABMS is to assist its member boards in developing and implementing educational and professional standards to evaluate and certify physician specialists. By participating in these initiatives, ABMS also serves as a unique and highly influential voice in the healthcare industry, bringing focus and rigor to issues involving specialization and certification in medicine. ABMS, and its website, is a designated primary equivalent source of credential information.

American Medical Association DoctorFinder: www.ama-assn.org/aps/amahg.htm

The American Medical Association helps doctors help patients by uniting physicians nationwide to work on the most important professional and public health issues. This online physician Locator helps you find a perfect match for your medical needs DoctorFinder provides basic professional information on virtually every licensed physician in the United States. This includes more than 814,000 doctors.

Best Hospitals: www.usnews.com/usnews/health/best-hospitals/tophosp.htm

U.S. News & World Report has ranked over 5,000 hospitals in 16 adult specialties and 10 pediatric specialties.

Best Hospitals: http://health.yahoo.net/articles/healthcare/best-hospitals-2011-12

Best Hospitals 2011–12

For clinical excellence, these 17 hospitals possess a rare blend of breadth and depth. A place on the Best Hospitals Honor Roll is reserved for medical centers that demonstrate unusually high expertise across multiple specialties, scoring at or near the top in at least six of 16 specialties. Just 17 of the nearly 5,000 hospitals evaluated for the 2011–12 rankings qualified.

Avery Comarow, US News & World Report, *July 19, 2011*

Besthospitals.com: www.besthospitals.com

A search engine of the best hospitals in America

HealthGrades: www.healthgrades.com

HealthGrades is the leading healthcare ratings organization, providing ratings and profiles of hospitals, nursing homes, and physicians to consumers, corporations, health plans, and hospitals. HealthGrades provides information and help for consumers, hospitals, health plans, liability insurers, and the community.

HospitalConnectSearch: www.hospitalconnect.com

HospitalConnectSearch is a complete source for reliable hospital information, organized by specific areas of interest.

HospitalLink.com: www.hospitallink.com

The HospitalLink.com website directory makes it easy to locate more than 6,000 hospitals and 1,700 websites by city, state, hospital name, and/or zip code.

American Nurses Credentialing Centerhttp://www.nursecredentialing.org/ Magnet.aspx

The Magnet Recognition Program® recognizes healthcare organizations for quality patient care, nursing excellence and innovations in professional nursing practice. Consumers rely on Magnet designation as the ultimate credential for high quality nursing. Developed by the American Nurses Credentialing Center (ANCC), Magnet is the leading source of successful nursing practices and strategies worldwide.

Massachusetts General Hospital: www.mgh.harvard.edu

The third oldest general hospital in the United States and the oldest and largest hospital in New England, Massachusetts General continues its tradition of excellence today. The hospital is consistently ranked among the top five hospitals in the nation by *U.S. News & World Report*. In 2008, Massachusetts General was redesignated a Magnet hospital, the highest honor for nursing excellence awarded by the American Nurses Credentialing Center.

National Practitioner Data Bank: www.npdb-hipdb.com

National Practitioner Data Bank is a bank of healthcare data with information about registering, billing and fees, disputing reports, reporting codes, Section 1921, and more.

INTERNATIONAL MEDICAL WEBSITES

Cancer Index: www.cancerindex.org/clinks5o.htm

The aim of the Cancer Index is to make it easier to find more specific information quickly. This is achieved by providing a directory of some of the key cancer-related sites and pages. Links are sorted into categories (by disease-type, medical specialty, country, etc.) and, where possible, annotation is provided to give the reader a brief description of each site or organization. In addition to links, the site presents basic information about cancer-related topics. Also, the site aims to draw the reader's attention to issues about cancer-related information on the Internet, especially those relating to the quality of information.

Union for International Cancer Control (UICC): www.uicc.org

The UICC is the leading international nongovernmental organization dedicated to the global prevention and control of cancer. UICC's mission is to connect, mobilize, and support organizations, leading experts, key stakeholders, and volunteers in a dynamic community working together to eliminate cancer as a life-threatening disease for future generations. Founded in 1933, UICC unites over 300 member organizations, specialized and engaged in cancer control, in more than 100 countries around the world. UICC is nonprofit, nonpolitical, and nonsectarian. Its headquarters are in Geneva, Switzerland.

World Health Network: www.worldhealth.net

World Health Network is the leading Internet portal for anti-aging medicine. This website provides links to, for example: Home, Events, Anti-aging Directories; Virtual Exhibit Hall; and Search link.

World Health Organization (WHO): www.who.int

WHO is the directing and coordinating authority for health within the United Nations system. It is responsible for providing leadership on global health matters, shaping the health research agenda, setting norms and standards, articulating evidence-based policy options, providing technical support to countries, and monitoring and assessing health trends.

In the 21st century, health is a shared responsibility, involving equitable access to essential care and collective defense against transnational threats. This website provides links to, for example: Health Topics; Data and Statistics; Media Centre, Publications; Countries; About WHO; Programmes and Projects; and WHO Reform for a Healthy Future.

World Medical Association (WMA): www.wma.net

The WMA is an international organization representing physicians. It was created to ensure the independence of physicians and to work for the highest possible standards of ethical behavior and care by physicians at all times. The WMA provides a forum for its member associations to communicate freely, to cooperate actively, to achieve consensus on high standards of medical ethics and professional competence, and to promote the professional freedom of physicians worldwide. This unique partnership facilitates high-caliber, humane care to patients in a healthy environment, enhancing the quality of life for all people in the world.

REFERENCES

Encyclopædia Britannica: http://www.britannica.com/

Articles are aimed at educated adults and written by about 100 full-time editors and more than 4,000 expert contributors. It is regarded as the most scholarly of encyclopædias. The *Britannica* is the oldest English-language encyclopædia still in print.

Merriam-Webster Online Dictionary: www.merriam-webster.com/

This website offers a full dictionary. Other resources include their unabridged dictionary, video, and the Britannica Online Encyclopædia.

Wikipedia: http://en.wikipedia.org/wiki/Wikipaedia

This is a free, web-based, collaborative, multilingual encyclopedia project supported by the non-profit Wikimedia Foundation. Its 18 million articles (over 3.6 million in English) have been written collaboratively by volunteers around the world, and almost all of its articles can be edited by anyone with access to the site. As of May 2011, there were editions of Wikipedia in 281 languages. Wikipedia was launched in 2001 by Jimmy Wales and Larry Sanger and has become the largest and most popular general reference work on the Internet, ranking around seventh among all websites on Alexa and having 365 million readers.

Since its creation in 2001, Wikipedia has grown rapidly into one of the largest reference websites, attracting 400 million unique visitors monthly as of March 2011 according to ComScore. There are more than 82,000 active contributors working on more than 17,000 articles. As of today, there are 3,661,176 articles in English. Every day, hundreds of thousands of visitors from around the world collectively make tens of thousands of edits and create thousands of new articles to augment the knowledge held by the Wikipedia encyclopedia.

Glossary

abandonment Unilateral severance by the physician of the professional relationship between himself or herself and the patient without reasonable notice when the patient needs continuing care.

abortion Premature termination of pregnancy before the fetus is capable of sustaining life independent of the mother.

accreditation An evaluative process in which a healthcare facility undergoes an examination of its policies, procedures, practices, and performance by an external sector organization ("accrediting body") to ensure that it is meeting predetermined criteria. This usually involves both on and off-site surveys.

admissibility (of evidence) Refers to the issue of whether a court, applying the rules of evidence, is bound to receive or permit introduction of a particular piece of evidence.

advance directives Written instructions expressing an individual's healthcare wishes in the event that he or she becomes incapacitated and is unable to make such decisions for himself or herself.

adverse drug reaction Unusual or unexpected response to a normal dose of a medication; an injury caused by the use of a drug in the usual, acceptable fashion.

affidavit A voluntary statement of facts, or a voluntary declaration in writing of facts, that a person swears to be true before an official authorized to administer an oath.

agent An individual who has been designated by a legal document to make decisions on behalf of another individual; a substitute decision maker.

Americans with Disabilities Act (ADA) Federal act that bars employers from discriminating against disabled persons in hiring, promotion, or other provisions of employment.

appellant Party who appeals the decision of a lower court to a court of higher jurisdiction.

appellee Party against whom an appeal to a higher court is taken.

artificial nutrition and hydration Providing food and liquids whenever a patient is unable to eat or drink, such as in intravenous feeding.

Aristotle A Greek philosopher, a student of Plato, and teacher of Alexander the Great. His writings cover many subjects, including physics, metaphysics, poetry, theater, music, logic, rhetoric, linguistics, politics, government, ethics, biology, and zoology. Aristotle is one of the most important founding figures in Western philosophy. Aristotle's writings were the first to create a comprehensive system of Western philosophy encompassing morality and aesthetics, logic and science, politics and metaphysics. See: http://en.wikipedia.org/wiki/Aristotle

assault Intentional act that is designed to make the victim fearful and produces reasonable apprehension of harm.

attestation Act of witnessing a document in writing.

autonomy Right of an individual to make his or her own independent decisions.

battery Intentional touching of one person by another without the consent of the person being touched.

beneficence Describes the principle of doing good, demonstrating kindness, and helping others.

best evidence rule Legal doctrine requiring that primary evidence of a fact (such as an original document) be introduced, or that an acceptable explanation be given, before a copy can be introduced or testimony given concerning the fact.

bioethics The philosophical study of the ethical controversies brought about by advances in biology, research (e.g., human cloning), and medicine.

borrowed servant doctrine Refers to a situation in which an employee is temporarily placed under the control of someone other than his or her primary employer. It may involve a situation in which an employee is carrying out the specific instructions of a physician. The traditional example is that of a hospital-employed nurse who is "borrowed" and is under the control of an attending surgeon during an operating room procedure. The temporary employer of the borrowed servant can be held responsible for the negligent acts of the borrowed servant under the doctrine of *respondeat superior*. This rule is not easily applied, especially if the acts of the employee are for the furtherance of the objectives of the employer. The courts apply a narrow application if the employee is fulfilling the requirements of his or her position.

captain of the ship doctrine A doctrine making the physician responsible for the negligent acts of other professionals because he or she had the right to control and oversee the totality of care provided to the patient.

cardiopulmonary resuscitation A lifesaving method used by caregivers to restore heartbeat and breathing.

case citation Describes where a court's opinion in a particular case can be located. It identifies the parties in the case, the text in which the case can be found, the court writing the opinion, and the year in which the case was decided. For example, the citation "*Bouvia v. Superior Court (Glenchur)*, 225 Cal. Rptr. 297 (Ct. App. 1986)" is read as follows: "*Bouvia v. Superior Court (Glenchur)*" identifies the basic parties involved in the lawsuit. "225 Cal. Rptr. 297" identifies the case as being reported in volume 225 of the California Reporter at page 297. "Ct. App. 1986" identifies the case as being in the California Court of Appeals in 1986.

case law Aggregate of reported cases on a particular legal subject as formed by the decisions of those cases.

charitable immunity Legal doctrine that developed out of the English court system holding charitable institutions blameless for their negligent acts.

civil law Body of law that describes the private rights and responsibilities of individuals. The part of law that does not deal with crimes, it involves actions filed by one individual against another (e.g., actions in tort and contract).

clinical privileges On qualification, the diagnostic and therapeutic procedures that an institution allows a physician to perform on a specified patient population. Qualification includes a review of a physician's credentials, such as medical school diploma, state licensure, and residency training.

closed-shop contract Labor–management agreement that provides that only members of a particular union may be hired.

common law Body of principles that has evolved and continues to evolve and expand from court decisions. Many of the legal principles and rules applied by courts in the United States had their origins in English common law.

complaint In a negligence action, the first pleading that is filed by the plaintiff's attorney. It is the first statement of a case by the plaintiff against the defendant and states a cause of action, notifying the defendant as to the basis for the suit.

Conditions for Participation (CoPs) Health and safety standards developed by CMS that healthcare organizations must meet in order to begin, and continue, participating in the Medicare and Medicaid programs. CMS also develops Conditions for Coverage (CfCs). These minimum health and safety standards are the foundation for improving quality and protecting the health and safety of beneficiaries. And, through a process called "deeming," CMS ensures that the standards of accrediting organizations recognized by CMS meet or exceed the Medicare standards set forth in the CoPs and CfCs.

Congressional Record Daily-published archive in which the proceedings of Congress are compiled. It is the first record of debate officially reported, printed, and published directly by the federal government. Publication began March 4, 1873.

consent See *informed consent.*

consequentialism A moral theory that determines good or bad, right or wrong, based on good outcomes or consequences.

contextualism An ethical doctrine that considers the rightness or wrongness of an action, such as lying, to be based on the particular circumstances of a given situation. The implication is that lying is acceptable in one situation but not in another, even though the situation may be similar. In other words, it depends on the context within which something occurs.

criminal negligence Reckless disregard for the safety of others; the willful indifference to an injury after an act.

decisional capacity Having the mental capacity to make one's own decisions. Mental capacity refers to the ability to understand the risks, the benefits, the alternatives, and the consequences of one's actions. Inferred in this interpretation is knowing that the decision maker can reasonably distinguish right from wrong and good from bad.

defamation Injury of a person's reputation or character caused by the false statements of another made to a third person. Defamation includes both libel and slander.

defendant In a criminal case, the person accused of committing a crime. In a civil suit, the party against whom the suit is brought, demanding that he or she pay the other party legal relief.

demurrer Formal objection by one of the parties to a lawsuit that the evidence presented by the other party is insufficient to sustain an issue or case.

deontological ethics An ethical approach that focuses on duty, rather than the consequences, when determining the right conduct to be followed.

deposition A method of pretrial discovery that consists of statements of fact taken by a witness under oath in a question-and-answer format, as it would be in a court of law with opportunity given to the adversary to be present for cross-examination. Such statements may be admitted into evidence if it is impossible for a witness to attend a trial in person.

determinism The view that nothing happens without a cause.

directed verdict A trial judge decision declaring either that the evidence and/ or law is clearly in favor of one party or that the plaintiff has failed to establish a case, indicating that it is pointless for the trial to proceed further, and directing the jury to return a verdict for the appropriate party. The conclusion of the judge must be so clear and obvious that reasonable minds could not arrive at a different conclusion.

discharge summary That part of a medical record that summarizes a patient's initial complaints, course of treatment, final diagnosis, and instructions for follow-up care.

discovery To ascertain that which was previously unknown through a pretrial investigation. It includes testimony and documents that may be under the exclusive control of the other party. (Discovery facilitates out-of-court settlements.)

dogmatic Stubborn refusal to consider challenges to your own ethical point of view.

do-not-resuscitate (DNR) order Directive of a physician to withhold cardiopulmonary resuscitation in the event a patient experiences cardiac or respiratory arrest.

durable power of attorney A legal instrument enabling an individual to act on another's behalf. In the healthcare setting, a durable power of attorney for health care is a legal instrument that designates and grants authority to an agent, for example, to make healthcare decisions for another.

ethical conduct Conducting oneself in a manner consistent with acceptable principles of right and wrong. Such conduct may relate to one's community, country, profession, and so on.

ethical dilemma A situation that forces a decision to be made that involves breaking some ethical norm or contradicting some ethical value. It involves making a decision between two or more possible actions wherein any one of the actions can be justified as being the right decision, but whatever action is taken, there always remains some doubt as to whether the correct course of action was chosen. The effect of an action may put others at risk, harm others, or violate the rights of others.

ethicist A person, often with an advanced degree, who specializes in ethics through the application of theory and ethical principles governing right and wrong conduct. Ethicists often serve on hospital ethics committees and are an excellent resource for aid in resolving ethical dilemmas.

ethics The branch of philosophy that seeks to understand the nature, purposes, justification, and founding principles of moral rules and the systems they comprise. Ethics deals with values relating to human conduct. It focuses on the rightness and wrongness of actions, as well as the goodness and badness of motives and ends.

ethics committee A committee created to deal with ethical problems and dilemmas in the delivery of patient care.

euthanasia A Greek word meaning "the good death." It is an act conducted for the purpose of causing the merciful death of a person who suffers from an incurable condition, an example of which would be providing a patient with medications to hasten his or her death.

evidence Proof of a fact, legally presented in a manner prescribed by law, at trial.

expert witness Person who has special training, experience, skill, and/or knowledge in a relevant area and who is allowed to offer an opinion as testimony in court.

futility Having no useful result. Futility of treatment, as it relates to medical care, occurs when the physician recognizes that the effect of treatment will be of no benefit to the patient. Morally, the physician has a duty to inform the patient when there is little likelihood of success.

Good Samaritan laws Legislative enactments designed to protect those who stop to render aid in an emergency. These laws generally provide immunity for specified persons from any civil suit arising out of care rendered at the scene of an emergency, provided that the one rendering assistance has not done so in a grossly negligent manner.

grand jury Jury called to determine whether there is sufficient evidence that a crime has been committed to justify bringing a case to trial.

guardian Person appointed by a court to protect the interests of, and make decisions for, a person who is incapable of making his or her own decisions.

health According to the World Health Organization, "A state of complete physical, mental, and social well-being and not merely the absence of disease or infirmity."

Health Care Financing Administration (HCFA) Federal agency that coordinates the federal government's participation in the Medicare and Medicaid programs.

healthcare proxy Document that delegates the authority to make one's own healthcare decisions to another adult, known as the healthcare agent, when one has become incapacitated or is unable to make his or her own decisions.

hearsay rule Rule of evidence that restricts the admissibility of evidence that is not the personal knowledge of the witness. Hearsay evidence is admissible only under strict rules.

holographic will A will, hand written by the testator.

home health agency An agency that provides home health services. Home health care involves an array of services provided to patients in their homes, or in foster homes, in cases of acute illness, exacerbation of chronic illness, and disability. Such services are therapeutic and/or preventative.

home health care Home health care is an alternative for those who fear leaving the secure environment of their home. Such care is available through home health agencies, which provide a variety of services for the elderly living at home. Such services include part-time or intermittent nursing care; physical, occupational, and speech therapy; medical social services, home health aide services, and nutritional guidance; medical supplies other than drugs and biologicals prescribed by a physician; and the use of medical appliances.

hospice Long-term care for terminally ill persons, provided in a setting more economical than that of a hospital or nursing home. Hospice care generally is sought after a decision has been made to discontinue aggressive efforts to prolong life. A hospice program includes such characteristics as support services by trained individuals, family involvement, and control of pain and discomfort.

Hospital Compare A government website (Department of Health and Human Services) developed to help the public find a hospital and to determine its rankings, including national comparisons. http://www.hospitalcompare.hhs.gov/hospital-search.aspx?AspxAutoDetect CookieSupport=1

hospital glossary An expanded hospital glossary developed by the U.S. Department of Health and Human Services and presented on its website. http://www.hospitalcompare.hhs.gov/staticpages/help/hospital-glossary. aspx?Choice=A

hydration Intravenous addition of fluids to the circulatory system when the patient is not capable of swallowing.

immoral Behavior that is in opposition to accepted societal, religious, cultural, and/or professional standards.

incapacity An individual's lack of ability to make decisions for himself or herself.

incompetent Individual determined by a court to be incapable of making rational decisions on his or her own behalf.

independent contractor One who agrees to undertake work without being under the direct control or direction of the employer.

indictment Formal written accusation presented by a grand jury charging a person therein named with criminal conduct.

informed consent Legal concept providing that a patient has the right to know the potential risks, benefits, and alternatives of a medical procedure or treatment before consenting to the procedure or treatment. Informed consent implies that a patient does in fact understand a particular procedure or treatment, including the risks, benefits, and alternatives; is capable of making a decision; and gives consent voluntarily.

injunction Court order requiring a person to perform, or prohibiting a person from performing, a particular act.

in loco parentis Legal doctrine that permits the courts to assign a person to stand in the place of parents and possess their legal rights, duties, and responsibilities toward a child.

interrogatories List of questions sent from one party in a lawsuit to the other party to be answered under oath.

Joint Commission See *The Joint Commission.*

judicial notice Act by which a court, in conducting a trial or forming a decision, will of its own motion and without evidence recognize the existence and truth of certain facts bearing on the controversy at bar (e.g., serious falls require X-rays).

jurisdiction Right of a court to administer justice by hearing and deciding controversies.

jurisprudence Philosophy or science of law on which a particular legal system is built.

justice The obligation to be fair in the distribution of benefits and risks.

Kennedy Institute of Ethics The world's oldest and most comprehensive academic bioethics center. The institute was established at Georgetown University in 1971 by a grant from the Joseph P. Kennedy, Jr. Foundation. Visit: http://kennedyinstitute.georgetown.edu.

larceny Taking another person's property without consent and with the intent to permanently deprive the owner of its use and ownership.

legal wrong Invasion of a protected right.

liability As it relates to damages, an obligation one has incurred or might incur through a negligent act.

libel False or malicious writing that is intended to defame or dishonor another person and is published so that someone other than the one defamed will observe it.

life support Medical intervention(s) designed to prolong life (e.g., respirator, kidney dialysis machine, tube feedings).

living will A document in which an individual expresses in advance his or her wishes regarding the application of life-sustaining treatment in the event that he or she is incapable of doing so at some future time. A living will describes in advance the kind of care one wants to receive or does not wish to receive in the event that he or she is unable to make decisions for himself or herself. A living will takes effect when a person is in a terminal condition or permanent state of unconsciousness.

malfeasance Execution of an unlawful or improper act.

malpractice Professional misconduct, improper discharge of professional duties, or failure to meet the standard of care of a professional that results in harm to another. It is the negligence or carelessness of a professional person such as a nurse, pharmacist, physician, or accountant.

mandamus Action brought in a court of competent jurisdiction to compel a lower court or administrative agency to perform—or not to perform—a specific act.

Marcus Aurelius A Roman Emperor from 161 to 180. He ruled with Lucius Verus as co-emperor from 161 until Verus's death in 169. He was the last of the "Five Good Emperors," and is also considered one of the most important Stoic philosophers. http://en.wikipedia.org/wiki/Marcus_Aurelius

Medicaid Medical assistance provided in Title XIX of the Social Security Act. Medicaid is a state-administered program for the medically indigent.

Medicare Medical assistance provided in Title XVIII of the Social Security Act. Medicare is a health insurance program administered by the Social Security Administration for persons aged 65 years and older and for disabled persons who are eligible for benefits. Medicare Part A benefits provide coverage for inpatient hospital care, skilled nursing facility care, home health care, and hospice care. Medicare Part B benefits provide coverage for physician services, outpatient hospital services, diagnostic tests, various therapies, durable medical equipment, medical supplies, and prosthetic devices.

metaethics The study of ethical concepts.

misdemeanor Unlawful act of a less serious nature than a felony, usually punishable by a jail sentence for a term of less than 1 year and/or a fine.

misfeasance Improper performance of an act.

monotheism The worship of one God who is immortal, omniscient, omnipotent, and omnipresent.

nasogastric tube, insertion of Involves placing a tube through the patient's nose, down the back of the throat into the esophagus, and then into the stomach. Its purpose is to suction out the contents of the stomach.

negligence Omission or commission of an act that a reasonably prudent person would or would not do under given circumstances. It is a form of heedlessness or carelessness that constitutes a departure from the standard of care generally imposed on members of society.

Neiswanger Institute for Bioethics and Health Policy Dedicated to the three-fold mission of research, education, and service, the institute serves students and faculty of the Stritch School of Medicine, healthcare professionals and patients of Loyola University Health System, and professionals from the regional community and across the nation. http://www.bioethics.lumc.edu

non compos mentis "Not of sound mind"; suffering from some form of mental defect.

nonfeasance Failure to act, when there is a duty to act, as a reasonably prudent person would in similar circumstances.

normative ethics The study of what is right and wrong.

norms Accepted rules and ways of doing things. Without norms, society would be chaotic and unpredictable.

nuncupative will Oral statement intended as a last will made in anticipation of death.

objectivism The belief that morality is based on some universal, external, and unchangeable fact. For example, murder is always wrong.

ombudsman Person who is designated to speak and act on behalf of a patient/resident, especially in regard to his or her daily needs.

paternalism A doctrine that literally means "rule by the father." In health care, it is the concept of physicians making decisions for their patients, whereas the more acceptable approach is autonomy, whereby the physician informs the patient as to the risks, benefits, and alternatives to care and treatment, and then the patient makes the final choice as to what is best.

Patient Protection Affordable Care Act A Federal act passed by Congress and signed into law by the President in March 2010. Its design and purpose is to provide better health security by putting into place comprehensive health insurance reforms that hold insurance companies accountable, lower healthcare costs, guarantee more choice, and enhance the quality of care for all Americans. The battle continues as to the costs of implementing this Act in its entirety. See: http://en.wikipedia.org/wiki/Patient_Protection_and_Affordable_Care_Act.

perjury Willful act of giving false testimony under oath.

plaintiff Party who brings a civil suit seeking damages or other legal relief.

polytheism Belief and worship in many gods.

privileged communication Statement made to an attorney, physician, spouse, or anyone else in a position of trust. Because of the confidential nature of such information, the law protects it from being revealed, even in court.

probate Judicial proceeding that determines the existence and validity of a will.

probate court A court with jurisdiction over wills. Its powers range from deciding the validity of a will to distributing property.

process A series of related actions to achieve a defined outcome. Ordering and/or administering medications are processes.

prognosis Informed judgment regarding the likely course and probable outcome of a disease.

prophet One who claims to be a messenger of God.

proximate In immediate relation with something else. In negligence cases, the careless act must be the proximate cause of injury.

rational Having the capacity to think logically.

real evidence Evidence furnished by tangible things (e.g., medical records and equipment).

rebuttal Giving of evidence intended to contradict the effect of evidence introduced earlier by the opposing party.

relativism The belief that morality is relative to each individual culture. What is right in one culture may be wrong in another culture. In ethics, it is a theory that conceptions of truth and moral values are not absolute but are relative to the persons or groups holding them.

relativist A person who is a proponent of relativism.

release Statement signed by one person relinquishing a right or claim against another.

remand Referral of a case by an appeals court back to the original court, out of which it came, for the purpose of having some action taken there.

res gestae "The thing done": all of the surrounding events that become part of an incident. If statements are made as part of the incident, they are admissible in court as res gestae despite the hearsay rule.

res ipsa loquitur "The thing speaks for itself": a doctrine of law applicable to cases in which the defendant had exclusive control over the thing that caused the harm and in which the harm ordinarily could not have occurred without negligent conduct.

res judicata "The thing is decided": that which has been acted on or decided by the courts.

respirator A machine used to assist a patient's breathing.

respondeat superior "Let the master answer": an aphorism meaning that the employer is responsible for the legal consequences of the acts of the servant or employee who is acting within the scope of his or her employment.

restraint Can be either "physical" or "chemical" (medication). A physical restraint involves a device (e.g., safety belts, safety bars, geriatric chairs, bed rails) that restricts or limits voluntary movement and cannot be removed by the patient.

slander False oral statement, made in the presence of a third person, that injures the character or reputation of another.

Socrates A Greek philosopher 469 BC–399 BC, renowned for his contributions to the field of ethics. One of his most important contributions to ethics was his use of what has been termed the *Socratic method* of teaching, which involves a form of inquiry and debate between individuals with opposing viewpoints based on asking and answering questions to stimulate critical thinking and to illuminate ideas.

standard of care Description of the conduct that is expected of an individual in a given situation. It is a measure against which a defendant's conduct is compared.

stare decisis "Let the decision stand": the legal doctrine that prescribes adherence to those precedents set forth in cases that have been decided.

statute of limitations Legal limit on the time allowed for filing suit in civil matters, usually measured from the time of the wrong or from the time when a reasonable person would have discovered the wrong.

statutory law Law that is prescribed by legislative enactments.

stipulation A concession of agreed-upon facts that must be in writing unless they are part of the court record and that are made by the parties in a judicial proceeding relating to the business before the court. A stipulation of facts is often made to avoid delay in judicial proceedings.

subjectivism A doctrine that says moral judgments are based on personal preferences.

subpoena ad testificandum Court order requiring one to appear in court to give testimony.

subpoena duces tecum Court order that commands a person to come to court and to produce whatever documents are named in the order.

subrogation Substitution of one person for another in reference to a lawful claim or right.

substituted judgment In the healthcare setting, a surrogate decision maker serves as a substitute for the patient in the event the patient becomes incapacitated and is therefore unable to make his or her own decisions. Decisions are made on the basis of the patient's known healthcare preferences. Such preferences are often described in the document that appointed the surrogate and/or other documents such as a "living will" or "durable power of attorney for health care."

summary judgment Generally, an immediate decision by a judge, without jury deliberation.

summons Court order directed to the sheriff or other appropriate official to notify the defendant in a civil suit that a suit has been filed and to inform them when and where to appear.

surrogate decision maker An individual who has been designated to make decisions on behalf of another person determined incapable of making his or her own decisions.

teleological ethics A theory of morality that derives duty or moral obligation from what is good or desirable as an end to be achieved.

terminal condition A medical condition that is incurable and in which death will occur.

testimony Oral statement of a witness given under oath at trial.

The Joint Commission (TJC) A not-for-profit independent organization dedicated to improving the quality of health care in organized healthcare settings. The major functions of the Joint Commission include the development of organizational standards, awarding accreditation decisions, and providing education and consultation to healthcare organizations.

tort Civil wrong committed by one individual against another. Torts may be classified as either intentional or unintentional. When a tort is classified as a criminal wrong (e.g., assault, battery, false imprisonment), the wrongdoer can be held liable in a criminal and/or civil action.

tortfeasor Person who commits a tort.

trial court Court in which evidence is presented to a judge or jury for decision.

unethical behavior Character that describes behavior contrary to admirable traits or a code of conduct that has been endorsed by one's society, community, or profession.

utilitarianism A moral theory that treats pleasure and happiness as the only absolute moral good. Acts that bring about happiness and pleasure are good, and acts that bring about pain and suffering are morally bad.

value Worth or usefulness. Intrinsic values are those goods that are valuable in their own right. Instrumental values are those goods that help us achieve another good.

value judgment A judgment that assigns value to an action.

venue Geographic district in which an action is or may be brought.

verdict Formal declaration of a jury's findings of fact, signed by the jury foreperson and presented to the court.

virtue A moral trait that refers to excellence and righteousness.

waiver Intentional giving up of a right, such as allowing another person to testify to information that ordinarily would be protected as a privileged communication.

will Legal declaration of the intentions a person wishes to have carried out after death concerning property, children, or estate. A will designates a person or persons to serve as the executor(s) responsible for carrying out the instructions of the will.

witness Person who is called to give testimony in a court of law.

wrongful birth Applies to the cause of action of parents who claim that negligent advice or treatment deprived them of the choice of aborting conception or of terminating the pregnancy.

wrongful life Refers to a cause of action brought by or on behalf of a defective child who claims that but for the defendant (e.g., a laboratory's negligent testing procedures, a physician's negligent advice, treatment of the child's parents) the child would not have been born.

Index

Rice v. Vandenebossche, 341–342
Riffe v. Vereb Ambulance Serv., Inc., 241–242
"right to die," 89–95
rights of patients. *See* patient rights
Riser v. American Medical Intern Inc., 74–76
risk, failure to disclose, 76–79
Ritalin, 266–268
Roberts v. Hunter, 205–206
Rodgers v. St. Mary's Hosp. of Decatur,
        63–64
Rowe v. Sisters of the Pallottine Missionary
        Society, 136–138
Roy v. Gupta, 181–183

S

Sacks v. Mambu, 199–201
safety
        employee, 321–322
        patient. *See* patient safety
salmonella poisoning, 345–347
Sander v. Geib, Elston, Frost Prof'l Ass'n,
        167–169
Sarivola v. Brookdale Hosp. and Med. Ctr.,
        245–246
Scaria v. St. Paul Fire & Marine Ins. Co., 85
Schauer v. Memorial Care Sys., 374–376
sciatic nerve injury, 253–254
scientific testimony, 211
screening and assessment, 115–159
        careless, 120–122
        definition, 115
        failure to assess and treat, 125–129
        failure to correct, 122–124
        failure to provide, 124–129
        inadequate, 129–134
        need, 117–119
        negligent and incompetent, 134–136
        nutritional, 145–146
        reassessment, 144–145, 147–150
        regulations and standards, 116–117
        standards, 117
        types, 115–116
"second victim" of medical mistake, 259
serial murder by healthcare professional,
        399–401

sexual abuse
        adult, 389–391
        child, 68–69, 389, 392–394, 400
Shelton v. United States, 230–232
Shields v. McLachlan, 300–302
shift duration safety, 326*t*
silent language, 27
6 CCR 1011-1 ch. V § 4.5.4
        (incident reports), 21
Smith v. O'Neal, 216–217
Smith v. Thompson, 186
Smith v. U.S. Dept. of Veterans Affairs, 164–167
Social Security Act amendments, 5–6
"societal obligation" to report, 364
Solomon v. Connecticut Medical Examining
        Bd, 134–136
Somoza v. St. Vincent's Hosp., 308–310
specific treatment, 209
"spoilation of evidence," 151–152
sponge count, incorrect, 250–251
squamous cell carcinoma, failure to diagnose,
        167–169
St. Paul Med. Ctr. v. Cecil, 221–223
Stacy v. Truman Med. Ctr., 338–341
Stamford Hosp. v. Vega, 98–102
Star Chamber (summary case), 407–447
State Ex Rel. Stolfa v. Ely, 266–268
State Operations Manual for the Survey
        Protocol, Regulations and
        Interpretive Guidelines for
        Hospitals, 4–5
state right, patients rights *versus,* 103–106
state standard, enforcement of, 11–18
State v. Cunningham, 70–72
State v. Houle, 391–392
statute of limitations
        doctrine of continuing wrong, 40
        fall from gurney, 336–338
        fall from nursing facility window, 334–336
        misdiagnosis of brain tumor, 180–181
        "plead around" dismissed, 122–124
        telephone-based care, 305–306
statute of repose, 313–316
Staub v. Proctor Hospital, 352–356
Stevens v. St. Louis Univ. Med. Ctr., 377–378
Stilloe v. Contini, 305–306